Central Banks, Democratic States and Financial Power

When the US Federal Reserve, European Central Bank and Bank of England purchased bank and state debt during the 2007–2010 crisis, it became clear, yet again, that when technically divorced from fiscal policy, monetary policy cannot revive but only prevent economic activity from deteriorating further. Pixley explains how the money production of the democracies and the immense money creation by capitalist banking put burdens on central banks, often neither socially useful nor peaceful. Central banks cannot be politically neutral and, despite unfair demands, are unable to prevent collapses to debt deflation from bank credit/asset inflations. They can foster debilitating depressions and hardships but not the recoveries desired in democracies, nor touch secret war finance demands. Drawing on economic sociology and history, this book appeals to readers interested in democracies, banks and central banking's ambivalent, if hopeful, potentials, via comparative and distributive perspectives.

JOCELYN PIXLEY is an Honorary Professor in Sociology at Macquarie University, Sydney, and Professorial Research Fellow with the Global Policy Institute, London. An economic sociologist, her fieldwork involves interviewing top officials in finance centres. She is the author of *Emotions in Finance* (Second edition, Cambridge, 2012), and edited a volume on the same theme (2012). With Geoff Harcourt, she edited *Financial Crises and the Nature of Capitalist Money* (2013).

Central Banks, Democratic States and Financial Power

JOCELYN PIXLEY
Macquarie University

CAMBRIDGE
UNIVERSITY PRESS

CAMBRIDGE
UNIVERSITY PRESS

University Printing House, Cambridge CB2 8BS, United Kingdom

One Liberty Plaza, 20th Floor, New York, NY 10006, USA

477 Williamstown Road, Port Melbourne, VIC 3207, Australia

314-321, 3rd Floor, Plot 3, Splendor Forum, Jasola District Centre, New Delhi - 110025, India

79 Anson Road, #06-04/06, Singapore 079906

Cambridge University Press is part of the University of Cambridge.

It furthers the University's mission by disseminating knowledge in the pursuit of education, learning and research at the highest international levels of excellence.

www.cambridge.org
Information on this title: www.cambridge.org/9781107122031
DOI: 10.1017/9781316402672

© Jocelyn Pixley 2018

First published 2018

A catalogue record for this publication is available from the British Library

Library of Congress Cataloging in Publication data
Names: Pixley, Jocelyn, 1947- author.
Title: Central banks, democratic states and financial power / Jocelyn Pixley,
    Macquarie University, Sydney.
Description: Cambridge, United Kingdom : New York, NY, USA : Cambridge
    University Press, 2018. | Includes bibliographical references and index.
Identifiers: LCCN 2017060049| ISBN 9781107122031 (hardback : alk. paper) |
    ISBN 9781107552340 (pbk. : alk. paper)
Subjects: LCSH: Banks and banking, Central—History.
Classification: LCC HG1511 .P59 2018 | DDC International finance.—dc23
LC record available at https://lccn.loc.gov/2017060049

ISBN 978-1-107-12203-1 Hardback
ISBN 978-1-107-55234-0 Paperback

V. J. Carroll

Contents

Figures

Tables

Acknowledgements

Fieldwork on this book started around 1998. My earlier work on the relation between citizenship and employment left me wondering why its importance became diminished in high policy circles, and why financial sectors had grown so fast. What were the connections to the end of full employment in these developments? I had pointed gloomily to the radical ideas of the 1970s that were converted into conservative policies. Central banks of the USA and UK sacrificed so many to joblessness; others followed but, the longer I interviewed those involved, the more I found things were not as they seemed. Modest improvement seems to be ruled out despite catastrophic financial crises that many informed sceptics worried about (to me). In consequence, I looked at histories of various dramatic central banking changes and different central bank models at the time when democracy held out promise to new generations, over depressions and world wars.

My turn to comparative monetary history is the reason I dedicate the book to V. J. Carroll, firm believer in history and sociology; and scholar of the Bank of England and the US Federal Reserve. Formerly editor-in-chief of the *Sydney Morning Herald* and *Australian Financial Review*, Carroll is respected as Australia's foremost intellectual defender of the Fourth Estate and honourable journalism. Vic's encouragement has substance: he also alerted me to Australian monetary histories about the extraordinary developments over the twentieth century. These show how a central bank constructed on social democratic lines grew from the 1900s under Labor Commonwealth Governments. It was different from most central banks, and faced incessant backlashes from Australia's banking sector, global finance sectors, the Bank of England and hegemonic pound sterling, which was rapidly taken over by the US dollar.

The relations of central banks to governments and to banking in war and peace – economic activity, stagnation or warfare – became more vivid with this counter example, about which Vic Carroll has discussed explanations with me. The Bank of Canada has a slightly similar model that broadened my comparisons, albeit mainly preoccupied with the US Fed.

Many gave terrific help; Geoff Ingham, as ever, with timely references, and importantly the work on central banks that I did with Shaun Wilson and Sam Whimster. We learned a lot from each other; Geoff Harcourt kindly gave his time in numerous phone calls and so on, as did Shaun and Sam. I mention my thanks (given elsewhere) to all the decent people whom I interviewed from the US Federal Reserve, the Bank of England, the Reserve Bank of Australia and later the Banca d'Italia and Bank of Greece. In fact, revisiting their transcripts, some of twenty years ago, has given historical insights to this book.

Dr Phil Good, my commissioning editor at Cambridge University Press, put his faith in my arguments and, with excellent advice from anonymous referees, I hope the book lives up to their hopes. Geetha Williams and Rashmi Yashwant Bhate my thoughtful adviser, were patient during its production, Harry Field and Sam Dawson were judicious readers, and many colleagues, friends and family were as ever my supporters in solidarity, with Louisa Dawson who designs my covers. Hector 'writes' the occasional blog on financial press articles, using my work thoughtfully, as one expects of Australian sheep dogs with only city parks to exercise their minds.

I Who Wanted Central Banks?

Central banks are ill-understood and most people – if they talk about money, its plenty and dearth, and its collapse in 2007 – focus their sights on banks and government treasuries. In many respects they are correct, as this book hopes to show. Central banks are the bankers to capitalist banking and to governments. Having said that, things get more complicated on the turf of central banks and money is that complicating factor. There are multiple understandings of money and, while none is perfect, some are deceptive or one-sided. Indeed, we have endured miserable ideas about banking and treasuries, or what it is that central banks do in *managing* money. After the last forty years, everyone wonders why civility is hard to find again whether in governments or in banks.

The era in which we live is divisive and unsettling. Once respected institutions devoted to doing little harm, work on principles that evade the rule of law. Banks are one case: far from serving their clients' best needs, financial institutions are devoted to plundering them. Line management runs from crassly well-off executives to ill-paid tellers ordered to deceive us and the authorities. Bank tricks are so dangerous that central banks and treasuries must rescue them. This book will not speak of a 'banking culture' where 'rogue traders' apparently flourish from nowhere. To the contrary, finance corporations are as indecent as they were in 1920–33, as I show. 'FIRE' (finance, insurance, real estate) appears to run everything.

Another tendency is that everyone has 'retreated into the present'; dignitaries and scribblers make long-term predictions based on yesterday's events.[1] The powerful take it as a right to lie, and this post-fact world is not new. Bank CEOs (dealing in or selling flimsy promises into the future most of all) demand certainty that no one can ever have. Efforts to squeeze uncertainty out of specific sources of unpredictability either fail or backfire as with the 2007–08 'sub-prime' catastrophe. For years, central banks had to help these banks try to control the future – with techniques that can wreak havoc on social and economic life, and above all must validate the past errors of banks. When that is obvious, central banks are easy targets of blame. Self-financing, dividends from their huge profits go to their Government's Treasury, an operation muddied with those few central banks that are still privately owned, or partially so. The US Federal Reserve System (Fed), the most dominant central bank in the world, is a mix of private and public ownership. Central banks – at arm's length from democratic states, but *not* from capitalist banks – are more financially secure than other independent government agencies.[2] Many democratic states are no longer trusted, whereas central banks are mostly unknown.

It may well be that central banks also deceive us, particularly the US Fed, which is, legally, partly directed for profit by Wall Street bank executives since its founding Act (the Federal Reserve Act [FRA]) in 1913. And yet, remarkably, since the Global Financial Crisis (GFC), the Fed has been speaking the language of civility, despite the Fed's divisions, its public forked tongue, and secrecy. The most recent former Chair, Janet Yellen, stressed that the interest rate should stay low until employment and wages improve, and inflation lifts off again. She has faced battalions of the ignorant and posturers, however, central banks are urging policies unheard of for two generations that the book recollects.

---

[1] A decent society *aims* not to humiliate. It requires a civil society which at the least is tolerant: see Markus (2001) and Pixley and Browne (2010). The 'retreat' into the present is a concept from Elias (1987) and see Elias (1970).

[2] 'Capitalise gains and socialise losses' is apt. The Bank of Italy is the other major central bank (CB) that is/was fully privately owned: Giannini (2011) gives an overall survey of CBs though my approach differs.

Instead of starting blandly with their functions or state mandates and remits, common in the central bank literature, I begin with the historical question of which social groups wanted central banks. Then the book looks at a number of central banks in the democratic times of the twentieth and twenty-first centuries. Before that, 'electorates' were tiny, exclusive. Bourgeois capitalist elites inside states and in banking sectors designed and controlled central banks. Semifeudal European sovereigns wanted them to fund wars, and capitalist merchants had interests in state protection: these earliest central or ersatz public banks were experimental, and many broke down (from Venice to Amsterdam). This is because money is always unstable since it consists in promises to pay (IOUs), of guarantees into the future by both creditors and debtors (to success or failure). The rise of nation-states and capitalist economies was actively sponsored by these close-knit rulers and classes, as Max Weber put it, for the state to rule and the merchant-financiers to make money. Central banks were the go-betweens, and populations had no involvement whatsoever in their inception.

Fast forward to the twentieth century, where a handful of the many new central banks were installed and designed by elected social democratic governments. In fact, the advent of democratic processes threatened to ruin the 'clubs' of state royalty, 'robber barons', of capitalist merchants that banked with central banks. *The twentieth and twenty-first centuries are this book's subject for that reason.* The US Fed is the focus, but the book stresses that different central bank models do exist; indeed, few copy the old Bank of England (BoE) model or the Fed's. This may surprise, and it is true that since Britain's overall decline, everyone watches the US empire/power-house and its Fed. The US imposes a 'one best way' that inflicts damage and crises in the different contexts of other countries' financial practices that are variously effective in coping with capitalist money, always difficult with mobile capital and US global currency fluctuations.

And yet, since 2007, elected leaders and executives locked in bubbles of privilege are utterly confused. Since the resurgence of activist financial sectors, many bank-supported political parties aimed to destroy democratic procedures and have removed the 'wets', the doves, the vulnerable and decent social democrats who were properly called civil servants to the people. 'Inflation' and state budget 'deficits' became alleged enemies. Then suddenly, incredibly, central banks begged for more inflation and keep harping about jobs and economic activity, although the European Central Bank (ECB) was busy creating more jobless even as the GFC spread. Prime Ministers and Presidents further weakened trade unions, waged wars, while agitators stir hatreds. History is constantly rewritten to abuse hopes for social democracy or any informed public. Who knows how wars are funded? Fact-checkers for scrutinising the chorus of lies or meaningless jargon streaming from corporate bank and government executives seem to indicate something worse. The slang used inside states and banks is far more value-laden than the terms I use in this book, like 'uncivil', 'humiliating', 'cruel', 'indecent', through to 'tolerant', 'civil', even 'decent'. Puerile dualisms of gang fights that give the power game away are 'hawks/doves'; 'wets/dries'; 'brown-cardigan losers'. There are feudal images of Darth Vader; big swinging dicks or Michael Douglas bad guys, whereas the slogan 'greed is good' *ad nauseam* is outdated because it is the norm. Misogyny, racism and vilification of the poor are out in the open, less original than children's chants of 'teacher's pet' or 'tittle tattle': the solidarity of tiny tyrants.

Governors or Chairs of central banks are not immune. My interviews in the 1990s to 2010s with the more civil, often truly decent informed central bankers did show anger, through to embarrassment, or cognitive dissonance, should one dare to ask why low-paid workers are sacrificed on the altars of austerity, joblessness and pitiful wages. Some denied central banks made political decisions in raising interest rates against people's social desires and desperate needs for money. Yet sceptics informed about money stressed, instead, decent methods to reduce inflation without such cruel, senseless results. Central banks could work strategically with their treasury: progressive taxes are known to reduce inflation, for example. Forget that: central banks were ordered to induce recessions, just like in pre-democratic times.

Central banks are in a harsh spotlight, as often before, partly because so few know what they do. Virtually no political leader or commercial banker (who cares not to know) understood or explained, when the GFC hit, how central banks suddenly created money, and so much. And saved the banks, which create far more money. When, in 2008, that bank money disappeared, everyone froze in fear. Was money so untrustworthy that it could vanish? The public had rare glimpses into money's previously unknown workings, operating behind our backs. States returned to full view and with their central banks became saviours: financiers had long dismissed states for 'repressing' banks. As it turned out in the GFC, the 'saved' was that exclusive crowd of fantastically rich in the vast financial sectors, parts of which we found out were corrupt. That varied across places; the smaller, but by no means poor countries often had the better central banks. There is even a modicum of egalitarianism left in, say, Canada, Sweden or Australia, the least GFC-affected countries. My favourite quote in 1998 was a US official who told me 'I do regret my advice to Sweden', for misapplying the US finance system to Sweden's.

In the OECD countries that created the GFC, the seeming order of things turned upside down, from markets, corporate (money-production) outfits and weak (if mean) states, to *money* at the centre of the whole show.[3] This cannot be stressed enough. Capital-labour relations, hardly congenial before, were further at the mercy of banking's reckless activities. Firms and households collapsed – the debtors – and the more criminal so called creditors. Since then, not one post-GFC politician has (publicly) argued that while central banks create money, so do private banks, which manufacture the bulk of the money that we use – except when they stopped in October 2008.

[3] My finance sector interviews are explained fully in Pixley (2004); my central bankers were mostly retired. The OECD is the Organisation for Economic Co-operation and Development.

Enter central banks onto the political stage (possibly to be sacrificed); these monstrous chameleons that, having cast workers and the jobless into humiliation for forty years, are begging their masters for the emphasis to be on job creation. Banks are not interested. States have resolutely refused, preferring austerity, yet governments previously improved economic activity through peaceful stimulus. That is the simple if correct and decent story that aimed for dignified meaningful lives.

My argument takes a different tack: Central banks are identifiable and (too) easy targets of attack. Who will dare take on J. P. Morgan given its 130-year banking history of dubious interference with the world? And wars still vie with peace: how 'pleasant' are states? Money is the social force that needs full recognition to the point of seeing that control over the production of money by banks or by states is the major social tension and historical conflict, as Geoff Ingham puts it. In between these two mighty forces, central banks are bankers to their governments and to capitalist banks, which are both harsh taskmasters. On occasion, in specific social-political circumstances, the forces of capital and labour – the producers – have intervened, but not in the recent GFC. Some question whether citizens really need central banks. That would depend on whether central banks are permitted to serve the public good (somewhat) rather than fund the old institutions of capitalist money and war mongering states exclusively. Some remain vital *and* decent. Usually they are not allowed to work with Treasuries for the public. If we want to see the naked power-dealers, we should not look first to central banks. To assess this, the book selects major incidents that affected central banks from mainly the sorry twentieth-century record to the abysmal GFC (2007 to the present), and including the mid-century moment when money was open to some democratic scrutiny.

The bones of the argument are unusual, although the obvious practices, centuries old, that all money is debt is continually banished, to the benefit of banks and states, unwittingly or not. That idea must not be lost or silenced to mystifying tactics.

- Central banks (CBs) are not rigidly similar: Some are/were exclusive and secretive, adjudicators of the clash of raw vested interests over the purposes of money; others attempt civil, public deliberation about their remits. Full employment (FE) and price stability are twin mandates of the US Fed and Reserve Bank of Australia (RBA), but most central banks are confined to price stability (anti-inflation) without FE (anti-deflation). By the mid-twentieth century democracy partly entered CB workings, with FE to stop them inducing recessions – but that emphasis later switched. CBs keep changing, then. The unexpected occurs that reshapes them for better or worse.

- The separation of form and content brings sharp dissonances – the form claims public good, but the content of central bank policies has major distribution effects, winners and losers that depend on the social distribution of political power over money. Treasuries can correct maldistribution, less so central banks, but both increase inequalities via public decisions. The funding methods of vast nuclear arsenals (say) is secret; unspoken.

- My precarious line is trod between uncivil, indecent doctrines, based on counterfactuals (not evidence) and on support for old exclusive social forces and, in contrast, the fragile social democratic practices and civil discourses abused for decades. This book explores evident pressures on central banks during civil and uncivil eras in the twentieth to twenty-first centuries, comparing typical capitalist-state patterns but in different contexts – of democratic norms, either welcomed, respected, or begrudged even blasted to empty shells manipulated by private money and state money production.

- Different CBs are selected, with diverse aims imposed under coalitions of the dominant interests of the time and place (that invariably change – and one cannot cover them all) – so the book gives a few comparisons. The mighty US Fed gets the most attention but a few outliers like the RBA or Bank of Canada (BoC) serve as energetic historical contrasts; the BoE too, but as the former hegemonic CB. If all kinds of purposes have been intended for central bank money creation, then there are no eternal rights or wrongs.

- The book draws on recent and past scholars (selectively), of note Karl Polanyi, who criticised those treating money as a commodity; André Orléan likewise argues liquidity is a term that denies money's social nature. These terms hint at the inequality in the opportunity to make liquid (or saleable) all assets. Most people have only one 'property' to sell: their capacity to labour. That is difficult in stagnant job markets. To Polanyi, land, labour and money were abused as commodities. Unlike money, the first two are obvious, thus climate change. Objectified labour is a 'hired hand' or a 'human resource'.[4] Just as humans, with our richly diverse capacities, are turned into objects for statistical analysis and sharp trading, so is money, which consists in mutual promises, contracts and obligations into the (uncertain) future. *Money is not a thing and involves generative relations.*

- The towering figures of Joseph Schumpeter and John Maynard Keynes must appear, because their social analyses are the start to explicate today's practices and production of bank money and state money. Some have brought the sociology of money into prominence, notably Ingham, Orléan and others. Works in political science, economics past and present, history and social policy are also discussed. Few outward-looking or socially alert meanings of money's creative power are ever free of doubt. Vicious counter-attacks arise, assuming a lofty bystander, which is impossible as everyone has a world view.

It is possible that central banks are duty-bound to defend 'state-capitalist money' and cannot do much else. Bearing in mind my entry-points on the crucial advent and impact of formal democratic procedures over money, let us reconsider the present. On 8 November 2016, a new US President was greeted in German press headlines with the phrase 'Horror-Clown!'.[5] The *Financial Times* ran a campaign against ideas of UK Prime Minister Theresa May and US President Donald Trump about central banks. No judgement is possible (so soon), except to say that jokers are part of any pack of cards, and this pack is tied to specific state and financial motives, that the book lays out. The vision of political leaders able to achieve anything

---

[4] Readers may find these approaches useful (I am not debating every teensy point theorists ever said, just what's suitable). My motto is beware of eternal 'universal' pomposities that Polanyi (1957 [1944]) criticised. He was hopeful that this nineteenth century trend was over by 1944. Social policy talked of the 'decommodification' of labour in the 1960s–70s; land became the scientific study of climate change. Money as a commodity is rarely analysed in Polanyi scholarship, with honourable exceptions.

[5] On the German press, see Lane 2016 and Sandbu (2016b). The *FT* was furious that the Fed and BoE were attacked, e.g. in Sandbu (2016a).

by barking out orders without diverse support is obsolete if it ever applied. As well, what a leader achieves, and whether she or he understood the implications, or not, are debated for centuries. I emphasise that in the twentieth century, politicians were gradually more separate from their usual allies in industry and/or finance (although less so for the last forty years). Before then it was difficult to distinguish their private from public interests. For example, the Bismarck family was, when Fritz Stern finished his famous work in 1977, the richest in Germany due to Otto's blurred lines of war finance and personal finance. Complex democratic policies to serve many walks of life suffer from any return to feudal patrimonial amalgamations.[6]

HISTORICAL MOTIVES FOR CENTRAL BANKS

Instead of hinting at mysterious social forces, I aim to call them forth; to describe the important private sectors' public roles and governments' duties to their electorates, in respect to pushing for changes to central banks. To compare with pre-democratic days, I briefly discuss a few bare bones of the semi-feudal motives for the creation of central banks. Depending on the central bank, sceptics among my interviewees were critical of them, but the more arrogant assumed that central banks should treat the downtrodden as expendable. We were not the citizens of the 1960s. Their friends on Wall Street, the City of London, or the Frankfurt stock exchange were executive traders, who spoke ironically in the language of warlords. They would 'rip off faces' of firms or governments waiting to be 'screwed'. Their surroundings looking over Lake Zurich or the Hudson River were lessons. To stroll (with care) on pot-holed Wall Street down below is to be among the street venders like old times.

---

[6] See McDonald (2016) on 'the joker'; I emphasise the disparate forces creating a leader, not only a voting base; on Bismarck, see Stern (1977). On patrimonialism in UK/Europe, see Weber (1978) or Louis XIV's absolutism in "l'état c'est moi"; like Chinese feudal lords who talked of 'their' state, in Osnos (2018). Semi-feudal states recur in weird forms and weeding out 'cronies' remains patchy. Industrial (debtor) sectors *have* supported democratic aims of general well-being, if rarely (in Chapter 4).

About 500 years ago, a handful of these central banks emerged from experimental bargains between sovereign feudal monarchs and the rising bourgeois capitalist classes in Europe. Capitalist money became the core social fact: in general, the motives of both sides were for some sort of public–private or central bank to manage their assets and liabilities to each other: each was mutually dependent. Gradually no one could survive without this money, but only a tiny fraction invented and controlled these deals: aristocratic elites of the rising nation state and new bourgeois class, which between them transformed a feudal economy of kings, nobles and serfs into a capitalist economy and nation states, of labour-capital and significant debtor-creditor money classes. The reader is saved the details of the great literature, since there is only one fundamental point needed to introduce this book. At the time when experimental central banks came into being, there was no democratic involvement in this 'symbiosis' of sovereign and merchant moneys that we all use.

In the central bank literature, a common theme is that in the twentieth century, these banks had to cope with 'the masses'. To some, that complicated central bank work. One cannot stress enough the elitism and disdain entrenched in the dominant central banks, those few that started ages ago. The Bank of England (1694) is a creature of kings and rich merchant-cum-aristocrats. The US Fed, founded in 1913 after a century of political ambivalence and bottom-up debates about money, and two defunct central banks, was created after the 'gilded age' by an exclusive state and a handful of 'robber barons' and financiers (Rockefeller or J. P. Morgan) in league with Congressional politicians.

Capitalism's violent origins was not the only source of immense global change. Change arose out of the fragmentation of lords and peasants, subsistence activity, person-to-person credit (IOUs) and local coinage. Far-reaching IOU trading systems were developing. Trading merchants funded European/English warlords battling to control territorial patches and, if their centralising aims were unintended, it was this partnership that made state unification and capitalist money possible. Both needed each other, the princes needed funds to fight wars and the merchants to receive 'royal' protection. One cannot look at the question of 'currencies' and labour 'markets', without recognising what state violence achieves. A central currency became imposed with the coercion of taxes only acceptable in that currency, and with (more) violent protection for bank money and its markets.[7]

Portugal was probably the first centralising state to ally with merchant-financiers and build heavily armed ships for merchants to collect 'far away' precious goods and to arbitrage – that is, to buy cheap and sell dear. These vicious systems, by far the biggest being the Dutch East India Company, were aloof from, but menaced local economies: luxuries went to 'royal' courts and to the merchants who funded state war finance and pacification over other warlord-mafia types and their subjected local peoples. Karl Polanyi rejects as fiction the orthodox view that from time immemorial people 'bartered' in markets for goods, and later with a 'handy' token – money – representing the goods. No: these bills of payment were promises over time. In contrast, the only barter in hunter-gatherer societies was equally long-distant trade that had little to no impact on their 'embedded' social structures. These reciprocal 'spot trades' between small stateless societies living thousands of miles apart in many cases (in Argentina, Australia, Canada), or feudal or caste hierarchical arrangements prevailed (with subsistence enmeshed in such complex societies), until the 'great transformation' around the late eighteenth century. Europe's virulent and dangerous merchant or pirate speculation in the New World, in Russia and India to extract huge concessions, also fatally weakened feudal hierarchical structures in a Europe that was also undergoing chaotic nation building, with the unending desires of princes for loans.

---

[7] Giannini (2011) on CBs is typical on 'the masses'; populism, ill-defined, is another charge; there were also some princesses. There is a huge literature on the 'transformation', such as Arrighi (1994), often recounted (e.g. in Pixley 2013). To Elias (2000), warlords aimed to keep territory, not centralise, he argued, but it happened inadvertently. Ingham (2004) makes the 'fusion' the most unusual aspect of 'state-capitalist' money, one that is used herein, and typically involved a central bank or proto one. See also Wray (2014a) on currency.

These civil or uncivil capitalist IOUs for distant trade, and nation state debts, often with tally-sticks recording the 'personal' sovereign's own debts, involved all kinds of deals with the bourgeoisie or *rentiers* – those who charged interest (for example hidden in land rents, or *rentes* in French).[8] Some deals with proto-central banks later proved unstable, such as the Italian city-states (Venice, Medici Florence and Genoa) or Amsterdam. It was only by chance that the English created the capitalist money–state fusion that remains to this day. War finance and protection for money producers seeking profit is one old motive; money for its own sake is the other old motive – but eventually they joined forces uneasily. Their new institution was the central bank.[9]

The earliest central banks often started as temporary 'solutions' to immediate problems posed by the specific social-cultural tendencies of the time and place, in which certain *ideas* were part of the prevailing habits and conflicts thrown up. This was the case of the BoE, chartered in 1694. A cash-strapped William III searched for ideas to pay for more wars, one of which was a state lottery. Instead, nearly by chance, the 'solution' gave the world capitalist money. Polanyi suggests English central banking ultimately offered protection to business enterprises from the disruptions of a *pure* market monetary system. The big issue – who is dependent on whom in state-money and bank-money relations – has fluctuated (it's rarely clear). That combination of public debt and private debt was forged after the English Stuart kings defaulted on merchants. William III's Bank Charter, instead, gave the BoE a privileged monopoly position. J. K. Galbraith explains the loan from wealthy creditors of the privately-owned BoE by noting that 'the government's promise to pay would be the security for a note issue of the same amount' to private

---

[8] Polanyi (1957) [1944] on markets: the idea of an 'economy' was irrelevant before capitalism; see Howell (2016) on the hiding of illegal 'usury' in rents as the origin of *rentier* (and she mainly refers to Joseph Fugger).

[9] Arrighi (1994) on the past 400 years; Ingham (2004) and 'fusion' as mentioned before. Chapter 2 explores central banks' roles in war finance, a vexed question that tends to be trivialised in much CB literature.

borrowers. Money doubled with this loan, as is evident in bank balance sheets. To Weber, it was an alliance: states would make war and 'merchant classes' would make money. The state set up markets in money and 'free' labour. The process was fitful, often brutal; it did not follow Dr. Pangloss's optimistic path into a glorious overdetermined future.[10]

A new type of 'capitalist money' developed states and economies in revolutionary ways, at times with decent results. How far state violence makes capitalist money possible is incalculable, since the (secretive) strong state is not going away, nor the weak states that are cash-poor and less able to pacify. The strongest early centralising states used the violence of policing powers, branding of counterfeiters and debtors' prisons, balanced by banks' political control over debtors like sovereigns who spend, and must tax if inflation or debasement threatens.[11]

Impersonal emotions were built into the institutional 'deals' – fear, distrust and self-righteousness on all sides. British governments tried to check the private BoE's abuses of government repayments and profiteering from paper money, with rare success. In Gladstone's view, in 1694, William III had put the state in 'a position of subserviency ... to induce monied men to be lenders', describing the imbalance as 'the money power supreme and unquestioned'. Britain's Bank Charter Act of 1844 tried to give the BoE's management of the national currency a quasi-public basis, but defined that as an 'automatic, technical' matter rather than a 'public responsibility'. The BoE's deals with its friends remained hugely profitable. Efforts to put a 'central' bank into

---

[10] See Polanyi (1957: 192); Galbraith (1975b: 31) who called this 'simple' practice repellent; Weber (1981: 264–5) and Ingham (2008: 32–4). See Tables 1.1 and 1.2. Here I refer to Voltaire's satire *Candide*, and his tragic Dr. Pangloss – against the liberal-capitalist 'Whig view of history'.

[11] Counterfeiting arose defiantly in the transition from local currencies, 'near money' and IOUs, to the state-capitalist currency. See Wennerlind (2001), Ingham (2004), and see also Wray (2014a): state spending in the currency is logically first, before taxes and debts are accepted only in that currency.

a role of public trust (that Walter Bagehot preferred) only lasted for a while in the twentieth century, as we see in numerous disputes.[12]

Nevertheless, the BoE came to regulate commercial banks with prudential supervision: the last run on a British bank was in 1866 – until Northern Rock in 2007. The BoE 'deal' looked attractive. The two sources of money fused, in a way, into one 'sovereign monetary space', the public debt of state bonds, and the private debt of bills of exchange. This kernel remains.[13]

The BoE is often taken as the universal model, partly because in the nineteenth century, Britain was the pound sterling hegemon, like the US and its dollar in the twentieth century. With the BoE established, and with Britain's land cleared of peasants over centuries, industrial (labour – capital) developments began before Europe, which set up somewhat different CB models. Their aims varied. The BoE combined to prosper with global London merchants (banks) mainly by funding war finance and advancing as 'loans' these notes (money) that relied on the Crown's security. Some states directed central banks to other sectoral approaches, such as to industry, which helped labour. Not all peaceful – the French example of Louis XV who was tempted by John Law's BoE model, but with a weak bourgeois class, was a drastic failure – unlike the ultimate bourgeois victors of the English Civil War. The British Crown was on notice to bourgeois Parliament in London, which promoted the City's merchant banks and the BoE.[14]

The BoE later had control over the dominant world currency, pound sterling, shared with treasury. Meantime the commodification

---

[12] See Kynaston (1995: 19–20), citing Gladstone; Bagehot on the 1844 Act is cited in Kynaston (1995: 22): there's a tongue-in-cheek in his recording. See also Tables 1.1 and 1.2. We usually don't notice money/central banks until crises and massive efforts to cast blame, or even to discuss money.

[13] On the 1866 'bank' run (one of many before), see Flandreau and Ugolini (2013); Ingham (2004: 128–9) on fused moneys.

[14] See Epstein (2006) on variations in central bank models, more on which is in Chapter 2; John Law is in Schumpeter (1954: 294; 311), Coombs (1971: 1) and Ingham (2004: 51; 211), who agree Law was correct about manufacturing money. Governor Coombs (RBA) said 'hard-faced' central bankers kept this secret, partly from the Law experiment's drastic boom and bust, but also, after Law explained he only copied the BoE's repellent money creating practices, French 'faith' in both disappeared.

processes (land, labour and money) introduced new relations of money classes, labour-capital classes and their specific stratification systems. These became embedded in global economic activity and countries – affecting all the hinterlands. Polanyi saw the late nineteenth century like this:

> Budgets and armaments, foreign trade and raw material supplies, national independence and sovereignty were now the functions of currency and credit. By [then] ... world commodity prices were the central reality in the lives of millions of Continental peasants; the repercussions of the London money market were daily noted by businessmen all over the world; and governments discussed plans for the future in light of the situation on the world capital markets. Only a madman would have doubted that the international economic system was the axis of the material existence of the [human] race. (1944: 18)

By that time, as he said, the British might send gun boats, but that was often less needed when the BoE could pull the thread of gold on a naughty colony or miscreant satrap, or the City of London might refuse to lend. The BoE was 'the conductor of the orchestra' (to Keynes) of international capital, currency exchange and global trade in the nineteenth century, which suited UK Treasury-imperial interests and English merchant–commercial classes (the City), but not the UK's industrial classes and county banks.[15]

THE COMING CAPITALIST CURRENCY HEGEMON: THE 'SETTLER' USA

The land clearances of peasants in Scotland and England and the complete conquest of Ireland (Cromwell and William III) meant that vast

---

[15] Ingham (1984) shows the nexus (or troika) of the City-BoE-Treasury was barely driven to favour British industry (ever) and the BoE focused on managing the international 'orchestra' (Ingham uses this loved quote of Keynes for his own argument). This was unlike the Continental emphasis, Japan's or even the USA's, on industry and its workers, for CBs (Epstein 2006).

numbers of displaced people sought refuge in, or were transported as convicts to, 'settler' colonies in the Americas. The slave trade from Africa became British-dominated in the 1660s (and the BoE was involved commercially).[16] Population movements reached their peak during the colonialising nineteenth century. British aristocrats' improved agricultural arrangements could not compete with the colonies' eventual output to Europe; keen to preserve their county estate comforts, many married into rich English families of the new capitalist merchant classes.[17] On the Continent, class transformations were much slower; the Habsburgs, for example, nurtured their peasants instead of clearing them off their land, to remain available for conscription into huge land armies; Napoleon won over the French peasants (to fight) via land rights. The UK's naval-based war power never required the extensive cannon fodder of Europe.[18]

A very diverse USA grew out of Europe's colonial carve-up, in the 1600s: an English agricultural economy in the south based on slavery; the French installed a semi-feudalism in Canada and the northern (US) lakes,[19] and similarly the Dutch West Indies Company further southeast; as well, aspects of modern finance (trades in stocks, banking)

---

[16] Ireland endured 600 years of English tyranny. England's early American cotton trade of settler-planters and slave trading began with Elizabeth I; later West Indies English sugar planters appealed for help to the House of Lords, attracting the City of London Corporation's interest, the Bank of England, Lloyd's insurance. All profited from the Atlantic slave trades, and built up ports in London, Bristol and Liverpool, which was the largest slave port ever in the world (see www.parliament.uk/about/living-heritage/transformingsociety/tradeindustry/slavetrade/overview/parliament-and-commerce/).

[17] The peak free migrations to the 'settler' Americas, Africa, Australia and NZ were from all of Europe, China and other countries in social turmoil; peasants cleared from rights to land in the British "Enclosures" benefited aristocratic land-holders until the mass migrations helped build up agribusiness competition of settler countries. See Schwartz (2000) on the rural aristocratic decline; the triumph of British bourgeois financiers over old aristocratic political/economic power we explored earlier.

[18] The contrasting Continental approaches to peasants are detailed in Pixley (2013) and, later in this chapter, the UK convict system. See Marx (1978 [1852]) on Code Napoleon and resulting peasants' debt peonage.

[19] Detail personally acquired, and to emphasise that orthodox economics has little interest in historical developments of class segments that vary greatly; and which influence the designs of CBs. French (Canadians) played a large part in opening the mighty lake-river system; also, some later became US 'robber barons', for example; but these old rich Dominions' CBs are rarely studied.

began in a tiny corner of New Amsterdam (Wall Street), whereas religious radicals escaped from persecution to Massachusetts. Trade with the Indigenous peoples ended in ghastly wars everywhere. The displaced of Europe migrated to the USA to be low wage labourers in eastern towns, or small farmers of the 'Westward Ho' movement. The US constitution's 'founding fathers' – wealthy capitalists, had numerous visions but the 'united' states had quite diverse economies, historical and ethnic traditions that hardly matched the visions. For example, Alexander Hamilton, the industrial warrior, took a pro-Wall Street, opposite position to Thomas Jefferson, a Rousseau-leaning small-farm advocate, and personally a slave-owner. Jefferson's argument was that wage labour was a dependency to be avoided in the free 'new world', as is evident in the US Constitution's 'self-evident truths'. Small farmers enacting the free society of independent white men (not a wage labour society, let alone unions), he proposed, would not be totally dependent on a monetary economy, but on mutual aid.[20]

For a long time, (white, male, free) Americans shared Jefferson's money views, and opposed a central bank. Whereas Jefferson said the banking establishment was 'more to be feared than standing armies', in contrast, and aiming to copy Continental Europe, Hamilton had pushed for war-finance and industry-promoting remits of an American central bank. His benign view compared to Jefferson's about Wall Street as a centre of 'the depravities of human nature', signalled America's long-held 'ambivalence and chronic culture warfare' against Wall Street. The tribulations of two different efforts at creating a US central bank in the nineteenth century demonstrated how merchants (sea trade and money) and federalism were tied up in conflicts between agrarian (south and west), manufacturing (north), also, local state versus nation-state building interests. In a nutshell,

---

[20] See Pateman (1979) on Rousseau's ideals and the US constitution debates; Galbraith (1975b: 28–9); and both on Jefferson. Women had no role in the constitution and the cliché of Southern slavery is belied by how slaves were more widely abused across the whole USA than is often thought.

US farmers and small businesses did not want a central bank or gold standard rule; Wall Street did, and eventually so did Washington DC.[21]

American 'exceptionalism' neglects the stark problem that during the century after the War of Independence, the USA was financially dependent on the UK. Former US Fed Chair Paul Volcker recently questioned the view of the USA as 'a huge and relatively self-sufficient country in control of our own destiny'. That view was shaken, for example, in the US 'first great' depression of 1837–44, which was a galling experience for Americans after winning independence from Britain. As recounted in Alasdair Roberts' sensitive history,[22] it was humiliating the US Administration had so lost 'credibility' abroad that it found no lender prepared to fund a war over British-Canadian territory – particularly not the British! In 1837, Treasury was broke, and the 'union' was far from perfect. Having engaged heavily in development and/or pork-barrelling, eight states defaulted on British creditors, including New York, which led to self-restrictions on local states borrowing from the City of London. Violence erupted everywhere, that is, not counting the tariff *versus* free-trade conflicts of the North and South, leading to the Civil War soon after.[23] US Treasury had no control of the few income taxes (except briefly in the Civil War) until a 1913 Amendment to the 1787 Constitution, in the same year as the US Fed was founded.

This abbreviated outline of the convoluted disunity in the US points to my argument in Chapter 7, that neither mono or federated monetary unions are so securely united as to blame the problems of today's ECB and Euro model solely on lacking a fiscal union.[24] Chapter 2, on 'war finance', discusses the key aims of the 1913 US

---

[21] These variations are heavily simplified. Galbraith (1975b: 29) had Jefferson's quote and see in Fraser (2005: xvi) on Wall Street. Also, in the politics, rural exporters wanted free trade; manufacturers protection.

[22] Roberts (2012: 1), citing Volcker, with a thesis that supports him. It's a good example to compare with the EMU, Chapter 7.

[23] The up-state New York Dutch peasants had a terrible time, still enduring indentured labour. Also, on how the (early) Monroe Doctrine suited the UK, see Roberts (2012).

[24] Tariff protection was/is a tax avoidance strategy, which hit the poor hardest. Comparing the United Kingdom with the US federation (in Chapter 7), the UK is not a federation nor

Federal Reserve System as it rose to prominence in WWI. Of importance for this chapter is that the well-informed small farm conflicts over money ended, farmers' sensible desires thwarted, in the 'gilded age' (from the 1890s onwards). Top bankers in Wall Street, like J. P. Morgan, straddled industry and banking, and the White House and Congress started to operate in an 'integrated' manner with bankers. They moved from lending for production, to consolidating and packaging corporate securities into 'Trusts' with huge corporations (General Electric, US Steel and many more).

Democratic participation narrowed. Although President Teddy Roosevelt tried 'to bust the 'Trusts', chances were slim, given J. P. Morgan was globally powerful, having helped to bail out the English Barings Bank that nearly folded in 1890. Furthermore, Congress members took bribes from big business (such as Standard Oil), and connections grew. A Senator and millionaire businessman, Nelson Aldrich, came to play a major role in the founding of the US Federal Reserve in 1913, along with Morgan and other Wall Street bankers. They had so increased their control over the US economy that the former nineteenth-century democratic disputes *against* a central bank were lost, to a US Fed that was pro-Wall Street and pro-American global ambitions.[25] And this came to pass in the 1914–18 world war.

Veblen satirised the gilded age. These financier-business men were always disruptive, inefficient and cause of depressions. The latter are a malady of the businessman, and central banks have rarely coped (well) with depressions. The BoE did not decline gracefully (examined in Chapters 2 to 4, also on CBs' roles in depressions), and it was founded in an entirely undemocratic context; whereas the US Fed

united or single, since this mono monetary non-system is run from the London 'nexus' to suit those interests not, say, Yorkshire's.

[25] Ingham (2004: 8) on the 'cross of gold' protests ending in the gilded age. Prins (2014: 14–16) describes the 'money trusts' e.g. J. P. Morgan's control of 70 per cent of the steel industry in 1901. Also, John D. Rockefeller with City Bank head James Stillman, combining with Standard Oil, Union Pacific and other railroads and banks. She describes Morgan's help to Barings (whose crisis had global repercussions). Teddy Roosevelt disliked 'muckrakers' – meaning a press critical of US Congress (Prins 2014). Bribes to say, the *FT*, were the 'done thing' in London too.

came at a time when grass-roots small farm options lost completely. Curious to note, the Fed's 'elite' founders met secretly in 1910, hiding from press critics, to design the only other CB like the BoE, to promote Wall Street. Only 60 per cent of Americans had effective voting rights to 1970.[26]

THE AUSTRALIAN MONEY STORY

Given its early, varied capitalist phases, America joined late the two most highly *urbanised* countries with full wage labour systems, in which dependency on jobs, money and state services was total: UK and Australia. Quite civil, often decent US scholars are convinced that the USA had the first 'Post Industrial' society in around 1970, but that is 100 years too late. Polanyi and Marx stressed how the English Enclosures created landless, 'free to starve' wage labour, also the prerequisite of the Australian agribusiness-labour scheme: post industrial.

The monetary (central bank) story of Australia herein was a surprise for an Australian to find, and I have no wish to advertise its current neo-liberal, indecent political class rule and capital investment strike. Medium-sized Australia never had BoE or US Fed ambitions, yet its unusual capitalist money development is unknown in the central bank literature (or Australia today); rarely mentioned either, are Canada's or India's central banks.[27] Another excuse for my Australian case study was a vivid 2010 example of the parochialism that always 'puts the US first', in some highly influential pro-austerity economists' work. Americans Carmen Reinhardt and Kenneth

---

[26] See Veblen (1904); further on I discuss voting rights and how these Fed designers wore disguises to travel to their meeting. That seems to show something more than what one would expect of ruthless leaders: perhaps a fear of the democratic process, even of mockery.

[27] I only unearthed Australia's monetary history in 2013, after decades of amassing primary material on the Fed and BoE; thanks to V. J. Carroll. (At the time of writing, the right-wing Commonwealth Government had a slim majority.) The Post Industrial thesis (Bell 1976) is about employment sectors: rural, industrial and services. In the USA, small farmers were a huge (informal, part self-sufficient) rural sector, and Europe similarly with peasants, cf. UK and Australia by about 1860.

Rogoff (R&R) presented debatable statistics on public debt to growth ratios, eagerly grasped by governments from Germany to Britain to justify more austerity.

Their survey of countries' records during the postwar years excluded Australia, Austria, Belgium, Canada and Denmark. R&R's second focus on selected years, to finger 'high debt countries', omitted Australia from 1946–50, New Zealand from 1946–9, Canada from 1946–50, former Dominion countries, from the very years that they – notably NZ – had full employment (FE), low inflation and very *high growth*.[28] This is no surprise if, in addition to R&R's 'threshold' not existing (countries with low growth tend to have higher public debt from reduced tax intakes), R&R conveniently knock out strong counter-evidence. These former Dominions, with central banks state-owned, had implemented their egalitarian traditions. In those postwar years, their rigorous low inflation: high growth/FE regimes taxed progressively to reduce inflationary trends in public debt. The result was vibrant activity with public debt used for successful long-term development. R&R's research was criticised, but such countries are dreary outliers. Austerity spread as the political fashion du jour, given that the US never *truly* produced traditions to support social democracy; elites kept union-related labour parties from developing seriously. It is far easier for US orthodoxy to knock out different countries' decent data.

However indecent it is (again), Australia's early white story is 'uncluttered' by white Canada's past feudal peasant relations (Québécois) or slavery-indentured labour (USA). The three countries had fitful, diverse federation processes. All settler countries had Indigenous peoples. Genocide was widespread in all these white

---

[28] Computational errors were uncovered in Reinhardt and Rogoff's "Growth in a Time of Debt" study, by less influential economists, Herndon, Ash and Pollin (2013) citing R&R's work in detail, on which I rely. NZ's real GDP growth rates to debt, of 7.7, 11.9, –9.9 and 10.8 per cent during the 1950s, did not appear; R&R only included NZ's *high debt* in 1951 when GDP was –7.6 per cent at lower growth. Other countries were allegedly cut on alphabetic grounds (!), so their statistical measure is flawed on their 'above 90 per cent debt danger' alleged threshold to 'low growth', however inadvertently.

invasions, with land stolen everywhere. On a blank-slate capitalist structure but a strong state, Australia's case shows money's perennial instability was experienced as a direct cause of white hardship, which gave rise to public debate and demands that quickly solidified across classes, sectors and political parties, for a well-designed, state-owned central bank that private banks neither wanted nor ever liked. It's a pessimistic story of egalitarian traditions and nation-building states attacked by intransigent capitalist banks. But a legacy survives in the Reserve Bank of Australia (RBA). It had fights with banks and right-wing governments – often to the latter's loss.

Primarily this example shows how cultural-political milieus make certain money decisions possible.[29] Australia became *modern* at its 1788 invasion, when Britain established a totally capitalist economy and, briefly, a military convict colony. The state was authoritarian, the UK Governor ruled by decree, but a ruling class (militia officers) formed instantly. Willing free labour was lacking. In common with other sparsely populated, huge land areas that developed to meet European industrial demand for rural products, UK officer-capitalists found that value is never added without labour. The Americas, invaded centuries earlier, used imported serfs and slaves, since (embattled) Indigenous peoples often refused. Argentina coerced peasant indentured labour but with less state monopoly of violence than that deployed in 'New South Wales' (NSW), Australia's first British name. Colonising European capitalist empires *created* markets forcibly.

Being a faraway, late starter (NZ after), Australia consisted in politically similar mixed-migrant colonies marked with disobedience

---

[29] To expand, the American 'post-industrial society' thesis has it starting in the 1960s, but UK and Australia were 'postindustrial' a hundred years earlier, i.e., in their very low rural and high service sector employment. The mass of US small farm employment only declined around 1930, in contrast. As Marx (*Capital* Vol. I: last section) said of Australia's UK invasion and a Lord Wakefield's scheme for South Australia, white migrant labour had to be priced out of land buying or squatting, for agribusiness to work labour and, in fact, find labour-replacing techniques.

to British domination.[30] Resistance included mutually destructive, hugely expensive Red Coats' wars against Indigenous guerrillas;[31] also costly officers' mutinies against (early) far-sighted UK Governors; and theft of Indigenous (aka Crown) land under UK *terra nullius* laws. Proto-agribusiness capitalists squatted on land, via primitive accumulation (murder) and capital (via profiteering on selling rum 'lifted' from Sydney's UK Commissariat).[32] They brutalized convict labour (that Governors kept freeing to class relations, small farms and elite jobs). Public-private partnerships (PPPs) began with the UK 'Rum Corps' (to sarcastic wits).[33] Capitalist money was installed from the outset.

The British had no clear rationale for invasion. Settlement, mainly urban coastal, was connected to state-built roads and railroads, designed to serve vast agribusiness stations in the outback. It proved monstrously costly. Britain ceded political rights to 'responsible government' at 1856, long before Ireland.[34] Having sent out radicals, highly-skilled convicts and 'assisted' free settlers, insubordination might have been expected. It was no accident that federation

---

[30] The USA, Canada, New Zealand, Argentina and South Africa were other 'land rich–labour short' large-scale developers for wool, cotton, timber etc.; see Schwartz (2000: his Chapter 9) on temperate zones.

[31] Early wars against the Aboriginal peoples were one-sided, e.g. white settlers and Red Coat losses in Sydney were comparable on average to the Somme; guerrilla tactics easily beat Marines' slow-loading muskets (Denholm 1979: 27–38), which was not the case later. Britain was not the only culprit in the Americas, Africa and so on; e.g. Finland against *white* Indigenous people.

[32] Illegal 'Officer-Squatters' initially depended upon convict servile labour, but in 1807's UK Act, could not import Indians as slaves; this UK 'Rum Corps' also hired 'Native Police' to kill other Indigenous peoples. Their total number was about 800,000 pre-invasion; deaths from murder/wars were (approx.) 20,000, and from white disease and resource-loss, 120,000; to leave 200,000 by 1850 (Hunter and Carmody 2015). These experts stress chicken pox. The 2016 Census has 786,689 Australians identifying as Aboriginal (abs.gov.au).

[33] Britain's convicts enabled UK officer-capitalist agribusiness. See McLean (2013) on the early PPPs.

[34] See Dyster and Meredith (2012: their Chapter 1) on Australian free labour: convicts were freed to become architects, accountants, farmers, lawyers and educators, compared with indentured serfs (in Argentina etc.). Free migration became the large growth factor to this day. UK Treasury gave up all claims to gold and to 'Crown land' in 1852, with responsible government from 1856 (larger colonies first): Butlin (1986: 30) and Cryle (1989).

in 1901 created the *Commonwealth* of Australia with slogans like
'Mammon or Millennial Eden'.[35] A unified, modern class-system of
high wages (perennial labour shortages, and from wage legislation)
and Australia-wide social movements started in no time, especially
unions, feminists and chartists. The lack of deference seemed to
exhaust Whitehall's Colonial Office and appalled City elites. Britain
nearly by accident settled on making money from debtors forced to
grovel (London assumed) and large-scale imports, and exports which
fluctuated.

Not lawless, it did not have the sizable excluded populations
of most settler countries. Military to early democratic authority – of
the European and US 'enlightenment' – was largely obeyed. Bustling,
substantial cities quickly grew, with chartists' demands met in 1855
and radical (capitalist) presses printing anything that mocked English
snobbery, banker and rich *squatter* lawlessness (theft, murder of
Aboriginal peoples) and pretensions to aristocracy.[36]

Most exceptional of the social democracies were demands for
state authority, not only for justice in unequal contests over land, life
chances, mooted workhouses and indentured labour, but also over
money.[37] UK Treasury tried to control money and banks to suit the
City, foolishly, nakedly. The initial convict colony quickly engaged
in exports, using expedients like 'miscellaneous coins, private promissory notes ... and bills on London ... of the UK Commissariat or
missionary societies', which led to a contrast between anything

---

[35] The Commonwealth was itself an English 1640s civil war slogan, and the anti-Mammon
slogan is around a Rotunda in Centennial Park, Sydney.

[36] South Africa excluded 90 per cent from all rights during Apartheid. On Australian
white male suffrage in 1855, see Butlin (1986: 30); cf. Canada had property-based white
male British non-Catholic suffrage (so excluding Catholic Quebecois); mostly in its
Confederation, 1867. Assumed groveling of Australians to the City is analysed in Butlin
(1961) from records of banking letters, 1828 to 1951, between London and Sydney of what
eventually became the ANZ bank. The local Bank of NSW started in 1817 (re-badged
Westpac in its near-fatal 1980s).

[37] On egalitarian policies, industrial rights and nation building, Pixley (2000) cites Beatrice
Webb, who saw Australia in the 1900s as 'a social laboratory'; see also Schwartz (1998).
See Cryle (1989) on Queensland's radical, pro-Aboriginal, anti-squatter presses of the
1830s.

convertible to 'sterling', and the 'currency'. The latter was not convertible except at a huge price (discount). As in other colonies, the *currency* became 'an Australian unit of account', not English money. In 1822, NSW tried a local currency with a Spanish dollar standard. Whitehall terminated that, contradicting its 1821 promotion of grazier squatters (cheap wool), versus state industries, nation-building Governors and parliaments.[38]

Persistent calls arose for a state-owned central bank: the *'People's Bank'*.[39] Each Australian colonial state controlled its fiscal and borrowing policies. 'Plural' voting for the wealthy was soon banned in favour of one vote, one value in the lower houses; by 1891 women and Aboriginal people voted in one state. That became universal *white* suffrage in the Commonwealth constitution 1901, after referenda and elite, racist male-chauvinist protests.[40] Each colony owned banks and enterprises and, pre-Commonwealth, competed tirelessly in building railways, grand Town Halls, assisted migration, R&D on (freight) refrigeration, agribusiness productivity and land conservation: on cheap public credit or London advances.[41] Australia's history includes (peaceful) conflicts against elites. NZ was perhaps firmer, and Canada even more so, later, although the English excluded French Canadians for some time, and it endured UK *and* US dependency.[42] The white 'Dominions' were open international economies with tiny domestic markets: debtor-capitalist developer countries. NSW's universally despised private bankers relentlessly argued *against* a state-owned central bank of budding Labor and Town Liberal design,

---

[38] See Butlin (1986: 27) on sterling versus currency as a local unit of account and the Spanish dollar incident.

[39] The People's Bank idea is stressed in Butlin (1983); Quiggin (2001) and Schedvin (1992); thanks to V. J. Carroll on Butlin references (etc.).

[40] UK assumptions of elite 'responsible government' and property rights were quickly democratised, but the Victorian Parliament was the most recalcitrant against Indigenous and female voting rights (cf. South Australia both), see in e.g. Pixley (1998) and specific voting details in aph.gov.au.

[41] On state credit and Australian colonies' R&D, see Dyster and Meredith (2012: 70–1).

[42] See Chapters 3 and 7 on Canada; its banks primarily used Wall Street markets; on its Bankers Ramp, see Ryan-Collins (2015).

whereas US small-farmer 'populism' opposed 'Wall Street' and 'robber barons', only to lose in the design of the Fed. Australia's story reverses orthodoxy's anti-democracy.[43]

The general nineteenth-century economic problem for settler countries reliant on exports was the gold standard. As Britain slowly gained leadership over this payment system (sterling), nearly all Western Europe benefited, and 'enjoyed persistently favourable balances of trade' from investing/lending and colonising overseas with those countries that used systems of 'holding fluctuating reserves of international currency'. For the latter, such as Argentina, Australia, or the USA to 1900, their 'volatile balances of trade' under the gold standard, meant any 'persistent imbalance was corrected ... by modifying interest rates, prices and incomes, to reverse the underlying causes of imbalance'.

These *distresses* and unemployment occurred in Australia early, given the vast distance and rapid growth of banks, local-owned (the first in 1817) and English-owned. Agribusiness and its city services sector of huge pastoral companies were politically dominant, unlike US small farmers versus Wall Street, but also met huge resistance from an urban civil society with advanced voting rights and trade unions. 'Circulation of gold coins was not an essential part of the gold standard', however, whereas freely convertible note issues, or 'making (national) gold coin an unlimited legal tender' were preferred practices.[44] Banks in Australia could issue their own notes, as in Canada – and faintly like the Scottish free banking system, and kept reserves (short-term sterling assets) in loans to London.[45] Perennial problems

---

[43] The Dominion nomenclature was disliked in Australia, which took the Commonwealth name, infuriating Whitehall etc. Orthodox theorems, say in Calomiris and Haber (2014: 298–312; 454–61), are incorrect about Australia.

[44] See Butlin (1986: 27) for both paragraphs. Argentina had an older rural system. Bruce Greenwald's unpublished paper on the USA as the 'first' service-sector economy and my counter-discussion were recorded at the 'Large-scale crisis 1929 vs 2008' conference, Ancona, Italy, Dec 2015.

[45] On note-issue and free banking, see Schedvin (1992: 5–7); this was highly restricted under UK directions and legislation, see Butlin (1986: 7–25; 26); he notes UK silver coins mainly circulated in Australia early on.

arose from banks' need to 'repress the lending enthusiasm' of their bank branches, the tendency to speculative booms and then withdrawal of lending to agribusiness during busts.[46]

Economists show in Australia's microcosm the capitalist patterns of conflict, less like Britain's industrial and service sectors so neglected by City–Treasury–BoE views. Gold was no fetter to banking sectors, save in countries inordinately reliant on overseas demand. Other countries (than the British Empire, with its vast markets of India) moved ahead from 1850 to 1900. What Australia needed was expansionary sterling *and* local currency (for local industry). Before NSW's and Victoria's gold discoveries (1851), British authorities were intransigent. Cheap food and raw materials were desired but also mobile capital seeks short-term profits, whereas anything involving sunk capital is costly. Each state (as in the USA) invested, specifically in shipping firms; infrastructure; town ports for wool, timber and leather classers; and marketing authorities. Australia was first to develop suburbs (with diverse jobs and coastal views). Skills, good health and their fixed costs give long-term returns. But the fragility of property speculation on infrastructure building (often from illicit insider knowledge of state decisions),[47] share pushing of start-up banks; of new pastoral financial companies and dubious trust firms, often English, suited the City and grazier-squatter interests.[48]

---

[46] See Butlin (1986: 28). This further refutes the line of Calomiris and Haber (2014) of alleged superiority of branch banks to unit banks, since branch banks were *renowned* causes of Australian busts about which, Eichengreen and Mitchener (2003) agree.

[47] We saw City neglect of British industry, whereas Europe's CBs were designed to foster industry. See Dyster and Meredith (2012); Schwartz (2000: 130–3) on rail lines. Property trading on inside knowledge was/is common with road and rail expansion everywhere.

[48] Colonial states had to rectify all the busts. See Butlin (1986: 7–25): eight banks existed before the 1851 discovery of gold: five were locally owned; (by 1860 there were 197 banks, swelling in Victoria's 1880s); English-owned banks had London head offices. Both types financed external trade. The bank branch system took off seriously after gold. On the Note Issue, the UK Acts of Incorporation and Colonial Bank Regulations prescribed it should not exceed paid-up capital, and all debts 'other than deposits should not exceed paid-up capital'. UK Treasury said post-gold amendments to such restrictions were 'quite unacceptable' (Butlin 1986: 9). Graziers (agribusiness) contracted *half* of Australian foreign debt, mostly City.

In 1825 Britain attempted to 'impose a sterling exchange standard on the entire British empire'. For NSW, this involved selling Commissariat bills for British silver coins. But British expenditure on NSW was not growing at the pace of demand for imports by the fast-growing NSW private sector. The experiment was abandoned within a decade. The gold discoveries gave Australia slight control over Britain's edicts against monetary expansion.[49]

Many players grumbled, mutually irritated, perhaps since Australia was so consistently redistributive and very wealthy. In Australia, cosmopolitan cities and busy presses created a public sphere in which not only the Irish thought of English elites less as enemies, than figures of fun. A somewhat inclusive education gave many Mary Wollstonecraft's feminism and for example Adam Smith saying it was unjust that capitalists marked down labour as a 'cost' (not dividends) when labour alone adds value to non-financial assets. More influenced with under-consumption ideas than with Ricardo or Marx insisting *ad nauseam* that bank money creation was 'fictitious' (when it was urgent), multiplier policies became common. Australia has remained in the top three wealthy countries *per capita* for 200 years with the USA and UK. Minimum wages are still better than in many countries.[50]

Before the 1851 gold finds, a bank crash and 'severe' depression occurred after a rural export boom that led to a NSW legislative 'Committee on Monetary Confusion' (how frank). It proposed a State Bank in 1843. Legislators (squatters and Town Liberals) criticised the

---

[49] Most British colonies resented the 'standard'; usually white ones could protest publicly. With the Australian goldfields, the City and UK Treasury lost potential gains (Butlin 1986: 28).

[50] On Adam Smith's ideas of adding value, see Collison (2002). Schumpeter (1954) thought 'A. Smith' was derivative, and Ricardo obstinate on money, aped by Marx – who in other respects was a 'top-notch economist'. In *Capital* Volume I, Marx wrote up Wakefield's South Australian (SA) scheme of pricing crown land out of reach of labour. Rowse (2015) notes under-consumption ideas influenced Labor and Town liberals also, Labor promoted state-owned enterprises to out-compete 'inevitable' capitalist corruption (Goot 2010). On Australia's consistent high wealth and redistribution, see McLean (2013); on minimum wages, see Wilson (2017).

'avaricious and incompetent' banker crisis, not as 'fictitious capital' but a social fact.[51]

Everyone volubly loathed banks beyond the usual: In 1851, the high-grade gold fields were 'an explosive force' in Australia. For that entire decade, gold replaced wool as the chief export and sparked a battle for a Sydney Mint. The NSW government devised the Mint plan that same year. Arguments in the *Sydney Morning Herald* (*SMH*) in 1851 were, first, that a Mint would make the Gold Standard 'work', but second, with the rapidly growing population arriving for the gold rushes, a 'large increase in coin' was needed for the huge expansion of trade. The *SMH* warned of 'monetary chaos' in California after its 1849 gold discovery.[52]

Whitehall's speedy assent to an 'unprecedented' NSW state Mint seemed inexplicable.[53] The Sydney Mint was to be a branch of the Royal Mint, not to control, and it appears the BoE was not asked, since Treasury (under Gladstone) kept both it and Parliament at 'arm's length' over Australia's monetary affairs, to quell (internal) debate. The BoE Governor seemed bemused at Treasury's approval to NSW's owning and running it, saying the Sydney Mint had no merit other than 'putting a little more money into the hands of the diggers'. One can *hear* it. NSW would fund the Mint, which implied UK losing control of 'royal prerogative over coinage'. Another battle over British coins being equal legal tender with Sydney coins was won by NSW, against Whitehall's demand that Sydney's minted coins circulate in the UK and all colonies.[54]

---

[51] Fisher and Kent (1999: 1) note this 'severe' depression. On the NSW Commission, see Gollan (1968: 15–18). Of course, neither type of legislator was free of those attributes either.

[52] The goldfields of NSW and Victoria, in Butlin (1986: 7) who therein notes plans for responsible government were underway before gold, and were completed, save for W. Australia, by the end of the 1850s; the *SMH* is cited Butlin (1986: 28–9).

[53] Despite the then advent of far faster steam ships for mail and gold, reducing colonial insurance costs too, the Sydney Mint was the most significant, Butlin 1986: 30–1 points out. Cable was not until 1872; other Mints soon developed, but outside these Australian ones, he says, Ottawa was only allowed a mint in 1908.

[54] The mystery of Whitehall is in Butlin (1986: 30–1); there he conjectures Whitehall was scared of Californian chaos and wanted total control over the Sydney Mint. The BoE, and a Tory royalist's fulminations are cited in Butlin (1986: 48; also 29, 32–3): Formal letters

Only banks opposed the Sydney Mint plan, to keep their gold dealing. On the goldfields in 'popular thinking, the local price of raw gold, and the exploitation of diggers by gold-buyers and banks, came to be seen as central points in the mint question'. The Eureka Stockade rebellion at one of Victoria's minefields broke out in 1854 (a rare uprising in Australia's white history), partly for the Mint. And, despite banks' 'specious' arguments against it, exchange rate fluctuations were much reduced once the Sydney Mint started operating in 1855 whereas, since 1788, currency – as notes and coins – and sterling, conflicted.[55]

With the Mint, Australia's money supply (bank notes and Sydney coins) expanded to great effect, while Europeans saw the gold influx as sufficient to give up silver (US small farmers did not).[56] Post-gold, English consortiums (usually with aristocrats on the Boards for alleged prestige to the trade in debt) were as keen move into Australian banking businesses as locals. After the UK Treasury's disapproval of various Australian-owned bank charters pre-gold, it 'rapidly processed' charters for British banks to get into the gold boom. It marked the London troika's disinterest in declining UK industry, too.[57] Chances for the City and distressed aristocrats were rosier elsewhere - too much so for banking's self-restraint. The number of

to and fro are cited between the Colonial Office and the Governor under NSW Parliament orders; UK Treasury finally lost control at least by 1855 when NSW gained responsible government (Butlin 1986: 48–50). As well, the Royal Mint was then in chaos, trying to get rid of titled sinecures (cronies), argues Butlin (1986: 31).

[55] Sydney's Mint was more trustworthy (than banks or the Royal Mint), and, what UK *and* NSW wanted, at NSW's cost. The diggers' quest for the Mint is in Butlin 1986: 32; Eureka was ostensibly about Victorian state charges on diggers. In Australia, banks gave specious arguments, according to Butlin throughout, because they lost control of gold deals to the state (of NSW), not only their exploiting of diggers.

[56] See Dyster and Meredith (2012: 42, 57) and Schumpeter (1954) also notes that the 'bi-metallism' of, say, France, acknowledged that the dearth-to-rush of gold was destabilising and that keeping both silver and gold supplies might maintain some 'stability'. The full gold standard destroyed US small farmers' effective economic and political clout (Galbraith 1975b; Gollan 1968: 44–5).

[57] On the 'favoured' UK banks, a detail I like, see Butlin (1986: 7, 12); on Board-stacking with dukes, marquises and baronets: V. J. Carroll (personal communication, 2015); also Cannon (2013). The case further proves Ingham's thesis (1984), since global industrial competition was outpacing the UK's.

banks, the branching, and shadow-banks in Australia swelled (to well over Canada's) but 'gold' was less a question than bank note issue.[58]

This case upends today's naïve monetarist 'histories'. Social movements turned to governments to correct the excesses of banks and rapacious agribusinesses. Squatters (graziers) used barefaced tactics, 'socialising their losses and capitalising their gains' (a typical phrase in muckraking) and profiteered from inside knowledge. A *populism of elites* supported UK control. Town Liberals, agrarian socialists, even the Country Party, often agreed with the growing Labor Party, which aimed to introduce democracy to the labour market and over the money markets and banks. The horror was bank money inflation, perhaps from Australia's high living standards since 1788. Several credit booms, deflations and depressions were not pinpricks in a life of grinding poverty to Australians (except the Indigenous peoples) but electorally shocking.

So it came to pass, that NSW *habitually* used effective demand policies and money supply expansion to counter depression from sudden 'floods/droughts' of international capital and speculation. (The multiplier, stressing services, operated long before Keynes.)[59] These were purposefully used in a *counter-cyclical role* as investment 'engines' to foster recovery, with programmes of public works on adequate pay rates to reduce hardship and prevent market stagnation. If public policy favoured rural productivity (labour-replacing), boosting export and service sectors for coastal cities' infrastructure created the jobs and helped factories. NSW tended to lead. Colonial government securities (bonds) were readily available by the 1860s

---

[58] Canada had forty branch banks between 1870 and 1914 (Ryan-Collins 2015: 17); Australia had 197 in 1860, and more in 1880. In Canada, a far older white settlement, banks served a mainly lumber-agricultural economy, highly stable in that period. Ryan-Collins cites 18,000 unit banks in 1890 in the USA, but Australia had a worse crash in 1890, even to Eichengreen the doyen (Eichengreen and Mitchener 2003), than in the rich also far older USA.

[59] See Dyster and Meredith 2012 on 'droughts' of hot money, and my Chapters 3 and 4 for details. A decade before Keynes, Australian economist L. F. Giblin codified the multiplier impact of production of local services (universities, hospitals, schools etc.), which were neither importable or exportable (then), cited in Coleman, Cornish and Hagger (2006).

to most private savings banks. Governments also devised their own
state-run models of the British post office savings banks (NSW's savings bank in 1832) for a 'steady flow of funds at low interest' in securities, and for states' avid 'borrowing for the public works' demanded
of a rising population and recurring 'financial crises'. They spread to
other colonies to meet 'government financial exigencies' and also
made *safe* 'savings bank facilities available widely', with government
savings banks by the 1870s 'sources of loan funds for governments'.[60]
Multiplier policies were perhaps a precedent in Australia although
not pork barrelling.

Laissez faire myths were publicly implausible. Excesses of
mobile capital drowned Australia in the 1880s and parched it in
the 1890s; so-called favours to Australia in the 1920s switched to
demands that foreign banks' profitable advances be remitted immediately in 1930.[61] NSW Treasury learned caution from its 1876–80
inflation (and contraction), to supervise strictly the massive growth
of building societies and land banks.[62] Pompous Victorian banks
were indisputably the cause of the major 1880s–90s boom and bust,
although miscreants liked to blame Barings' crash. In global comparisons, this reckless credit boom is to this day called 'dramatic'.[63]

---

[60] On NSW's 'effective demand' and safe local banks, see Dyster and Meredith (2012: 70–1,
137) and Butlin (1986: 69, 71, 76, 85). Victoria, Queensland (QLD), Tasmania and South
Australia (SA) became separate, 'responsible governments' during the 1850s with NSW;
Western Australia (WA) three decades later. Northern Territory and ACT (Canberra) are
still not states.

[61] See Dyster and Meredith (2012: 356) on 'surges' of mobile capital; also, Dyster and
Meredith (2012: 42) on the BoE/English banks that controlled the growing outflow of
global funds (hot money) from 1890 to 1914.

[62] See Cannon (2013: 119) on the 1878 NSW inflation: £8 million of UK investment; £12
million from NSW selling more Crown land; the 1884–5 drought bankrupted graziers; that
bust made NSW Treasury tighten bank controls, unlike in Marvelous Melbourne.

[63] On the boom/bust, see Cannon's racy text on bank corruption and ostentatious buildings
(Cannon 2013, in its fourth edition since 1966). Pastoral expansion onto marginal land is
always fragile; Barings' collapse was minor to Melbourne's rout. See Gollan (1968: 29) on
careless banks; see Fisher and Kent (1999: 32), of the RBA, on bank branches, managers'
incompetence, dodgy building societies and vast losses to depositors – so 'dramatic' that
for Eichengreen and Mitchener (2003: 34) it is singled out in their extensive survey of
major global credit booms.

A Melbourne land and grandiose building boom, over-investment in the pastoral industry; trade and price fluctuations brought a far longer depression in Australia than elsewhere.[64]

During this calamitous bust, over half of all Australian deposits were suspended and over 61 per cent of all note issue ceased to be 'freely negotiable', but that varied in each colony; New Zealand decided not to join the Commonwealth in consequence. The 1880s' land boom had 'disregarded all caution', blindly assumed rising prices, and 'crumpled' with the banks, after a vast expansion of bank branches with low 'internal control', fraudulent practices and 'fringe' banks. British-owned banks were particularly blithe in their advances, buoyed on a mass of English and Scottish deposits in these banks that paid double the Consol rate. Public derision of the banks' imposed depression barely lifted. 'The share capital of some banks bore the scars of their 1890s reconstruction right up to the 1980s, when the Bank of NSW put a final one out of its misery'. Banking policies, furious topics in the labour, liberal 'protectionist' and 'free trade' agribusiness-socialist movements, left banks cautious for 100 years, although rarely benign politically.[65]

Even before NSW Labor joined a quasi-coalition government in 1891, it aimed for a national, state-owned central bank.[66] Of Victoria, Butlin said, 'the sudden and complete loss of spending power on the

---

[64] It was longer than Australia's Great Depression, 1930s. See Dyster and Meredith (1990) on Argentina's recovery well before Australia, and McLean (2013: Chapter 7), on the length of Australia's 1890s depression.

[65] Gollan (1968) discusses the fraud too, on the banks' 1980s misery, V. J. Carroll (email, 2015). The 1890 crash's immensity in global comparisons, is ignored in Calomiris (2013), who prefers 'bank branching', whereas in Australia's 1880s they were utterly reckless! Australia's 1930 Bankers Ramp is in Chapter 3.

[66] On Labor bank plans, see Edwards (2005: 79). See Butlin (1961: 302) on understating averages, e.g. Tasmania not hit by fraud; on the 1890s bailouts, which to many was 'financial legerdemain', see Butlin (1961: 302); Isaac Isaacs, then Victorian 1890s Solicitor-General and MP, charged one bank and, after (gentile) MPs refused his lawsuit, resigned: Gollan (1968: 39–41). Returning with a larger majority a month after (no surprise), Isaacs later became a Governor-General. NSW Protectionist MPs needed the Australian Labor Party (ALP), which saw tariff as a tax on the poorest (until ALP MPs later bargained for fair wage legislation in return).

business community and on private lives' in three states, left a long legacy:

> Suspicion of financial institutions had long been endemic in
> Australian thinking, becoming active at times of economic stress;
> but a tradition of unscrupulous motives and maleficent policy
> as the normal characteristics of 'the banks' ... a major strand
> in twentieth century politics, owes much to this apparently
> obvious deduction: in the 'nineties [1890s] the banks' *escape by
> reconstruction* was made at the expense of their customers.[67]

In the banks' reconstruction in Melbourne, when that avoided bank-ruptcy, imposed creditor or shareholder losses, depositors were paid, at worst, a few pennies in the pound to, at best, seven shillings and six pence, if they withdrew rather than have deposits 'suspended', and wait years for mergers or better times. Note issue was no longer freely negotiable. British critics enjoyed castigating Victorian state debts, ignoring profligate (UK) private hysteria, Barings' collapse and marked differences to older colonies (Quebec was near feudal, India the ancient 'jewel'). But the pitifully few radical, uncorrupted MPs could not stem 1890s' Victorian Parliament excesses and ersatz *laissez faire* bank policies, since MPs were not paid (NSW initiated a MP allowance in 1889). Both Victorian Houses were stacked with bankers and squatters. One State Premier, mired in milking depositors' funds in the dubious bank he also headed, rushed a Voluntary Liquidation Act through, to prevent his and other Melbourne companies from compulsory liquidation and public court examination. He thereupon appointed himself Agent General in London, to which he 'fled'. Cartoonists were in hot demand.[68]

---

[67] Butlin (1961: 302, my emphasis), also cited in Gollan (1968: 27). In comparative policy literature, the cliché Australia was as neoliberal as Anglo-America, is incorrect. NZ and Australia, to social policy experts, had 'Wage Earners Welfare States'; plus, it put no strain on state budgets. On Australian wealth, we saw McLean (2013) and see Schwartz (1998; 2005), on social democratic aspects in Australia.

[68] See for the fraud in so-called reconstruction to cartoons Cannon (2013: 33, 49–50, 62–3, 189) and Butlin (1961: 302), also on British hypocrisy.

This scandal of 'reconstruction' is worth noting for the GFC fallout and on to Europe (in Chapter 7). And, like 1890s Britain and the USA, the Melbourne public was shocked to find 'the Elect', and Anglicans, had committed banking frauds. Ostensibly religious capitalists aimed to squash male workers' freedoms, and instil virtues of thrift, savings and trust in banks.[69] Calvinist and 'Temperance' religiosity did not endure its 'shameful controversies' thereafter.

Unlike Victoria, NSW Parliamentary reforms had earlier enabled the Labor Party to stand candidates to voter acclaim. In NSW's distress of 1892, not comparable to Victoria's, NSW Premier Dibbs, allied with Australian Labor Party (ALP) MPs, issued a proclamation to prevent a run that began on the NSW Government Savings Bank, stating that NSW would guarantee that bank's deposits. It did not stop Melbourne banks from dragging down their Sydney 'connections' who 'refused to make bank notes a first charge upon bank assets'. Dibbs declared bank notes legal tender anyway.[70]

MODEST MODELS, SOMEWHAT LESS ELITE

This Black Swan case destroys orthodox efforts to find innocent banks. Australians endured years of bank rackets and foolishness, aided handsomely by ruling elites of agribusiness and politicians with nefarious connections to the City and Whitehall. Britain's designs fooled few. Early political coalitions were fluid; their 'counter-cyclical' policies had wide support. The ALP and the unions opposed corruption and, understanding money so well, later aimed to prevent bank *money and asset* inflation, than provide a lender of last resort (let alone to repeat the 1890s 'reconstruction').[71] In an 1893 NSW Royal

[69] On a Temperance hotel of a (dubious) capitalist, see Cannon (2013: 367–9). See also of the many *public embarrassments* the 'Elect' faced: in 1894, a Rev. P. J. Murdoch, father of Sir Keith, grandfather of Rupert, suggested that a home for destitute children in Melbourne, run by a Presbyterian woman, should give preference to, and feed only Presbyterian children; she refused.

[70] Cannon suggests NSW was somewhat 'inoculated' from Victoria's *laissez faire*, including he says (2013: 119 – 128) by Dibbs.

[71] Australia's Black Swan is not a counterfactual (see Chapter 3) but *counter-evidence* (the idea that 'all swans are white' is falsified); Bernanke (2000: 95) mentions a recent populist,

Commission, a national bank proposal wanted all private banks to invest in government securities by law, to be held in reserves, and to nationalise the note issue.[72]

A novel central bank model grew fitfully,[73] earlier than Canada, NZ and India in the 1930s–40s. These states created distinct CB models too. People's well-being demanded they all gain national monetary sovereignty from the UK or USA: a thankless task. After the 1934 BoC Act, Canada's Liberals declared a rebellion against US Fed functions and BoE war finance; the BoC would not be a 'banker to the banks' but to government, although to 1938, it was a private share-ownership (BoE) model.[74] Stricter, given the colossal 1890s' crash, and older, consensual aims for prevention, Australian Labor wanted a *strong, intrusive* State-owned central bank to work against banking's pro-cyclical habits of lending aggressively in a boom and contracting harshly in depression. The ALP proposed currency and bank reforms to bring 'profound social changes to the advantage of workers'. Banks could be generative, but instead proved recalcitrant. From 1901 at federation, before Labor took majority office in 1910, private banks told short-lived Commonwealth governments that under no circumstances would they accept a Canadian system. Canada's Treasury required banks to hold 40 per cent cash reserves in government notes

not Karl Popper. Calomiris and Haber (2014) insist that all bank fragility is from populist (non-elite!) demands. They finger US small farmers, and pose a counterfactual on French-Canadian ('peasants'), arguing that had the Québécois been early included, politically, they "would have" wanted unit banks – something which Calomiris and Haber cannot prove or disprove since French-Canadians could not vote then. They are incorrect in seeking support for their flimsy (anti-democratic) counterfactual in Australia, given its bank branches and the 'populist elite' 1890s' crash.

[72] See Butlin (1983: 122) on the NSW Commission of 1893; the City and Whitehall loathed all this, but with 1901 federation, the note issue was crucial across parties.

[73] 'Fitful' is in Coleman et al. (2006: 229), citing L. F. Giblin's Commonwealth Bank of Australia (CBA) history. Inquiries/debates on the 1890 crash *and* the Constitutional conventions for federation (1901) consumed the 1890s (Gollan 1968: 72).

[74] On the ex-colonies, India was not independent until 1947, and on Canada, see Ryan-Collins (2015: 4, 16, 17).

(so lacking in Melbourne's disaster), that may account for Canada's bank stability, given similar bank note issue and lacking a central bank.[75]

But Australian banks *knew* that 1901 federation would entail legislation over banks. Despised, and more concentrated after their 1890s disgrace of reckless note issues, banks wanted government excluded yet feared all politicians; probably why they dared not *demand* lender of last resort (in a CB), nor dared protest losing their former Note Issue rights.[76] Since they gained 'more criticism than profit', banks accepted that federation would involve Treasury commanding their note issues – it was a handy public 'free loan' to the Commonwealth. Andrew Fisher's ALP majority government passed a Note Issue Act in 1910. Fisher also engaged in modest (specified) debt financing for public infrastructure, which banks complained 'treated the note issue reserves as a convenient fund to raid when in need'. To mollify alleged 'wild experiments in paper money', in 1911 a cautious state-owned Commonwealth Bank of Australia (CBA) was founded under Fisher (that is, not a central bank but a *public competitor* to banks).[77] Private banks whinged about the Bank ever after, but states

[75] In Gollan (1968: 70), and Schedvin (1992: 46) described fairly Labor's counter-cyclical aims. Gollan cites well-informed ALP debates (1968: 74; 48) such as using Bagehot's BoE critiques as a model; or how the US demonetising of silver in 1873 meant the US gold-based dollar rose in value (but US small farm remedies could suggest either a quantity theory: dig more silver too, or preferably, a managed currency: 'greenbacks'). As well, Gollan cites bank resistance to any state control; how political opponents said the ALP and/or workers were 'unfitted' and unable to know banking's 'mysteries' (1968: 60; 84); banks' refusal of the Canadian system is in Gollan (1968: 75–6). Canada's high reserve requirement is *counter-evidence* to Calomiris (2013).

[76] See Gollan (1968: 60; 90–1) on unanimity in the new Commonwealth parliament against banks. Another aspect of the BoE model, Lender of Last Resort (LOLR) had 'political complications' to Schedvin (1992: 54). I suspect Schedvin meant the scandal of 'reconstruction' in the Melbourne crash of 1893. Discounting of treasury bills (at a rate for LOLR to work) was not until June 1931; cf. Norges Bank was LOLR by 1890, with a similar export economy; see Ugolini (2011).

[77] See Butlin, on 'more criticism' and a 'free loan' instead of to banks (1961: 330, 347–50), who therein argued that parliamentary CBA debates were not very contentious, nor were the Note Issue 'raid' or 'paper money' fulminations linked to bankers' carping about Treasury's Note Issues to be held at 25 per cent of gold reserves. Prime Minister Fisher ignored the carping to build railways and defence (WWI). The Notes were Australia's legal tender, although if presented to Treasury were exchangeable for gold then, but not later (Gollan 1986:86).

had major tax powers (to 1942) and already owned savings banks for 'cheap' loans and securities for public finance. Monetary expansion/ contraction already had fruitful remedies.[78]

Labor's aim of the 'People's Bank' started with a state 'monopoly' of banking in 1911, to be gained not by nationalising banks but by founding a competitive (state-owned) trading bank that, Labor alleged, would improve, even drive out private ones. The Bank took two decades to become a central bank despite such old demands, and states' regular use of the multiplier.[79] Its initial function was to undertake commercial or trading banking and to run the Commonwealth's business. This alone was contentious for capitalist banking interests – their dubious refrain, *ad nauseam*, was that a non-private yet profitable bank made them face unfair competition. During WWI, the CBA's London branch manager said he faced 'repugnance' to the Commonwealth Bank from the 'monied interests in the City', and its borrowing from the City was not helped 'politically' by UK Labour's keen interest in its state-ownership.[80]

In sum, powerful threats and strikes of the major finance centre and currency hegemon of the day always causes difficulties for all countries and are hard to separate from domestic questions. Australia's case, purely capitalist through Britain's invasion and total land theft, with unions able to meet on relatively fair terms with

---

[78] Ironically, in the 1914 election, conservatives campaigned (and sadly lost) for the Note Issue to be *included* in the CBA Act. Bankruptcy laws, bills of exchange and promissory notes would be uniform by general consent (one difference from the EMU of 2001; see Chapter 7). On that, and savings banks, see Butlin (1961: 352) and Schedvin (1992: 21–2).

[79] Not-for-*commercial*-profit meant the profits went to one shareholder, the Commonwealth. See Fisher and Kent (1999: 14–18) on the 1880s–90s savings banks in colonial states, which were also customers' 'safe havens' during the 1893 crash; on CBA's competition aim, see Gollan (1968: 57). Decades for a CB were bank and right-wing opposition; thus, the 1910 Notes Bill faced hysteria including snobbery about the hygiene of Notes used in the 'slums', and the 1911 CBA innovation aroused 'bitter' and 'intense partisan feelings' about, say, the manipulation of banking by 'John Fat Esq.' said Gollan (1968: 92–4).

[80] Bank whining (Butlin 1983) and detail, Chapter 4. A London manager to his CBA Governor in Sydney during WWI, cited by Gollan (1968: 150–3). The Bank came to prominence in WWI. War and postwar debts preoccupied state and Commonwealth governments (Gollan 1968: 128–45).

large-scale employers, demonstrates the following. 'State-capitalist money' is the primary mover for good or ill, for economic activity or stagnation. Well understood in that context, the Commonwealth state (also NZ's) that democratised quite early had a role in taming this much-needed if critical money.

Eventually, the 'upstart' central bank became a stern Commonwealth Government's and banks' banker to work against deflationary and mostly inflationary tendencies of private banks and states – successfully, yet banks and Anti-Labor political forces fought it bitterly and decades later, mostly won (by 1960). Immense difficulties in many countries, also from the peak money-centres, are explored in Chapters 3 and 4. This case study confirms that even with social forces aiming to *tame capitalism* peacefully with a democratically controlled central bank, these driving factors rarely survive unchanged.

The logic and social justice that may appear in monetary policy can easily turn into the harsh opposite when state, financial and economic forces combine to reverse them. Control over the production of money is the major conflict that constrains central bank authority over money. Central banks with social justice mandates will mostly end in cognitive and emotional dissonance in balancing policies between the relative strengths of governments and of financial sectors, global and local. Price stability and FE were achieved in many OECD countries in the 1945–70s era, which had never been seen before. That ended by about 1980, although Sweden was the longest standout for everyone able and willing to work. Note also that current employment statistics count as 'employed' anyone who laboured for pay for an hour in the reference week. That is not a 'job'.

Since the logic of the full employment (FE) period is so rarely analysed – not even after the GFC and its further inequalities – a brief discussion is in order. It is a 'standard' by which the capacities of central banks, their policies and operations, are assessed in this book. The logic cannot rest on monetary policy alone, but must combine with fiscal policy openly and, above all, broad democratic social support.[81] Unpleasant or optimistic situations are therefore the running motif in the book. Far from orthodox ideas of a thing-like economy and of central bank techniques as a slow 'evolution', the book takes a different tack. It attempts to look at social *contexts* of central banks, since the advent of some democratic norms, with this undemocratic, mysterious, *quasi-global* arena of money creation of states and of financial institutions.

CENTRAL BANKING'S COGNITIVE AND EMOTIONAL DISSONANCES

'Dissonance' is another important concept running through the book. I relate it to new democratic processes and to central banks' typical, recurring functions. These are, in brief, that central banks can easily induce a recession and great hardship on the various inflations thrown up from social or literal (war) conflicts, to the benefit of banks and *rentiers*, but can rarely specify war financing methods (in Chapter 2); likewise, they perennially find it *difficult* to control bank money (see Chapter 3). As for getting out of Depression, they cannot do much but 'reflate' (to deflate *more* is disastrous): this refers to their interest rate policies (cheap or dear money). For ameliorating Depressions, CBs can do little but support and combine with the sources needed for FE and social investment, which have only been seen once (see Chapter 4). Later chapters show how that ended in the 1970s when socially-useful private bank money switched to reckless money creation. Chapter 9 worries that if this is uncontrollable with democratic procedures further abused, CBs might best seek the absurd: to do their best under whatever bleak cards they are dealt.

The concept of 'dissonance' under FE meant that CBs must avoid inflations, but not deflate into depression. Dissonance arose

---

[81] A well-known macabre joke that emerged during Wall Street's great 1929 Crash put the problem of inflation-deflation well. If central banks only use rate changes, they are 'pulling a string' with terrible incalculable results like depression, but one can't 'push a string' at all, to get out of deflation. Often fiscal policy is better equipped (and other institutional mechanisms) for both problems.

when they deflated to increase unemployment rates. It is not to claim the 1945–70 era was perfect (!), just to stress FE had never existed before and, after 1975, decent jobs dwindled. However, central bankers now know what is possible and desirable *logically and ethically*, if impossible for them alone to achieve. In practice, the 1945 FE era did not welcome women – half the population; so, jobless rates excluded 'discouraged workers', as women and others were in fact. They didn't count. Given that great leeway for the authorities and employers, and, in many democracies, segmented discriminatory markets of low-paid casual workers, in hindsight it is puzzling that FE created such a *backlash* – without underlying anti-democratic forces. But thereupon, cognitive and emotional dissonances set in (see Chapter 6).

Second, FE did not end for over determined reasons insisted on by (some) central bank advisers (e.g. the mythical 'Philips curve', in Chapter 6, was a tall story) or allegedly shocking wage demands alone. Lacking any designer of harsh policy, old financial patterns reappeared, yet under near irreversible changes (oligopolies; urban life; nuclear war states) and (reversible) precarious democratic processes. Postwar social mobility of male FE, open universal education, pensions, often with security of health systems and cash benefits (neither universal in the USA) were quite contrary to the severe contractions after WWI (see Chapter 2). The 1920 reversion to deflationary austerity, an obliterated public scandal, and banks and central banks imposing further austerity in the deeply depressed early 1930s, even in countries that remained democratic (see Chapter 3), resulted in capitalism's near-collapse and World War II. In the 1940s–50s after such a terrible era, fairer policies tempered money elites' resentments at so-called upstarts and unions desiring money as well (in Chapter 4) under always-weak democracies. These upstarts were not all white or male. Not that women and blacks ever ran the show, but life-chances slowly improved until the 1970s. FE was thereupon lost and the dual remits of two central banks barely applied, least of all in the Fed: a cognitive or legal dissonance (see Chapter 5).[82] William Greider calls Fed Chair Paul Volcker's drastic contraction starting on 6 October 1979 'a behavior modification' over the entire USA: A 'pact with the devil' formed against Democrat President Jimmy Carter (and many others).[83]

Third, policies for FE, minorities, and female majorities are not luxury irrelevancies to central banks, as some assume. Dissonances first arose after normative and practical constraints on bank money were abolished. This is because central banks (and their states) require – in logic, democratic and ethical considerations – FE for peaceful social integration of varied lives and a tangible sense of citizenship; not bank lending to socially useless asset deals. Central banks know but (often) publicly repress how harsh policies give rise to stigma, inability to make ends meet, social disintegration, violence, and costs on trustworthy, state money in rising private debt and crises.[84] Elites grabbed chances to disparage those who desire money to work with *pay*, security and work-hours of their choice. Meantime, elites claim their 'rights' to obsequious workers and servants, to tax minimisation, to unheard-of wealth: illogical for a CB. These coalitions of interest groups perfected the art of whining. Despite forty people searching for each vacancy, abuse of dole bludgers or cadgers became tabloid news and further disgraces everywhere. US policy added to the illiberal meanness of 'food stamps'. Implementing the vote for blacks caused outrage: US Fed Chair Arthur Burns said he was 'anguished' in 1979 (the year new Chair Volcker crushed FE). Really?

---

[82] Anti-democratic forces, FE defenders, bosses, banks and states did not 'design' the post-1970s outcome inflicted on so many, though CBs were flattened by the Phillips 'invention' (myth), see Chapter 6. CB literature exaggerates the shock of 1970s 'stagflation' we see, whereas I stress the entire 1914–45 era was truly frightful. Cognitive dissonance: a simple way of putting it: a man can say he believes in gender equality, but his practices belie his beliefs, his emotions in favour of women's rights, or for *even* legal restraints on violence.

[83] See Greider (1987), including his Chapters 3 and 4 titles cited. (He gives copious evidence on Nixon's destructive role, we see in my Chapter 5.) Volcker knew he was causing a recession; he masked it publicly, spoke of 'wage deceleration', yet did not support banking's new freedoms. Greenspan did; see my Chapter 7.

[84] The Nixon-Burns period was crucial, but Wall Street went global from the 1950s (see Chapter 5). See Table 8.1 on bank liabilities.

> As the income maintenance programs established by government
> were liberalized, [Burns claimed] incentives to work tended
> to diminish. Some individuals, both young and old, found it
> agreeable to live much of the time off unemployment insurance,
> food stamps, and welfare checks.

Chairing that meeting, the former Chair, McChesney Martin thanked
his Fed successor for stressing

> ... the psychology of inflation and the fact which we are all aware
> of, namely, that *money is a social phenomenon*, and a great deal
> depends on what people think it is or what they think it ought to
> be.[85]

Who had a clean conscience? Martin had a social analysis of money
whereas Burns resorted to abusing the insecure and jobless he
created. By the 1970s many more women were actively seeking
work for money; this increased consumer demand and, in downturns,
increased formal jobless rates, and more child poverty. 'Stagflation'
as Burns (or CB historian Curzio Giannini) had it,[86] was a term that
in fact combined harsh monetary policy against jobs and wages, with
price-wage and asset inflations, to deny those new chances for half
the population: women; and also, US blacks who had escaped indentured labour somewhat – black women most precariously. Women
also tended to work in the growing service sector; Congress attacks
on 'black mothers' living (how shabby) on food stamps grew vicious.[87]
The service sector still dumbfounds central banks since its productivity cannot be 'counted'. Pathetic metaphors – like the incidence
of what Keynesians called 'hysteresis' (note the sexism), meaning
skill loss, or the FE term 'lubrication', a time for re-skilling for new

---

[85] Burns et al. (1979: 14) (just retired to Volcker) and Martin, Burn's predecessor, quoted from
Burns et al. (1979: 26, my emphasis). Burns 'not afraid of prosperity' too, was a stab against
Martin's sternness to banks. See Chapter 5.

[86] Stagflation was the cliché of the 1970s with exaggerated carping; notably Giannini (2011)
argued it was 'as bad' as the 1930s.

[87] On 'black mothers' and southern white senators – 'who will iron my shirts?' – see Pixley
(1993). Anti-food stamp campaigns aimed to force labour to drop its price.

jobs – were excluded later for the 'Philips Curve myth' (see Chapter 6). After being told there was 'no such thing as society', this instrumental masking lexicon of 'hysteresis' vanished. Instead, recourse to household and consumer debt rose as unemployment rose, inflation dropped as wages declined and unions were crushed: elites would 'part pay – part lend' to workers. This entailed illogical, unsustainable household debt.[88] Central banks' denouement beyond the GFC is in Chapters 8 and 9.

Apart from welcoming young people into the adult world or running the dangers of millions of despairing (indebted) people, FE offers instrumental (logical) advantages to the authorities – now a cognitive dissonance in central banks. Milton Friedman's view of FE is hardly worth debating, save monetarism's 1980s onwards impact on central banks, which mostly insisted (again) money was 'neutral'.[89] Another idea he quietly dropped after harsh measures succeeded was a negative income proposed during the height of the 1960s–70s US Civil Rights disputes. Nixon nearly got it through (desperate for popularity).[90] States will never give away money already taxed (HPM) to the able-bodied: even *decent* treasuries need them to work (usefully) for taxable pay. Equally, non-monetarist central bankers rarely touch 'helicopter money' (in Chapter 8). This point is lost on the well intentioned who propose a similar 'basic income'. People do not want 'sit down' money, as Indigenous Australians dismiss it, rather a sense of social purpose and shared citizenship.[91]

Budget deficits always rise when jobs collapse, even in the absence of unemployment benefits (in the USA), because of loss of

---

[88] This is not to denigrate re-skilling, only the terms. Margaret Thatcher's infamous denial of 'society'. On part lend/part pay, see Palma (2009: 858); its lack of logic did worry some central bankers.

[89] Inflation of money's value hurts rentiers most, and see McChesney Martin's methods, showing money is always political, in Chapter 5.

[90] See Craig Freedman (2007), on 'dropped'. Friedman's monetarist ideas of 'negative income' herein draws on Pixley (1993).

[91] HPM is high-powered (state) money, and validating it is via taxes on labour market earned wages and incomes, and on *rentiers*, if not tax evading unearned income. Basic income plans are reported daily; little on why they won't happen.

income tax revenue, and consumer taxes drop from decline in effective demand. Prison expenses have risen sharply, although FE is far *cheaper*: the US shamelessly locks up a quarter of the world's prisoners.[92] The authorities have *logical* interests in FE for full wage-labour societies, unlike employers and financial elites, basking conveniently with no dissonance.

Instrumental interests of producers (employers), banks and Treasuries do however exist in renewed generations of consumers, debtors, workers and taxpayers. Mass migration on the cheap (Gastarbeiter from Turkey or Hispanics to the USA and so on) has extra bad faith – disaffection, poverty and divisiveness.[93] Elites retain a feudal delusion that people will provide a replacement population without modern FE and services. In Great Depressions, of 1930s, and the 1890s when birth control was widely used, populations declined rapidly. There is no hope for children in adults' futures; in other words, people subsisting on wages-only cannot include parenthood in their lives, *and* society suffers. The French, on a nakedly pro-natal drive after the huge losses of the 1871 Franco-Prussian war, provided free childcare to unmarried and married mothers, not mere propaganda. Just in time, sadly, for that new generation to become WWI's cannon fodder, and women to give cheap labour until sent home after both world wars. Only Scandinavia followed very soon with childcare. Most rich countries took decades. Corporations need new workforces and consumers; society its continuation.

Inter-generational debates carp illogically against an ageing population less supported by new generations of taxpayer-workers; pro-war, anti-abortion double standards are back. Many elderly comprise women also most in poverty. *What do central bankers think?* Well, Gary Becker of the Chicago School of Friedman's time sought

---

[92] On US prisons' take-off (1970s: no surprise), see Western (2006). US benefits depend on being previously employed and are short-term.

[93] However, the full UK citizen rights of West Indians and Pakistanis migrating to Britain did not improve their plight much either, as seen to this day; Australia has recently descended to this too.

an economic argument for locking women to unpaid domestic labour and sole caring. He only improved orthodoxy's classing of households as consumption sites, a 'grazing on kitchen floor' model, with a 'small factory' model. His 'household utility function' is incoherent; he relies on a circular line that lower female wages cause women's domestic commitment that create lower wages. It is apologetic. Worse, children are commodities produced in this factory purely as a choice. The 'Demographic transition' is ignored: in societies of wage labourers, beloved children are *personal* financial liabilities and our collective future.[94]

With no empirical economic argument to justify female deprivation and submission to 'century of the child' moralism (worse for non-white women), the authorities copied Becker (ignoring other economists like Hyman Minsky) in scotching 1970s feminist debates. 'Money passing hands' (GDP) and its 'sound value' (CPI) *versus* social security spending, progressive taxes and jobs, are the main (narrow) counted indicators. Unpaid labour has enormous economic value, uncounted, while firms, and lack of pre-school and aged care provisions pass on more tasks; credit raters ignore it. This is not 'informal cash economic activity' that evades tax; it is not paid at all, yet it raises living standards and adds value. Double standards abound: grandparents often make parents' paid work possible, yet they are hounded; the unpaid labour of making a meal nutritious needs purchasing power to buy kitchen fixed capital and fresh produce. Taxes (e.g. VAT) are imposed on people surviving (just, but in housing?), in reciprocal arrangements (maybe) – which reduces effective demand and domestic harmony. The USA is consistently low on UN scores

[94] Australia's birth rate dropped savagely in 1890; Italy's and Japan's are now the lowest to a low OECD base. Household consumers do not eat raw potatoes. Utility is 'individual', but Becker has a Head *mysteriously* called 'M' and another adult 'F'. Becker assumes resources are pooled, altruistically, as if F maximised the head M's 'preference function'. In sum, this reduces biology to destiny; ignores power differentials, foregone earnings in care, M's exit threats; and extols 'skills' e.g. managing garbage. Children are individually *and* collectively vital in all other social-economic formations (feudal, hunter-gatherer etc.), hence the fallacy of composition in modernity. The references and self-citations are in Bittman and Pixley (1997: 174–209).

of OECD states' support, decent wages, housing and health. But this is all in the realm of logic and decent institutions.

MONEY'S LOGIC WITH FULL EMPLOYMENT

However, to recognise in *logic* a FE policy of social and democratic integration – jobs, 'value adding', decent security, services and regeneration – one can use the 'taxes drive state money' argument about High Powered Money (HPM) that the population of able-bodied must be employed taxpayers because they are vital to servicing or retiring state debts and to (financially) supporting their personal dependants not capable of taxable work. Without pensions, low-wage adults are tormented about frail parents' needs. Central banks (*cognitively*) measure how elites pass on costs of responsibility for money.[95] One can combine this *instrumental* logic for FE (i.e. policies to stop CBs' savage deflations) – fostered via public spending on a high-quality 'working' economy – with the fact that banks compete via their privately issued debt to produce money, too: Bank balances are in Tables 1.1 and 1.2. In later CB public talk that avoids how all money is debt (even US Fed Chair Bernanke), crises are allegedly not possible (but befell Bernanke. See Chapter 8). A plausible account knows banks create money, but, like states which tax to service or retire their debts under inflations, healthy economic activity is a must for retiring commercial bank debts too, so that both can 'serve as money'. This compares ill with contortions of Burns to Bernanke.

In Perry Mehrling's subtle argument that 'taxes drive money' but not exclusively, neither state debt nor bank debt is 'default free'. Money can become unacceptable, non-transferable or untrustworthy in both cases. The payment system can collapse, as in 2008. Why did central banks applaud near money's explosion? The previous Fed Chair, Greenspan, seemed to fear while praising markets (see Chapter 7). Bernanke? He did urge jobs (see Chapter 8), with a monetarism

---

[95] References to GDP, CPI, 'Informal activity': Pixley (1993); Bittman and Pixley (1997), also with cited data Janet Finch on UK pensions ending 'torment'.

manqué, which entails excluding bank money, yet knew the Fed created money since he did it publicly (under huge pressure) to save banks, as per monetarist 'histories' of the Great Depression (in Chapters 3 and 6).

An old term, 'Real Bills Doctrine', is defended in Mehrling not because these commercial bank bills are 'safest' (see Chapter 3) or, least of all that 'free banking' without a central bank is possible because banks are allegedly self-regulating. He argues the Real Bills Doctrine's 'main truth' is that some proportionate bank portfolio of such 'self-liquidating bills' gives a bank the liabilities that 'serve as money'. That is, commercial bills are tied to hope that the debts of firms can be serviced and retired with the proceeds from actual economic activity. Schumpeter, similarly, saw its merit *versus* consumer debt. Thus, the *capacity to repay bank debts* resembles how state debt also needs to be 'self-liquidated' by employed taxpayers.[96] Quality debts then, are about the pattern of payments in public and private that rest on inclusive economic activity – FE for all: not charity (as rich tax evaders assume), instead reliable money we all use.

In the USA, after the 1970s calamities, private debts eventually turned (partially) into securitised loans (such as on NINJA) – later proving unsustainable in banks' main portfolio, off balance sheet (see Chapter 8). Everywhere banks became 'egalitarian' in vulgar form: women could borrow as much as they wanted.[97] In one pitifully rare triumph which improves people's capacity to service, or avoid taking unsustainable debt, Fair Work Australia decided in 2010 to award the community sector workforce a big pay rise. In public debate with orthodox economics, heterodox unionists refuted claims about

[96] See Mehrling (2000: 401–4) on state and bank debt, and on the Modern Money Theory (MMT) of Randall Wray: he argues Minsky does not 'conflate' money and state finance as Wray, although Hayek's absurd 'free banking' is anachronistic both ways; Schumpeter (1954). Ingham (2013) on bond vigilantes' impacts on state debt (which the Fed could resist). At present, there is too little central bank or regulatory impact on banks' debt.

[97] NINJA was well-known in 2007–08, an acronym meaning debtors with No Income, No Job, No Assets; i.e. dangerous US bank advances (to the poorest, often female 'NINJAs') that were commoditised, 'packaged', sold on globally, allegedly 'safely', see Schwartz (2009). 'Real Bills' as above are safer.

'gender-neutral market institutions' since they systematically under-value the services produced mostly by women.[98]

So, the logic and ethics of multiple collective actions and beliefs (to Durkheim, 'social facts') are always present in demands for improvement. However, *what came to pass* was the opposite: illogical regression to pre-democratic doctrines. Injustice bred central bank cognitive and emotional dissonances, most of all for or against money as collective desire and need, an institutional social relation between three parties. This became unspeakable: money classes' indecencies became dominant again. In practice, but rarely sayable since the 1970s, central banks have ever more limited control over 'the money supply'. Bank novelties create (or restrict) new money, to disrupt the (*control*) definition of 'money' CBs deploy at any one time, as in 'Goodhart's law'.[99] Employment and useful investment are affected, and speculative behaviour is enhanced.[100] Even the massive pressure from employers' penchant for the lash of hunger is qualified (in logic) by higher profits in FE with its enhanced purchasing power, and the contrasting disaster of debt deflation to active businesses. Banks' and rentiers' interests in *low economic activity* returned, and this now includes corporations tied to financial practices (see Chapter 7). *CBs were suddenly divided into hawks and doves* or rather, the illogically indecent and the decent clear thinkers.

This introductory sketch shows the *growing dissonances in central bank policy* – plain logic contradicted in actions, or twinges of conscience about stagnation, newly created jobless and rapid decline of life chances.[101] Capitalist finance evasions and disruptions, and

---

[98] See John King (2013: 22): orthodoxy ignored 'social structures, social roles, and power relations', these feminists argued. Since then, regression returned.

[99] Simmel (1907 [1990]) rightly spoke of 'three parties' in money creation, debtors, creditors and the state. As Sheila Dow (2006: 38–44); Pixley (2004) say, banks are 'adept' at CB evasion, as in 'Goodhart's Law' of how a CB 'definition of control' shifts to expand or contract money at banks' own pace.

[100] On 'desire' and 'output': the most Durkheimian, sociological economist is André Orléan – see Orléan (2014).

[101] Some officials spoke of betrayal in my interviews, also Abelson, of Barrons, cited in Pixley (2004) said Americans disparaged Wall Street as a Casino from the 1930s to 1980s.

government war interests (we see) recreated this harsh situation. There was a time when 'banks were banks' and thoughtful advances for producers the norm.[102] Forget that. Impersonal forms of finance aimed for control (not decent service) that dismantled the central bank of the 1940s–70s era of (limited) democratic and ethical control over money. As evasive financial deals rose, financial hubs – like the old City of London, Tokyo, Zurich, perhaps Paris – became semi-autonomous from their national hinterlands. Wall Street had ups and downs that dominated. CBs transformed under their globalising (militarising) states, as mobile capital re-gathered force. Logic had nothing to do with it and nor, heaven forbid, bank balance sheets.

CENTRAL BANK AND BANK BALANCE SHEETS

Bank statements do not deceive unless aspects are hidden. Undoubtedly the fact that all money is debt – although not all debt is money, it may be 'near money' as in less transferable, or non-negotiable personal IOUs (credit) – has long been frightening; thus, the fiction of the gold standard. Economists like Léon Walras refused to include the basic practice of the deposit-creating loan in 'theory', because although he knew it, he thought it 'immoral'. At much the same time, in 1909 the no-nonsense editor of *The Economist*, Hartley Withers, outlined an 'imaginary' balance sheet to demonstrate the process of manufacturing money, and to show the mutual indebtedness of banks and bank clients. *The practice is dependent on mutual trust into the future, mutual responsibility*, but shows the fragility of banks. Loans are advances on the back of reserves.

A simplified 'Bank Balance Sheet' stylised after Withers (with Schumpeter), as 'fractional reserves' is below, in Table 1.1. Banks' and Bank Clients' obligations are entered on each side, and the way

A BoE official publicly attacked Thatcher's intent to destroy unions and create a vast reserve army of labour, cited in Palma (2009), on Budd.

[102] Greider (1987: 96) shows the US FE Act was too late and ignored; Kaufman (2015) on the former bank behaviour to clients, business and households. It is moot whether wars increased as politicians became less popular domestically; causal factors are hard to prove but nuclear arms funding is concealed, we see in Chapter 2.

Table 1.1. *Simplified private bank balance sheet*

Private Bank: LIABILITIES		ASSETS	
Deposits: At 'call', due to client		**Loans: Accrue interest from borrower**	
Owing to Jamil	$1,000	(Cash or notes in hand or now electronic. No interest accrues to bank from Jamil)	$1,000
Owing to Louisa	$900	Loan to Louisa if reserve 10%	$900
Owing to 'Others' – Sam and Joc	$810 $729	Loans to 'Others' – Sam and Joc	$810 $729
Other deposits; equity etc.		Other loans; other transfers, etc.	
Totals:	$3,439		$3,439

Source: Withers 1909: 25-36

mutual indebtedness occurs through creating money also appears. The opposite of firms and household balance sheets, which include non-money, unlike banks. In contrast, financial statements always 'equal' (double-entry rules), since bank buildings (e.g.) are a tiny fraction of assets (or 'non-money'). 'Jamil' is the 'saver' who deposits his wages or windfall. The others are bank borrowers.[103]

---

[103] On balances, loans deposited, and on Walras, see Schumpeter (1954: 1015, 1026, 1116); Withers (1909: 25–36) also on cheques, as 'evasion' of the UK 1844 Act (1909: 56–84).

The bank and the client have mutual obligations into the uncertain future; the downsides are that the borrower may default, or the bank may renege on its promise to clients' ability to spend freely from their deposits (as in the GFC). Withers uses this over-simplification to show how a bank manufactures money; the scale in large established banks is vast, but the procedure the same for this slice or handful of depositors, and for other banks which also receive proceeds as deposits from loans spent. Withers built on this to show how from notes (and early disasters), cheques were used in his day, whereas today electronic transfers are most common; he then considered the BoE's balances. The procedure is the same – the BoE's clients are other banks and the government.[104]

In the central bank balance sheet, too, patience is needed to read double-entry bookkeeping, but it cannot be avoided. This is because partisan positions only enable one to unearth clues by comparing their debates; that is, by assessing the logic, norms and evidence of different arguments: unlike balances. Schumpeter's statement about fiscal policy, that 'the budget is the skeleton of the state stripped of all misleading ideologies', applies equally to banks and CBs as creators of money.

The 'skeleton' in CB statements is found in their interactions with treasuries and with private banks. Their historical statements bring 'to the realm of sociology' the social relations of central banks,[105] but they cannot show changes over time in any specific asset and liability statement. Since banks hold no non-financial assets to speak of, the two sides in double entry bookkeeping equal zero. So, one can only see money expansion or contraction over a series of statements.

Ultimately (in the 5th row), from $1,000 (Jamil's representative 'reserve'), $9,000 is created through loans or advances in a 10 per cent fractional reserve banking system. More dubious bank practices emerged, notably after the 1970s. Savings banks (fixed time deposits not 'at call' in some rules) and mutuals, thrifts and building societies (not 'banks') changed or vanished.

[104] Prompted by the GFC (probably) McLeay et al. (2014) of the BoE also depict balances and money creation; as do Ryan-Collins et al. (2011); and speak of 'non-money' in non-bank balances of firms etc. These are non-liquid or less liquid. Withers' balance sheet example is simple, possibly easier to follow.

[105] Schumpeter (1991 [1918]: 100). His approving quote on sociology is an Austrian's at the time of WWI. He thus challenged orthodoxy which, to this day, avoids remarking on the deposit creating loan.

The ease with which banks and central banks create money (permitted with state licence, and charter) with advances (loans) entered as both liabilities and assets, is remarkable. In contrast, for firms and households, one can spot a deficit or a surplus in each statement because they have either more, or less liabilities (debts) than income flowing in from employment or non-money assets. Further, in the case of banks, 'the cost of production of money is a negligible factor in its price' (it is 'penmanship' or, today, keystrokes),[106] whereas producing goods or services (hard work) always has a cost more than merely the price of a loan. As well, banks are not money lenders since they do not have money to lend. Shown in double entry, all banks create a loan as both an asset, interest stream into the future, and a liability, deposit to be honoured by *banks*. Table 1.2 below is

Table 1.2. *Simplified central bank balance sheet*

Central Bank:	LIABILITIES	ASSETS
	Due to Treasury or private banks 'at call' or at their whim	*Accrues a stream of interest payments*
	L1 – Deposits or reserves held by private banks (to create money)	A1 – Loans to private banks of, e.g., Treasury bonds
	L2 – Deposits held by Treasury *	A2 – Loans to Treasury * or purchases/sales of T-Bonds
	Deposits held by 'others', e.g. foreign	Other securities, e.g. other states' bonds
	Net worth; equity; 'funds' or 'owner's capital', or none	Cash or notes in hand etc.
Totals:	10,000,000	10,000,000

Sources: Timoigne, 2014: 87; Wray 2014b: 117-119; Withers 1909: 261; 213 on BoE (* see the footnote on page 55)

[106] See Withers (1909: 233) on 'penmanship' and the tiny 'cost'.

a simplified central bank balance sheet, partly drawn on the US Fed method (with far fewer zeros). Balance sheets importantly show what 'the game' is.

Licensed private banks need the CB reserves at Liability 1 (L1) as a 'required' fraction for them to create more money (or not). Banks use these reserves 'as cash'. To prevent reckless expansion, there used to be strict bank requirements on holding permitted reserves in the Fed.[107] Nevertheless, loans create deposits, and banks are merchants of debt: some economists don't look, others find it so 'obvious' they don't mention it.[108] L1 bank reserves are usually used to the max, except under quantitative easing (QEs) of 2009–10 (see Chapter 8) when reserves were awash because there was little demand for loans except for speculative asset purchases. The expansion of Wall Street banking's Fed reserves that happened in WWI was also typical (see Chapter 2): their profits come from selling debt (off the fraction in their Fed reserves) and thereby creating money. As a rule, to replenish the deposits in L1, banks must borrow from their CB, so Asset 1 (A1) rises as L1 does. The rate of interest charged on these borrowings is called the Fed Funds Rate in the US, or the CB interest rate. It is meant to control the amount of money that banks can create.[109] CBs use a movable 'target' in the rate they charge, since central banks routinely 'accommodate' private bank demands this way. Despite central bank control over their interest rates, Hartley Withers denied the BoE had control in 1908 'over the extent to which its banking customers create credit', saying that the private banks ruled the BoE.[110]

---

[107] Table 1.2's asterisks are explained in the chapter's last footnote. The FRA (1913) required gold reserves of 40 per cent banks' outstanding note; 30 per cent deposit liabilities: Bordo and Wheelock (2013: 75, 97). The 'deal' was so banks could gain LOLR (this is not quite QE). In 2008, Goldman Sachs asked the US government for a licence (for QE). See Figure 7.2.

[108] See, however, Minsky (2008: 55) on banks as 'merchants of debt'.

[109] See Timoigne (2014: 87), Wray (2014b: 117–19). Private banks also set their own interest rates.

[110] Withers (1909: 213, 261) about the BoE. It relates to Mehrling (2000) on bank debt (discussed earlier).

Hard money people (hawks) exclude these revealing statements, in the sense that a mere look at balance sheets contradicts the innocent role neoclassical economics gives to private banking. The uncivil, in other words, only look at whether Treasury is in debt – that is, creating money, but – again – rarely look at the way central banks cannot avoid monetising state *and* private bank deficits.[111] It would spoil their story of state profligacy alone, whereby they can depict banks as 'perfect'.

These discussions of the various motives of governments in establishing a central bank, the pro-finance motives, the war funding or pro-industrial aims, and even desires for social well-being and economic development, are the book's themes. The ways democratic procedures interacted with central bank possibilities and disputes from the twentieth century onward are stressed throughout. One question is whether central banks are comparable to the judiciary, which I argue against. Understanding money-creating processes, in contrast, is essential for assessing central banks: not about typical

---

[111] Drawing on Tymoigne (2014: 87): US Treasury and bank activities over any single year that expand/contract the Fed's balance sheet in stylised Table 1.2:

> L2 amounts of taxes/bond proceeds go down * when Treasury spends from CB liabilities on the 'at call' side
>
> L1 amounts go up as Treasury pays for activities; payments deposited in private banks and other economic units to increase banks' creation of credit if demanded = money supply increases
>
> L2 amounts rise when tax receipts and bond issue proceeds come in (seasonal)
>
> L1 amounts decline (also throughout the private banking sector): L1 is the 'base money' = money supply decreases
>
> A2 * In the past, but not with the US Fed in WWI or now, US Treasury might ask for a loan, and the CB made this direct advance; when the Fed buys T-Bonds or Securities, A2 shows an increase, and entered/deposited in L2, increases the money base; if it sells bonds, A2 shows a decrease *over time.*
>
> The Fed in WWI was not bypassed: even if the 1913 Fed could not 'lend' directly to Treasury, it held T-Bonds to lend to banks or to sell. See www.federalreserve .gov/releases/h41/Current/, the section 'consolidated statement'. Withers (1909: 243) said one must 'use caution' and only make 'guarded deductions' from BoE statements. Wray (2014a: 13–14) emphasises this for today too, in querying the 'fiscal discipline' of T-bonds (or 'bond vigilantes').

'functions' but their variations, despite the old money-creating patterns. It arms the argument with further complexities to explore as CBs must shift their sights in larger, usually contested contexts. The first is the earlier (under-examined) major motive of war funding that wrought many unexpected changes in the terrible occasion of WWI, to which I now turn.

2 War Finance, Capitalist Banks: Shared Monetary Sovereignty

War finance is a critical element in central bank relations and capacities. The earliest central banks' founding and history was usually about arranging their sovereign state's financing of wars although, like so much about money, public knowledge is scant. In the endless 'war against terror', the quest to find out who is funding ISIS, or al Qaeda, has not been top news. Nonetheless, questions are rarely asked at all about the sources of funding for President G. W. Bush's invasion and occupation of Iraq. The literature is sparse. One cannot blithely assume that the 'coalition of the willing', the USA, Britain and Australia, destroyed Iraq (further) with no debts later. A major expert on the economics of war, William Nordhaus, agrees and lists the copious stupidities and costs of wars. Inevitably, the 1914–18 Great War scores very badly, as does the 2003 Iraq War. His main concern is with the destruction of the economy: war has terrible costs on victors and vanquished alike. Nordhaus sounds like a peacenik: old slogans, 'winning the war and losing the country' come to mind. This chapter examines how only the USA benefited spectacularly from WWI, in building its economy on its allies' huge war debts and in becoming the world's major creditor country. The US's main allies (mostly the Entente) suffered grievously, except for Japan, despite being the victors. That included Britain which was not invaded unlike France; also Italy and Tsarist Russia.

As bankers to states as well as to banks, central banks are involved the moment a government needs to find sources for war funding. However, the two World Wars changed central banks in quite different ways. This is my focus, to tease out central banks' relations to their states when they demand war funding. The methods of managing war costs show us ways to assess the preferable *peacetime* functions of central banks that are promising rather than harmful.[1]

People assume taxes fund wars. To collect taxes, states need a monopoly of violence for pacification, and that has costs too. Defence budgets in semi-peacetime are rarely questioned in legislatures, unlike social line items, and many states pay hidden subsidies to the US for the nuclear umbrella. Mysteries around money (touched on earlier) multiply. Least discussed openly, war costs are mostly met through political-private borrowing, semi-hidden in central banks balances (in Table 1.2). Early central banks were designed to be go-betweens in the creation of this specific capitalist money for states to fight wars, and for banks to use this secure state debt for multiplying their bank loans. It was a public-private shared monetary sovereignty.

How does that work? Political elites made deals and contracts with merchant bourgeoisies, and this relation often became a club. A few 'central' or 'public' banks supplied war finance for centralising and warring states. Sovereign debt gave a fairly secure guarantee or protection for private sector money creation from their reserves in the central bank; for expanding capitalist development in trade and industry. The deal required that the state collect taxes to service its debt payments, to retire or redeem its IOUs (money) and roll over some (or most) perpetually. Banks also depend, likewise, on receiving interest, and repayments to cancel (some of) their debts (money). Merchants and banks with shaky IOUs preferred their central bank to nurture their needs and, even when the lending for the state's fiscal needs lay behind old deals managed by central banks, private banks often insist on limiting fiscal spending by raising their rates. It then appears that Treasuries were (or are) separate from monetary policy (CBs). War funding, however, makes an 'independent' central bank a

---

[1] Large wars in the nineteenth century include the Napoleonic wars and US Civil War. Napoleon founded the Bank of France in 1800, and the far older BoE played a contentious role for the English side. There was no central bank at the time of the US Civil War: the north's funding was run by US Treasury. In WWI, Japan also lent to the Entente.

more open fiction. They exist to meet the demands of their states and commercial banks.

Capitalist money creation, frequently originating in war debt, gave an unheard-of freedom of movement for the rising bourgeois-merchants: they could inspect state debt to decide whether to lend – although never wholly 'free'. The repressed factor is that mobile capital is reliant on territorially fixed state entities and 'the community' that accepts their money and pays taxes (say, on bank bailouts). Bank assets are (usually) the profit from charging more than they pay interest for money, but banks frequently expand and contract their money creation in unstable ways. States were under strict bank-lending rules set in bourgeois parliaments, and won or lost wars and conducted unscrupulous invasions of pre-modern regions. Banks, however, could refuse to lend. Wars give a clear insight into the pushing and pulling for advantage of these two forces, states and finance, with central banks the fragile institutions caught both ways. Monetary policy is always on two-way paths: states spend money into existence, and banks deposit advances (loans) to create bank money, with central banks behind both as their banker. If all debt is paid back all at once, there is no money. The problem is the purposes of all this money whether for businesses or for states.

This chapter explores how the norm of state dependency on capitalist money for war finance changed after the 1914–18 War and the Interwar miseries.[2] For the USA and others, WWII and its post-war period was the only democratising era of money, linked with the warring states' needs to mobilise entire populations for total war. Unlike WWI, governments did not grovel to the finance sector for WWII funds. Indeed, global clubs of capitalist finance lost significant

---

[2] War lotteries were considered before the BoE was founded. See Simmel (1907[1990]) on 'community', a vague term for (usually) the state that accepts a specific money (its currency) in payment of tax (debts to the state). Legislatures create/change the mandates for CBs (mostly; or the Executive). Ahamed (2009) is one good reference for re-introducing war finance to central bank histories; Tooze (2007, 2014) as well. The Great Depression is in Chapter 3, and WWII finance in Chapter 4 on governments that tried to democratise central banks.

control in WWII (also unlike WWI). When not under fascist or communist states, civil society had some ability to hold governments (and their central banks) to account; this spread post-WWII. In contrast, WWI was no finance sideshow – it seems likely that each state's war finance methods helped to rearrange nations, classes and sentiments, rather than politicians and generals alone.[3]

WORLD WARS AND CENTRAL BANKS' CHAMELEON NATURE

My entry point at the twentieth century World Wars is to explore this intertwining of democratising governments and capitalist finance through the central bank (CB). Rosy stories of CBs' slow evolution belie the evidence of central banking wedged by class and state conflicts over specific circumstances nationally and globally in that century. So, I put the World Wars to the forefront and not as mere interruptions in orthodox accounts. It is not to diminish the democratic gains and terrible losses but to emphasise this other major role of central banks, their continuing relations with governments. The state has been the object of loathing in recent decades, compared to markets on one side, social movements on the other. But the 'total' wars expanded governments greatly in depth, domestic reach and as the greater sources of technological change than before. The former 'small' wars were different, as Karl Polanyi said about the nineteenth century, compared to these two world wars. Contemptible as war is and rarely decided upon democratically, financing and payments varied greatly for each War (we see). The global impacts on money class relations included a major expansion of voting rights in the 1920s, Germany notably, USA one of the least, as America came to

---

[3] The German reparations focus, we see further on, shrouds the debts of America's Allies (Entente, colonies and Dominions) in WWI. Nordhaus (2002) notes war histories ignore faulty cost forecasts. Sociological world histories on wars are useful but rarely about central banks. Some draw on money theorists like Polanyi (1957 [1944]), later, notably Ingham (1984, 2004, 2008, 2011).

dominance from WWI's turmoil of debtor *versus* creditor countries. For democracies, the process was less unjust in WWII.

If war finance is understudied, even more peculiar, it is merely a 'field of tension' in the CB literature. Compare it with state and bank spending on peaceful, cautious, socially useful projects (unlike today). The World Wars show that the question of state sovereignty and capitalist money is a chicken and egg problem, and any one-sided view is misleading. Central banks represent the political-economic conflicts of the time and place; and exercise some influence with their banking activities. Violence is expensive for centralising forces: their internal and external defence or aggression must be financed. Nuclear arsenals are not cheap.

Logic is hard to find. Many social arrangements are vulnerable due to mutual dependencies, taken for granted, between states and economies. It follows that these structures cannot be separate objects of study. At the centre is the money that we need for purchasing power for goods and services, without which capitalist economic life cannot proceed, given money is also the means to pay legal obligations and promises that create and destroy money (so it is never a 'thing'). Were central banks a solution to these vulnerable promises? War funding linked to bank profit motives in creating more (not less) money, were the old drivers for symbiotic relations between the capitalist and the state institutions of money and their markets. Capitalist bank money can expand from lending for anything, speculation or war included. Whereas the ghastly WWI proved to be a lovely deal for private debt-holders if not a 'gift', *and* for the USA (we see), in contrast, strenuous efforts in WWII were made to avoid the inequalities of WWI funding and its grim Interwar aftermath.[4]

Important to note so far, then, is that neither party is reliably *benign* or intended that democracy would expand through state deals and capitalist institutions. Democracy is now frail; however,

---

[4] Funding for nuclear arsenals is partly a WWI model. Before the CB war finance 'deals', (from late 1500s) war loans to states took money *out* of economic activity; on 'symbiotic' capitalist money see Ingham (2004). But what economic activity, what 'activity' is left after nuclear war?

its expansion was fostered by both 'total' wars. As well, under total war, private banks were far less 'free to roam' (than now). States could claim patriotic duties were owing from banks, and citizen-armies and workforces became infuriated that bankers profited by dealing with enemy countries and their bankers.

The few central banks in existence by 1900 were privately owned, thus also driven to increase shareholder value at their population's expense. This kind of 'independence from government' became a 1980s fad, to try to copy those pre-democratic days. Yet the common factor of all nation-states is their monopoly of violence, which political philosophies accept more or less.[5] The corollary is capitalist money tends to falter without the state debt that drives this monopoly. In the absence of a monopoly of violence, we talk about 'failed' states (unable to pacify, tax, or save banks).

WWI launched the major twentieth century upheavals, as an outcome, in hindsight, of capitalist finance, industry and key states catching up with Britain. The social forces and national coalitions varied enormously. Some countries were so abused from invasions and plunder, or 'open doors' to China and so on, or fragmentation (in the Middle East), that establishing national sovereignty with independent local coalitions and democratic demands was difficult. Britain still 'ruled', just, although WWI effected the switch. Thereafter, the hegemonic currency passed from the UK to the US *de facto*. WWI belligerents had few 'near total war' histories – only partly the Napoleonic or US Civil wars. The World Wars, in contrast, suddenly put ruling classes into a proto-dependency on populations. Appeals to patriotism roused democratic questions that elites loathed: accountability at the ballot box. The US, claiming it was the beacon with a 'manifest destiny', only allowed 60 per cent to vote

---

[5] Global trade did not recover for thirty years after WWI. In Hobbes, states are Leviathans to keep peace; in Locke, they may just build roads, which if used implies a 'contract' with the state; see also Mann (2010); Pateman (1979); Macpherson (1962). Libertarian economic and anarchist theories are anti-state. Economic libertarians tend to political authoritarianism; e.g. Milton Friedman, see Freedman (2006, 2007), neglected war finance talk.

until 1970. Former slaves were one part of the excluded, the other were the desperately poor Irish, Poles or Jews: displaced peasants. Not every American claims their country is 'exceptional', but it resurfaces. It is only fair to recall, though, that 'Land of Hope and Glory, Mother of the Free' (of 1902) is still played at the British Proms.[6]

'Total war' included civilians as well as armed personnel, and it called up more claims than capitalism as usual and anachronistic alliances could handle. And, whatever rulers fondly think, money is socially unifying, affecting most people. This became obvious as mighty swings in the hierarchies of credit-debt domination in world monetary affairs took place before their eyes.[7] This is stressed, because the impact of WWI on the Bank of England's supervision of the old currency hegemon, and the US Fed's takeover with the new hegemon, is vital to understanding the specific conflicts of these central banks and their governments. Typically, German war reparations are the key topic in the literature, and yet Britain's war debts to the US initiated the counterproductive struggles of the 'British Empire' and the City of London to maintain world dominance. The BoE tried every possible tactic to preserve British monetary world power.

Today state costs of keeping the world on continual war alert are self-censored inside central banks (even) and private banking. The question is rarely asked, and the ever-present horror of nuclear war is different from the World Wars. In a nutshell, WWI was the shock to the nineteenth century capitalist-state order, and to central banks and treasuries, which were forced to fund full employment (FE) for

---

[6] President Obama tried to play down US 'destiny'; Obama, cited in Watson (2016), was howled down. During 2016, sociologies of demagoguery (in the *New Yorker* alone) exposed treatment of desperately poor migrants. In 1900, the richest 1 per cent (10 per cent) owned over 50 per cent (90 per cent) of US and UK wealth. On US voting, see Therborn (1977); Elgar wrote the music to 'Land of Hope'; lyrics by A. C. Benson were written in 1902, about extending the British Empire 'Wider still and wider ... God who made thee mighty/ make thee mightier yet'. Still wildly popular in Britain; the Proms are held annually at the Albert Hall, London, with so-called promenaders draped in flags and jingoistic clothes.

[7] Money's unifying nature is found in its absence mostly (the GFC e.g.), also with increased numbers using banks, e.g. in Johnson (2011); also, see Chapters 6 and 7.

the first time. WWII hastened a general acceptance of democratic FE, whereas the Vietnam War helped to end those hopes.

After Vietnam, government peace or war financing was ruled out in central banks' formal duties (in the Fed's 1913 founding too) forbidding deficit finance *de jure* despite their long history of monetising the sovereign debt mostly for war. Yet *de facto* state financing via central banks still goes on, as against private finance's 'plebiscite' – that is, to refuse to lend except at ruinous rates.[8]

Continual interests of states and banks (creditors' cartels) in gaining control of money creation (and of people) can be conflicting or mutual. Yet there is no 'technical solution' through a 'central bank' to instability and disruptions. War funding models remained much the same for nearly 400 years – once rulers were prevented from defaulting (banks now are the main defaulters not governments), through the imposed 'deals' of banks, and often ended in acrimony. The high demand for loans in WWI meant that the IOUs of states enabled private banks to expand their advances in lucrative ways. (WWII funding made fewer concessions to banks.) Bank money can always endanger economic stability. Indeed, since 1975, the volume of private bank money and private debts overwhelms the relatively small amount of public debt (including debt for war) that only rose significantly for the 2009 bailouts to funding levels of WWII, except the public debt declined quickly post-1945. These public facts gain no publicity, even from central banks (which collect this data). What, then, is the role of central banks?[9]

Although it is depressing to use the World Wars as a 'natural experiment' to test this case, states and banks both devastate

---

[8] On Vietnam, see Chapter 5. See Giannini (2011: 129) on the 'tension' between state debt and bank profits (far too tame a term!) and I discuss his term 'plebiscite' or veto right in detail later. Defence costs in 'peace' are not always vast; the problem (nuclear arms races worse) is how private (and central) banks are involved in complicated ways, often covertly.

[9] States still can default but banks tend to 'veto' state social spending (e.g. schools) more than for war. Treasuries often make cut-backs to 'please' financial demands for predictability; social wages (e.g. healthcare or pensions) give populations some independence from controls of employers and banks, cf. privatisation. Schularick (2014) gives copious data on public debt; see also in Chapter 8 on the 2009 bailouts.

countries with their money creation and contraction. These ghastly wars show how central banks interact with both sides, with social-political effects, globally and locally.

Central Bank Models and the Masked Ball
Creating the US Fed

Despite the apparent uniformity of central banks, the BoE (1694) model was rarely copied by choice. Central banks are experimental in their national aims, with rules modified in face of social disruptions. In the nineteenth century, the brief English gold sterling standard rule (a nice subsidy to City banks) was suspended in 'small' wars, but especially when bank bubbles collapsed. The 'National Debt' and 'War Loans' were *hot topics*. These practices were at odds with naïve 1914 ideas that WWI would be over when the gold 'ran out'.[10] Powerful parties (during war or peace) have tended to disrupt the prevailing rules – to break out into ventures that become uncontrollable – or to use the rules to immediate advantage, like the private Bank of England during the 1847 railroad 'ventures'. In 1866, it formally became lender of last resort, reluctantly.[11] In efforts to keep state money and bank money in some believable balance, the functions of central banks can be either reduced or augmented, so flexibility was common despite and often because of the gold standard.

At nineteenth century's end, Europe was the main region with central banks. Its elites were inordinately wealthy, few people could vote, and domestic bottom-up protests were quelled violently, as

---

[10] Ugolini (2011: 3–4) cites Howard Davies, Forrest Capie, Charles Goodhart, as wrongly saying the BoE model was copied. The BoE tried to *impose* its model on the Dominions (1930s) but see Chapters 1 and 3. See Ahamed (2009: 73–85) on the 'smug', antiquated 'sound money' idea of gold running out, notably since the Napoleonic and US civil wars used all 3 (listed below) non-gold methods of funding.

[11] See Ugolini (2011: 15–16) on deficit finance; and Gollan (1968:7); Hawtrey (1962 [1932]: 138–9). With the 1844 Bank Charter Act, the BoE was to manage its 'Banking Department' like any private bank (cf. its 'automatic' gold standard 'Issue Department'). Its 'Banking Department' competed for discount business in the 'dangerous' time of British railway development and the BoE was blamed in 1847. See Flandreau and Ugolini (2013) on the 1866 crisis of the London firm, Overend-Gurney, and the BoE reluctance and bank stonewalling over lender of last resort (LOLR).

they were in the USA. Many areas of the world were either colonies (of Europe) or feudal fragments not 'sovereign'. North America was colonial until the 1775–83 war saw the eastern USA created, with a population of 2,210,000. Former German kingdoms were partly feudal until Bismarck as Chancellor spent money through his personal banker Gerson Bleichröder on the unification of Germany by 1871. Russia was a feudal backwater, yet Japan modernised after 1861. Japan's central bank (1882) was partly modelled on Belgium's. German (1876) and French central banks (1800) did not copy the BoE either; since to catch up with the UK, the Reichsbank and Banque de France financial support went to industrial more than financial sectors. That had different effects on distribution, to labour, or to *rentiers*. Many central banks were designed to finance the state, taking its debt issue for redistribution to creditor cartels (banks) to multiply bank money. Only the BoE and the Fed used 'indirect tools' to boost the City and Wall Street, Epstein argues.[12]

Central banks spread only during the mid-twentieth century but still varied, with mixed political motives, some aiming to free colonised regions from Dutch, French, and mostly British political and economic yokes, and to promote development and/or to garner mobile capital. Rules and legislation varied, and not only to suit governments or bankers. They critically expressed the outcomes of conflicts between primary producers, industrialists, service sectors, banks, *rentiers* and political elites, and free and unfree labour. International banks and merchant houses were often the forces to push for central banks, and sometimes (although rarely) labour movements.[13] Wall Street got 'its' Fed in 1913, the first of the new

---

[12] See Stern (1977) on Bismarck's lucrative, bigoted relation; Giannini (2011: 90) who said Bagehot's 'model' with LOLR, was not 'the essence' of central banking. Ugolini (2011: 11–13) slightly disputes that claim (and LOLR required countries to lift a cap on usury to raise CB interest rates on banks); as do others, see Chapter 8.

[13] See Epstein (2006: 2, 5) on variations in central bank developmental aims for finance or production, and how the US and British 'indirect' sectoral support to finance is played down in the orthodox literature to castigate 'direct' support to industry among early European CBs. The Bank of Spain (of 1874) was like Germany and France.

century and rapidly the most dominant, aided by the 'explosion' of war finance.

Like the BoE, the US Fed's design was to promote its finance sector and international role. The USA had two central bank experiments in the nineteenth century, driven by acrimonious struggles over the nature of money and agrarian fear of Wall Street control. Against opposition, one old 'founding father', Alexander Hamilton saw advantages in European models in supporting economic development and a strong state. The latter (with its implications for war finance) was submerged in the 1913 Federal Reserve Act (FRA), which somewhat ignored the BoE's private bank supervision role too. Rather ludicrously (in wearing disguises for the travel), a secret meeting of select senior Congressmen and private bankers assembled at a Jekyll Island resort in 1910 to draft the FRA. It was a cosy deal among financiers, secluded from critics well-versed in public knowledge of money.[14]

The FRA mandated a separation of fiscal finances from Fed operations, which 'technically' ruled out deficit financing. As well, the FRA called for the Fed to supply 'elastic currency' to banks so they could fund economic development, although this was still under the rigid gold standard. The Fed was clearly a banker to the banks through the twelve privately-owned District Feds, with certain limits to lending of last resort, and it 'dealt in' Treasury bonds. The amount and discretion to hold government paper was strictly limited in the Fed's Act. Nothing seriously changed until the legislation of Roosevelt's Administration in 1933 to 1935. J. P. Morgan and Wall Street criticised the Fed model at its inception as being 'far too politicized' (a tedious refrain ever since), since the Washington DC Fed Board was not exactly based on the privately-owned BoE. Morgan appealed in vain to the Fed Board to underwrite J. P. Morgan's war

[14] See Chapter 1, introducing the diverse US social forces. See Johnson and Kwak (2011: 14–30) on how Washington and Jefferson opposed a central bank, also others in Chapter 1. On the Fed, see Ugolini (2011: 16), and on bank supervision, see White (2013), citing Hartley Withers. Montagu Norman travelled under a pseudonym and disguise during his long BoE term. CB secrecy, as with the 1913 FRA designers, reversed radically in the 1980s, see Chapter 7.

lending to Britain and France in 1916 when the US was not at war.[15] Wall Street aimed to compete with the London banks, Senator Carter Glass declared in WWI. FRA proponents like Glass never aimed to impair 'the rightful prestige' of Wall Street. Rather, he said, the Fed's aim was 'to assist powerfully in wresting the scepter from London' to make Wall Street 'the financial center of the world'. This Fed would create (semi-guaranteed) markets in private bank and trade 'accept-ances' (depersonalised commercial IOUs) with the Fed to discount them. That 'discount' was often a Fed subsidy (a low interest loan 'discounted' beforehand) and included hopes for global use of the US dollar to enhance Wall Street bank profits. Jobs held no interest.[16]

With 'total' war finance, most central banks had state-imposed roles, yet from 1914, the Fed gained influence more from Wall Street's financing the Entente, and less from the war-shy US Administration. Yet time and again, war finance makes demands on central banks because decisions of war are never theirs to make. They are caught in a domestic and global hierarchy of bank dominance and national patriotic domination and hysteria. War finance overrules their equally 'political' monetary decisions for depression or inflations, whether privately owned or not, when they have power to create large num-bers of losers in unemployment and bankruptcies of firms.[17] But the World Wars required FE. The thesis herein is that the only undisputed example of *(part) democratic governments directing central banks to serve populations' needs and global monetary stability* was out of the dreadful circumstances of WWII, after the 1914–18 War and

[15] The FRA rejected original war finance purposes of the (private) early central banks, but T-Bonds in its 1918–20 balance sheets show it had been buying state debt; Tooze (2014: 38–9) on Morgan views; Wray (2014b: 115) on fiscal finances; Bordo and Wheelock (2013: 72–5) on the Act (FRA) 1913; Eichengreen and Mitchener (2003: 46) say the 1914 Fed assumed gold would dampen borrowing cf. war inflation and bank expansion; for the Fed post-1933, see Sayers (1949: 199) cf. the BoE.

[16] See Epstein (2006: 8) (my emphases), citing Glass and Paul Warburg, another FRA architect, on acceptance markets so common in Europe; these enabled open market operations, also bills of exchange, to compete with London. Epstein (2006: 9) argues New York banks were rent seeking and pushing the Act.

[17] Political decisions and political outcomes of the main power of central banks, are not the 'blunt tool' that economists criticise tamely; rather a covertly murderous blunderbuss.

after the 1930s Great Depression, deflation and WWI debt conflicts. Supporters of this thesis are mostly forgotten today; central bank ruses, blasted in wars, returned in the 1970s.

This introductory discussion leads up to showing how events of the twentieth century makes central bank purposes obvious and brings forth CB dissonances. World War I shattered so much, but it was lucrative for capitalist bank models. Since 1975, war finance has mutated, and the now vast size of the (often warrior) state is contested: to a point. Namely, war finance *methods* are barely discussed in debates about states or banks, or even behind closed doors of US Fed meetings.[18]

World War I was the beginning. The previous century's liberal European utopia – 'small wars' of global trade (debt) and domestic police forces – by 1918 looked vicious, a delusion in its fervent hopes of a peaceful global order, whether effected through capitalist money for development, speculative markets or gun boats. Many hoped that financialised global trade, with luck, might foster peace. Other global 'counter' movements, feminist, socialist, environmental had emerged, active for democratic peace. Liberalism used the term 'night watchman state' about mere peace keeping (defence). Representing a male bourgeois class, 'economic liberalism' was divided over money's value – depreciation benefits debtors (industry, state services and other borrowers) but throws *rentier*-guarantors down to 'lower stations'. Reversing inflations (with deflation) to favour *rentiers* and banks always excluded and exploited 'the masses'. Behind liberal terms was state violence towards peoples forced to speak alike, and to use and labour for a uniform currency with which to pay taxes to a central authority that would thereby be able to retire (some of) its money creation and maintain its control over artificial territorial boundaries. In answer, Marx fondly hoped for a peaceful reduction ('withering') of the state through direct democracy, the 'universal'

---

[18] The Federal Open Market Committee (FOMC) meetings have been transcribed since the 1980s, see on federalreserve.gov. Today's CB literature tends to neglect state roles in money creation (for war) or to over-emphasise states (cf. see, e.g. Palley (2015), and below).

proletarian class and unions, instead of 'universal' bourgeois operators and financiers.

These dreams were not to be, but everyone was correct in insisting that resort to war is a huge miscalculation and a breakdown of diplomacy. Memories frozen into economic 'theories' from that liberal era rose (from graves?), despite a huge growth of states and private conglomerates in size and spread. Tenacious patterns in money creation continue, and central bank policies are mute on war finance, as if the nuclear arsenal did not exist. War costs are notoriously underestimated to gain popularity and assent. Victors' spoils are invariably *less* than claimed in 'wooden-headed' aggrandisement, even given the huge losses of the vanquished. MAD is different.[19]

WAR FINANCE OF THE 1914–45 'THIRTY YEARS WAR'

World War I would be over, leaders declared, in five weeks! No one needed to worry too much about funding, since old central bank methods had served well: borrow from banks and deficit finance. Admittedly there were expensive Dreadnaughts but, as the UK Liberal, Lloyd George satirised in 1911, one Duke cost more to sustain than two warships. Europe had its huge continental armies ready for a new build-up since the 1870–1 Franco-Prussian war; Britain had its navy and the colonies to trawl for more troops and so on. The model of warfare most relevant was the American Civil War of 1861–5, plus Henry Ford's production lines. WWI was not lucrative like the capitalist colonising Boer War or the Opium War models. It spelt brutal mutual slog, debt to the USA, and dashed Panglossian hopes for technology's 'progress' in logic and principles, although war R&D

---

[19] Nordhaus (2002: 78–80) lists failed cost forecasts, with reasons like elites' innumeracy, refusal of facts, patriotic faith, against obvious economic evidence that war is a negative-sum game; e.g., the US's 'short, cheap, bloodless' 1991 Persian Gulf War seemed to predict it 'would be the same' in the 2003 Iraq War. He mentions the greater costs of a 'botched peace' than of bloody war, as at the Versailles Peace treaty in 1920, since German reparations cost the indebted victors too. MAD is Mutually Assured Destruction, but now 'questioned'.

grew then and now. As for financial miscalculations, all the WWI victors lost except the USA.[20]

Old ways of financing wars became new ones but at a fantastic scale, quite beyond the typical scope of central banking's hidden secrets. In the first place, virtually every belligerent went off gold and used paper notes only. This scandalised the gold bugs, although the same thing had happened in previous wars (e.g. the Napoleonic war). For that war, the UK also introduced war taxes, inflation was mild, although writers who wanted to 'indict inflation' and blame the BoE stirred up controversies.[21] Gold was also regularly abandoned to cope with severe financial scandals but that had little effect on the deflationists.[22] The gold standard was supposed to be 'knave proof' against the temptation for banks to create near money and/or to limit state spending. Hardly any ruling elites cared about jobs. Yet, the 1850-1 Australian and Californian goldfield discoveries that kept Europe economically active up until WWI were not mere chance. With the gold standard as the rule (to be broken), motives to find gold led to great openings for the poor and desperate from Europe and Asia, with some democratisation of money in Australia if not California. During and after WWI, one central banker, Ben Strong of the New York District Fed, tried partially divorcing US monetary policy from gold. The treatment of these 'grand facts' is spartan in some literature.[23]

In 1914-18, funding sources suddenly became semi-visible, a fraught problem. For the first time, whole populations had to be

[20] See Sawer (2012), on dreadnaughts. The Boer War was largely about South Africa's gold. Few dispute WWI's anti-democratic stupidities across Europe/UK's heartland. Ford's $5 wage bribery was a brutal, 'effective demand' strategy to enforce conveyor belt work. The US Civil War was copied and its R&D (research and development) but its four-year slog was not heeded.

[21] See Butlin (1986) on gold; Schumpeter (1954: 690-1) on Napoleonic war finance debates 'indicted' in the UK as allegedly inflationary; one prelude to the 1844 Bank Charter Act, which aimed for the BoE to be knave proof as the cliché had it.

[22] See Morgan (1943); Gollan (1968) on lifting the gold standard in the nineteenth century, mostly to save banks.

[23] See Hawtrey (1962 [1932]) who favoured Strong's policies, as had Keynes earlier for India's system; Ahamed (2009) on controversies; on technical 'terms' see Calomiris (2013); Bernanke (2000).

mobilised for a war effort that no one (in 'charge') imagined would be so extensive. War expenditure and revenue sources cannot be neglected, as they are in conventional central bank thinking today. WWI was both a radical augmentation and a capitalist variation of ancient wars of mercenaries and continental peasant conscripts. WWI finance immensely advantaged the banks, as shown in debates on how to finance WWII.[24]

In comparison to old wars, the massive resources needed for 'total' war mobilisations in both World Wars comprised four main sources over the entire economy: 'i) increased production; ii) reduction of civil investment (private and government); iii) reduction of current consumption; and iv) overseas resources'. After WWI, Ralph Hawtrey said that the UK Treasury had not 'relaxed' financial control at all, in contrast to what many then supposed. Rather, the 'fighting departments' of Navy and Army had had a 'free hand', but civil expenditure virtually none. In the USA, civil spending (like pensions) was low during WWI, but as we see on, capitalist industry did fabulously, and employment and financial sectors boomed to Wall Street's further benefit. This was how private US lending and US investment transformed the global hierarchy.[25]

Direct funding for war usually has three main sources in modernity. The first option is taxation to pay for the current war-related expenditure on the spot. The second option is the 'perfected' 400-year-old government war borrowing, which pays the present war costs, either by the central bank monetising state debt or by state direct borrowing short-term or into the never-never admitted. The third option is for the state/central bank to resort to rolling out the printing presses. This option vied with ancient plunder for first place in history. Each had problems at the time, but some left terrible

---

[24] Of course, peasant conscripts were time old habits not only in Europe. There was certainly devastation: see later on Ingham (2008), about how Hitler's aims of plunder were anachronistic to capitalism. Economic debates on WWII funding focus on what to avoid of WWI financing; cf. a rarity in today's non-peace.

[25] See Butlin et al. (1941: 3) for their list of funding methods. Also, see McLean (2013: 149); Hawtrey (1921: 64); and Chapter 5.

hangovers into the future. This is not the case with taxation (which somewhat retires or cancels the printing press option, rarely used today), but tax is terribly unpopular across all classes.[26] If the war (or nuclear arsenal) is also disliked, a state may be reluctant to tax, as Presidents L. B. Johnson and R. M. Nixon were for the Vietnam War. Banks cannot profit from war taxes at all, nor do wealthy elites *enjoy* progressive taxes. WWI was barely funded by taxes.[27] There were other or additional methods:

> The 'greenbacks' issued by the US government during the Civil War and the 'Bradbury' notes issued by the British Treasury to avert a crisis during the First World War were free of particular debts.[28]

That is, the notes issued paid no interest rates; a marked contrast to the high ones that were paid to banks/*rentiers* on government bonds, which was the huge problem with the next option in WWI.

In borrowing, central banks played a key role, and this influenced how the postwar beneficiaries were banks (discussed below). Monetising deficits through short-term central bank credit creation does not debase the currency, nor destabilise the payments system, the evidence shows. WWI government bond issues (borrowing from banks at interest) were different. In early 1940, Keynes devoted a pamphlet to the case for a new path for war finance in the UK for WWII.

---

[26] Ugolini (2011: 16–17) shows how the printing presses destroyed the payments system and, although early on central banks took up deficit finance instead (short-term credit creation), that fairly safe option for 'sudden' costs like war is still taken incorrectly as debasement and printing presses in orthodoxy.

[27] Indirect finance depends for viability on winning and global creditor status. See Dyster and Meredith (2012: 81); McLean (2013) and on war debts and taxes; and see later Butlin et al. (1941). Few countries imposed higher taxes (the UK did), see Tooze (2014: 22) who does not *list* all sources of finance and Ahamed (2009) on taxes mainly. LBJ did raise a war tax; it stopped **with** Nixon, the most reluctant (see Chapter 5).

[28] Ingham et al. (2016: 1252) on Bradbury bills – backed by the credit of the state to later accept (pay) them back. This is rarely mentioned, e.g. King (2016). Ryan-Collins (2015: 20) shows in WWII, the Canadian government had an 'interest-free loan' from the BoC's money creation, which gained profits to pay it back to the state, its sole shareholder.

He hoped funding would be 'conceived in a spirit of social justice ... for moving ... towards reducing inequalities', and not as excuse for 'postponement' of social justice such as by cutting the consumption of the poorest to increase returns to 'lenders'. This alludes to how Treasuries had cut back on civil spending in WWI and, postwar, by CBs raising inequalities as well. As in WWI, WWII was (rightly) expected to involve major shortages of all imported and consumer goods, the prices of which could be chased up by the increased purchasing power resulting from huge expansions in civil and military workforces. Borrowing from investors (including banks) is the problem because:

> a deferment of money expenditure must be made by someone. This will not be avoided by allowing prices to rise, which merely means that consumers' incomes pass into the hands of the capitalist class. A large part of this gain the latter would have to pay over in higher taxes; part they might themselves consume thus raising prices still further to the disadvantage of other consumers; and the rest would be borrowed from them, so that they alone, instead of all alike, would be *the principal owners* of the increased National Debt – of the right, that is to say, to spend money after the war.[29]

Post-WWI, the exclusive few had the right 'to spend money'. During the war, 'profiteers', a 'limited class' whose individual incomes rose the most, along with trading and manufacturing companies, benefited (not through their 'fault', Keynes added). The system of borrowing via voluntary 'savings' during WWI led Keynes to exclaim: 'what a ridiculous system with wages and prices chasing one another upwards ... [when] no one benefited except the profiteer ... And we ended up with a National Debt vastly greater in terms of money than was necessary and very *ill distributed* through the community'. Other wartime economists had similar worries, although during WWI, UK employers

---

[29] Ugolini (2011: 16–17; 23) shows deficit finance is not currency debasement; it is common; the norm for wars and intriguingly, when commercial banks are not trusted; and see Keynes (1940: 1) on postponement; and Keynes (1940: 6) my emphasis.

paid low wages or brought in women to undercut male wages, so perhaps Keynes exaggerated wage rises in Britain, compared to high wages in Canada, NZ or Australia, like the City's *rentiers* – the bond-holders. In contrast in WWII, politicians hardly cared if they offended bond traders, given most Allies set far lower interest rates than the ruinous ones that were set in WWI.[30] The postwar effects of each of the finance options are discussed in later sections. One option, taxation, avoids states having to deal with private banks.

The old plunder that helped pay for victory had become anachronistic and untenable compared to state-capitalist money control of war funding. It enabled private capitalist money to develop the economies of conquered areas that Britain et al. exploited profitably (*some less by naked plunder*). Those states and their classes that combine and hold the most debt are those which usually win. Most governments assumed, for example, that the USA would 'win' WWII. In contrast Hitler decided upon plunder with (costly) policing to quell resistance across Europe, and the death camps starved prisoner-slaves to secure German war needs. Japanese fascism between 1930–45 did much the same to the SE Asian countries and POWs.[31]

Money creation for war finance has none of the benefits of that for peace finance – if it is creatively used for enterprises and jobs. War finance is obviously aiming to destroy public and private wealth (at least, of the enemy). The economic growth resulting from government spending for war activity is not renewable, even if (peace) industries

[30] See Keynes (1940: 64; 73–4 my emphasis) on 'fault'; and on 'chasing up'; albeit elite conflicts over War and the 1920s were evident in Keynes and Hawtrey's hostility to 'cruel' classical theory, instead urging workers' purchasing power be raised. Ahamed (2009) suggests 'old money' saw war profiteers as 'vulgar upstarts'. See B. Friedman (2005) on low female wages; and Tily (2015), on WWII T-bond rates at 3 per cent UK and 2.5 per cent USA, were much lower than WWI.

[31] The Soviet Union's role in WWII is not disputed; however, it was helped by the US Lend Lease programme. Plunder (of Nazis) is in Ingham (2008: 176); Evans (2016) argues French Resistance grew as Germany plundered its domestic economy in WWII and for slave workers (a mark of ancient plunder). Arendt (2006) argues of Europe that the Danish were the 'least prone to anti-Semitism'; the next least was Italy, but the French were 'prone' to it. See Tooze (2007) on Reichsbank notes for industry rearmament; Speer's murderous 'Hunger Plan'; Tooze argues Germany was less wealthy than thought in 1939.

develop too, as happened in the US monetary space (from tanks into cars). In war, social needs must be curtailed (so: shortages, inflation); states want low interest rates (to keep their expenses down); banks want profits and, if not controlled, expand to whatever activity they want. The World Wars needed domestic FE, in fact, greatly expanded employment of those formerly excluded: women, minorities and the retired. This was new, but wartime job expansion is unlikely to be repeated on such a scale now that drones, nuclear arms and R&D displace the labour (cannon fodder) of the armed forces, and civilian workers.

The increase in entire populations' spending (purchasing) power among all combatants was a huge shock in WWI. Along with the severe shortages of goods, some could exploit 'bottle-necks' in goods, labour and services by raising prices. Speaking of the 1940 Battle of Britain, a Londoner told me war was her first chance to escape poverty and gain a skilled job.[32] Such 'surprises' expose the savage money class nature of former eras of 'peace'. While households' purchasing power was not as miserable as it was in peacetime, it tended to outrun the workers and consumer materials that could be supplied to the private sector: it inflated prices and war-industry profits, and hence detracted from the war effort. The alleged recovery after WWI reversed the positive changes, and cruel demobilisations increased poverty (we see below).

Out of the 1914–18 war and Great Depression experiences, alternative theories and politics of money strengthened, resting on demands for democratic inclusion and fiscal-central bank *consolidation*. The Labor Prime Minister of Australia in WWII, John Curtin, famous for his policy making, always aimed to control private-bank expansion, state pork barrelling, and their inflationary effects. However, in a speech he gave in 1917, he also said:

> Governments which could raise millions for the prosecution
> of this fearful war merely by lifting their little finger, when

---

[32] The previous paragraph draws on Gollan (1968); Butlin et al. (1941); Ingham (2004). On the 'surprise' of (mostly) FE, Butlin et al. (1941), on classes see Ingham (2004: 81); on the Battle of Britain, my personal discussion in the 1970s.

confronted with the problem of saving from semi-starvation the many millions of their people existing in abject poverty could do nothing but unearth reports from pigeon holes to prove their *utter inability* to improve the situation of the people.[33]

Central banks and treasuries only changed this 'inability' *after* their tenacious support for the finance sector at the expense of people in the 1920s and 1930s, when the democracies noted the unequal, inefficient, anti-democratic methods of securing WWI finance. WWII funding changed and, notably, the US postwar debt relief was fairer than ever before (and hugely beneficial to America). The democracies' treasuries and departments fostering renewal and innovation became more important than central banks. In what follows, I turn first to the finance tragedies of WWI. The pattern suggests states can neither be assumed to be benign nor irrelevant to 'the economy'. Central banks must change with the emergencies and social hysterias of the day. The national traditions and class divisions are influential, and the relative strengths of social forces change CB policies and mandates.

FUNDING WWI BY WALL STREET AND UNCLE SAM

The clearest (if rarely debated) example of the problems arising from financing the 1914–18 War is the subsequent monetary and military world dominance of the ambiguously 'reluctant' USA. Violent conflicts marked world economic history for thirty years, and international trade did not fully revive until 1945, when an amicable relation between debtor-creditor states and, partially, organised workers, was at last established. What was the role of central banks in WWI? Combatants 'chose' borrowing. One year into the war, the Entente's war finances had to be augmented with heavy borrowing from the US.

---

[33] Curtin, cited in Edwards (2005: 92), my emphasis; Edwards, who was on the RBA Board, puts the case for the WWII Prime Minister Curtin unknown to me four years ago. Curtin in 1917 (WWI) wanted a counter-cyclical policy against deflation, and with the Australian Labor Party (ALP), and economists, opposed bank money inflation; indeed, all inflations (also see below on the US, and Chapter 4).

Although constantly revised war histories are hugely popular, today's accounts of central banks overlook war. Only economic-social historians give a vivid sense of the acrimony of peace, let alone war, but CB war studies are meagre.[34] War finance historian, Adam Tooze, focuses on American war involvement and its interwar isolation, casting the greatest aspersions on President Woodrow Wilson. Tooze admirably includes the Soviet Union, Japan and China. But which 'facts' to select? This ubiquitous question is most troubling in the case of money. A good CB counterpoint to Tooze's ambitious sweep is *Lords of Finance* by Liaquat Ahamed, which examines four central bankers who allegedly 'broke the world' into the Great Depression. I try to avoid personalising these office bearers and stress their constraints, as did thoughtful analysts of that time, exasperated with the institutions. The 'march of infamous men' across history is not my thesis. A UK Treasury official, Ralph Hawtrey, tried, and thus regarded the 1922 Genoa Conference failure with regret and the BoE with scorn.[35] One cannot avoid selection in looking for the political conditions that allow certain officials to gain acceptance for their monetary proposals while others are locked out, and in seeking patterns in the vicissitudes of central banks *vis à vis* their relations with sovereign states and financial power.

The original 1904 Entente, with private 'informal' financial networks 'acting' for their Banks and governments, had reasonable balances at war's outset in 1914, like most combatants. But Europe's trade collapse meant France and Britain quickly became heavily in

---

[34] We saw Nordhaus (2002) confirms neglect of costs; and see below the neglect of war funding methods!

[35] See Tooze (2007, 2014); Ahamed (2009) compares the US Fed, the BoE, Banque de France and the Reichsbank (also in context). Indeed, the 1910s–40s was so fraught that records and data rarely complement. For example, Tooze (2014: 207–8) citing Keynes's attack on the gold 'fetish' and cited in Ahamed (2009: 155) on gold as a 'barbarous relic', agree, but neither holds a debt theory of money. While Hawtrey who did (1962 [1932]: 209), praised the NY District Fed's Strong saying it was 'a disaster for the world' that Strong died in 1928, Ahamed (2009: 318–21) agrees; whereas Schumpeter (1954: 1121) citing Hawtrey, was not impressed with Strong's policies; Hawtrey praised Schacht in ending German hyperinflation; the BoE is Hawtrey's main culprit; next the Banque (cf. Ahamed 2009). See below for the Genoa Conference.

debt to Wall Street. Japan also lent to its Entente allies. Combatants issued war bond IOUs. France's middle class bought more war bonds than the UK's (this led to constant disputes, we see).[36] In the case of foreign borrowing, the City funded Italy, France, Russia and far more, Wall Street funded the Allies, before and after America entered the war in April 1917. Since 1915, J. P. Morgan & Co had been 'spending in America on behalf of the British government' to buy armaments for the UK, for which Morgan was paid fees. So, Morgan mobilised the US armaments industry privately. Britain and France borrowed from Wall Street in dollars, therefore, could not later inflate their way out of debt, unlike Germany, postwar. Total Allied war loans from US 'private investors' amounted to $28 billion in 1919; the Fed and the Administration demanded that US financiers be paid back in full.[37]

October 1916 saw war dragging on ruinously (and without the USA). The Entente tried to raise a further $1.5 billion from Morgan & Co whereupon (to Tooze), it asked the Fed for help on the grounds that it had 'bankrolled' the Entente's side since 1915. But Morgan got no 'reassurance' either from the new Fed or from President Wilson. The Fed announced the US 'public' should no longer invest in the Entente, and Wilson is on record for drafting a letter to the Fed to refuse Morgan.[38] After the Fed's (or Wilson's) warning in late 1916, and with no backing for Morgan, sterling was offloaded by speculators on Wall Street. As a consequence, 'J.P. Morgan and the British Treasury were forced into emergency purchasing of sterling to prop up the British currency'; while Britain suspended support for French

---

[36] On private networks, including the privately-owned BoE, see Tooze (2014: 36): he is hardly precise (what does 'acting for' entail?). Tooze also claims the Entente 'printed money': if that means the UK Bradbury bonds, it is not so, see earlier. On the trade collapse and debt to their ally Japan, also see Tooze (2014: 96). See Ahamed (2009: 84) on French bonds as mainly middle-class purchases.

[37] See Dyster and Meredith (2012: 85) on the debt chains; see Tooze (2014: 36–8); on Morgan 'spending' in US dollars on allies' debt, thus also how finance leadership switched to USA.

[38] On J. P. Morgan: see mostly in Tooze (2014: 50–1); Paul Warburg is also cited drafting the letter for Wilson (Chernow 1993) as a then Fed Board member and part designer of the Fed. His time on the Board was marked by WWI bigotry due to his double exclusion, a German-Jewish background. Of interest is that the Fed cannot be called 'independent' in this case.

purchasing and made demands on Tsarist Russia's gold. The British cabinet 'concluded ... that Wilson meant to force their hands and put an end to the war in a matter of weeks'. To be fair, the President had just been re-elected to keep the USA *out* of the war, but the Allies were still shocked at what they perceived to be this funding horror.[39] (I do not believe the Fed directed US foreign policy.)

Just then, Germany's Chancellor put in 'a pre-emptive demand for peace negotiations'. Wilson sent a 'peace note' on 18 December 1916 asking *all sides* to explain their war aims. Armaments shares plunged on Wall Street; the German ambassador to the US and Wilson's son-in-law, William McAdoo, then US Treasury Secretary, were 'accused of making millions by betting against Ententeconnected [US] armaments stock'. The Central Powers faced bankruptcy but rejected Wilson's offer to 'mediate'. It seems Wilson was delighted with the US rise to creditor ascendancy; and he got a navy larger than the Royal Navy despite his anti-war mandate.[40]

J. P. Morgan's financing of the UK and France had the effect of 'carrying out a mobilization of a large part of the US economy' to build armaments, and of creating a boom that might become 'too big to fail'. America got further power over debtor countries, but that power did not necessarily belong to the US Administration. 'Was Wall Street too independent?' asks Tooze, a question President Wilson seemed to have acted upon when he refused Fed support to further J. P. Morgan lending. Morgan's loans suggest that private banks here took a directive role in economic development, unlike Hamburg or Berlin bankers who regularly had to ask permission of the German

---

[39] On UK Treasury, Cabinet, and again Morgan, see Tooze (2014: 51–2) and on the Entente's war finance, also influx of their gold to the USA, see Ahamed (2009: 73–95 and 130–53).

[40] The Central Powers comprised the Austro-Hungarian Empire, Germany and Turkey. In late 1916, Germany's money supply 'ballooned' (Ahamed 2009: 88) and its civilian cut backs saw starving. On McAdoo, and on Wilson's trying to impose 'peace without victory', 'George V is said to have wept', see Tooze (2014: 52). Keynes (1920) saw another Wilson in person; warrior Teddy Roosevelt and his Republicans opposed Wilson, and Clemenceau spoke of Wilson's 'sanctimonious' manner. Wilson's was a vision of the USA as a moral exception in promoting a civilised world *run by whites*, to Tooze (2014: 60). Herbert Hoover and Strong spoke of 'dark' old Europe; in Ahamed (2009: 132).

Foreign Office first. Wall Street banks profited nicely, yet they did build up America's industrial strength.[41]

When the US joined the war soon after, the Fed became a going concern (somewhat), devoted to war finance – allegedly not in directly purchasing government bonds, merely in selling or 'marketing' them to 'investors': that was the argument anyway.[42] In April 1917, the US Administration conducted a drive to create mass buying of war 'Liberty Bonds'. Congress insisted that 'the dollars lent must be spent exclusively in America', like J. P. Morgan's war loans. But US lending hardly covered the Allies' war needs. Robert Self explains:

> US neutrality [pre-1917] precluded anything other than the flotation of private loans and these obligations were all repaid in full. Immediately after the US declaration of war, however, the Congress passed the first of five Liberty Loan Acts authorizing the sale of bonds to the US public. With the finance raised by this appeal, the US treasury was empowered to receive 'certificates of indebtedness' from Allied governments in return for credits with which to finance their essential war purchases in the United States.
>
> While Britain was the largest debtor, with outstanding obligations to the United States of $4,227,000,000, in its turn it was also owed $6,753,000,000 by its allies, of which a large proportion had been advanced after April 1917, owing to the refusal of the United States to finance anything other than dollar purchases in its domestic markets to the benefit of its own producers and own tax revenues.

[41] See Tooze (2014: 38–9; 52–3) on Wall Street and on Wilson's second refusal to Morgan; Stern (1977) mentions Bismarck's lack of interest in colonialism; also on Germany and WWI, Friedman (2005: 279–84); Chernow (1993) on the Warburgs' visits to Berlin; cf. Ingham (1984), on the British empire and City banks' global investment, also agrees: Wall Street was usually more 'independent' than the case in Britain.

[42] 1970s neoclassical revisionists, we see further on, *hate* the Fed's war links to Wilson; also later, a dispute about whether the Fed did monetise the debt, against its founding FRA. Ahamed (2009: 94), disagrees (no 'direct' bond purchases), but others suggest it was via the private bank 'war loan' accounts: see Palley (2015); Wray (2014b: 115); Tymoigne (2014: 87; 94), and also Table 1.2.

The novelty in this arrangement was the extraordinary coordination of public credit and protection of US industry, to an extent unparalleled among the hegemons of former centuries.[43] The Administration recruited its most influential central banker, the Governor of the New York District Fed (privately-owned), Benjamin Strong, for the Liberty Bond advertising campaign. In all cases of this type of financing, central bankers are behind what Treasuries are doing, but, given the US Fed's strict FRA remit the Fed *seemed* to be distanced from buying these Bonds; also, from banks' typical expanding the money supply from their lending for war. By the end of WWI, the Fed had the largest reservoir of gold bullion in the world; France the next.[44]

Keynes argued in 1917 that Wilson's Administration enjoyed this chance to put the UK in a state of 'complete financial helplessness and dependence', while France and Italy were far more decisively indebted to both creditors. The Entente *chose* to aim for a brutal final 'blow' to Austria-Hungary, Turkey and Germany, via the Entente's credit dependency on the emerging US hegemon, but without any later currency depreciation option to devalue their US dollar loans. This was the occasion when Keynes said to the UK Treasury that 'we have made a fetish of the gold standard'. But on no account, could Britain afford to leave it – in that near-bankrupt situation of a war to which Keynes was a conscientious objector.[45]

DISPUTES TODAY OVER THE FED'S WWI

Stepping back to claims and counter-claims, the effects of war finance and the US Fed's role remain disputed – if they are mentioned at all (I compare two positions here). It is difficult to tease out a basic

---

[43] In Self (2007: 284–5); also see Ahamed (2009: 94–5) and Tooze (2014: 206–7) for claims about US financial hegemony and the protection of industry.

[44] Strong, formerly at J. P. Morgan, was allegedly influenced by Warburg to Chernow (1993); the gold imbalance was (to Hawtrey (1962 [1932]) a key problem postwar (thus his hopes for collective ways to manage gold at Geneva) and later the gold standard returned in Britain in 1925. See Self (2007) also Tooze (2014: 207), on the novelty of the US loans.

[45] Keynes, cited in Tooze (2014: 207–8) and see for Tooze's view on the 'final blow' aim.

story, since economic analysis heavily influences central bank policy now, and disputes are unresolved because capitalist money is contentious. Early central banking experiments hint at their context-driven nature. Just because Sweden's Riksbank was the first money-issuing organisation to *survive*, earlier than the BoE of 1694, their practices did not invariably apply to those of earlier or later CBs. Economic orthodoxy developed 'theory' through winning some loud public quarrels over central bank founding Acts. Political winners and losers were often temporary, however, and the legislation revised. Orthodox economists' claims to superior theory implicitly relied on the seemingly settled nature of battles won that were specific to some national elites not others. From that (messy evidence), they deduced a timeless model of neutral money that made WWI finance as anomalous as financial crises. Keynes said of classical economics, of its 'virtue' of austerity, its logical 'beauty':

> That it could explain much social injustice and apparent cruelty … afforded a measure of justification to the free activities of the individual capitalist, attracted it to the support of the dominant social force behind authority.[46]

As this suggests, WWI had not shaken orthodox assertions that (mundane) relations of the BoE and UK Treasury, to the 'social force' – *the City* – were timeless and neutral. Alternatives offered by Keynes or Hawtrey did not prevail against the 1920 deflation or the 1925 British gold standard revival. Their ideas were heeded somewhat only after Britain suspended gold in 1931. US and British commercial banks dominated their central banks, either through the Fed's 1913 design

---

[46] On the Riksbank, and on how the orthodox line that acceptable ideas of CBs only emerged in 1850–1900 is 'a myth', see Ugolini (2011: 3) or referred mostly to the BoE and Fed alone. Many, from Schumpeter to Ingham, agree economic analysis *was influential* and very much tied to political disputes. See Keynes (1964 [1936]: 33; 32) who explains, just before this quote, how a 'Ricardian victory' (e.g. in the BoE 1844 Act) was from 'a complex of suitabilities … to the environment into which it was projected'. Keynes's passage is also cited in Ingham et al. 2016: 1248 for being 'contentious'. That is, Keynes spoke plainly of who benefited from 'cruelty'. Ricardo's influence is discussed in later chapters.

or the BoE's favourite practices. Orthodox economics usually attained 'policy relevance' with axioms that conveniently ignored diverse conflicts of state executives and legislatures, central banks and banks, and producers of goods and services. The desires of populations must be unspeakable to preserve this logical 'beauty'.[47]

Armed with an inherently anti-democratic logic, then, in today's economic debates about the 1910s to 1930s, typically either private banks or governments are targets of attack, rarely both. The social sciences (including economics) tend to be more even-handed.[48] Economic claims to 'natural' scientific progression give orthodoxy an unwarranted certainty about how, for example, the BoE or the Fed made 'mistakes' and 'errors'. It would be nice if this were tongue-in-cheek, given that central banks bow to the social forces of the day. US Treasury had performed many central bank functions and borrowed from banks long before President Wilson established the Fed in 1913. Even then, relationships between the Administration, the new (divided) Fed, and Wall Street are obscure, partly from secrecy, so claims of institutional blame continue. Others argue Washington DC and Wall Street were vehemently opposed.[49]

One dispute has been whether the 1913 Fed was just a Wall Street instrument (heterodox left) or that it had 'too much' Washington 'influence' (libertarian right). Both sides talk about 'politicisation'

---

[47] Howson (1985: 177) compares Keynes and Hawtrey; both disputed 'neutral' money. Whether US banks did 'dominate' the Fed, the exception we saw earlier was the Fed/ Wilson refusal to help J. P. Morgan in the WWI disputes. Perhaps it was an exception to prove the rule.

[48] For example, in sociology, students are schooled in Durkheim, Weber and Marx, Wollstonecraft, (etc.), and are begged to make up their own minds; the economics in Polanyi, Weber, the *sociology* in Schumpeter or Keynes are included. Economics is no natural science.

[49] Exceptionally, Calomiris (2013) accepts class/sectoral/state disputes and empirical details (i.e. less axioms) but with orthodoxy, blames democracy as 'populist'; see Chapter 3, on disputes about 1820s practices of the 'real bills' doctrine, by which the Fed focused on bank money creation from lending for trade through the 1920s, to Calomiris (2013). We saw, Chapter 1, that the doctrine was safe; but missed *innovations* in bank money expansion. So did Calomiris.

in a disparaging way, but very differently. Two contrasting 'just so' stories circulating today show the background to the suspicions of 'Washington DC' in WWI. The right criticises the Fed 'support' of Treasury in both WWI and WWII as political, although all monetary policy is unavoidably so.[50] For example, Fed expert Charles Calomiris was present with Bernanke and Greenspan in 2010 (not wearing disguises this time) to celebrate the Fed's secret conception at Jekyll Island in 1910. His arguments are exactly like the 1913 Wall Street views of the FRA. WWI finance needs, Calomiris argues, served to 'politicize' the Fed in helping Treasury to market its Liberty Bonds. This was sin enough, but worse, it reduced bank reserve requirements and the 'penalty' discount rate for Lender of Last Resort (LOLR) activities of the Fed, all of which set up, to Calomiris, the 'short-term inflationary binge of 1917-20'. Conveniently, he avoids how the owners of private District Feds (i.e. private banks) reduced the terms of LOLR to *banks*, because the toothless Fed Board (in Washington DC) only had veto powers over District Feds, and it did not use it in that case. Calomiris argues that 'politicizing' paved the road to perdition in 1933, when F. D. Roosevelt made the Fed 'a fiscal instrument of the U.S. Treasury'. He says nothing about private banking's WWI profits; nor about Treasury's weakness in having to entice banks to buy war bonds. His most scandalous omission (apart from war itself) is the American Economic Association's 1918 criticism of US Treasury for not relying more on taxes (to reduce war price inflation).[51]

[50] Balance sheets as simplified in Table 1.2 show no CB can avoid working for its state and the finance sector. So, cf. Calomiris (2013); see Ugolini (2011) on US Treasury tasks pre-1913 and Wray (2014b). See also on obscurities, Greider (2014: 8) and Johnson and Kwak (2011: 26–7), also both on Benjamin Strong as a 'leader' of J. P. Morgan's 1907 alleged Wall Street 'bailout' that US Treasury apparently helped secretly, thus a view of the 1913 Fed as 'instrument' of Wall Street. But which Fed: the President-appointed Fed Board based in DC or the District Feds (New York above all), appointed by the local commercial banks?

[51] Calomiris explores how cabals and political alliances differed over the centuries, yet he loathes changes like the democratic character of states in the twentieth century. My quotes are in Calomiris (2013: 172–3), his chapter from Jekyll Island Fed's centenary. There is little on bank profits in either Calomiris (2012) or Calomiris and Haber (2014), which *avoids* the GFC, and greatly admires Reagan and Thatcher. Giannini (2011) often

The left, on the other hand, tends to assume that the democratic state 'misunderstands' the political opposition to forms of state control from banking sectors and anti-union employers, as do citizens. Randall Wray, who urges a fiscal-led and Fed recovery for today, alerts us to how governments finance themselves by creating demand for the safest money (HPM), via imposing obligations to pay taxes. 'Logically, the state must issue its currency through its spending or through lending before it can receive its currency in payment' Wray says. He is correct, so too on misunderstandings of all sides, except that democracies do not always produce well-meaning states. As he says, semi-feudal sovereigns spent by '"raising a tally" or by minting new coin to finance a war' – both more 'transparent' methods than the state offering bills for private banks to discount, or than states creating a central bank, which are obscure or 'opaque'.[52] Bank discount practices subtract part of their loan (bill sale) as pre-paid interest. However correct his logic, states can refuse to 'understand'; bond and currency trader sell-offs are constant threats, as in the non-benign WWI sequence.[53]

What occurred was the financial sector could expand further when demand for loans was high, even to create speculative panics and 'rule' politically. That 'obscurity' was the WWI problem, also ignored by orthodoxy which harps on the sins of state debt and (wage) inflation, but not bank asset or their money inflation fostered (for example) by state war debts, both ignored in orthodoxy. Name one

disparaged 'mass politics' more openly than with the loose term 'populism' of Calomiris; the District Feds and taxes of the AEA proposal are cited in Shull (2014: 21).

[52] HPM = High Powered Money rests on 'chartalist' views which recall 'the tally', so as Wray (2014a: 11) puts it, the state's currency and CB's reserves are at the top of the hierarchy of 'monetary IOUs', thus, the exchequer submits bills to banks, which supply deposits to finance sovereign spending; if banks 'refuse' to buy bonds, the typical answer was to create a CB. Wray (2014a: 17) adds there is a 'remote' chance of a 'bankers' strike' against a 'democracy'. That is a concern (perhaps only the Fed could resist), though his logic is fine cf. Chapters 3 and 8; see Ingham (2013) on the Fed here, and cf. Palley (2015: 56).

[53] Discounting is a loan where e.g. $100 must be repaid later at interest, but only $99 is lent so 1 per cent is 'discounted'; Withers (1918 [1909]: 143) is clearest. Central banks came to use the discount rate practice to reduce instability e.g. after the BoE discount rate during 1830s–70s had little impact on market rates (Giannini 2011: 90–1).

belligerent *state* in WWI that was benign or democratic. It cannot be assumed that banks are inherently benign either (or that they would be if only the state stopped interfering or taxing top income brackets).

These crisscrossing arguments, described as simply as possible in the following chapters, include the evidence that states are perfectly capable of producing money for FE with inflations kept low. Banks can foster employment too. The total wars achieved that regardless of finance sector and mobile capital opposition. By WWII, the terrible legacies of the 'thirty-year war' provided the circumstances to produce forty years of peaceful FE. It was also a time of rising wages, low inflation and hopes for extending distributive justice to all. Logic played no part in the later substantial attacks on the livelihoods of citizens, workers, young and old in the 1970s on to the 2010s, in which mobile capital won the world, and nuclear-armed or nuclear-protected states displaced most cannon fodder.[54] Central banks adjusted to conditions at every changing set of circumstances. Dissonances grew later, since their FE remit (against deflation) had equal importance with their 'price stability' remit (against inflation) for the Second Wartime exigencies, and for socially useful purposes of money creation after 1945.

WAR INFLATION AND DRASTIC DEFLATION: 1920

From my (gross) caricature of libertarian right and statist left ideas, and bleak prognosis for central banks to see any future alliance with social democracy, we return to an earlier time when opinion was

---

[54] On FE, see Chapter 1. Having given a taste of two opposing economics in Calomiris versus Wray, let me say the so-called orthodox right has too many permutations to list here; generally anti-democratic, there are social conflict approaches (Calomiris), deductive Rational Actor, pro-markets and substance theorists of money. On CB mandates, the right favours the illogical, indecent, socially unjust path (price stability but heavy deflationary costs); the heterodox left does not. Usually fiscal-CB consolidation; welfare and FE with price stability (mild inflations if at all) are their favoured mandates. 'Heretical', heterodox economics debates, as discussed in Ingham et al. (2016), are often just as 'obscure' as the Orthodoxies, and as heated, also about benign/malign governments. That varies on both sides.

also as 'impervious to argument' as it is today.[55] The dismal facts of the sudden 1920 deflation are as consistently avoided today as the facts of war finance, except by staid economic historians and some heterodox monetary approaches. The enormity of the post-WWI fall-out (deflation) is unrecognisable in Calomiris's loose talk of an inflationary 'binge' in 1917. Added to theorems that central banks must follow 'rules' against (wage) inflation alone, with no discretion, he neglects the US and UK deflation at that time, of countries that were, after all, the rising and declining hegemons. The German hyperinflation has been the sole horror story even after the GFC. It *was* horror and destroyed rentiers and savers, but deflation prevailed among the victors and, soon after its hyperinflation moment, in Germany.

An exclusive fixation on (wage) inflation alone represents the 'hard money' hawk of indecent rule for central banks – so 'soft on banks' is this rule that private banking's inflationary role (money or assets) is rarely mentioned. Banking's faults (if any) are due to governments, 'populists' and 'weak' central banks. For this position, terminology for CBs such as Public Bank or the truly renegade term, 'People's Bank', is a scandal. The pro-market nostalgia for a private CB has resulted in a rewriting of history from deduction not evidence, that pretends all its opponents are 'soft money' types.[56] The 'neutral money' attack is against (cheap) money as politicised, as if sound (dear) money policies were apolitical. Keynes is painted a leftie, post-GFC, regardless of the fact that he criticised inflation. For example, in his Versailles Treaty pamphlet against war reparations, *The economic consequences of peace* (1920), Keynes quoted Lenin on how the surest way to overturn a society is 'to debauch the currency'. Keynes's 1940 work on war finance was tough on wage inflation, while insisting that WWI's beneficiaries were the 'capitalist class'. Other renegades

---

[55] As Schumpeter (1954: 694) called the Ricardian 'victory' that led from 1815, to the UK 1844 Bank Charter Act, an allegedly technical move aiming to stop the BoE monetising state debt or consolidating with fiscal policy.

[56] Niall Ferguson stooped (post-GFC on TV) to improper remarks on Keynes; the People's Bank was the Australian Labor Party (ALP) aim, see Chapters 1 and 4. It is not comparable to the People's Bank of China.

being difficult about private banks can end in naïve hopes for govern-ments' technical ability to control financial power. Some students of monetary-fiscal policy (e.g. sociologists) doubt that states can do this without some shift in the political and social arrangements that benefit private banking and *rentiers*, or state war interests.

The reasons for the savage US postwar deflation in 1920 (unlike the milder one of 1866–79 following USA's Civil War) are therefore hard to pin down, due to familiar backroom deals and dubious claims on all sides. Between 1914 and 1920 the US price level nearly doubled, but it dropped by 22 per cent in 1922. Wages rarely rose, particu-larly after demobilisation forced ex-soldiers to compete for jobs under deflation. In 1919, some of 'the regional Feds raised discount rates sharply ... and a deep retraction followed that led to deflation of farm prices'. The NY Fed's Discount rate in June 1920 went from its war-time 4.25 per cent to 6 per cent and then hit 7 per cent, an increase of nearly 50 per cent – other District Feds increased rates by 70 per cent. Ben Strong (NY Fed) kept it there for a whole year. There were many local, non-Wall Street bank failures between 1921 and before the 1929 crash. To heterodoxy it was an 'unprecedented deflation', which saw a steep rise in farm foreclosures.[57] Historians agree that 7 per cent was 'dramatic', and mention the fact that Japan started the deflation move, and that the BoE had increased rates to the same 7 per cent.[58] Strong and the NY Fed had apparently opposed Treasury's

[57] This is barely acknowledged in Calomiris (2013) or Calomiris and Haber (2014) yet stressed in e.g. White, who also shows 766 US national banks and 4,645 state banks failed between 1920 and 1929 (2013: 40–1). Elsewhere, White has written with Calomiris; both defer to Meltzer's Fed history (noted in this book) and also cite Friedman and Schwartz's history. On high rates and farm price collapse, see Wray (2014b). Paul Warburg was one of the few bankers stressing how to control bank expansion, see on supervision: in White (2013), since Warburg knew the BoE and Reichsbank well, but was ignored; Calomiris and Haber (2014) fail to cite wrongdoing by banks, only fragility from unit banks (and not, they insist, banks with branches: see Chapter 1's contrary 1890 case on that). This is despite their impressive sweep of 300 years of insufficiently 'liberal' and allegedly too 'populist' economic policies.

[58] See Tooze (2014: 360; 216; 344; 349) on the dramatic deflation, and Ahamed (2009: 157; 161; 157–8) who stresses Germany and France at 1920 chose *devaluation*; Germany succumbing to hyperinflation in 1921, France later. Tooze suggests the Bank of Japan (BoJ) considered it too difficult to deflate savagely; that France *refused* to cut back state

insistence on such a sharp rise in rates: Tooze cites Treasury officials saying that they did not 'care if [Wall Street] crashed'. Strong had earlier disputed the Fed Board over Treasury's determination to keep rates low, since he claimed Wall Street banks were in 'danger'. He reduced banks' reserve requirements in 1920. The main reason for the 'fragility' of Wall Street banks postwar appears to be a decline in their gold reserves, owing to their money expansion and stock market speculation.[59]

A Congressional inquiry of 1921, convened partly due to what became a huge political crisis in 1920 (on many fronts), criticised the Fed's delay in restricting 'the expansion, inflation, speculation and extravagance'. Moreover, one Fed Board member, Adolph Miller, said that the Fed's duty should be to avoid such sharp contractions, and to make the 'extremes' of the 'business situation ... less pronounced and violent'. Miller asked why the public should accept this severity and unemployment when moderation was preferable.[60] One problem was the Fed's alleged 'apolitical' design, so much so it neglected the effect on the nation of its extreme contraction in raising rates. The Fed's lack of a macroeconomic employment vision was obvious in the postwar period, as was also the case with the Bank of England, which saw only the City.

From such various partisan accounts or the personalised focus on heroes and villains, it appears that, despite raging war price inflation and wilful bank money expansion, US Treasury was frantic to

---

spending, unlike UK and USA; it stopped *expanding* state money supply. That they rejected the savage 1920 UK and US deflation may have lessened the impact of 1920–1 on world recession compared to that of 1929–30, to Tooze (2014: 358–62). Hawtrey (1962 [1932]) disputes the last point, see below.

[59] Strong is cited in Tooze (2014: 344). For Wall Street and alleged NY Fed motivations, see Bordo and Wheelock (2013: 75; 97). So, there are disputes in the literature.

[60] In Wray's edited collection, based on Modern Money Theory, see Shull (2014: 21–2), and Wray (2014b: 111). Miller is cited Shull (2014: 22) as a renegade. The small farm sector barely recovered in this contraction of 1919–20 (and sank after 1930), but apparently, Congress reduced its concern in the 1920s: see in Dyster and Meredith (2012: 83–5); Friedman (2005: 94), who also discusses the 1920s demagogues, Ku Klux Klan revival, wage cuts and demobilised troops.

keep interest rates low after WWI ended. This seems a general pattern of war borrowing: low interest to reduce Treasury's immediate servicing payments (which mainly go to private banks), even if the related bank money inflation lowers the value of taxes. Again, it appears that a 'political' argument emerged to justify this narrow state interest: another war pattern. Thus, according to US Treasury, 'savers' had bought Liberty Bonds, and a rise in interest rates would reduce the price and resale value of these Bonds, and allegedly affect 20 million people. This argument ignored the fact that loans create deposits, not the other way around, and that buying Liberty Bonds had little to do with 'savings' but banks. Nonetheless, high rates indicate the market 'thinks' state debt is 'weak', and that reduces the Bonds' resale value (even if traders make guesses). Treasury claimed that patriotic household lenders and the Bond market would lose out with any drop in the resale value. Tooze argues that bond buyers were mainly banks, not 'savers' both during and after the war. It is in that sense that the Fed 'underwrote bank credit', an argument which has diverse support. Wall Street entered via these balance sheet back doors and increased inflationary pressures. Specifically, the Fed's help towards financing the war was its offer of 'preferential discount rates on loans ("advances") to member banks secured by government bonds', with banks' purchase of a billion dollars' worth in the open market. This story is not clear-cut since banks and US Treasury stood to benefit on opposing but shifting fronts. France and Britain stood to lose as large US debtors. Generally, little of what was claimed by states, central banks or private banks can be taken at face value.[61]

One American peculiarity, dating from April 1917, was that the banks, and not the Fed, held 'war loan deposit accounts' for US

---

[61] See Tooze (2014: 216) on Wall Street purchases – his is not a Schumpeter line; also see Bordo and Wheelock (2013: 75; 97), on the 'preferential rates' to those banks which were Fed members and so able to borrow from District Feds, which they owned. War finance is 'pro-cyclical' since states and banks are spending crazily on various 'ventures' going nowhere economically (save for the US car industries), into consumer price inflation, asset speculation and war destruction.

Treasury. These accounts received the proceeds of Treasury's Liberty Bond offerings and, up to 1929, private banks could monetise Treasury debt when told to buy T-bonds and credit these bonds to their special Treasury accounts. Perhaps this was how the Fed could avoid (or try to avoid) being accused of monetising state war finance. Government bonds show up in all central-bank balance sheets (Table 1.2), but the Fed's weird and cumbersome system is anomalous. The US requirement to this day is that the proceeds from taxes and state debt are first placed in private banks, and banks enter them as 'cash or notes in hand' in their balances. Formally, banks cannot touch the deposits. When Treasury wants to spend, it requests that its proceeds be transferred to its Fed deposit account. Why bother?[62]

The efforts with 'quantitative easing' (QE) to refinance bank balance sheets after the 2008 collapse, resembled what happened during war, in that CB war finance was usually intended to monetise sovereign debt, and QE did that for banks. The Fed tried to do this in a way behind the backs of many (making it more alarming). Recall the original Federal Reserve Act 1913 (and central banks today), ruled out monetary financing to the state (and not QE to banks). Banks expand their advances on such deposits, often creating money inflation that might not be serviced; whereas taxes reduce or retire government base money expansion. The point (see Figures 5.1 and 5.2) not mentioned by hard money people is that many WWI belligerents hardly taxed, unlike the situation during the Napoleonic Wars when UK inflation was only slight. Still, what was involved in the WWI T-bond 'marketing' by the Fed is obscure. In such balance sheet manoeuvres the Fed still monetises debt, whether of the banks or US Treasury. In the process of Treasury *spending* on its Fed deposit account (see Table 1.2) and *filling* its Fed account when loan (and now tax) proceeds come in, the Fed debits or credits the private banks' reserve deposits at the Fed

---

[62] This partly contrasts with accounts in Tooze (2014: 216; 342–5). The special accounts are in Tymoigne (2014: 88; 94) and Moe (2014: 47); and are now called Treasury Tax and Loan Accounts (TTL). These MMT proponents take the US TTL accounts held in private banks for granted. But why if no other CB bothers?

as well. Debits lower the amount of private bank Fed reserves (more so when Treasury is spending *less*) and the 'base money' amount or fraction on which banks are permitted to create money.

In the final analysis (whether monetising is forbidden or not), the Fed ends up holding government debt – CB's lucrative interest-paying assets in any case, and they are entered as liabilities to private banks too, through the double-entry balance sheet norm.[63] Private banks can indulge in 'off-balance sheet' adventuring, as well. In WWI, one clue to 'adventuring' was a dispute between US Treasury and the Fed about the rebadged postwar 'Victory Bonds' (issued in spring 1919).[64] These bonds were designed to reduce the public's now excess purchasing power (and thus reduce price inflation). But there is no agreement about what happened. Tooze says it was 'misguided'. The dispute between Treasury and the Fed could be related to how private banks deposited the proceeds of the Victory Bonds into their 'war loans accounts' for Treasury later (nothing is clear), or to how banks bought Victory Bonds in greater quantities than 'the public'. Undoubtedly banks created money with this expansion, and the 'public' was not sacrificing anything but instead was on a spending spree.[65] This mess is matched nicely with a scholarly dispute about who was the champion and who the wrongdoer, US Treasury or Strong's NY Fed.

Calamity came when the District Feds finally raised interest rates in late 1919, while at the same time reducing banks' reserve

---

[63] See Chapter 1 and Tables 1.1 and 1.2: There are two entries for any one debt or deposit, as an asset and a liability. Banks and central banks both practice fractional reserve banking on their deposits to multiply their deposit-creating loans or advances. On QE see Chapter 8.

[64] This 'adventuring' in bank balance-sheets to Minsky (2008 [1986]: 279) is always possible without strong CB supervision.

[65] Wray (2014b: 117–19) on (US) Fed Liabilities; Tooze (2014: 342–5). To Withers who puts things clearly, banks have reserves in their central banks which they 'use as cash' and, when money is 'abundant' (as in WWI), banks use it 'as the basis for the manufacture of more credit'; Withers (1918 [1909]: 109, 249); Schumpeter (1954) also uses the term 'manufacture' money. Withers did not trust BoE 1908 statements (see Chapter 1); it was a private bank.

requirements.[66] Jobs collapsed during America's and Britain's tightening. Which institution was responsible for the rate rises? Was it the huge bank expansion that led to Wall Street 'fragility' and then its steep contraction of money? Why did US Treasury choose not to raise taxes at the war's outset in 1917? Why did Victory Bonds fail to cut back consumer purchasing power? Was the Fed to blame or private bank expansion? Which arm of the Fed was involved? The original Fed design meant that local private banks owned the 12 District Feds (as they do to this day), not Treasury, and the Fed Board in Washington DC only had a veto at that time.

WAS THE FED'S STRUCTURAL DESIGN A FACTOR?

The postwar inflation of 1919 severely tested the 1913 Fed's governance, in that decisions had to be made under a 'checks and balances' design. The idea, which was partly Woodrow Wilson's (who fondly imagined he was above dirty politics), was to *divorce* the Fed from mud-slinging by establishing 'clash of interests' through a complicated and fragmented authority structure, which (it was thought) would avoid 'partisan' policies: but many partisans were excluded. At least one of the original Fed designers, Paul Warburg, thought it would be 'a paralyzing system' that gave powers and took them away.[67]

At that Congress inquiry of 1921 into the abrupt rise in inflation to harsh deflation, the Comptroller of the Currency claimed that District Feds 'discriminated against the rural banks'. Congress suggested in its 1922 report that the 'clash of interests' approach could not counter general economic instability. But it did add another agricultural, sectional interest to the membership of the Fed Board. Thus conflict between the various policies of twelve District Feds (the only policy initiators), and between them, the Fed Board, White House

---

[66] See the Fed balance sheet of 1920, in federalreserve.gov; evidence cf. Calomiris (2013) above; Tooze (2014: 216).

[67] Warburg is cited in Shull (2014: 20–4) and Shull here on governance. Johnson and Kwak (2011: 26–30) give evidence of considerable 1913 FRA conflict (e.g. financier-Senator Aldrich backing Strong; Louis Brandeis wanting democratic control of Wall Street).

and Congress, continued through the 1920s right up to the Fed's 'futility' in the early 1930s.[68] Detailing the Fed's founding, William Greider cites the few bank 'populists' remaining in Congress, who described the 1913 FRA as a central bank 'wholly in the interests of the creditor class, the banking fraternity' and commerce, with no provision for debtors and 'those who toil'. Others insist the moderate Louis Brandeis, critic of Wall Street had some, limited influence over Woodrow Wilson's muddled 1913 FRA.[69] To the 'hard money' people, the Fed was too 'political' until it 'regained' independence in 1919. Privately-owned District Feds created the 'intense depression' (as Hawtrey put it critically), stopping the economy and creating political havoc, while Wall Street became more concentrated and profitable.[70] The postwar 1920s then started grimly for most.

CENTRAL BANKS AND THE 1920S DISPUTES AND DISTRESS

How much did the Fed versus US Treasury dispute matter, either to postwar USA or the world? Wall Street was now global. The Bank of England, Reichsbank, the Banque de France and Fed were fighting among themselves when they were not conspiring against populations. Why was CB authority so influential? The war debts were a critical component. After all, it was Uncle Sam (crudely 'Uncle Shylock' to Europe) less the Fed, which insisted that France, Britain and Italy pay back their Wall Street 'creditors' to the max.[71] Why had the BoE/Treasury agreed to this US war-debt settlement? What of world imbalances of gold holdings? Was war financing the only thing? These are the disparate factors that made the 1920 Versailles Treaty

---

[68] On this futility, see Ahamed (2009: 172). See Shull (2014: 22–3) on Congress only increasing the 'clash of interests'.

[69] In Greider (2014: 9); who writes for *The Nation* (left wing), Greider's *Secrets of the Temple* on the Fed's history saw no evidence, for example to call Paul Volcker's Fed a group of wealthy financiers (unlike the 1913 Fed).

[70] See the Jekyll Island debates, earlier in this chapter, such as Calomiris (2013); cf. the post-1920 'intense depression' is in Hawtrey (1962 [1932]: 208).

[71] See Ahamed (2009: 169) on 'Shylock'. On in-fighting, see Hawtrey (1962 [1932]) and throughout, Ahamed (2009).

and the Entente's demand for German reparations more vindictive. So-called old Europe wanted to return to pre-war times despite their huge borrowings. Karl Polanyi insisted that the 'nature of the international system [of the nineteenth century] ... was not realised until it failed. Hardly anyone understood the political function of the international monetary system'. No one viewpoint can take in the interdependencies. Polanyi said of the 1920s that it was 'the democracies that were the last to understand the true nature of the catastrophe'.[72]

Global trends between 1914 and 1918 were everywhere inflationary: Africa, India, Egypt and South America had 'bitter social conflicts over shares of purchasing power and wealth'. Tooze argues that the British Empire rigged its markets;[73] peasant farmers in Europe started refusing to sell crops for disparately-valued currency, women were being used to undercut high war-time male wages and, from Japan to Tsarist Russia, rice or bread riots toppled elected states or regimes. This inflationary wave came from the expansion at the monetary centres – Europe and America. 'As war expenditure surged, in none of the combatant countries did taxes keep up. Nearly everywhere, the state skimmed off purchasing power by issuing government bonds repayable long after the end of the war', according to Tooze. Yet purchasing power rose![74] France paid the least for war expenditure from higher taxes, with only 5 per cent more tax taken for WWI.

Prices rose, and at war's end, the war stimulus to the US economy stopped (if not before). Treasury terminated contracts as war goods were no longer wanted; the demobilisation of troops was welcomed with a small government surplus by 1920. This shabby

---

[72] In Polanyi (1957 [1944]: 20, 22), but this was said in hindsight.
[73] To add here to Tooze (2014: 212–15); Dyster and Meredith (2012: 85; 100–11) show that Britain's preferential clause in Australia's 1906 tariff as special treatment, was not reciprocated and including the war indebtedness to the UK, an Australian pound was cheaper than Britain's (when it followed UK's 1925 gold return) increasing that debt's value.
[74] Purchasing power rose due to FE and bank expansion. It is weird that Tooze assumes that war bonds did 'skim' effective demand off households, above, since Tooze says banks were involved (2014: 212–15).

budget cut was unnecessary; pointlessly harsh on industry, workers and troops (notably the maimed), but good for Wall Street well-off *rentiers*, bond holders, as Keynes said of the UK as well.[75] Waves of strikes took place in 1919, mainly for wage increases. The US Attorney General and other officials treated these as a 'Red Scare' (as also happened in the UK), by using hired thugs with which to beat up unionists to 'rival the McCarthy episode' 30 years later. The Ku Klux Klan rose again in the early 1920s. According to Benjamin Friedman, all of this marked a new era of slow economic growth after the US prosperity of the 1890s. Immigration restrictions and high tariffs from early 1920 rose further, to the Smoot-Hawley tariff of 1930. The fact that the world's major creditor, the US, imported so few goods in the 1920s had a substantial impact on the global economy in terms of gold imbalances. Only Germany's Great Depression was worse than that of the US.[76]

Some argue that the central bank great 'Deflation' of 1920 largely imposed by the US (as the major creditor) is vastly under-reported in current texts, compared with constant refrains about 1921 German hyperinflation. Considerable confirmation is given by the economic historians, who now divide the 'global economy' into two stages, pre-1914 and post-1945. The selective histories of neoclassical economics avoid the 1920 deflation.[77] Churchill referred to the 'thirty years war' of 1914–45 and said he regretted the BoE decision (it was his, as Treasurer) to return Britain to the gold standard in 1925. A key motif then, and since 1975, is the harping against German

---

[75] See Ahamed (2009: 84) on French low taxes for WWI; and Tooze (2014: 216) on stimulus. Earlier this chapter, Keynes (1940), who also said taxes should not be endured by low income groups (for WWII), and Hawtrey (1962 [1932]) were both cited on the 1920 shock of central bank induced deflation and treasury harshness in the UK and USA.

[76] See Friedman (2005: 145–56): thus, we see the UK's first (1921) Labour Government was sacked after 'red' scares (in Chapter 3). In 1955, I saw severely incapacitated soldiers of WWII begging in London and Paris streets, shocking for my childhood visit from well-off Australia. Europe's and USA's First World War demobilisations were worse.

[77] See Tooze's criticism of the 'neglect' of the 1920 deflation (Tooze 2014: 216); this shows in Calomiris's glass eye (2013), above. For relentless inflation 'scares' to date, the parrots are recounted in Chapters 6 and 9.

hyperinflation in 1921, to ignore CB promotion of global deflation – of 1920, 1925 and 1929–33.

Tall stories about inflation disguised the preferences for deflation's distress. The Fed and BoE relished it.[78] Both Ralph Hawtrey and Irving Fisher in the 1930s emphasised that private banks and bond buyers (Keynes's creditor 'capitalist class') benefited fantastically when the value of debt grew, at the expense of debtors. In more tedious choruses, it was said that the problem stemmed from the 'imprudent' borrower. Hawtrey objected to blaming 'credit' for the 'business cycle', because the banking system increased the supply of *money* and war raised effective demand (for the few goods).[79] Central bank rate rises on bank money production operate primarily against consumers' (workers') wages and jobs, in harming all debtors (producers).[80]

The 1920 deflation tried 'to even out' the gold imbalances directly due to the war finance the US provided to the Entente. It should be strongly emphasised that the borrowing and the US terms for war funding (along with tax neglect) created so much later trouble. So did the major finance centres. In 1919, Hawtrey, then a rising star at the UK Treasury, wrote a paper on the urgent need for a stable value for money, given that the wartime 'displacement of large quantities of gold from circulation in Europe' to the USA had reduced the world value of gold. But 'remedies' were worse: 'If the countries which are

---

[78] Churchill's chameleon roles are cited mostly a few pages on.

[79] See Hawtrey (1962 [1932]: 204–7) on the nineteenth-century confusion of money with credit and of blaming 'imprudent' borrowers for a 'herd instinct'; of central banks ignoring money and the trade cycle, with 'mere symptoms' being uneven build-ups, precarious profits leading to speculation, 'over-trading and over extended industries' leading to crash, contraction and 'persistent depression'. These attributions are presented as new 'theory' from 1999 to date!

[80] The confusion of bank money with credit is another choir song. Banks do not 'credit' their borrowers, they create money (on fractional reserves) in advancing and depositing these loans (advances) as assets and banks' liabilities (Table 1.1). Minsky (2008 [1986]) points out that money-lenders/pawn shops have money to lend or to 'credit'; banks do not. Debt was not much on offer to workers until the 1920s, see Chapter 3. *Bankers can always refuse to make advances.* Industrialists were always the top debtors, so jobs/wages are indirectly hit with rate rises. Hawtrey (1932: 207) separated injustice to debtors from instant sackings by bosses, as another injustice. Bosses rarely appeal to CBs (cf. Chapter 4).

striving to recover the gold standard compete with one another for the existing supply of gold, they will drive up the world value of gold', resulting in more 'deflation and unemployment' (via high bank rates). He suggested global cooperation on a 'gold exchange standard to economise gold'. Hawtrey had 'high hopes' (as an active player) for the 1922 Financial Commission of the Genoa Conference, which urged the Bank of England to call a conference of central banks to regulate credit and the purchasing power of gold. It came to nothing; there was no conference on exchange-rate stability. In 1932, the 'catastrophe foreseen in 1922 had come to pass, and the moment had come to point the moral', he said. In his view, restoring the gold standard without global cooperation on money was the cause of the disaster.[81]

On the actual 1929 disaster, Hawtrey insisted, the BoE played a prominent role throughout the 1920s with the City of London. The BoE had divided responsibilities and it lacked 'far-sightedness'. Its most 'vital' Banking Department had been entrusted to a 'chartered company' (for profit), but the issue of currency was 'automatic': limited by 'gold' and thus against expansion (when needed) through its Issue Department ever since the 1844 Act.[82] The BoE 'tradition' was to govern by a 'directorate chosen from the financial and mercantile houses' most influential in the City. But 'technical understanding' was neither required nor a recommendation, although the 'art of central banking is something profoundly different' from familiarity with banking practices. The general view, Hawtrey said, was that 'a central banker should be like a ship captain who knows nothing of navigation'. Worse, he said this: 'Nothing but complete scepticism as to the power of central banks to do anything whatever promises *a quiet life*

---

[81] Hawtrey (1932: xiii–iv) citing his 1919 paper for the 1922 Genoa Plan, a League of Nations offshoot; its failure pointing to the 1932 'catastrophe', he said. Keynes by 1922 wanted an end to the gold standard altogether. The US did use a gold exchange standard, and Eichengreen and Mitchener (2003: 53) agree that central bankers failed to agree to new rules. See also Fisher (1933), and Ahamed (2009: 170–2) on the extent of gold building up in the US.

[82] The gold standard limited the Issue Department; the Banking Department was for profit. Withers shows the 1908 balance of the latter was over £78 million, of the Issue Department (gold), £55 million (1909: 244).

for their directorates'. The 1914–18 war debts magnified with the failure of the 1922 Genoa Plan, compared to BoE successes in controlling banks since the 1866 run on Overend-Gurney, he said. The 1929–32 calamity was due to the 'disastrously synchronized unwisdom' of the main central banks.[83] Yet states and financial sectors directed them so – and in the US too.

There are many sides, then, to the world deflation of the 1920s. On one side, there was the domestic monetary chaos with its divisive hatreds. On the other side, there was the USA's world financial and economic dominance and it was this that put the world onto its deflationary path. Tooze asks 'would America's own institutions prove adequate to the challenge of an entirely new kind of financial leadership?' Many stress US isolation policies and low imports from high tariffs, yet to explain the entire 1920s depression, banking crises and monetary disasters were also major factors.[84]

SAVING EMPIRE: 'WILD' MONETARY FLUCTUATIONS, HYPERINFLATION AND UK'S DEFAULT

We saw that reliance on borrowing for WWI finance later met savage monetary-fiscal decisions that worsened the shocks (except for banks). The immediate inflations arose from war shortages and bank expansion on treasuries' war-borrowing. But war itself stopped the 'global economy' and its old monetary arrangements. Global trade, investment and the payments system thereupon had postwar 'structural weaknesses' – Japan and the USA were the most economically advantaged from WWI. Yet Japan was politically fraught by battles between social democrats and rising fascists, and skirmishes against China at Britain's urging during WWI. The USA indeed had four

---

[83] Hawtrey (1962 [1932]: 246–8), my emphasis of 'the quiet life'. He praised Strong for a domestic stabilising policy in 1922 (Hawtrey 1962 [1932]: 209); Schumpeter (1954: 1121) dismissed Hawtrey's hopes in CBs and reflation; but praised his work on endogenous bank crises.

[84] See Tooze (2014: 211) and Dyster and Meredith (2012: 85). The depressed 1920s exacerbated the Great Depression's spiral down from a weakened base. Hawtrey stressed monetary disasters over tariff (Hawtrey 1962 [1932]: 208–9, 244).

separate recessions between 1918 and 1927, not counting the Great Depression.[85]

One postwar case – the Bank of England's dealings with the US Fed – exemplifies this harsh reaction against the expanding electoral interests. With the cessation of the 'first global economy' proving anything but temporary, new entrants with democratic demands were anyway most unwelcome to all those elites that had launched the war carnage. They tried to crush feminist, trade union, civil rights, socialist party and peace activists directly, or they looked away when Klansmen or Freikorps appeared.[86] Violence, domestically, was widespread: war's victors were the first to impose austerity and deflation on the bulk of their populations. While the defeated were so crushed that the only unified support was for reducing the value of reparations via a disastrous hyperinflation (albeit halted overnight, we see below), the victors' induced depressions were foolishly cruel.

British industrial and rural export sectors were priced out of world markets, and unemployment was high from lack of recovery, cutbacks, and the Bank's harsh deflation of 1920–1, which kept rates at 7 per cent for a whole year. These troubles were probably a 'side effect of a high degree of financial piety and rectitude' and surely motivated by desires to revive the unequal past. The City 'imposed' a high interest rate regime to compete with New York for funds. Some British authorities urged 'delay' in returning to the gold standard, but the BoE Governor, Montagu Norman, spied opportunities in the 1924

---

[85] Hawtrey 1932 used the term 'wild fluctuations'. Dyster and Meredith (2012: 81–2); and B. Friedman (2005: 144–5) give macroeconomic and social data; cf. Tooze (2014: 361) argues that the Bank of Japan and Banque de France partially made up for 1920s global imbalances, but not of the 1930s. Tooze (covering the years 1916-31) is an excellent source on Japan, China and extreme disorder created by the French and British carve up in the Middle East.

[86] An understatement: McAdoo, Woodrow Wilson's son-in-law and former Treasurer opposed 'anti-lynching laws' with Klansmen in the 1920s. The German Social Democrats' Weimar Government was depressingly weak: not only to the Freikorps fighting against democracy and 'the Reds'. Who killed Rosa Luxemburg? Tooze (2014) and Friedman (2005) explore these, with class and KKK resentment ably explained by Hofstadter (cited in Friedman 2005: 144). Friedman argues economic growth fosters progressive reforms; decline to regression, his exception the progressive FDR from 1933.

election of Baldwin's Tory government, with Churchill as Chancellor. Norman raced to consult his best friend across the Atlantic, the NY Fed governor, Benjamin Strong, who with 'the Morgan bankers', campaigned for Norman to get the pound back on gold pronto (with enticing loans too). The reasons the Fed advanced were: to improve world trade under 'Britain's leadership'; to reduce UK inflation that was still 'too high'; to prevent the US 'draining the world of gold'; and (secretly) to counter those with 'novel ideas for nostrums and expedients other than the gold standard'. Strong wanted a long UK shock therapy even though he knew that further hardships would ensue. The BoE (and Treasury) *wanted* hardships; the gold standard was a big subsidy and sector support to the global City. Lacking was any macroeconomic (inclusive) vision.[87]

Opponents in London dubbed these 'American pressure tactics'. A close friend of Churchill's, the press baron Lord Beaverbrook, decried the 'absurd and silly notion that international credit must be limited to the quantity of gold dug up'. Keynes agreed. Hawtrey criticised the 'undue fluctuations in the purchasing power of gold', and the BoE's 'mechanical system of gold reserve proportions'. Churchill's position varied. At first, he criticised American 'incentives' to wield their huge war gold reserves over world finance and Britain *and* objected to the City's 'interests' in gold. Montagu Norman replied saying that, if he returned to gold, Churchill might be abused by 'antiquated Industrialists' but not by 'posterity'. To this Churchill said: 'The Governor of the Bank of England shows himself perfectly happy with the spectacle of Britain possessing the finest credit in the world

---

[87] On 'piety' Ahamed (2009: 218–19) and Hawtrey agree. On Strong urging the UK return (mysteriously or was it Morgan influenced with its London branch, Morgan Grenfell?), see Ahamed (2009: 226–8). To add to Ahamed's story, Hawtrey agreed the BoE needed 'cheap' money for a 'trade depression' and, after 1925, UK workers' incomes were 'compressed'; US trade suffered; Germany had a severe *depression* straight after hyperinflation. The Fed had opposed Britain's credit restrictions pre-1925 and in 1927, the Fed 'intensified' its 'relaxation': the defence of Strong in Hawtrey (1962 [1932]: 210–11). Against Hawtrey on this, Ahamed's sources on Strong are newer releases of classified records; he explains the 'nostrums' were Keynes's and other renegades; see Epstein (2006: 10) further on the gold subsidy to the City.

simultaneously with a million and a quarter unemployed'.[88] Those groping to analyse the war changes and to promote a more equitable monetary policy for domestic social relations (such as Fisher, Hawtrey or Keynes) had varied arguments, but as seen above, they were shut out.

Churchill gave in, possibly to Treasury and Empire. One aspect of this decision involved higher rates for over a year in 1925 which 'compressed incomes', intensified unemployment, and led to the 1926 general strike. The other aspect was that returning to gold was so 'costly' – the incoming money was 'hot' speculative, which offered no permanent investment, and required high interest for the entire 1920s while the trade depression continued and spread. And what was the City doing meanwhile? It was as usual lending overseas, not to Wales or the Midlands.[89]

Norman was a rigid gold bug like Treasury. He took no heed of the 'cheap money' policy for trade depressions that the BoE had used since 1844; and, like his milieu was indifferent to 'lower orders'. The BoE's macroeconomic understanding was minimal and it wilfully despised (UK) industry. Norman was enthralled with the City, American central bankers and – after German hyperinflation was halted 'miraculously' via the Rentenmark (in late 1923) – with Hjalmar Schacht. He became President of the Reichsbank after his Rentenmark triumph. Few know why this German 'miracle' was so effective. Today's central bankers pretend that letting 'the inflation Genie out' is unstoppable, but a new currency did the trick in 1923

---

[88] Beaverbrook, cited in Ahamed (2009: 230); see Hawtrey (1962 [1932]: 209) who had hoped for a 'co-operative' gold exchange standard: see also Howson (1985: 156–9); Norman and Churchill are cited in Ahamed (2009: 232).

[89] Treasury pressure is often mentioned. See on 'hot money' Hawtrey (1962 [1932]: 210–11) and for the next paragraph on trade depressions and the BoE's former approach. To Ahamed, in this 'futile attempt to retain the primacy of the Bank of England and the City of London, Britain had now tied itself irretrievably to the United States', Ahamed (2009: 238-40), cites Keynes's opposition to Norman, and how Churchill later called it 'the biggest blunder' in his life, saving his greatest venom for Norman.

Germany overnight.[90] Norman's prejudice against the French (even the food) is recorded in all his dealings with the Banque de France. The BoE was allegedly above politics. It assiduously supported the City and Wall Street (with Norman's naïve faith in Strong). Treasury allies of Norman, like Otto Niemeyer, promoted the gold standard as 'knave-proof' against political rigging. Niemeyer had 'the faith'. They *knew*. In effect the Tories accepted they were knaves to be punished. No wonder Churchill loathed Montagu Norman.[91]

The war debts spelt vicious monetary conflict (not 'diplomacy') in the 1920s, and from the perennial intransigence of private banks. To generalise from the personalities, the 1920s 'wild' monetary fluctuations were fuelled by rational emotions such as economic and political fears that mostly only hindsight could assess as tragedies. Terrible hyperinflation was a result of Germany's war reparations and the new democratic German (Weimar) state's inability to monopolise violence to keep peace. It then endured the deflation inflicted world-wide, with Schacht agreeing and prodded by Rudolf Hilferding, the Social Democratic Government's finance minister in 1923 and 1928–9.

These harsh fiscal and monetary policies of the German state expressed fears of Germany's creditor, the USA, also of flattened German *rentiers*. By 1928, unemployment rose from 7 to 30 per cent. Later, Chancellor Brüning's deflation was worse than Hilferding's, but Hilferding was a product of a Marxism that saw production as primary, and money as secondary or minor. In his *Finance Capital*, he had industry and 'finance' merging, and he claimed absurdly that interest rate changes had no real effect on the business cycle.[92] Hilferding's

---

[90] See Ahamed (2009: 184–92) on Norman's prejudices, cf. to me ordinary in elite circles. On the Rentenmark, a notable sociological explanation is in Orléan (2013), who discusses how money rests on pure belief and confidence as with the new Rentenmark currency. It was called a 'miracle' at that time in Germany.

[91] On knave-proof, see Ahamed (2009: 234–5); to Ahamed, France was assessed harshly in these high circles. See Ugolini (2011) on the 'faith' in Treasury, and Chapter 3 shows Niemeyer's further roles as the bailiff for the Empire.

[92] Henwood (1998: 229–31) says Hilferding's book contains 'something obsolete, misleading or wrong on every page'. Schumpeter (1954) argued Marx was as devoted to Ricardo's

policy errors were partially derived from a position opposed to orthodoxy however, both positions claimed, 'money doesn't matter', it's
neutral, it's a mere 'veil over the real'. Similarly, with hyperinflation
(as Ingham says) Reichsbank governor Havenstein's apology for not
printing money fast enough expressed a 'quantity' approach, i.e. that
prices 'determined' the quantity of money and not vice versa.[93]

War debts had ended in Hitler's Germany (June 1933) and
Britain by June 1934, when both defaulted on US loans. This UK
default is hardly mentioned today (neither is France's), but British
officials had wrangled with the Americans since 1919. One account
said that the discontent worsened in 1930 when President Hoover
reduced Germany's reparation payments to France and Britain, to
ensure that Germany repaid its Wall Street loans. France and Britain
had been recycling these reparation payments to repay the USA.[94]
This poisonous British-US war debt controversy was part of the struggle to win the peace. Robert Self suggests the tactics of Treasuries
and Foreign Offices always oppose each other. Treasuries tend to
think first of brinkmanship, whereas Foreign Affairs officers prefer
diplomacy. One side of the conflict viewed it as US 'intransigence',
the other, as British 'welchers'. There was hypocrisy on both sides.
The 'Official Mind' consisted of prejudice, stereotypes and 'covert
value smuggling'. Elites turned to pejoratives, the UK alleging that
the 'adolescent' greedy US was in a 'temper tantrum', whereas the US
feared being cast as 'suckers to the world'. After the final suspension

---

obsession with calling non-gold money as 'fictitious capital' as Hilferding. This problem is
explored in later chapters.

[93] See Ingham (2004: 49); Germany's hyperinflation had nothing whatever to do with
'heterodox' money approaches (Keynes had no influence!) as later claimed, speciously.
It expressed total political and economic breakdown. Hawtrey (1962 [1932]) adds the
huge reparations demands, the assassination of minister Rathenau, and Ruhr occupation
prodded that hyperinflation.

[94] The British and French said the Young Plan of 1930 was unfair since they relied on
German repayments to repay to America: on Britain's default, Tooze (2014: 488–9; 507);
Ahamed (2009: 467); France also stopped payments to the US.

of repayments in 1934, the Americans were apparently the less bitter after a decade's petty dispute.[95] US supremacy was clear.

War Finance in General

Financing the First World War by borrowing (primarily) was, above all, chained to refusal to recovery afterwards. Borrowing had such an adverse effect that it dampened the chances of later prosperity among active economic groups in most countries. For example, despite its wealth Australia (like many others) found that servicing its war debt to Britain consumed half of all spending up to 1922. It continued for years and added zero to current output. In the US Midwest, farmers who increased food output to meet war shortages were hit by the slump in their rural export prices and rural indebtedness from the 1920 deflationary shock. This rural glut was also due to European countries that encouraged greater food production to ameliorate high postwar unemployment. Before the Wall Street crash of 1929, the general situation was only 'less bad' than what was to follow in the 1930s.[96]

The enormous damage of states' choosing the borrowing route (so much), to pay for the 1914–18 carnage, and the postwar *choice* to inflict the worst outcomes on populations was aligned with bank profit motives. This is something no central bank could or can acknowledge. Governments kept falling during that time but, along with the now extremely wealthy, private banks consolidated post-1918. Bitterness and *ressentiment* about the reparations flourished; there was also careful criticism about the war borrowing and the troikas of states-central banks-finance sectors determined to regain their former power. Anti-democratic sentiments also grew among 'democratising' states. War shows that the 'solution' of a central bank giving 'security' (of T-bonds) to bank-created IOUs is not self-evident. Most central banks were neither able nor willing to curb bank excesses in

---

[95] See Self (2007: 292–305) who also suggests the UK official animosity and default may have pushed the US further to isolation and Neville Chamberlain to a vigorous anti-American stand.

[96] The politics and economics of war debts were inseparable; see McLean (2013: 149–50).

WWI; and afterwards, they were only interested in saving the banks. What learning that did take place in WWII and post-1945 gave hope, which was lost later.

The ambiguities in central bank purposes, as bankers to the state and to the banks, are exaggerated in war but this is now unmentionable. I suggest that the command economies (of all combatants) necessitated by the total wars, with the inflation of credit and prices, and the demand for war workers, are a significant reminder of money's contextual nature. War also shows vividly the consequences of money inequality in ordinary times.

In a recent history of the Nazi war economy, *The Wages of Destruction*, Adam Tooze shows Nazism had narrower options for war finance than the economically developed, less peasant-based countries.[97] Reichsbank President Schacht found ingenious inter-firm methods for Germany's pre-war rearming, but the balance of payments grew worse. He was sacked or resigned in 1939. The 1939 Soviet pact rescued the Nazis, when Germany only had two weeks of supplies to conduct any invasion; Germany later gained plunder from France, Belgium and other industrially-based nations. Japan also took loot as it swept south, but only Indonesia had rubber and oil. Starvation was widespread in both 'empires' and at the end in Germany, for example, through Albert Speer's murderous Hunger Plan.[98] Savage barbarism (the holocaust was also economically illogical) and looting were behind the times to methods of capitalist finance. In the USA well before, Wall Street's control over money invested industrially and offshore was far more lucrative, and secured

---

[97] Recall the pleas for peaceful developments of John Curtin, about the terrible 1914–18 war (early in this Chapter). Hitler saw Germany's time was running out for American world dominance to be complete; in Tooze (2014: 18), on Trotsky and Churchill seeing this too. Ingham on anachronism (2008: 176); Tooze (2007) on Germany as poor and backward. The Soviet Union knew more about money to rely on plunder alone, as built into Nazi war strategy; possibly as Kulaks were decimated because of their inflationary interests in raising food prices, as protest.

[98] Speer argued that the Hunger Plan would keep paying for the war. With food so scarce, wages and food prices could be kept low through working all able-bodied prisoners to death in the 'war effort' (Tooze 2007).

America's global dominance. One question never asked is whether Wall Street funding helped foster WWI's slog, since none can accuse the US Administration of willing that war.

Central banks were tools for managing state warfare in WWI for the benefit of banks to manufacture more money. Banks stopped that when debts started inflating away until the CB deflation of 1920. In WWII, Allies tried to avoid WWI finance methods. This central bank function still defines these institutions, but sociology suggests that an analysis of functions on its own tends to ignore the social motives for these institutions and to see them exclusively in terms of their current functions. But 'functionalist' analyses neglect the interests that are served by any one function. With central bank war finance, the interests of the state are glaringly obvious but banks' profitable benefits are hidden. After WWI's lavish finance, the 'function' of central banks later in peacetime to keep economies in depression for 'as long as it takes' to save the finance sector – is not a logical economic function, in principle or in democratic terms, as the next chapter shows on the Depression. Qualms or dissonances were rarely heard.

Democratic demands grew in many countries before or after WWII, the other 'total war' of that century. But today, the FE shown possible from the total mobilisation type of warfare is no more, and the finance sector is no longer 'the servant' it was in WWII.[99] Central bank operations are not technocratic but always political, depending on relative balances of social forces. State warmongering is ever present; its funding is obstinately overlooked.

---

[99] To the best of my knowledge: my view is Wall Street made advances for WWI for profit and to gain more control over the City and Paris (etc.). On dissonances, see Chapter 1. See Helleiner (1993) on the control of finance of WWII, quite absent in and out of WWI or today.

3 Peace Finance of Bankers' Ramps, 1920s–1930s

Nearly all recent monetary histories blame central banks for the Great Depression. This chapter suggests the exaggerated versions conveniently avoid identifying the main actors. Refrains like Alan Greenspan's that "history tells us" some technical "monetary lesson" are rubbish.[1] Historians tell histories. Orthodoxy tells the Depression story as a policy error that "could have been corrected" – even that since the 1990s central banks became immaculate from "what if" type "lessons". Attacks directed at central bank decisions alone, but not at the Depression's brutal results on people, remove political and financial influences in favour of unwarranted historical guesses. Orthodox "lessons" are about saving banks. They omit volatile bank money production and repudiate the obvious: commercial bankers make political decisions about winners and losers (nearly) as much as governments and central bankers. Similarly, orthodox tales of the financing methods of the 1914–18 War applaud the outcomes. Under an equivocal badge of central bank *independence*, deceptions multiply. Their audiences (today) learn nothing about how banks and money classes became owners of the huge National Debt, with the sole right to spend money after 1920. Central banks protected these lucrative war-assets of a tiny elite with deflation – at populations' expense and dire effects on politics and economic activity. Having

---

[1] Chapter 2 did allude to this blame of CBs, though it focused on war finance, which is equally not CBs' decisions! Monetary (orthodox CB) histories from the 1960s onwards do not provide social-economic histories. Double inverted commas are used to denote "typical ideas or clichés" not 'actual' quotes. In Congressional and Federal Open Market Committee (FOMC) meetings, Fed Chair Greenspan chose specific counterfactuals from many central bank decisions to suit or justify his political opinions for different contexts. He was merely exemplary.

avoided inspecting that actual result, orthodoxy's science fiction then hits upon central bank "technical errors" spied in 1928–33 monetary policies, to blank out the hysterical political conflicts of the Great Depression.

"FOG OF CONFLICT" – NOT "MONETARY LESSONS"

Using the methods of social science instead, my argument is that central banks were fronts for the copious money class and state money conflicts of the 1920s. No dissonance back then, CBs enjoyed waging war on decency and logic. Fights intensified as the Depression spread, climaxing in *Bankers' Ramps* that capitalist bank-money forces, with central banks, won against social democratic labour governments. That term typically refers to bankers colluding in price manipulation, market-rigging, or insider trading of stock or currency – perhaps to force some lucrative showdown. While still common in markets (even when illegal), these practices of Bankers' Ramps in 1929–32 ballooned into *public*, political-financial attacks of outsized proportions. They forced well-meaning governments to impose austerity or else; central banks openly banded together and, with powerful banks, resentful parties and politicians, colluded to abolish the (new) democracy. Their overt aim was to stop the most timid governments from acting on the pleas of 'lower orders'. Widely recognised as scandals at that time, Bankers' Ramps 'ruled through panic' of financial markets with 'tory' parties and the press.[2] They ploughed a toxic field for fascists. Demanding profits and survival at all costs, in fury against their victims – the millions of jobless and bankrupt firms – Bankers' Ramps created public legitimation crises and played with the fire of global social-political fractures. These 1929–33 Ramps opposed elected governments that dared to provide modest improvement on behalf of the people through state money creation. Ramps purposely made the Depression far worse.

---

[2] Polanyi (1957 [1944]) on 'panic' is cited on this scandal in full below. The point, as we see further on, is that economics tends to dismiss the political wrongly, since politics is at the heart of monetary policy, in this case determining that economic life suffered.

Bankers' Ramps are brazen evidence. Instead of non-evidence, such as the counterfactuals that still influence central banks illogically, this chapter shows how alleged technical problems like the "gold standard" or "errors" of central bank policies skate over the deliberate destruction of people's miniscule hopes and desires. Public institutions of the day opposed the cruelty in vain. Under badges of "independence" and "neutrality", harsh policies were intentional, not errors. Orthodoxy picks minor mistakes to argue these "could have been" corrected: imposed as today's central bank lessons, they are partial (in only supporting banks) and antidemocratic. These counterfactuals ("what ifs") dominate today's literature, but few spot the consequences. Inconvenient Bankers' Ramps are dismissed to maintain the fiction that central banks merely erred. In 2009, one economist claimed these 'lessons' helped 'central bankers to come to a superior understanding' than that of the 1930s–70s, basing his argument on fact-free counterfactuals that would permit technical central bank perfection.[3]

Historiography is clear that historians must be selective, and interpretations vary. Catastrophes of the past fill vast dossiers. One cannot pick one lesson and cook.[4] History's sole recipe is that the future is uncertain. But this over-riding condition is denied when monetary mistakes are transformed into prescriptions, in which the contexts of the old alleged errors are excluded. Counterfactuals, such as "the Fed should have done this or that", are meaningless and dangerous. In contrast, recounting obvious, major events and refusing the

---

[3] See Chapters 4, 5 and 6 on CB 'independence' with publicity (jawboning) for active economies. To warmongering, but still democratic states, CBs could suggest financing methods. Independence from finance centres is desirable, rarely practiced. James (2009: 25), even though he spoke during *deflation*, says 'superior' policies such as inflation targeting gave monetary stability. (At a cost.)

[4] This chapter does not pretend to cover the vast literature on the Depression (e.g. global trade), just central banks' roles in context. Hawtrey (1962 [1932]) omitted the UK's Bankers' Ramp, yet reiterated CBs' deliberate cruelty; Keynes (1940: 6) was quite explicit. Many wars are justified on flimsy grounds to "avoid" repeats (e.g. not *appeasing* some new 'Hitler'), not current contexts or the unknowable future; the same with banks, see Kyrtsis (2012); and Bok (1978) on lies.

cover-ups reveals the intense social-political pressures that pushed central banks towards the calamitous Depression. This is not "the sole Truth" but strong evidence to expose lies. The cases are barely known today, and even heterodox economics plays down the large-scale, vivid public clashes against law-abiding social democracy for fear of sounding "political".

Bankers' Ramps are not conspiracies of behind-the-scenes murders, such as President Nixon's top-down order relayed secretly to the CIA (in 1970) to 'make [the Chilean] economy scream' in response to the election of Allende; or Stalin's order to massacre Kulaks over food price inflation. Today the IMF, backed with bond vigilantes, is hardly better (such as in SE Asia in 1997).[5] In the 1929–33 Ramps, central banks supported private banks – shamelessly, in countries that (merely) aimed for social improvement. In the old capitalist democracies (the selection discussed here), Bankers' Ramps publicly fought the norms of diplomacy and democracy. Loans were called in and CB interest rates raised, thus creating further joblessness; property was foreclosed through bank decree, there were riots, frantic swings from short- to long-selling, and further loans were refused to cripple these governments. Suicide rates increased. The press screeched the messages emanating from banks, ruling classes and central banks, and governments were replaced, despite the results of the ballot box. These vicious Ramps dominated public debate; violent fascist groups roamed streets unmolested. Interdependencies, however, finally brought unintended consequences, as events of 1933 and onwards proved.

Neither right nor left governments were innocent. Most had reasons of state for acquiescing to private control of money production, whether from colonial rule, or ghastly global debtor positions, invasion fears, or financiers who held high political office. My

---

[5] The Nixon/CIA incident is cited in Pixley, Wilson and McCarthy (2013), thanks to Shaun Wilson. Stalin sold Hermitage paintings to financier-US Treasurer Mellon (Ahamed 2009); Mellon wanted to 'liquidate labor, etc.' (see below); cf. Kulak price resistance and liquidation is generally known. On 1997 SE Asia's crises and riots, see Pixley (1999).

comparison herein of the Bankers' Ramps against the British Labour Party government, with the Ramps against the Australian Labor Party government is also noteworthy because Australia's central bank was never designed to copy the BoE or the Fed model in slavishly serving war interests or banks. But it did in 1929. The BoE also tried imperial strictures against Canada, NZ and in India murderously. The entire US establishment detested social democratic aims such as Britain's or Australia's. Although the two Ramps succeeded (fascists roamed these countries' streets too), banks later lost the economy and the politics – luckily to inclusive social democracy, not to fascist, totalitarian regimes.[6] We see later that post-1945, central banks' interests in economic activity were shared with their sovereign currency issuers, nation states, large-scale producers and populations, to provide hope and some security for four decades.

Thereupon, orthodox, revisionist monetary stories aided the 1970s reversals, and altered CB policies. Re-adopted equilibrium models see no incoherence like bank instability within the system. Events like WWI are just outside "shocks", and finance conflicts are deemed "anecdotal".[7] Equilibrium allows orthodoxy to see time as logically timeless, and economic life as a series of market equilibriums of either the short run or the long run. Large historical changes – like the collapse of feudalism – are trivial to humanity's "propensity" to bargain selfishly in markets. Politics is dispensable in favour of perfection unfolding: not *capitalism* or necessities like a *state* monopoly of violence, but a gorgeous "market". Equilibrium excludes social democracy and, as that extended in the twentieth

---

[6] On Canada, see Ryan-Collins (2015: 4–5); and on the Dominions, see Cain (1996); I am paraphrasing 'winning the war and losing the country' about the Ramps. We saw in Chapter 1 the US state does not pay cash benefits to unemployed people to this day. In 1929, Germany meekly obeyed harsh global rules; the US capital flight from it started in 1928.

[7] Equilibrium has a feeble escape clause, *ceteris paribus*; capitalism is a rude word, everything stays 'the same'. On 'system' factors 'ignored or posited out of consideration': see Minsky (2008 [1986]: 114–28, 126); see Heilbroner (2000: 210–11) on Alfred Marshall's equilibrium: he was 'compassionate' but WWI 'passed him by'. See Kindleberger (1989) on 'anecdotal'.

century, orthodox proponents revolted against a scent of social justice with counterfactuals.[8]

Stepping back to the 1920s money elites, the Great War had changed little of importance for profits, which rose. Habits of total bourgeois power and pre-war worldviews contrasted poorly with war's results in destruction, economically useless debt repayments, weakened world trade, yet increases in the suffrage (a scandal to elites). It made worse the jobless trends and the dead-ends of central banks. In the 1920s, global elites were barely civil – not only in central bank rivalry but everywhere – and indifferent to social disasters and their roles in imposing them. Peace movements, suffragists, minorities and unions met mounted police, who were also ordered to put down demobilised troop protests. Britain's control of the global monetary system was fading but it hardly seemed inevitable back then, either to Labour, or to the City, Treasury and the BoE. Nor did hopes for restoring the UK's 'political functions' of global finance seem the delusions they were found to be in retrospect.

In contrast to war finance, when central banks obeyed Treasuries, this chapter examines the "peace finance" of 1920 to the early 1930s, the Interwar years. It asks what happened to money creation in "peace" (my sarcastic contrast), after the nineteenth century gold finds, the pre-war credit booms/busts, the rise of the USA, and further post-WWI democratic expansion. Monetary affairs in the 1920s cannot be characterised as a "return of central bank independence" that ahistorical claims insist. Most central banks were still privately owned and, like banks, they benefited greatly from government

---

[8] Democracy is reversible, but its legacy is hard to repress. Cf. Bordo and Wheelock (2013: 60) also dismiss WWI as a 'shock' and cite Friedman and Schwartz's history, of 1963 on *the Fed's failure to save banks, as 'a principal cause of the Great Depression'* in 1931, adding 1913 FRA 'defects'. During the GFC, the *saved banks* foreclosed on debtors. The interwar German Weimar state, we saw, unable to monopolise violence to keep peace, had near 90 per cent suffrage; in Giannini (2011).

war finance. Unregulated Wall Street hot money was a major factor during the 1920s.[9]

In peacetime, a central bank has, to a limited legal extent, a free hand in negotiating banking services for its demanding superiors, the state, but threats posed as advice from financial leaders are often more forceful. Never independent from either, central banks have few monetary choices. Hyman Minsky argued that they play a game 'loaded' against them, which qualifies the stories of their guilt for the Great Depression. (The remaining democracies reformed them greatly soon after that, and WWII broke the bank clubs.) Mired as peace was in war legacies of reparations conflicts between victors and vanquished, and war debts to a hegemonic USA, the *victors' squabbles alone* show the pernicious effects on populations of conflicts between creditor and debtor countries. No one was blameless.

1920S ELITES CLUNG TO THE STATUS QUO ANTE

Ever more publicly bitter, the multiple interdependencies – global and national webs of affiliations – were mired in distrust. Some claim that the US/UK money classes 'wrote policy' in 1920 to restore money's value, yet political chauvinism, trade and gold exchange imbalances were factors.[10] The gold standard had never performed as intended in reducing bank excesses. Nor did the 1850s gold discoveries

---

[9] The treatment of returned soldiers was despicable – although a few Dominion countries were slightly better. 'Independence' is, among others, in Bordo and Wheelock (2013: 75). My criticisms of current terms projected onto the past, like 'independence' from now democratic states, are not like the cheap-shot blame for past actions taken: we know the later outcomes which incumbents could not. Orthodox narratives instead *excise* democratic changes (and wars). They urge CBs to act today as the autocratic private banks they once were; e.g. in many chapters of the Fed Jekyll Island volume. The idea resembles Montagu Norman's ludicrous claim that CB decisions (on dooming millions) were made 'on other than political grounds', cited in Giannini (2011: 132–3).

[10] See Minsky (2008 [1986]) on central bank problems. The claim they 'wrote policy' is in Blyth (2013). Economists look at the economy as a separate entity, 'hit' by ideology. The 'webs' and 'interdependencies' are in Simmel (1907 [1990]) so too social theorists Elias (2000) and Polanyi (1957 [1944]); see Kaldor (1970) on exchange imbalances and further factors Higgins (1949).

completely explain the swings from depression to prosperity (or wild speculation), given other, albeit disputed factors.[11] Elites forgot the path dependencies of pre-WWI booms and busts, and instead stared in utter horror at the first-time-ever full employment of the 1914–18 War. The rise of UK's Labour Party was an outrage. Social democrats in Australia dared to reform *timeless* money rules biased against populations – and unemployment as capitalist discipline – and met the first Bankers' Ramps. Deadlocks resulted from these civilising movements clashing with decivilising ones.[12]

After the 1918 armistice, central banks faced price and credit inflation. Instead of productive reconstruction postwar, the victors chose 'undue' deflation, high real interest rates, stagnation and unemployment (as contemporary Irving Fisher criticised in the US), against civilising inclusion. (Fisher had great hopes for Roosevelt's reversing of the US 1929–33 deflation.) Yet, was deflation central banking's exclusive choice to make? Banks owned the state war debts that created billions for waging war, and could call in these debts instantly. In 1920, the Fed and BoE gave their finance sectors huge profits – which was what they wanted. In modest places like Australia, deflation of the note issue was opposed by banks and all political parties alike.[13] Central banks rarely looked for economic recovery, indeed British elites' attempts to restore the gold standard created more economic distress, and City profits. Armed with Churchill's 1925 Treasury 'gold' decision, Montagu Norman set a sterling value that priced UK exports out of world markets; the French set low exchange rates yet,

---

[11] See Schumpeter (1954: 1101–25), on theorists from 1870–1914, and who stressed bank money creation as 'manufacture' (inflationary/expansive). This view of money gives little role to gold or to the savers-depositors so glorified in quantity theories that depict money creation 'rigidly' coming from one direction, the state (see Chapter 6).

[12] See *The Civilizing Process* (Elias 2000) for the concepts; Polanyi (1957 [1944]) similarly used the 'double movement', such as for/against UK imperial/domestic cruelty of the debt-owning class. WWI's extraordinary increase of jobs to FE, today hardly known, upset orthodoxy's line that joblessness is voluntary; workers must drop their market price to get jobs as if by magic.

[13] See Fisher (1933) and B. Friedman (2005: 145), on how US deflation in 1920 detracted from democratic progress. See Butlin (1961: 367–8), on the Australia note issue, which was decivilising all round! Further, see Fisher on 'avoidable' deflation (1933: 348–9); Tily (2015) on the high real interest rates paid to WWI bank profiteers.

like the US, "sterilised" or hoarded gold, thus reducing global demand for goods. The victors' conflicts reached a peak in the 1929–31 Bankers' Ramps against labour governments, in the UK, but more brazenly in Australia with its existing counter-cyclical programmes and older (near) universal suffrage. Central banks did not destroy such governments of labour alone; stronger forces loathed labour. History doesn't appear in counterfactual monetary stories such as the Fed "should have saved" banks – that is, even more.

The global social catastrophe of 1929–33 consisted of further deflation under the existing 1920s depression. As we saw, in 1920 neither Germany nor Austria could choose the deflation of the victors. Reparations aimed to destroy Germany's economy. In response, its capital markets opened to hot 'foreign' speculation to pay reparations. A fledgling democracy, besieged and weak, gave in to calamitous hyperinflation followed by deflation as savage as the UK's.[14]

If one picks the blandest "facts" from thousands of "events", one might feel pessimism. What did the money classes, Treasuries and the banks do in the 1920s to destroy economic life so thoroughly? Central banks were cheerleaders. It is salutary to note that Wall Street's 2008 crash was far worse than its 1929 crash, but in 1931 the US unemployment rate was nearly as bad as Germany's. Private bank money creation is today directed to trading financial assets, far less to economically useful ends. From 1880 to 1970 it was fairly in line with GDP, but not now, as discussed later (see Figure 5.1).

Here follows the depressing interwar tale. Hope emerged during WWII; gone were central bank verities and the 'easy life' of claiming

---

[14] Recall Chapter 2 on the UK 'gold' controversy. Tooze (2007) criticises Keynes's (1920) on reparations using a counterfactual, cf. the *only* position Montagu Norman shared with Keynes and the Reichsbank of Schacht, was to oppose reparations of Versailles. See Dyster and Meredith (1990: 72–81) on world economic conditions and Australian policies. See Ahamed (2009) on Keynes-Norman clashes on BoE harshness and H. M. Schwartz (2000: 166), on UK's disastrous 1925 gold valuation and its terrible impact on British industry. On Germany's open capital markets (to Wall Street mostly), see also Ryan-Collins (2015: 12). *Hyperinflation ruins those in credit, rentiers/debt-holders and those on fixed incomes and very low incomes.*

helplessness.[15] The gold standard, Australian economist S. J. Butlin agreed, relied totally on how nineteenth century 'western societies were prepared to accept the subordination of economic stability to exchange stability' and 'levels of unemployment and degrees of insecurity which would leave late twentieth century man incoherent'. Central banks urged exchange stability in the 1920s–30s too. The post-1945 *economic stability* was scotched by 1980, when insecurities returned; Butlin and hopes were dead.[16] Austerity mimics the US's 1920 harsh budget surplus and Britain's 1920 'balanced' budget. But now we have a successful *democratic* model to recall, lasting from the mid-1930s to the 1970s (although crushed thereafter), as *one way* of managing the production of money. That *legacy* implies new democratic strategies for today's impasse.[17] After the global bank crisis of 2008, austerity returned, but monetary policy *is not deflationary*, unlike the bleak interwar years. Nonetheless, despite central bank U-turns, deflation persists. Should we say, so much for "monetary lessons"?

Central banks rose to inordinate prominence in the 1920s for vast financial clubs enjoying others' sacrifices. (They also seemed to be stars in the 1990s–2000s.) Montagu Norman and the other *Lords of Finance* (Ahamed cites four) did not cause 1930s' Great Depression although they played a role, brashly political. The BoE and the 1913 Fed had no remits for growth, economic stability or jobs, unlike the Reichsbank and Banque de France (faintly); even exchange stability rarely concerned the finance markets. What were central bank responses in "peace" before their "disgrace"?[18]

---

[15] See Ahamed (2009) comparing the 2008 crash data. Recall Hawtrey's attack on CBs 'easy life' (1962 [1932]) and his admitted hopes for CBs, in Chapter 2.

[16] Butlin posthumously (1986: 27, 'man' is left in); Butlin's comment is also unimaginable with today's finance sector control over money creation. The 1920s–30s saw no exchange stability either, rather vicious financial anti-diplomacy.

[17] Thatcher's "There is no alternative" (TINA) was demagogic. By "legacy" I do not mean nostalgia for a "return". Alternatives emerged successfully, but under specific circumstances that are not replicas of the last ones.

[18] See Chapter 2 for Ahamed's (2009) marvellous personalised, yet broad social history of the four Interwar CBs shenanigans (the Banque, Fed, BoE and Reichsbank). See also Sayers (1949: 210) on burdens of 'adjustment' of those years (so like austerity today).

INTERWAR CENTRAL BANKS AND THE 1929 CRASH IN HINDSIGHT

Views on central banks vary, but rarely are class and political divisions or social change discussed. Giannini and Calomiris are unusual economists in discussing the political implications of money, yet their theses are anti-democratic.[19] Hardly remarked upon is the financialised nature of the US recovery in the 1920s. Bank profits come (mostly) from interest payments, so the greater the demand for loans the better. An investment boom took off in those huge US corporations producing very expensive consumer items such as cars and radios (churned out from war R&D and US war-loan stimulus, via mass production). How did a boom happen? Few could afford to buy cars outright, given the 1920 deflation to dear money and depressed wages. The unequal distribution of US income was more marked than before the war, although the situation was worse in the Continent and UK. Bank investment in production was patchy, particularly in the UK. In the richest countries (by then USA, Canada and Australia), the "answer" to weak consumer demand by 1925 was 'hire purchase' or 'instalment credit'.

To the banks this debt seemed safe – a car could be repossessed – but on a large scale it was fragile. The authorities ignored this mysterious form of bank money expansion (the deposit-creating loan), though Australian ones started 'worrying' in 1927. Central banks faced powerful elite forces – Ford, General Motors, other oligopolies – that connected with bank credit by setting up specific go-between hire-purchase/instalment credit companies. But in 1926, fixed capital re-investment in US industrial firms started to slow. US workers were laid off, while this income stream (sensitive to wage falls) from instalment interest kept up somewhat. The industrials' share prices and dividends rose, and an exciting building boom took off. Wall Street

[19] The blamed 'masses' is in Giannini (2011), similarly in Calomiris (2013: 168) on the 1913 FRA remit and approval of Fed independence regained in 1920 after WWI, to slash wages (see Chapter 2). In this and Calomiris and Haber (2014: 184–7), the thesis is bank "fragility" arises from "populism" not *big banks* (or Ford, GM et al.). Neither is an economic or social historian. See also the latter on the 'superiority' of bank branches, cf. Chapter 1 on branching, a calamity in 1890 on, of a "populism" of huge branch banks and political *elites*.

became a gamblers' paradise and US banks retrieved short-term hot money, from Germany most critically.[20] In this speculative bubble, margin (call) loans were another huge credit expansion for trading shares. Reliant on asset rises, margin loans were called instantly when the crash came, and bankruptcies increased.[21]

In the denouement to the 1929 Crash, one sees an uncanny resemblance of those usurious, risky "credit innovations" to ever more of them today. In pre-crash 1929, the Fed Board and Treasury wanted margin loan controls, but the NY Fed preferred "moral suasion" or jawboning. Some question the efficacy of this tactic, given Wall Street's other, near money sources for stock trading. Wherever a democratic hope appeared, bankers and central bankers stepped up to destroy it, while ignoring bank money inflation and the global hot money of the 1920s.[22] States were not innocent: bankers gained confidence from *laissez faire*. Wherever a social, religious, political or ethnic group could be blamed, they were vilified. (J. P. Morgan and Henry Ford were notoriously anti-Semitic, and "Red Scares" raged). Woodrow Wilson sacked Paul Warburg from the Fed Board in 1918,

---

[20] Henry Ford's $5 wage rise to force workers onto conveyor belts pre-war – although unions resisted – did not help purchasing power by the 1920s. B. Friedman (2005: 160) on US investment and decline; Sayers (1949: 208), on the mid 1930s–40s Fed 'quality' controls over both credit forms; Greenspan eschewed margin loan control in 1994 (Pixley 2004). See Dyster and Meredith (1990: 100; 115), on Ford dealers' 1925 hire purchase firm allied to the Bank of NSW in Australia, just like USA, Canada and NZ. On 1927 Australian 'worries' and a tiny start in UK nineteenth century instalment credit for pianos (etc.), see Eichengreen and Mitchener (2003: 38; 41) then mindful of the dot com bust. See Butlin (1983) on the Commonwealth Bank (later RBA) *banning* hire purchase in WWII and controlling it postwar. 1990s warnings of central banks/Treasuries on consumer credit were ignored, to Schularick and Taylor (2012: 1058); see Friedman (2005) on the 1920s US investment.

[21] Margin loans are for taking shares on loan at call: the control is the requirement to own from 99 per cent to say 40 per cent of the stock outright (100 stops these loans); other 'credit' is in Ahamed (2009: 321–2); near money "innovations" are recounted daily in the *FT* or *Barrons* or its daily *WSJ*.

[22] Jawboning can have benefits, which itself is another CB debate. Killing off "green shoots" reappears. Wall Street was *long* renowned for dodgy "bucket shops" selling 'near money', less negotiable. Recall, double inverted commas denote the clichés, also the masking jargon like "sterilise" for hoarding.

a loss of his emphasis on productive credit:[23] Examples of wilfulness and bigotry.

Economic records are muddled by omissions and counterfactuals about potential lost influence and better monetary policies that "could have" worked. No one will ever know. Hawtrey argued that during 1925–8, the Fed relaxed credit and the BoE restricted it. 'British industry was in much the same state of depression and American industry in much the same state of activity' as in 1925, albeit weaker in 1928. Wall Street's bubble "would have" ended sooner or later, Hawtrey guessed, but the Fed's and BoE's fault in 1929 was 'to hasten it by methods that would *make it worse*'. Hawtrey's is a partial counterfactual: US real interest rates spiked to over 15 per cent, causing instant collapse of the margin debtors.[24] Orthodoxy seeks excuses: central banks "could have" halted the bubble. A belated, less orthodox, treatment of the credit expansion of 1925 and of the 1990s, wonders '*whether the financial system itself creates economic instability through endogenous lending booms*'. Of course. People like Hawtrey had said bank money creation is internal (endogenous), elastic and unstable. High demand for advances swells bank profits. Money is not a creature of government spending alone (as monetarists claim), but primarily bank money.[25] Even when the central bank supplies reserves at a strict rate, banks remain difficult to control. Hartley

[23] Chernow (1993: 130–6; 186–8) in *The Warburgs* argues Paul was sacked for being German and Jewish; 'productive credit' is cited in Tallman (2013: 102). Morgan banker before his NY Fed job, Strong learned from Warburg's knowledge of European/UK CBs. I did a general google of the US Fed recently: depressingly, there are articles about 'who owns the Fed?' with charges that Rothschild does (it is now a small-scale, diversified group).

[24] Hawtrey (1962 [1932]) (see the detail in Chapter 2); and Fisher (1933: 347) argued that Strong's death was a pity, cf. Kaldor (1970) only criticised what Strong actually did do when alive. My point is who knows what he "might have done"? No one. See also Hawtrey (1962 [1932]: 77; 82) his emphasis. UK hire purchase credit was minor (at 2 per cent of car purchases), while *two-thirds* of US cars were on instalment in 1927, about which Hawtrey may not have known (my conjecture). See Tily (2015), on the real corporate and government interest rate spike; cf. Volcker's 1980–3 was less at 10 per cent.

[25] On 'endogenous' credit expansion: Schularick and Taylor (2012: 1042), my emphasis. On booms, Eichengreen and Mitchener (2003: 38); see also Goodhart (2003b: 88) (in answering them), rejecting their idea that bubbles are easy to stop, and stressing supervision of banks.

Withers told the 1910 Fed founders of this English pattern; the US experienced bank failures.[26]

The consumer credit "solution" to low purchasing power can be lauded as a "choice" on the part of workers (as the Fed claimed in the 1990s too), only if one ignores the fact that, with loans and oligopoly, people paid more (say for a car), while higher wages were damned as inflationary. But people are not fooled. Of the 1920s, semi-orthodox economists (e.g. Eichengreen) cite as reasons for the crash the 'ease of entry' of highly dubious 1920s US credit instalment firms, and the extent that a financial sector is 'aggressive': both points with merit. Typically, no one knows anything under a riotous boom but gossip flies. Probably the best US economist of that time, Irving Fisher, said stocks had reached an all-time "plateau" just days before they toppled.[27]

The price-earnings ratio before the 1929 crash, at 32:1, was far less than the P/E ratio before the 1999 dot.com crash, at 45:1. In other words, no company producing radios or cars had earnings (profit streams) by late 1929 anything near their high stock prices.[28] An asset bubble raises public ire against bank gambling, but the most critical issue is the major banks making advances for extreme speculation (as a chastened Fisher stressed in 1933). Traders are under delusions like

---

[26] Withers was asked to submit a paper to inform the Fed design debates at Jekyll Island 1910 (White 2013); also see his 1909 *The Meaning of Money* in my Chapter 1, bank money then was greater than UK state money (cf. Figure 5.2). Controls are rejected by Meltzer (2013: 219–20) in contrast, and constantly by Fed Chair Greenspan. He thought the trick was to avoid deflation after a bust, the Greenspan 'put' (Pixley 2004).

[27] In 2008, sub-prime *debtors* were blamed, and in 1998-99 the modest dot.com buyers entered that market too late. A defence of "smart traders versus diffusion traders" compares poorly with the 2001 court charges of "dot con" Wall Street "pump and dump" collusion – typical in the 1920s too, see Cassidy (2002). Eichengreen and Mitchener (2003) provide a long list of ways that 1920s Wall Street firms were aggressive. It is useful against the Greenspan group's illogic and see Chapter 8. The sad Fisher tale of his foolish prediction in 1929 is cited in Ahamed (2009: 353).

[28] On P/E ratios see Ahamed (2009: 278). The problem with the exit hope is that the doors become clogged in seconds. 'Financialisation' and booms are allegedly because "the people" want these (e.g. Calomiris on "populism"). In 1929 only 3 per cent of the US population owned shares; some data suggest less, see B. Friedman (2005: 470–1); see Calomiris (2013); Calomiris and Haber (2014) on how US banking "fragility" was all about rural unit bank "populism".

the gamblers "curse" of exiting just in time. Hawtrey said that moralism about roulette was not a central bank concern, only (bank money) inflation. The general point is really that all ventures are "speculative". Schumpeter argued that it is hard to make distinctions between banking's creative destruction and 'destruction without function' if there is reckless bank lending in either case. He urged the authorities to use controls. But in 1928 short-term US foreign capital moved out of Europe to throw at Wall Street's boom, just when productive US industries cut back. In 1928 Germany sank into depression. Britain lost more gold too. Finance sectors were in close mimetic networks.[29]

Historians point out that, while no other country enjoyed the American boom, the crash hit nearly everyone. Once capital was urgently repatriated to USA after the crash, bank collapses took off, first in Austria, then Germany. This told against the City, which had lent heavily to Germany and Austria on borrowed French money. The older US industries (agriculture; steel) were already weak, while construction and new consumer industries all sacked workers. No more long-term loans were made; economies sank further. The slump destroyed one-third of the global monetary base, 1929–32.[30]

Records of the dubious banks of Wall Street and the City in the 1930s are plentiful, but neoclassical "history" ignores them in favour of counterfactuals. Monetarist lines about 1930–3 argue that the problem was the Fed failed, either to expand the money supply, or it didn't lend to banks because of its poor design, or its "flawed policies". Another line argues that the Fed was "constrained" by the gold

---

[29] The 1990s dotcom bubble weakened sectors as trader 'opinions' diverted investment from economic activity, but it did not leave major bank distress (since stock brokers, not banks, were most involved). This was unlike the debt-deflation of 1930 or the 2008 sub-prime crash. For the Fed's role in the Dot Con under Greenspan; and the asset/credit housing boom, see Chapter 8. Hawtrey on roulettes although not US margin loans (1962 [1932]: 80–3) that fed the casino; Schumpeter (1934 [1911]), 'creative' is for new jobs whereas 'destruction without function' is a crash with nothing positive afterwards. On the German depression see Ahamed (2009: 320).

[30] Dyster and Meredith (2012: 88–92) the boom was only in USA, but whose banks' global impact was at their bust. See also Galbraith (1975a); Ahamed (2009) on City lending French loans on to Germany at higher interest; pure hot money. On the destruction of money, see Eichengreen and Mitchener (2003: 46). On monetarism, see Chapter 6.

exchange standard and, after Britain's gold collapse, the Fed "could have chosen" expansion. Both opponents and defenders of Benjamin Strong, the NY District Fed Chair, fall back on: "if Strong had lived" a year longer, he "would have" done something. He died in 1928! Counterfactuals are dangerous because the orthodox (and today central bank) view is that monetary policy was the greatest single factor in the crash and subsequent Depression.[31] M. Friedman said 1920s American monetary policy was good, but the 'big error in Fed policy was that of 1931'. This view casts "events", shocks or social disintegration as extraneous, whereas the social sciences are more catholic in credit and blame. Central bank rates were indeed damaging, but what prompted this?

Friedman's answer to the question of what caused the Great Depression is unbelievable: he (finally) argued the (whole) Great Depression 'was produced by government mismanagement rather than by any inherent private instability of the private economy'. His extreme *overestimation of central banks* in creating the Great Depression avoids the fact that their structural position makes them bankers to finance sectors just as much as to states: these are fraught, *partisan structural positions* for CBs.[32] Instability and demands from banks are interminable. Thus, trade during the 1920s was still

---

[31] Blaming the 1929 Fed was M. Friedman to A. Meltzer, B. Bernanke and so on, all listed in Tallman (2013: 100) also useful below; Johnson and Kwak (2011: 32–3) and Minsky (2008 [1986]: 112–36). Attributions of blame on the gold standard is from Barry Eichengreen to Peter Temin; Eichengreen (1990: 246–7) suggests the Fed 'could have chosen' in 1931, not *why* no Fed expansion took place. B. Friedman (2005: 163) agrees, however he instead worries about *democratic progress*. On Strong, Calomiris (2013: 175), citing Meltzer; as also Hawtrey (1962 [1932]) cf. Kaldor (1970) on Strong's not living to the end of 1929. Of course, we long for our wise friend or family to still be alive to help with new disasters, sadly but rather selfishly. To Calomiris (2013: 169) unit banks were a creature of 'populism' and, just like those old days, Clinton's US Administration was to blame for 2008's GFC. Clearly, if one takes one theme alone, it's easier to stick with it *ad nauseam*.

[32] M. Friedman is cited Cherrier (2011: 353; 354) who also cites Temin that Friedman 'assumes the conclusion and describes the Depression in terms of it'. That's the problem of those who think predictions are even slightly possible in the fog of conflict. I accept that MF changed positions many times, but specific "lessons" are used for 2007's GFC onwards.

teetering from WWI. Credit-debt relations between the US, UK, Japan, Italy and France or Germany were not amicable. Bob Self, on the UK's default on its US wartime loans, said: 'Few issues more clearly demonstrate the complex nature of this ambivalent relationship between the wars than the vexed question of Britain's war debt to the United States'. The USA held the most gold, making it expensive to attract it to Britain.[33]

Nevertheless, being privately owned, these CBs acted for and with large private banks (e.g. the NY Fed District bank, and its member banks comprised J. P. Morgan and so on) to drag repayments out of Britain; and the BoE did the same (for Barclays, Morgan Grenfell et al.) to Britain's debtor countries. Thus, nicely aided, private banking's aggressive lending ended in drastic cessation of industrial production and foreclosures. To argue that central banks are solely culpable for the Great Depression ignores financial forces, productive firms, trade and hapless households. As well, US Treasury wanted liquidation (aka austerity). That country endured no Bankers' Ramp, since hope was not on offer to anyone but the usual suspects, at least until Roosevelt's U-turn on taking office.

Granted, at the 1929 crash, the BoE and the Fed did reduce rates very slowly, and cruelly so into 1930. This sluggish pace worsened the situation for the British people in a 'grave depression'.[34] Brüning was Germany's 'hunger Chancellor', even more destructive. Hawtrey said Norman's delay until May 1930 in reducing the Bank rate to 3 per cent was unprecedented in comparison with BoE rate cuts since 1870 and given Britain's 'state of pre-existing industrial depression', with a world depression 'imminent and obvious'. (However, the UK's

---

[33] As the book argues throughout, CBs must be chameleons, purely as official bank/state bankers, or less when democratic principles and a vigorous civil society are in place. In contrast, many take the state's side or the banks' side, both in an authoritarian way. As I defend, the more general ambivalence is in Self (2007: 283–4).

[34] Friedman on CB culpability is cited Cherrier (2011: 360). See Hawtrey (1962 [1932]: 81) on 'grave'; Ahamed (2009: 365) gives background details. See Chapter 4 on FDR's U-turn, prompted by industrialists. Greenspan 'learned' Friedman's trick of speedy rate cuts for 1987, but it is by no means a fool-proof solution, if economic activity is low, wages collapsed, and housing and stock bubbles the order, for example before/after the GFC.

Bankers' Ramp was boiling, we see further on.) By May 1930 'the opportunity for escaping from depression by cheap money alone had passed'. The BoE was not prepared to purchase securities for fear of losing gold. The Fed did, but 'too late'.[35]

Hawtrey harped rightly against deflation: 'The kind of caution that spares water during a conflagration' does not support the thesis that the BoE made an "error", but rather it was deliberately cruel. His counterfactual – that lowering interest rates "would have" eased the problems – ignored the possibility of other consequences and yet he used actual nineteenth century comparisons with evidence of benefits. In 1930, deflation *governed*. Bank money expansion and price inflation of WWI finance were 'cured' when the USA and the UK imposed the 1920 deflation by restricting *economic* activity, while US *financial* activity took off. But economic activity was restricted in 1930 when *deflation*, not inflation, were severe world problems.[36]

The way to include all the relevant factors is to ask what the City or Wall Street wanted (and got). Generally, inflations are easily tempered, but debt deflation is far less easy to reverse, and it increases the value of debt – and hence bank profits. In fostering deflation, banks hamper loans granted so lavishly just weeks before and want instant debt servicing to repair the mess they themselves had made. Margin loans are first to be called, resulting in bankruptcies as asset prices shrink and debt values rise. In early 1929, *banks* opposed Fed discount window borrowing (lender of last resort), in public rage when the Fed Board dared to control margin call loans to try to foster *productive* lending.[37] Banks wanted only to feed the

---

[35] At the Crash, the central banks of France, Germany and Britain welcomed Wall Street's descent, Keynes too; Norman that it might 'rescue' sterling; Schacht in hope to end reparations. On huge pressures on Germany (e.g. Brüning), see Ahamed (2009: 369–70); see Hawtrey (1962 [1932]: 234–5) on the BoE cuts, 1870 onwards, also on 'imminent' and 'cheap money'.

[36] Hawtrey (1962 [1932]: 238) on sparing 'water' (to save banks). Recall states tried to save on war interest expenses to banks until 1920. James (2001) and Eichengreen and Mitchener (2003) show US industry collapsed the most.

[37] The US 1930 Smoot-Hawley Act raised tariffs further: US *exports* also collapsed. Fisher (1933: 345) cited the call loans as the fastest to spiral down; Tallman (2013: 104–5) refutes

bubble. Wall Street foreign flows reversed; more gold returned. By then, France appeared to be hoarding gold, with a large accumulation (relative to the US), in comparison with the UK and Germany, which had little. A sympathetic account of France argues that Washington struck a harsh WWI debt repayment deal in 1924; that hyperinflation was growing by 350 per cent in 1926; then, with Poincaré returned as 'trusted' President came a *miracle cure* like Germany's. Gold and foreign exchange reserves accumulated: to free France from the 'yoke of Anglo-Saxon finance', claimed Poincaré. His were defiant words, although no reflation took place.[38]

Norman's 'standing' wavered at the new Labour Government's Macmillan Committee of late 1929–30 for refusing to explain his policy, despite Britain's chronic high unemployment and critical economic state. He tried to launch a kind of 'world bank' to "manage" gold, but neither the Americans nor French trusted the English to advance large sums. Nor did the Dominion countries enjoy the BoE's imperial, opportunistic designs for their central banks. They refused the BoE central bank model (sooner or later) and UK Treasury's fond ideas that Dominions must cripple their domestic economies further, to save the UK.[39] That episode ties in with the Ramps against

the Fed's alleged "flaws", in showing banks borrowed a lot from the Fed during the early 1920s, but 'direct pressure' it applied against margin [call] loans in the late 1920s turned banks against asking for lender of last resort, which *required their books be examined* in Minsky (2008 [1986]: 357). Bernanke (Chapter 8) said banks must be spared its "stigma". That is, monetarists ignored CBs looking into banks' books until banks preferred borrowing via anonymous markets. In 2007 and on, the Fed knew nothing of banks' balances. 'Real bills' doctrine guided Fed fears (Chapter 1); but reckless bank credit was 'a thorn in its side', Sayers (1949: 208); *not* as Calomiris (2013: 174–5) says on Real Bills as the Fed's key "error".

[38] 1920s US tariffs worsened countries' war debt, too, when they were unable to export to USA; Schwartz (2000: 167) argues that the hundred years of the Dominions' 'cheap loaf' to the UK both cushioned the British against domestic distress and finished off the landed classes. On France in the 1920s–1930s, see sympathetic Ahamed (2009: 374–80) and on the 'yoke'; cf. Tooze (2014: 469–72). On France's similar 'miracle' to Germany's with the Rentenmark, see Orléan (2013) and on collective trust in money.

[39] See Ahamed (2009: 371–3) on Norman's callous views and how Labour obeyed the gold standard; on Norman's 'world bank' (in a new BIS founded for reparations), Ahamed (2009: 381–2); on the Dominion plan see Cain (1996). Hawtrey (1962 [1932]) on the 1922 Genoa Conference to manage gold, about which the BoE (then) showed no interest (to Hawtrey's dismay/anger), is in Chapter 2. Keynes and Hawtrey differed on monetary policy, in

the Australian Labor Party Government and the British Labour Party Government to which I turn.

BANKERS' RAMPS – THE FIGHT TO CONTROL MONEY PRODUCTION

Theories are value-laden, and accusing central banks neglects the cacophony of struggles over uncertain outcomes. The search for cause-effect factors or motives is hazardous, yet one can glean how stated ideas defended either private or public control of the production of money. Instead of bellowing "had central banks known ...", I ask what ruling institutions did.

If central banks were culprits in creating the Depression (or partly), orthodoxy's list of counterfactuals demonstrating their "errors" shows no such thing. Milton Friedman's critics, even, blandly accept his use of "counterfactual evidence", but a *counterfactual is not evidence*. The data show that central banks increased deflation to raise the value of debts, thus adding to the millions thrown into poverty. That helped the banks nicely. Friedman argued that Wall Street was innocent; that government intervention and the Fed caused everything.[40] Partisan counterfactuals never explain why money supply stayed tight nor why elites defended gold. Nor is "tradition" an answer since Hawtrey and Victor Morgan showed the Bank of England often lifted gold. Another pernicious habit is to personalise failings as though stupidity or greed of office-holders is a cause. Both traits are tediously old. The chief Fed official in 2013 did not use either argument: Bernanke plainly declared the 1930s US policies were 'harsh', unlike how the Fed managed the GFC calamity. Yet Bernanke also neglected the dubious roles of private bank money creation and mobile capital, although staunchly defended

---

Howson (1985), yet both agreed the problem was economic stability, instead of hysteria over exchange stability that crippled production and populations.

[40] Cherrier (2011: 535; 360) equates "what ifs" with 'evidence' and see on Friedman. France had deflation after 'the Blum experiment' of 1936 failed, a potential Bankers' Ramp (Woodruff 2014). Calomiris and Haber (2014: 84) even praise Disraeli's horror of democracy; Friedman avoided such talk.

jobs.[41] Ramps that include appointed public officials as well as private sectors seem crucial. In the incomparable 2010s, central bank counterfactual "solutions" lacked effectiveness, however refused the cruelty of 1920–33 and of today's Treasuries and private banks.

The most telling argument against orthodoxy that follows is governments of labour (social democracy)– not 'demagogues' – dared to improve the fate of so many suffering the Depression but were dismissed, aided by CBs under no "error". After the UK Labour government resigned in 1931, a so-called national government straight away abandoned the gold standard. Labour Parliamentarians thereupon claimed they had been the victims of a 'Bankers' Ramp', a partisan claim hardly known now. Whereas counterfactuals have gold and CBs big technical culprits, by neglecting perennial instability inside a "Wall Street" orthodoxy must dismiss "outside" disturbances as "political". Gold is now emphasised as the trouble not the political power of Wall Street,[42] and the fate of social democracy is unmentionable.

Accordingly, Bankers' Ramps are censored out of history. The evidence, however, shows as the Depression began, Ramps had gained a new, broader application than just fraud and market manipulation. What were they? What are the strongest explanations for these Ramps? The most flimsy ideas must be dismissed. For example, bankers did not directly, cunningly exploit the 1929 collapse, because no financial sector has ever welcomed state control: even a modest left-wing government is "Commie" anathema. 1920s ruling elites saw communism as totalitarian yet flirted with fascists as they desperately clung to profits by destroying mild, elected democratic governments, which happened to be easy targets.[43] Capitalist money is not

---

[41] See Morgan (1943) on gold and Hawtrey (1962 [1932]) just earlier. Stupidity is ubiquitous, so it's hardly a causal factor for a specific calamity. See Chapter 8, and Bernanke's lectures (2013b) about 1930s USA.

[42] Gold (Hawtrey 1962 [1932]: 234–5) was then a part of the 'trilemma', discussed in Chapter 7. Minsky (2008 [1986]: 127) criticised Wall Street's alleged 'perfection'.

[43] With the USSR established after 1917 and political turmoil postwar (see Chapter 2), elites were aghast. However, decades later, Milton Friedman had a minor part in the hunt for

democratic: the logic in relation to sovereign states is for control to milk them: opportunistic. Moreover, at that time, America's dominant creditor status upset the City-Whitehall-BoE troika. Fraud was also a minor point in these 1929 Bankers' Ramps (although Ponzi unravelled in Florida, with bankers), rather the Ramps were public tactics to wrest back control over money creation.[44] Polanyi, on reforms that he hoped to be long lasting, recalled the rising fascism during the Great Depression. His analysis stresses unintentionality of the Ramps:

> [But when] ... the United States went off gold ... the political dispossession of Wall Street was the result. *The financial market governs by panic.* The eclipse of Wall Street in the thirties saved the United States from a social catastrophe of the Continental type.[45]

Finance markets do not exercise political control because a market conspires, or even less because it "thinks". Did bankers purposefully exploit their own panic, which entailed shorting state debt, arbitrage on gold, price swings and switches to illusory 'safety', foreclosures, moralism and public denouncements? This should be taken case by case, since bankers are like any other social group seeking political advantage and survival. Ramps were not for the public good. André Orléan suggests (expanding on Keynes) a precise formulation of panic. Logic does not exist in 'the social institution of liquidity' when each main player – bank, or fund manager – is trying to avoid loss. Traders

communists – he is reported asking if Galbraith was a 'Commie' (in Freedman 2006); and today's orthodoxy speaks likewise of Keynes.

[44] Capitalism was early on based on 'rigging', e.g. the life insurance industry originated in betting on people's longevity: that was later banned (more in Europe than England) because some people 'hastened the death' of the living 'object' of the gamble – a meaning of 'going short'? (Clark 2002). Also, Minsky (2008 [1986]: 127); Ahamed (2009) and Tooze (2014: 487) stress finance sectors' evasions and imperfections, less fraud, at the heart of the problem. Charles Ponzi ran a pyramid scheme; then 'Ponzi finance' became a general term (Minsky 2008 [1986]. After drafting this chapter, the Greek crisis of July 2015 erupted: Evans-Pritchard (2015) said the EU troika ran a *Bankers Ramp* (see below).

[45] For a 'technical ramp', see Ahamed (2009: 428) and herein. The quote is Polanyi (1957 [1944]: 228–9), my emphasis, also cited in Woodruff (2014).

in money and 'near money' have no clue about what might be sellable but try anything and must copy each other because the 'desire for liquid goods' is shared between these simultaneous sellers and buyers. 'Mimetic desire' stifles dissent.[46] This is not 'collusion' but an internal competition in which 'the News' in Keynes's sense, hints at each competitor's new definition of liquidity. The more fragmented the beliefs, the wilder the swings and the more authoritarian the disputes. If states and legislatures are unable or unwilling to control banks and disrupt their panic, or order their central banks to do so, the fallacy of composition (each becomes a seller) worsens a bad situation. Markets simply cease, unable to 'correct' their own messes, because buyers vanish. Players calculate minute-by-minute, taking bizarre positions down self-fulfilling spirals.[47]

To these eminently social, uninformative copycat finance panics, industrial and agribusiness capitalists did not or could not take opposing political roles to wedge against a full-blown Bankers' Ramp till later. They were sacking workers. In 1929–33 bankers blocked modest labour party policies with exit threats, flights to 'safe' assets and demands for debt servicing. Economic stability always threatens bank control, but it was (then) a scandal for any government to try to restore stability and jobs. In many cases, banks stared at self-immolation on an exit treadmill, since the moment buyers vanish, a market stops. What drove central bank or treasury policy towards the unfolding crisis? The authorities feared banker threats, fretted for their global (nationalistic) reputations, and worker protests were impertinence, except to labour governments.[48] Given subsequent knowledge of the calamity, their destructive policies cannot be underestimated.

---

[46] FOMC members often ask what the market "thinks". On trader copycats; mimetic desires for liquidity, see Orléan (2014: 206, 111, 118–21).

[47] The 'News' is of the last second's market moves; it is of traders making guesses of guesses. These depictions of Keynes are amplified in Pixley (2004) on the financial press as trust agencies.

[48] On Polanyi's meaning of panic, also see Woodruff (2014) on the EU. On competition, see Pixley (2016); and Veblen (1904) on capitalist disruption.

The BoE and UK Treasury wasted years trying to impose 'discreetly' the BoE privately-owned central bank model on the self-governing Dominions, in attempts to get instant debt repayments and 'indirect' political control over the governments of South Africa, India, New Zealand, Australia and Canada. The Dominions were not fooled one bit. All instead aimed to raise their own prices and reflate. They resisted Montagu Norman's aims in 1932 to revive the old dominance of the City, and sterling over the US dollar, through his envisioned club of 'Imperial Central Banks' that would subordinate their domestic needs under a 'sterling bloc'.[49] Disparate states, sectors, political parties and paramilitary organisations also sought to benefit from crisis, but the BoE's by then absurd tactics backfired straight away and in the long term.

In economic disasters, like 1928's collapse of prices, one can say that a Bankers' Ramp occurs when a legitimation crisis is visibly, loudly evident – which it rarely was in the nineteenth century, since few could vote or stand for office. Stonewalling and ruling class outrage expresses political conflicts over state or bank control over the production of money. If states oppose banks (and the US did not, until after Roosevelt took office), central banks usually appease states. They had to in financing WWI: states by definition were the guilty parties to declare war, although banks enjoyed lucrative advances. But at the end of the 1920s of "peace finance", what loomed well before Wall Street's Crash, was a total economic collapse of global demand and domestic activity. The primary exporting countries of Argentina, Australia and Brazil had to devalue, but UK industry had already declined. Germany was in depression by 1928, all of Europe and the US had sunk by mid-1929. All this happened before the crash. In 1933 the Nazis took over the Reichsbank with its head Schacht

---

[49] The Canadian literature picks up this story: Canada had larger debt repayments to the US than UK, than the others, thus 'prised' to a BoE chafing at US creditor status. Its Ottawa conference of 1932 did find *one unity* among these vastly different countries: namely a collective desire for the opposite, 'alleviation', to UK Treasury and its later Chancellor Neville Chamberlain's horror: see Cain (1996: 342–3).

favouring rearmament. In contrast, in moderate democratic countries, Bankers' Ramps are always obvious. A peacefully elected Labor
Government in Australia had implemented policies to revise the
terms of the production of money, while a Labour Government in
the UK only tried to defend unemployment payments (anathema to
UK and US elites). Canada tried to give relief but had a divided government and was in a major debt dependency to Wall Street, and the
City, during that time. It was not just routine bond or gold vigilantes and banks which fought state protection of the people, hysterical
elite-political coalescences did too.

These two vivid cases, the UK and Australia are notable because
these large-scale monetary attacks on social justice policies are still
repressed, in general and in monetarist histories. Both countries were
as wealthy as the USA, and their labour parties – social democratic –
had taken office in 1929 (a Canadian version was in 1935). On the
complicated, fraught Continent with (older) labour parties, Bankers'
Ramps were one horror of many. They were also less stark in a US
of two pro-Wall Street parties of government, until banks failed seriously just when FDR took office.

So, the obvious Bankers' Ramps against social democratic efforts
to combine fiscal and monetary policy – with a host of schemes old
and new for alleviation in Australia – include the 1931 one against
British Labour, discussed next. First, I take the earlier, 1929 case
against Australian Labor. Both are good tests of the narrow analysis
that isolates central banks from social, cultural and political forces.

CASE ONE: AUSTRALIA'S BANKERS' RAMP OF 1929

The broad social economic approach to central banks looks at wider
cultural and institutional struggles over the production of money
from which central banks cannot escape. Narrow blame is the lazy
path of academic battles waged over petty points in a narcissism of
small differences. The actual conflicts were glaring cases of private
bank resistance to losing any control of money, achieved by political-
economic destruction of the legitimate governments that tried to

ameliorate the Great Depression. Counterfactuals rarely compare, but rather universalise with mere conjectures, whereas even the UK and Australia were very different.[50]

The Commonwealth Bank of Australia (CBA), founded in 1911 under the first federal Labor (ALP) majority government, started as a state-owned commercial bank to rival private counterparts. Labor had long dreamed of a 'People's Bank' to control banking and monetary fluctuations. Earlier I recounted the struggles against Australia's first 1890 Great Depression, and Labor Prime Minister Fisher's 1911 gradualism, and how banks and Anti-Labor parties, and the City, BoE and UK Treasury loathed this "upstart" CBA. Eventually it became Australia's central bank (later called the RBA): banker to the (federal) Commonwealth of Australia and to the banks, with the intention to work against the deflationary and (mostly) inflationary tendencies of both the private banks and the state – which it did. Labor's aims of democratic control over the monetary "system" for full employment, via the CBA with Treasury, were fought bitterly. The idea of a central bank as a way of *controlling banks* for social justice ends erupted in prolonged class battles. Today's smoke screen analyses of 1929 compare poorly with analyses of Australia's earlier economic disasters in the 1880–90s, widely agreed to be the result of bank recklessness, fraud and deception.

Having gradually gained central bank remits, during the 1920s, however, the Commonwealth Bank stooped to damaging everyone. One Anti-Labor government created a Note Board separated from Treasury but ludicrously not inside the CBA. One Note Board member, a businessman who headed an Assurance firm that competed against banks, and preferred to restrain banks' cash resources, insisted the Board restrict the money supply, allegedly against inflation. After wide public criticism and genuine bank difficulties, a 1924 Act allowed the CBA control of the Note Issue, with the supposed aim of converting it into an "expert-run" central bank. Again, Cabinet put

---

[50] See McLean (2013), for data of the three most wealthy countries for 200 years (UK, USA and Australia). To add, I cannot cover every minute detail, and instead give sufficient to show the silencing of these massive political conflicts.

its business friends on the CBA Board, against the wishes not only of the Labor Party, but also the Government's coalition partner, the Country Party.[51] The Act also gave this state-owned Bank complete independence of government by preventing the CBA from taking any direction from Treasury, thereby 'giving away the Government's right to determine policy', such as fiscal stimulus. This Anti-Labor Act, deeply 'flawed', meant that 'the Commonwealth Bank refrained ... from active competition with the trading banks'.[52] Labor's aim that state-owned enterprises be 'set up to provide genuine competition to private companies which would otherwise cooperate with each other to defraud the public' vanished from the CBA, despite the many state-owned enterprises in Australia.

Maybe 'defraud' was too robust a term to describe scared, still despised, uncreative banks of the 1920s. Unlike Wall Street's reckless 1920s, or Melbourne's 1880s, banks were less a source of financial crisis than Australia's patchy Interwar global trade; the 1920 note issue deflation, WWI debts and the CBA's doctrinaire and self-interested tightness.[53] Indeed a UK-owned (later the ANZ) bank was, in the 1920s, constantly being criticised by its London headquarters for timidity: recklessness was desired. The CBA had expanded in WWI and was itself 'aggressive' in taking over banks owned by the states. State governments, whether Labor or Anti-Labor, loathed the CBA since their savings banks were 'regular sources of cheap borrowing for capital expenditure'.[54]

[51] See Chapter 1. The 1920 Note Board was deflationary; the Country Party (agribusiness, not small farmer) Treasurer opposed it; but the 'hawk' prevailed; banks protested the Board's restrictions and controls on minimum notes in deposits, involving the CBA too, see Butlin (1961: 367–75). On turning the CBA into a central bank, for details up to 1929, see Gollan (1968: 100–2; 146–7; 152–8) and Coleman et al. (2006: 230).

[52] On CBA independence, see Edwards (2005: 116, my emphasis); also, on not competing, in Butlin (1983: 104); on 'flaws', see Cornish (2010: 122).

[53] For the ALP's state-owned competition against 'fraud', see Goot (2010: 80). Neither Schedvin (1992) nor Fisher and Kent (1999: 32–3) explain cautious 1920s banks, beyond their poor standing since the scandals of 1893.

[54] ANZ is obviously the Australia and New Zealand bank. See Butlin (1961: 351–3), on two UK-owned banks that later merged into the ANZ and also, CBA's WWI 'aggression' to the states' banks.

The post-1924 Commonwealth Bank was designed to support Anti-Labor sectional interests. But this was not where the Act's "flaw" lay (e.g. later CBA–RBA Governor Coombs rightly called for a theory of the state and of sectional interests). Rather, the perennial problem is that no one can predict what any sectional or government interest might be in new, unforeseen circumstances. The Commonwealth Bank's all-businessmen Board controlled its Governor, but it failed the Anti-Labor aim for agribusiness to expand the money supply (on the Country Party's side), just like the harsh 1920 Note Board. The CBA Board knew zero but, politically defending business "communities" (they assumed) and to try to look mature, they asked BoE Governor Montagu Norman for advice. He leapt at the opportunity for hectoring colonials on 'his gospel', dispatching the BoE's Ernest Harvey for three months in 1927. Here started the Bankers' Ramp part of the BoE, later combined with the BoE's Otto Niemeyer. Both officials aimed, like the BoE Governor's Dominion Conference, to force the CBA and Commonwealth Government into slavish support of UK/City domestic interests.[55]

Harvey's 1927 advice – to make the Commonwealth Bank a BoE replica – was worse than useless (it backfired on the BoE by 1931). He told them a central bank must be privately owned, independent from government, not in competition with other banks, instead only supervising them and holding bank reserves. Little happened from Harvey's 'shibboleths' like his 'fatuous inference' about a CBA privatised ownership, beyond local bank resistance to reserve control. Anti-Labor amended its 1924 Commonwealth Bank Act to insert a Rural Credits Department, which scotched the BoE model, and the

[55] On the 'state' theory of Coombs, see Rowse (2015). Schedvin's history of the RBA, contrary to his own evidence of domestic private banks and local ribaldry at BoE carping, says of the 1920s: 'The pressure for reform came not from within the financial community, as in the United States, but was championed by ideologues who were politically opposed to the banks, and by practical politicians ... seeing a central bank [as part of] ... a mature capitalist system' (Schedvin 1992: 51). His quasi-monetarist charge in 1992 was the 'done thing'. Schedvin (1992: 50–2) said Norman had 'a gospel', Harvey was later Norman's Deputy; to Schedvin the BoE model was an irrelevant joke.

CBA's own business fatuity. Harvey's visit resulted in the opposite of his intentions, except that the (crude) influence of the BoE – always politicised – stiffened the 'orthodox' in the CBA, which sided with a local Bankers' Ramp against Labor to make the Depression far worse. Harvey's 'genial' wining and dining left Keith Murdoch (and others in the press) furious that the BoE later refused 'trifling' debt concessions in 1931. Anti-Labor governments had bungled the CBA's remit into poisoned legacy, further mangled in a mutual pomposity.[56]

This composite near central bank (state-owned and a commercial arm) with sole control of the note issue thereupon led Australia's 1929 Bankers' Ramp. That was far more important than the BoE's absurd meddling. When ALP Prime Minister, James Scullin took office in late 1929 (Labor's government split in 1932), Australia had been in trade depression for years and its 'massive deflation' was glaring. Unemployment reached 21.3 per cent by 1932. Schedvin argued that the public debt of states and Commonwealth was 'crushing' but, against that, no bank could borrow long-term from London from January 1929.[57] UK's problems lay in its further decline to the USA and City recklessness; its creditor moralism (to the Dominions, while itself in deep debt to the USA) ignored that 'certain City houses', one used by the BoE, had subjected Australian debt securities to 'an assiduous and well-planned campaign of *denigration*' in 1926–7. This campaign, as an Agent-General for Western Australia in London reported in 1927, was prompted by City shock at the "principle" that a state-owned firm, an Anti-Labor government's Commonwealth Oil Refineries Company of 1926, competed with private firms and allegedly harmed UK's oil business. Of course: never compete with

---

[56] See Cornish (2010: 122–3) on how 1924 Act 'erred'. Giblin's CBA history on 'fatuous' is cited in Coleman et al. (2006: 229), also citing Murdoch, father of and more interesting than Rupert; and Butlin (1961: 375–6) on BoE moralism.

[57] Schedvin (1992: 26, 52) on the 1929 situation in Australia; states' public debt was on further large-scale urban and industrial development. See Dyster and Meredith (2012: 89) on 1932–3 unemployment data. The UK was at 22.5 per cent, the USA 25.9 per cent and Germany 30.1 per cent; Canada also was hit hard. Australian recovery started in 1937 (by 1939, 10 per cent were jobless among unionists).

capitalism. This classic Ramp ignored Australia's (top) creditworthiness, wealth, huge purchases of UK products rather than sterling and sound developmental debt. Australian securities fell instantly. The *FT* dismissed the attack: UK enjoyed 51 per cent of all Australia's imports under 'imperial preference'.[58] Also in the 1920s, ALP Queensland Premier Theodore endured a credit boycott engineered by grazing and financial interests with the City, for his raising the rents of grazier squatting. That informed his time later as Labor's Commonwealth Treasurer.

These London Bankers' Ramps ballooned out to the BoE and City in 1929 but were run most vigorously inside Australia's banking and right-wing politicians' opposition to Labor's comprehensive anti-Depression policies. 'The struggle to *capture the history* of the Depression' in Australia thus began in the 1920s.[59] In 1929, local banks refused to lend to the new Labor federal government, defending 'sound' doctrine and their profits (irrelevant to the non-commercial profit CBA). All resisted devaluation until January 1931. Money stayed ruinously dear. The banks also objected to Labor's programme for revival through Treasury and central bank: to use the multiplier practiced from Australia's early years; to consider the national interest; to give local industry support and provide social benefits.[60] In Canada (struggling to UK *and* US creditors), no policies like the ALP's were yet afoot, save evidence of collusion between Canada's

---

[58] Coleman et al. (2006: 114) cite the City's 1926–7 Ramp. Colebatch (1927: 222–3) cited City 'prejudice' towards 'the subscription by the Commonwealth, then in Anti-Labor hands, of £318,750 towards the capital of Commonwealth Oil Refineries Limited "to fight the established oil-importing companies"' that is 'so much disliked'. The City claimed (cited Colebatch 1927: 220) 'over-borrowing' with 'few' details. Yet Australia was first to arrange war debt settlements to UK; statistics showed a 'sound wealth' ratio to credit in Australia, in the *FT*.

[59] On the Queensland Premier's conflicts, see Dyster and Meredith (2012). See Coleman et al. (2006: 231, my italics) on 'capture the history'.

[60] See Fisher and Kent (1999: 40–1; 7) on banks versus devaluation, and love of tight money (in a conflagration), which 'prevented' active fiscal policy; cf. Edwards (2005: 98–9) is stronger. On the multiplier via the creation and maintenance of markets and jobs (early in Australia), L. F. Giblin codified the practices in the 1920s, see Coleman et al. (2006).

three largest banks 'to artificially constrain the money supply'. At this stage, Canada had no central bank. We saw the BoE attempted to impose its own 'traditional precepts' of central bank models on the Dominions, but far more so after the US 1929 crash, to try to revive British 'financial imperialism' while Wall Street conveniently sank. Australia's domestic banks formed a 'hypocrites' chorus' of moralism while also demonstrating 'steady-eyed devotion to their own advantage'. The BoE didn't stop Commonwealth Bank reforms, a few years after Australians deplored the CBA's very own Bankers' Ramp.[61]

The Ramp occurred in 1929, when the Commonwealth Bank's Board Chairman (a businessman who controlled its Governor by law) imposed a harsh quantity theorem, insisting on budget cuts to 'guard' against *inflation*. This federally owned bank followed to the letter the local private banks' debt deflation. The Chair told brand-new Labor Ministers that the Bank was *'entirely independent* and he would accept neither advice nor requests from the Scullin government. He would give Scullin and [Treasurer] Theodore another five weeks to show how spending would be cut to reduce the growing government deficit', or he would not finance the Commonwealth thereafter. With the foreign exchange 'crisis', when Australia finally devalued, the CBA was led by a large Australian-owned private Bank of NSW (itself with rates being undercut by the City). The CBA Chairman 'nearly tore out his hair'. Yet in 1932 'gold had disappeared from Australian banking' and was earlier token, despite press attacks on Treasurer 'Red Ted' Theodore's 'printing presses'. UK Labour in contrast clung to the gold standard.[62]

---

[61] See Ryan-Collins (2015: 17) on Canadian bank collusion; Cain (1996: 343; 336–8) on BoE pressure on Canada. Coleman et al. (2006: 128) argue *domestic* banks stymied the CBA, less the BoE's irrelevant orders; Butlin (1961: 375–6) suggests similarly on Australia's 'hypocrites' chorus'.

[62] On the CBA quantity doctrine, see Schedvin (1992: 52). The CBA Chair's threat is cited in Edwards (2005: 98–9) my emphasis; and on Theodore, we saw Wall Street imposed higher rates on 'Red Ted'. The Bank of NSW is in Dyster and Meredith (1990: 134, 2012: 134).

But the banks' victory forced the Commonwealth government to deflate in 1930; also, the local states were in class wars – Labor versus stridently Anti-Labor held states. Then, as if the Commonwealth Bank Chair's political refusal to increase the Note Issue to its sole shareowner, and banks' facile view of citizens were not enough, the BoE, 'acting on behalf of the [City] creditors engineered an adviser' to be sent to Australia. Sir Otto Niemeyer, former UK Treasury 'sound money' (indecent) type helped local bankers 'close the ranks' with Anti-Labor opposition parties. Total debt satisfaction to the City was his priority (like an IMF mission, except with no capital on offer). He assiduously cultivated Anti-Labor states and NZ from July 1930.[63]

Niemeyer's 'performance' was a 'weird episode' that 'raised tensions' during yet another BoE 'junket'. His edicts were 'asinine': that Australia was 'overpopulated' (at around 7 million); that secondary industry would not create more jobs than agriculture, when it already did. He was 'staggered' by the CBA's suggestion that Britain would soon leave the gold standard. Australia's keenest economist, L. F. Giblin, fought him 'from the day [he] landed'. Niemeyer's deflationary 'decrees' of a balanced budget, wage and spending cuts; higher interest to English creditors, simply copied the CBA's orders. Nauseating sycophancy towards the UK from banks and Anti-Labor states ignored the fact that Niemeyer's plan of wage cuts benefited British consumers of primary goods. The BoE's difficulty, and obstacle for Australians irritated by Niemeyer's pomposity – he was dismissed as 'the bailiff' – was the City's 'hysteria'. This was how the City behaved even though Australia strictly repaid.[64] The BoE's low

Coleman et al. (2006: 118) on 'tore out his hair'. See Butlin (1961: 403) on gold 'going' and Cornish (2010: 24) on the embargo on gold, when the standard was 'effectively abandoned'.

[63] See Dyster and Meredith (1990: 134–6, 2012: 134) on the BoE's 'advisor'; Butlin (1961: 396) describes Niemeyer's tactics (cf. IMF) in Australia and NZ.

[64] Coleman et al. (2006: 112–14) on 'weird 'junket and citing Giblin's fight over Niemeyer's 'asinine' edicts. Butlin (1961: 391) adds the facile 'equal sacrifice' plan. On repayments to the City, see Coleman et al. (2006: 114), and see Schedvin (1992: 28) on Niemeyer being 'the bailiff' and 'hysteria'. Boyce (2012: 275) is inaccurate on Niemeyer: esteemed by the City, not 'helpful' to Australians. The City was repaid, see Coleman et al. (2006: 114).

reputation in Australia is unknown outside this country, but the farm closures that came from BoE demands did not please Australia's huge multinational agribusiness sector either. Canadians still complain of Niemeyer's drive to educate 'colonial savages': Like the USA, Canada had some agribusiness then, but mainly prairie small farmers and French 'peasants'. In Australia, Niemeyer achieved 'an apparent triumph' that was short-lived.[65]

ALP Treasurer Theodore's final challenges – his Central Bank Bills of 1930 and 1931 – were 'successfully defeated by the banks' led by the CBA (via the Senate). The Bills were allegedly 'a gross intrusion on the private sector', and the fact that Theodore proposed a 'substantial' (but modest) rise in the money supply that had no 'gold backing' was deployed as a scandal. Theodore said that bankers' whining about a 'shortage of money' only created high interest rates (to banks). His response was, 'Very well, let us increase the supply'. Theodore's 1931 'fiduciary' notes Bill aimed to include funding for depression relief, public works and industry, and to stop further wage cuts. Expansion was killed in the Senate, with opportunist parties bizarrely undermining Niemeyer's backing. They soon came to regret their opposition to Theodore. In retrospect, his Act more resembled the BoE model than what later transpired.[66] After that, the ALP government had few tools left to deal with the Depression except tariffs (to raise the multiplier in lowering the volume of imports). The Depression in Australia was less severe than its terrible 1890s one, and it didn't last longer than in other affluent countries. Unlike 'perennially poor primary producers' (e.g. South America), Australia had substantial, modern industrial and service sectors. As for emergency funding, all states' money creation lost out to the CBA, the City, the BoE and

---

[65] 'Savages' is in Cain (1996); and on Niemeyer's failed visit, not to him! see Coleman et al. (2006: 114).

[66] Butlin (1983) said the whole incident was an 'irony', as we see in Chapter 4. See Butlin (1983: 98); Dyster and Meredith (2012: 138), who describe the passage of Theodore's Bills; quotes of Butlin (1961: 399). Citing Theodore on increasing money, see Coleman et al. (2006: 119; 94–109; 124) and on U-turns.

local rentiers. Their engineered political-speculative panics, refusals and crises backfired soon after.[67]

In 1932, to public cheers in adversity, the indebted Sydney Harbour Bridge went up; the span met! In further defiance, PM Scullin appointed the first *Australian* Governor General, Sir Isaac Isaacs, before the Labor Party split, and its government resigned that year. Also, in 1932, the NSW 'crown' Governor sacked NSW's Labor Premier for threatening to default on London, while fascist groups (led by graziers and ex-army generals) grew violent, and tent cities of the homeless spread around Sydney Harbour. The NSW Labor Premier had suggested a debt renegotiation, publicly copying Britain's prior 'revisions' with the US (before the UK default in 1934). Despite the BoE's attempted financial imperialism and Anti-Labor's 'spiteful' destruction of Australian credit on gaining office, these Ramps were overturned in 1934, and state money creation won earlier. In its interests of socialising agribusiness losses and farm foreclosures, the Country Party, a coalition partner of Anti-Labor parliamentary forces, campaigned *with* Labor in 1935 to set up a Commonwealth Royal Commission investigating the Bankers' Ramp.[68]

No 'technical mistakes' created this Depression. Today's orthodox claim that independent central banks are "apolitical" and in 1930 made "errors", was publicly contradicted in this Ramp's authoritarian aim to demolish reform, even the mildest efforts to stave off collapse. Central banks are all creatures of governments. Thus, Anti-Labor nearly destroyed Australia's 'People's Bank' for ten grim years:

---

[67] See Schedvin (1992: 54) on the forced Scullin deflate; and tariffs increased substitution. See Eichengreen and Mitchener (2003: 34) on the 1920s Australian banks, also in Schedvin (1992: 56); Butlin (1961: 391–2) argued the Bank of NSW was better run, cf. the CBA and other banks. Dyster and Meredith (2012: 130–41) add Australia's recovery was like the US's (not 'poor' countries'): since the Depression was from the 'drying up of capital in highly capitalised economies' for both of them Dyster and Meredith (2012: 125).

[68] See the UK default on the USA in Chapter 2, and Dyster and Meredith (2012: 137–9) on NSW Premier Lang, the NSW debt, and fascist leaders; Coleman et al. (2006: 124) cite the spiteful Anti-Labor government (Giblin said). See Cornish (2010: 9–10, 138) on Australia's 1934 election, and the RC terms: to 'inquire into the monetary and banking system' for 'changes'.

a hostile bequest to the in-coming ALP Government. Its election timing in late 1929 was unlucky. Economists dithered politically; politicians, central bankers and 'vested interests' fought with each other. Reflation and regeneration lost – to banks, Anti-Labor, the CBA, the BoE, only briefly, whereas fascists quickly became figures of mirth. As joblessness increased, the CBA legal powers to contract the money supply reproduced, in the eyes of the Labor Party and many other Australians, the long-held 'intransigent resistance to any fetters on the unqualified freedom of the banks'. There were no "mistaken" central bank flaws: Australian capitalist banks and UK bailiff interests used thumb-screws.[69]

We cannot impute motives to the Commonwealth Bank's resistance to rediscounting treasury bills against banks (or the ALP government's regarding it as 'an attack on democratic principles'); nor to Niemeyer's objections to the ALP Government's 1930 Central Bank Act. Whatever influence Niemeyer had on CBA appointments backfired: his 'blessings' for its 'deflationist' Chief Economist resulted in the latter's U-turn *from* the gold standard, revaluation and from deflation. Of Giblin's 1951 history of the Commonwealth Bank, the BoE protested that Giblin did not 'pay the deference' due to Niemeyer, 'a man of pedigree'. Like most officials, Niemeyer was multi-tasking into confusion and an Australian figure of ridicule, still.[70]

The legacy of the 1890s – and high unemployment from 1928 to 1938 – left Australians feeling bitter that the private banks and state-owned CBA had 'delayed and obstructed recovery'. It was publicly

---

[69] Of the 'dithering' nationalistic economists, one was Keynes, that UK's interests should deny Australia's, another in the US was Viner on 'cheap money'; Giblin and others also switched to dear money, wage cuts, etc. then back, in Coleman et al. (2006). The quote is Butlin (1983: 113) – his favourite term is 'intransigence of banks'.

[70] Schedvin (1992) took the banks' side (cf. Butlin), only on their 'performance' as better than Wall Street's (!), against the CBA's refusals and Niemeyer's bailiff role, and said the ALP was 'bitter'. By mid-1935, banks finally used T-bills as 'cash'. He notably admitted the CBA's successful 'attack' on Labor was 'on the right of an elected government to determine its own budgetary policy'. Niemeyer's asinine aims backfired, to Selwyn Cornish, personal email in 2016; Melville was Chief Economist CBA; the 1951 citation of BoE official Kershaw on Niemeyer's 'pedigree' is in Coleman et al. (2006: 114; 228).

argued that the banks ranged from villainous to incompetent, and a 1935 Royal Commission (RC) proposed what wartime Labor Prime Minister Curtin later achieved. It condemned bankers and the CBA for overruling Scullin's Labor government by withholding funds. The RC wanted bank licenses to be conditional (as in Canada to this day), and the CBA to accept publicly, with reasons, government authority after a specified time for finding consensus with Treasury, in force still. It favoured the 'composite' central bank to direct the Commonwealth Bank's commercial arm to expand or contract money as needed. Against imperial demands of a sterling bloc, the bipartisan RC said

> ... stability of exchange rates with sterling [was] wise policy ... but we do not consider it should be the single or even central aim [of the Commonwealth Bank, rather] that ... it should be subordinate to another policy.

Instead of this grim policy, fluctuations in *economic activity* must take precedence (the RC said), with Treasury and CBA *consolidated* to achieve stability. Canada followed suit against the 'Norman conquest'. Aghast at the Australian RC's harsh publicity, in 1937 the CBA started open market (limited) operations to buy national debt.[71] The RC said that 'modern industrial conditions' required 'adequate bank credit'. Banks' 'privileged position' as 'public utilities' needed profit regulation. Comically, Anti-Labor in office switched from screeching about free (aka reckless) enterprise, to the idea of *compulsory* minimum deposits of private banks into the CBA, prompting one Anti-Labor Treasurer, Richard Casey, to say that banks 'will give vent to piercing screams' (because voluntary deposits suited bank

---

[71] On the RC, see Fitzgerald (1990: 63); Schedvin (1992: 55–8); the RC slammed the CBA, see Cornish (2010: 9–10), who cites the RC. See Schedvin (1992: 57) on compromise with Treasury and in Chapter 4 and see Coleman et al. (2006: 51) on open market operations. Cain (1996: 343; 353), on 'the Norman conquest of Canada' overturned in 1938 and the BoC's nationalisation.

money control). Yet Casey's Bill was postponed and, with the 1939 war imminent, he removed the bank licensing idea (of Canada's).[72]

For future reference, the Commonwealth state's lack of a full Treasury from 1901, and local state non-sovereign borrowing (with no control of the currency) to mid-WWII – on the open market – resembles the 2001 EMU (European Monetary Union) structure of member states taxes, debts and vigilantes. Secession of states from the Commonwealth festered with 1929's deflation; yet 'fiscal equaliser' transfers to the states (starting 1934) staved off secession and break-up threats. Centralised federal income tax was only introduced in WWII by Labor PM Curtin. A unified labour market from 1901 federation – Arbitration of unions and employers with wages based on *need* not just profits – compared well with other nations (and the EMU). In 1937, Arbitration Court judges granted a wage rise to dampen Australian employers' inflationary optimism. I do not know if this was a world first.[73]

This Bankers' Ramp fought Labor's efforts to stimulate activity and establish a democratically-controlled central bank, the 'People's Bank'. Its viciousness shocked Australians so much that the Ramp backfired on private banks and the BoE. Neither got the central bank of their (different) designs or anything like the US Fed's. Well-formulated policy, strong public engagement and political party compromises finally won. After conflicts over bank control of the

---

[72] 'Public utilities', to the RC, is cited in Schedvin (1992: 57). Coleman et al. (2006: 164) cite Treasurer Casey.

[73] On the EMU, see Chapter 7. Cornish (2010: 51) says the open market was limited. The Commonwealth had customs/excise duties for costs of pensions, defence and foreign affairs; states kept the rest. cf. Calomiris and Haber (2014: 456–8) are inaccurate on Australia's 1901 constitution. Mono-state New Zealand founded its central bank in 1934. The NZRB used 'heretical' Major Douglas ideas, but (Niemeyer) orthodoxy prevailed, to Butlin (1961: 391). Anti-Labor switched, see Butlin (1983: 98), perhaps when W. Australia (WA) as usual and New England (in NSW) agitated to leave the Commonwealth; Arbitration vs. employer inflation came from economist W. B. Reddaway's public evidence, cited in Rowse (2015: 155).

production of money in 1929 (not "errors") by 1931 the CBA was monetising the Commonwealth state debt.[74]

CASE TWO: BRITAIN'S BANKERS' RAMP IN 1931

The similarities between the UK's Ramsay MacDonald Labour Government experience in 1931, and the James Scullin Labor Government of 1929–32, reinforce the thesis that money has always been 'a space of exception'. Both governments took democratic, moderate stands against bank and central bank demands, to defend 'common wealth' interests during the Depression. Their defeats led to internal splits, betrayals, Cabinet resignations and collapse. Bankers bet on destroying legitimately elected labour governments, states that were quite unlike either fascist or communist ones. The British story is as conveniently hidden as Australia's. The Depression worsened, not from monetary "mistakes": US orthodoxy is untruthful about this. Hard-nosed, right-wing coalitions stopped labour governments from saving citizens, to give private banks and *rentiers* a profitable deflation.

The main difference between the two Bankers' Ramps was that, in Australia, Labor never promoted orthodoxy. It had long put money into a public space to demand democratic control of inflationary-deflationary bank money with a People's Bank. British Labour promoted the gold standard just as Australia dismissed gold and BoE imperialism. Perhaps MacDonald was scared of this insubordination. However, Australia could not dismiss the bailiff's demands since the Ramp of Australian private and public bankers was far worse for the ALP without a full Treasury, than BoE pettifogging. The 'mono-state' UK Treasury dominated from London since feudal days.[75] Perhaps

---

[74] See Cornish (2010: 51) on the CBA's 1931 monetising state debt; the 1934 Commonwealth fiscal equaliser began, Coleman et al. (2006:155–60) while *states still controlled* most fiscal policy (until 1943, see Chapter 4) though dependent on bond vigilantes. Theodore, when Premier of Queensland had to pay higher rates on Wall Street after the City boycott. Banks much admired the US Fed model, not the BoE's.

[75] Mann (2013) argues capitalist money's control over labour and distribution comprise the monetary exception, in that it occurs behind our backs. UK Labour seemed less alert to

UK Labour self-censored (its treasurer so unlike the ALP's 'Red Ted'), although its Cabinet resigned because some dared to try to prevent jobless Britons from starving. A single humane policy was surely not too much to ask. Also, unlike the ALP's lengthy majorities or Liberal-Labor in government (often Labor since the 1890s, supporting town liberal or agribusiness parties), the first UK Labour Government (in 1924) was a minority government, and fell in the same year, due to a rigged 'Red Scare'. Its next government, also minority, lasted from June 1929 to August 1931. It needed Liberal support for reforms such as the unemployment assistance included in its 1930 Poor Law Act that abolished the workhouse test (that Australians derided a century before). Labour knew little of monetary economics, save some (ignored) unionists, unlike Australian Labor's lavish traditions.[76]

Australia's Commonwealth Bank being state-owned was the most contentious to private banks and to the UK (to Keynes even). Also, multiplier policies had been common for generations, and were revived even under Anti-Labor governments post-1932. In Britain, austerity and free trade were the 'done thing' for so long, compared to protectionist USA. The money class/club with the BoE and Treasury, looked down on workers, unions, industrialists and Labour, whereas UK unionists, feminists and chartists were (often) Australia's defiant freed convicts and settlers. Deference to Britain was deplored as a pompous class affair. In Europe, older social democrat parties and unions had far worse sufferings than either country. In the US, unions were barely allowed (strikers regularly shot) until F. D. Roosevelt's presidency. No party of the labour movement has ever taken US Federal office, and there are still no cash payments for the jobless

---

the possibility of secure, socially just money creation with Treasury and BoE than, e.g., the ALP's Treasurer Theodore (who was, incidentally, a part-time capitalist *rentier* too).

[76] UK's treasurer is Chancellor of the Exchequer (London's feudal moneybags). Labour's 'Red Scare' involved a forged 'Zinoviev letter'. The Tory and Liberal party dominance for so long gave Labour a difficult entry; in Australia right-wing parties frequently changed names unlike the ALP.

(apart from short-term insurance for the previously employed).[77] The US had no Bankers' Ramp because Administrations cravenly kowtowed to the banks until 1933.

The British Bankers' Ramp, then, was somewhat different from Australia's. Economists sympathetic to workers and wages had little impact on UK's Labour Party. It was piously with gold, whereas Keynes and Hawtrey saw bank money and speculative panics as inherently destabilising. Hawtrey charged the BoE with needless, intentional cruelty (as had the Australian Labor Party of its CBA). His 1932 account shows how grim the situation was by September 1929, not long after Labour took office. The BoE's expensive money (officially at 6.5 per cent, but in real deflationary terms well over 10 per cent) had reduced financial transactions in London due to the high rate's impact against reviving world trade. After the late-1929 Crash, BoE and NY Fed rates declined slowly, 'deplorably' so, Hawtrey charged, when deflation was already unstoppable without 'vigorous reflation'. All countries on the gold standard competed to 'compress' consumers' income (in Australia less from gold *per se*). Britain's unemployment grew; prices fell, except gold. Labour set up a 'Macmillan Committee on Finance and Industry' of 1929 to 1930, some argue, to justify the gold standard and BoE policies. Others show Montagu Norman failed under sharp questioning, especially Keynes's. Its Report during the crisis of 1931 estimated that 'the City's short-term liabilities to foreigners' were $2 billion, although they proved to be far worse.[78]

There is little case to be made for a unified or planned exploitation of the monetary chaos, whether in Australia or Britain. It erupted. Collusive strategies fell apart; alliances collapsed. Indeed, the literature varies: Robert Boyce alleges that steps that "could have been taken", but were not, included UK industry's debates with

---

[77] Roosevelt's Wagner Act only accepted a tame unionism; and it excluded Southern 'farm hands and servants' (Blacks) (Katznelson 2013); private agents like Pinkertons shot unionists for nineteenth century oligarchs 'robber barons'.

[78] Hawtrey (1962 [1932]: 217–19) on rates; wage 'compression' to price falls except for gold; see Boyce (2012: 317) on the Committee and City debts; on Norman versus Keynes, see Ahamed (2009: 424).

unions about monetary reform – a managed currency – which built up 'enormous pressure' from UK agriculture and industry for reform. Deflation destroys jobs and firms suffer, unlike the City's so, big banks were quite indifferent.[79] A British ICI industrialist 'impressed' on Montagu Norman in 1927 the urgency of Britain going off gold: clearly to no avail! The US and France were "sterilising" (hoarding) their large holdings of gold *against* increasing the money supply, prompting more price deflation worldwide. All other central banks on gold were immobilised in mutual distrust, fearful of their reputations under criticism from industrialists, and shorting from bankers, anxious to attract gold (or loans on high interest) and maintain control over 'politicians'. But as gold imbalances, economic activity and price declines worsened, the Fed and the Banque dithered, unable or unwilling to pursue price stability; countries desperate for loans begged New York. Central bankers, united only in loathing Norman, quarrelled over a League of Nations 'Gold Delegation' on exchange stability, with inquiries in 1929 and 1930. During Britain's crisis of 1931, Norman suppressed the Delegation's critical report of all central bankers and, 'fearing the adverse publicity', he refused to have bilateral talks with the Banque. In contrast, City bankers urged 'unilateral domestic action' in a campaign against the 'disorder' of Labour's budget. Labour's Chancellor/Treasurer (Philip Snowden) supported *Norman* and in 1931 appointed 'City men' to a committee of 'retrenchment' that predictably concluded in favour of starvation.[80]

Hawtrey showed there were no "errors" during the pound sterling crisis on whether it was 'over-valued'. Asset values dwindled, profits turned into losses, bankruptcies were 'epidemic', and bank

---

[79] See Boyce (2012: 150–2; 244–5; 319) on industry pressure; argues for 'a ramp by [British] bankers' mostly, cf. Labour's 'incompetence': To industry (debtors) – in logic – inflation reduces money's value and if modest, helps economic activity.

[80] Boyce (2012: 244–5) describes the ICI industrialist aims; see Hawtrey (1962 [1932]: 215–19) on deflation, USA, UK, and gold. On 'pressures' for reform, industrialists versus Norman; on central bankers 'vulnerability' and the League of Nations' report 'suppressed'; on Snowden, see Boyce (2012: 151–2, 212–20, 274–6; 314–15) and Ahamed (2009: 381–2; 425); on loathing of Norman, also Snowden's 'retrenchment' Committee.

advances to traders and industrialists became bad debts. UK industry largely never recovered. Credit Anstalt, an Austrian bank, failed in May 1931, German banks in June. MacDonald tried to distance the UK from Germany's distress, made worse with 'hunger Chancellor' Brüning's austerity, Reichsbank credit restrictions and penal interest rates. The UK and the US blocked later French efforts to improve Europe's situation or to lend to Germany: 'Again and again be it said: France is the enemy', MacDonald said in July 1931, as life worsened in Germany and Britain.[81]

A foreign creditor panic ensued, as Hawtrey said, a 'storm of distrust beat in succession' upon the principal creditors to Germany: namely American and British. But in Britain, where London banks had not invested in industry for decades, mostly conducting 'business' abroad, financiers 'feared' suspension of gold after the 1931 German bank defaults. 'London was both a short-term debtor and a short-term creditor on *a huge scale*'. Its bank assets could not be called up quickly without 'loss' – Hawtrey did not specify the extent. A 'panic-stricken' withdrawal of deposits saw more gold leave the BoE; further foreign loans were raised from the NY Fed and the Banque in August. How much was Labour's 'portentous' budget deficit due to 'the crisis'? Hawtrey only said that the 'political upheaval' (Labour's split), and the 'drastic' budget (still Snowden's) of the "National" government that replaced Labour, did little to assuage foreign loss of confidence. The 'crisis had gone too far to be checked': continental countries believed Britain was bound to devalue. Panic withdrawal from holding pound sterling balances became a 'torrent', until the suspension of gold on 21 September 1931.[82]

The basis for the hooha that dismissed the idea of threats, even a Ramp against Labour to allow the market to 'govern by fear',

---

[81] Account of Hawtrey (1962 [1932]: 214–19); on dear money and 'epidemic'; on sterling's value, also see Schwartz (2000); on MacDonald and the French 'enemy', see and cited in Boyce (2012: 314–15) and Ahamed (2009: 381–2), sympathetic to France.

[82] This is the rest of the story in Hawtrey (1962 [1932]: 220–4) on 'storm', on London debtor-creditor excesses (my emphasis) on crisis 'too far', and a 'reconstructed' national government that finally suspended gold.

was shaky. Indignant responses from those reluctant to criticise banks, and/or dogmatists opposing this Labour-run state, were hot. Hawtrey merely referred not to a Bankers' Ramp, but an 'upheaval'. No dogmatist or 'orthodox' (on money), he was just another economist neglecting politics, the state and vested interests. In his favour, he damned the idea of 'confidence reassurance', perhaps alluding to the large cuts in the already pitiful support for UK's unemployed. Reassurance failed to convince sterling holders. True, but that strategy cast Labour into oblivion. He claimed the main panickers were only international bankers. Some commentators today (e.g. Ahamed) allege that foreign fear started the sterling exit from London too. With half its gold reserves gone by July 1931, Norman borrowed, then collapsed into ill-health. On 31 July the City group's report exaggerated the deficit in order to 'alarm traders'. It proposed savage budget cuts of 30 per cent off jobless benefits. While Keynes told MacDonald that it was 'a gross perversion of social justice', Cabinet divided.[83]

A stronger story suggests both the BoE's Governor and Deputy, among others (industrialists and the TUC), knew the problems with the gold standard, but the BoE then panicked (at the foreign run), and definitely engineered the final 'political' crisis of Labour. However, MacDonald fully agreed with the cuts. Indeed, Ramp stories vary partly because of the polemical uses to which they are put and self-serving denials of the "reconstructed" government and BoE. Also, relative responsibilities of City bankers, international financiers, the NY Fed and private American bankers are hard to untangle. *Their* attacks on Labour were loosely worded. Budget cuts would somehow restore 'confidence in sterling', a vague projection, or, exacting cuts as the terms for foreign loans would 'reassure' creditors. Williamson notes that Richard Sayers, official historian of the Bank of England,

---

[83] See Hawtrey (1962 [1932]: 220–4) on 'confidence' and that the 'reconstructed' Cabinet did no better than Labour's, which is correct. For counter claims, see Ahamed (2009: 425) and Williamson (1984) on Norman; on the City's budget horror (the 'May Report'), Keynes is cited in Moggridge (1992: 523); see too Ahamed (2009: 426), and on Labour's split. Williamson (1984) gives copious sources on the 'Ramp'.

'suggested that the Bank's activities were not quite so blameless as has sometimes been claimed'. Few doubt that Treasury was a driver in defending gold and austerity under Snowden. This was unthinkable to Australia's Labor and its constituency, about which the ALP's defectors were treacherous.

One view (in 2009) looks at MacDonald and the BoE trying to secure a 'secret deal from Morgan' (sending the request via the NY Fed). They hid from Cabinet the weeks of discussions about J. P. Morgan's demands for more budget cuts, with an elaborate 'smoke screen'. Morgan bank allegedly told BoE Deputy Harvey on 22 August 1931 of a *conditional* loan approval. This puts the Americans to the forefront.[84]

Before anyone knew such details of behind closed-door negotiations, the Fabian Beatrice Webb insisted that the City was involved with Wall Street. She said that when the City firms

> found that they could not get back from Germany and Austria
> the sums [lent and] ... were driven to draw gold from the Bank of
> England, ... [the BoE] itself borrowed ... from American bankers
> [but gold kept 'draining'] ... and these capitalists appealed for help
> to the Labour Government, which had known practically nothing
> about the matter. [City firms insisted] the whole City of London
> would go bankrupt ... Meanwhile the American Bankers refused
> [to help] unless the Labour Cabinet did two things ... "balance
> the budget" [and effect] a drastic "cut" in Unemployment
> Insurance.[85]

To Webb (unimpressed with MacDonald), the City wanted a bailout regardless of people's survival. One Bankers' Ramp historian argues that Cabinet was not 'dictated to' by the BoE. Rather, MacDonald

---

[84] See Boyce (2012: 319) on 'engineered'; Williamson (1984: 771) on 'self-serving' and Williamson (1984: 776) on the BoE and Sayers; Ahamed (2009: 426–8); on the BoE Deputy Harvey, of 1920s Australian ridicule, and MacDonald's secret deal with Harvey.

[85] Webb was wife of dour Sidney Webb (in that Labour Cabinet), she enthused about Australia's 'social laboratory' years before (see Chapter 1) and wrote this two months after the Labour collapse, in Webb (1931: 482–6).

and Snowden loathed the TUC proposals for abandoning gold (e.g. of Ernest Bevin), and possibly agreed with extremist views of Liberal and Conservative leaders (e.g. Chamberlain). MacDonald did withhold from Cabinet knowledge of secret discussions with J. P Morgan & Co about the public loan terms. This suggests that it was not Morgan that called for specific budget cuts, but Cabinet which, save for a few dissenters, wanted the cuts *despite* the Depression. The picture was not obvious either to Webb or to Cabinet, and authorities' hopes of 'respites' remained to early August apparently.[86]

Nor did the left-wing *New Statesman and Nation* know the full picture even later in 1931, but instead blamed France, and the City's own mess for creating the panic:

> What the City did in fact was to borrow from the French at 3% in order to lend to the Germans at 6% or 8%, after that the Vienna and Berlin banks crashed and according to this line, the French saw more banks going in England: Acting on this vision they started a run on the Bank of England; in plain words they called in their deposits ... The "dole" has nothing to do with it.

Yet the BoE did not keep the Banque informed in August 1931, whereas the Fed and BoE had constant discussions, so perhaps France was more a fearful panic candidate than conspirator.[87]

In contrast, Boyce in 2012 starts by denying there was any Bankers' Ramp from foreign sources. Using private letters (released decades later), he makes a serious charge that the City and BoE conducted the Ramp 'alone'. He argues that Norman refused the help offered by the Banque, then a year later, during the July 1931 crisis, Norman repeatedly asked the Banque 'to sell sterling for gold' when sterling was *already* under huge pressure. Also, the BoE Deputy told

[86] See Williamson (1984: 798–800; 801–3; 778) who says of all the British trade unionists, Bevin was least concerned about abandoning gold; and see on 'negotiations' secret from cabinet; also, on 'respites'.

[87] The *New Statesman*, perhaps October 1931 (cited undated in Ahamed 2009: 428); the Banque kept in the dark, is in Williamson (1984: 774).

the NY Fed chair, Harrison, that City bankers had decided to engineer a sterling crisis, he confided, 'to make the British government understand the seriousness of their position'. Another BoE official told the Banque that Cabinet needed 'a serious warning'. MacDonald and Snowden warned (ludicrously) that 'sterling could go the same way as the German mark in the hyperinflation of 1923', yet still resisted cutting jobless benefits.[88]

There were also two differing views *inside* the BoE on the foreign run on sterling. One wanted an extreme rate rise (even 7 per cent) with an increase in the 'fiduciary issue', allegedly so its 'announcement effect' would stop the gold run. The other favoured more foreign loans and credits (even). With further BoE panic, the Banque told it to stop raising rates – and on the 6 August 1931, the BoE decided it was the budget's fault. As Williamson sees it

> ... thereafter Bank directors helped to ensure that pressure upon ministers was sustained ... [as] Norman [said] ... (privately) the country would pull through 'if we can get them (the Government) frightened enough'. In this they were evidently successful, for on the 14th Grenfell noted that the leading ministers appeared to be 'at last properly frightened'.[89]

On the (risky) loans asked of Wall Street, US bankers probably were reluctant – American elites loathed UK Labour's jobless benefits as well. Harrison (NY Fed) recorded Norman's chats: on Labour 'we must force an economic adjustment now ... sufficiently drastic to

[88] Officials and political leaders are cited in Boyce (2012: 319–20); Moggridge (1992: 525) agrees: Labour had to accept cuts to gain loans from 'overseas financial markets (i.e. the City)'. Boyce is cited in Cain (1996), about 'imperial finance'; to Cain a huge gap existed between BoE aims and effects.

[89] See Williamson (1984: 791; 780), on BoE views, and citing Norman 'frightening'. Also, about Grenfell, J. P. Morgan and Co. had a London partnership in Morgan, Grenfell and Co.; Edward Grenfell was senior London partner, a BoE director and Tory MP. Soon after, the BoE stepped up complaints to Snowden, and talked to everyone – Keynes, *The Times* – to declaim Labour 'extravagance'. Moggridge (1992: 524) also says Eichengreen misinterpreted the 'fiduciary issue' like markets at the time; it was not to increase money supply but to 'release more gold' to stem panic, which failed. We saw Strong died in 1928: Harrison took his place at the NY Fed (privately owned).

place the cost of output and wages on a competitive basis' with the world. (Note Norman's fantasy about 'restoring' UK global trade.) The BoE reported that Harrison would rely on BoE advice and help arrange credit; interpreting this offer as a needed ultimatum, the BoE took it to Cabinet on 23 August 1931, the same day that Cabinet resigned.[90]

Whether or not it was 'brutal foreign bankers' laying down terms, the Banque and the Fed did favour a joint loan to the UK Government, and one BoE official proposed an import tax to Labour, a morsel ignored: 'The Bank directors [and] ... Conservative and Liberal leaders – thought that what would best *restore confidence* in sterling was the spectacle of the Labour government reversing its expenditure policies and committing itself to "sound" finance'. To Williamson, 'the bankers did not want the Labour government to collapse during August 1931. The Bank of England directors brought the Conservative and Liberal leaders into the discussions ... to increase pressure upon ministers to take immediate action - *not in order to replace them*'.[91]

After Labour's resignation, the loans from Morgan's US 'consortium' and some French banks were used up within three weeks; the budget cuts failed to 'restore market confidence' and a 'mutiny' occurred among Royal Navy sailors. That was when the (new) government and BoE took the UK off gold (19 September 1931). A NY Fed official claimed this would 'leave France and the United States high and dry, and then return to gold at a lower level'. Evidence has UK Treasury 'the diehards'.[92] At least Labour resigned honourably, split like the Australian Labor Party Cabinet.

> [The] other Cabinet ministers did not challenge Snowden's and MacDonald's statements – even the ... eventual dissentient ministers accepted that the gold standard should be defended.

---

[90] Harrison's diary is cited in Boyce (2012: 321; 322); see Ahamed (2009) on released records and note the BoE's lack of interest in economic activity beyond improving the terms of trade, to preserve UK's gold dominance, or rather, the remaining fragment. Recall Chapter 2, the BoE's disdainful policies to UK workers, and disastrous return to gold.

[91] The Bankers' Ramp accusation as Williamson sees it (1984: 805, my emphases).

[92] This is as Hawtrey also said (rightly), we saw, about 'confidence; in Moggridge (1992: 526–7), also the 'mutiny' against wage cuts; Ahamed (2009: 429) cites the Fed official.

> This acquiescence of the Labour Cabinet to the views of the
> authorities has been expressed, notoriously, in the reported
> statement of a former minister, when the National government
> suspended gold payments in September - 'they never told us we
> could do that'.[93]

This account omits the 1927 industry and *union* debates about going
off gold, not that the BoE and bankers said anything but nag about
budget cuts. Some unionists knew. Later the BoE wore *the odium*,
but broader considerations remain. Apart from the standard lines –
the UK was no longer the hegemon but the US, the British economy
slightly "improved" – there are institutional relations. When was
the City's influence dampened, given its prominence in the 1950
Eurodollar deals? Was going off the gold standard a diminution of
City manipulation by a showdown of 'foreign' vigilante traders and
banks? Or was WWII more significant in ruling out global financial
deals? WWII prohibited trading with the enemy and was stricter on
war finance than WWI. Treasuries took over most central banks.
The BoE, nationalised in 1946, did take a 'firmer' approach to banks
but, Sayers argued, not as pointedly as the US Fed, nor, I would add,
Canada's and Australia's central banks.[94]

   In the Bankers' Ramps of Australia and the UK, the same sectors and institutions performed similar operations. The CBA sided
with commercial Australian banks and the BoE acted as debt collec-
tor there for British banks: Australians dismissed 'asinine' Niemeyer
as an imperial repo-man, busy being mocked by Australia's press, like
BoE Deputy Harvey beforehand. The City extended itself everywhere,
choosing far more dangerous advances (than to the Dominions), never
UK economic revival. Webb put the situation of the 'financial world'
this way. She said, 'they first make an appalling mess of their own

---

[93] Williamson (1984: 777); Williamson says this maybe apocryphal but shows 'their
   acquiescence' or ignorance. As in Britain, the ALP Cabinet went in various ways;
   Theodore knew the most about money, and started disengaging, another went straight to
   the new right-wing Cabinet, and so on.
[94] Sayers (1949) on the BoE-Fed differences postwar; further of the above is in Chapters 4 and 5.

business ... and then by the most barefaced dissimulation and political intrigue they throw out one Cabinet and put in their own nominees'. Not in "error" then.[95]

Censored now, elected labour governments of wealthy countries endured these Ramps. Central banks and trading houses campaigned in disorganised ways to remove the target of their abuse, namely social democracy, by refusing state money creation and inflicting extreme disruptions. Panic selling of the Euro from 2009 was also a Ramp. It won the ECB's lavish support to EU financiers and frightened the German government (possibly most) into committing troubled member states to years of austerity. French and German banks were quietly bailed out. Ambrose Evans-Pritchard in *The Daily Telegraph* put the 2015 EU crises most atypically: 'We conservatives have watched in disbelief as one Socialist party after another immolates itself on the altar of monetary union, defending a "bankers' ramp", as the old Left used to call it. We have seen the Left apologise for 1930s' policies and defend a pro-cyclical regime imposed on Europe by a handful of "Ordoliberal" reactionaries in the German finance ministry'. This (alleged) Left 'meekly endorsed ... a formula for permanent recession'. In July 2015 (re Greece) 'the cruelty on display in Brussels trumped all'. He hoped for change and thorough rethinking by the Left.[96]

In 1931, BoE and Treasury threats against Labour were both imperialist and deferential to market panic, somewhat like the panic selling of the Euro from 2009 that frightened the ECB, IMF and EC troika into imposing years of austerity on the remnants (really) of social democratic states. Conflicts rage, even more savagely when there is selective ignorance of the nature of bank money creation and

[95] The 'bailiff' is in Schedvin (1992: 28); some cited above thought Niemeyer "might have" helped in the UK crisis were he not in the "colonies". How deferential. Note the City's arbitrage on French low interest loans to charging high interest to Germany: see Webb (1931: 470) extract of her Diary, 23 September 1931. Webb has no theory of money but acute points.

[96] For most EMU details, see Chapter 7, also, Evans-Pritchard (2015: 32) and bailouts Streeck (2014).

its power of expansion and contraction, whatever the costs to citizens and to banking's socially useful purposes.

SO MUCH FOR COUNTERFACTUALS

Banks had thorough control over money creation in the 1920s. They intensified their countries' unequal social fabric and injured hopeful democratic economic agendas. The WWI deadlock led the Entente to borrow from the US. The City lent to Treasury and thence to France, Italy, and UK's Dominions. Japan also lent, as did Russia until the 1917 revolution. The gold standard, said to constrain money inflation, had *never* minimised credit booms and busts. Innovations of credit IOU 'commodities' that Schumpeter neatly called 'near money' via analogy with 'near beer' of the US Prohibition, enabled money's expansion. Hartley Withers showed in 1909 how central banks could not control bank manufacture of money, since banks used their reserves in the BoE as 'cash'. He stressed strict supervision to the Fed Founders, futilely.[97]

Gold was always suspended in English bank crises, and the gold standard did not prevent Barings' collapse in 1890 or Melbourne's 1880s recklessness. So, going off gold in WWI was not the source of problems in war finance, instead, the extreme war finance borrowing was due to heavy state dependency on banks (despite belligerents' efforts to tax and/or garner resources from voluntary 'savers'). Armistice revealed bank money inflation, speculation and obvious inflationary effects of goods shortages (rarely mentioned now). Banking did nicely from war debts: Wall Street rose. My case opposes arguments that place all the blame on central banks or on gold standard 'constraints'. What counterfactual "might have" tempered the Great Depression? Let us not be naïve: banks wanted total control

---

[97] On WWI debts to USA see Chapter 2. An argument against the constraining role of gold (Hayek's love) is in Eichengreen and Mitchener (2003: 25; 45–6); cf. Schumpeter on 'near money' (1954), less transferable and unregulated than CB guaranteed bank money. See Chapter 1 for more on Withers (1918 [1909]) and to White (2013).

over politics, gold simply served as a proxy of financial power. The BoE and Fed enjoyed being tools of both masters.

Drastic deflation in 1920, not reconstruction, or help for maimed troops (how shabby and cheap), expanded financial power to those who were "owed" war debts. Reparations exacted from the vanquished were thereupon failed states. Some central banks were concerned with economic activity under 'peace', hardly the BoE. Whether the NY Fed and its dealings in foreign exchange and gold (a 1924–8 build-up) under Ben Strong made a difference is debatable. Less disputed is the fact that UK's reinstating of the gold standard proved disastrous. For what reasons: Empire? Norman's personality? Is it implausible that gold was banks' key source of control?[98] The Fed kept its eye on economic activity as the Wall Street boom took off. It is worth recalling that the truly massive US investment in conveyor belt technology in 1915–18 were from conditions placed on the Entente's war borrowing, care of J. P. Morgan and later the US Treasury, to the delight of Ford and GM. Unions started sit-down strikes in the 1920s; corporate concentration grew in the US.

The 1925 US credit boom grew from consumer credit too; its 1929 crash exploded on a world economy to which peace finance had contributed zero. Economic stability with enhanced purchasing power appalled central bankers and their financial patrons. France and its Banque were peculiarly objects of attack, as US authorities obsessed about exchange stability. Disarray masked financial sectors' *globalisation of indifference* against any economic activity. For Hawtrey, central banks countered every plan for cheap money with inflation scares. Their argument was that 'improving the ventilation of the Black Hole [of Calcutta] is rejected on the ground that it would admit air'. He hardly focused on states or 'his' Treasury. His reflation

---

[98] Recall my double inverted commas denote facile explanations. See Chapter 2, and for Hawtrey on the League's 1922 Genoa meeting; Eichengreen and Mitchener (2003: 45–6) say a 'hybrid interwar gold-exchange period' operated, cf. Ahamed (2009) argues the US hybrid made it difficult for the BoE and other 'gold standard' countries.

counterfactual cannot be 'predictive', but it is not the shameless, naïve neoclassical prescription that banks, not people, should have been saved (more) in the Depression. Banks and CBs exacerbated Depression.[99]

By 1930, central banks and Treasuries had one task, self-imposed or imposed, which was to restore the confidence of banks in the then frantic global trading of gold and foreign exchange. Central banks chanted the evils of inflation to any suggestion for increasing the purchasing power of 'near people'. State money expansion and the multiplier were banned via sacking elected governments; debt deflation brought great suffering. Current orthodox debates about central bank errors deny that they and banks actively imposed the Depression. In hindsight one can ask why traders would believe that Britain could 'recover gold', when its economy was in depression for the entire 1920s. Hawtrey said (rightly) that trading was based on fears of what *might* happen, not on 'reassurances' beforehand. Restoring 'confidence' prohibited labour governments from gaining any power of money creation.

Acknowledging that banks 'govern by panic' through a lucrative 'destruction without function' makes more sense and fosters better social science than narrow monetary histories. The arguments of M. Friedman seem somewhat quaint in the light of 1930–3. Friedman suggested that flexible exchange rates and Forex speculation in the 1960s 'would be' stabilising, thus implying that gamblers can narrow the gap between 'over and undervalued' Forex rates. How fatuous. In 1931–2 attempts to restore confidence with more borrowing, or by subjecting populations to more deprivation, failed to stop traders, since speculation on sterling 'ramped up'. More banks collapsed, only increasing the fear of those still in the game. Friedman's assumptions,

---

[99] I suspect that a mark of the global control of money by Wall Street and the Fed was the extreme attribution of blame on France, not that Ahamed (2009) quite says that. The 'indifference' phrase of Pope Francis; and see Hawtrey (1962 [1932]: 271).

Thomas Palley argues, denied volatility and extreme instability.[100] In 1932 no trader thought of 'gold' (flexible or inflexible), but rather of liquidity and its loss: disbelief became a downward spiral. Puny moves to increase budget spending were quashed. Vigilante traders expressed implicitly the key actors' fight to keep control.

In this book's focus on central banks, of most pertinence is the complete omission of Bankers' Ramp cases from conventional monetary policy thinking. Ramps removed elected governments and wrought havoc and suffering. In Britain, such thought processes (joblessness as 'the done thing') were only exemplified in a long-time BoE official, Edward Grenfell: a Tory politician and senior partner of J. P. Morgan's London outfit, Morgan Grenfell. *Lords of Finance* rightly makes these typical connections, although its thesis is central banks 'broke the world': surely, they were pawns of banking and the Right, collectively active against decent social democratic governments.

The City, BoE and Treasury also ignored the pleas of industrialists. Wall Street refused to borrow from a Fed Board that dared put 'direct pressure' on bank lending via the 'call loan market'.[101] It is lazy thinking to ignore unpleasant incidents, to excuse banking, finance clubs and their powers of money creation and destruction, by blaming the gold standard – 'the cross of gold' as rural Americans earlier called it – or central banks alone. Treasuries blasted WWI's full employment and promoted banking's triumphs but, since high interest is costly to treasuries, austerity, anti-democracy and mass unemployment were the order. And, as wilfully cruel as banks, governments were responsible for that terrible war. Australia's Labor governments dared challenge total banking power and aimed for counter-cyclical policy, to find control of the note issue by its state-owned CBA put it on a par

---

[100] Palley (2015: 55) citing/and on Friedman and cf. also on Randall Wray, a Keynesian-Minsky approach: see in Chapter 2 and cf. Ingham et al. (2016). I also suspect confidence boosting turns into a con game (Pixley 2004).

[101] Ahamed (2009); on Fed pressure, Tallman (2013: 104) who was the sole voice in the Fed Jekyll Island Volume to criticise Wall Street. Brave guy.

with BoE intransigence. UK Labour did not pose Labor's challenge, but Labour's stress on purchasing power, feeble perhaps, was disallowed too. Australian Leslie Melville's account shows how orthodox economists who experienced the Great Depression saw the issues. It applies equally to recent monetary histories. He said (decades later) overseas loans simply 'closed up completely' in 1929 because

> that was the free market at work. It wasn't a government decision in Britain or anywhere else that [Australia] shouldn't get any more loans. The market simply closed up.[102]

But that constitutes rule by panic. Melville asks us to believe, too, that the Depression was caused by "errors" or that a state-owned CBA's Chair (a businessman), or, by implicit extension to a Montagu Norman, or a Niemeyer, or members of the private NY Fed, were 'obsessed' and 'limited' men. How professionally insular to impute ignorance on central bankers when as office-bearers – *not* as private personalities – these men had the power to refuse to monetise the debts of elected governments because they held central bank state-granted legal powers, with independence from government but not from banking pressures. US Treasurer Mellon (a financier) said 'liquidate labor, farms, industry, banks'. The BoE was in a path dependency of slavish support for the City, and purposefully opposed industrialists, unions and Labour. It feared Wall Street's hegemony; although Treasury and the BoE were imperialists, they needed US loans. The Interwar period in Canada saw, but only after 1935, another inventive democratic challenge and the BoC's reform. No monetary "lesson" allows us to conclude that today's central bankers have a greater understanding now, than they did in the 1920s and 1930s. They understood very well, as do CBs again independent from

---

[102] Melville also said of the CBA Chair Robert Gibson: 'He didn't have any real understanding of ... central banking ... [but] an obsession' with gold. Interview, Sir Leslie Melville 23 May 1996, by Evan Jones, with kind permission to quote. Another (English) gossiper, Lionel Robbins said Australian delegates like Melville at Bretton Woods were 'surly and unhelpful', demanding detail 'it was not convenient to give' – for UK delegates in spite of FDR's call for consensus. This gorgeous quote is cited in Cornish (2013).

elected governments, and that is dangerous but differently. Allan Meltzer (a Fed historian) believes that Fed 'discretion produced the Great Depression, several recessions' and the 1970s 'Great Inflation'. Central banks must abide by 'rules' and stop neglecting 'long-term consequences' (inflation). Really. As a monetarist, Meltzer cannot see Japan is unable to *reach* inflation (1990 to date), because his doctrine has no theory of the social forces of money, far from it. These 'economists' choose to ignore contrary, glaring events, since that would undermine their methodological individualism, their loathing of the social sciences.[103]

The Depression is not about *what might have been* had the gold standard not operated, or had central banks not *erred*, because no one can know that. Rather, labour governments, having clearly improved the fate of working people (there is no "what if" about it), were sacked for expanding state money for jobs. Purchasing power rose in WWI, but monetarist historians detest stimulus and full employment. It is not that state powers are always more trustworthy to electorates than financial powers. The way for states to gain trust is to be extensively democratic, honest and inclusive: that constrains stupid wars and fosters economic activity. Financial power from WWI to 1933 had no constraint from social democracy; those desired controls only extended thereafter, for those spared fascism. But, by 2008's crash, the US authorities took those counterfactual fantasy lessons to be accurate evidence and threw state money and QE at any dubious bank or near bank, unconditionally. Everyone else endured the 'Great Recession'. The Fed's 2010 counterfactual proponents at Jekyll Island were thrilled, less so those inside divided central bank boards that, with legislators harped about jobs.[104]

---

[103] Meltzer (2013: 223–4), at Jekyll Island; also, Bernanke (2013b) citing Mellon. Meltzer crops up again in Chapters 8 and 9. Orthodoxy usually refuses that it is just one among the social sciences; see Chapter 6 on monetarism.

[104] Bernanke (2013a) at the Jekyll Island Fed celebration had a hard time, I suspect because elsewhere he repeatedly and scathingly cited Mellon's Stalin-like screeches for liquidation (e.g. in Bernanke 2013b) and see Chapter 8. What, after all, does a Fed Chair

The social fact of Bankers' Ramps shows how banking's political governance exercises control over money, states and economic life: it looks like a blind opportunism. Central bank policy is inevitably political in altering the social distribution too. Ramps show the power resources of financial sector activities over money classes and labour-capital divisions, political parties, legislatures, governments and their authorities. Any 'variables' for a Ramp are irrelevant to new ramps, which are always possible. Rising suicide, homeless and prison rates all imply twenty-first century widespread despair, as do quality attitude surveys on what electorates feel about austerity or private banking's lack of social purposes. These are preferable sources among many, and certainly to unwarranted evidence-free rules for central banks if democracy is to prevail. The Ramp concept refutes anti-democratic counterfactuals on the Depression's central banks.[105] Later public legitimation crises were different, as democracy spread: Ramps resurface not quite like the Great Depression's.

say to Congress or to students? See also, Chapter 1 on CB dissonances in the democracies and others.

[105] Schwartz (1998) gives a useful comparison of countries in his 'pluck, luck and stuck' idea, for conditions of *possibility* of new policy, 'stuck' meaning path dependencies. In top quality surveys, attitudes are correlated (cross tabs or statistical analyses) with all the social/demographic data and divisions, e.g. in careful policy work of Wilson (2013). Such attitude surveys show extremely few trust banks, but no one understands central banks, e.g. in Pixley (2007a) in Australia, and with unpublished UK (IPSOS) data I collected with Sam Whimster; see also Whimster (2009).

4 Central Banks, Democratic Hope, 1930s–1970s

Roosevelt's Administration is the major representative of the ensuing chances that opened to social democracy after other countries' hopes were smashed. Reactions to the 1929 central banks aiming for crisis 'adjustment' – today's euphemism for imposing distress and starvation – were mixed. Central banks took implicit or direct orders readily, not in error, from the turmoil of Bankers' Ramps. Those who controlled the situation assumed a prerogative to dismiss democratic claims. Ralph Hawtrey attacked the moral and intellectual short-comings of CBs' cruel refusal to expand money and reflate. His employer, the vicious UK Treasury, and the City of London escaped that charge, although he believed private bank money caused inherent instability. His hopes lay in central banks that would serve economic activity; however, governments of labour looked critically at treasuries too.

After FDR took office in 1933, his broad reforms had world significance, and included the US Fed's *raison d'être*. The historical period that followed shows the contested nature of central banks. Most had just pushed unemployment higher, on top of employers' cutbacks, and refused to fund social democratic government policies. Their masters in opportunistic financial sectors and treasuries gave the divide and rule politics and persecution of minorities an easy entry. Countries with old electoral rights, democratic procedures and defences of people's needs proved the less violent. Fascism, war fears and revolutionary communism tore countries apart. Few escaped this close call, as Philip Roth's *The Plot against America* or D. H. Laurence's *Kangaroo* fictions show, by alluding to actual but luckily failed fascism in countries large and small.[1]

With fascism so forceful by 1933, peaceful reformers knew central banks were not the sole players that needed drastic revision. Harsh public lights shone into secret clubs of high finance and politics, to temper prejudices that the ills of capitalism and communism were due to Jewish bankers and labour's social democrats – bigotry that let gentile banking houses and anti-Semitic central banks or WASP treasuries off the hook of their secret money creation.[2] In remaining democracies in the mid-1930s, inquiries collected evidence from all sides to find out what was 'wrong' with money. Indictments of culprits were helpful for proposals to prevent past and pressing evils, which this chapter explores.

Its aim, though, is to look thoroughly at fiscal-monetary *consolidation* as devised then. That gives the book a comparison for debates on CBs today, to find links (if any) between treasuries and CBs that are democratic and relevant now. These two bodies have different logics, as do executives versus legislatures whether decent or indecent. Accordingly, aims, mandates and public service vary in the quality of how they manage money.

What might be needed to rectify the indifference and humiliation just imposed? Given the unknowable future, about which everyone knows zero, could central banks do much? The power of private banking lies in their state licences to manufacture money. Banks are not money lenders since that assumes they have money to lend.

---

[1] Understandably about Treasury, see Hawtrey (1962 [1932]: 271). The point about openly fictional counterfactuals, like Roth's, is that no one would dream of taking these 'what-if' stories as evidence. Hitler did not manipulate a US Administration. We often dream of 'what ifs', but only monetarist counterfactuals direct CB policy, we saw in Chapter 3, by excluding key evidence like Ramps opposing any help for populations.

[2] Chapter 2 recounted 'Red Scares' re labour. See Arendt's *Origins of Totalitarianism* (1967 [1951]) on Jewish financiers. On reflection, Fritz Stern in 1977 said the Bismarck family was the wealthiest in Germany; Stern shared the blame around. Chernow (1993), on how Hitler via Schacht 'had' to deal with Max Warburg for war funding until the Warburgs in Hamburg fled, some too late. WASP does not say male, white Anglo-Saxon protestants, yet WASMP is appropriate.

Central banks never seem to admit that, yet CBs also create state money and guarantee bank money. State spending, deposited, creates the hybrid private-state money. Banks have no heavy work of the industrial and service sectors. They create money in advancing loans, which are deposited at the stroke of a pen or keyboard: their assets are their loans and their liabilities the deposits, many of which are deposited loans (Table 1.1). Although financing techniques unexpectedly change, old adages still apply. Money is a relation by which one person who cannot pay gets another person who cannot pay to guarantee that she/he can pay. Writ large, that suggests banks be cautious. One bank cannot create money without an eye to other banks, since loans are spent, and their proceedings are deposited in other banks. These are guaranteed on state High Powered Money (HPM). No theorist of money, Mark Twain grumbled that banks always lend out umbrellas on sunny days and recall them at the onset of rain. Keynes put the matter simply – 'banks march in step'. Money expands with demand for loans but in 1929–33, banks contracted it excessively. After a few hundred years, a wild pattern seemed visible. Money is created in treasuries, central banks, and banks yet, whereas governments usually have the monopoly of coercion to service and retire their debts through taxes, firms and households are reliant on economic activity, on profits and wages to service interest payments to banks. Banks can choose not to lend for job creating enterprises and instead for useless deals that only profit the few, and banks. Depression is prolonged.

Bearing these practices in mind and also, by 1933, the shaken state of (often fledgling) democracies in face of fascism's rise, this chapter examines CB changes in the 1930s–1940s to assess their merits. Resistance to democratic processes was strong. Thus, the Bank of England tried to impose a financial 'imperialism' on the Dominions, to push its model on the central Bank of Canada established in 1934, but soon after the BoC was not a 'banker to the banks', nor was the Reserve Bank of India later. Australians argued for the People's Bank from the 1890s, nearly gained in 1930 via its 1911 state-owned commercial bank. Australia's later became a stern Banker to banks and states. In Britain, the 1929–30 Macmillan inquiry petered out with the Bankers' Ramp against Labour. These parties of labour did not go quietly after they lost government. British Labour had less influence until post-WWII: the pre-war National Government devalued but allowed stagnation.[3]

Compared to Britain and least of all the dominated colonies (e.g. India), the US was 'lucky' with Roosevelt in 1933, Canada 'lucky' with a new government in 1935, Australia 'lucky' that a strong Country Party supported Labor's demands from opposition in 1934. Farm foreclosures were no more endearing to agribusiness than bank contraction to town businesses, the unions and jobless. This pattern hit the US and the world badly. The City or Wall Street institutions were proudly resistant to public outrage. Of the commissions and public inquiries into failures of banking, the US Congress's demand for a far-reaching investigation into the 1929 Crash, the Pecora inquiry, was the harshest light. Australia held a 1936 Royal Commission into its state-owned central bank. Germany was beyond public debate by then; in France, the socialist Leon Blum endured a Bankers' Ramp in 1936; Germany invaded in 1940; Canada installed a state-oriented, deficit-financing central bank in 1938.[4]

Luck in the timing of elections played a role. Nevertheless, Roosevelt's 1932 campaign espoused gold orthodoxy, despite economic chaos and Britain's break with the gold standard a year before his election run. Unlike British Labour, Roosevelt's electoral timing was perfect, since bank collapses rose to the day he took office. Whether industrial billionaires, like the anti-Semitic Henry Ford or a Marriner Eccles public reformer, would influence the Administration was not clear. It appears that FDR was easily persuaded to reflate and more.

[3] In Chapter 3 on Australia's and Britain's Bankers' Ramps; farm and firm foreclosures; banks refusal to extend such loans worsened the Depression. See Sayers (1949) on the BoE; Cain (1996) and Ryan-Collins (2015) on Canada and India.

[4] See Woodruff (2014) on France's Ramp; Ryan-Collins (2015: 4; 13; 37–8) on Canada (citing full studies of the BoC's creation after bank crashes, and thorough state reorientation after BoE's failed interventions).

I do not dwell on the 1944 Bretton Woods easing of Interwar international creditor-debtor conflicts – that so obsessed central banks – except to compare its problems with the 1971–3 dollar 'float' of President Nixon. Instead I show how the grim 1914–45 years of wars and depression, along with changed social-political alliances, finally saw remarkable reforms in OECD Treasuries and central banks. Since the 2008 crisis, any similar reform looks unlikely in today's different contexts.

THE RISE AND RISE OF ECONOMISTS' INFLUENCE

Deflation is far less easy to curtail (if at all) through monetary policy, than inflation: 'it is easier to prevent people from creating money by borrowing for production and consumption than it is to induce them to do so'. Thus, inflations are reversible whether via creating millions of jobless into deflation, or far more moderate measures like raising asset reserves and taxes, and by wage-price controls. Orthodoxy's counterfactuals on the Great Depression (deflation) mystified what CBs 'might have' achieved. Full employment (FE) to monetarists is only a *trickle down*, free-to-starve market by-product.[5] Roosevelt's backing from corporate industrialists who promoted decent paid work, against the by then despised financiers of Wall Street, needed new approaches to redesign the Fed. Whereas booms and depressions were taken for granted, momentarily CBs became less overtly elitist and stressed economic activity, ideally in the public interest.

Economic imperialism dominates in our era of central banking, which took over from FE economists serving the state. The old classical, allegedly scientific model – predictive, apolitical, class neutral, with which to mystify *all* political, democratic and social questions – is defunct but dominates. Previously elites had not listened to economists but the key actors, namely themselves and their

---

[5] See Chernow (1993) on Ford and see Chapter 5 on Bretton Woods' end. See on 'inflation', Ingham (2008: 88–91) who wants rigorous testing of the efficacy of central banks. The jobless said to be 'voluntary'; trickle down is the Laffer curve, see Chapter 6: a job means poverty wages, hourly labour; lock-outs and wage theft.

most important friends or foes. A few 'radical' economists such as the American Thorstein Veblen (also sociologist) went so far as to say in November 1919 of Woodrow Wilson, that there was no 'failure' at Versailles. Rather 'upholding the vested interests of the established order was always the true purpose of the peace'. Neither Schumpeter, also historian and sociologist, nor Keynes, also a philosopher, were as forthright as Veblen. In 1920, Keynes, in *The Economic Consequences of the Peace* used logical and psychological analyses. None influenced reparations or hard deflations that only benefited high finance in the 1920s.[6] Most importantly, democratic rights were brittle and under attack.

After the worst events took over in 1933, US economists who understood 'reflation' and 'the multiplier' were suddenly invited to policy tables. *Infinitely more significant*, influential industrialists collectively switched FDR's policies into an admired turnaround. This powerful class of US debtors slapped the old claims of Wall Street and forced governments to turn their attention to employment. Where would profits come from, if not workers adding value and as consumers? America took the lead beneficially. Governments became major economic actors whether wanted or not, although both world wars were significant in the rise of the corporation and the state. Much public emphasis was on fiscal stimulus, with inaccurate clichés such as how Mussolini got the trains running on time (by making third class passenger trains wait in the sidings with goods trains). Indeed, prejudices against hyperinflation, Red Scares against unions and social democratic governments looked ever more feeble, once fascism was reflating. Schacht at the Reichsbank was both reflating for rearmament, and pressing the dangers of inflation, the printing press, and balance of trade consequences on Hitler, up to Schacht's 1939 sacking.[7]

---

[6] Veblen is cited in Tooze (2014: 521); the others are used selectively further on.
[7] See Chapter 1. On FDR's global influence, see Ahamed (2009: 435–6), and also Tooze (2007, 2014); and on the fascists and Schacht: forget 'independence' there.

In other words, CB reforms occurred due to changed social-political forces. Economists concerned about people's well-being, and for proving that more efficient and democratic economic policies were socially just, were heard. These mid-century economists opposed the tediously claimed natural science 'laws' of orthodoxy. To RBA Governor Coombs, their 'rebellious arrogance' opposed the 'mean-spirited chaos of the great depression'.[8] Rebellion was vital, but a superiority grew as they became self-congratulatory; central banks followed suit. Post-1970s, mean-spirited economists (again), in the wilderness after the 1930s, took over these newly-entrenched policy chairs to repress further any other social science approaches.

In the British case, 'everyone' was said to follow Keynes or Hawtrey by the 1930s. Yet BoE historian Richard Sayers, in comparing the Fed in 1949, said the BoE barely changed. One cannot stress enough, then, that the 'force of ideas' such as Keynes's or orthodoxy's is insufficient to explain CB reforms, compared to the structure of conflicts with the state over money production, and banking's terrible disruptions. In insignificant Australia, Labor politicians gained electoral support in their economic policy commitments to a modicum of state control over the production of money and labour markets. But their *ideas* got nowhere for decades, until WWII gave the only opportunity to democratise money to *some degree*, post-war. In contrast, Roosevelt either did not know of heterodox views or chose not to know, before taking office in 1933. His Democrat Party relied on southern white supremacist votes, as a history of Congressional disputes in the 1930s–50s shows. Roosevelt's New Dealers compromised.[9]

---

[8] 'Mean', to Nugget Coombs looking back in 1970, (cited Rowse 2015: 145) who was firm, we see later, also self-doubting. Sayers (1949) said the BoE did nothing positive until nationalised (1946). Recall in Chapter 3, UK industrialists had less influence than US industrialists.

[9] See Chapters 5 and 6, post-1970s; Howson (1985) on Keynes. Katznelson (2013) shows the New Deal did less for southern US Blacks but it did achieve far more than what previously was not politically possible. It is always a thin line between compromise and sell-out.

NATIONAL CENTRAL BANKS, CLASS AND 'INDEPENDENCE'

The thinking of Keynes, Hawtrey and their contemporaries on a 'new role' for central banks deserves a mention, before recounting changes to CBs during and after the Great Depression with two case studies: the mighty US Federal Reserve and the marginal player the Reserve Bank of Australia (ex CBA). One charge against Hawtrey was that he had 'too much' hope for the efficacy of central bank interest rates and possibilities for reflation, whereas Keynes was more jaundiced about monetary policy. Keynes's model of independence for central banks included strong control over bank money creation. Hawtrey saw central banking as 'art' not science for coping with changing circumstances and used semi-counterfactuals; Keynes stressed the 'science' and home of technical expertise. Both agreed expertise and even a sliver of social justice were lacking from 1914–34.

A problem in theory-driven recipes is that nobody can pick the future 'situation-to-be' of financial activity, therefore of relevant political controls over banks. Sayers pointed out that in the UK mid-nineteenth century, mercantile credit was the 'sensitive' quantity in the English economy; later that century, English long-term foreign lending influenced the entire world economy, and in both periods, these areas of 'sensitivity' were highly affected by Bank Rate 'technique'. In effect, the BoE could maintain the gold standard, he said, without much 'theory' behind it, and to 'force the burden of adjustment onto the borrowing countries … with little bother for England itself' via this interest rate technique. Writing in 1949, he saw the more 'sensitive' points were stock exchange speculation and consumer credit. Sayers supported CB discretion over any one situation, and quality controls over banks. A brief reduction in finance sectors' political control during WWII offered chances for greater democratic state control. But what might be next? No one can ever say.[10]

---

[10] See Howson (1985: 164; 172) further; Sayers on the nineteenth- to twentieth-century eras (1949: 210–11), as we saw Butlin (1986) on 'burden of adjustment' to Empire, in Chapter 1.

With admiration for his analysis of 'the inherent instability of the modern credit system', Schumpeter was critical of Hawtrey's over-reliance on central bank policies. To explain 'cyclical fluctuations' in trade and employment, Hawtrey left out 'new orders' for industrial equipment (i.e. job growth) and looked only to wholesale trade in stocks 'that react to small changes in loan rates'. Schumpeter implied that reversing deflation is difficult, which it is. To be fair to Hawtrey, the political-economic relationships and conditions in Britain meant that industry was neglected in the City-BoE-Treasury nexus and understudied in economics. Geoff Ingham suggests that UK industry was under-funded and under-invested during most of the nineteenth century. Britain's industrial dominance was more to being 'the first' to impose machinofacture. Hawtrey stressed the US industrial engine, France, Germany and Italy too, and the primary producing debtor countries (Argentina, Australia) but put too much hope on monetary policy. His influence waned, said Howson. Still, he damned the *natural experiments* of CB cruelty.[11]

And counter-*evidence* (not theorem-driven counterfactuals) against the hard-nosed role of central banks was stunning. Inside FDR's Administration were left-wing to neoclassical economists and political scientists, like Laughlin Currie and Gardiner Means proposing democratic state planning. Means, famous for *The Modern Corporation and Private Property* 1932, he wrote with Adolph Berle, reported in 1935 on 'administered prices'. In contrast to blaming CBs alone for deepening Depression, Means said that concentration and corporate control in some industrial sectors disrupted market price adjustments, exacerbating the slump. Berle and Means made quite clear that US corporations were un-owned, and shareholders could not control managerial 'abuse' such as the 'power of confiscation' of

---

[11] See Schumpeter (1954: 1121); see Ingham on the weaknesses of the UK (1984; 2004: 150–1); and e.g. Arkwright chained small children to work his machines. See Hawtrey (1962 [1932]: 50) on inherent 'autonomy' of money disorders in booms/slumps. *Natural* science can do experiments on water's boiling point: orthodoxy extends that to humans, excluding their fabulous selves.

profits/dividends to refinance growth (later, CEO salaries). Berle, a conservative jurist, argued in the 1950s that government's role in corporations (R&D and demand management) meant that private profits were nearly 'alien'.[12]

Keynes cast the most blame on dithering, nostalgic governments and (unlike neoclassical anti-state views) the control exercised against fiscal stimulus from the *rentier* classes' liquidity preference, and for low wage inflation and capacity to escape taxes. His aims for central banking were to abolish the 'despotic' gold standard for a managed currency; and to oppose undue inflation *and* deflation. In other words, the CB should stabilise domestic prices not exchange rates. Control of bank credit creation was important as a joint Treasury-Bank role. Keynes argued for *structural* reform of central banks in which governments be responsible for setting the overall policy, and thus accountable to electorates, but central banks should have, as is said now, operational independence based on their 'science' that, unlike orthodoxy, was evidence-based. Elected legislatures would set CB 'goals'. There must be no secrecy in the BoE either: 'We do not want to be governed by masked men in false beards'. Treasuries and CBs cannot be antagonistic, Keynes argued, and the BoE should 'not stand for the interest of the City' any more than other national interests.[13]

Keynes's loose class analysis suggested central banks be independent from *finance sectors*. Historical and sociological analysis shows that WWI horrified the old elites because of state control needed for conducting total war and its FE. The tiny *rentier* class,

---

[12] See Stapleford (2011: 6–17) on Milton Friedman, neoclassical, and Wesley Mitchell, Hegelian Marxist, having a mutual conviction that hard predictions (Friedman) or soft historical ones (Mitchell) could be made: They both worked in FDR's National Resources Committee in 1934–9. Stapleford (2011: 14), cites Means on prices. See also, Berle and Means (1932: 8; 247), and Berle cited in Henwood (2003: 4). 'Un-owned' firms free from stockholder directions (not dividend demands) is in Pixley (2012: 46–7) – the un-owned 'money manager' phase was due to a rise of pension and superannuation firms.

[13] Relying on Bibow (2009: 130–1; 146–7; 134); Keynes is cited in Bibow (2009: 136; 141). We see further, Keynes hoped *exchange rates* would be reformed with his global bancor idea (that failed).

today represented in a huge way (a kind of contradictory class location) in pension, investment and money market funds, aimed to overturn democratic stirrings. 'Old money' found industrial profits coarse, 'common' and prone to war 'profiteering'. Active *rentier* and bank resistance to any minimisation of their fabulous war benefits squashed governments from positive action. Keynes exposed the stagnation this demanded.

Later his views became an object of reverence, Cambridge the 'Keynesian Jerusalem'. He downplayed the slender chances for maintaining social improvement, in that historically, employers oppose FE, not only the band of *rentiers* seeking 'sound money' (dear money). 'Keynesians' gradually lost sight of money during the postwar, but anti-FE economists dumped social structural analysis altogether. The latter ignored how the previous century's owner-managers had long given way to hired managers of un-owned oligopolies who later battled with hired managers of un-owned pension funds, and, via ahistorical 'theory' tried to refute any power relations or democratic processes. As all this methodological individualism rose again, heterodox economics was somewhat diverted.[14]

Keynes, unlike neoclassical 'village fair' individualists, refused predictions. But to one great sympathiser, Geoff Harcourt, Keynes saw a role for 'philosopher-kings' like himself, and for those trained at Oxbridge to run government industrial/fiscal planning. Jim Crotty also suggests that Keynes hoped for 'a gentlemen's revolt' and feared mass agitation.[15] Central banks would use 'beneficent scientific control' like electrical engineers. Any vested interest would meekly accept technical expertise. Keynes had no objections to central bank public ownership that Labour proposed in 1932. On UK Labour's policies (Jörg Bibow points out), since Keynes did not put the 'ultimate' blame on the BoE for the 1920s–30s poor conduct of monetary

---

[14] See E. O. Wright (1997), on class location. Jones (2003b) looks critically at Keynes's deification; Chapter 6 explores these debates on the smashing of FE.

[15] Minsky (2008 [1986]) spoke of the 'village fair' view of markets in this resurrection. Harcourt, personal discussion; see also Crotty (1999: 563; 574).

policy, but on 'the higher authorities of the state', there is a 'tension' in Keynes's idea of 'independence'. I'll say! He sidesteps the problem of central banks' 'ambiguous' structural position whereby monetary decisions side (politically) with financiers or politicians or both. Would that be a Tory-run or Labour-run state?[16] Wider social sciences and the informed public tended to lose, then, in the postwar, to pompous experts, which produced a stable of economists inside the state and central banks, leaving an established space into which narrow-minded economists opposed to FE (but possibly not warfare) installed themselves from the 1970s onwards.

Monetary-fiscal consolidation differed among analysts. Hawtrey blamed central banks and disputed Keynes's fiscal measures, on original not socially harsh grounds, in favouring 'reflation' over direct stimulus. He did not oppose treasury stimulus if that was more rapidly effective, but overall, cheap money would be the answer to 'induce' banks to invest in job creating industries, and to increase workers' purchasing power (i.e. effective demand). However, against a deflation, cheap money does not always achieve more than 'pushing a string' without business demands on banks for loans. Also, bank advances can be diverted from long-term business and trade, and to consumer debt, equity, property and other asset bubbles. Schumpeter's analysis of 'destruction without function' applies. Open market operations (that Hawtrey favoured), in post-WWII UK, fostered a bond market bubble, and strenuous City lobbying against Attlee's Labour Government aims succeeded, when Chancellor Hugh Dalton gave up cheap money, also from an attack on Labour by one of Keynes's 'gentleman friends' keen to reinstate the City and evidence-free 'theory'.[17]

---

[16] On 'engineers' Keynes is cited in Bibow (2009: 139); on ambiguous CBs see Ingham (2008: 50); Bibow (2009: 141) on UK Labour, and (2009: 146) on 'tension'. If Keynes was personally sympathetic during Labour's Bankers Ramp (in Chapter 3), it's hard to see the political attacks on governments of Labour, and the ALP, which was better informed about money, fitting in. *Ideas* made no difference. Logically, CBs cannot be 'neutral' engineers.

[17] See Howson (1985: 165–7) on Hawtrey; Sayers (1949: 198; 205–6) on UK, postwar. Evidence of the City's resistance and Dennis Robertson the faux 'friend' is in Tily (2015); see also Higgins (1949).

Richard Sayers argued that the US Fed moved straight away, after FDR's 1933–4 changes, to qualitative (and quantity) controls of credit expansion, whereas the BoE from 1932 onwards only used cheap money, which fostered a housing boom. Economists started debating how the quantity control of raising or lowering the interest rate was such a 'blunt tool', against industry and jobs. With the job-creating effects of WWII, and central banks reduced to *passivity* (to neoclassicals, but not really) during war, Keynesian fiscal policies postwar, took centre stage; the BoE was nationalised in 1946 (and it gained some controls) by Attlee's Labour Government.

Two economists were politically active in their specific times. Keynes and Milton Friedman, global public intellectuals, pushed political barrows and shifted positions opportunistically. Firm believers in the power of ideas and 'science', Friedman told employers and financiers what they wanted to hear (and would never talk of 'class'). Did Keynes give succour to the labour movement? Keynesians and others rarely contemplated money class and labour class analysis, like say, of Max Weber (on the 'memorable alliance' of states and money-merchants, and the whip of hunger). Australian economist L. F. Giblin, colleague of Keynes who developed a multiplier theory, remonstrated in 1930 with John Curtin (later the ALP Prime Minister). Curtin criticised Giblin for leaving 'the money question sacrosanct' and ignoring 'the economic structure of society'. Giblin said, 'I am not convinced that "private interests" have *hitherto had very serious effects*. The question of technical competence is more important.' Giblin's colleagues constructed analyses of agribusiness 'interests' and tariff boosts but got no further.[18]

---

[18] See Sayers (1949: 202; 207) on Attlee's changes; and Freedman (2006, 2007) on the publicity minded JMK and MF, and Chapter 1 on Weber (1978), and (1981 [1927]), which, funnily, F. H. Knight translated in 1927, Knight being a conservative *bête noir* of Friedman's). Coleman et al. (2006: 136–8): cite Curtin and Giblin, my emphasis. The vested interest was protection of Queensland's sugar industry. Giblin said he agreed with Curtin on the 'existence' of social structure – hardly – Giblin imbibed a ruling class world view yet was well-meaning.

Keynes's somewhat philosopher-king and/or technical approach became precious to many economists who operate with no theory of the state or class. Consider empirical detail on central banks and their relations to governments and 'vested interests'. To Ingham, central banks' difficult position means Keynes's idea they could be semi-independent scientist-engineers leaves out CBs' structural position and the contingent changes in social groups and governments. How this is characterised in diverse eras is the clue to understanding CB decisions.

One way to illuminate their structural position is to mention how one central banker experienced those problems. Nugget Coombs, the Governor of the CBA (1949–59) and RBA (1960–68), had serious doubts in 1936 about Keynes's *General Theory*, which led him to worry (privately) if he could work in the CBA 'and retain my integrity'. Central bank work is never like Keynes's idealised electrical technician. Coombs imposed sociological questions on the 'propensity to consume' idea, arguing against either aggregating 'schedules of individuals whose actual incomes are widely different', or using a non-Keynesian, even more 'doubtful concept ... the representative individual'. Attacking economists like Hayek expressing the interests of a former dynamic capitalist class, historically, capitalists were now bent on keeping 'large scale monopolistic units' and so, to Coombs, Hayek futilely promoted 'free competition'. Instead, Coombs called for 'the adoption of a theory of the state' and not the 'fictions of liberal economics and the limited interventions of Keynes, Meade, Harrod and co.' In 1944–5 he wrote most of Australia's White Paper on FE – a pragmatic support of Treasury management of effective demand. In its drafting, Labor's Cabinet ruled out his concern that capitalism's discipline over workers would go with FE, and bosses' demands would return. Unions could press for higher wages, but how would the state respond? To Coombs, Keynes 'seemed to bypass the most divisive issues within our society'.[19]

---

[19] At the LSE, Coombs was partly taught by Hayek, also Laski; cited in Rowse (2015: 150–2) from private letters. Also, Rowse (2015: 158), on Curtin's refusal to talk of FE; Rowse

This is fascinating. Coombs was no Marxist and he rightly included the vested interests of the *military* too; WWII and Bretton Woods were preoccupations. How he fared in Australia's mid-century CBA/RBA is further below. Fast forward on, where his principles seem just alive in the RBA: central banks have a very modest role and independence is awkward. So, if an elected government makes a complete mess of everything, it can in principle lose office peacefully via the ballot box. 'Politicians will never change their spots and they will say ... when interest rates are rising, "The Central Bank is doing it". When interest rates are coming down they'll claim the credit for it', RBA Governor Fraser told me. He unusually hectored everyone on how financial sectors prefer low economic activity.[20] A statutory central bank cannot be electable, yet the danger is also in the anomaly of the European Central Bank, and hysterical drive for independent (but dependent on finance sector assessments) central banks. Recall that states have separate (war) interests, which cannot be reduced to classes or (absurdly) to individuals. Social and political divisions are inevitable although change can occur unexpectedly, not in binary contrasts that, say, paint FDR a hero *versus* villains, or vice versa. Fiscal-monetary consolidation is desirable if fraught. It suggests some independence of CBs *from banks* not only from states (both thorny problems).

THE US FED FOR THE PUBLIC INTEREST?

Before Roosevelt took office, US Administrations largely supported Wall Street, and so had no stark Bankers' Ramps of elsewhere (we saw). Moreover, monetarists ignore US banker resistance to control. For example, the Press trumpeted how in early 1929 Charles Mitchell, head of National City Bank had defied NY Fed Harrison's

suggests Coombs drew on Kalecki and Barbara Wootton. Coombs's 1981 memoir is also cited Rowse (2015: 164; 163).

[20] War debt however lingers after electoral change. Many RBA officials opposed 1990s 'independence'; also, on his FE remit, in my interview B. W. Fraser, Former RBA Governor, Canberra 28 June 2002 (in Pixley 2004); cf. Blinder et al. (2001) *How do central bankers talk* is self-congratulatory; see Chapter 7 on 'pseudo-independence'.

dampeners. Despite (or because of) his membership of the NY District Fed, Mitchell propped up the shaky bubble in March 1929 with much publicity and Wall Street cheers, like the Hearst press that if a share market was 'wrong' as 'alarmists' said, the government should either close the NYSE, or the Fed should 'mind its own business'. The US Great Depression was stark by October 1931, when President Hoover proposed that private banks 'save' Wall Street. He talked (secretly) to nineteen bankers (the heads of the largest Wall Street banks) with Treasurer Mellon and Harrison, NY Fed. The bankers instead demanded the government or the Fed – created to be their lender of last resort, they said – must bail them out. The nineteen did 'try' to gather 'funds' but the plan, 'paralyzed by its proprietors' ultraconservatism and fear of losing money, folded'. Private banks wanted to 'govern through panic' as Polanyi put it, to pass on all losses.[21]

Yet the Fed did intervene – ducking and weaving around the two forces. Irving Fisher argued debt-deflation under the Depression 'could have' been stopped earlier, but saying: 'In fact, under President Hoover, recovery was apparently well started by Federal Reserve open-market purchases, which revived prices and business from May to September 1932'. The efforts were not kept up and recovery was stopped by circumstances, Fisher said, including a political 'campaign of fear'. What was this *fear campaign* against legislation enabling the Fed to put $1billion of Treasury securities into bank reserves held at the Fed? Roosevelt's!

To J. K. Galbraith, Republican Party ideas of balanced budgets were 'high doctrine', but the Democratic Party platform of 1932 called for a 'federal budget annually balanced' and worse, 'an immediate and drastic reduction of governmental expenditures'. In reply

---

[21] See Chapter 7 on the ECB; Hawtrey (1962 [1932]: 237) on US bank failures; currency hoarding by 1930–1; see Dyster and Meredith (2012: 127) Australia devalued in January (1931); dating the 'Great' depression is in Ahamed (2009: 438; 436–7), who says the '19' included Lamont and Whitney of J. P. Morgan, Wiggin of Chase National, and Mitchell of National City, to Ahamed the *usual suspects*, rather like *13 Bankers* in 2008 (Johnson and Kwak 2011).

to Roosevelt's vigorous campaign for a 'sound currency ... [as] an international necessity', and his criticism of 'fiscal recklessness' (the Hoover dam and Fed reflation), Hoover promised he would not 'exhaust' the budget 'in the issue of securities'. Perhaps his open market issues were 'too late', or ineffectual since monetary policy was 'pushing on a string' and big banks used their larger Fed reserves for their own recovery. With pitiful loan demand and banks reluctant, no 'useful' money was created. Bank closures grew scarily, exactly when Roosevelt took office in 1933. Luckily Roosevelt's fondness for banks reversed quickly.[22]

FDR declared a 'bank holiday' closing the banks and took the US off gold. The 1932–3 Pecora-led Senate investigation into the Crash reported Wall Street abuses so beyond public doubt that disgust settled in. Wall Street banks' dramatic halt to investment from 1928 had serious impacts worldwide and, with Treasurer Mellon's austerity, on the USA. Probably influenced by its powerful US creditor, Germany's 'Hunger Chancellor' Brüning and the Reichsbank imposed that fatal deflation in 1930. Hitler took over in January 1933, Roosevelt too. Fisher discussed the 'cruelty' and 'starvation' in the US debt deflation, whereas today's verdict on FDR of harsh money's camp followers is vicious. Monetarists welcome the 'shake-out' of American industry of the Depression, sounding remarkably like Andrew Mellon of that time.[23]

So, initially, did Roosevelt's remaining grim aim for a 'balanced budget'. However, that *raised the public ire of industrialist groups.*

[22] Fisher (1933: 347) like Hawtrey (1962 [1932]: 236–7) favoured CB buying of securities, and only gestured at the politics; never Galbraith (1975a: 200–1), citing Roosevelt and Hoover; see B. Friedman (2005: 162) on Hoover's dam; and Ahamed (2009: 439) on the Fed's 1932 purchases. FDR was from New Amsterdam 'old money'.

[23] *Barrons'* editor told me Wall Street was seen as a casino for fifty years afterwards, in Pixley (2004). Against Fisher, Calomiris says (2013: 178) 'The Fed had not expanded its open market operations [in the 1930s] because it did not see the point'. Calomiris (2013: 174–85) cites Meltzer on the Fed's 'real bills error', and the huge *benefits* in Depression's 'shake-out' (liquidation to Mellon) of 'backward' US firms (2013: 180). Moe (2014: 40), on FDR's bank holiday: two days after his inauguration; his Emergency Banking Act got through Congress four days later.

Marriner Eccles (a Utah millionaire) warned that further 'drastic deflation', 'decrease in purchasing power' and greater unemployment would ensue. Invited to Treasury where he loudly promoted government-planned deficit financing, in 1934 Eccles was invited by FDR to chair the Fed. He refused, saying Wall Street banks were dominating the Board in DC, since the private District Feds could 'ignore' Board decisions. Roosevelt asked Eccles to propose reforms. These industrialists' challenge to excessive finance control over the Fed thus began, and Eccles became Chairman of the Fed.

'Banks must make longer-term loans to justify their existence'. An outrage to Wall Street (but like Australia's 1936 inquiry) Eccles wanted political control of the Fed, deficit financing, and removal of banks' control of open market operations. Eccles accused them of taking a 'narrow banking rather than a broad social point of view' and urged the 'public control ... [of] issuing currency and by regulating the volume of bank deposits'. The Washington Fed Board must take the 'national interest'. Even Chicago economists agreed.[24]

The Board had its powers strengthened, but the District Feds were never nationalised. The Senate watered down Roosevelt's Banking Act of 1935 (as FDR had ghoulishly expected) to ensure (allegedly), the Fed was no 'adjunct of the Treasury' complained Senator Carter Glass.[25] Perhaps it was also hard to push supervision onto the (old despised) Fed after those shocked days of 1933 bank collapses.

---

[24] Moe cites Eccles' and other industrialists' Association demands (2014: 40–1) and his assistant Lauchlin Currie who, on 'justify', is cited in Moe (2014: 44–5). On 'narrow' banks, Eccles is cited in Shull (2014: 24); and on 'public control' cited Moe (2014: 46). In 1930, Chicago economists like Frank Knight, Henry Simon, Aaron Director, had urged an end to the privately-owned District Feds, as had the American Bankers Association and Congressman Wright Patman; see Ryan-Collins (2015: 8) on the 'Chicago Plan' for a 'public monopoly on money creation' (dropped by MF later).

[25] Senator Carter Glass, pro-Wall Street 1913 FRA promoter, opposed state ownership; and got the treasury secretary and comptroller of the currency removed from the Fed Board in the 1935 Act; despite FDR hiding that section in a longer Bill, cited in Shull (2014: 24–5). So much for consolidation. Roosevelt relished battles with Congress but said that reforming the Fed was an uphill task. The NY Fed is owned by Wall Street, so dominates among District Feds.

So, the Fed, like all central banks self-financing, amply funded to supervise, has little tradition of effective supervision except via the Discount window (last resort) and critically, margin loan requirements. The private NY Fed could still 'supervise' the Fed Board, thanks to Glass; while separate New Deal finance regulators, and Glass-Steagall rules, became institutionally entrenched (but the SEC's distrust strategies after the 1970s were inadvertently counterproductive). Public hostility to Wall Street lasted at least until the 1960s, and the Fed did gain controls over bank advances in the late 1930s (than the BoE, we saw) of a quality kind, not just quantity.[26]

In WWII, the Fed lent directly to Treasury (this was not revoked until 1981) and bought its securities on fixed, very low rates. Treasury dominated the Fed; less so after the postwar 'bank credit inflation' with the Korean War. Yet Eccles never relaxed from the Fed's duty to counteract 'the twin evils of inflation and deflation'. Coordination of fiscal and monetary policy should aim for FE and 'a decent living for every man and woman'.[27]

Wray points out QE's monetising of private bank debt from 2009 is the same process as war finance (of WWII), although QE's type of 'printing money' (reserves really) aims only to *induce* banks to lend (pushing on a string), not to give Treasury any *direct* funding. The similarities of QE and WWII financing are in the impacts: First, very low interest rates on state debt; Second, the Fed's books are packed with most of this debt, and Third, private bank reserves grew 'to historic levels' from QE, and from the Fed's buying and lending against private debt. With WWII, the Fed's purchase of Treasury securities was designed to avoid the way banks manipulated WWI Liberty

[26] See on the service of Fed chairs: www.federalreserve.gov/aboutthefed/bios/board/boardmembership.htm; See Sayers (1949: 202) on the Fed gaining more bank advance controls; Shull (2014: 24) on Fed margin loan powers. The Glass-Steagall Act separated investment from money creating banks. The Securities and Exchange Commission (SEC) was established, and accountancy firms checked bank balances.

[27] T-bills were less than WWI's, at 3/8th per cent interest and long-term T-bonds at 2.5 per cent, Moe (2014: 47); after Eccles' 1951 modest break with Treasury and on 'decent' FE, Eccles is cited Moe (2014: 38-9).

Bonds. Banks had delayed purchases in hopes of future higher rates (leaving greater postwar burdens for citizens and taxpayers). Fixing rates seemed a solution to these tricks; lower than WWI's rates, 'when the "hard-faced men" of the City and Wall Street profiteered from the carnage'. But this time, 'private investors' rebalanced their portfolios to the higher rate of long-term T-bonds, and away from the low rate short-term T-bills. The extent of this practice was so great that the Fed held nearly all the T-bills at WWII's end. As well, banks offered cheap finance to the public to buy T-bonds, only to buy them back later at a profit. US Treasury did little to prevent this.[28]

However, and even if the USA was again the main creditor to the Allies (with Lend Lease) during this war, the Allies turned to price controls and taxes, totally unlike WWI. Terrible inequalities of WWI's aftermath were to be avoided. Keynes proposed a system of 'deferred pay' and allowances (means tested) since it was unfair to tax workers to withdraw some of the 'increased purchasing power' (during a wartime FE). As well, if taxes to reduce inflations were only on 'the rich', they would still benefit from price (shortage) inflation, and taxes would be insufficient. His plan for 'social justice' would put the steepest progressive tax on the top incomes and the most deferred pay downwards, to go into Post Offices at interest paid later. However, rations and price controls were more successful in reducing those war inflations; in Britain, many in the working class ate better than ever before. During the Korean War, Eccles moved, in 1951, to reduce that wartime bank money inflation, not pleasing US Treasury, but that did not decrease the Fed's commitment to FE, unlike the savage deflation imposed in 1920, or later battles in the 1970s.[29]

The devastated countries had the worst of it, and staggering debts but this time short-lived. Like WWI, war gave a huge stimulus to

---

[28] See Chapter 2 war finance; Wray (2014: 107); 'hard-faced' is in Keynes, cited in Tily (2015); Moe (2014: 47–9) on T-bills and banks.

[29] Keynes (1940: 8; 21) on the low-paid and 'rich'; (1940: 31; 41–3) re plan of Post Offices; on WWII price controls see Galbraith (1981) who ran some; and see Chapter 2.

US industry; Canada and Australia built up large industrial bases too. This retired state debts quickly. That joint state-private investment in production in both wars was remarkable. If there is one excuse for orthodoxy this was it. Never interested in the direction of bank loans, orthodoxy still assumes banks actually lend to non-financial firms (hardly now) and that only state or CB-money is inflationary. By the Vietnam War, banks were lending for asset investments (going nowhere socially useful or repayable when booms collapsed) and productive loans became unfashionable. The household sector became major (private) borrowers. Central banks stopped looking while the mixed economy dwindled (except Defence). From public debt at its highest levels in WWII, that dropped straight after. Useless dangers to today's public debt are the costs of bailing out banks.[30]

Generally, US Treasury and the Fed worked together (from 1933 to 1980) and, until President Eisenhower (R.), there were few government moves towards 'undue reliance' on monetary policy with its maldistribution, Galbraith noted. The Fed considered economic activity and thus avoided imposing such high rates for lengthy periods as to risk deflation. The District Feds were not nationalised but, with Bretton Woods arrangements to stabilise the global dollar (see further on), the few US currency threat points enabled numerous controls of banks (more than Britain's). Governments introduced, then later abolished, these reforms. The central bank in Australia, to which we now turn, also shows the extent that they are creatures of the state. Pressures to maintain FE were higher than in the US but, similarly, that depended on (social democratic) governments being less beholden to the financial sector than the interwar years. The story is hardly known today even in Australia: the struggles were not pretty.

---

[30] All of Europe, Japan, UK had devastation and debts, until the US plans, see later. On state-private spending, and Vietnam, see Ryan-Collins (2015: 13) and Chapter 5; on public-private debt ratios, cross-country, see Schularick (2014: 195, 198). Unconditional bank bail outs are a licence to plunder.

AUSTRALIA'S RENEGADE, DEMOCRATIC
CENTRAL BANK MODEL

The curious tale of Australia's CB model, effected in WWII, shows private banks hated its social democratic, allegedly 'anomalous' features. Its design implied compromise, in that politics and economics are linked (practically) to inevitable 'vested interests'. The Commonwealth Bank became a full central bank and, through its state-owned banking arm from the 1911 founding Act, a competitor to capitalist banks. By WWII, the CBA's commercial arm tempered its money-creation, guided by its central banking arm. That double role describes the CBA's uniqueness, unacceptable to banks. Its part-independence from banks was by owning one! Institutional conflicts in 1945–9 involved the typical suspects, which spread into a 'national hysteria'. Banks used (some say bank executives coerced) their staff and tellers to engage in what was called the 'battle for the banks'. The rebadged Reserve Bank of Australia was compromised further, yet with an unusual legacy than most central banks, out of the nearest Australia reached to a money-class war, and a constitutional and legitimation crisis. Whereas Australia's 1929 Bankers' Ramp left Australia in bitter depression, the post-WWII class war saw the ALP triumph even after losing office.[31]

This ruling class conflict against a majority Labor government was regarded as such, although few, save the monetary economists of that time show that banks opposed any CB. In response (e.g. to court cases), Labor's intervening proposal for complete bank nationalisation fed the 'unbridled imagination' of banks and press, to mixed public hostility. The ALP government's central bank design stayed, partly, and its 1945 FE policy; the twin mandates were both strong.

---

[31] 'Anomalous' to capitalism per se – and to economists who are listed in Beggs (2010). L. F. Giblin said 1947 'hysteria' was 'unbridled', cited in Butlin (1983: 15). On paying tellers to protest, see May (1968); Butlin (1983) and McLean (2013). The RBA was an entity legally continuous with the state-owned Commonwealth Bank Act of 1911. The CBA was separated off in 1960 under the right-wing Menzies government.

Compromise after the 1970s inflation scares was also unusual. Slight independence from banks and the state remains.

The conflict was over the conditions of control over the production of money, however modestly civilising that was. As Geoff Ingham says, 'the state's direct participation in the economy is its most contested activity'. The ALP believed a strong central bank was one key to control private banking excess, backed with labour market reforms for the stability of money. The CBA/RBA strenuously aimed at minimising all kinds of inflation (within FE), using quantity and quality controls, and urged progressive tax to retire state debt. Its original make-up (by 1943) is forgotten and hardly mentioned in UK or US comparisons, for obvious reasons that Australia is a minor, ignored, rich country *and* it upsets most central bank models.[32]

Clearly a constructive context since the US set the postwar global tone; economic conditions became rosy. Yet, as war ended, policy makers (wrongly) feared a slump even in countries spared war's destruction. Unlike some, the CBA rapidly changed course to fight inflation; Governor Coombs was often alarmed by cheap money.

Another extraordinary feature was that what the ALP wanted was not to come out of secret, cosy deals with big finance. It was to be a central bank that would guard the *banking and state* conditions for social justice for citizens (more than Eccles' dreams). A 'composite' of a state-owned, Labor-introduced CB *and* a not-for-commercial profit bank – was the reason private bankers were grimly determined not to have any central bank at all, even if banks would benefit from lender of last resort. In the absence of 'expensive Dukes' battling against British Lloyd George's 'People's Budget', in the ambitious Australian 'People's Bank', money was less the space of exception from democratic control.[33] But an enormous amount of energy and

---

[32] I have stressed before that FE and price stability mandates can prevent a CB from being relentlessly deflationary. See Ingham (2008: 178), the Australian model amply supports his statement, as we see below.

[33] The Australian economists cited here are exceptions today. Calomiris or Giannini's *raison d'etre* is undone with this counter-example remaining in the RBA (since a democratically

propaganda was consistently applied against Australians to deny the People's Bank, if banks had truly had their way. The CBA Act passed in 1949 (later modified in 1960) yet, given the vicious and exhausting nature of opponents since 1911, few remarked in 1949 that the ALP had won the main battle for their chosen model. The RBA remains quite a beacon, albeit subject to global currency vigilantes and today's reckless local banks.

This case compares starkly with the top-down EU attempt to impose the ECB on Europe, and earlier CBs. The RBA was primarily a bottom-up creature of Labor, a party that back then understood how banks create money. The differences to FDR's (limited) reforms of the Fed are striking, even against the far stronger BoC's.

Just before he died in 1977, S. J. Butlin left a wistful optimistic message. Australia's century of major and 'debilitating conflict' over central banking's very existence was over by the 1960s. To him, 'the principle of a substantial degree of control and restraint over the [private] trading banks, of the existence of an effective instrument for the exercise of monetary policy ... had been taken out of politics'. The politics of recalcitrant banks from 1911, the 1929 Bankers' Ramp, and class war 1945–60 were bald-faced. Class war politics only diminished about specific CBA/RBA decisions; in particular, Butlin argued that depoliticising money would not be 'a good thing', because '**politics is of the essence of monetary policy**'. Butlin did not, then, see 'neutral' central banks of Keynes's Oxbridge elite.

Albeit more sociological than most CB histories, Butlin's successor to the RBA's history, Boris Schedvin, gave a long sigh. 'The Olympian ambition' of Labor's 1945 central bank was to override the market not 'use' it. Thereafter began 'the long descent from this ambition'. Coombs saw the Bank as 'a vehicle for social advancement',

inspired central bank controls bank inflation and dangers, but not to deflation: See Chapter 8): there is no meaning of 'populism' though the 'masses' is ominous. Sawer (2012) cites dreadnaughts (in 1910–11), when UK Liberals stacked the House of Lords.

which, Schedvin said was 'refreshingly' free of the 'lofty pontifica-
tion' and 'Delphic utterances' of the Montagu Norman style.[34]

Butlin's stress (like the youthful Coombs) that CBs make political decisions is supressed today. The Melbourne bank crashes in 1893,
and its depression, saw state commissions on bank reform, all proposing a national bank, but bills failed. Politicians busied about constitutional design and redesign in several referenda for the federation of
1901 (cf. the EU had few). At that time, many (often ALP) had taken
sustenance from the US bi-metallism controversy and the US ('populist' small farm) movements, later around Jennings Bryan, although
the ALP did not pursue bi-metallism (rightly) and focused on banking's
social purposes and on theorising the multiplier.[35] John Curtin was the
ALP's and in fact Australia's twentieth century intellectual leader. He
developed under-consumption approaches to money and later drew
on Keynes. He was not dogmatic and *not alone*: his stark examples,
when capitalist elites consistently opposed state money creation in
both depressions, but which magically, dangerously flowed from bank
advances in WWI, were no odd coincidences. To anyone who was
Labor, social or 'Town' liberal, often Country Party cum rural socialist, Curtin's political-theoretical approaches were sensible and denied
rigid 'causes and effects'.[36] Reading Coombs-Curtin debates is a revela-
tion; it was an experimental mixed economy approach that opposed
inflation and deflation (FE partly code against undue anti-inflation).

After the Bankers' Ramp of 1929 (like UK's Labour Government
fate), the ALP split three ways when its legislation to control

---

[34] In Butlin (1983: 115–16) my emphasis; cf. asociological, e.g. Giannini (2011); see Schedvin
(1992: 71; 204).

[35] See also Chapter 1. Theoretically bi-metallism was a dead end, Gollan argued (or still
deflationary, unlike managed money), cf. ALP state bank and Post Office banking. The
'Money Power' theme in the US argued 'English, Jewish, and foreign; the American
plotters were bankers, city men and easterners' (Gollan 1968: 46; 47–58). In the ALP,
Bellamy's 'absurd' plans died: to favour Bagehot and 'the money power' only as 'John Fat
Esq'. not an anti-Semitic figure, in Gollan (1968: 95).

[36] See Chapter 3 also Fitzgerald (1990); Edwards (2005) citing and explaining Curtin's
approach; and Sawer (2012) mentions ALP-British Liberal links (not just UK Labour).

monetary policy was blocked in a hostile Senate. Deflation worsened. ALP Prime Minister Scullin spent a futile six months in Britain trying to 'reassure' London creditors; meantime Labor had bitter state-level Premiers' battles. The ALP Premiers who spent to keep the domestic economy alive and provide unemployment benefits were blocked; NSW Premier Lang was sacked in 1932 for his 'go-slow' on interest payments. The CBA and private banks' behaviour was anti-democratic: even so, a Royal Commission on banking was forced on Anti-Labor in 1936 (we saw).[37] Curtin used its report later. Local private banks were cautious since their disgrace in 1890, but their political and economic negative carping rose in defence of total freedom for bank money creation.

The Anti-Labor Government mismanaged rearmament finance before war's start in 1939; taxes were regressive. It struggled, unable to implement 'a politically acceptable policy of war finance' with a two-seat majority up to late 1941 when it split and the ALP took office. Everyone expected that a war to defend Australia would be mainly waged against Japan. But the 'phoney' war gave Anti-Labor a laziness and Menzies was deferential to Churchill's troop demands (from 'his' Empire). Plans for further centralising the federation and moving the economy drastically towards a war economy failed, as banks and the states constantly stonewalled. In the dying days of the Anti-Labor term of Menzies/Fadden, its Budget included the ALP proposals. Banks refused to give up an inch of their profit-oriented focus; Anti-Labor states opposed income tax centralisation even as a 'temporary' war measure.[38]

---

[37] Scullin's government fell in 1932. Niemeyer (personal email Selwyn Cornish) helped block even a BoE model (Treasurer Red Ted's 1930 CBA Act); Lang's literal sacking in 1932, for copying UK's tactics of revising down its debt to the USA, was a constitutional crisis like PM Whitlam's sacking in 1975; the 'regal' Governor of NSW said Lang could not control the fascist 'New Guard' – a hypocrite's charge.

[38] See Coleman et al. (2006: 193) on mismanagement of war finance, about which Butlin (1955: 352) agreed was a nice business 'earner'; Churchill is treated with little reverence in Australia (save for those who distort), since his little Englander mission and disastrous battle schemes (e.g. the Greek campaign), *continually* left Australia terribly exposed

Menzies also made a 'fatal error' of appointing far too many 'expert-businessmen', with no clue about public service in the national war interest (and so unlike US Marriner Eccles and co). Butlin excepts Essington Lewis, the otherwise infamous head of BHP Pty. Ltd., whom the Labor Government kept for organising munitions. Criticisms grew of Anti-Labor's over-reliance on bank borrowing, and how the progressive nature of income tax had been 'in decline since 1932'. Labor argued war finance should come mainly from steep progressive taxation and from (some) money creation of the CBA. ALP Cabinets were particularly unwilling to bring out the printing press and argued war monetary expansion must be controlled to ward off bank money inflation; also, price controls were essential.[39]

Labor was fully aware that 'inflation' is best defined in a contextual sense since without distinctions, typical 'inflation' claims only serve sectional interests (to Butlin). In wartime, it was the classic inflation of too much money chasing very few goods and services. Wages were easily controlled with Australia's central Arbitration, but not profits and not bank inflation. Purchasing power rose quickly as FE 'over-reached' when more women gained jobs. War shortages in plain and luxury goods were inevitable, import restrictions were 'essential' to the war effort but, as it seemed to the ALP, banks irresponsibly used monetary expansion to create more money for consumer lending or via hire purchase firms. The wartime press, relentlessly hostile, grumbled about limits on pink icing for cakes, yet gaily promoted voluntary Australian troops in Europe, or rather Changi POW camps in the event.[40]

(to Japan), though India fared more badly. See Butlin (1955: 379) on how banks resisted holding reserves, and investment controls were evaded under Anti-Labor.

[39] Business 'men' feathered their own nests, but the Managing Director of BHP rode around 'his' mines with a riding whip, not for his horse. See Butlin et al. (1941) on tax decline, also Giblin's fiscal equaliser is cited Coleman et al. (2006: 145–59). Having shared revenue with states, the ALP hoped that Curtin's later state controls for war might meet less complaints.

[40] See Butlin (1955: 349–51) and Butlin et al. (1941: 33). American, British and Australian troops were all POWs, although only the Australians set up reciprocal prison arrangements, despite Japanese control. The 'press' grumbled ruthlessly. On Rupert's

The 1936 Commission into banks unanimously proposed 'the principle of prescribed minimum deposits by private banks with the central bank, which ... was the most important direct control in the wartime banking regulations and of the 1945 legislation' of the ALP government. Curtin's election promise 'National control of the means of exchange is a fundamental principle of the Labor Movement', saw the ALP returned to office with a landslide. The legislated control over the currency and heretofore 'taxing' states remain. Central banking powers that accrued during WWII, only when the ALP took power, were consolidated in the 1945 Acts on Banking and challenged immediately to no success.[41]

The timing of elections was a crucial component (like FDR earlier) ignored in economics. The war was in a ghastly way a most auspicious occasion for Labor to implement FE and effective central banking in Australia. PM by late 1941, when Japan bombed Pearl Harbour the next month, Curtin used the constitutional 'war powers' to impose central banking under threat of imminent invasion. After the Allied troops including ANZACs evacuated from Churchill's disastrous campaign in Greece, the fall of Singapore (February 1942), to UK's shame, prompted Churchill's demands that ANZACs *en route* home be sent to fight in an already collapsed Rangoon. Curtin refused. Along with bomb attacks on Australia, the Changi POW capture lent fury to anger at Menzies' deference to Churchill; his maintenance of iron exports to fascist Japan in 1938 earned him jeers of 'Pig-Iron Bob'. In the UK, a Tory Party-National *coalition* was in power, whereas Curtin, informed and active, consistently refused all

---

father Keith Murdoch's retail advertisers 'He'd never knock them', said V. J. Carroll – in the 1950s a journalist on one of Keith's papers (Interview 1999).

[41] See Butlin (1983: 98), citing the 1936 Commission. The first, 1941 Curtin government took over Menzies/Fadden's after it collapsed; ALP's 1943 election landslide gained 49 over 12 Menzies' Party seats in the House; Robert Menzies is disliked for: (1) Selling pig iron to Japan just pre-war; (2) his pre-war pro-Hitler comments and (3) his nauseating monarchism and Red-Scares. Curtin, cited in Edwards (2005: 117). His monetary and economic programme was attributed to Ben Chifley, PM after Curtin died in 1945, but they shared it. Another war finance factor was hosting US troops *en masse* and Lend Lease, Australian production of goods and services took off.

proposed 'national alliances' before taking office. He was the first PM to control income tax fully, that also prevented states bidding tax downwards. The fiscal 'equalisation' policy of the Commonwealth already gave support for weaker states. He kept on Dr H. C. Coombs and called in 'liberal' experts to direct Curtin's focused monetary and FE reforms during the war *for the postwar*.[42]

In bringing this unusual central bank story to its climax, recall the tame, not for commercial profit CBA that opened its doors in 1913, became the hated target of all private banks, but loved by clients for its allegedly 'unfair competition' as an ordinary bank. That was briefly disallowed in a 1924 Act. By WWII's end, the struggle transformed into bank resistance to the sovereign Commonwealth state's right to control bank money (and its inflation) at all. During war, Curtin's ALP government was incessantly concerned (rightly) that private bank lending would foster consumer inflation. Shortages of virtually every aspect of life gave banks lucrative opportunities. Bank controls that the CBA and Treasury imposed revolved around whether the banks were lending for 'essential' measures to further the war effort, or not. (This did irritate bank clients and postwar, Governor Coombs amiably agreed.)[43]

Rather like other WWII allies, in Australia the commercial banks were '*de facto* arms of the state'. Obviously by 1945, Butlin argued, a transition to postwar conditions backed with ALP 'reconstruction' must occur. And as war ended, Bank legislation was passed to regularise state-bank relationships. Labor did not propose its old bank nationalisation policies, although directed the (commercial) CBA to compete *actively* for business, and to retain the Special

---

[42] See mostly Edwards (2005: 117) – like Roosevelt, Curtin played up war invasion threats (Darwin was bombed; Japanese submarine attacks took casualties even inside heavily guarded Sydney Harbour with mini-subs). Rangoon (now Yangon) fell after Singapore but Churchill demanded ANZAC troops even after Darwin's bombing, and Indonesia, New Guinea invaded. Nearly post-war, Churchill let 3 million Bengalis starve to death.

[43] The changes occurred under Labor. It was clear once the US entered war, the allies would win, for Curtin to start postwar planning, in Edwards (2005); on banks and essential lending, see Butlin (1983).

Accounts banks had to hold. One bank missed the purpose of Special Accounts, wanting a clause to permit banks to use their Accounts 'automatically' – 'if deposits fell'. But the CBA's discretion to raise levels of Special Accounts was intended to *make deposits fall* if banks seemed dangerously aggressive in their business or to lower them if too reticent.[44]

Stupidity aside, private banks opposed a trivial section in the 1945 Banking Acts that declared 'the central bank should be the banker to governments' and not only to the Commonwealth state. This, Butlin said, was 'the fuse for explosive political events'. Since the Bank of England had been created for that purpose in 1694, it was not 'radical'. Even Victoria (banking with eight private banks) was 'acquiescent' to by then PM Ben Chifley's 1947 proposed transfer of their business to the CBA. But an immediate response from Melbourne City Council challenged the entire 1945 Act and the Commonwealth High Court declared it unconstitutional for any *government* authority to be denied 'free choice' of its banker. Against capitalist bankers' jubilation, Chifley proposed legislation to nationalise all banks three days later, furious that banks rejected basic central banking.[45]

Banks wanted their cosy pre-war situation. A state-owned, 'composite' central bank was suspicious 'heresy' deeply rooted in Labor's past. Nationalising all banks sparked a 'hysterical campaign' of banks, the press and Pig-Iron Bob Menzies' Anti-Labor party, which tried further legal action. Their case won in the Privy Council in

---

[44] See Jones (2003a: 10), on 'arms of the state'; Chifley and Curtin disliked bank nationalisation; Butlin (1983: 116) on a bank's 'inadequate appreciation' – Special Accounts was less 'blunt tool' of interest rate policy.

[45] See Butlin (1983: 111) on the 'fuse': the CBA did federal state business from 1913 and most states, but less local councils' banking. Butlin cites the Non-Labor Banking Commission (RC) of 1936 (1983: 144–5). Butlin called the name-changing right-wing coalitions 'Anti-Labor' to prevent confusion, but the RC had Country Party *and* ALP support, so it was dubbed a 'Non-Labor' inquiry. Melbourne City Council took up the 1945 challenge; the main press like Murdoch Snr took banking's side to extremes yet promoted Curtin's biggest (1943) landslide ever. Butlin recounts the hysteria of 1947 (1983: 152); that May (1968) took the bank side in the 'battle'.

London (with dubious claims, never tested). Labor lost the 1949 election to Menzies' coalition, not just on banks. Menzies promised to outlaw the Communist Party: that Referendum failed, but Labor's catholic anti-Reds split the ALP until Whitlam's 1972 government.[46]

Some argue PM Chifley threatened nationalisation after the banks' refusal to *accept* a central bank, which the ALP in 1945 wanted primarily to control private banking's 'loose money' inflation. Chifley was infuriated with bank stonewalling on central banking most of all because he and the late John Curtin had not favoured bank nationalisation beforehand, nor was it included in Labor's 1945 banking Acts. Evan Jones remarks of a 1946 meeting on reconstruction generally, that 'Chifley displayed a cautious mentality regarding discriminatory action' in both stemming inflation and fostering postwar reconstruction. Chifley, he quotes, had emphasised 'the great importance of caution in handling any suggestion to private enterprise for a deferment of new investment'. Also, the Governor of the CBA from 1949, then RBA, for a total nineteen years, Dr Coombs, was relentless about fighting inflation postwar and was quite puritanical:

> Coombs shared the blame around – governments with their
> unrestrained developmentalist ethos, business with their
> unprincipled pricing, banks with their undisciplined lending,
> workers and their union leaders, individuals as consumers.
> He saw all groups as selfishly taking advantage of the boom,
> unprepared to collectively make sacrifices for the 'greater good'.[47]

Long before, Coombs had despaired privately of the divisiveness of 'vested interests'. Yet the remarkable aspect was that ALP governments' legacy was not to strengthen central banking powers to 'print money' for a 'totalitarian state' – private bank allegations. Far from

---

[46] See Butlin (1983: 101; 147) on 'heresy; Schedvin (1992: 77–8), on the Privy Council and the dubious claims. Menzies did not win a 1949 landslide, but good enough. The ALP split with a new DLP as another regressive anti-democratic force; 3 out of 6 states opposed outlawing the CP, as did over 50 per cent of the Australia-wide vote.

[47] See Beggs (2010) about 'loose money'; and Jones (2003b: 6) citing Chifley's caution; Jones (2003a: 28) on Coombs's blaming everyone.

that, it aimed to prevent state boondoggling and to dissuade banks from inflationary money creation on consumer or speculative lending. Bankers battled to remove wartime 'Special Accounts', the CBA's commercial arm and, in the constitutional crisis, a CB altogether. Three decades later, Milton Friedman accused all these FE authorities of fostering inflation.

Coombs defended the CBA's dual functions as practical substitutes for his unattainable ideal – that 'a successful monetary policy apparatus required the banks to internalise central banking prescriptions as appropriate norms for private banking practice'. Intransigence and refusal to take the 'national interest' ruled that out. As well, Coombs knew central banks had very limited control over bank money creation. *Owning* a commercial bank might help the CBA control the money supply. It was 'not unthinkingly modelled on the Bank of England or beholden to its values ... The commercial arm could also be used for regulatory purposes, including for aggregate demand management, and the central banking personnel could learn from the hands-on experience'. Coombs said the commercial CBA

> provides a channel through which Central Bank policy can
> directly affect the working of the economy. In inflationary
> conditions, direct control over the trading sections should make
> them more responsive to the need for restraint than the private
> banks which naturally are anxious to find profitable employment
> for their funds. Even more important, in a situation where
> the economy is threatened with a recession and widespread
> unemployment, the trading sections of the Bank can be used
> directly to stimulate and maintain production, investment and
> employment.[48]

---

[48] See Chapter 6 on Friedman's inflation hysteria (in theory these bankers were 'Hayekian' free money types); Jones (2003a: 29–30), on CBA 'dual functions'; Coombs in 1952 is cited in Butlin (1983: 170); 'trading banks' usually meant commercial banks in Australia, with the CBA state owned.

Coombs used that control against the CBA's banking sections which, postwar had expanded its industrial hire purchase debt, becoming the biggest player. In 1950, for monetary policy reasons Coombs told it to cease expanding this credit. Banks' animosity towards the trading bank arm as 'unfair' was, the *SMH* screeched, because the central bank has 'the power to commandeer a very substantial part of their assets in the form of Special Accounts and other compulsory deposits – and to use these assets partly to the advantage of the Central Bank's trading interests'. Banks whined about how terrible it was that their lending policies should be 'burdened' with an anti-inflation policy. Equally, under deflation, private banks would enjoy this 'unfair' competition, in that the trading CBA was *disadvantaged* by Coombs's policy. A secret grudge was the (non-capitalist) CBA's being their large and much trusted competitor.[49]

The triumph was Australia gained the Labor-designed central bank, still with its competitive trading bank. Curtin's FE policy was so widely supported that Menzies never dared contest it and he continued all of Curtin's reforms. PM Menzies and Treasurer Fadden kept the newly appointed Governor Coombs whom, in the election, Anti-Labor labelled a LSE 'socialist'. Yet at the LSE until 1933, his PhD preparation included Hayek, Laski and Robbins; Coombs was eclectic, unlike many economists.[50]

[49] See Beggs (2010: 33) on hire purchase (or instalment credit); *SMH* (not Murdoch owned) of 14 October 1954 is cited in Butlin (1983: 177); Beggs (2010: 28) and Jones (2003b), on bank complaints of being 'burdened'. Their grudge is my conjecture from experience.

[50] See Jones (2003a) on the socialist charge; Coombs's LSE doctorate (1933) was on central banking in white settler countries; Hayek perhaps noted on money creation (Rowse 2015); Coombs criticised Keynes, we saw earlier. Butlin (1983: 117) suggests the previous CBA Governor was a constructive influence for postwar transition under the 1945 Act and Coombs's appointment in 1949. Governor Armitage 'combined a sturdy insistence on the principles of effective central bank control' with sympathy for private banks' problems; he opposed confining 'experienced' banks to tiny advances for small retailers. But with one bank's liquidity mess, Armitage said: 'The bank must help itself if they want us to help them. They will not make advances to building societies nor will they purchase anything but short-dated government securities. If they are not prepared to take the same reasonable risks as other banks they must abide by the consequences of their own policy' (cited Butlin 1983: 117).

Under Coombs, now with the (weak) right-wing Menzies/ Fadden government, the CBA was ordered to separate its sections (to a state-owned Glass-Steagall). Private banks never trusted their own demand, always assuming huge advantages between the monetary policy arm and the commercial bank arm. Butlin was 'sympathetic' yet had no evidence to suggest that the CBA did anything heinous; the reverse. Even Menzies argued there was 'abundant room for both', telling the press the government was 'no more prepared to damage the Commonwealth Bank' than private trading banks.

It never dawned on the 'free enterprise' parties or bank propagandists that they actually wanted irresponsible private banking, or their populism in favour of cheap money might create problems by 1960. No – just unfettered capitalism. Banks were happy to 'exploit' a backlash against inflation controls in 1952 and some felt private banks largely won the postwar transition. They appeared, to Coombs, to be unable or unwilling to 'restrain advances that the central bank desired'. Every time the Governor held his meetings with the bankers, they complained about 'unfair' competition. V. J. Carroll, talking to the ANZ bank managing director in the early 1950s, asked where he was going after. He said; 'Oh, to Sydney to have my wrists slapped by Nugget', Coombs's nickname.[51]

After constant disputes, Menzies' Cabinet gave in to banks; in 1960 it separated the CBA off from the rebadged Reserve Bank of Australia (RBA). Butlin argued 'the effective power of the Reserve Bank was not significantly changed', and that it was a 'formal victory only' since the CBA could be more competitive afterwards, only equally subject to tax as other banks.

Amidst this furore, inflation increased from 1955 and relations of Treasury and the CBA reached a bitter stalemate. In 1960 that culminated in the *worst postwar 'credit squeeze'* and Menzies' near loss of government. The conflict was over Treasury ('stop-go') aims of

---

[51] Controls were on Korean War wool price inflation. See Butlin (1983: 173; 174; 177; 166) as 'sympathetic' and citing Menzies; Coombs, and Butlin on cheap credit, respectively. Carroll: former editor in chief *SMH* and *AFR*; Personal email in March 2015.

high immigration, public investment and low interest rates, against the CBA's monetary aim of the 'highest possible full employment consistent with low inflation' using 'sensitive reactions to key indicators'. Treasury 'trenchantly opposed' Coombs's call for a rate rise in 1955 and ignored CBA advice due to its right-wing government's cheap money 'doctrine' and 'reluctance' to tax. Funnily enough, banks accepted a few CBA controls just as they were 'gearing' for their final 'assault' on this dual central bank. Fringe banking was growing, about which in 1959, Coombs achieved his desired official short-term money market. But by 1959–60, consumer demand was surging to cost-push inflation, while a bubble in property and shares plus the trade deficit were 'out of control'. Treasury further ignored CBA advice and kept delaying, with a 1960 budget containing little of 'the strong deflationary medicine' urged by the CBA. Coombs did not invoke the Reserve Bank Act to inaugurate a 'formal dispute' with Treasury – Schedvin regrets – and by late 1960 an emergency Treasury budget was brutal; and unemployment rose to over 3 per cent, unheard of since pre-war. Menzies nearly lost the 1961 election. Treasury was obsessed with cheap money to reduce its debt servicing costs *and* regarded the CBA as a mere 'subordinate' doing 'mechanical tasks', which it wasn't. It was sophisticated and 'independent'.[52]

A right-wing government, wildly pork barrel expansionist, with Treasury unwilling to raise taxes or help to control banks and fringe banks, ignored a cautious central bank that aimed for FE, social justice with low inflation. Coombs was also ignored when urging a rapid

[52] See Butlin (1983: 188–90) on 'formal victory'. The Korean War played a role; and Schedvin (1992: 297; 239; 241; 248; 311; 297; 309; 311), respectively, is the source of the quotes in this paragraph; Harold Holt became Treasurer in 1958, and was even weaker than Fadden to Secretary of Treasury, Roland Wilson the 'cheap money' supremo (taught in Chicago by Viner). Coombs, aware of hire purchase, the rise in equity finance and fringe banks (in a 1958 lecture, published (1971: 40), a year later was losing the 'dual' central bank, *and* his battle against inflation (unlike Eccles's US Fed earlier). In 1959 Coombs (1971: 120; 121; 124) warned that terms of trade were close to 1930s 'depression years'; and the pricing policies of 'monopolistic' industry were rising to a wage-price spiral. Policies for infrastructure to support high immigration (in poor urban areas) had to wait for the Whitlam ALP period. Coombs did advise PM Whitlam but was shocked at the 'loans affair' (Rowse 2015).

reflation post-1961. He argued taxes be applied for inflationary state borrowing, and for cheap/dear money management by an effective central bank with a commercial arm. A Bank official at the time said: 'Yes that was a firm belief of Coombs and it was a thing that upset him immensely when [in 1960] separation came. As well, he would have retired then except for ... other motives.' Butlin saw a 'reluctance' of senior RBA officials to accept separation for years. They later scorned Menzies' edict in effect to 'be kind to banks' it was said. Retiring in 1968 Coombs went on 'Obliged to be difficult' to work for Indigenous rights, pro-feminist and green concerns.[53] Unfortunately, he had not invoked the CBA's 'formal dispute' mechanism to make the matter public. It seems that the most decent CB mandates also suffer from external pressures (the most? – right-wing governments are also intransigent).

This composite CB model was, Coombs proposed, quietly enlightened: more advanced than the 'blunt tool', or quality controls of the US Fed imposed on banks (externally). CBA's banking arm gained no advantage when ordered to minimise credit inflation, and was at a competitive disadvantage in minimising deflation, probably not in the long term, with (taxable) jobs created and businesses maintained and expanded. It was a logical, specifically monetary role that had ways to reverse deflation, the far more crippling problem for capitalism than inflations. Thus, a novel way of reining in, or expanding the money supply and multiplier to economic activity in distressed times was lost. The Australian model showed an acute understanding of bank practices and sympathy for the profit motive. RBA Governor Stevens often quoted Hartley Withers on private bank reluctance to serve 'national interests' in employment, having tried to counter Australia's 2016 imbalances from the mining boom and bust. Governor Fraser publicly stressed the RBA's dual remit on FE

---

[53] Coombs (1971: 41; 30) and from an unpublished interview of Evan Jones with ex CBA, Robert Scott in 2002, Canberra: I am grateful to Evan Jones for permission to share this material with me. See Butlin (1983: 115); Schedvin (1992: 323) cites the edict 'be kind'; and Jones (2003a) on a review of Coombs's work on retirement.

and price stability against banks' desire for weak economic activity in the 1990s.

And, thinking of Coombs's criticisms of Keynes, it is not clear that defining a 'national interest' is possible. Coombs hinted he wasted his years as a central banker, and his legacy was that the most 'divisive' structural issues were insoluble. Central banks, then, take the blows from conflicts of capital-labour and bank money–debtor class disputes, and try to defend twin remits, a legacy that survives somewhat in the RBA, less so the Fed until after the GFC. Australia's egalitarian central bank is a threat to rehashed neoclassical doctrines, so that ignorance of the RBA appears to be bliss.

IS THIS A HELPFUL MODEL FOR FUTURE?

The RBA is publicly-owned, and the CBA was solely owned by the Commonwealth until an ALP government (Prime Minister Keating) part-privatised it in 1991–6. The (fully-private) CBA is now as disgraceful as its other competitors, nearly in the same league as US and UK banks. Few Treasuries are brave although one worked well with the RBA in 2008.

The Curtin-Coombs legacy, after the decades of conflicts to build it, perhaps holds hope if social democracy ever revived to temper capitalism. This central bank composite model was not to my knowledge copied, to direct a large banking arm against credit inflation or severe contraction, and to be cautious in serving clients' interests, another appealing trait loathed by private banks. The CBA banking arm created safer types of bank money advances. The US Administration never imagined nationalising banks in 2009–10 but put banks under 'conservator' policies: how useless that proved. US Treasuries were soft on bankers. Many German and French banks were state owned; not like Australia's model. In Britain, the Royal Bank of Scotland was the largest GFC bailout of the largest corporation ever; it still fails its clients. Tory Cabinets are trying to sell it, when it could be directed to lend for industrial and service sector regeneration. In Australia, once Menzies crippled and weakened the RBA's hand, and deregulation followed, its remits remain. But, as elsewhere, late-1990s right-wing Treasuries hived off prudential and supervisory functions to under-funded bodies, just like the US's SEC. The RBA tracks their work in a duplication.

Other options in monetary-fiscal policy consolidations, specially of note for the EMU, lie in the Commonwealth's control of income taxes, which lessens bond vigilantes (somewhat) from either attacking the national currency or trading down the profligate bonds of NSW or WA, busy front loading on empty stadiums: wild pork barrels going nowhere. The fiscal equaliser remains so that there are less 'quasi-third world' regions like northern England. The City and the US state of Delaware are 'off-shore' tax havens, with direct links to Panama (etc.). So is Ireland in the EU; federal Australia controls corporate tax, but hardly at present.

Furthermore, Australia's centralised industrial (arbitration) courts, predictably attacked under right-wing governments, are a double-edged monetary sword against both wage inflation and corporate inflations. In 1930, having savaged workers' wages in terrible circumstances, in 1938 Arbitration raised them to rein in industrialist exuberance. The minimum wage is still higher than in most countries. It could go higher, and dampen asset and property inflation, even correct the heavy imbalance of the shares between capital and labour. And the RBA is not alone in sharing fiscal-monetary controls; the BoC is differently interesting and, including the Riksbank, none of these countries had the full GFC shock.

Not only, but state ownership of a commercial bank and centralised union-boss arbitration decisions, both monetary policy 'quality' tools, have no negative impact on Treasury budgets: higher wages give higher taxes. It means the currency issuer benefits from unified positions on labour market and employer inflation-deflation, and on local state inflationary boondoggling with the fiscal equaliser. Positive impacts via the composite CBA's dividends to its sole share-owner, Treasury, were greater in that model. Inflation is never solely in wage claims that dear money (soft on credit) guys see. There are also costs to Treasury in servicing 'dear money' bond debts.

The capitalist norm is that banks and shadow banks always find routes to inflationary escape, and disrupt with fringe tricks in mimetic competition. Banks took over consumer credit instalments, they lend to money funds and credit card corporations. Coombs stopped the CBA increasing consumer credit; it was trusted and more prosperous for its caution, even loved by children in its state-owned days. That was the composite central bank. Banks hated it as did Menzies, even after Cabinet's self-induced 1960 credit crunch. Now private, the CBA has a scandal-prone 'insurance' arm, it has laundered drug money, rigged the market, cheated clients along with the ANZ, NAB and Westpac. The 'four-pillars' expanded to ill effects (like NAB in Scotland), and make foolish advances. Two banks nearly collapsed in 1980 (some controls came back). I am not proffering a counterfactual. We know what the composite CBA achieved: counter-evidence. Nationally owned firms were supported even in right wing governments, to compete against huge foreign-owned corporations engaged in price rigging. Forget that now.

In CB general histories, the Australian model rates no mention. Giannini's *The Age of Central Banks* is less monetarist than the American fables. He calls the US Fed a 'dirigiste' model and claims that post-1945 every country followed the Fed model. Why? Hardly any had privately-owned CBs like the District Feds – the reverse to the public CBA composite – nor did Canada or Britain. Italy did. Monetarists later sainted New Zealand's Reserve Bank (RBNZ) model of NZ Labour Treasurer's 'Rogernomics', which preceded Reaganomics. A country with a unicameral parliamentary model, harsh NZ reforms swept the place rapidly. Equally they were overturned as fast: renationalising got under way; a multi-party electoral reform won easily to check executive abuse. Few note such switches (or refusal to give entry to US nuclear warships). But NZ banking is dominated by Australia's dubious 'four-pillars'. Mostly, such countries are of no interest to those following the *real central bank action*, the Fed. Central banks have different models but 'so what'. Of course, the hegemonic currency and Fed affect all CBs, to which we turn.[54]

BRETTON WOODS – EROSION OF ITS HELP

When war ended, central bankers looked across borders to the 1944 Bretton Woods agreements about global currency that gave a calming boost to central bank domestic policies while they lasted. And today, Bretton Woods is again a beacon, but another World War cannot be like WWII. The 2016 Trump candidacy put the stalemate of Mutually Assured Destruction under question and the 'small wars' are not 'total' on the home front. States' reasons for another Bretton Woods do not press. The question for this section is whether mobile capital was indeed controlled by the 1944 rules and institutions, or by war. WWII and national controls tore apart global banking networks and old liaisons, and with wartime laws against 'trading with the enemy'. In WWII, finance sectors complained about restrictions on their profits, but effectively re-gathered after 1945.[55]

In other words, Bretton Woods may seem less a 'beacon' fondly imagined post-GFC. Still, the 1944 monetary agreements spread from the OECD 'bloc' and reduced currency fluctuations (the Interwar) – to avoid 1920s–30s cross-border speculation and beggar-thy-neighbour devaluations of 'exporting' joblessness. The two 1944 negotiators, Dexter White, pursued US interests for Treasury, as did Keynes for the UK, yet the US Administration, Fed and Wall Street opposed both men's inclusive plans and both plans lost. Conformity to the US dollar was set. In the 1950s–60s, a Eurodollar market was the first contrary

---

[54] Perhaps Menzies' Treasury secretary was enraged that Coombs was correct; its Minister too busy with pork-barrels. I know the recent numbing detail of Australia and NZ off by heart. In general central bank histories, Australia's exception might be mentioned but not to my knowledge and if anything, what is said is wrong.

[55] Corporations and banks broke this law: Prescott Bush and his Wall Street firm was never prosecuted for trading with the enemy; the presidential Bush family wealth came from high finance, in Salant (2003). Ingham (2004) on war and banking networks, and Dyster and Meredith (2012: Chapter 2).

trend showing US banks were breaking out from grumbling into action. Under the Bretton Woods deal that extended America's sovereign authority, Wall Street never endured capital controls like others, and US capital dispersed in ingenious ways, making the Fed's tasks difficult. But whereas some like West Germany had a close-knit *lending-productive* relation between banking, industry and unions, other countries' finance sectors looked to internationalise away from domestic legal or ethical controls over bank money creation. States also globalised in expensive ex-colonial military adventures and nuclear Cold War.[56]

At micro level central banking, the BoE simply lacked the staff to cover the minute requirements of the UK's own post-WWII 'credit controls' over the City's evasive techniques, Geoff Ingham argues. City novelties turned towards Eurodollar markets. Hyman Minsky showed how, from the end of the war, Wall Street banks expanded their 'position making possibilities' with repurchase agreements, Eurodollar loans, sales at new overseas branches, which lessened the impact of Fed restrictions, albeit stronger than the BoE's.[57]

Pitifully few established central banks, post-1945, noticed how the ex-imperial and US corporate 'development of underdevelopment' divided the world. Dismissed as 'backward' some countries remained partly pre-modern or at least pre-industrial; peasantries on systems of feudal (absent) landlord tenure were not all overthrown, and 'modern' peasant production in France, Italy or Japan was newly 'protected'. In Japan, the unemployed could return home to an informal, unwaged 'rice-grower welfare state'. It was not until the 1930s that the US small farm sector collapsed forever. America joined late, then, the

---

[56] On Germany, see Kurzer (1988); and Bhaduri (2014) argues by 1980s at least, states competed on unit labour costs not so much on joblessness of the 1930s; also see Schwartz (2000: Chapters 8–9).

[57] Ingham (2004); Minsky ([1986] 2008: 86; 67): cf. the US Treasury-security market (former) monopoly, these alternatives for bank financing limited the Fed, expanded the money supply and increased potential for instability. Franklin Bank nearly failed in 1974, had it not been for the Fed. This prevented a run on the Eurodollar market or bank CDs (certificates of deposit), but the Fed (then under Burns) did not 'propose significant reforms of the overseas operations of American banks' Minsky complained ([1986] 2008: 67) and see Chapter 5.

two highly urbanised countries with full wage labour systems in which total dependency on money, jobs and state services was old (UK and Australia). FE was a welcome peacetime experience, compared to Interwar humiliations; the use of banks was not yet widespread. Comparisons known to practical bureaucrats and in social policy, politics and demographic research passed the Fed by, with some countries loath to bow to US triumphalism.[58]

Financial sectors and CBs are always in political-social relations, then, whatever they claim and do. Looking at OECD countries, by 1955, the City was a huge competitive financial hub to Wall Street busy colonising it, yet these bank challenges only looked anomalous and even controllable to those who worried (CBs) at the time. Wall Street had the most constraints (if free from capital controls); Tokyo also has the US Glass-Steagall, Sydney the stern RBA and Canada's Parliament decides bank licence renewals regularly, Zurich manages personal wealth (globally). Most banks were staid: US bank collapses were rare. Central banks worked closely with Treasuries, with inevitable tensions, and elected governments 'managed' their economies. States took responsibility for upsets. FE was an ethical or legal constraint. Central banks, no longer the 1920s stars, were to avoid economic instability with treasuries. Or try to do so.[59]

The global arrangement of 1944 gave national democratic sovereignty some space to control each country's domestic economic affairs under the US dollar's 'rule'. Yet uncertainty and capitalism's inherent instability makes monetary management difficult and, lacking huge

---

[58] 'Underdevelopment' is in the Marxian global literature; cf. oil corporations' roles for example, compared to jingoistic 'modernisation' theses, and a Technological Determinist 'march through the sectors', say in Bell (1976), cf. Winner (1993). Reform of land tenure in Japan, S. Korea, Taiwan, Singapore postwar is rarely discussed. Yet Giannini (2011: 147) gives an average from *1900* to 1995, for G7 agricultural employment: e.g. France 43.4 per cent; Germany 39.9 per cent; Japan 64.8 per cent; **UK 13.0 per cent** and USA 38.3 per cent. **Britain stands** out *(like Australia)*. Absentee landlord classes still exist in South America. A formal service sector (uncountable productivity) developed unevenly.

[59] Minsky ([1986] 2008) US banks; On Canada's banks see Cain (1996); Calomiris and Haber (2014) and Ryan-Collins (2015). On Zurich, Pixley (2004) interviews: it mostly offers banking services to the wealthy.

electoral support, conservative governments tended to pork barrel to retain 'favoured regional' votes: the supremacist US South enjoyed huge military bases; state money poured into London and nuclear arms. Less status bound than the centralised UK, America's vibrant civil society and individualism of former small farmers, meant that people were unwilling to subordinate life to the maintenance of US dollar supremacy.[60] Rebuilding Europe and Japan under the US Marshall and Dodge Plans gave hope – although 'free enterprise' propaganda of US corporate expansion worked against collective policies. The baby boom expressed a new enthusiasm or relief, while the threat of the Soviet Union forced OECD elites to associate capitalism with democracy. Darker (inflationary) currents existed (variably), with oligopolistic administered prices, 'new' financial tricks to evade sensible bank controls, the costly Korean War, Red Scares and permanent spy agencies seeking any hint of social democracy (as Commie), in anti-colonial movements and domestically. For example, when J. K. Galbraith was Ambassador to India, he asked President Kennedy to remove the CIA from causing the same 'insane' troubles in India, as in Vietnam. The US Administration mushroomed further. After WWII, banking had room to manoeuvre in funding the US military presence and/or industrial stability sweeping the world. Women, US blacks or other minorities, and ex-colonies hardly saw a 'golden age' but OECD wages improved immensely. Social research turned to 'pockets of poverty' work to seek further helpful measures.[61]

The post-1945 period was, overall, less a transition to peace in the democracies. The US was the superpower to build the alarming

---

[60] Katznelson (2013), on the US deep South. To US small farmers the UK and Wall Street had imposed the 'cross of gold' (nineteenth century) and London usually subordinated labour/debtors to pound sterling that the US, and (in exchange rates) France, Japan, Germany, others were never prepared to do: see Mehrling (2000: 402) and Epstein (2006). On 'pockets' research, see Pixley (1993) and on Michael Harrington in the USA and John Stubbs in Australia.

[61] See Galbraith (1981: 396–8) on the 'insane' CIA (how wise to save India), and Allen Dulles's by then 'Bay of Pigs' fiasco: the dark underside seemed to be nakedly visible as decades went on. In South Africa's apartheid, that former Dominion of 10 per cent Whites (cruelly rich), was no formal democracy at all.

'military industrial state' that President Eisenhower cited from his watch. Funded less by the tax and price-wage controls of WWII methods, it increasingly came via the war finance convention of borrowing from private banks, said to be a reason for the USA's diminution of plans of both public negotiators at Bretton Woods, Keynes and Dexter White. Yet for the first time in the US (far earlier elsewhere), unions at last had a voice in corridors of power with corporations and governments. Democratic expansion coincided with the build-up of states, banks and corporate oligopolies under the stable currency gift to CBs from Bretton Woods (to 1971).

At this huge meeting in 1944 in wartime, the U-turn from CBs' 1930s rigid support of 'gold' was remarkable in its desperation. Even the BoE's Montagu Norman worried that Bretton Woods *might not* abandon gold.[62] Europe was not just in hock to the USA but, post-1945, America's massive industrial 'peace' surplus would need more consumers – from then ravaged combatants – despite USA's large internal market. That was Keynes's point about creditors and debtors having mutual needs. American officials in quantity and commodity money camps accused Keynes of trying to welch on Britain's debts and, behind his back, of double standard lies. It was as though no other delegate plotted or schemed.[63] Dexter White also tried and failed. The 1944 meeting holed up in a lonely, derelict hotel in New Hampshire that Moggridge describes makes me wonder why Keynes and White were the only members dead so soon after.

No agreement of creditor versus debtor nations occurred to improve central banks' long-term possibilities. For example, was 'gold' *per se* the big fetter that Barry Eichengreen claims? Were not

---

[62] Everywhere progressive taxes were still high (80–90 per cent at the top scale) also under Eisenhower. See Amato and Fantacci (2012, 2014) on war finance. Moggridge (1992: 732) on 'the [BoE] Bank's tendency to claim the Washington scheme was similar to the gold standard' and to let 'Keynes's stuff "percolate where it will"', i.e. to let both monetary plans die; and citing Keynes's thinking. UK Treasury and BoE worried about sterling indebtedness and weakening of sterling's global position.

[63] Australian CBA chief economist Melville loathed Keynes at Bretton Woods (mutual); he alleged Keynes said one thing to the US camp, another to UK's gold standard fears; cited in Evan Jones's Melville interview of 1996 he kindly made available.

the inequalities and arguments of treating international currency as a commodity (store of value) globally, worse than a technical manacle? Competing definitions of money clashed, with Keynes's idea of global mutual obligations in the 'bancor' facing the mighty creditor power of the USA. White proposed a similar 'euthanasia of the *rentier*', of that 10 per cent of populations enjoying unearned income. Critics saw both as threats (implicitly to capitalist money).[64]

THE FED'S INFLUENCE ON BRETTON WOODS

Assessments of Bretton Woods (BW) still clash with 'true believer' approaches to central banks since the 1970s, when gold became totally irrelevant. After that, the dominant idea was that *rules* must tie CBs to set interest rates to inflation targets: just like *gold*. A prominent proponent of targets, J. B. Taylor, praises BW for its rules of 'adjustable pegs' for exchange rates, and of no exchange controls (this was not so). With this 'magnificent American blueprint', 'the IMF would provide assistance in the form of loans with the help of outsized contributions from the United States'. To Keynes, in contrast, his proposed unit of account (bancor) was no 'Red Cross philanthropic relief scheme' but a 'rule' to prevent trade imbalances to the mutual benefit of creditor and debtor nations – the peoples of the world. Keynes's principle was for an international currency that cannot be stored and hoarded to augment creditor country control.[65] *Mutuality*? The Fed ended up scotching the Keynes and White plans, seeing both 'a starry-eyed normative exercise'.

If Bretton Woods (BW) was a collective collapse to a US 'blueprint', why did it take place? Roosevelt was the internationalist who desired rapprochement with forty-four countries (Allies like USSR

---

[64] Eichengreen (2011); see further in Chapter 5 on the breakup of Bretton Woods. Cf. de Cecco (1979: 51) comparing Keynes and White. Keynes drew on E. F. Schumacher (1943), a plan that favoured the 'end of capitalist money'.

[65] See Chapter 7 on targets; Taylor (2015: 3); Keynes is cited in Amato and Fantacci (2012: 123). To Giannini (2011: 137), *exchange controls*, currency 'blocs' just *pre-WWII violated the game's rules* cf. 1944 should not give legitimacy to 'flight capital' though WWII stopped 'flight', not primarily Bretton Woods in Ingham's view, above.

included); and thirty years of war urged a peaceful deal. For central bank themes, Bretton Woods can be credited with making domestic control easier with the US dollar the global 'reserve' currency. But it could be hoarded, to continue inequalities for debtor nations, which become unable to buy the creditor countries' goods (and brings creditors down, in turn). The capital controls desired, applied not to Wall Street (care of US authorities' bargains) and gave it a postwar head start against rival centres and their CBs. Other authorities, then, had the burden of stopping their own *rentiers'* capital flight to US freedom from controls. And the US economy to 1960 at least, completely dominated; trade surpluses were so high that US authorities controlled the international monetary system at will (to the prevalent market conformity). But from closed economic models in both the 1930s and BW years, unintended consequences built up. Benign compared to the 1930s when each country viciously tried to protect its currency, the later remnants of BW, as with sterling before, rested on US 'perceptions' of its global interests, which shifted under challenges. The US needed to control its domestic fiscal and monetary policies to keep a stable exchange rate. That was politically 'costless' during postwar US economic power, as was its 'generosity' to the devastated countries. Loans were a handy global control for the US but, 'costless' sacrifice did not last.[66]

De Cecco argues America's position firmed up not at BW but in the Fed's 1944 proposals. The Fed started from a desire to avoid sterling's old hierarchy, yet to give England 'latitude' and, since the US should not devalue (cf. Nixon later), the UK and West Europe must do so. A Vice-President (New York Fed) damned the Keynes and White

---

[66] De Cecco (1979: 55) cites the Fed report on 'starry-eyed'. Of those who rue the failed Bretton Woods, see e.g. Amato and Fantacci (2014); Schwartz (2000: 197–214) and de Cecco (1979). See D'Arista (2009: 638; 640) about the 'apolitical' bancor ideas, and she lists how at 1945, the US had 60 per cent world's output, 60 per cent of world's gold reserves and low import needs. US production lines faced little competition for decades; on exchange rate balances, costless, 'the Triffin Dilemma' especially see Schwartz (2000: 201) and the next Chapter 5. On loans, the IMF's demands on the UK alone were often worse than the 1931 Bankers' Ramp.

plans; and criticised the Gold Standard's hierarchy that he said, both plans purported to reinvent as a democratic 'adjustment mechanism'. He urged the US should not practice exchange controls or vary the dollar in *peacetime*. Meantime the BoE was trying to construct (or reconstruct) a Sterling Area ('a Schachtian web' to de Cecco) but most Dominions rejected the BoE's effort to repeat the 1930s. As well, UK's new Labour 'socialist' government appalled US authorities. Devaluation of sterling appealed to 'all shades of American opinion'; threats and inducements applied.[67] De Cecco says of the 1950s–60s the US was brutal to Britain and Europe about devaluing, which forced them to focus on exports – an imbalance good neither for the US, ultimately, or Europe.

On further developments that disabled Bretton Woods, Amato and Fantacci argue that banking's extensive new role was a 'market niche' by-product of the low 'quantity' of resources allotted to the IMF in the 1944 deal. Explicit limits on capital movements were difficult without a Eurodollar market to help revival, since international *trade* demanded far greater money than the Fund's $8.5 billion over Keynes's opening bid for $26 billion (but in 'bancor', a point orthodoxy cannot imagine). It was less that the US gained seigniorage or even held the greatest voting rights on the IMF, but more that global imbalances cannot be absorbed in a *commodity money system*. So, dollar balances were either in glut or shortage (de Cecco suggests) and could be 'indefinitely hoarded as reserve assets by foreign central banks'.[68]

The logical next step is to consider BW's actual collapse in what looked at the time like an *anomalous* US Nixon Administration. That was not to be by President Reagan's watch and ever downward, when the Fed gained more if delimited powers *against* a different, less

---

[67] De Cecco (1979: 55) citing a J. H. Williams' NY Fed report (cf. Taylor) with the USA *only* to have no exchange controls. The Fed won apparently. Also, de Cecco (1979: 56–60) on the BoE and Sterling, through to devaluation outcomes in the next paragraph.

[68] To Amato and Fantacci a bancor 'would have' cured this: (2012, 2014: 136–9); cf. Eichengreen (2011: 47), enjoys the limited IMF funding; he implies opposition was to US seigniorage of BW, that is, a small clip, or profit that accrues to the currency hegemon. The Hayekian Jacques Rueff went far further in advising de Gaulle. Eichengreen trivialises the Triffin dilemma (see Chapter 5) that he says is curable by the US avoiding 'policy blunders'; and says Triffin knew 'this one big thing' (2011: 7; 50). Ho Hum.

inclusive, more military state that enabled and welcomed (via free market slogans) private financial power. The Fed then endured rule by Wall Street's panics to an exploding global financial sector. In the 1980s, most CBs attempted to ignore what they wreaked on citizens – unemployment – the RBNZ first; the BoC and RBA less so. Pressures were severe. BW's demise eroded the consolidated Treasury-CB relation. It only exists in the secret, less democratic corridors of power than in the 1935–70 years, now the true anomaly: when money was a social relation, feebly, under very limited accountability to citizens or, simply put, 'when finance was the servant'.[69] The problems of money, then, are not what they seem.

From *de facto* or *de jure* state control through CBs and Treasuries, or Fascist/Soviet war finance for the two World Wars; and with peace amazingly, in 1945, eventually *de facto* capitalist control resurrected. Today's politicians rarely understand this since social democracy is debased, partly from fear of nuclear war and abuse by finance markets. The irony by 2016–17 was that CBs finally talked the tune of the old social democracy – that great if doomed effort played in many postwar CBs. Today, they plead for the FE on decent wages they had systematically destroyed, albeit demanded by the capitalist finance sector and productive sectors that imposed austerity. The postwar era shows how central banks' reviled location Interwar, moved briefly to democratic governments for creating the safe money we all use. Citizens had some influence; confidence spread. In the 1970s, appalling braying to mask shabby and cheap disputes returned central banks to financial sectors not, as variations show, to obey meekly in either location but not unaffected either, we now see.

---

[69] See Helleiner (1993) for his 'servant' quote. Here I look to Chapters 5 and 6; also the US state's need for massive war finance, spooks, jails and policing.

5 Vietnam War, Dollar Float and Nixon

Karl Polanyi's concept of 'embeddedness', and its remarkable transformation around the eighteenth century, only shows that the possibilities of twentieth century democratic public engagement or solidarity were always slender. Optimism for decent and civil arrangements in the institutions of money seems the most futile. Banks and governments do not accept cautious controls by central banks willingly. States want war finance; banks seek profits – no matter the damage and humiliation imposed.

Polanyi wrote in 1944 when chances were high and yet, his overall argument did not assume reforms to be permanent. Long-term changes in social structures were his emphases. Thus, Polanyi's work on the origins of markets disputes orthodoxy's position that 'in the beginning there were markets'. The record is that 'the great transformation' instead involved

> … no less than the running of society as an adjunct to the market.
> Instead of the economy being embedded in social relations,
> social relations are embedded in the economic system.

His argument to support this assertion – that status rankings or reciprocal relations (whole ways of life) were overwhelmed by modern market relations of money-class and capital-labour – is often over-looked. Former non-capitalist 'markets' did not change the 'internal organization of an economy'. It was the formation of nation-states and a rising bourgeoisie – capitalist financiers – which built impersonal markets that, he argued, commodified old face-to-face social interactions of 'money and labour' and old attachments to 'land'.[1] Capitalist class relations thereupon were structurally 'embedded', but these often-cruel forces do not completely dominate, politically or culturally. It is not only that Polanyi's economic anthropology gives us overarching distinctions of market, status hierarchy and reciprocal relations, but also that norms of reciprocity or decency – 'counter-movements' (he said) – can qualify the embeddedness of market (all against all) institutions. Markets cannot destroy blindly without resistance. Money's relations that enable markets to put a price on all human relations and on land become unsustainable. The money we use can vanish.

Or, in Norbert Elias's terms, there were civilising processes in the rise of nation states over warlords at the same time also 'decivilising tendencies' of old plunder and slavery, then modern war, nationalism, money- and labour-markets. European imperial ambitions and class divisions in various states brought forth such tendencies in habits and ways of life. Hannah Arendt discussed (decivilising) money relations, split by a specific anti-Semitism. In Europe, nineteenth century Jewish financiers had few investment choices (only for states' warfare and civil innovations, not capitalist industry). Savage discriminations in financial sectors can always recur.[2] In Polanyi's discussion of the embedded reciprocity in hunter and gatherer societies, mutual caring went with sometimes strict rituals and a sexual division of labour to maintain conformity to the whole way of life. These are not comparable to *hierarchy* or to *markets* (both with brutal norms), although norms of reciprocity are known to temper or civilise both;

---

[1] Polanyi (1957 [1944]: 57–8) looked at Indigenous societies, cf. the cruelties of child *labour markets*, the working of people to death, and the selling of land and money to be abused and treated like 'things' as well. England was the first. Markus (2001: 1019–21) explores how *decent* or just *civil* society can ameliorate these processes; Pixley (2010) reworks these two thinkers' ideas, drawn on above.

[2] See Elias (2000) e.g. warlord-dukes became polite, servile to the king; Arendt (1967 [1951]) pointed to how gentile, rapacious bankers, enjoyed letting blame and mystery for money's vicious outcomes be cast on Jewish bankers for financing terrible wars *and* civil improvements. This book (and see Chapter 4) stands against conspiracies, about Jewish profiteering war mongers and 'like Bolsheviks', building 'socialistic' roads, still revived by some gentiles. For example, Murdoch's media empire and Hungary's PM Orbán campaign against decent George Soros; see also Stern (1977); Chernow (1993). The hypocrites' chorus lives in blaming anyone else really.

so too, enlightenment values, like the French slogans of liberty and equality. The democratic movements established the major foothold. However, 'fraternity' is a solidarity only different from patriarchy in being authoritarianism of the (bourgeois) brothers and less the father-rule over the sons. Nineteenth century capitalism amplified fraternal (gender) domination that is tenacious. Age-old solidarities in discrimination against 'out-groups' are easily exploited. These arrangements are not natural but created, and thus it is important to avoid idealising the postwar social settlements. They were a great improvement on decivilising times though.[3]

And Polanyi's specific argument was against the dour, cruel doctrines of nineteenth century classical economics, against which he posed 'counter-movements'. By the time he wrote as WWII was ending, these counter-movements were effectively institutionalised in governments and civil society. Not for long.

Gradually, land, labour and money again became unprotected commodities, fictional 'things' though they are. Labour must find its market price, no matter how low. The renewed treatment of money as a 'substance' and not the social relation that is the heart of money, informs this chapter on the 1970s decivilising revivals with drastic changes (again) to central banks.

During the 1940s–60s, central banks shared monetary tasks of avoiding deflation and inflation with treasuries and legislatures, even central industrial courts in some OECD countries.[4] Were there already challenges that grew so noxiously that, after the 1971 decision of President Nixon to break the 1944 Bretton Woods deal, the democratic full employment era was choked off? In addition, the US Vietnam War finished off the postwar era in more ways than one. This chapter explores how this switch in central banking happened,

---

[3] Pateman (1979) on patriarchs (Trump, e.g.), implies the fraternal bourgeoisie gained equality and liberty. Status/caste rankings are blurred by capitalist money power, and in-groups also exclude certain ethnic groups and nearly always half the population: women. Repression is common because we resist.

[4] The 1890s had proto-Green movements too. Bibow (2015) singles out labour/employer 'pacts' to defend labour/wages; also, even in the US are state/states minimum wage laws; see Wilson (2017), cf. the EU, see Hancké (2013); Debelle and Fischer (1994), and see Chapters 4 and 7.

from the fairly decent views towards banking and governments during McChesney Martin's long reign at the FDR-modelled Fed, to that of Arthur Burns, Fed Chair from 1970. Chapter 6 explores why CBs became heroes to banking, less picturesque compared to those we saw in Chapter 4.

It seems uncertainties about money's value before 1970 were manageable, and central banks could maintain the logic and ethics of stable economic activity without much dissonance, in that high finance and its anti-democratic cheer-squads were discreet. That meant monetary problems existed (as usual), for which decisions were less uncivil or fraught than under their former, and later clearly illogical, harsh duties.

Central banks had to cope with expansionary, US-led banking trends that sought new external and domestic deals; also, with states ramping up military expenditure (so soon). The modicum of welfare provisions (if shabby in the US) and treasury fiscal policies supported central banking. However, low wages in the USA and UK notably, amidst prosperity and protests in general, shook workers out of deference to corporate heads and ruling officials. Postwar promises to citizens unravelled but, in 1971, central banks stared at a wild social landscape after President Nixon ended the link with gold and global finance took over. By 1980 many central banks, prodded by conviction politicians with growing war motives, took harsh steps against citizens. FE ended.

Big changes were afoot, then, mostly through *reactive responses*. At least three running histories of the monetary upheavals of the 1970s exist, in which 'battle of ideas' and nationalist sentiments clutter my attempts to follow the action of war finance, wage claims and mobile capital. Scholars of empires often universalise their states and central banks, whereas less tunnel vision accounts of central banks, such as Curzio Giannini's include the Depression's influence on the 1930s 'wave of distrust of central banks' and against Wall Street and the City; also, the welcomed (or loathed) postwar 'new settlement'. Yet as economists are wont to do, Giannini called the postwar central bank policy era 'Keynesian' and he is anti-democratic. That era to 1971, as I see it, was instead an open, experimental time for central banks, varying with countries' social democratic conditions of possibility.[5] Thus, 1970 marked 'the attainment of democracy' (universal suffrage) in the US superpower. On a darker note was the fate of Europe's ex-empires. France behaved just as badly postwar, say in Vietnam, as the British in India or, gradually, the American empire.

The postwar was the first era of central banking that opened to broader needs and demands from citizens, through formal bridges to democratic states and their treasuries.[6] This is the social democratic story. The 1970s mark how heavy battalions became entrenched against these democratic processes – the US state (IMF too) and Wall Street leading. The subsequent 'Friedman monetarist' turn similarly suggests a planned redesign of central banks, but relative strengths of states, right wing or social democratic governments, and economic sectoral balances were the far more basic *agents of change* that pushed central banks to wreak havoc or, rarely, to slightly democratic compromises over perceptions of money's value. Treated as a *thing* not relation, Wall Street dealt in money again, more lucratively and frantically.

VULGAR CENTRAL BANKING STORIES

According to central bankers and monetary historians like Bernanke and Meltzer (parochial) or Giannini (more catholic), and efforts of Mervyn King, former BoE Governor, and Fed Chair Arthur Burns of

---

[5] See Giannini (2011: 135–7): albeit couched in narrow economics, his book has no time for Hayek's idea of 'free banking' nor for monetarists. Giannini ran the international research of the Banca d'Italia. His 'settlement' (2011: 145) barely includes FE. See e.g. 'von' Hayek (1982) on LBJ's 'Great Society', and anti-discrimination laws to benefit women and minorities. Hayek argued that all social policy disrupted allegedly spontaneous market 'law'. Even given that transfers to unemployed and discouraged workers are short, food stamps patronising to humiliating, Hayek and co aimed at their abolition well before the first US transfer went out.

[6] Voting for US Blacks came after brutal fights, and 1970 was the year that nearly the entire adult US population could vote; poor immigrants were excluded in the north too (literacy tests etc.), in that from 1900–70 an estimated 60 per cent of the US population voted, in Therborn (1977). Of OECD countries, Switzerland was the last in 1971 to include *women*. Therborn argues the USA's was a deliberate 'one-party regime of the upper bourgeoisie' (1977: 17); registration rules, intimidation and poll taxes meant the Fifteenth Amendment, post-Civil War waited for hundred years. See www.infoplease.com/ipa/A0781453.html. Furthermore 'Nearly 6 million people to date are prohibited from voting because of felony convictions. Today voting hours and voting places are restricted, misinformation about voting rules handed out. Our record is dismal' (Personal email, June Zaccone, Hofstra University NY, 24 June 2016).

that time (a self-serving account), there was either no consensual FE era worth mentioning, or it has faint respect. Expensive anti-communism may as well not have occurred. These omissions influence neoclassical economics in its dogmatism. As Fed Chair during the GFC, in one of his accounts Bernanke left out the postwar decades altogether, an omission unavailable to Burns forty years before. Far better, Giannini (before the GFC) said this of 1945–75: 'The mission of government was to promote the general will; safeguarding the national currency was considered one of the fundamental tasks of the democratic order.' Pointing to doubts about 'confidence' in the new fiat standard, Giannini argued the IMF was effective in providing confidence, saying this was *'a far cry from supporting the confidence of holders of money against the risk of abuse ...'* Moreover, (he said) the monetary order inaugurated at Bretton Woods did work, becoming 'the most long-lived system, and most successful in terms of economic growth and expansion of trade, in the monetary history to this day'.[7] He despised monetarism and slavish pro-market views.

Giannini unusually admitted the benefits of banks alleged 'financial repression' too and yet, more typically orthodox, he thereupon painted an alarming 1970s scene. 'In the history of both economic thought and monetary institutions, stagflation played the same role that in the 1930s fell to the Great Depression: that of indisputable indicator that the existing monetary arrangement was degenerating'. In contrast to Giannini's even-handed mercies (the postwar) and wild exaggerations (the 1930s to the mere 1970s), Bernanke's has omissions. In his 2012 lectures as Fed Chair, the full employment era did not rate a word. Reagan's desperate urging of the Fed's reflation for

---

[7] Bretton Woods IMF's top shareholder is the USA. Bernanke's (2013b) efforts follow next. Giannini (2011: 142–3 my emphasis) adds the 'original design' bore little resemblance to Bretton Woods' architects; despite Giannini's valuable attacks on money holders above, FE is not mentioned; the 'general will' is too Rousseau-like (a kind of economic authoritarianism); and he refers to the 'masses' or an undefined 'mass politics' just like Burns et al. (1979).

economic revival in 1986 after the disastrous 1980 shutdown of Paul Volcker's deflation may as not have happened.[8]

This seems to reflect an institutional cognitive dissonance, due to the undemocratic central banks by 1980. Postwar hopes, capitalist disruptions and states' nuclear preoccupations (Cold War), vanish in Bernanke's omissions, but not brutally like Burns's rewriting of (his) monetary history. Bernanke described three 'economic eras' in America: the 1930s 'Great Depression', the 1970s 'Great Stagflation' (Burns's watch), and the 'Great Moderation' of 1987–2006 (Greenspan's watch).[9] In (BoE) Mervyn King's account, the era of praise is the Great Moderation too: he calls it the 'Great Stability'. Although Bernanke was a rare appointment to the US Fed, an economic historian, the WWII and 1940s–70s full employment years vanish. His most vaunted era was in fact *a great immoderation* for banks, and rising job insecurity and poverty.[10]

Yet Bernanke's Great Depression research criticised how creditor nations and banks of France and the USA benefited hugely at the 1930 debt deflation.[11] This implies that central banks cannot be 'independent' of powerful political and economic forces. He warned of the 1930s' gold standard faith and US Treasurer (also Fed Chair) Mellon's austerity policies: central banks accepted the 'heartless' discipline 'no matter how bad unemployment got'. Even-handed, civil, *not counterfactual alleged facts of 1930s monetary history*. But FE, its low inflation, bank stability, and golden age era is unsayable.[12]

[8] Giannini (2011: 150), in which stagflation is an exaggerated scare cf. the terrible 1930s. Pixley (1993); my lectures to undergraduates compare the FE era, why not Bernanke (2013b) to his students? See Greider (1988: 568) on the indubitable facts of Reagan's reflation; later tightening, a cause of Wall Street's subsequent crash of 1987. That year saw the Greenspan 'put' emerge (to save banks).

[9] Dissonance is in Chapter 1. Economic history was neutralised by the 1980s. Bernanke (2013b) devotes his lectures to these eras; perhaps FE is discomfiting.

[10] King (2016); and Paul Krugman 'Money: the brave new uncertainty of Mervyn King' in www.nybooks.com/articles/2016/07/14/money-brave-n.

[11] In Bernanke (2013b: 37–9) presented in 2012; also *inter alia* in Bernanke (2000) on the creditor nation France; see Bernanke and Parkinson (2000: 255–75) supporting US wage rises as stimulus. On 1930, see Chapter 3.

[12] Pixley, Whimster and Wilson (2013) criticise individualist views of independence; Bernanke (2013b: 20; 25), on heartless, cf. Bernanke (2000: 250) argues the New Deal is best seen as clearing the way (with reflation and saving banks) for a 'natural recovery' and was

Bernanke even avoids the 1970s 'stagflation': specifically, its frantic financial and currency disturbances, wage-price inflation; the renewed 'heartless' job losses partly due to Burns' self-styled 'anguish'; as well, Volcker's tight money and the capital strikes from 1979 onwards, to chronic unemployment and stagnant wages. Bank money expansion is avoided despite continual financial crises during the allegedly stable 'Great Moderation' (GM) years. Bernanke's hero is Milton Friedman as saviour of stagflation. Although the 'GM' ended in the GFC just months after he took Fed office, he only said banks were 'overconfident' and it was somewhat due to lack of Fed supervision and neglect of consumer protection. Naturally defensive, Bernanke did not believe the Fed could do much to 'solve' the GFC: true; but just when *public jawboning to urge Treasury was most needed*. I discuss justifications later, noting that FE was not Bernanke's expertise, which hardly helped young Americans be better informed.[13] In contrast, Greenspan, whom Bernanke defends, and Mervyn King both flirted around Hayek's 'free banking'.

In exploring these tunnel visions, my argument seeks logical and normative considerations. Bernanke's words like *harsh* compare to decency, but few talk about how central banks make social-political decisions. The US Administration and Wall Street were the global influences on the 1970s outcomes. America never quite had the memorable alliances between states and capitalists as in Europe. Wall Street and US industrial capitalists often acted against the US Administration and Congressional interests (Wall Street by 1920 to dominate the world), and against the chameleon US Fed. The 1944 hegemonic US dollar aided America's less 'territorial' (colonial) world control, whether political elites preferred isolation or not. The Fed stands between more

---

not 'engine of recovery' itself: the 'lesson' for the GFC he says, cf. Chapter 3: No surprise, Hawtrey in UK Treasury blamed the BoE; Bernanke in the Fed, vice versa.

[13] He seems to be driven to defend Greenspan, perhaps for the office of the Fed to students, not just as Greenspan's successor. See my Chapter 8 on that; and Bernanke (2000: 42–3) citing Friedman on crises; and who says Hyman Minsky and Charles Kindleberger, in arguing for 'inherent instability', 'depart from the assumption of rational economic behavior'. But cf. Pixley (2004); Pixley et al. (2014) on rational fears of crashes versus irrational non-logic. Bernanke (2013b: 88–90) is weak on banks and (2013b: 49–51) on consumer protection. Crises in the GM were in faraway 'crony' countries it appears.

autonomous state *versus* capitalist interests than, say, the last century's BoE,[14] and it was founded to promote Wall Street. Nixon was an unwitting fulcrum of lethal changes: he abused the Fed as well.

HINDSIGHT'S REVISIONS TO THE SOCIAL SETTLEMENT

The end of the FE era requires us to explain central banks' forced return to non-democratic policies known and said to have failed miserably, complicated in the 1960s amid established oligopolies, growing finance firms, with (suddenly) grass roots protests. How scandalous, said the bourgeois fraternity (about feminism, civil rights; unions); hence, dissonances appeared. Central banks and banks were in a postwar 'club', sceptics told me. The BoE 'told' clearing banks of policy changes yet ordered them to behave in person. Bankers were public spirited and 'decent'. That English club give-and-take did not always apply to the Fed, since the formal 1933–4 rules set up external distrusting scrutinisers (like the SEC) with high expectations of banks. Yet those public interest aims (not perfect, e.g. Australia's brutal money-class wars of 1945 to the 1970s) twisted, when finance centres became impersonal and vast. US hedge funds fought central banks and states (such as UK's currency). Once despised 1950s' 'corporate raiders' became routine job-cutting M&As. Money fund firms and money markets took off. Unlike banks, they knew nothing of their market borrowers. A corporate form of free riding froze out old banking, which had kept big clients going in good *and* bad times, unlike money markets, and complexity made collapses likely.[15]

How did this happen? Monetarist central bank histories are most appalled that postwar authorities could 'repress' banks. Yet, the Fed may have lost control of bank inflation the earliest. 'Stagflation'

---

[14] Ingham (1984, 2008: 176–7) on UK industry and Schwartz (2000) also on US sectoral clashes and the dollar; see also Chapter 2 and my Nixon argument in this Chapter 5.

[15] Budd and others told me the BoE Governor invited bankers to tea: interviews cited, and distrust strategies explored, in Pixley (2004); Bell (1976), cited a Bank of America (BoA) president opposing Friedman's view of shareholder value for tearing up the *social fabric*; this president Dan Clausen of the BoA was also nearly chosen by Jimmy Carter instead of Volcker, Fed Chair: in Greider (1987: 45) and Crotty (2012). Minsky (2008 [1986]); Gibson (2009); Gibson and Tsakalotos (2006) discuss the money markets. M&A refers to Mergers and Acquisitions; the SEC is the Securities and Exchange Commission.

according to tales like Burns's, needed right wing governments committed to strong-arm tactics. Burns was Fed Chair in 1970 under Nixon's watch of 1969–74, and Nixon was a strong-arm President! Giannini argued we must blame 'the masses' for breaking 'the post-war settlement'. In his words, recovery from WWII was 'based on a "social pact" that called for wage moderation in exchange for high investment and an expansion of social expenditure by the state'.[16] Giannini the central banker spoke with a forked tongue. Insecure people did not sign a 'pact' to negate their desire for money to make ends meet or to gain a modicum of life control. He ignored Scandinavia, Britain, Australia, NZ, Canada that had *White Papers on Full Employment* implemented. The UK, France and Germany spent sensibly on public housing, national health, and nationalised industries; many more spent on jobs, education and jobless benefits. NZ and Australia spent less on social services since they had wage-earners welfare states of male pay high enough to service home mortgages. State ownership competed (successfully). On UN social scores, Scandinavia does best, USA worst. Parochial stories of 'stagflation' miss these economic successes.[17]

Yet central banks were invaded with converts to monetarist (US imperialist) faith, and monetary tools came to favour banks and shadow banks against governments and electorates. Impacts varied; some decent non-monetarists (aka doves) remained. Governments were not innocent, nor were big financial centres after explicit WWII laws ended. Banks renewed their liaisons and, with state largesse like the UK's for Euromarkets, rebuilt global finance markets. Geoff Ingham argues that the rebirth of financial power was inevitable. Nothing was

---

[16] Hayek continually exaggerated bank 'repression', using a Prince-serf model. Giannini (2011: 145), whose social pact idea at least finds the Triffin Dilemma too determinist; cf. collective assumptions (shared beliefs in Durkheim's sense) in many OECD countries about fairness in this thirty-year 'settlement'.

[17] Sociologists and social policy experts are attuned to comparative work, unlike so many economists and central bankers, usually more nationalistic; see Pixley (1993) and Wilson (2017) for a sample. NHS is Britain's National Health Service; UN (HDI versus GDP) Human Development Indexes for OECD countries.

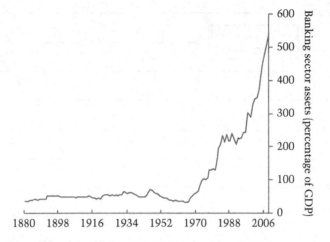

FIGURE 5.1 Size of the UK banking system 1880–2007
Source: Haldane 2010: 6 [Annex], from Bank of England data

planned to bring the result of the City (or Wall Street) so dominant, so carefree in, and with, economic and political life. Vicki Chick shows that UK banks often 'regretted' their demands for parity rules with building societies; the same occurred with the 'Thrifts' in the USA.[18] Bank money clearly took off from the 1970s. Andrew Haldane of the BoE gives ample retrospective data.

Figure 5.1 shows the size of UK bank assets was 50:50 to underlying economic activity from 1880. After 1970, bank assets grew to about 500:30 in Britain by 2006 (and Switzerland), USA's to 100:50 to GDP (a diversified economy): thus, banks expanded against active sectors across the OECD. Other data, the same in Australia and Britain (for example), indicate the huge take off in M3 or 'broad money' (commercial bank money) and a flat line for M1 or 'base money' (currency). Well before the 1970s, the ratio M1:M3 had been 50:50, and by 2012 it is 3:97 as Figure 5.2 shows. In Britain, with Quantitative Easing from 2009, the 3:97 ratio does not change. Questions are why central banks

---

[18] Ingham (1984; 2004: 156) on post WWII; Burnham (1999: 46) on UK boosting Euromarkets; Chick (2008), on how UK banks regretted 'parity', but then securitised their loans; both took on more dangers; also to Minsky (2008 [1986]) on US Thrifts.

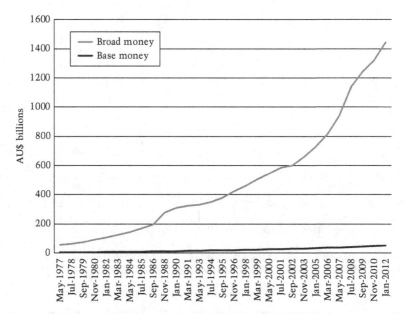

FIGURE 5.2 Australian money supply ratios 1977–2012
Sources: Reserve Bank of Australia in dollars, Excel sheets; Pixley, J.
and Blaxland, M. for ratio calculations and design

did not ring alarm bells by the 1990s, when this trend was obvious.
Were they ordered not to complain or (doctrinaire) true believers?[19]

The increase is so great it scotches the fairy tales. The former
state to bank money 50:50 ratio, and the size of UK bank assets from
1880 (Figure 5.1) did not imply economic stability, due to pre-1940s
inequality, gold standard austerity and rigid class divisions. The Great
Depression is a blip, although Haldane generally argues 'the rise to
heaven and descent to hell' was the same, 1920s–30s, as in 1990–2008,
and shows monetarist claims about the 1930 collapse of the money
supply (M1) are exaggerated. Consumer credit and other types of
'near money' also consolidated after the 1970s with more securities.[20]

[19] For the British M1:M3 ratio, see also Alessandri and Haldane (2009); my Table 1.1 on
bank balances, and, in Ryan-Collins et al. (2011) the BoE calculations are the same as for
Figure 5.2 of Pixley and Blaxland's work on RBA's Excel sheets. Both Figures omit further
M/s, which are 'near money' that also took off, so that counting up 'M/s' became difficult:
see Figures 7.1 and 7.2 for further statistical evidence.

[20] See Haldane (2010: 22) on 'descent to hell', and Chapter 3 herein on the 1930s. M1 is High
Powered Money.

What is striking is how capitalist bank money was lost from central bank public debates just as its manufacture and institutions grew. Skyscrapers of finance from the 1980s grew with bank executive pay.

This decade is scrutinized as a mess, not the forgone conclusion the above data of hindsight shows. How did the switch take place? Fed Chair Burns's crocodile tears in his 1979 'anguish' over feminism and US civil rights, his shock about Americans allegedly 'idling' on food stamps (when most OECD had proper cash transfers), tell us nothing of the Fed's twisted roles from 1970. It was shabby that Burns blamed those just enfranchised in the USA – asking for fair adult wages, also given women's unpaid economic contributions – and the distressed or plundered ex-colonies raising oil prices. Inclusive democracy and fair wages reversed after that decade. Years later, Stephen Roach, a cynical Wall Street analyst, said at the Dot Com bust in 2000 that the share of income from labour to capital had gone way too far. Not only unjust to labour but economically unsustainable. Data above (of CBs') showing that economic activity sank as private bank-money exploded, became taboo.

The nation-building central bank ended because the nation-building democratising state collapsed, consolidation along with it. Previously treasuries had larger fiscal roles to pursue experimental approaches, and monetary policies were complementary or 'ancillary'.[21]

This was the 'social view' and 'national interest' of the eclectic Fed Chair Marriner Eccles, with aims to influence interest rates, bank money creation, quality of credit and Forex rates, for employment, never *solely* the state/Fed's money creation.[22] Likewise, RBA Governor Coombs was wary about inflation of all types and any likely deflation; in Australia caution ceded, somewhat, in a 1962 order to 'be kind to banks' as RBA officials mocked their tory government; the Fed and BoE weakened in 1960. Who could imagine that by the 1990s,

---

[21] Burns et al. (1979) also cited in Chapter 1; Roach cited in Pixley (2004); Giannini (2011: 136; 138) argued central banks were *demoted* to 'ancillary': i.e., macroeconomic FE policy was consolidated CB-fiscal state policy.

[22] See Chapter 4; Kaufman (1986: 27), Wall Street analyst (and cited Pixley 2004, interviews) defends an Eccles Fed against 'doctrinaire' monetarism: saying central banks should not ignore 'fiscal policy, debt management, the volume and composition of credit, and union and corporate wage-price policies'. Amen to that.

US Fed officials would ask cravenly 'what the market *thinks*?' Most central banks had to follow the Fed, with its (new) populist devotion to markets and banking.[23]

In marked contrast to the 1940s–60s, by the time of Fed Chair Ben Bernanke's nightmare stretch, 1870s practices (as 'new') were re-established. Having ignored data perhaps too embarrassing to admit, he told students a bank run occurs only because 'no bank holds cash equal to all its deposits'. But *most* deposits are loans; his Fed deposits its loans too. His blind spot is to claim that banks derive funds from saver-depositors that Schumpeter criticised as 1830s bankers' 'professional ideology'. It kept bankers cautious, even though inaccurate since banks create money. The social effects of Bernanke's loanable funds 'fallacy' are to give 'savers' a magisterial role that they do not have. Ideological support in vaunting saver-pensioners, not rapacious fund managers, marked central banking.[24] The next question is how such anachronistic central bank policies returned in the 1980s.

Compared with Bernanke's fishy tale, Hyman Minsky showed of the 1960s–70s that the 'normal functioning' of a capitalist economy with a 'Wall Street' bred conditions that are conducive to financial crises. To Minsky *instability* festers during 'tranquil' stable times. He also compared US finance eras, from commercial 'real bills', to financial capitalism (by the 1870s) to *money manager capitalism* (post WWII). That eventually included mutual, hedge, money market funds, university endowments, sovereign wealth and other leveraged investors' funds. Replicating the 1870s securitising of stocks (alone), it took off into property 'securities' such as Real Estate Investment Trusts (REITS) in the 1960s with a speculative bubble in REITs partly responsible for large US bank failures in 1973–5. Central banks followed behind.[25]

---

[23] FOMC transcripts in 1994 onwards; note the personification of 'the market' a 'thinking' entity. In the 1990s, 'globalization' was the fad; Thomas Friedman of the *New York Times* put out a popular book praising the market's 'golden straitjacket' (Wall Street).

[24] See Bernanke (2013b: 5–6) on banks; and Schumpeter (1954: 730) on 'savers', and loanable funds in Chapter 8:Table 1.1 too.

[25] Minsky (2008 [1986]: 72) on 'normal'; and Minsky 'eras' are cited in Pixley (2012: 43; 50); King (2013: 23) on money funds etc., and on REITS see Minsky (2008 [1986]: 68–71).

One can ask if Bernanke's curious timeline is the embarrassment of central bankers shielding any *hint* of social-political structures, full employment remits, and the character of money production. Congress had threatened to impeach him for 'printing money' (QE), but his weak justifications compare poorly with Minsky's analysis that banking's 'good times induce balance sheet adventuring' aka bank 'liability management'. How did central banks switch from trying to constrain bank money production? Full employment remains a Fed duty and, if other, somewhat decent central bankers later told Pixley how much 'easier' it was with one remit of price stability, some of Bernanke's contemporaries (silenced in the Fed) were more critical. Retired financiers like Henry Kaufman of Wall Street or Mike Lazar of the City of London are still angry. RBA Governor B. W. Fraser hectored the press that he had full employment remits too. Where was McChesney Martin's commitment to the Fed's 'leaning against the wind' of inflations and deflation? They complained Keynes was ignored. So, what happened? If economic *theory* was a minor driver of actual changes (as I argue), monetarist nostrums promoted in the 1970s seriously affected central bank policy, to banking's vast advantage and to sceptical financiers' fury. In the 1980s Kaufman was bet against as Dr Gloom of Wall Street.[26]

Timidity of the 1960s Fed

To Minsky, a 1966 'run' and credit crunch showed the US Federal Reserve had no 'guidelines' of economic theories to watch out for financial instability. McChesney Martin's punch bowl jokes appalled the reviving orthodoxy too, for his 'imprecision'. Some postwar

---

[26] Minsky (2008 [1986]: 48); e.g. *Alan Blinder* v. *Greenspan*, in Pixley (2004): interviews 1998–2008 (City, NYC, Washington DC, Zurich, Frankfurt, Berlin, Sydney and Paris); Athens and Rome 2013, and London with Sam Whimster; Bank of England officials favoured the one remit in 2001; financier Henry Kaufman worried about credit expansion, deregulation of banks from the 1980s; Reagan's tax cuts. Interviews on FE also cited in Pixley (1993); all with permission to cite. Kriesler and Nevile (2003) and Pixley (2004), cite B. Fraser on the FE remit; Pixley (2004) with A. Abelson (*Barrons*) and Lazar; Martin is cited in Greider (1987: 328).

central bankers stressed 'humane' economic ideas: one argued that since governments, politicians and central banks are 'dependent on the intelligentsia' to understand what is happening, where it 'stands is pretty critical'.[27] Others agree that central banks are conduits for economic theories of the day, in policy *reactions* to interpretations of previous central banking 'disasters' to avoid.[28] A neoclassical 'synthesis' of US Keynesians, the significant economists then, dimmed the focus on money creation as a social institution. That CB joking subverted a renewed naturalising of capitalist money and yet, Paul Samuelson's 1958 article 'An exact consumption-loan model of interest with or without the social contrivance of money' is boringly silly, especially when the desire for money became universal in the newly urban, wage labour US society. The UK and Australia long had full wage labour, urban societies (non-subsistence). Capitalism is not dynamic without banking and finance, but it seemed forgotten how bankers make a living as 'merchants of debt' and how this 'normal functioning' throws up 'highly disruptive forces'. Wall Street grew, to have domestic and global consequences on a larger scale than before.[29]

Did the Fed ignore this or was it lulled because Wall Street was so quiet? McChesney Martin was tough on banks and wages. Before 1966, *no serious US financial crash* had occurred since 1933; domestic inflation was low, full employment widespread; each sector held mainly US government debt. Old doctrines abhorred the *social* existence of money while 'neoclassical Keynesians' focused

---

[27] In Minsky (2008 [1986]) cf. the RBA was unheeded in 1960, Chapter 4. Then RBA Governor Coombs (1994: 9) about the UK and USA intelligentsia of 1940s; replaced in the 1980s by those 'who identified with the system', who had another 'picture' of how economic activity works that, he claimed is inhumane and inefficient; Greider (1987: 328) on Martin's quip 'taking away the punch bowl before a riot breaks out', to the horror of Friedman (1953) naturalising like mad.

[28] Pixley (2004) cites interviews with Blinder, Goodhart and Budd (who said experiencing CB disasters 'gives you a very different take on central banking' and on 'life'); also, John Flemming (BoE) on a CB tendency of 'avoiding the odium' of 'pricking a bubble'. So much for precision.

[29] Synthesis also in Chapter 6; Keynesian Samuelson is cited in Ingham (2004: 23); 'desire' is explored in Orléan (2014), on bank disruption, Minsky (2008 [1986]: 278–9). See Chapter 1 on full wage labour societies and the US a late starter.

(overly) on fiscal intervention. Bretton Woods gave Wall Street alone the freedom from capital controls, and hence the ever-likely financial instability, and need for the Fed to act as lender of last resort. The US authorities had 'no theory' to assess relentless changes in US banking and finance. Minsky also tirelessly complained that open market operations to give banks credit left the Fed with less 'power to affect member-bank behaviour'. In contrast, the Discount window (last resort at high interest) gave the Fed oversight on banks' business and balance sheet standards. It became 'much diminished' post 1945. Open market policy emanated out to the world.[30]

The Fed's 'permissive' approach to *domestic banking's* new securitising techniques started in 1960, when banks began trading in Certificates of Deposits (CDs) at Fed banks. This was a position making (near money) that increased lending to an investment boom brewing that, in 1966 met a sharp Fed slowdown of the reserve base, to reduce bank money inflation: removing 'the punchbowl'. A run on CDs resulted, until the Fed opened the Discount window. But it 'legitimated the use of negotiable CDs' said Minsky, the juggling to make position *and* reassured money markets that banks would be saved. Increased spending on the Vietnam War *saved* that actual credit crunch. The next disturbance in 1970 (care of Burns) came from another 'near money' instrument of commercial paper to finance the expansion of the corporate sector. As it 'exploded', the Fed curtailed that inflation in 1974: bankruptcies and a run on this market ensued. Both Fed Discount window and open market operations protected the market in commercial paper, which became a 'covert liability' that was 'off bank balance sheets'. Minsky warned it became an 'additional component to the effective money supply'. Between 1970 and 1982, American financial 'innovations' listed by Henry Kaufman grew to thirty-eight – in cash management, investment contracts in primary markets and for various consumer loans, in market securities

---

[30] See Chapter 4 on Bretton Woods; crashes and the discount window (LOLR), see Minsky (2008 [1986]: 50–3; 87); whose work grew out of Schumpeter and Keynes.

and finance organisations. In 1985 *alone*, thirty-eight new ones were added. Since his firm Salomon Inc. traded them, he would know.[31]

1960s Global Balances of Trade

Turning to the international influence of Wall Street, one question is whether the US Treasury and Fed were the craven tools of Wall Street expansion during the 1960s–70s that Minsky implied. Some suggest Bretton Woods was fatally flawed and recount each step of banking's evasions as an inevitable end to the 1944 deal. These are left wing counterfactuals – albeit with logic and ethics lacking in orthodox work. One could equally argue, also with zero evidence, that a Bretton Woods 'bancor' said (foolishly) to be 'apolitical', 'might have been' subverted from inter-state rivalry or in financial revolts against a bancor's definition of money.

There was no bancor. Compare my above conjectures with other views. A more moderate US monetarist than some, Barry Eichengreen has devoted his work to the 'international monetary system'. In *Exorbitant Privilege* (2011), we find patriotism but neglect of money creation. His American parochialism – common under the British Empire too – at least implies the monetary conflicts generated in central bank policies. Yet he insists on a mono-causal direction for a hegemonic currency:

> There may be an association between the economic and military
> power of a country and the use of its currency by others, but
> it is a country's position as a great power that results in the
> international status of its currency.

Eichengreen disregards capitalist money creation for military power and multi-causal processes. In respect to sterling's waning hegemony by the 1870s, he says: 'Great Britain was a small windswept island off the northeast coast of Europe. The United States, in contrast, was a

---

[31] See Minsky (2008 [1986]: 50–3; 98; 102–3) on CDs and bank runs; Kaufman (1986: 22–7) on new tricks.

continental economy'. So what. War finance, the City of London and the vast British Empire have no reference.[32] Indeed, the US went cap in hand for City loans up to 1900, then, in financing WWI, it gained most gold reserves (Chapter 2). Somewhat parallel to the US dollar's trend from 1945, the UK's bargaining power had 'worked' when the BoE held the 'only gold reserves of the huge British financial system', de Cecco argues.

However, as more countries joined 'gold', Britain increasingly borrowed gold from other countries as its gold reserves declined. City banks sought more outlets abroad (multiplying off their deposits of overseas sterling). Such financing gave Britain 'a financial income in excess of the interest it had to pay on borrowed funds' – a kind of global seigniorage.[33] It shamelessly exploited India, which was by far its largest colonised market (contra Eichengreen), squeezed Britain's other colonies and Dominions, also forced Japan to buy pound sterling through their exports. The British put India on the gold standard; compelled it to keep reserves in British government paper and deposits in the City. UK accounts balanced, but soon global doubts about convertibility became realised. Barely months before WWI broke out, sterling had become 'incredible' since Britain was unable, visibly, to convert sterling to gold after Wall Street put a moratorium on the City calling back its loans. The gold standard stopped three months before WWI.[34] This crisis is mostly a foot-note. Hawtrey did admit the 1914 'acceptance crisis' led to the fiduciary limit being suspended. Treasury actually issued 'Bradbury' currency notes because of the

---

[32] 1944 'flaws' are discussed in Chapter 4. Eichengreen (2011: 6) cited; and see Chapter 2 on war finance, via which Wall Street rose to first place!

[33] De Cecco (2009: 124) on UK gold, which is little known (or admitted), since Eichengreen (2011) dismisses US$ hegemonic subsidies too; the US is seen as the great martyr (a cliché today).

[34] Amato and Fantacci (2012: 161–72); de Cecco (2009: 129–30) further explains the BoE-Treasury managers of 'gold' found difficulties, as more countries went on gold and City banks became more leveraged. The UK's use of India, first with silver, reduced the rupee value and created an export boom 1890s–1900s, then India was forced on gold: de Cecco on Wall Street's moratorium in (2009: 133). Not even Hawtrey (1921) names the 'Bradbury Bills' of Treasury (see Chapter 2).

'paralysed' discount market, which needed advances.[35] The saga partially resembles Nixon's in 1971.

America was loath to build its military very much before both world wars. The Allies' WWI debts owing to the USA expanded Wall Street, the Fed and US industrial strength. Eichengreen argues that the euro cannot be an alternative today 'because' its member states are 'inclined to pander to their domestic constituencies' and the ECB tempted to print money 'to monetise government debts', which will 'not inspire confidence'. **Nixon-Burns did that** not the shabby, deflationary ECB. Eichengreen could be giving Montagu Norman's lectures to British Labour in 1931. Critical scholars argue a mere chronicle of events side by side with Eichengreen's rosy *America is Great* glasses and correlation (not causation), hide his brash selection. Who benefited from US 'stimulus' and 1944-dollar bargaining power but the US?[36]

This was clear to RBA Governor Coombs at that time. Roosevelt's death saw a 'change in tone of American international policies' from Lend Lease and Marshall plan 'generosity', to a 'determination to extract ... the full price of its war time support for the Allied cause'. US firms increased ownership of global resources and enterprises, and the Truman Administration imposed a modified 'free trade pattern' to allow the US and the few very well-established 'industrial, commercial and creditor Nations' to dominate the global economy. This and free capital mobility were increasingly promoted in the IMF and GATT, two 1944 creations. An Australian-led group

---

[35] Hawtrey (1962 [1932]: 134), said 1914 was like the 1825 crisis. Victor Morgan (1943: 231–3), gold was always suspended in crises, 'riddled with exceptions' (1943: 102); there was a growing 'problem of gold reserves'; any 'major drain of gold' had one remedy, raising Bank rate (1943: 217); the Wall Street crisis of 1907 caused 'an immense drain on the Bank of England' but he rejects 'some writers' who say there was a 'serious' embarrassment in a 'scramble for gold', which to Morgan (1943: 222–4), was improved in 1913; all was 'calm' before the Great War. Amato and Fantacci (2012) above suggest the 'threat' of war did create gold hoarding in other, later combatants, but the G. S. had virtually collapsed by the 1890s, some date that earlier.

[36] See Chapter 2 again. Eichengreen (2011: 7; 17) knew of ECB actions; and cited on 'fetters', in Amato and Fantacci (2012: 153–4) and see their comments. Rose-tinted glasses are unavoidable, but willful?

of 'less developed powers' made efforts to 'limit the power of the IMF' with a proposed 'International Trade Organisation' to foster global demand and help maintain full employment, but Washington blocked it. Kaldor joined a second Australian call in 1949. Early on, the IMF became a *hard-nosed lender* and mouthpiece for finance and US interests, said Coombs. Thus the development of underdevelopment.[37]

The 1944 'structure' lasted for twenty-five years while the US switched from being the main creditor to debtor. Many argue US postwar success was less from Bretton Woods, and probably more about America's huge and thriving economy, from banks being cautious and drastic reconstruction elsewhere. Dollar hegemony enabled central banks to pursue domestic concerns. Herman Schwartz stresses the US competitive advantages in their assembly line methods, perfected in churning out war materiel, but these methods spread under the Marshall and Dodge plans. Gradually, Germany, France and Japan became strong competitors.

Nixon abandoned gold in 1971. Ironically, the US, Europe, UK and Japan thereupon made strenuous efforts to slow mobile capital at 'grim-faced' meetings. Each monetary disorder after Bretton Woods ended was a 'dirty float' as in 1973, and saw officials suddenly trying Keynes's 'bancor' idea so despised at Bretton Woods. But by the 1990s, remnants of control vanished (mostly); volatile mobile capital resumed its nineteenth century path at a far more disruptive scale. Nothing natural here, then, and much unintended.[38]

The great gold hoard of the USA since 1914 had so shrunk that in 1971 it was insufficient to meet external demand for dollar conversion

---

[37] Keynes also pursued a similarly failed global plan for holding commodities rather than accumulating money (cited in Amato and Fantacci 2012: 131). Nugget Coombs (we saw in Chapter 4); Coombs (1994) argued the 1944 global trade plan would impose 'obligations on the major powers ... to establish employment and trade policies' for high demand for globally traded goods but became 'a footnote in history' (1994: 7–8). He said the IMF and GATT (later WTO) helped 'to intensify the polarisation of economic power', and not an 'environment for human and economic diversity'. On Kaldor's joining Australia's team, see Turnell and Ussher (2009).

[38] See Helleiner (1993) on the 'servant', and Schwartz on this (2000: 200; 203–5) and on 'grim faced' efforts on a bancor, way too late; and Chapters 6 and 7.

to gold, volubly from French protests. Stepping back, in about 1958, more dollars were held as 'Eurodollars'. British authorities were tempted to use them (apparently) because this free space or off shore Eurodollar market reduced pressure on balance of payments and on sterling; the City regathered. Wall Street banks had evaded Fed and US Treasury supervision by opening foreign branches in the 1950s, and the profits enticed expansion and more adventures. Unregulated, 'no questions were asked and no information was given', Eurodollars gave opportunities for 'shell' (investment) banks off-shore, and increased banking's change of profit sources. Proto-Forex deals grew and generated income from fees charged (in addition to loan interest streams) that did not foster economic activity. The rearming of 'vigilante' bank traders against government social justice plans and *central bank* controls began.[39]

The US industrial sector had challengers now revived from WWII's catastrophes. America's terms of trade turned against it around 1960, and speculators started attacking the US$. Banks lobbied strenuously against 'financial repression' but the Kennedy Administration tried various 'soft capital controls' and fostered revaluation of the deutsche mark and Dutch guilder. And the mid-1960s saw greater financial instability from cross-border lending. Inside Kennedy's and Johnson's Administrations, arguments were aired for deregulating Western European capital markets, and the Fed overtly agreed to keep Eurodollars free of reserve requirements. Against that growing susceptibility, the main central banks in 1962 *agreed* to support each other from speculative attacks, but in 1967 nothing prevented a run on pound sterling and an attempt on the US$. Nixon went off gold and by 1973 nations and firms were exposed 'to exchange risk for the first time in four decades'.[40]

---

[39] See Burnham (1999) on Eurodollars and Galbraith (1975b: 294–99) on gold; Eurodollars were just dollars held in European firms or deposited in banks, which grew as firms sold more to the US whose firms' equipment had become relatively obsolescent to France or Japan; see also Amato and Fantacci (2012: 103; 104) on the unregulated Eurodollar market, also citing Paul Einzig, 'no questions asked'.

[40] On US banks changing, see Isenberg (2006: 374–6) also Dymski (2006: 391) on President Kennedy; and Schwartz (2000: 204), and exchange risk.

Collective revolts, then, against the central currency grew in non-regulated or non-banking near money IOU schemes: difficult for central banks required to supervise and attuned to coping with banks. McChesney Martin was Fed Chair from 1951 to 1970. He 'leaned against the wind' of bank inflation, but eventually seemed to give in, Minsky claimed. This was nothing to Arthur Burns, Chair, 1970–8, however, monetarist histories despise Martin's efforts (and JFK/LBJ's) most. In addition, the Fed had a negligible record of supervision. Hartley Withers stressed supervision, and how difficult the BoE had found that, in his advice to the 1910 Fed founders that they ignored, as did a few commentators at the Fed's 2010 centenary. FDR's 1933–4 reforms, I argue elsewhere, were distrust strategies that allotted supervision to agencies like the often-underfunded SEC (given whims of presidents or Congress), and to accountancy firms. The response to distrust in more impersonal relations can prompt those so distrusted to live down to that suspicion and to behave dubiously: I made a social argument added to 'Goodhart's law' of evasion. Impersonal ties are too distant to maintain boys' club cooperation.

After the Fed started avoiding the Discount window just as Wall Street dominated worldwide, other central banks' states followed suit, with SEC-type regulators. By 1970 finance secured a break out, and the dollar float institutionalised Wall Street's global reach.[41]

The Nixon Administration under Vietnam War Inflation

The second important factor for understanding the US fracture of Bretton Woods and alleged Great Stagflation is the Vietnam War and underplayed monetary roles of the Nixon Administration. The saga is an example of Geoff Mann's position that central banks are part of a profoundly anti-democratic monetary regime; to him, aspects of capitalist money 'operate at a super-distributional level' (against labour; regions, etc.). The regime is not 'shaped by competitive market

---

[41] See Chapter 2 on Withers; collective revolts see Orléan (2014: 123–7); see Minsky (2008 [1986]: 54–6) on Martin, and see Pixley (2004), cf. to Goodhart (2003b), on distrust of the SEC. The Discount window is lender of last resort.

forces' but structured by state authority that is, in the '"democra-cies", non-democratic'. Central banks had first-hand experience of WWII and Korean War inflation. Yet rarely in today's 'stagflation' lit-erature is the US Vietnam War excess demand inflation (price hikes from shortages) mentioned, nor its main mode of finance – of bor-rowing privately and not raising taxes. It is extraordinary how little that war inflation is researched, given Vietnam became so unpopular. James Galbraith is one, who argues that Johnson and Nixon never put Vietnam on a 'total war' basis with price controls and tax. The results included runaway bank and corporate inflation. His father recounts LBJ's modest efforts at both, but in central bank histories, blame is cast on Democrat Johnson's Vietnam War. And LBJ's 'Great Society' has the odium over Nixon's 1970s inflation. Republican Nixon's external adventures, escalation of the war to Cambodia (versus LBJ's peace plans) are as *pianissimo* as the domestic bank money inflation care of Burns's Fed. We see Nixon's desperation far outshone an obse-quious Fed.[42]

Nevertheless, hindsight is a wonderful view never available in the fog. I do not single out "Nixon" except as the joker in a pack of unexceptional politicians inside the CIA and Pentagon, central banking, in Wall Street, Congress, Treasury, the IMF – self-serving as usual, and reacting to short-term problems. My argument weaves a story to stress no one cause – for what we now see as a chaotic tan-gle. Nixon, Burns, Volcker et al., had they known, *could have* acted other than how they did, namely applying old pack-gang tactics to democratic institutions. Not only, but 1970s politics were strange across the world too. Engineered and stupid UK fake coups, flexed ex-colonial muscles; greens, war protests, union strengths, femi-nism, masked a main player. 'Wall Street' figuratively revolted and

---

[42] Mann (2013) and also see Mann (2010) on the state's roles. LBJ is blamed e.g. in Burns et al. (1979); in Giannini (2011: 148); yet LBJ implemented the social plans that Kennedy could not persuade Congress to pass, to Galbraith (1986: 337), bringing the US *barely near* the social democracies, he said correctly. Also, unlike many economists back then, JKG opposed Vietnam. His son James Galbraith (1997) on 'total war' financing.

succeeded. The *unruly masses* was a simple-minded whining, but the 1970s turned I think into a critical juncture, but that judgement may be decades too early to make. Central banks were enmeshed in multiple institutional changes that, again, who could guess in 1970, created the Washington-Wall Street consensus that forbad CB-treasury cooperation for public benefit only 'Defence'.

Moving to Vietnam War finance and the state a main player, Greider's account is how, at the end of WWII, the US 'government did not demobilise for peace. Defence spending grew, as did its permanent contribution to aggregate demand'. Demand for credit also grew, and Eisenhower tended to over-rely on Fed monetary policy with 'its discriminatory, even reactionary effects'. Minsky emphasised military expenditure 'makes no useful contribution to current useful output'. Conventional stories irritated J. K. Galbraith too. He said the Nixon economists invented the cliché 'fine-tuning' and harped about Johnson's 'fiscal disorder' as 'an alibi' for the Nixon serious inflation. Nixon inherited a fiscal surplus after LBJ's (war) surtax of 1967. It was in 1970 that the deficit regrew, Nixon having ended the surtax and reduced other taxes. He also rejected WWII-type controls on wage-price spirals as the idea of 'extremists' (such as Galbraith).[43]

On social transfer and defence costs, Minsky shows US national military expenditure at $14.0 billion in 1950, and in 1969 at $76.3 billion (or in 1950, 4.9 per cent of GNP, doubled to 8.2 in 1969). In contrast, US *transfer* payments to GNP were 3.8 per cent of GNP in 1950 and 5.4 per cent in 1969; transfers only became pronounced during Nixon/Ford's watch (to ease the 1974 crash). Given that 1950

---

[43] Greider (1987: 325–6) on defence; the monetary policy of Ike is in J. K. Galbraith (1981: 348). Minsky (2008 [1986]: 23–8) agreed war is inflationary; Galbraith (1975b: 284–8) said, in the 1967 calendar year, US Treasury deficit = $12.4 billion; in 1968, the deficit = $6.5 billion yet, in 1969 it was a surplus = $8.1 billion, the year Nixon took office, inheriting 'a remarkably sound fiscal position'. 'As well fine-tune a Mississippi flood' snorted Galbraith at Nixon's turning to monetary policy. He also (1975b: 292) lambasted Greenspan's 1974 vision of controlling 'the genie of inflation' with 'a (capitalist) god' who could 'exorcise' inflation 'forever' with enough requisite pain. During WWII Galbraith managed to much success some of the US price-wage operations, rationing and rent control, described in his *Life in our times* (1981), with comparisons to Canada's more successful controls.

was the middle of the Korean War; similarly, 1969 was mid-Vietnam, social transfers are modest, then, against claims to the contrary.[44]

Eisenhower neglected fiscal policy and, although a moderate, the expensive anti-communism led by the Dulles brothers, Nixon, and McCarthyism took off during his presidency. Martin, Fed Chair throughout the Eisenhower-Kennedy-Johnson years, imposed three short recessions during Republican years, and a credit crunch in 1966 on a Democrat. In the late-1950s, Martin tightened monetary policy briefly, to help disable union demands (Mann argues) in the industrial core.[45] Nixon blamed Martin for not giving easier credit during his 1960 election campaign, which he claimed was the *reason* he lost to Kennedy. It became Nixon's obsession.[46] CBs may be chameleons but not then.

Kennedy-Johnson tax *cuts* (on high rates) started in 1961 which saw great domestic prosperity, Minsky argued, due to these and also to JFK investment credits aimed *conditionally* as corporate inducements (unlike Reagan's unconditional tax cuts). State spending grew, which Martin reined in. Although everyone at the time blamed Johnson for his lies about Vietnam War escalation, inflation was also from Cold War (nuclear and CIA) spending. The size of government was far larger than the 1930s, and the failure to tax when needed was one cause of many of the problems. And yet, we saw President Johnson introduced a Vietnam War surtax – a 10 per cent flat rate on personal and corporate incomes that lasted until Nixon. Greider argues this surcharge was 'too little, too late' although Galbraith's

---

[44] Minsky (2008 [1986]: 26–8) gives the Gross National Product data.

[45] In hindsight, Eisenhower (not V-P Nixon) was a comparatively moderate Republican; Trump is 'merely' outcome of decades of Republican political melodrama. See Galbraith (1986: 348–50) on the Dulles brothers, John Foster, Secretary of State and Allen Dulles, Director CIA; how they 'liquidated' the US global 'fund of goodwill' from WWII and postwar. Mann (2013: 198; 211; 209) on unions also Dickens (1997: 81) show that in the 1960–1 recession the Fed T-bill rate rose to 3.2 and on to 3.4, held for about three months. A full 9 per cent rate at the 1969–70 recession lasted three months (cf. see below, *crippling* durations under Burns and Volcker).

[46] Greider (1987: 328–9) on Nixon's blame of Fed; and Minsky (2008 [1986]) on the 1966 crunch.

data disputed that. Nixon was in the White House in January 1969; Martin's Fed rate rose sharply in that December. In 1970, there was a short recession with joblessness *and* inflation: stagflation was Fed-induced. Collective faith in the global US currency dwindled.[47]

A short debate recalling Vietnam War finance occurred, after G. W. Bush launched the second Iraq War *and* reduced taxes. 'The Kennedy tax cuts were proposed, and then adopted by Congress, before the Vietnam War was a big expenditure item' said Gary Burtless at the Brookings Institution. Furthermore, he said:

> Vietnam initially did not require much in the way of additional outlays; it was not like either World War II or the Korean War, which started out with a huge runup in military spending. It was not until 1968 that the Johnson administration proposed the surtax to help pay for the Vietnam War ... Still, the Vietnam era surtax went into effect within five years of major spending on that war. We are now more than eight years into the 'war on terrorism', and we've had only tax reductions; no tax hikes.
>
> 'Traditionally countries raise taxes to pay for wars, then cut taxes by a portion of the amount raised once peace descends' [added a J. D. Foster of the conservative Heritage Foundation].[48]

But 'traditionally' taxes were patchy. To expand on the four 'typical' methods of war finance, the first is state borrowing from the central bank. This process is technically unlimited although often limited legally (e.g. the FRA 1913), and it causes an immediate \$ for \$ increase in spending power.[49] That increase in the volume (or supply)

---

[47] See Greider (1987: 331) and Schwartz (2000: 205) on Kennedy's tax cuts, and Minsky (2008 [1986]: 141) on prosperity and cf. Reagan using the infamous Laffer Curve (in Chapter 6 next); Greider (1987: 334) on Martin's 1970 recession.

[48] Farley (2009) cites Burtless and Foster. Further proof that by the Iraq wars, Wall Street dominated funding.

[49] See also Chapter 2 and the BoE's founding in 1694. To amplify, there are also four kinds of sovereign state borrowing from the CB: advances; discounting of treasury bills; central bank subscriptions to state bond issues; and purchases of securities from the public to enable private individuals to subscribe to new loan issues, Butlin et al. (1941: 32). The last one (the Fed WWI?) is like direct central bank expansion given the same effects as the other operations.

of money means private banks have more cash. In the usual fashion, once the government spends the new funds (cheques drawn on the central bank), the supplying firms deposit their proceeds in private banks. This money is added to the banks' deposits with the central bank (banks use them as cash). With greater liquid resources, banks multiply on that if the demand for loans exists, that is, create further deposits (see Table 1.2).

Effects of war finance are not clear-cut. Although there is no clear line between mild and runaway price rises, at the extreme they are inflationary. Thus 'unlimited credit expansion' is dangerous and difficult to manage (but not impossible) with controls on investments and prices when all profits are rising.

The second method of war finance is to borrow directly from private banks by selling government securities. If banks must cut back their private advances to do so, spending is transferred to the government. But if banks can continue their private advances (as back in 1694), buying government bonds leads to a modern expansion of spending in 'the *same way* as central bank subscription to loans'. The 'ideal' solution is to reduce banks' 'non-essential advances' as their advances from war finance rise (like in WWII), while CBs cater to private bank cash needs. Bank resistance and intransigence is a typical reaction.[50] From 1970, control of banks was further declining under Burns's Fed.

The third method, borrowing directly from the public, only reduces purchasing power and bank expansion if banks are not involved. But by the 1970s many more people used banks. Butlin et al. argued that WWI showed that 'self-sacrifice' by the community or banks was highly unlikely. Because lending is 'voluntary', the effects on banks are rarely seen; further advances to 'profiteers' are

---

[50] See Chapters   2 and 4, and Butlin et al. (1941: 34–6; 37–8; 62–7) on banks also, on limiting advances: the British method in 1941. The WWII Australian case required banks to keep 'Special Accounts' at the CBA to limit 'non-essential' advances. The private banks were, in 1942–9, loath to 'support government policy' 'voluntarily' in Butlin (1955) on war finance, banks' intransigence; also, in Butlin (1983).

available from private banks, as Keynes mentioned in 1940, while others on low/fixed pay must cut back due to higher prices. In Vietnam (1970s), unions wanted wage rises, which fed the corporate sector's price-wage spiral.

The fourth method, taxation, directly reduces the money supply and the public's spending power, and so it gives *the least opportunity for price and credit inflation*. Tax minimises the steep interest payments that overwhelmed post-WWI budgets. The 'recipe' for WWII was to limit 'expansionary' borrowing, to gain much war finance from a steeply progressive tax system, and price controls.[51] Keynes noted in 1924 that the French resisted the higher taxes needed 'to pay the claims of the French *rentiers*' and of Wall Street's: the Banque de France chose to devalue, rather than deflating or inflating ruinously.[52] LBJ's war 'surtax', a flat rate, was not quite an ideal 'recipe' as it hit lower earners most. Yet Nixon inherited a budget surplus and ended the surtax altogether. Burns dismissed price and wage 'controls', so effective in WWII. His Fed involved both inflation and deflation, and Nixon devalued. 'Fine-tuning' was an empty claim in this chaos. If it was hard to win democratic support to pay for WWII, in contrast, states are silent about funding permanent nuclear arsenals and grotesque military interferences.

However, President Nixon's break from Bretton Woods in 1971 is often given determinist (balance of payment) causes. To my mind that is only half of it. For example, Fed Chair Burns (afterwards) mentioned 'loose war finance' of 1968, and not Nixon's ending the war

---

[51] See Butlin et al. (1941: 39–43), cf. Keynes (1940) favoured steeply rising taxes from the middle and top income brackets but 'deferred wage payments' for the low bracket. This deferred portion would be deposited in Post Office or other savings and returned with interest after the war (today's superannuation in Australia was the ALP 'solution' to 1970s inflation). But Butlin et al., while interested in Keynes's scheme, did not support deferred pay. I suspect they trusted neither governments nor banks, which might likely be predators on low-income earners/savers. Whatever, the latter came about in due course.

[52] Keynes is cited in Ahamed (2009: 264, 219; 261–8) on the Bank of France; also see Chapter 2, on the high number of middle-class French subscribers to war bonds in WWI. Current war funding methods are so little discussed that in my view suspicions of state war motives and magical funding tactics need much more research.

surtax, or inflation's explosion, 1970 onwards during Burns's watch (also deflation). He was Nixon's appointment after McChesney Martin. Demands on America for gold from foreign suspicions of the dollar's value increased with Burns's and Wall Street money inflation.

Nixon the 'Fine Tuner' with Burns's Fed

Of all the disasters of Nixon's presidency, the Burns relation is often missed. Slogans helped: We are all Keynesians now, Nixon preached, 'fine-tuning' for everyone (Wall Street to white trade unionists). One later tall story (anti-democratic) assumed wrongly that left-wing politicians 'interfered' with central banks. No one can say Nixon was democratic in his South American tactics, or virtuous in his Campaign to Re-Elect the President (CREEP) set up in 1971. The Senate voted to impeach him in July 1974; Nixon resigned a month later. Giannini talked sympathetically about Burns's 'stagflation' fears, omitting Nixon's corruption of democratic processes.[53] Monetarists blame the Fed for 'accommodating' Johnson's deficit, and mention Nixon's 1972 'political business cycle'. Really. Nothing is said about Burns-Friedman-Nixon-CIA's mutual *political anti-Red views* nor how, faced with 'unprecedented working-class power', Nixon's crisis-management took an explicitly 'inflationary form' with Burns's help in 1970. He was the profligate 'faux-Keynesian' President. Nixon seemed to ameliorate distributional conflict, allegedly to win (white) unions' votes with veiled tricks. Although Friedman did advise Nixon, and his colleague George Stigler served on committees during Nixon's years, neither was happy with Nixon's 'price guidelines' that monetarists reject. *Friedman favoured a dollar float.*[54] In the 1990s, that 1970s

---

[53] To Galbraith (1981: 346), 'Nixonland' was 'a land of slander and scare; the land of sly innuendo, the poison pen, the anonymous phone call and hustling, pushing, shoving ... anything to win': in Galbraith's speech for Adlai Stevenson in 1959; later cited he says, in the Watergate years, for Adlai's 'prescience'. See Chapter 6 on Friedman's influence on CB changes; we saw Giannini fudges, earlier in this chapter. LBJ left Nixon a surplus; the Fed raised the rate too.

[54] Pro-market: see Dickens (1997: 82–3): New Classical economists differed from monetarists about workers' inflation expectations, but for both, the ire is at Johnson,

inflation was mainly claimed to be from wage demands, but not to monetarists or rational expectations people, who just blamed weak 'money-printing' authorities and democratic pro-job governments. These remain the alleged reasons central banks must be 'independent', however, implicitly not from warrior, pork barrel ones or from Wall Street rent seeking. In contrast, those opposed to Volcker when he 'decelerated wages' and virtually stopped economic activity in 1980, tended to by-pass 'Nixon'. Volcker was target of their critical (rightly shocked) disputes. So, except for Greider's work on the 1970s Fed, little more is said of Nixon-Burns, nor the state interference of a divisive Administration into a peculiar, secretive Burns-led Fed.

But much can be said.

Looking at Burns's background, he taught Friedman at Rutgers and it was because of Burns, and more to Homer Jones (of Chicago) and influential for years at the St. Louis Fed, that monetarism entered Fed views. To Greider, Jones ran St Louis Fed research as 'a kind of guerrilla outpost for monetarism'; Kaldor had similar charges. Friedman continued to respect Burns. It is not certain how the influence flowed: perhaps mutual, Burns as his senior.[55]

Nixon did not draw on Burns for any monetarism, just the opposite. We know he was obsessed with *divide et emperor* popularity but consider this: Still blaming McChesney Martin for his 1960 election defeat, Nixon had to wait for Martin to retire before he could appoint Burns to the Fed on 31 January 1970.

"I respect his independence", Nixon assured the White House gathering. "However, I hope that independently he will conclude that my views are the ones that should be followed". Vigorous

and only at Nixon's 1972 re-election 'cycle'; less the War, tax cuts or CREEP. Nixon's 'inflationary bias' to (white male) unions is stressed in Mann (2013: 209), as the anomaly in central banks. My colleague Craig Freedman has kindly summarised for me Stigler and Friedman's relations with Nixon; on Friedman's floating exchange view, see Friedman (1997) and Greider (1988: 581–2).

[55] Eisenhower, Kennedy and LBJ *wanted* the Vietnam War, Nixon the *nuclear option*. Kaldor (1970) and Greider (1987: 97) on the St. Louis Fed; from Craig Freedman (who interviewed Friedman, Stigler etc.) with thanks.

applause. Nixon went on, "you see, Dr Burns, that is a standing vote for lower interest rates and more money"'. Two weeks later, the Fed provided a lower interest rate and more money. Outside the Fed, not inside, due to internal cynicism at Burns's 'pious rhetoric', Burns cultivated a reputation as a 'stern enemy of inflation'.[56]

Nixon exploited countless domestic disorders and protests, promoting a 'silent majority' in a polarising fashion. LBJ's increased electorate would assess Nixon first. Accordingly, as Greider says 'when Arthur Burns erred, his errors were always tipped in the same direction – providing a prosperous climate for Richard Nixon's re-election campaign' CREEP. As inflationary pressures mounted Burns assured Fed governors there were no 'political constraints' on Fed policy. 'Nevertheless', he added, 'the Federal Reserve System is part of the government'. Nixon's White House staff also put pressure on Burns, probably unnecessarily.[57]

After Nixon's dollar float on 15 August 1971, Volcker, then Treasury under-secretary for Monetary Policy and International Affairs, 'spent two years in globe-trotting negotiations, trying to patch back together the orderly system of international currency exchange but the efforts failed'. 'Afterward, Volcker saw the breakdown of Bretton Woods ... "as a failure of American leadership, unwillingness to confront the nation's excesses and to impose self-discipline"'. That moralism is no endorsement of Burns.

Burns cast himself as marvellous. When he took over the Fed, the CPI was at 116. When he left, it was at 195 and rising like his jobless rate. In retirement, he lectured on the 'anguish of central

---

[56] Greider comments on, and cites Nixon, elected late 1968 and how Martin refused to go prematurely, in Greider (1987: 340–1); also, thanks for email on 29 June 2016 from V. J. Carroll on the Burns fiasco and his fear of 'posterity'.

[57] LBJ aimed for cohesion in pushing effective Civil Rights and some welfare (undone with Vietnam). Packer (2014) on the psychologising of Nixon in the literature, and that Reagan was more insidious; Wheen's *Strange Days* (2009), recounts the 'paranoid style' of the times among left and right; in the US Kent State U National Guard shootings, May 1970, with Nixon calling student rioters 'bums' and V-P Spiro Agnew 'permissivists ... traitors and perverts' in Wheen (2009: 24–5). See Greider (1987: 342–3; 344) citing Burns, and on 'pressure' and inflation rising with Burns.

banking'. In 1972, he quashed Fed Board concerns about bank-money inflation by saying 'he was not afraid of prosperity' (a barb at Martin) that is, to give banking a free rein. He was afraid of *posterity*. Burns abolished the practice of keeping verbatim minutes of FOMC meetings, only summaries. The FOMC did not make its meetings public until 1993 during President Clinton's watch; it was pushed by Congressional Democrats critical of Volcker and Greenspan. Transcripts are kept secret for five years. Congress wanted appointment of minorities to the Committee and release of videotapes of meetings. That failed.[58]

From this evidence, Nixon's Administration cannot be a side-note on the Great Stagflation critique that fingered Johnson's promotion of the Great Society, or the mounting opposition to 'Keynesian policies'. McChesney Martin had been especially tough on LBJ, the Eisenhower-Nixon Administrations, and *unions*, JFK, banks, all in marked contrast to the possibly 'sordid' relations of Burns with Nixon, and later attempt to 'ingratiate' himself with President Carter, who refused to reappoint Burns. Formal records show that in early 1976 on Carter's taking office, the Fed eased the Discount rate when US 'stagflation' reached its peak. Burns retired in January 1978, having left the Democrat a poisoned chalice.[59]

None of these Fed stories vindicates orthodox accounts. The Nixon Administration instrumentally used any force it could find but no matter because, to monetarism, neither the banking sector nor unions are disruptive factors in deflation or inflation. Neither Martin's nor Burns's Fed (notably) opened to 'a wider participation in, or oversight of, monetary policy' (to Minsky). Nixon's corruption was ignored. Overstepping typical exclusions and exceptions of money's social relations was part of a chaotic interplay. Incredibly, Burns's Fed accommodated white union *and* bank power,

---

[58] Greider (1987: 335) citing Volcker on 'excesses'; Burns et al. (1979) on 'anguish'; on secrecy, Greider (1987: 345–6); and Pixley (2012: 124; 168) on how House Democrat Henry Gonzales (Chair Banking Committee) had a bill to impeach all Volcker's Fed members.

[59] A Fed aide on Burns 'ingratiating' himself to Carter, is cited in Greider (1987: 346), leaving Carter an ugly gift.

Vietnam War costs, CIA dirty work, then switched off, to unemployment (more than Volcker's) and stifled debate. Civil society started to unravel. What were the outcomes for the Fed?

A capitalist economy's survival is threatened, Minsky said, if it 'oscillates' between 'an imminent collapse of asset values and employment' and 'accelerating inflation and rampant speculation'.[60] Nixon-Burns did both. Democracy's so-called 'inflationary bias' came not from any democratic drive. White House orders and (as CREEP handmaiden) Burns's switches to win posterity's accolades with dear *and* cheap money, tried everything. In monetary histories, the ignored fact that from Nixon's legacy, *stagflation* became Democrat Carter's problem and a political opportunity for the Chicago monetarists, since stagflation settled in, partly care of Burns's unemployment in President Ford's years.

Greider shows from his interviews that Burns was criticised during Nixon's time behind Fed doors and Congress joined in, with the 1974 (recession) when Burns stopped the Fed's record taking. Perhaps this secrecy excuses Giannini's brief mention of Burns, apparently 'accused years later' of his 'overly complaisant' view to Nixon's re-election. But Giannini cited Burns's 1979's 'defence' thus: 'What is unique about our inflation is its stubborn persistence, not the behaviour of central bankers'. Naturally not! Giannini also cited Burns (and others) on indexation as a 'counsel of despair' to the 'discipline needed' for the *'permanent welfare* of our people' but nothing on Nixon's feeble price 'guidelines' compared to America's WWII controls, and in other countries during the 1970s–80s.[61]

---

[60] Nixon at least had a Secretary of Defence who stopped Nixon's late-night direction of a nuclear war. Mann (2013: 209) on 'oversight'; Minsky's (2008 [1986]: 6), point being no matter how unfair and inefficient, warding off such threats, including monetary threats, is vital to maintaining capitalism. Mann (2013: 209) fingers Nixon on fulfilling the alleged 'bias', and thanks to Craig Freedman (July 2016) for comments on Friedman's triumph during Carter's term, delivered by Burns's unwanted inflation following Burns's 1974 creation of mass jobless.

[61] My emphasis, given people's 'permanent welfare' was to be hardship (again) in Giannini (2011: 148), citing Burns et al. (1979: 21). Giannini (2011: 276) also cited Burns's *Reflections of an economic policy maker: 1969–1978.* See also Giannini on President

Nixon was divisive yet the economic expansionist, anything for his re-election, his war (and 'Red China' legacy, or whatever else). It gave Wall Street *and* wages huge boosts. The 'explosively speculative 1970s' started with the 'commercial paper fiasco of 1970', Martin's liquidity squeeze, and recession of 1969–70 after which, under Burns *no reform of banking took place.* This 'commercial paper' was off balance sheet and a new component to the money supply. CREEP in late 1971 with the Watergate burglary were perhaps due to Nixon's reviled war expansion to Cambodia. Asking for unpopular taxes for a hated war seemed too hard (not for LBJ who retired decently). Without substantial taxes and wage-price controls, Nixon-Burns endangered the value of the Fed's liabilities to function as money, in either government debt or private business debt. Few outsiders trusted the US dollar. During Nixon's landslide 1972 re-election, there was a 'strong' recovery (bubble) and Nixon suppressed its inflation with price and wage 'guidelines' after publicly despising JK Galbraith's 'extremist' scheme barely days before imposing them.[62]

Burns-Nixon Messy Fallout

Recovery was not for long, since a large growth in corporate investment after 1971 put upward 'pressure' on market interest rates. Abruptly, in early 1973 just when the Senate inquiry into Watergate began (urged with a 70-0 vote), Nixon's second Administration removed price controls (after Fed-provided 'easy money' for CREEP). Talk about counterproductive. It set up huge hoarding of corporate inventories; the United Steelworkers' 'Cost of Living Adjustment' (COLAs) also rose. A 'virulent inflation' stripped assets of their 'safe margin': Burns's Fed tightened (late 1973) and the REITS were

---

Gistard d'Estaing's sacking of a resistant Banque de France governor in 1974 (missing how the USA was the influence). Ignoring Greider, Galbraith and so on, Giannini also cited arch libertarian Ronald McKinnon opposed to indexation on whom, for trite recanting aka financial deregulation after 'faraway' crises, see McKinnon's *The Order of Economic Liberalization* (1991).

[62] 'Speculative' and 'fiasco' is in Minsky (2008 [1986]: 55–8; 103) and about the US dollar. Also see Galbraith's earlier comments; more classified records may turn up.

'walking bankrupts' by 1974. Bank failures set in and unemployment rose to 9.1 per cent by 1975. OPEC's embargo on oil in September 1973 (Yom Kippur War) saw a fourfold increase in its price.[63]

Contraction started exactly when Burns' Fed raised the T-bill rate, and ever further, to 12.9 per cent in July 1974; on monetarist accounts because the Fed must stop monetising the budget deficits. To others that makes no sense of the Fed's behaviour between mid-1974 (just before Nixon resigned) – to early 1975. For a start, a deficit has a surplus elsewhere (in corporations). Second, the M1 ratio to M3 (bank money) had already dropped (Figure 5.2 on similar ratios). Explanations less orthodox suggest the Fed kept unemployment high to compel workers to give up their wage gains or COLAs, suffer hardships of the oil and food price rises, and, once wages were lower to reduce the Administration's transfer payments. Minsky shows these exploded to 'nearly 200 per cent' only then, so saving a depression. Meantime New York and other states nearly shut down in bankruptcy.[64]

Burns listed the weaknesses in 1974's banking and finance, although these had emerged earlier. Instead of seeing financial instability as inherent in a capitalist economy, Burns argued for regulators to be more 'zealous' and better organised (the Fed having avoided that). Also, foreign exchange transactions (exploding in 1973) exposed large banks, Burns said. That was Nixon's dollar float.

A final point to these forgotten details is electorates' assessments of the Vietnam War included revulsion to state lies – the South Vietnamese alleged invitation; Johnson's and Nixon's secret

---

[63] On price controls and COLAs see Dickens (1997: 88); and, further on the Burns hike, a big data set is in Schwartz (2000). See Minsky (2008 [1986]: 31) again, on REITs.

[64] Minsky discussed bank failures, the largest since the 1930s (2008 [1986]: 59); also, Minsky (2008 [1986]: 205) on Nixon price controls and on REITS see earlier. Compare with accounts like Dickens (1997: 86–7) and Mann (2013), since Minsky was a FE, pro-union, yet anti-transfer guy; he exaggerated transfers in his own data of 146 per cent (2008 [1986]: 27–8) although he admitted they saved the US from two depressions at that time (adding Volcker's of 1980–2), and he neglects the weak US state welfare compared to most OECD (less Japan); also see Wheen (2009: 98–117). Of note, NYC's collapse was Trump's real estate chance. Volcker's 1980–1982 recessions are in Greider (1987: 344; 346).

war expansions. The loss of America's reputation and decline of trust in the democracies grows.[65] Experienced Republican Nixon, paranoid about so much, preferred dirty tricks at home and abroad, and pressure on Burns. Having promised to end the war in the 1968 election, Nixon also foiled outgoing LBJ's Paris *peace efforts*. F. D. Roosevelt, as Sisela Bok recounts, possibly told a 'white lie' up to Pearl Harbour. She assesses Nixon's lies differently: the Watergate burglary was a petty tit for tat for the 'disloyalty' of Daniel Ellsberg's 1971 leaking of the Pentagon Papers. Was Nixon a pathfinder to a 'post-fact' world, or a continuation?[66]

Monetarists and libertarians loathed Nixon's price guidelines because democratic consensus was an outrage. The oligopolies kept passing on wage rises to prices, to keep production strike-free; to secure more profits. No patriotism there! Nixon's resignation in 1974 was at Wall Street's crash. This clever if inconsistent President, who lacked confidence; indulged his conspiracy fears and was obsessed with electoral success, changed the US Administration. The Fed moved to greater 'independence' (internal dissonance and grim rates) out of the disastrous Nixon presidency. Misinformation became widespread. Posterity does not give the due emphasis to Burns's Fed, for neglecting controls on banks and their new securitising, of the monetary and historical professionals like Minsky or Greider. My 2001 interviews of BoE officials only found bland remarks about how manipulation of central banks was a fault of 'left and right' governments, naming Nixon's. Surely his was the large-scale example, since all the former postwar presidents accepted the Fed's discretion.[67]

---

[65] Burns cited Minsky (2008 [1986]: 57–8). Nixon's continuation of the Vietnam War (a civil war) helped to fan impatience of democracies that were less inclined to indulge US war spending.

[66] Detail (Kaiser 2016) is on *Nixon's illegal engineering*, allegedly with Kissinger, against a beaten LBJ's near-peace treaty with North Vietnam in Paris, and shows Nixon was determined to win against Hubert Humphrey in 1968 at any cost. It is argued that LBJ called it treasonous. Also see Bok (1978) on this example.

[67] Giannini (2011: 148–50) kept repeating critics of price guidelines with approval. In contrast, Nixon's tapes, vindicating so many suspicions were assiduously ignored in Burns et al. (1979). Minsky, see earlier on the REIT run and 1974 crash. Pixley interviews

No Determinist End to Bretton Woods

The unintended consequences during Nixon's watch mounted up. Well before Nixon resigned to avoid impeachment, much had gone wrong with the jaded, undermined Bretton Woods deals and institutions of 1944. Its original flaws, in sum, included how the US alone could break the rules (capital mobility), which gave Wall Street a huge start. America's superior position post 1945 – the enlarged US industrial might and vast surpluses in trade and gold (1944) – dwindled once former debtors were able to compete. American orthodoxy sees only US strength. As Schwartz argues, 'Bretton Woods' future ultimately rested on US perceptions of its national interests', ones that gave little acknowledgement that America had no closed economy or capital controls. By 1970 'Eurocurrency deposits amounted to five times US gold reserves'.[68]

In August 1971 Nixon abolished the arrangement. The prevailing reasons for the breakdown are US balance of trade factors, which switched against America, democracy and US workers' wage claims; rarely Nixon's active promotion of wage rises and Wall Street's rise, also of Tokyo and the City. The awkward evidence of banking and Eurodollar markets, however glaring, is often wished away. Wall Street took over. The first two large US bank crises up to 1970 showed not only Goodhart's law was well into operation – evasion of regulations, but also banking's 'near money' profit seeking regardless of rules.[69]

---

cited (2004) Budd, Graham Ingham, John Flemming, BoE. Right-wing Menzies is another cunning inflationist contender in Australia, see Chapter 4. Governor Coombs's struggle, (perhaps) too overwhelmed to activate the CBAs' independence remit, didn't occur with Burns's Fed, rather the reverse.

[68] In Schwartz (2000: 198; 205) on US national interests and on 1970; cf. Amato and Fantacci (2012: 154–5) on a similar collapse of gold with the Fed's 1928 restrictive rate, to single out CB tricks (2012: 167), not the warring camps including labour but their main project, the 'market' of settling and destroying debts to make peace. As they say, we do not have 'peace'.

[69] In Goodhart's chartalist view (e.g. 2003a) CBs can focus on a definition of money that is promptly evaded; Minsky or Kaufman emphasize that 'good times' normally breed 'explosive' balance sheet adventuring to respond to demand/booms, not just evasion of existing rules.

More determinist accounts include how the country that issues the reserve currency (sterling formerly, the US dollar since 1944) has an awkward problem, which radiates out to the world. Known as the Triffin Dilemma,[70] the hegemon central bank cannot achieve domestic goals and meet other countries' demand for (fixed) reserve currency at the same time. This did not apply to the BoE during sterling domination since Britain's domestic needs and its colonies' needs – for jobs and effective purchasing power – were *always subordinated* to maintaining the value of sterling. Electorates hardly existed. Any hegemon central bank either fails to provide 'sufficient' global liquidity if it stems domestic inflations; or it creates 'too much' untrustworthy liquidity internationally if it tries to stimulate domestic demand in tandem with Treasury. Moving beyond the Triffin point, new definitions of money, such as Eurodollars and disruptive assessments of the value of money in finance sectors are always destabilising.[71] Moreover, the US was *the laggard* in voting rights.

During 1970 when voting effectively included blacks and other impoverished minorities (at last), Nixon appointed Burns as Fed chair. Countries suspected that the US dollar's global value had been further diluted while Burns's monetary expansion went up. Was the US$ to be accepted into the future? Were market actors scared or seeking to profit from the uncertainty? US Eurodollars (IOUs of the USA) had exploded; those with the bargaining power deemed the dollar unsafe, collective faith in its liquidity broke down. What Nixon's dollar float 1971–73 meant was a kind of devaluation not permitted to the US under Bretton Woods. Yet, US industry needed help in the 1960s (obsolescence *versus* France, Italy and Germany), and

---

[70] Triffin, a Belgian economist of the 1950s–60s, only stressed the non-democratic nineteenth century world that trading countries always suffered under sterling: as in Chapters 1–3. On the nineteenth century UK 'nexus' see Ingham (1984, 2004) and UK elites' indifference to populations, cf. the USA.

[71] See also Chapter 4 and Eichengreen (2011: 47–50) on Triffin cf. Amato and Fantacci (2012: 153–4); Schwartz (2000: 198; 201–6). In some contrast (to Eichengreen especially) Orléan (2014: 123–4) discusses disruption.

labour disputes rose. Other countries could devalue: *How unfair* said Nixon's Secretary of the Treasury.[72]

While Nixon railed against challenges with an ill-judged closed economy view, the experience of other countries was the reverse. At that time, British economist Nikki Kaldor said of the growing US balance of payment deficit in 1971, that the Triffin problem was manageable while 'countries preferred the benefits of fast growth to the cost of part-financing the US deficit'. The US could also manage if it could maintain employment and real income increases, even as European and Japanese goods displaced American. But Kaldor said of America's path in 1971, 'if it continued long enough it would involve transforming a nation of creative producers into a community of *rentiers* increasingly living on others, seeking gratification in ever more useless consumption'. Others add that America's nuclear umbrella was also a political bargaining card. And as it came to pass, *rentiers* rarely invested in USA's 'creative' economic activity but property and more asset booms, care of bank money creation; Reagan with *unconditional* regressive tax cuts and Star Wars.[73]

John Connally, Treasury Secretary in 1971 said: 'It's our dollar, but it's your problem'. Apart from domestic US motives and imperial grandiosity, internationalising of other states developed, such as Britain's interest in Eurodollars. And, since US Treasury decides dollar policy, it gives instructions to the Fed. To Volcker then in Treasury, Nixon didn't understand the float: 'poor old Nixon', he said, just wanted the Fed and Treasury to 'make sure the best interests of the United States are taken care of', whether fixed or floating. Maybe this accounts for the schizophrenic hostility in monetarism to social democracy: Nixon's life-work was Congress and the White House (not the global US$). Conspiracies via spending (instrumentally)

---

[72] See Mann (2013: 209) and Schwartz (2000: 204–5) on faith in the US$.

[73] Kaldor in 1971 articles in *The Times*; are all cited in D'Arista (2009: 645); also note he compares a 'nation' with a mere 'community of rentiers'; see Bhaduri (2014) on the nuclear bargain; Helleiner and Kirshner (2009) and Helleiner (2010) on huge problems imagining another 'Bretton Woods'.

for a vastly expanded US electorate care of LBJ, spurred Nixon's parochialism.[74]

These more and less sociological monetary stories complicate the question about Bretton Woods' impact on central banking's effectiveness, roles and losses, and whether further factors were traumatic for the Fed. Burns in 1979 did not mention Nixon's name though he admitted the 'devaluations' in 1971 and 1973 were damaging. Everyone agrees the 1944 agreement consisted in aversion policies to the 1920–33 disasters. Postwar collective and manipulated beliefs against communism (Nixon's pet) and public optimism for democracy were crucial. Today's dominant accounts refuse to look at *money's sociality* or an informed public sphere that can criticise the jargon in less populist ways. With Nixon's *divide et emperor* populism, attacks on the players not the ball rose again. Although Bretton Woods aimed to prevent the hot money of Interwar years (making life easier for central banks), and to protect semi-closed economies for a benign FE order, Wall Street hot money rose postwar. Whatever the failures of Bretton Woods, it did diminish currency wars. Some assume social democratic processes created the inflationary dangers, the 'popular masses' that Giannini exaggerates, since needs for wellbeing and stability are hardly revolutionary. Bargaining power grew (over wages somewhat) but never over the instability of global and other local forces.[75]

The Impact of Nixon's Float and Onwards

Wall Street and the City conflicts grew after the 1971–3 float, as did banks' creation of more money (Figure 5.1). To a handful of central bankers (not to orthodoxy) the breakdown of Bretton Woods reduced their options because Wall Street banking took over the international monetary 'system'. The explosion of Forex transactions exposed Wall

---

[74] Connally is cited in Schwartz (2000: 197) also see Henwood (1998: 54); Volcker is cited in Greider (1987: 339).

[75] Blinder et al. (2001), the key central bankers of that later time, suggested the public likes economic stability, unlike a Wall Street on which their sights were mainly set. In contrast see Goldthorpe (1978).

Street's banks, Burns said. But to Jane D'Arista, the private sector thereupon *ran* global finance, not the public authorities; a point supported in Giannini who argued that states are weaker now, under financial shackles whereby the finance sector is 'free' to rule states by 'plebiscite'. Orléan insists this is *relative* to the bargaining power of different parties, also to the prevailing values, types of distribution and public deliberation involved. Workers asking for security infuriated a Wall Street now less shackled. The Nixon Administration's behaviour suggests that Keynes was correct – central banks should be slightly 'independent' of rabidly expansive states, as the RBA's Coombs attempted against another wily, pork barrel, right-wing government.[76] If CBs are overly independent, a social democratic state has weaker logical intelligent public potentials (the fate of those are seen in Bankers' Ramps). The downside of CB 'dependence' is a 'Nixon' pursuing a (warrior) nationalism that, unlikely his intention, gave Wall Street strength to undermine peaceful nation-building and semi-cooperative states, and former ways that CBs consolidated with treasuries. Later some governments preferred to lose public responsibility.

The next chapter delves further into central banks' reversion to pre-1930s policies out of a virulent project to counteract very different circumstances of democracy, FE and duties to people's wellbeing. The postwar era had many faults; the most dominant central bank, the Fed, has never been fully state-owned, although its successes with FDR's model contrasted well to the 1970s mess. By many twisted routes, central bankers' political *art* transposed into an alleged science (for public consumption). However, against the natural science's exhaustive non-predictive research on climate change, for example, money is a space of exception from peoples' livelihoods, the declared work of economic research. The art of central banking's former public

---

[76] See Amato and Fantacci (2012: 92–5); Chapters 3 and 4 on Ramps; Coombs's loss; and Pixley (2004) citing RBA Governor Fraser on Bretton Woods; and D'Arista (2009) on public control cf. Eichengreen's insistence there is a 'system'. Burns is cited in Minsky (2008 [1986]: 57); Giannini (2011), on a plebiscite but rarely on war finance – he died before the Italian original was published (in 2004); Orléan (2014: 124) on bargaining power.

service became detached but never *scientific*, the effects of which masked or (weirdly) individualised the money class disputes, capital-labour conflicts and state interests. We can understand impersonal-to-object relations, like the natural non-reflective weather, but no one can predict money's relations (impersonal-to-impersonal). That is the situation despite ceaseless efforts to *naturalise* capitalism. Central banks try to manage class conflicts and collective desires for liquidity (by verbal avoidance?): these desires can be as meagre as asking for one's only 'product' or 'property', the capacity to labour, to be sell-able. After the 1970s, few central banks were to care for full employ-ment, and the market in labour lost to equally fictitious commodities in money markets. (Land may be irreparably commodified.) Central banks became benumbed and *seriously divided*, due to financial sec-tor control and anti-democratic demands from the mighty forces of competitive warrior states. With Vietnam, the float, and so on, the US state and its Fed lost control over money. CBs adopted as new, appar-ently scientific techniques, (under pressure) the pathways to which we move to next.

6 The Great Inflation Scares of the Phillips Curve

Inflation of many kinds was a major concern of central banks during the postwar stability of tight labour markets and social democratic developments, with deflation quite rare. Suddenly in 1970, Burns's Fed stopped worrying about any inflations. Wall Street enjoyed a boom until Burns induced a long harsh recession in 1973–5. It was not a depression partly thanks to the new US transfer payments, but far more people were jobless and huge US cities bankrupt. With the 1971 dollar float, un-owned corporations were exposed to exchange rate dangers for the first time in decades, as were central banks and treasuries. Meantime, bank money expansion dropped from CB sights – exactly when disruptive asset inflation and securitising of loans grew. The funny thing was that an appearance of objectivity, under stable market values and prices post 1945, namely, of everyone's expectations of money as a peaceful means of exchange (for goods and services) and for payment of debts like taxes had, by 1970, come under enormous dispute. Debts dropped in value. That gave a weird boost to pre-1930s doctrines about *natural* prices, claims that resolutely ignored the oligopolies and banking. How the 1970s conflicts over money affected central banks is this chapter's challenge.[1]

ECONOMIC FAIRY TALES ABOUT INFLATION

'Inflation' became a singular cry. How was purchasing power affected? Benjamin Friedman argues that the American post-1973 'slowdown', as he calls it, is still a 'puzzle' since 'the OPEC 1973 recession' was stark, but oil price volatility had little shock-value later. Western

---

[1] See Minsky (2008 [1986]: 54–9) on the boom-bust 1973–5; Orléan (2014: 124–5) on disputes about value; see also Chapters 4 and 5 (the float's impact is explored further, below).

Europe and Japan experienced similar 1970s slowdowns, though perhaps from causes like the end of postwar rebuilding. The postwar US wage rises and moves to a 'more progressive society' reversed in consequence of this economic stagnation. *Ben Friedman argues the decline in wages put an end to democratic progress.* This is surely correct; many protested the loss of employment's security and of hope in governments and firms. New partisans declared citizens were ungovernable (ignoring corporations' price rises). Yet the era was not hyperinflation or even a 'dangerous' 20 per cent (for *rentiers*). Inflation fighters conceded, years later, that a 10 per cent CPI inflation is manageable (without sacking millions), and the 1970s did not reach 20 per cent inflation. Yet the 'inflation scare' became a public term to frighten pensioner-savers, to replace debt deflation, that far worse threat than inflation to authorities –and to capitalism.[2]

Full employment was lost, so too effective demand (later 'replaced' by consumer debt), not under deflation but a price-wage inflation that was manageable (unlike banking's *inflations*) with consensus proved in some countries – but not tried in the US. Central banker dissonance grew as economists like Milton Friedman tried to force defunct 'quantity' money ideas onto what was a battleground over control of the production of money. Monetarists said states were the sole producers of money, and 'too much' created inflation. It was a *congenial justification*, just as banks expanded money and *rentiers* complained of negative rates on unearned income. Banks' economic allies grabbed the opportunity and destroyed the old decent central bank as well.

---

[2] Effective demand, purchasing power and the multiplier are related. See Friedman (2005: 197); *no relative, Ben largely follows Milton*, save on democracy and the evils of stagnation! Cited in Kriesler et al. (2013: 59), Barro studied a hundred countries' CPI inflation experiences (in 1996), covering over thirty years. While consumer price indexes look at a 'basket of shop goods' they don't count bank money inflation (etc.): CPI is code for wage inflation, only for *price*-wage spirals though. Also see Forder (2014: 117) on Barro, a proponent of RatEx in the 1970s, at least did this U-turn.

The Vietnam War, bank money and asset inflation, the currency crisis, wage-price rises and OPEC all suggest M. Friedman's focus was untenable. Few accepted it for years. Hayek's *The Road to Serfdom* exaggerated a slight change in the balance of influence. He said elites were 'serfs', to a vicious 'Prince' who disrupted the individual 'order' of the market, such as LBJ's 'Great Society' and other monstrosities. Hayek wanted to abolish central banks: absurdly, Fed Chair Greenspan and BoE Governor King flirted with Hayek's 'denationalised money' ideas.[3] Yet like the 1930s–40s social democrat economists, these indecent anti-state money economists (soft on bank money) had a profound impact on *central bank aims and structures* and *the IMF; World Bank; BIS;* on their institutional relations to governments and banks. Unlike 1940s 'disinterested' public servants who were committed to FE, new-old guard policy-makers claimed 'neutrality'. They did not openly demand the abolition of FE yet anti-democratic indecencies took off. What was this extraordinary switch about?

I give less emphasis to a 'conspiracy' of economists and central bankers, that others propose about the 1970s onwards, or a 'revolving door' between lucrative bank jobs and central bank, treasury or academy jobs; or a neoliberal 'ideology'. These were long 'the done thing' of capitalism, unlike democracy, which was the new social-political movement to modify 400 years of economic bourgeois liberalism. Conspiracies and dystopias are partial explanations. As I see it, from economists in service to the state and citizens postwar, another economic type began to act as handmaiden to a rising financial sector aiming to control state money. Luck played a huge role: not claims to natural science status, rather, celebrity photo-ops and slogans blared at 'the masses'. The social sciences disappeared from policy debates since a narrow-eyed definition of the situation was lauded for its *rough accord with the effective players*, the banks and money

---

[3] See Pixley (2014) and Orléan (2014: 162) on Hayek (1945; 1982); Giannini (2011) also and on 'the masses'; Greenspan and King used long time-frames, cf. Offe (1980), on bridges between citizens and their governments, now gone; see below.

manager capitalists' complaints of excessive state controls and (shocking) wage demands; of *rentier* profits dwindling. States decreed *laissez faire* as well, hoping to globalise. The idea of central banking as a 'slow evolution' ignores these forces: deflation went to a bottom drawer until it shattered OECD central banks in 2007 and thereafter.

Global financiers' and states' aims to return to 1920s policies stumbled repeatedly. The context was wildly different, and citizens did not accept that FE be abolished. In central banks and treasuries, resistance held out (unlike in 1920) although opposition to FE grew in producer corporations too. I earlier explained this new battle as a finance utopia (dystopia if you wish) that drove a (wealthy) social movement, using the tactics of 'upstart' (poor) feminists or unionists. Economists only played chorus to political fights against the 'wets' and 'brown cardigans' in banking and governments, with battles against electorates said to be 'ungovernable'. Whining about losses in profits, wealth and status implied (rightly) that democracy was incompatible with (raw) capitalism. After all, 'new peasants' – rich employers and bank managers – were doomed to serfdom. Major players chanted to end the 'politics of envy'.[4]

Looking back, it was clear that economists in the wilderness (first fighting inside academia) would have no effect on civil society, states and CBs in 'freeing' banks from 'financial repression' (code for removing ethical and legal constraints), while using fallacies of personalising global banks and conglomerates into 'serfs'. Hayek was incredible. No, despite loathing 'Commie' welfare states, but not the expensive, snooping, war-mongering authoritarian states, rising orthodoxy had to capture 'policy relevance'. It thus fingered not

---

[4] See Chapter 2 on the savage deflation post-WWI. See Burns et al. (1979) citing Huntington on ungovernable masses and in Offe (1980); Wheen (2009) *Strange Days* in the US and UK 1970s, and Friedman (2005) cite the aggrieved white entitlement claims in Richard Hofstadter's work. A UK military coup was planned against PM Harold Wilson, by retired generals. An Australian constitutional coup in 1975 against the Labor government under Whitlam, which was like later attempts of the Republican Tea Party: Senate refused supply. I fleshed out in Pixley (2004) a totalitarian market dystopia that emotionally drove 'the revenge of the rentiers', a phrase of Smithin (1996).

'Nixon', but allegedly tired and misguided Keynesians in treasuries and CBs (of the 1950s). That banks were disrupters to money's value – in not lending, in capital strikes with huge money expansion or contraction (booms and busts) – was passed over. Contra Giannini or Bernanke, 'Stagflation' was no catastrophe like the Great Depression. Confusion helped those making asocial 'scientific' claims for the efficacy of monetary policy (alone) and damning of fiscal policy. It was a vast project to get states to impose that on hapless authorities and citizens.

This chapter examines central banks' internal policy changes away from thinking. But there's more to that. My self-selected central bankers never presumed that neutral expert scientific or technical predictions were possible. After all, one hardly agrees to talk on record to a sociologist about emotions of uncertainty – fears of odium, distrust, regrets, or anger about fanatic monetarists or the Mont Pèleron octopus – and defend the indecencies and cruelty expected of CBs. This absurd predictive approach towards human 'atoms' broke through in OECD countries that refused to build on practical knowledge, and jettisoned modest 'Keynesian' economics as unscientific.[5]

Unlike the natural sciences, social action is too complex, reflective or 'self-referential' to permit academic or CB scribblers to view a world in which they are unaffected. What happened during the 1970s was a political reversion called 'neutral' that denied breakthroughs in biology and physics (even) about research, results of which depend on the question put. Just when natural sciences admitted to 'social constructions' of reality, it became forbidden in central banks that formerly talked gaily of taking away punch bowls.[6]

Further, it was extraordinary how the battleground that the rising economists marked out excluded Wall Street type money

---

[5] See Chapter 7 on the 'project' (of ICBs and IT) and experts in Pixley (2004, 2012, 2016); Pixley et al. (2014). I think central bankers who ignored my request assumed that sociologist meant socialist-commie. I also only sought the retired, see my methods, Pixley (2004). Mont Pèleron comprised von Mises and Hayek notably; it spread everywhere. Primarily, (indecent) ersatz 'scientific laws' are used to quell (decent) dissent still.

[6] See Gould (2003) on natural science; cf. Friedman (1953) trying to evade this.

creation just as bank crises rose. Central banks – less the crucial figures in Schumpeter's analysis than banks (since like Keynes or RBA Coombs, he queried CB capacities) – became divorced from historical changes in banking and governments. To be superheroes to monetarists, we see. Although they are bankers to states and to banks, central banks then neglected the money creating capacities of banks or their need for restraint. They reverted to 'technical' nostrums that deposits create loans where the saver is king, despite bank balance sheets and CB balances showing loans create deposits. To those refusing monetarist economics – *anyone using logic* – it is bizarre. But how congenial these 'reactionary' policies were to 'the rich and powerful' Galbraith said.[7]

So entrenched these became that even central bankers like Bernanke seem convinced that the 'loanable funds' (of savers) drive investment and credit. Based on quantity or non-money substance theorems, policies dressed that most unpredictable social relation into a thing for probability measures. This money side of the story for central banks did not heed Schumpeter's outstanding *History of Economic Analysis*. The fence sitter who never relinquished his profound analysis of the manufacture of bank money was, in afterlife, hardly known; less demonised than his counterpart Keynes. Meantime, banks were turning away from 'creative destruction' (now lauded incorrectly) to the 'destruction without function' (a distasteful, thus ignored term) that Schumpeter identified in 1911. Schumpeter's optimism for a reunification of the social sciences took a posthumous U-turn.[8]

---

[7] See Tables 1.1 and 1.2, and the discussion there; a participant at the time, Galbraith (1981: 348) insisted on inequalities created by 'simplistic' monetary policies that never restrained the oligopolistic, only small business sector. M. Friedman etc. went back to 'competitive free markets' just when *corporate domination of the market* was entrenched.

[8] See Schumpeter (1954: 1101–25) – whose patron was Weber, died 1950 and Keynes in 1946 – and Bibow (2009), on the 'loanable funds' fallacy; and in Chapter 8 thus, according to Bernanke (2013b), Chinese savers who ramped up US banks' 'loanable funds' were culprits in America's 2007 crisis, not Wall Street.

THE PHILLIPS CURVE MYTH AND CENTRAL
BANK DISSONANCES

Central banks started to exclude (to the public) private bank balance sheet evidence or off-balance sheet activities. Schumpeter insisted balance statements are 'the skeletons ... stripped of all misleading ideologies'.[9] What happened to central bankers' expertise, part 'art', practical and theoretical, yet political and difficult mission to rise above narrow sectional demands and serve public interests? Private banks' drive to reinstate their control over money creation (whether understood as such or not) succeeded under the despised Burns; only made 'respectable' in 1979 with defunct *obscure* doctrines that to Minsky 'ruled out the existence of money and uncertainty'. Thus, a failure of thought.

The bank saver as capitalism's 'driver' implied banks were passive: the logic of bank money expansion disappeared.[10] That idea was frightening and, to financial elite common sense it seemed obvious the value of 'their' money (unearned income) declined because of full employment: ghastly social democracy. British elites complained of the inconveniences of full employment and dearth of obedient staff. But how could economists claim a neutral *science* for central bank policy, that state directives for CB remits focus on (wage) inflation in the singular, and mask sectional interests and desires? Central banks divided, they tried and failed with various nostrums to present in public. Congress slammed Fed bankers saying inflation was from 'too many' people in jobs. The Fed did destroy jobs! Yet Volcker's Fed opposed deregulation; the bank money collapse on Mexican speculation scared him, since Wall Street was no US domestic affair.

---

[9] Tables 1.1 and 1.2, and Schumpeter (1991: 100) on fiscal sociology and (1934 [1911]) on two types of 'destruction'.

[10] Minsky (2008 [1986]: 50). Debate on 'the bank saver' – see in the 'monetarism' section below. The 'saver' is in the pension funds and life insurance industry; their role in economic activity (shareholders alleged as 'owners') is hotly debated. Bibow (2015) argues these pension industries are reactive, and in the Eurozone crisis 2010 on, suffered from bank foolishness and EU austerity. Minsky and others said cf. that fund *managers* ruled: to me, both are correct, via stock value pressure on firms, not to pensioners' benefit.

US authorities assumed that 1970s America was a closed economy; but the icons of industry also left US shores.[11]

A desperately needed central bank obscurity, really alibi, could silence ghastly complaints. The actual alibi is in James Forder's careful, witty history of the Phillips Curve 'Myth'. His choice to study the 'Curve' is inspired and his method is to hold previous statements to account, rather than wasting time on every absurd claim.[12]

Forder's 'myth' research is highly pertinent to explaining central banking's reversion to centuries-old doctrine, akin to defending Ptolemy. This myth is still CB policy. Anyone who experienced the politics of the late 1970s remembers Milton Friedman's televised denouements with the slogan 'fight inflation first'. The Phillips Curve (as myth) was 'truth' Friedman said and 'free lunch'. Central bank dual mandates of full employment (FE) and price stability vanished, keeping only half the latter by excepting deflation. The battle was overtly Keynes's followers versus Friedman's, and both men were masters of persuasion, taking every opportunity, so one cannot demonise either on those grounds. The social battles that counted most, not in hindsight either, were mobile capital's triumph over workers' desire to live.[13]

To set the academic scene, submerged in macroeconomics there was quite a debate – in about 1955 – that worried about inflation, not from 'war finance' but FE, although CPI inflation was low (2 per cent). At the same time, many turned to econometrics.[14] Involved in

---

[11] Reference to 'too many' workers was an FOMC member, 1990s; Volcker was not reappointed under Reagan who installed Greenspan, the banks' cheerleader, see both in Pixley (2004) and Chapter 5.

[12] Forder (2014). Ironically, Keynesian or social democratic ideas remain economic policies in various twisted forms (Bibow 2009), but rarely include the social sciences now; monetarists do not listen to either.

[13] Copernicus reversed our view of the sun rising; as had 400 years of analyses of the *social* in money (Schumpeter 1954). On values and logic, the pair shared nil; see Freedman (2006: 90–1) *passim*, on how Friedman casually dropped his fads, U-turning from deflation to inflation. In Chapter 3, Keynes U-turned back to gold-sterling – perhaps patriotically in 1929–31.

[14] The 'bastardised' micro Keynesians compromised their defence against monetarists. The BBC's Commanding Heights quoted Friedman saying his first Mont Pèleron meeting was when Hayek/von Mises charged him with Keynesianism (Freedman 2006). Francis Wheen

both trends, A. W. H. Phillips, a New Zealand economist did a spot of doodling ('quick and dirty analysis') over a 'wet weekend' in 1958, he said. His result, 'the Phillips Curve', was wrong on every assumption and it was sloppy empirical work, published too hastily in a prestigious economic journal. It was ridiculed instantly and rejected by Phillips (even) soon after. Twenty years later it became the [in]famous 'inflationist fiction', far more politically successful than monetarism in destroying CB deflation concerns (if not internally).

It is a peculiar story, since it shows how economics and thence central banks revived harsh theory but through overturning Phillips's 1955 'curve' into an alleged brute fact. The idea that unemployment and inflation were negatively related could not be proven from Phillips on how low unemployment allegedly went hand in glove with some wage inflation from *1861 to 1957* using UK data. Although this data wrongly assumed labour structures were *unchanged* for a hundred years, Bill Phillips also never said there was a 'trade-off' between the two. And he died before distortions crept in.[15]

As the show-pony in a field of morose carthorses, Milton Friedman performed a miracle in its transformation (from mostly luck externally given), far more startling than his usual argument that Keynes had nothing 'new' to say. Forder goes back to the 'curve's' origins to demonstrate that Friedman's retrospective story of 1977, now taken as fact, is incorrect at every point and contradicts Friedman's earlier publications. Friedman often let his former ideas quietly die. He slid away from his Chicago teacher Henry Simons' proposal for 100 per cent bank deposits (too revealing), not because it (sadly) neglects *near money*, and from another teacher, Frank Knight, who refused economists the claim to make predictions. But on Phillips, Forder shows, Friedman's was flagrant distortion and went like this.[16]

in *Strange Days* recounts the London *Science* museum entrance hall had Bill Phillips' economic machine: stuff of cartoonists' delight, Bruce Petty the master.

[15] Forder (2014: 13; 24; 243) on Phillips' rainy weekend, his denial of a 'trade-off' and its results.

[16] 'Nothing new' is in Freedman (2006). Milton's switches are telling examples of Chicago 1970s rewriting crashes 1929–33 and the Great Depression – Henry Simons opposed bank

The date was crucial for Freidman's 1977 paper, with 'stagflation' marked, care of Fed Chair Burns, with his gift of electoral arsenic to President Carter (Democrat). Burns said in 1979 that after 'benign neglect' for thirty years, 'the international monetary system' in the 1970s 'has been in almost constant turmoil' (the float). Friedman stepped away way back from the Nixon-Burns stop-go. He alleged economists of the 1950s–60s were ignorant of adaptive 'expectations' in 'inflation'; they fell upon the 1958 Phillips curve and 'Keynesian' policy makers used it as a *choice* of inflation-unemployment combinations. Voters might prefer one or the other and in effect policy became inflationist. Friedman declared he and a colleague 'revolutionized' economic thought in triumphantly proving that expectations (of inflation) changed the 'curve' so much that there was no 'trade-off'. In response, Forder says each component should be dismissed and so should Friedman's overall implication that 1950s–60s economics was 'primitive' and practitioners 'slow-witted'. Friedman claimed falsely in 1977 that 'some of us were skeptical from the outset'; and, since the 'age-old confusion between absolute prices and relative prices gained a new lease on life', the Phillips curve filled 'a gap' in Keynes's theory. These 'economists busied themselves' seeking the 'right' 'trade-off' in work that Friedman claimed failed abysmally.[17]

Friedman's fiction is still received wisdom and became the indecent post-1980 consensus. That this fake history is tenacious as a technical truth of twenty-first century *central bank and treasury*

money. Freedman (2006: 95) cited Samuelson, on how 'Milton' let the 100 per cent idea die, though not to Martin Wolf with *FT* pieces in 2008. On Knight (1964 [1921]) also see Pixley (2013). Craig Freedman (a colleague tireless in his advice to me) is *the* historian of George Stigler's ideas; he interviewed Friedman, colleagues, opponents: Stigler was austere, 'morose' and refused the public stage; Forder (2014: 24) summarises Friedman.
[17] Burns wanted Carter to reappoint, not exclude him, in Chapter 5. Friedman cited in Forder (2014: 3); Forder's charges (2014: 1–3); Friedman (1977: 455) thanking his colleague E. Phelps, cited also Friedman (1968). But 'the 1968 Friedman' said the 'curve' is not always 'well defined' *yet* is in 'reasonable' accord with the 'experience of the economists who have explored empirical Phillips curves … and [they] have found that it helps to include the rate of change of the price level', since only sometimes do 'nominal wages and "real" wages move together', Friedman (1968: 9): all reversed in his 1977 paper; smuggling back his (1953) ancient 'natural rate' (seed corn etc.).

policy assumptions is the concern. More effectively (than Friedman of course), since bond vigilantes will destroy governments that defend employment (supposedly via the despised Phillips Curve), the aim to preserve bank profits put central banks in a straitjacket.[18]

Forder takes the story to 1979, the year when Thatcher took office in Britain and Carter appointed Paul Volcker Chair of the US Federal Reserve. Policy was to change drastically. Economists aping Friedman denounced the 'Keynesian approach' as a 'naïve faith in a simple, exploitable Phillips curve', so that a 'new' macroeconomics must now sort 'through the wreckage' of that Keynesian era. The 1950s approaches, to summarise allegations, were responsible for *promoting* inflation – of 2 per cent.[19]

Readers of my previous chapters know that this was all a sham. In the USA, Fed Chairs Eccles and Martin had major battles to restrain postwar rapid bank money expansion. In postwar Australia, RBA Governor Coombs's battles against *all types of inflation* were more widespread, successful – and specific: bank money inflation, asset and price inflation, the Korean War inflation, wage inflation, consumer credit inflation – and his hostility to (inflationary) unproductive, pork barrel right-wing government spending. Coombs had separate battles with the Treasury Secretary, who insisted on 'cheap money' to keep Treasury expenses down (on debt servicing). One anomaly was a combined Treasury-Cabinet strategy (cheap money/pork barrels: *so* Nixon), for which Menzies nearly lost Government in 1961. Treasury stubbornly refused Coombs's request to tighten under bank inflation, delaying to extremes, and refused RBA requests to loosen when inflation subsequently dropped dangerously. The public was outraged as the accompanying *credit squeeze* hit mortgagees, jobs and firms. Afterwards on a two-seat majority, Menzies began making concessions to intransigent

---

[18] Influence on CBs: Forder (2014: 4–5) says this is not a minor error of uncertainty. My worries about Keynes's *technical* truths (in Chapter 4) are nothing to Friedman's indecent lies.

[19] Forder (2014: 7), citing Lucas and Sargent, later 'famous', with no understanding that their denunciation was Milton's myth; Forder cites Meltzer likewise: Phillips allegedly 'filled a gap' in Keynesianism.

bankers, *maybe* to beg them to invest in job creating firms (than consumer credit). This Treasury/Menzies rapprochement was what RBA officials called 'be kind to banks'.

To Boris Schedvin in his RBA history, it was a pity that Coombs did not use the Act's provisions to make the dispute public and show Treasury's counterproductive interests and banks' inflation.[20] Eccles won against Truman in 1951. This public measure of independence of the Fed or RBA from banks and states was ending into secrecy and internal dissonance. Fed Chair Burns argued banks became unstoppable but did nothing, nay, fostered bank money growth for Nixon. Menzies nearly lost government, rightly held responsible to the electorate. Everywhere, a fragile ideal of democratic bridges between citizens and accountable states ended.[21]

Beforehand, governments however incompetent, opportunist, 'stop-go' or war-like, never supported or deployed the Phillips Curve. Indeed, Thorstein Veblen in 1904 argued business inflation *expectations*, their 'money illusions', were the causes of 'exuberance', and ensuing 'depression' was 'a malady of the businessman'. Ralph Hawtrey stressed 'confidence' or fear; Forder also describes the 'inflation expectation' positions of David Hume (back in 1752), and evidence that no major government ever 'promoted' inflation during the 1950s–60s. Mid-1970s governments (e.g. UK; NZ; USA, Canada, Australia) promoting *unemployment* made no reference to a 'Phillips curve' or its 'breakdown'. Inflations in plural remained, until the

---

[20] See Chapter 4. I doubt Menzies knew much. A treasury's 'ideal/logical' interests are low inflation to maintain tax's value; but cheap money to reduce state interest rates. Taxes also help. Between 1960–2, Australian CPI inflation went up to 4.1 per cent, down to 0.4, and unemployment rose from 2.4 per cent to 3.2 per cent, in Dyster and Meredith (2012: 199), and see Schedvin (1992: 323–4). In 1951, Australia had a bubble for its part in, and supplying Korean War US troops with agribusiness wool; Coombs solved it. For years, Menzies cravenly followed the US (war finance, lower taxes) and Britain in its Suez Canal adventure that Eisenhower stopped.

[21] Burns et al. (1979: 19–20) recounted the 1960s US banking in Eurodollar markets, and 'ingenious' structuring 'liability management', yet Burns did zero (in Chapter 5). In 1979, he wanted reductions in top taxes! My point about 'democratic bridges' is not to have elected CBs, but the reverse: fully responsible and accountable elected governments.

target of wages alone took over. On the inflationary Korean War and nuclear arsenals, monetarists were silent.[22]

The economists I cited on war finance warned against the myriad types of inflation from war borrowing and its bank expansion; the expanded full employment and goods shortages (urging war taxes; price-wage controls). No one wanted to repeat WWI debts in WWII, but elites loathed wartime controls. WWII's social economists – Butlin; Keynes; Galbraith; Polanyi and co – also railed at central banks, treasuries and financial sectors that claimed (pathetically) that any domestic spending in the 1920s (UK) or 1930s Depression (global) debt deflation, would bring hyperinflation the next moment. To 1930s authorities, the old whip of hunger would cure the global competition that mattered (save starvation). After this past shrank from memory, then, the Phillips 'myth' could mystify brutal conventions. And to push this, Friedman was no gloom merchant. Giannini claimed (without including wars) that 'expectations' became the 'moderate' solution for central banks to cure 'stagflation'; compared to truly defunct ideas of returning to gold, or Hayek's impolitic promotion of inequality, or *monetarism* he said. Let us see.[23]

Forder cites an early inconsistent debate on the 'curve', which had no instant impact at all. Further, it was rarely clear whether the 'curve' referred to excess aggregate demand inflation – for labour, goods and loans so obvious in war, that is, greater than supply

---

[22] Coombs lost monetary tools of controls of the commercial arm CBA (in Chapter 4). For that postwar era, to Butlin (1983), Australia was 'cheap money'/heavy controls on all inflations; also, see Veblen (1904: 237–8); Forder (2014: 146–7), on how Friedman (1977) assumed UK Labour PM Jim Callaghan to be admitting (in 1976) the Phillips Curve was a 'failure'. Forder suggests (2014: 152) that Callaghan instead agreed with Peter Jay (his son-in-law, speech-writer) on how the inflation-unemployment problem was due to 'aggressive trade unions' and 'cost-push' (union and corporate power) inflation. Phillips was ignored in Nixon or Heath, Ford, Wilson, Menzies or Carter administrations. Labour's Callaghan and Wilson dealt with balance of payment, currency speculations: *unemployment* was their policy, NZ worse. Fed chair Burns was attacked for 'aiding' Nixon (war, CREEP) to *The Economist* writer, Graham Ingham, cited in Pixley (2004); not to Giannini (2011).

[23] This is partly a summary of Chapters 2 to 4. Weber (1978) repeated the 'whip of hunger' often, not approvingly since he included a proto-Keynesian 'multiplier' discussion. See Giannini (2011: xxi–xxii) approval of Friedman. Also, Galbraith (1981) opposed Vietnam, disappointed with JFK and LBJ.

capacity – or 'market power' inflation, that is, without excessive over-all demand but with corporate and employee 'cost-push' inflation. Postwar Keynesians burrowing into this 'market power' type price-wage spiral inflation, far from ignoring this mild inflation, studied that, as did central banks. The postwar Bundesbank and Germany's consensual corporatism kept wages low with job *security*. Anglo-Saxons didn't look, while Germany (etc.) outpaced US industry.

Phillips 'Curves' cannot prove a determinist 'law of motion' between 'some' full employment (or unemployment) and 'some' price or wage inflation below excess 'aggregate' demand (e.g. excess war inflation). Monetarists also rejected 'market power' inflation in seg-mented markets (to meet, say, surgeons' pay demands, but female theatre nurses' cut-backs; or white not black workers).[24] Why not?

Not only did Friedman (MF) and co exaggerate old insights on expectations into their own amazing new findings. But also, the for-mer focus on bank money expansion and contraction, and on asset inflation, was lost up to this day. Monetarists finally won, but only via the 'myth' and ignoring the uncertainty of firms ever finding profit in new fixed investment. Earlier 1950s–60s economists knew all about 'gentle' price/wage inflation from high employment, when labour demand shifts from one sector to another, or they used a more menacing idea (Veblen's before) of corporate profits 'looking rosier' with price markup inflation (or J. S. Mill's on the 'delusions' of trad-ers in 1844). The myth overlooked these debates about causes and 'expectations'. To Coombs (RBA), Keynes had missed the divisive social issues: the last thing postwar Germany wanted. Then entered US economists with whom we are more familiar. In 1972 James Tobin (of Tobin tax fame) summarised these wage inflation discussions with extra ideas, like George Akerlof and Janet Yellen, later Chair of the

---

[24] Forder (2014: 22–4; 208–9). Also, Crotty (1999) argues Keynes was aware of wage demands from less than full employment, and supported 'effective demand' policies, whereas 'stimulus in aggregate' tends not to 'trickle down', because inflation in top salaries, houses, luxuries comes first, thence to 'brakes', but against low paid workers. Also (low paid, often 'feminine') service jobs are difficult to 'quantify', so authorities apply brakes in absence of 'productivity' measures of a well-taught pupil.

US Federal Reserve, who argued about pay cuts damaging worker 'morale'.[25]

Later, Yellen was known as a 'dove' on the Board to malevolent (manly) 'hawks', although when Fed Chair, like former Chairs, she used the Phillips Curve 'constraint'. The Fed had a dispute about it in October 2015, when two members of the Board of Governors contested Yellen's use of the non-'trade-off' Phillips Curve. Maybe they had not read Forder's book.[26]

Forder concludes that the myth need never have gone further (i.e. in the academy). Interpretations of the Phillips Curve were neither 'Keynesian' nor 'anti-Keynesian'. Yet by the mid-1970s, opponents of 'Keynesian' orthodoxy took to accusing 1950s–60s policy-makers of promoting inflation on the dubious basis of a refuted Phillips Curve trade-off, and Friedman's charges in 1977 were the most thoroughgoing. Forder upholds a cogent intellectual argument. But *ideas and logic* are not ultimately decisive; monetarists fuelled banking's deeper desires; Anglo-Saxon corporations wanted certainty in worker discipline, not uncertain new projects; embattled states agreed. Institutional cognitive and emotional dissonances grew in central banks, thus divided into 'hawks and doves' or rather, the indecent and decent.

Of those economists who had other explanations for, say, a price stability of 2 per cent inflation, that is, a reasonable, but not zero price stability, which is highly dangerous – deflationary – *the myth peddlers never said*, one could say that the postwar economists were no more 'inflationist' than the ECB and Mario Draghi's view in bleak 2013. 'It can hardly be that the story is to be summed up by saying that the weakness of the macroeconomics of the 1960s was that it was just as inflationist as the European Central Bank', says Forder.

---

[25] See Frank Knight's thesis (1964 [1921]): the unknowability of firms' profits; and see Veblen (1904: 137); so too, Forder cites Mill (in 2014: 83) on how a price rise 'persuades all dealers that they are growing rich'. On Yellen, Tobin, Akerlof, see Forder (2014: 76–7).

[26] Irwin (2015) *FT*, on Yellen, however, the two Fed members only said the Curve didn't work *now*! Yellen defended the FE mandate: forcefully at the GFC.

To take Forder's point on, in 2013 there was stagnation; wages had sunk, some but not all inflations (in plural) were low. Friedman falsified stated claims and economic theory. Europe with zero inflation drifted in and out of debt deflation; 2 per cent is a hope. Yet poor Bill Phillips curve is still dragged out in central banks.[27]

What is more, Friedman never thought inflation would increase in the 1970s. In 1968, he did not see inflation; instead he said, 'there is always a temporary trade-off between inflation and unemployment; there is no permanent trade-off' (a free lunch). As for MF's meaning of 'temporary', in the USA, 'a full adjustment [expectation] to the new rate of inflation ["a reversal"] takes about as long for employment as for interest rates, say, a couple of decades'. Decades! In 1973 Burns crippled US jobs in one year. For 'much more sizable' changes in the 'rate of inflation' in South America, MF said the process 'is greatly speeded up'. That depends on what speeds.[28]

Luck – that the political myth of the Phillips Curve, to dismiss Keynesians who 'still cling' to a crude trade-off Curve which Friedman himself did in 1968 – appeared suddenly. The 1970s had Nixon's float, high inflation/s *and* Fed-induced joblessness, OPEC, bank expansions and busts. The financial crisis and Fed-imposed recession of 1973–5 after speculative bubbles, built up unemployment. *Burns* left President Carter with the 'stagflation'. Friedman ignored financial instability: central bankers like Stanley Fischer, Meltzer – all those

---

[27] See Forder (2014: 200–2); Kalecki (1943) on bosses and 'discipline'; Draghi used old 'lubrication' arguments, but there were no price-wage spirals then: decent wages were dead and buried. Australia in 2016, had a 1.5 CPI inflation overall (0.5 if property inflation is subtracted). See later, Chapter 7 on the ECB and targets.

[28] cf. US Vietnam 'loose financing' was wrongly alleged to be 1968 by Burns et al. (1979: 9, 12). No forecast is in Friedman (1968: 11) cited in Forder (2014: 209). MF's 1968 paper was monetarist, but in his 1977 'Nobel', a Central Bank 'prize', the Phillips 'myth' lecture said little. In Friedman (1968: 8), Phillips is 'celebrated'; the Fed accused of 'first expanding the money supply ... unduly ... then, in early 1966, stepping on the brake too hard' until November 1967. MF preferred the US 1920s system without an 'erratic' Fed; he introduced 'the natural rate of unemployment' (on top of 'natural' interest rates; Friedman (1968: 8; 12). Also, Nixon's 1970 order to the CIA to 'make the economy scream' in Chile (in Chapter 5): Friedman colleagues 'advised', not MF, thanks to Craig Freedman about the latter.

hostile to 'Keynesian' policy – joined him in finding a 'rationale' for specifically linking unemployment and (wage) inflation (as in the Fed dispute of 2015 on Phillips, Fischer as Yellen's deputy).

Broader 'myth' research was spun out of the 'presumed existence' of the Phillips Curve – allegedly 'corrected' of a long-run 'tradeoff' – that Keynesians had *not* deployed. Rather, Friedman alleged a brief pain (to the jobless), with lovely gain (FE) *later*. Spin-offs, also very important for central bank policies, came from anti-democratic research on 'the *political* business cycle', then RatEx and optimal currency areas. Friedman in 1977 enthused about RatEx research for its predictive rationality (under 'risk' – although Friedman only talked of adaptive expectations).[29]

The 'natural rate' smuggled in with the Phillips Curve 'myth' implied that job creation ('unnatural') was from democratic states actively promoting 'inflation' using Phillips. Yet states/CBs had just *prevented inflation* post WWII. Friedman (1977) triumphed through distorting the 1950s, citing only Carter's 1978–9 'brute' experience, whereas Forder's work supports my position that central banks also use monetarists' fantasy counterfactuals (of MF and co) as history lessons 'about' the Depression, not just Friedman's blatant deceit. Market forces are 'natural' and, in a trivial truism, central banks found a 'non-accelerating inflation rate of unemployment', politically a tad milder than 'natural rate' of workers taking any price. Forder suggests the NAIRU moved away from Friedman's presumption that all unemployment was voluntary. MF implied democratic governments were 'unnatural': A slump cannot be from lack of demand for labour (at market prices of employers' decree). Workers 'voluntarily'

---

[29] Friedman (1977: 459) on 'cling'; Minsky (2008 [1986]: 50–1) on the 1973 crash, the Fed was using open markets then. To Forder (2014: 211): 'It is a peculiar consequence, but whereas Friedman and Phelps are believed to have killed off the idea of a long-run exploitable relationship, it is nearer to the truth to say they invented the idea of a short-run exploitable relationship.' Forder (2014: 194–5; 200–1; 210) on NAIRU; Orléan (2014: 196) on RatEx, the appalling 'markets are always correct' Rational Expectations, against Knight (1964 [1921]); see also Chapter 7.

decide to be jobless (also to Burns: forget WWI). Under NAIRU, central banks applied deflationary brakes even under by then deficient demand for now deskilled workers, if (wage-price) 'acceleration' is spotted, because the Curve myth refused all *other* causes of inflation than its unproven 'causal link' to employment. To James Forder, Friedman's 'historical failure on a grand scale' is like claiming that the attack on Pearl Harbour started the Vietnam War.[30]

True, but the *lucky chances* for monetarists of finding powerful coalitions of interests against FE and legal bank controls, indeed social democracy, was like the reflationists' luck in finally gaining audiences in the grim 1930s. Bankers' Ramps had scotched any expansionary policy of treasuries trying to create jobs and raise effective demand via minimum wage rises. That never applied before the US New Deal, and instead central banks pleaded for 'business confidence'. 1970s partisans negated a benign thirty years. Lost to this triumph were postwar specific controls over different types of inflation and a profound wariness of financial instability, to 'doves'. Stagnation *with* asset inflation set in, and central banks turned to 'expectations' (of financiers) and confidence management (under the NAIRU and Phillips 'curve' that remain).[31] The Hawk-Dove distinction became a new institutionalised central bank dissonance. Before 1933 no central banker supported full employment. FE supporters, after the 1970s scares, found CB life hard.

[30] See Chapter 3, also Forder (2006: 231) on NAIRU; Galbraith (1997). Burns et al. (1979) was conservative (like the 1977 OECD report cited below); he did not use 'a natural rate': voluntary joblessness was from 'Great Society' provision of food stamps; 'wholesome demands' in the 1960s–70s were also inflationary, in Burns et al. (1979: 13), saying 'welfare' removed work incentives. Thus, unlike Friedman in Forder (2014: 205) on Pearl Harbour, Burns took harsh 'cause-effect' positions, cf. Friedman was free lunch.

[31] In Friedman's 1977 lecture, he said his was no 'ideological' view; he wanted FE and price stability but only via his story of what 'brute' events 'told us'; Forder (2014: 192–3) stresses few Keynesians challenged Friedman on deflation. I add the 1930 Bankers' Ramps (see Chapter 3). Effective or aggregate demand policies were not 'lost' after MF; Reagan had a vulgar Keynesian warfare/tax cut/trickle down, not effective demand but *aggregate* demand-type reflation (Crotty 1999, 2012; Bhaduri 2014). Juggling reflation or a modest (quick) deflation is preferable; the problem for central banks (or fiscal policy) is picking the timing/length of either.

INFLATION IN THE 1960s TO 1970s

It was noted in Margaret Whitlam's obituaries that during Gough's tumultuous years of 1972–5 as Prime Minister of Australia, she did not ask but declared: 'What's all this hooha about inflation.' It was a good point: official historian of the RBA Boris Schedvin calmly recounted: The long 'successful' era of 'internal balance – the combination of low inflation and low unemployment – ended abruptly. Inflation surged to an annual rate of about 5 per cent in 1970 and remained stubbornly at or above this figure for more than a decade'. Australian unemployment reached 2.5 per cent in 1972, and grew far higher, Schedvin said, in 1983 to over 10 per cent; CPI inflation was 12.9 in 1973–4. Wages actually rose *more* in Menzies' 1960s of *laissez faire* upwards and censorship down.[32]

US and UK wages were feeble compared to other OECD countries. Yet US data might as well show hyperinflation to Bernanke who spoke of the Phillips Curve 'myth' as fact and 'savings create loans' fiction. We saw Bernanke excepted from his monetary 'eras' the heyday of full employment (FE) of over thirty years that raised living standards markedly, without anything but a modicum of 'slow' CPI inflation about 2 per cent. US employment rates were jobless 2–3 per cent of short 'frictional' unemployment; the US not with the stalwart FE-low inflation records of Sweden, Canada or others. Price inflation only started rising during late 1960s bubbles, Vietnam War, oil in 1973 to recession in 1974 when unemployment rose and stayed. Friedman took to globe-trotting with his 'message'.[33]

[32] M. Whitlam obit, *SMH* 17 March 2012. Schedvin (1992: 419) used other calculations to Dyster and Meredith's 6.8 per cent unemployment on RBA data in 1972–3 (2012: 199). Schedvin compares (1992: 419), the 1961 'peak' 2.5 per cent in unemployment when PM Menzies got a two-seat majority.

[33] McLean (2013) on Australian wages – then better than US or UK and see Bernanke (2013b) and Chapter 5. Coleman (2007), on Friedman's stopovers in Australia, shows he 'respected' Whitlam who refused to meet MF [!]; Friedman loathed PM Malcolm Fraser, mutually felt as with PM Bob Hawke. MF visited care of right wing think tanks and Mont Pèleron devotees. Schedvin (1992) listed MF as a RBA visitor; Kaldor and others; noting economic 'types' started to change. I bet.

To continue Forder's 'myth story' briefly, familiar names of the 1960s were dead set against inflation: J. K. Galbraith, somewhat a renegade (too 'tame' to OECD Marxist sociology, yet 'Leftie' to Friedman), argued in 1960 that 'to do nothing [on reducing inflation] was not a tolerable choice'. International reports summarised the entire postwar economic thinking as anti-inflationary – the OECD ones of 1977 and 1970 – back to the United Nations report of 1949, which stressed full employment enhanced the need for 'continuous and continuing action [of governments] to preserve price stability'.[34]

With the great 'scare' of the 1970s, an OECD report of 1977 that Forder cites argued 'controversially' (to monetarists and sociologists differently) that perhaps social conflict was at the heart of the 'inflation' problem. *Of course, it was a factor.* Forder is correct to mention it because monetarists attacked the thought that politics is intrinsic to central bank policy. Forder only mentions in passing the 1980 'change of regime' and the 'historical episode' of a 'change in power relations' towards banking.[35] As I see it, monetarism helped in breaking up postwar bridges to democratic legitimation of policy, but the effective forces to change central banks and states were capital/ investment strikes, bond traders and IMF views against lending, with a switch from internal to external (global) markets in currencies and financial assets. Also, governments.

OPEC and Oil Corporations

The OPEC cartel price rise is in Friedman but his 'natural rate' fiction took precedence. This collusion shocked the OECD countries; here were entire countries that dared to have ex-colonial 'aspirations' in fixing oil prices flagrantly. Monetarists disliked this causality of cartels. Needless to say, the political motives of oil prices were less

[34] Freedman (2006, 2007) on Friedman's 'Commie' charges; the rest is cited in Forder (2014: 108).

[35] Forder (2014: 109) cites these OECD reports, and social conflict, e.g. also in Forder (2006); cf. Butlin (1983) on 'political' monetary decisions; Forder (2006: 229) on regimes, and power also in (2006: 239).

remarked. The *pianissimo* on OPEC may also be due to the structure of oil ownership in the Middle East: namely Esso/Exxon, Royal Dutch Shell, BP. That is, a few 'American and European oil companies combined with governments of the oil-exporting nations to impose sudden and enormous price rises' and, later, reduced supplies truly at will. The IMF and monetarists played a different tune in *forte*.[36]

Perhaps a cunning PR stroke of the free lunch 'myth' was to exclude any inflation of wages and its implicit damning of full employment (neither admitted as such), the latter being the Fed's stern focus, not some Phillips Curve myth. Friedman ignored political attacks on unions. War finance sank from sight as the nuclear arms race rose with bank money. OPEC's shock was not an emphasis in the monetarist story.

Up to the 2007 Financial Crisis, only CPI inflation concerned central banks. Mobile capital took charge over, and scrutiny of, state money production and CBs between 1971 and 1980.

For central banks and everyday understandings, Forder notes that 'types' of inflation disappeared in the 1970s. Food shortages, mining stock or REIT bubbles had no place. Despite OPEC rises 1973–4 being partly 'excess demand' for oil, and part 'cost-push' market power inflation, US/UK price-wage 'guides' or income policies had allegedly failed. Australia's 'Accord' was never heeded.[37] The collapse of Bretton Woods in 1971 and *fortuitous* slowdown – to no one but Wall Street and monetarists in the mid 1970s; the convenient *high* political dramas – gave Friedman his chance out of the blue to invent his myth. The Phillips Curve became useful, then, since MF's efforts to 'rehabilitate' the 'quantity theory of money' since the 1950s had

---

[36] Friedman (1977: 464) on OPEC; cf. Dyster and Meredith (2012: 234) said OPEC was with OECD oil oligopolies.

[37] Forder on inflation types (2014: 194). US unions were weak cf. in most OECD countries; UK unions' real strength was marred from lacking an overall bargaining structure. Elsewhere was different: German corporatism or Australia with a judicial system of arbitration gave a central independent structure for income/price policies. But oligopolies were the least obliging (another ignored point). J.K. Galbraith promoted US income/price policies from his WWII successes; Australia's success was down under the PR radar of monetarists.

not fared well. Forder also argues Solow, Tobin and Samuelson didn't put a good case after 1977: by then the attack mob was in full force – employers, high finance, *versus* (unions, recession, oil) state costs (for poor people, not warfare). Friedman in 1968 linked the 'inflationist state' to FE and no one refuted that; by his 'myth' of 1977, econometricians gave up work on union/corporate power or income consensus that Friedman's side dismissed.[38]

Resistance to monetarism, which Forder criticized as too 'vituperative' (when lives were ruined), lost to events.[39] What moderate economists said beforehand of union pressure on wages under corporate price inflation was barely sociological (such as workers' not CEOs' 'money illusion') – also among Marxian economists like James O'Connor on *The Fiscal Crisis of the State*, less so Claus Offe.[40] The unconventional Galbraith in 1952 said a 'conspiracy' of concentrated industries and large unions pushed up wages and prices; this was like O'Connor's comparison of US oligopolies with the low-wage small business sector. US assembly line dominance lost in the 1960s to Germany, Italy and Japan, and finished by Volcker's shattering of domestic monopoly capital to more off-shore outfits.

The far-left demanded collapse of the 'System', an amorphous attack. They made no compromise to fend off conservatives who said, well yes, why do anything for 'the poor' if decent schools and jobs only 'reproduce capitalism'? Governments' social policy departments (urban planning, housing, health etc.) shrank under proudly named 'razor gangs' of Treasuries. Divide and rule set in among many groups: male WASP 'workers' against 'shirkers'; state debt

---

[38] See Chapter 5. Many argue monetarism per se failed; Forder (2014: 192–6) on Solow, and (2014: 194), on the few refutations; the press also reviled 'Keynesians'.

[39] Forder is excellent in scholarly debates with orthodoxy: he sees critics as intemperate (2006: 238); however to social policy and analyses other than 'economics', political and bank powers are crucial (tediously so), not 'vituperative' claims.

[40] Moderate economists (often doing econometrics) were hurt or infuriated about 'intransigent' unions (e.g. English miners), Forder agreed; labour market segmentation (etc.) were too sociological (as I noted on Giannini (2011), even Keynes cf. Coombs, see Chapter 4). Cf. to Marxists, a 'fiscal crisis' might bring the end of capitalism; but see Offe (1980) on a democratic legitimation 'crisis' and rise of economic 'experts'.

'inflationary' – always omitting war finance – while a reasoned public sphere declined.[41]

Challenges from Everyone

The only Trotskyite permanent revolution was in the boardroom. One has a sense of a switch in public beliefs or mutual delusions. Important then is to consider the accounts during that time. Robert Keohane and John Goldthorpe were rare 1970s sociological and political science exceptions in the USA and UK who explained (wage) inflation as *social conflict, above all*. Both countries had few egalitarian traditions, and their deferential workers finally rebelled: Why so? Surely one factor is how the enhanced democracy stopped at the factory gate. It was not a state 'fiscal crisis' given capitalist *rentier* screeching about low shares of profits and 'excessive' taxes. Few connected wars to war finance; instead to Vietnam conscript protests, hippies and feminists. The democracies rarely dared use conscription again (cannon fodder from reserve armies of labour suffices, given nuclear technology). Moderate economists hardly worried about the Phillips Curve; rather whether 'excess demand' or market power created specific inflation, and under what permutation. Sadly, few central bankers looked at bank inflationary expansion either.

Add to that how Milton Friedman rejected the 'union power' (weak in the USA) and corporate profits ideas, indeed arguing that union-led inflation would not 'continuously rise' (accelerate) even if 'high', since to a monetarist, 'acceleration' was states 'printing money' (for jobs!). Forder argues another idea that retail price rises might tempt banks to create 'extra purchasing power', was less pertinent to his thesis.[42] True, but hire purchase or credit instalments

---

[41] The Marxian literature of the 1970s–80s is too voluminous to recount (Forder 2014 cites O'Connor) but the implications of that to me and others at the time (see also Frankel (1979), who cites most of them) was that radical critiques of the 'capitalist *welfare* state' were a gift to the rising neo-conservatives. Looking back, the other gap in the Marxian literature was about money and its value.

[42] See Goldthorpe (1978); Keohane (1978); cf. Swedish or German corporatism linked somewhat to worker democracy, it was attractive in Australian unions etc. (Pixley 1993).

swelled into Credit Card securitised systems. This new bank money creation proved a profitable rising prop for sagging effective demand, yet more fragile than state demand management.

Governments even of labour (UK) turned against unions. Another chilling factor was the surprise of earlier (moderate) economists that unions might be 'aggressive' (or less 'responsible'). Evidence (contradicting MF) of 'Keynesian' fights against wage inflation, ignorance of living standard disparities, even indifference was plentiful. A battle against unions came just as banks demanded their freedom. Forder cites UK economists (e.g. Phelps Brown, Roy Harrod; J. R. Hicks) on certain 'social groups' having 'aspirations' to better incomes and the 'unreasonableness' of wage demands (not of academic salaries or, later, about consumer debt). English Keynesians recall 'intemperate' miners' wage demands of the 1970s. (I visited the mines: wages and conditions were dreadful.) Former heads of the Australian Council of Trade Unions still castigate their renegade unionists, but the ACTU helped arrange the consensus Accord. 'Deep down, Rowthorn [in 1977] had the same kinds of ideas' against wages, says Forder. By the 1980s, Cambridge economist Bob Rowthorn seemed slightly pleased that the British working class worked harder. Notably, Labour PM Callaghan aided by Peter Jay, a 'social market' journalist, set the British tone against 'aggressive' unions, preferring them 'rattling on bosses' doors'.[43]

Under Thatcher there were three million unemployed by 1983, City Hall told us from its black flag that taunted Parliament across the Thames. Economists' knowledge of comparative social public policy was scant: for example, in the 1970s the Yorkshire minefields were still cruel places, but Thatcher turned the police onto miners.

Citations in Forder (2014: 111–12) and see debate in the next pages. His citation on banks of Fritz Machlup of 1960 is useful for seeing how CBs used the 'Myth' – to neglect banks; Forder discusses monetarist and 'independent' central bank flaws in other work.

[43] Citations of Harrod to Jay in Forder (2014: 114–15), and on Callaghan; see also Wheen (2009). As well, a Keynesian English academic; Bill Kelty former ACTU leader also RBA Board member (both in 2012); and FE Keynesian Rowthorn in the 1980s, spoke similarly about the 1970s at conferences I attended.

The US assigned Blacks to any awful casual job. Yet 'full employment' economists charged that UK unions were too 'calculating'; only historians, sociologists, a handful of economists looked either at money's social injustice, or the US oligopolies raising prices to further profits.[44] It meant (Forder rightly says), there is no evidence that 1960s British or US economists promoted wage or any other inflation (Friedman's charge): far from it. The most democratic analysts saw that market power-induced inflation could be remedied by consensus led by governments, and not the *blunt* tool of interest rates, which can stop the economy. Treasuries could raise progressive taxes and CBs make short-term advances, rather than fund wars. FE is decent, cheaper to states, less inflationary than unemployment benefits rises, which do keep effective demand going somewhat, but reduce the value of taxes. Whereas the feat achieved by US Fed Chair Paul Volcker most dramatically in 1979 nearly *stopped America*, in 1983 the ALP incoming PM Bob Hawke gained consensus on a price-wage 'Accord' between unions and firms, with a greater social wage, of all sides debating it at special Parliamentary sittings. With Australia's central union Arbitration structure, wage inflation declined, but less employer price-fixing.[45] Geoff Harcourt played a role in formulating the union-corporation consensus; a federal-run Medicare ensued; also

[44] Australian Labor was attuned to bank money inflation like the RBA (Schedvin data 1992). Living in the UK 1973-9 was gloomy: ACTU unions were more aggressive on weaker grounds than the UK's, where schools and public playgrounds (etc.) were run down; students told me they had 'no hope' in 1975. I toured the Yorkshire minefields in 1973. Miners' wages were £17 a week for surface and £19 for face workers (ill health; injuries common). City Hall's Mayor 'Red' Ken Livingston ran the 'flag'. In Australia, a wave of 1970s Social Policy studies and a Royal Commission (and economist Chair) found 'pockets' of poverty among migrants, sole parents and Indigenous peoples; it was less the upper-class indifference and reciprocal mistrust of the quality UK research on 'deferential workers'. In the US, research was on poverty of American blacks, sole parents etc.; Friedman proposed a negative income tax, with no clue [!] of its inflationary effects. Nixon tried to introduce it, failing to hysterical white supremacist Congress members (Pixley 1993).

[45] Forder (2014: 138-9). By then the ABS used the term VLTU, 'very long-term unemployment', later dropped, but added under-employment while VLTU grew ever more (Pixley 1993). ALP Prime Minister Bob Hawke, the Accord architect was a former head of the ACTU (he mocked airline pilots' wage demands as a bunch of glorified bus drivers).

wages partly in superannuation (pension funds, half now subject to bank abuse).[46]

In debates on the 1970s' recession, critics said a 1977 OECD report was less 'scientific' than Friedman's. Its historical interest is that it shows the efforts needed to break the postwar 'social settlement' that Giannini argued was the major source of economic success until the 'masses' finally demanded 'too much'. Neither the determinist positions of Friedman's myths, nor these debates bother to compare different country efforts to resist. In a review in 1978, Robert Keohane accused the 1977 OECD Report of being anti-democratic. It relied not on 'economics per se but unexamined political or ideological assumptions' and urged democratic states impose 'discipline'.[47]

The OECD Report included plain Phillips Curves, non-economic debates on rising 'aspirations' and the wage-price spiral. 'Shocks' discussed were food and oil price 'explosions' and the end of the fixed exchange rate regime. The Report alleged policy 'errors' of 1970–2 in the US monetary expansion of Burns, not Nixon, nor related stock and asset booms to 1973. (Recall Friedman alleged the 'errors' were back in the 1950s–60s.) Most pertinently to us, the Report did stress global inflationary factors in the *1971 Bretton Woods collapse*, with rapid increases in official liquidity (mostly of foreign exchange reserves), and how domestic authorities failed to 'sterilize' them. A deeper-down 'laxity' according to economists writing the Report, relied on their explaining the causes for inflation in a sociological and political fashion (e.g. OPEC, the Vietnam War and social aspirations)

---

[46] Stopping the US is in Smithin (1996); Geoff Harcourt in personal discussion; 'deferred wages' was in compulsory Superannuation (split into decent union-run with former RBA Fraser as Chair; and private gouging); the Accord; praised in Bibow (2009: 169); in Australia, the 'tory' Fraser government never supported universal *progressively taxed* Medicare. But PM Fraser 1975–83 never followed Thatcher, NZ treasurer's 'Rogernomics', or Reagan, that 1996 neo-liberal PM John Howard later aped, with supply side, trickle down tax cuts, still extant. Schwartz (1998, 2005), sees the Hawke-Keating years as a triumph against bond vigilantes over a small rich country, to cease after. We saw views of Giannini (2011) in Chapter 5.

[47] As I said, Forder (2014) introduced this literature to me. See Keohane (1978: 109) who takes an American not UK view, cf. the OECD Report's indifference to social democracy was a shared effort. Burns et al. (1979) partly repeats the OECD Report.

that they did not bother to verify, Keohane charged. In a contrasting criticism of the 'ungovernable' carping, Claus Offe pointed to 'insecurities and structurally induced need for jobs' in increasingly urban, wage labour societies, poison to anti-democratic opinions.

Restrictive policies and recession in 1974–5 (stagnation), the OECD said, are curable via reducing 'inflationary expectations' and improving business 'lack of confidence' – both unanswerable, uncertain assumptions of social psychology to Keohane (or to Veblen). He charged the report with 'external' misuse of social sciences, whereas its 'economics' could explain properly only the large increases in the money supply after 1971, that is, from private banks – Wall Street.[48] At last, evidence such as in my Figures 5.1 and 5.2 are noted.

The *entry of Friedman's myth came right at this point* of the OECD Report and similar strident demands. Nothing like that, monetarists only insisted old Keynesians were lax, not 'democracy'. They closed eyes at the few attempts at falsification (in the 1960s) that the Phillips Curve might not exist, which apparently succeeded! No matter, the 'myth' was based in economics (so-called); Friedman's notion of 'accelerating inflation' due to inflationist Keynesian monetary policy and dumb politicians was cast as 'pure science' *thereafter*. Neither money conflicts nor the disastrous Nixon years, or domestic social-economic upheavals had a role in Friedman's sunny non-science.[49]

Yet, hardly much of a contrast to the monetarist 'free lunch' (notoriously long-term never-never), the OECD Report explicitly wanted global 'constraints' on democracies and insisted on the dire necessity of considerable unemployment.[50] Avoiding actual strife (as did Friedman) of states' own making, such as installing dictators

---

[48] Keohane (1978: 110–12) gives this summary; I've heard one had to reject the first MF premise, since he trapped people on trivial points; a kind of tabloid TV journalist. To me Offe (1980: 7) was more sociological; the OECD Report, cited Keohane (1978: 115).

[49] Forder (2014: 215) on the non-existent 'curve', and as discussed above.

[50] Keohane (1978: 117). Like Friedman, though, this 1977 OECD McCracken Report is called 'Towards Full Employment and Price Stability'. It stated there *could* be an outcry, to which Keohane agreed. But if radicals argued high employment-low inflation was not feasible – music to conservative ears – therefore capitalism should be scrapped, the outcries lost. See also ibid. p. 120, on the 'disciplinary state'.

in Iran to Chile, or Nixon's prolonging war and near impeachment (in 1974), the Report claimed the welfare state and public sector had grown 'disproportionately'. Price and income policies only diverted 'social and political institutions from their natural functions'. The 'natural' aspect was not defined, but the dubious transition to (unstated) normative imperatives insisted that democracies adjust to capitalist profit and its other 'needs'. What a PR disaster, when social democracy still prevailed, when everyone knew capitalism was not naturally given: Friedman was more cunning though lots were not fooled.[51]

Most revealing, the Report discussed how governments borrowed far more from the quickly growing global capital markets than before Nixon's Bretton Woods break. Keohane said borrowing grew mostly for the 1973–4 OPEC oil rises, but evidence is mixed given Nixon's war failures, bank bubbles, wage demands, and food stamps in the aftermath:

> Consequently, the limits of reserve-creation have become ill defined and fluid, being *set now by the private market's judgment of the credit-worthiness of individual countries* rather than by official multilateral evaluation of the needs of the system as a whole. In this sense, the private market has taken over functions and responsibilities that used to be thought more appropriate to national and international authorities, and *the international monetary system* has taken on some of the characteristics of a *domestic credit system without a central bank*.

Remarkable: not monetarist, this Report said central banks and treasuries lost important 'multilateral' possibilities of making assessments of global capital market money creation and its viability, democratic sovereignty over the monetary system having outsourced to private markets. Keohane stressed the Report's 'remedies' (now ubiquitous) required

---

[51] OECD 1977 cited in Keohane (1978: 118). Many still knew capitalism self-collapsed in the 1930s adjusting later with FDR, Keynesian ideas and others including central bankers!

not *laissez faire* but a 'disciplinary state', vigorous in promoting capitalism. It must be international, with some global 'Federal Reserve' counterpart supported by national sovereign authorities, since private money's 'interdependence' was a huge complication. This implied that bailouts must be offered. Central banks rarely stated these trends in public.[52]

Keohane had just completed work with Joseph Nye on President Carter's valiant but failed attempts to persuade Germany and Japan to reflate, so he was surprised that the Report implied a 'global Fed' was feasible. Keohane had hopes for then current sociological work of Goldthorpe, Fred Hirsch and Charles Maier, and harked back to Schumpeter's 1911 argument about how far economics could go before sociology and politics were needed. Economics, in his *Theory of Economic Development*, was quite narrow.[53]

So, what was so clever about the Phillips Curve 'myth'? The OECD Report was far too honest about global capital's breakout. Brutal prescriptions for overthrowing the postwar settlement proliferated, screeching that electorates (not banks) were 'ungovernable'. The inadvertent windfall was that Friedman and co never accepted sociological or political factors at all. They loathed the OECD Report, since MF ignored banks and went for neutral science as a huge improvement on Keynes's. But it was anti-democratic, secretly, and the old guard merely renewed. Monetarism (as though 'new') retrieved 'quantity of money' theories debunked for centuries. No wonder Friedman liked the Phillips Curve: monetarist doctrine held that when the 'quantity' of money changes, price movements occur and not vice versa. One could ignore 'social groups' and 'social types' of inflation. They were too collective. More urgent than Friedman and followers' claim to science, was

---

[52] The OECD 1977 quotation is cited in Keohane (1978: 121), my emphasis and on OPEC. See Chapter 5 on the Nixon stop-go.

[53] Keohane (1978: 124–7) noted that the USA, Germany and Japan might be wealthy, stable and vigorous enough to impose the appalling 'economic medicine' (1978: 123), but smaller countries like 'Britain, France and Italy' might find populations and unions baulking at medicine purely for increasing capital accumulation. He looked less in the Report on bank money's 'plebiscites' i.e., rise of the bond vigilantes.

their extreme anti-Communism, regardless of cost. Any economic upset to demote these suspiciously 'Commie' sounding Keynesians could have done. Carter and the Curve *myth* did very well; it was the 'only alternative'.[54] Central banks seriously divided.

Monetarists took great care to hector politicians, insisting governments were irrelevant to their *neutral science*. States after all, had to implement this. But it suited now despised politicians perfectly. Nixon disgraced the office of President (Burns, the Fed). His successor Gerald Ford gave speeches trying to manipulate inflation expectations: we must think it away! By 1974 Burns's Wall Street bubble burst, manufacturing departed, and cities were bombsites for riots.[55] Friedman was ready. The Phillips Curve myth masked their nagging about monetarism that, before the 'myth' triumph, convinced very few, whether central bankers (e.g. Volcker) or Schumpeter-Keynes type economists. The Fed's Arthur Burns agreed unemployment was voluntary – people luxuriated on US food stamps. What a clean conscience was promised.

Monetarism

At its simplest, the 'quantity of money' is only what economists call an identity: there is at any point in time a 'quantity' in use in one or more sectors. That says nothing than if government is in surplus, other sectors are in deficit, or vice versa. Over time, however, money varies in 'amount', or it expands and contracts. How and *why this happens* is the political-economic battlefield. And the measured 'quantity' depends on what 'type' of money is 'counted'. The US Fed used a 'quantity approach' in the 1920s and 1930s Schumpeter said, like the 1870s when this mere 'theorem' gained another 'lease of life' (and another, a hundred years on). One question is whether explaining

---

[54] See Freedman (2006) on how 'micro-foundations' were necessary. True believers' avid anti-Communism is linked to any whatever collectivism. Friedman went anywhere he was invited: thanks to many personal discussions, also on how US state welfare rises were less costly than the Vietnam War (and see Chapter 5).

[55] During the US Presidential primaries of 2015–16, the press dug up Trump's grab for Manhattan's 1974 'bomb sites' via generous NYC tax relief.

the value or the purchasing power of money is kept separate from other (economic analytic) uses. If not, it is 'the quantity theory' with the causal direction of change pointing 'rigidly' in one way. Another recurring problem, Schumpeter and other objectors showed, was how Walras (e.g.) used assumptions that rendered his theorem or equation 'of course true' but *'trivial and quite valueless'* to analysis.[56]

Under a 'different institutional set-up' than 1870 – the Fed of the 1920s was under a 'gold exchange standard' – it picked up the 'mechanical', already anachronistic quantity doctrine 'with a vengeance' more 'than is generally realized'.[57] The Fed assumed it could control or 'stabilize' business (in open-market operations). Money was just a commodity, a 'circulating medium' and 'banks are *normally* "loaned up"'. This meant banks extend loans right up to their legislative limit, a Fed theorem making 'the quantity of "money" (deposits) strictly dependent upon the action of "monetary authorities"'. But banks were (are) far more than 'loaned up', said Schumpeter.

Ignoring or denying *the deposited loan*, the 'quantity' argument stated when prices rise, that is caused by increases in 'money', whether from weak legislation or the Mint, or gold discoveries or state 'paper' money. Even with Irving Fisher's 1911 approach, price rises were not separate from the authorities' build-up; to Fisher,

---

[56] Schumpeter (1954: 1095): Understanding money hinges on *explaining money's shifting value*; describing a 'quantity' is easy. The social relations/conflicts between bankers and business debtors were vaguely represented in the Currency vs. Banking 'schools', which resolved to the former in the UK 1844 Bank Charter Act; and not to the US greenback dollar or bi-metallism debates of farmers versus 'cross of gold' Wall Street, until the 1913 Fed (banker to banks). Schumpeter defended Irving Fisher's work of 1911 as not as 'rigid' as many claimed (or *liked*, in Friedman 1968); and said Walras was 'a victim of the delusion' that his theorem (marginal utility; fixed and circulating capitals 'determined' by the interest rate) backed his currency reform ideas (1954: 1100). Forder (2014) shows Friedman's 'natural rate of unemployment ... would be ground out by the Walrasian system of general equilibrium equations', MF said in 1968. *'Ground out': people asked how?* Another e.g. of Friedman's tabloid journalism (I think). Schumpeter classified Pigou and Marshall as quantity theorists.

[57] Schumpeter (1954: 1100), my italics ibid.: (1101–2) (for next two paragraphs, his italics), including the 1940s, he cited Currie not seeing the 1920s quantity theory at the Fed; a mistake repeated, e.g. Currie, uncited in Friedman (1968), to whom it was just an 'oral tradition' that Freedman (2006) criticises.

'industrial or labour combinations' exerting 'pressure' was irrelevant. The theory also maintained a distinction between money and 'credit'. Although Schumpeter retained sympathy for Fisher, he agreed that the Fed avoided the 1920s–30s economists who 'rightly' said the 1920s *currency troubles are but the reflex of deeper things*. All in all, the rigid view gave 'money' in circulation 'an altogether unjustifiable role in economic therapy'. This was exhumed in the 1980s: by then banks had won, to silence how money is created through debt with legal obligations for clearing it.[58]

Another confusion was Keynes and postwar Keynesians. Keynes was influenced by the 'quantity of money theory' but mostly opposed it. He could be said to have reverted, in a sense, in *The General Theory*, although Schumpeter agreed the dividing line was often hard to draw in many cases. To emphasise the liquidity preferences of *rentiers* gave Keynes an out from attacking money creation, he thought.

Whatever, monetarists picked up this tired rigid quantity idea as perfect 'therapy'. Friedman talked about 'an oral tradition' rarely citing specific sources, with additions like (unknowable, nice) long-run and (harsh) short-run effects. If people knew the despised 1920s–30s Fed was 'monetarist', that could expose his great fib that the causes of 1970s inflation were 1950s 'Keynesian inflationist' authorities expanding state money, via 'wrongly' taking a Phillips Curve 'trade-off'. Regardless of banks and wars (!), the authorities of state money (not 'gold' anymore) could *easily* reduce its quantity held in central bank reserves for bank lending ('loaned-up banks' not the bank money creation it entailed). In other words, blame treasuries

---

[58] Fisher cited in Ingham (2004: 21) on union 'pressure'; Schumpeter (1954: 1105) on troubles, my emphasis. This quote was about those worried about WWI inflation and its awful 'cure' 1920. Schumpeter (1954: 1100–3) defended Fisher's 1911 work: he over-simplified a 'misleading form of his own thought ... for statistical work ... to serve a piece of social engineering'. Thus, if 'Velocity' of circulation and the volume of 'Trade' do not 'vary' so much in extreme 'Price' fluctuations (up or down), price is 'passive', then 'Money' in circulation is the only, or 'normally' the 'active' explaining variable ($M \rightarrow P$). Sometimes he admitted to other 'indirect influences', and thus *other* 'real' causes ($P \rightarrow M$), which 'shelved' the quantity theory. Fisher often looked at 'disequilibrium', and debates trying to explain not only inflation but deflation too (Fisher 1933), unlike MF on Phillips.

and central banks, said Friedman, as the source of inflation and not the conflicts in money, or bank demands for CB to accommodate them. Geoff Ingham argues the stability of money only represents some form of stability in the balance of power.[59]

Subsequently Peter Jay said of Thatcher that when monetarism was explained to her, it was like someone unfolding a map of the world to Genghis Khan. How appealing to the 'iron lady' or the 'Star Wars' movie actor US president was this (dubious) science? They needed slogans – the free lunch – to cover brutality. Fireside chats and false 'housewife budget' analogies were easier (cf. Table 1.1) than enduring outcries about massed police marching across Yorkshire moors to beat the miners. 'There Was No Alternative' to alleged science. This rhetoric was to avert public embarrassments of constant Bankers' Ramps against state welfare and FE; hedge funds betting against the UK pound; or via IMF bodies doing the job for bankers, and CIA-engineered coups in Latin America, Vietnam and on. Friedman did not need to know that UK Labour PM Harold Wilson, with a brilliant '12 Alphas' Oxford degree, feared the Soviet's spooks most; or retired UK generals were also plotting. Also, one cannot accuse the worst conspiracy theorists (like Wilson!) for perhaps being unaware that Stalin's destruction of the Kulaks was less about their 'bourgeois-peasant' class control, and more likely due to their rural power to keep food prices high. If Lenin debauched the currency to remove a real bourgeoisie, the final solution to food-price inflation was the gun and gulag. No, monetarism merely said stern expert parents would be in charge. A pitiful few put counter-arguments that became acceptable only with GFC hindsight.[60]

---

[59] Bank money also see Kaldor (1970: 10) below; on 'oral tradition', Freedman (2006), and Ingham (2004: 81).

[60] Friedman appeared on TV everywhere; I saw him silencing Joan Robinson over a trivial knot he'd tied; see Coleman (2007). PM Wilson's paranoia is in Wheen (2009); Alphas at Oxford are like firsts; two Alphas is good. Thanks to Sam Whimster alerting me to Thatcher's new biography (also Lloyd 2015). That cites how Gorbachev teased Thatcher for wanting nuclear war: 'flustered' at this charge, 'her expression hardened', an onlooker said. See Keynes (1920), on debauching; and Chapter 2.

What won *central bankers* over was the Phillips Curve Myth, whereas Friedman's monetarism had a short-lived time in actual monetary policy. In the 1970s, opposition saw 'the System' not 'money'; 'strange days' included the Baader-Meinhoff, IRA, and Weatherman terrorists; critical analysts saw labour market struggles; the hippy movement was more libertarian than monetarists. The 'System' would be overcome by refusal, and retreat to communes. Money had precious little mention; Keynesians were beaten – many hardly Keynesian just empiricists. The economic libertarian dystopia was brutal against political freedoms, say in social movements of the 1960s–70s. No, orthodoxy's entry-point to theory was not wishy-washy altruism, peace, social coordination or plurality, but universal self-interest in pin-striped suits or cashmere cardigans and pearls.[61]

A prominent UK critic of monetarism at the time was Kaldor at Cambridge University, with strengths and originality, often criticised for attacking the monetary approach of Keynes as much as Friedman's. Kaldor's attack on Keynes, for his weakness on endogenous money (that Bibow denies) resembled Schumpeter's 1954 *History*, which said there was a slide in Keynes's 1936 *General Theory* back to giving the 'saver' a role. To Schumpeter, Keynes's 1930 *Treatise* with the 'deposit-creating bank loan and its role in the financing of investment *without any previous saving up of the sums thus lent*, have practically disappeared' in the *General Theory* of 1936. In that and in 'Orthodox Keynesianism', the 'public's propensity to save' – aka rentiers' psychological 'liquidity preference' – became the 'central facts' of the money market.[62] It gave a re-entry to 'expectations and 'confidence' too.

---

[61] Wheen (2009); and Pixley (1993) on communes etc. Cardigans teamed with jolly skirts.
[62] Bibow (2009: 121; 95). The gossip is Schumpeter was jealous of JMK's success, loathed FDR (in Swedberg's jaw-dropping 'Introduction' to Schumpeter 1991; Freedman 2006). Keynes in Schumpeter (1954: 1113), his emphasis; and wonders if this was 'progress or retrogression'. It follows Schumpeter's section on quantity theories. He discusses Wicksell, Hawtrey and other aspects of Keynes; later (1954: 1110–17), on the bank 'creation' of deposits, and his treatment of 'real bills', as anachronistic, not 'evil' re Meltzer (2013); or 'mistaken' in Calomiris (2013); more like Mehrling (2000) see Chapter 1,

Kaldor's 1982 *The Scourge of Monetarism* was blindingly direct, so too his remarkable arguments in 1959 that the Phillips Curve was 'wrong and dangerous' (about inflation) because profits were excluded from explaining wages, and a Phillips type 'demand policy would prevent inflation only if it lowered profit'. This would damage growth since business demand for loans could drop off. That same 1959, at British Radcliffe Committee hearings, Kaldor pressed his point of linking mild inflation with spurring *economic growth*. With 'more panache but certainly less finesse' than others, Kaldor urged the Committee acknowledge the UK economy so lacked dynamism that it should be 'doping it with inflation'.

Apart from despising the Phillips Curve, Kaldor had few illusions about money: he was aware that inflation might prompt the well-off to capital flight, but under Bretton Woods in Britain, only minimal.[63]

In a 1970 lecture Kaldor gave to Lloyds Bank, there is no mistaking his dislike of the monetarist 'counter-revolution' already 'winning' against views of Wicksell, Myrdal, Kalecki, Keynes and later Cambridge scholars. The latter all couched economic management according to the key problems of inflationary *and* deflationary tendencies, over which they sought 'to regulate the economy'. But the monetarist doctrine, Kaldor charged, had been

> ... assiduously propagated from across the Atlantic by a growing
> band of enthusiasts, combining the fervour of early Christians
> with the suavity and selling power of a Madison Avenue
> executive ... And one hears of new stories of conversions almost
> every day, one old bastion of old fashioned Keynesian orthodoxy
> being captured after another: first, the Federal Reserve Bank of
> St. Louis, then another Federal Reserve Bank, then the research
> staff of the IMF, or at least the majority.

since banks formerly financed 'the needs of trade' but now less so; Schumpeter's demolition of the 'middleman' view of banks praised Keynes's *Treatise*.

[63] Kaldor with 'panache' and cited in Forder (2014: 16; 118) on 'Phillips' and capital flights or strikes.

Aside from his 'panache' or exaggeration (which applied to MF),
Kaldor argued that structural analysis of different sectors, that is, the
use of all the social sciences to understand money, was displaced in
Friedman, with a (then) wishy-washy monetarist brand in the UK,
and an 'extreme' US form. To wit, Friedman claimed there is 'a stable
demand for money' proven by regression analyses, of select data that
has no bearing on inter-relationships: thus, Friedman just said more
money to 'the population' comes as it were from helicopter drops.
(There are governments and there are lone individuals.) Kaldor asked
who are these 'people' – Rentiers; Wage or Income earners; Businesses –
and asked which way the causal relationship ran. The extreme gen-
eralisation in Friedman and his co-workers was a truism – money
to GNP correlates with 'money supply' but so does everything else
(wage-bill, investment, consumption, wealth 'etc.'). Kaldor continued
with English conventions (pre-feminist):

> Every schoolboy knows that cash in the hands of the public
> regularly shoots up at Christmas, goes down in January and
> shoots up again around the summer bank holiday. Nobody
> would suggest (not even Professor Friedman, I believe) that the
> increase in note circulation in December is the cause of the
> Christmas buying spree. But there is the question that is more
> relevant to the Friedman thesis: Could the 'authorities' prevent
> the buying spree by refusing to supply additional notes and coins
> in the Christmas season? ... But [if so] would it stop Christmas
> buying? There would be chaos for a few days, but soon all kinds
> of money substitutes would spring up: credit cards, promissory
> notes, etc., issued by firms or financial institutions which would
> circulate in the same way as bank notes. Any business with a
> high reputation – a well-known firm which is universally trusted –
> could issue such paper, and any one who could individually be
> 'trusted' would get things on 'credit'. People who can be 'trusted'
> are, of course, the same as those who have 'credit' – the original
> meaning of 'credit' was simply 'trust'. There would be a rush

> to join the Diners Club, and everyone who could be 'trusted' ...
> would still be able to buy as much as he desired.

Thus, the quantity theorem is legless. His point was not (logically) that central banks are powerless; it accepts that inflationary bank expansion can be created from say, government borrowing for war finance. We know that. Central banks can also raise interest rates to much damage. However, Kaldor's happy example of spending up for big holidays, shows that by creating other IOUs to include nearly all the population in forms of 'near money', he said, 'a complete surrogate money-system and payments-system would be established, which would exist side by side with "official money"'. To Forder, 'Kaldor was viciously critical' of the monetarists for reversing the causality of inflation, on grounds that their policy ignored how a central bank's narrow definition of money might induce banks to create 'near money' advances and increase the money supply. That they did.[64]

It is hard to understand why Kaldor's (or Galbraith's) lack of diplomacy was such a sin. Countries were treated dreadfully: in 1990 post-Soviet Russia, Friedman true believers applied 'shock therapy': the 'market' would sort out new capitalist prices; money was irrelevant. Instead, a huge industrial nation resorted to 'surrogate money' and barter between (say) oil and paint businesses, to appalling results. IMF shock therapy assumed away a 'Fed-like' capitalist CB and emergent capitalist banks, too fragile to create sufficient money endogenously to keep industrial and service sectors surviving. Political scientist David Woodruff showed that surrogate 'bad money' drove out *good money* (central bank HPM Roubles) as Gresham's 'law' argued.

Central Banks end Full Employment: The Real Purpose

Money is endogenously created inside banking, not to monetarists. Forder argued that apart from Friedman's monetary targets proving

---

[64] Kaldor (1970: 1–2; 3) on Wicksell to 'structural'; (1970: 6–7) on holidays to surrogate money; Forder (2006: 228) criticises his panache; I think it's clear *and* witty. See also Figures 5.1 and 5.1.

unworkable for CBs, 'the greatest failure of Friedman's theory' was that after Thatcher was elected in 1979 and 'when inflation was controlled, unemployment did not fall'. Britain's bank liberalisation also set off a property bubble in the Tory heartland. By the inflationary boom of 1990, unemployment was higher than the entire British postwar history. Forder says he cannot imagine a more 'categorical refutation' of Friedman's optimism – his free lunch. True, but few social democrats had believed this. The Bundesbank became the harsh central bank model with technical expertise claimed for reversing the high employment, low inflation era of some democratic accountability of the state to its citizens. The new external context of private banking's take-off switched central banks to trying to please markets. This market 'plebiscite' (to Giannini), implied wage reductions via more unemployment. Monetarists promoted bank deregulation with an unworkable 'theorem'.[65]

Kaldor also criticised the monetary history of Friedman and Schwartz and their bemoaning NY Fed Ben Strong's 1928 demise. Kaldor implicitly supported Schumpeter's contention that the Fed used a 'quantity theory', that is, a 'rigid' monetarism in the 1920s and early 1930s. Friedman and others turned this round into a non-provable counterfactual to argue for conservatives (Strong or Montagu Norman replicas) to run the Fed in 1980. Kaldor's view was harsh, in hindsight with good reason:

> I do not believe that the Great Depression ... *would have been saved* but for Governor Benjamin Strong's untimely retirement and death in 1928. Indeed, ... Governor Strong's policies in the years prior to 1928 [may have] ... contributed to the financial crisis following the crash in 1929. For he kept the volume of reserves – the supply of 'high-powered money' – rigidly stable in the years 1925–9. This occurred at a time when the U.S. *economy*

---

[65] Woodruff (1999, 2014) on Russia. Endogenous money was accepted in a Bank of England paper, McLeay et al. (2014). Forder (2006: 230) on how the option to 'end FE' after Friedman's 1970s propaganda, met huge opposition. Giannini (2011) on the Bundesbank, which was harsher on Germany than Volcker's Fed on the USA at that time and see Chapter 7.

and the national income was expanding, with the result that the banking system became increasingly precarious: the ratio of bank deposits to bank reserves, and the ratio of deposits to currency in the hands of the public, rose well above the customary levels established prior to the first world war, and to very much higher levels than these ratios ... attained subsequently.[66]

Shortages in nineteenth century British colonies had similar effects (Ratio HPM: bank money, Figure 5.2) as did 'rigid' roubles to surrogate currencies in Russia 1990. Fed Chair Volcker's 'dear money' *stopped American industry.* Later, unconstrained 'cheap credit' grew. A refutation of monetarists when UK and US authorities attempted to apply monetarist policy in the late 1970s to mid-1980s was that the 'theory' of freezing the monetary base (state money: HPM) could not be operationalised. This followed Kaldor's points on holidays. Central banks were meant to 'target' M1 or M2 'base money' according, Friedman said, to 'natural rhythms' of the 'real economy'. That obfuscation left out bank money (i.e. credit is not distinct from money if it is 'accepted') and near money so easy to create in IOUs of globalising business networks. Few looked at new credit instruments that evaded central banks. CBs found they had M4 to even M10 and abandoned the policy. Giannini argued the policy had 'no significant application'. The RBA's caution to bank expansion helped in Australia: more decisively, PMs Malcolm Fraser and Bob Hawke opposed monetarism. A Fed FOMC member of 1980 told Pixley that Volcker had not 'really' applied monetarism. The Fed, like the Bundesbank, induced crippling Recessions nevertheless, and the USA did not give consensus a try.[67]

---

[66] Kaldor (1970: 14), my emphases; I removed most *double negatives.* Compare with Chapter 3 on Strong. Giannini (2011: 152) – also, to Friedman's defence of Ben Strong or Montagu Norman, Giannini cites Rogoff's similar line, proposing conservative central bankers 'averse' to inflation, as if McChesney Martin et al. were not.

[67] Smithin (1996) on 'stopped' the USA; Tily (2015) on 'cheap credit'; Ingham (2004: 8) on the BoE with M1–M10: what 'counted'? Giannini (2011: 151) and FOMC member Lyle Gramley (interview cited Pixley 2004): both seem to prevaricate, Gramley, convinced inflation must be slashed, said Volcker was reacting to monetarist publicity; which implied Friedman and co were screeching at the Fed, cf. Australia had a wage-price Accord.

Central bank focus on bank and financial fragility (even Burns, Fed Chair, noted it in 1974 and 1979) was lost from view, since monetarists claimed the Fed was 'all-powerful' in controlling 'the money supply' and via that, price stability, jobs and income. But stability leads to instability. Burns said Fed rates to control banks were less 'onerous' under inflation and the 'explosively speculative' 1970s. What?[68] *He and Volcker then created mass joblessness.* The monetarist failure ignored central banking weakness at controlling bank novelties. So, no 'textbook monetarist' direct and 'neutral' effect on monetary aggregates occurred, rather, full employment ended, banking took over. To Sheila Dow:

> The banks innovated extensively to diversify from traditional banking activities in order to minimize the risk posed by the financial instability of the [1970s] period. The nature of the impact of monetary actions depends on the structure to which they are applied. But that impact in turn spurs on innovations, which change the structure [in banking].

Friedman's therapies did not die, though they failed, because the Phillips Curve 'myth' lived (a simplistic job ratio to CPI). Banking gave up normative-ethical rules over financial practices and tricks while, as wages and jobs plummeted, private bank money swept to heights never seen (Figures 5.1 and 5.2).

If I may be as vituperative as Kaldor, the most obtusely consistent was Hayek. His dour idea of money had none of the shared collective fun of holiday demand for good old trustworthy money. Public faith in money was 'heretical', an outrage to Hayek's individualism

---

[68] Fragility to Minsky (2008 [1986]: 54–5) and citing Burns also (1986: 57), for failing to see that 'financial stability is destabilizing'. Also, reverse logic is in Fed Chair Burns et al. (1979: 20). Minsky used the REITs and insolvency of the Franklin Bank as 1974 examples. Minsky (2008 [1986]) *never* monetarist, swallowed Friedman's 'curve' *myth*, though argued state welfare transfers were inflationary (and saved recessions) and *not* full employment (with union consensus).

way beyond Friedman's (or Jacques Rueff in France on ICBs). Hayek thought far better to abolish money and central banks; instead permit private agents to issue 'rival fiduciary instruments', amongst which 'the market' would decide the best. As Orléan says, Hayek's is 'a counterfactual model' of a utopia of rational market individuals. Well said: Efficiency 'decrees' that supply and demand laws and competition *would be better* than untrustworthy state money, to 'free society from the tyranny of a disfiguring monstrosity' of a monetary unit subject to collective disagreement, 'to agonistics'. That the social 'authority' of money won from major disputes of those with more social bargaining power *must be masked via neutralizing*. Hayek sided here with monetarists who understood money the least. In evidence *against* such counterfactuals, the de-national 'free banking' that issued the notes in nineteenth century Australia had disastrous outcomes, except for banks. In 1910–11 Treasury took over note issues and a state-owned Commonwealth Bank was founded. The People's Bank as central bank is a Hayekian nightmare.[69]

Hayek's authoritarian libertarianism was too Stalinist to be copied to the letter. Central banks turned to 'inflation expectations' and how to control inflation 'credibly' for fickle banks; it was a 'moderate' solution to inflation (Giannini said, compared to Hayek's extremism). Beliefs in money's neutrality became vital 'in shaping today's policymaking environment' of central banks ignoring bank money. Friedman's 'natural rate of unemployment' directed against Keynes and 'Keynesians' is a strong tenet in many divided, central banks. The absurd 'natural rate of interest', based on a model that pretended we lived/survived in a corn seed economy,[70] with historical social relations assumed away, worked similarly to Friedman on unemployment. He dismissed central bank experiences of the 1930s that 'the unmanaged

[69] In Dow (2006: 43); see Pixley (2014) on Hayek's other work too, banks; Orléan (2014: 162–3) deals with Hayek and Rueff; bargaining power see Weber (1978, 1981 [1927]), 'free banking', 'People's Bank': Chapters 1 and 3.

[70] 'Credible' policy: Ingham (2004: 29–31); 'moderate' cf. Hayek or Friedman, to Giannini (2011: 150–1); Forder (2006: 224), on neutral money beliefs. Seed corn [!] and 'natural' interest is explored in Hayes (2013); 'natural' assumes (away) wage labour.

capitalist system might deliver permanently high unemployment'. Freeing capitalism from financial repression went hand in glove with unemployment. Statistics now conform to Friedman's claim. Across the world, formal jobless rates exclude people who worked for pay for *one hour* in the 'reference week'. It's a job!

The *results for central banks* of monetarism and RatEx, and impact for democracy and global-domestic poverty, started in the 1970s, creating crisis by crisis to the 2007 great 'North Atlantic' crash – GFC. The failure of money supply *targets*, subverted with the move to global markets for financial assets (Mexican crisis) and wild currency volatility, saw a huge rise in joblessness. By the early 1980s, non-financial US corporations moved to low wage countries and taxes declined. Amidst these costs, central banks had larger difficulties, with greater global private banking control and rise of shadow banks. In 1981, the Banca d'Italia Governor sternly called for 'a return to a stable currency'. Even if central bank focus already switched substantively, formally in the Fed or Australia with dual remits – to dismissing (quietly) full employment, how could they then achieve price stability?[71] They dismissed *non*-Anglo-American bubbles and crashes; these were 'crony' capitalists faraway, so unlike the City or Wall Street.

By the early 1980s 'rational expectations' (RatEx) was a further gift to demands from banks and money markets. For central banks to prove their 'reputation' to allegedly all-seeing 'markets', they must display 'a lack of concern for unemployment' through a firm and 'unwavering pursuit of price stability'. If policy-makers believed this was 'essential to economic wellbeing' it could legitimate 'an attitude of great distain to the plight of the unemployed'.[72] The Fed and BoE

---

[71] Forder (2006: 225) gives a useful summary, and citing Friedman on jobless (and counting it, in Pixley 1993); see Giannini (2011: 155) tables and (2011: 72) on central banks of 1980–9 with dual or sole or no remits and cites Italy's Governor (2011: 154) saying, 'independence' from monetising the government deficit 'might' stem currency instability. Why would it? – enter bond vigilantes and US war finance.

[72] The 'North Atlantic' crash was an RBA term, given proximity to the 1997 SE Asian crash. Citing Barro and Gordon on CBs to be 'unwavering', see Forder (2006: 234) and his comment on plight; to Giannini (2011: 152): RatEx only aped a 1974 'model'.

had *already raised unemployment* so *RatEx central bank policies* only copied monetarists 'fighting inflation first'. As central banks gained a starring role to markets they also increasingly took public blame, such as the furore over Volcker from US Congress to builders' unions. This led central banks to provide 'transparency' (the new jargon) demanded from a shocked Congress, to see more democratic oversight.[73]

As Forder explains well, if Friedman assumed 'misfeasance' by the Fed (the rarely spoken Nixon), in RatEx this was not the case. 'Suboptimal outcomes' apparently result when the policy-maker is 'perfectly public-spirited'. Thus, inflation continued, according to this line (Barro and Gordon), because *the central bank acted in the public interest*. This 'anguish' was to be banned. In effect, as central banks gave up on monetarism, private banks could simply demand central banks be solely concerned with what financial markets desired. Not only that, a range of politicians took these 'theories' to their electorates (e.g. Lawson in the UK), spreading panic about the impact of bond and currency market assessments or harsh IMF conditional loans.

Governments could apply rules to central banks, which could 'reassure' global markets of 'a form of commitment' and 'prevent the policymakers' good intentions from harming the public': thus the forked tongues. Forder recounts the first 'rule' applied in the UK was an exchange rate target as 'credibility-enhancing' since, if it were missed, CBs faced 'public embarrassment'. This came to pass, because a 'recession-inducing', overvalued exchange rate of the pound in 1992 was as hard to meet as the previous 'money supply' targets.

Forder said the British ERM disaster was 'the moment to bury' RatEx and its theorem of CBs' (slavish) efforts to give credibility. Never enough for traders, so the City kept up pressure (not theorists) and BoE inflation targets were adopted. This copied a 1990 New Zealand target, which if not met, the RBNZ Governor faced possible

---

[73] See Blinder et al. (2001) on CB transparency and blame, and they refused to accept charges such as CB 'inflation surprises' of monetarists et al.

dismissal. Forder slightly underplays political and financial sectors' might over any prospects of modifying central bank CPI inflation targets (recounted in Chapter 7). [74]

Limitations on states came, also, in their freely adopted 'Laffer Curve' to hobble Treasuries. The economic literature is on the heavy-handed 'influence' on central banks of monetarism and rational expectations ideas. It explains much about their later 'Great Moderation' up to 2007, better called 'The Great Excess'. But at the same time, right wing governments introduced other measures, which also made central banking policy difficult, by rapidly increasing inequality. Reagan and Thatcher wanted to 'roll back' the state, not for their own war-mongering (unstated) but to slash social security. When JFK reduced taxes (Chapter 5), the investment inducements and *conditions* put on firms revived (taxable) economic activity, but not this time.

Far more than a 'laffing' matter, easier for Reagan (or Thatcher) to understand and promote to electorates (than RatEx) was from Arthur Laffer, who in 1974 sketched 'the napkin doodle that launched the supply-side revolution'.[75] Laffer just picked a spot on a curve between 0 and 100 per cent tax rates, arguing the government gets no revenue in either case. We'd never have thought. The chosen point aimed to maximize individual endeavour and tax revenue, he alleged. The unproven claim was regressive tax cuts for savers-rentiers, would trickle down in higher growth: *rentiers* would work harder with more mollycoddling, and workers with far less! With a Fed-induced recession and global instability, unemployment worsened yet Reagan reduced the marginal rate from 70 to 28 per cent, with no conditions; Thatcher employed Laffer.

---

[74] Forder (2006: 233) for these three paragraphs, with my commentary on social questions on top of Forder's clear demolition of the theorems/jargon. The Exchange Rate Mechanism (ERM) was a UK agreement with the EU, the pound betted against by US hedge funds; it all harmed the public and was a nice earner for banks.

[75] See the 'Great Excess' earlier this chapter; and note a creeping totalitarian tone in 'anti-state', warrior-state politics. Bloomberg is cited in Seccombe (2016) on Laffer's story. Laffer came to Australia to help craft the May 2016 budget; Seccombe cites a meeting of Laffer with young Republicans Dick Cheney and Donald Rumsfeld in 1974. President George Bush Snr later called it voodoo economics: once again the fad.

For employers, 'discipline' needed sackings, and the wealthy hated FE; so 'inconvenient', so few servants. To Burns 1979, Fed interest rate rises proved useless (as in the 1920s), since banks could find novelties under these inflations, until Volcker really stopped the show.

The OECD's 2015 report on rises in government debt showed that the US debt-to-GDP ratio had fallen sharply from its peak in WWII. With Laffer cuts and Star Wars of the 1980s, it rose briefly, but in 2010 it trebled on bank bailouts. Other research in 2012, such as the US Congressional Research Service found no correlation between taxes of highest income-earners and economic growth. So, benefits of tax cuts are pocketed, particularly corporate tax cuts.[76] Laffer is back to influence Trump. Laffer reverses all logic: namely high progressive taxes make state investment/stimulus safer since taxes are obligations (not charity) that reduce state money (HPM) inflation.

Nation-states, then, were not innocent. They comprised the other key force that suddenly switched during a conversion of central banks to nostrums of the 1920s. Were social democrat or labour governments seduced or torn apart? The *luck* of the anti-(wage) inflation and anti-FE troops in succeeding, only at this time, produced further effects. Nixon's end of Bretton Woods in 1971–3 had freed finance everywhere. Power over now flexible exchange rates moved from public authorities to private finance, while central banks converted to ancient 'loanable funds' quantity theory and Treasuries to failed defences of exchange (ERMs) and risible Laffer approaches, and ignored banking developments. Most unsayable, war finance ramped up in the USA, UK (elsewhere too), so that (state) war inflation continued, on and off, producing asset inflations/bubbles, more unemployment, and mean-spirited austerity. Most nation-states turned

---

[76] On FE as 'inconvenient', see Robinson (1978). Seccombe (2016: 4) cites the OECD's 2015 'Sovereign Debt Composition in Advanced Economies'; the US Congressional Congress compared low US tax rates at 2012 with postwar rates above 90 per cent; the Australian Bureau of Statistics found *since* 1960, private business investment trended down as a share of GDP in Australia (trickle up was Laffer's result). Costs of bailouts after 2007 sent state debt up, while economies sank into deflation.

from domestic to foreign markets in a different beggar-thy-neighbour than the Interwar gold exchange aggression. The superpower status of postwar USA left surplus countries 'defence dependant', so countries like Japan, Saudi Arabia and Germany were less likely to sell off the US$ (than the vicious 1931 US and French 'diplomacy' that drained the vicious deflationary UK and Germany of gold). This time, trade rivalry became competitive reductions of labour unit costs and disinflation with more jobless, to try to improve real exchange rates.[77]

Central banks lost to sainthood. To Forder the overall prescription that 'central banks need to be controlled and constrained' was unsayable, more so after the failures of monetarism and RatEx. Next is further proof that governments were the actors that hobbled central banks, under fear of private or IMF loan or bond vigilante refusals, and/or to cast off political responsibility (secretly to fund war or policing). Some central bankers took time to relent to de-regulation of banking, for which this apparently mysterious 'stagflation' gave spurious justification. The 1980s saw financial freedoms from logic and ethical norms added to the above listed new constraints on central banks. Wall Street gained in competitive strength from Nixon's 1971 break with Bretton Woods; Thatcher introduced 'Big Bang' in 1985 (what a term), and central banking shifted: from democratic accountability to their treasuries, and instead, to 'communicating' to markets. Giannini said before he died in 2003, 'careful monitoring by the financial markets has become a "permanent plebiscite"'.[78]

---

[77] See Chapters 1 and 2 on the tax logic, and Burnham (1999) on state guilt certainly about the UK case. Few were fooled by Laffer curves, but labour governments either self-weakened or succumbed, often split. Further to Chapters 2 and 5, on the Interwar deflation versus WWI's FE/shortages inflation, for the 1980 switch to unit cost aggression, see Bhaduri (2014: 391); naturally Trump/Republicans turn blind eyes to defence dependency impacts.

[78] On CBs losing control, Forder (2006: 233); see Pixley (2004) on 'Big Bang' in interviews with Budd, Flemming, Lazar etc.; these decent BoE and bankers told me it merely opened the City to overseas financial firms; and the BoE stood back from London's property bubble of 1990; also Blinder et al. (2001); Giannini (2011: 156–7).

Collapse of Central Bank Decision Capacities

Pork barreling and rent-seeking in the finance sector, for which monetarist and RatEx types excoriated governments (never markets), were disingenuous and inefficient. The real success in removing democratic legitimacy from CBs was accomplished via traders up-ticks. But the financial sector, having amplified the most divisive social issues, kept demanding more ways to reinforce central bankers' steely resolve by the later 1980s to 1990s. 'Certainty' became an order, not a hope. The move from trade in goods and services, to global trade in financial assets grew and, finally, CBs had zero to do. Sir Alan Budd and Governor B. W. Fraser implied publicly they either felt betrayed (Budd); hounded (Fraser) or silenced: the central bank decent 'wets' were concerned with employment. Apparently Budd was a monetarist, who later criticised Thatcher for wanting a reserve army of labour.[79] Any public spirit aim in central banks must be crushed. As Ingham says, there is no social and political structure in quantity theories that would generate disputes. Central banks using its nostrums flailed under class and nationalistic conflicts, and private finance demands. They accepted credibility rules, then an independence (not *freedom from markets*) that harried or vicious elected governments decreed. Some felt it a perfect evolution.

Monetarist die-hards assumed a neutral individualistic world by falsifying what their 'left' collectivist Keynesian and other opponents argued about how to control inflations. Monetarism was criticised immediately, but the 'myth' of Phillips was Friedman's winning blow. Inventing a myth that falsified what Friedman himself earlier said should surely go into history as a con-job. It still influences central banks and states many years after the GFC. States refrain from seeking state money expansion, from fostering taxable jobs or any wage inflation. Instead, austerity seeks lower real and nominal wages,

---

[79] Fraser did not succumb to hounding (Pixley 2012); neither was silenced. Budd's 'Marxian comments' are cited in Palma (2009) also Palma on how 'part pay-part lend' is the new norm. My CB sceptics knew that few were fooled; see earlier on quantity theorems.

under real and nominal price declines. Exceptions are asset, credit inflations and tax incentives to the already rich with inherited wealth or for primitive accumulation of CEOs. The plebiscites of the bond and currency vigilantes, ruling states with slogans like 'states don't pick winners', are implausible.

When monetarists rewrote the Great Depression, this falsification comprised more than the counterfactuals *ignoring* Bankers Ramps, poverty, stagnation. Postwar democratic processes opened states to institutional bridges linking them and their statutory bodies to citizens. The battle against that democratising was infinitely harder; citizens noisier in opposing the revived coalitions of interests creating mass unemployment, and central banks were thereupon divided. Only 'hawks' – the 'manly' – took CB office before 1933, afterwards 'doves' – thereupon ordered to endure indecent PR guys after the 1970s. Central bankers acted the 'credibility' part for bank confidence, while requirements to refrain from defending public aims kept them divided: indecency overruled. The cognitive and emotional dissonances in central banks were entrenched. Central banks could hardly send a hawk to legislative questioning, but the financial sector rejected decency, even tolerance. Performing to these lions and tigers is one thing but its dissonance is significant. Making trivial judgements under a 'rule' or 'target', above all to appease global financial markets, they in fact give *discretionary* justifications using probabilistic data, tepid jawboning and 'Fedspeak'. Yet the rule was imposed to *remove* CB discretion.

We saw how the con-job penetrated central bank policies, as political leaders helped destroy the reputation of states, which scotched democratic hopes of greens, feminists, civil rights, unions and Vietnam conscripts. Wages moved backwards as *money* became scarce (but not cheap advances). After that, as monetarism failed and ancient *divide et emperor* spread, central banks took the stage. I next ask on whose stage did they perform? Which key actors forced the 'independence movement' and 'rules not discretion' onto central banks? Forder is alarmed theoretically, and finance was surely dominant. Debates in central banks *after the GFC* suddenly found that asset and bank credit inflation, and evasive banking tricks were *relevant*, after all those years of *clubbing the economy*, their new role in indulging finance sectors. 'Moderately' because Volcker's recession went too far for everyone; 'deflation' was banished for stagnation of very low 'inflation', the type that always suits finance sectors.

Remote or probably negative chances that capitalist money could be democratically controlled disappeared. After the conflicts to the calamity of WWII, central banks were reformed although the Fed not so much. Yet, even if the District Feds 'had been' nationalised, and Board members appointed with union, medical or social work backgrounds, other central banks had unionists and excluded bankers. They too changed under the weight of the 1970s–80s events.[80]

That highlights my line that central banks are creatures of governments (as used to be said). If 1970s states were weakened from finance plebiscites (Giannini's term, or better, Bankers' Ramps), from stock exchange and credit (money) expansion crashes, there are other trends. States vary in military strength, many depend on (pay) the USA. Domestic policing rose while governments took to globalising themselves. Demands by industrial and service sector CEOs for cheaper labour and removing red tape *constraints* increased electoral disaffection. Each to their own became the order, with governments competing as tax havens, attracting finance sector growth and passing off their problems and blame onto allegedly independent central banks. Global banks also cast blame on these servants who cannot carry that weight.

---

[80] My discussion draws on Forder (2006). 'Bridges' is in Offe (1980: 8); stagnation can teeter to deflation; for doubts re unions on CB boards, see Mann (2013); The RBA must exclude bankers, see Pixley (2004) from diverse central bankers' interviews, and recently on CBs 'clubbing' to stagnation.

7   Pseudo-Independent Central Banks and Inflation-Target Prisons

Money is a unifying force of an implicit social fact and binding power. But this force is rarely felt unless electronic transfers stop, ATMs and bank doors close. If money vanishes overnight, the payment system has broken down. A breakdown in social unity. An external social fact provides an objectivity to everyday social interactions and trust in money, but when not, relations fragment, fear and distrust are widespread. The GFC sundered collective but barely consciously held beliefs. Yet for years, banks had not bothered to care for the liabilities and obligations of their licences. Central banks had to act on money vanishing.

This chapter looks at how central bankers passively oversaw the build-up in 'securitised' advances, to busts in the GFC. Many acquiesced but critics grew, as had populations forced to use bank money (and less the currency).[1] Moves to make CBs 'independent' of treasuries and prescribe 'inflation targets' were orders, this chapter argues, with the European Monetary Union a 'logical' continuation. Governments sided with the global finance sector to decree *inflation* the enemy. They prevented central bankers from worrying about deflation and jobs. Jawboning about fractional bankings' dangers was rare, although many central bankers knew, against myths, that money is never fixed in value: stability gives rise to instability; inability to meet mutual obligations. Breakaway definitions by financial actors that

---

[1] Who seriously worries that a shop – actually a bank – might refuse to honour the content in one's debit card to buy a pack of cigs? Or that cash (currency) to pay debts will not be available? Cash-earners may last a day longer. The payment system is a catch-all term for money as both means of exchange (buy/sell) and of payments (debt/tax/wage obligations). One bank may fail, but 'too many' mean that entire economies stop. Durkheimian terms are used brilliantly in Orléan (2014) on money's 'binding force'. See also Table 1.1 on bank *liabilities* (to keep bank money deposits freely available on call) and bank assets.

became hot in the 1970s, showed central banks shackled or torn, as happens in total war finance too. Conflicts ended in the OECD when the fashion became markets. Deflation became unmentionable (while Japan's began). Reagan and Thatcher weakened treasuries; others copied their iron glove attacks. Rules ensured that treasuries could not be economic players with central banks, and the latter were rendered 'independent' of democracy, with neither its stalwart defenders. Murmurs of public distrust – that this 'independence' (ICBs) was bogus – exploded in the GFC when both acted jointly. But protest rarely used Geoff Ingham's terms of 'the control of the production of money'. Control passed to the financial sector more thoroughly than ever, including over war finance spending about which nothing was said. State spending for peace is in a cul-de-sac.

J. K. Galbraith, never a friend of inflations, wrote about 'the pecuniary nexus between an undue reliance on monetary policy and the people who so ardently approve its use'. To him, the applause of the 'rich and powerful' accorded to Milton Friedman aptly reflects their self-interest. Whenever monetary policy is invoked against inflation, the 'primary effect is on the small man not the large corporation' (with capacities to raise prices or absorb higher interest with retained profits not available to small business). By the 1980s, undue reliance on monetary policy created independent central banks, forbidden to negotiate with treasuries. Fiscal policy (of a specific sort) was damned even if CBs cannot avoid *de facto* public debt monetising.[2]

One impact for ICBs was that public-private debt ratios from 1970 to 2007 saw a drop in public debt and dramatic rise in *private debt*. Markets were said to determine winners in the race to substance definitions of money, via assuming a rabidly unattached individual. A celebrated actor free from scruples, values or shared obligations, the good guys left: corporate low life was embedded in global society. Collective experiences of job losses and humiliating monetary

---

[2] See Ingham (2004), and Galbraith cited his own work of 1957 (in 1981: 348–9), critical of Eisenhower (Galbraith was more feminist later). Few other OECD members cared about Japan, the big (hated) competitor of the 1980s.

policy transposed into protective measures for self-survival. If one cannot beat such forces or protect households from their ravages, more institutions and people must join them (into debt). In a 'winner take all' society, attacks on social democratic policies succeeded. Growing inequalities arose partly from state-imposed 'inflation targets' that dictated one CB operation, we see, which *removed* operational independence.[3]

THE CB INDEPENDENCE MOVEMENT AND ITS DISTURBING ANALYSIS

Independence, in Durkheimian terms, could equally be read as 'anomic', a detachment from established norms. In the idealised terms of advocates of independent CBs, however, freedom to act independently could enhance impartiality, technical competence and policy caution. But such independence can be re-interpreted in organisational terms as self-importance, superiority and the absence of constraint – constraints that encourage both caution and accountability to publics. Research in the sociology of organisations shows that the modification of the 'rules of the game' can have unintended as well as intended consequences. Dissonances inside CBs magnified with so-called independence, circumscribed by targets. To critics like Dow, central banks abandoned the social democratic settlement, though to my mind orders were out to be kind to banks (and blame the public, and yes, all the fair postwar settlements).[4]

Compare that to total war, when CBs are not permitted to undermine patriotism, and must monetise state debt. In WWII, they set cheap rates on bond issues via pegs on interest payments of treasury and ordered private banks to buy these bonds. Today, bank finance

---

[3] Nothing was said of military finance, nor, as inequality rose, the policing, prisons or refugee camps, murderous and wasteful. Schularick (2014) on private debt. ICB decreed operational independence, states would set the policies. IT gave no discretion to operations! Michael Douglas (*Wall Street*) stressed he was the bad guy: financiers aped his role, loved it (Pixley 2012).

[4] Thanks to Wilson's points on anomie, as we said partly in Pixley et al. (2013). See Dow (2013) and Chapter 5 about 'being kind' or craven.

for nuclear arms is hidden, funnily. This section discusses the equivocal badge of 'independence' imposed to make CBs indifferent to, and
unable to work publicly and formally with, treasuries. And, as suited
private banks admirably, central banks were to ignore HPM's relation to rescuing capitalist bank money, while their routine practices
did the opposite (Table 1.2). Central bankers said: 'We are islands'.
Informed ones saw through this.

A 'Dynamic Stochastic General Equilibrium' (DSGE) model
came to be used in central banking that, incredibly, excluded any financial sector from CB considerations; ignoring their *actual provisions to
banks*. Neat! Some talk of a 'performative' element in central banks, but
such economic influences, framing, oversimplifies. The 'style guides' to
appease finance markets, such as in *How Do Central Bankers Talk* are
a mixed script. As well, CBs did not 'perform' to *imposed* policies when
urgent, but used the postwar, civil policies. Did (private) bank CEOs
understand this DSGE, or merely that CBs stopped jawboning and left
them free to roam? Traders were taking orders down the line. Revolving
doors of central bank, private finance and treasury jobs mounted, with
a global increase of the same in IMF-BIS top jobs into global banks.
One can point to numbers of CB Governors and Treasurers who were,
or moved on to be, GS&Co executives. In my view, this is only a reversion to pre-democratic club ways of central banks. *Money* is firmly
exceptional and, although 'independence' opposed deficit financing *de
jure*, monetising happens *de facto* anyway.[5] Promoters of independence
used substance analogies for money which exempted banks from actual
money creation, an excuse demolished with banks' massive 2007
contraction of that same manufacture of money.

While the EMU was slowly coming to fruition, a steady, bleat-
ing demand for independence of central banks (ICBs) from financing
treasuries grew voluble. But (we saw) these demands are difficult to
separate from the 1970s–80s private finance plebiscite on states, the

---

[5] Blinder et al. (2001) blur lines of 'talk' and secrecy: to big market players or the public
(?); the press always called traders 'investors', lone and 'rational'. See Ingham (2004)
on performative, and Goodhart (2013) on DSGE. See Table 1.2 and Wray (2014b) on
monetising. (This is how nuclear military finance occurs.)

result of national-international political and social conflicts. Bank competition (into oligopolies) and the reduction in CB bank supervision took off. Social democracies, FE and inflation (of wages) were cited as the only restraints. The charge that politicians had *always interfered* in CBs (some told me in 2002 well after independence) was a vague 'left or right'. A few central bankers accepted it of labour governments, only naming Nixon's Administration; they seemed diffident, or opposed *this* independence. Inflations do not suit, logically, state interests in a stable tax value (to Chartalists) as, ironically, the post-1945 era showed.[6]

EXPLANATIONS FOR ICBS AS ATTACKS ON SOCIAL DEMOCRACIES

Many commentators call the process after 1971 an attempted 'depoliticising' of money. Wolfgang Streeck poses stages of major social conflicts, starting with the rise of wage inflation in the 1970s – a 'compensation' for the modicum of democratisation and welfare state provisions. Social democratic processes lost with the FE commitment overturned, the devastation from which, in policy-flailing, was soon compensated by the increasingly foolhardy maintenance of effective demand via 'easy household credit'. One can ask what, given central bankers always love long memories, brought them to accept that banks could create as much money as they liked?[7]

Social action is the most important. Some debate whether scrapping full employment was a 'revenge of *rentiers*' or by accident from Nixon's exploits. John Smithin takes the 'revenge' line, whereas Greta Krippner suggests, rather, the coincidences of many different US interests pushing their own barrows, and not design. To Schumpeter (a kind of revenge thesis), savers do not have the ruling

---

[6] Substance analogies rely on seeing money as a mere 'veil' over 'the real' economy of 'utility' or 'use-value' of goods and services (Chapter 2). The EMU is discussed further below, and the plebiscite is in Chapters 5 and 6. Chartalists, who give *primacy* to state money (often as HPM), range from Goodhart, note, a central banker, to Wray in all their texts. Keynes, and Ingham today also, are mostly Chartalists. See Chapter 4 on postwar CBs.

[7] See Streeck (2014) and compare Figure 5.1 on 1970s bank asset growth.

role as was (wrongly) claimed on behalf of modest pension holders; banks create money, but for what purpose? Politicians recused themselves from electoral responsibility for monetary policy (or tried to) in the name of the exigencies of the global economy (as argued by Peter Burnham) and in 'third way', allegedly social democratic politics, which relinquished state sovereignty to markets, and urged that workers deserved 'easy credit'. Political leaders included Keating, Blair and Clinton. CBs let the sector do what it wanted: and how could social democratic governments flout capital strikes?[8]

Public conflicts over the purposes of money were never openly about capitalist money creation: 1980s rhetoric was 'greedy workers' destroying the value of sainted savings. Increases in bank competition imposed by US and UK governments above all, and the contradiction in the loss of CB supervision and reduced lender of last resort (LOLR, called the 'Discount window' in the Fed), distanced central banks from what was once a core concern: trying to supervise, even monitor private money creation. Separate supervision copied the US system, while banks became the main producers of money with control over the direction of loans – whether for economic activity or for consumers, speculation (etc.). Virtuous savers were left defenceless.

Some central bankers opposed hiving off supervision. Since CBs do 'accommodate' and bail out banks, in Reserve Bank of Australia Governor Fraser's view, a vigilant central bank would 'shadow' and duplicate the work of separate regulators, in case LOLR were needed. He also opposed independent central banks because fiscal policy works in tandem with monetary policy. Fraser is a democratic FE central banker, a 'take away the punch bowl' type. He urged that the RBA should stand up against 'markets', not merely jawbone, and give

---

[8] Citations are of Smithin (1996); Krippner (2011); Burnham (1999), and Schumpeter (1954) (Figure 1.1). General claims are in my interviews, Pixley (2004). In Chapters 5 and 6, the disputes were over whether Nixon's 'inflation' was via Fed Chair Burns; the notion of 'inflation surprises' is denied in Blinder et al. (2001); few spoke of pressures from the rise of Forex markets (international). A wishy-washy tone to labour governments was promoted in many of Anthony Giddens's texts: Third Way was marvellous cf. Schwartz (1998; 2005); Bill Clinton swore about bond traders too.

'the markets' short sharp 'shocks' not lengthy rate rises (discussed by Ian Down as a 'sacrifice ratio') to avoid destroying economic activity. The sacrifice ratio measures the cost, in terms of either output or unemployment, of a point reduction in inflation. Down found the most independent central banks appeared to conduct more costly disinflations than their politically dependent counterparts. Evidence suggested the 'more conservative (i.e., inflation-averse) central bankers will deliver lower inflation than less conservative bankers but will likely impose higher welfare costs on society in the process'.[9] That is, unemployment.

While some CBs, then, tried to avoid costly disinflations, calls for independence of CBs were nearly realised by the end of the 1990s, except *parts* of Asia or others. The globalisation of trade, towards free capital movements and computing of bond trading and derivatives were further pressures or threats. For example, with 'globalization', an ICB was 'respectable' to a global cast of creditors including authorities like the IMF. So, they applied pressure too.

1980s–90s political scientists looked at the decline of OECD manufacturing and cite CBs as a direct cause of unemployment – from the Netherlands to USA. Other countries held out, but the trend was clear. One exception was France with state-owned industries, another was relationship banking in Germany. It meant that big business and labour unions were less excluded from money's heartland in North Europe, than in the UK or USA. Kurzer suggested 'when financial institutions have vested interests in manufacturing, as in Germany, the central bank will be less opposed to fiscal expansion and relaxed monetary policies'. The Bundesbank was hardly *relaxed*, although the informal relations of a CB are partly dependent on the strength of the financial sector and German unions were business-linked. The production of goods and services is logically at loggerheads, not

---

[9] The 'Discount' is the Fed's interest rate to lend to banks, see also Minsky (2008 [1986]). Fraser is cited Pixley (2004); and see Down (2004: 401–4) on 'sacrifice' which meant stagnant economic activity, and high unemployment. Stringencies on social security, health and education spending were treasuries' counterpart.

with banking's *money* production *per se*, but a strong finance sector demanding *low economic activity*. This systemic logic became less obvious to capitalist production of goods/services because business disliked the lack of discipline of full employment. The largest US corporations became financialised first, and engaged in currency bets, corporate raiding and offshore production.

'Comparative political research that focuses on ICBs as institutions made it very clear that "independence" arose out interest coalitions that favoured low inflation' – the financial industry with significant political and economic influence. Independence, seen in this light, was a rhetorical device to persuade policymakers and the public to give CBs greater influence over monetary policy to obtain low inflation at the cost of greater unemployment, the latter being undesirable (logically) to governments with any ability to influence monetary settings.[10]

If this account is true, it leads to interesting questions – with near-deflation since 2007, is the coalition favouring low (wage) inflation still intact and as influential? And, more importantly, do the benefits of independence and inflation targets equally exhaust themselves with the demise of inflation as the overarching economic goal? Many central banks are pleading for more wage inflation and state stimulus to little avail (see Chapter 8), whereas the BoE (for example) has been ducking and weaving both before and after the 2016 Brexit plebiscite, we see below.

Indeed, independence during the 'fight (wage) inflation' dominance gave some CBs the sense they were masters of the universe, despite cautious efforts such as Basel 1, while deregulations occurred during the independence push. The Bank for International Settlements (BIS) in Basel gave central bankers a 'camaraderie' given their

---

[10] See Kurzer (1988: 30; 28–9); for her extensive comparative ICB research and 'interest coalitions'. Posen is cited in Goodman (1991) on the political influences of the finance industry. I stressed (Chapter 1) treasuries lose from (taxable) workers cast into unemployment, and from stagnation. Logic was thereby lost, not only political popularity from a large voting base (workers).

unpopularity (in destroying jobs), I was told; other central bankers said BIS's luxury dinners wasted money. Public suspicion about their back-patting photo ops rose. 'Basel' only gives guidelines that need state enforcement; commercial banks evaded Basel 1. Independent CBs became ever more fearful of market 'odium' once they could no longer blame treasury. By the 1990s, CBs relentlessly worried about 'what the markets think' in US FOMC transcripts: the standard for CB decisions became financial market criteria. They lost the nerve to 'prick' asset bubbles and 'lean against the wind', quickly, rather than slow the entire economy.[11]

How are CBs implicated in what has gone so wrong, in social democratic terms, and in social market consequences – including capture of policy by investment banks, anti-unionists and their spokespeople. Models that CBs still use, whether with inflation targets or later QE, are based on the exclusion of a financial sector (we saw). FOMC meetings obsessed about the opposite. A problem, Dani Rodrik's analysis of cross-country surveys showed, is that twenty years of ICBs 'locked in' to price stability objectives, meant any response to governments was weakened by independence. Many were reluctant, or *disallowed* to take concerted action with treasuries, in opposite situations of *no* growth and debt deflation. He cites Argentina in the late 1990s, and there are evident strains in many CBs in what Rodrik calls institutional lock-in. Thus, the 'credible fixed rules' imposed on *operational* independence, of inflation targeting, become 'rigidities' when policy goals change and there is a need for 'flexibility'. That was hardly the word when the GFC hit central banking 'art' with a horror-scape.[12]

'Democratic politics is the bridge between the citizen and the state' in formal liberal democratic theory. To Claus Offe, debates and

---

[11] See Pixley (2004) for central bankers' interviews about Basel and FOMC transcripts confirming the opposite to DSGE 'framing'. Greenspan tried once to control a bubble, never again! Also, Ingham (2011); Chick (2008) and Haldane (2012) on Basel.

[12] Rodrik (2008) is excellent on 'institutional lock-in'; thanks to Wilson's permission to draw on his thoughtful points and on Offe, in our joint segments, most unpublished; and in Pixley et al. (2013). Also, to my colleague Dick Bryan on CB 'art' – a Landscape or The Scream, on my *Emotions in Finance* book.

conflicts, or their resolution, rely on these institutional 'bridges', but the location of politics and the formulation of state policies had shifted, Offe said, during the 1970s. For example, governments *rely increasingly upon criteria and standards of performance that are derived from other sources than the democratic political process'.* Democratic theory posits mediations between the state and individual, which are breaking down, some virtually abolished.[13] And unlike other arms' length public entities, central banks are self-financing (always, then, with *an* independence).

Early central banks were also privately owned, and some profited with the financial sector. Some were bankers to the government, others supported industrial sectors. Yet in the 1950s–60s, despite day-to-day *consolidated relations* between treasuries and CBs committed to full employment, surveys of economic and political measures show that dependence on governments was never total, with a fairly desirable independence, which is also discussed in the postwar Fed and RBA cases (Chapter 4). It is far too simple, or populist, to blame *all ills* on financial elites, given the ICB movement had large corporations, anti-tax drives, and government promoters too, noting bank funding for war is largely hidden from view.

But the dogmatic central bank independence movement assumed that in liberal capitalist economies, the main risk against rational economic policy came from the profligacy and political self-interest of government administrations, which "would have" a bias towards monetary expansion, low interest rates, and full employment, and would not be sufficiently mindful of the costs – the inflationary pressures on money's value, public debt and industrial unrest. As Forder shows, the Philips curve 'myth' helped to give a justification for what we saw was not so. And two perversions of the orthodox account of the political economy of monetary policy eventuated. In the US, an independent central bank was equally capable of generating

---

[13] Offe (1980: 5; 8), Offe's emphasis, since he talks of 'mediations' or 'arms-length' entities, although not CBs in his examples.

a monetary expansion, by the 1990s mainly to accommodate a financial system that had become dependent on easy money (private debts) to fuel loans, for rescues of share markets (e.g. Greenspan at 1987) and housing markets. In Europe, in contrast, the emergent ECB adopted such austerity-generating monetary settings that it added to unemployment and fiscal vulnerability of governments. In both cases, CBs *appear* as central actors, producing problems in both directions.

The argument for independence made assumptions about the role of 'big government' in the chain of causality that produced the slowdown since the 1970s, but not to financing defence. In their independence, central banks assumed greater technocratic responsibility for the economy. But unlike the case of political administrations, independence rules meant CBs have no democratic responsibility for policy errors (the Fed *de jure*). This asymmetry creates a schism in authority and accountability for such institutions relevant to the problem of democratic design. Assessment of policy effectiveness, in the era of independent CBs, was further dismissed. If anything, 'technical problems' merely awaited correction and adjustment. These were (dishonestly) detached from democratic problems subject to institutional and public pressures such as elections that throw governments out of office. To further illustrate – other 'independent institutions', like courts for example, are subject to potential judicial review and legislative correction. But monetarists' counterfactuals for the Great Depression (CBs had made technical 'errors') were influential, ones that (conveniently?) disregarded Bankers' Ramps (see Chapter 3). One must wonder in imposing independence, what new procedures for review need to be invented for ICBs. Do these exist, or does this political- and monetarist-driven independence, from treasuries now removed of social responsibilities, need revision?[14]

---

[14] We saw Forder (2014) in Chapter 6; these two paragraphs rest partly on Pixley et al. (2013) and Pixley (2004). Posen (2008), not known for being left wing, is explicit on how the finance sector controls states/CBs. The alternative problem is erratic, far-right governments such as Trump's, or see Chapter 5, Nixon's never-spoken.

Whether formal independence from financing treasuries reduces the impact of other economic and institutional influences pressing on CBs, or increases them, is moot. Parliamentary committees call their head central banker to account regularly for CB decisions, but once independence is set in legislation, what can committees do about policy favouritism in this equivocal independence? Legislation can be changed ultimately; governments can appoint a different CB Chair who, like judges, might be unpredictable, but *under orders* and *events* far more than judiciaries.

Inflation targets were also imposed on CBs by governments for similar motives, and the more stringent, the more central banks were in a straitjacket negating *independence*. Since deficit financing occurs inadvertently, as CB balance sheets show (Table 1.2), and instability towards deflation is always likely, the imposed targets appear to give the greater scope for errors or rather, stagnation, save for defence.

INFLATION TARGETS: 'ALL THE FREEDOM OF THE PRISON YARD'

Whatever views inside central banks prevailed, often from non-democratic eras, the switch to independence, combined with inflation 'targets', cannot be cast in error over achievements of economic science but *despite* any science.[15] Money is political, a complex social relation. Neither coincidence nor intentional design, these 'targets' came less from epistemology but financial market and insatiable military actors' worldviews, from bank demands (a few regretted) for revived control, whereby states should have little control over the production of money and its uses, banks would. Under enough public agreement (the sanctified 'savers') but implicitly, finance sector domination over government debt, many states foisted rules on central banks in the 1990s, the tightest to target 2 per cent CPI inflation or if it went *below* 1, to 'prevent' deflation (somehow). Combined *oddly* with central banks

---

[15] Bibow proposes that Keynes had not fully revolutionised 'our ways of thinking' (2009:10). But did 'science' influence finance sector and other vested interests, or whatever was appealing? Often that posed as science.

independent of governments, demand management via fiscal policy vanished (treasuries!) in favour of disinflation, joblessness, lower wages, private debt-driven demand and asset price inflation (instability rarely publicly debated). Volcker self-started the process on a less equal US than other OECD countries.

When James Forder studied the Philips Curve and concluded that the fiction of 1950s 'inflationism' was all that survived, he wondered why inflation targets, independent CBs, efficient market claims et al. did not quietly die after (wage) inflation and FE were dead. Better than orthodox monetary analysts (since he harped about problems of causation versus mere correlation like Forder), Curzio Giannini suggested that central banks played an *active* role. Yet he cast governments as in a difficult time between 'market integration and mass politics' and 'therefore' central banks turned to 'holders of money and not to holders of political power' in promoting market liberalisation, 'seconding [the financial industry's] needs and promoting its growth'. Giannini also said none of that *could have* happened 'without the rise of mass finance'. His counterfactual implies, perhaps, repeated slumps in demand until household debt rose. Savers had to trust private pension funds too. Although warning that market self-regulation was impossible, Giannini died before US households lost $18 trillion in wealth by 2010.[16] Some but not all central banks were forced to attack wage inflation alone – squeezing household loan servicing. Who worried about that logical inconsistency? With private banks, the IMF loved targets, ICBs and fiscal cutbacks (re wellbeing) as conditions of loans to states; state money was constantly undermined. Political fears of bond vigilantes grew.

Looking back, conflicting demands magnified the chaos building up. When governments, also congenial to banking, removed CB supervisory tasks to underfunded agencies, it turned out agencies were played off with regulatory arbitrage among Wall Street operators.

---

[16] Forder (2006); Giannini (2011: 253–56); note his messy position; see Blinder (2013: 354) on US household wealth-savings lost between 2008 and 2010 was over a year's US GDP. So much for 'mass finance'. People lost; recession ensued; policing, prisons and wars continue to grow.

States decreed inflation targets (IT) even when high interest forced up treasury costs, or the RBA had a formal remit for employment (a dual Fed mandate too). In his final 2016 speech as RBA Governor, Glenn Stevens remarked:

> I can recall being asked by an IMF official during the mid 1990s whether, if inflation rose above the target, we were prepared to create a recession to get it down again. The implication was that we should be. We insisted on *not being obliged to have a recession to shave a few tenths of a percentage point off inflation* in a short period. We were not believers in the idea of destroying the world to save it.

Pressures were heavy. Bankers, central bankers and politicians were often so ill informed that they pleased neither citizens (in 'destroying the world') nor financial sub-sectors. Banks had major collapses in Sweden, Canada, Australia in the late 1980s, although were saved on stricter terms. Some said UK treasurer Nigel Lawson thought he knew all about money. Martin Wolf argues most elites are innumerate. The UK's ERM disaster followed by a housing crash in the London region proved ruinous (to the Tories). Right-wing Treasurer Costello assumed closing the government bond market would enhance Australia's credit rating. What a shock to bond traders, who told him HPM and state debt were essential to bank money creation and their profits, not before the Press ridiculed the Treasurer.[17] Such stories are found across the OECD; hindsight assessments of BoJ officials and Greenspan are unflattering. To many RBA officials at that time, targets 'seemed undesirable'; not only to their FE remit (economic activity):

> [Thus] former Governor Johnston, speaking in 1992, described the combination of central bank independence and a single (inflation)

---

[17] Levin Report (2011) on regulatory arbitrage. See Stevens (2016) my emphasis; Wolf (2016); we saw the ERM disaster in Chapter 6; and Tories lost power for years; see Pixley (2012) on Costello: evidence of reactive and dumb strategies.

objective as 'bestowing on the Bank **all the freedom of the prison exercise yard'**.

Comparing inflation target (IT) regimes, the Fed (non-IT with a FE remit) had a 'covert' or 'eclectic' target; the Swiss National Bank said it was not 'an IT-er' but did so; Japan was in deflation. The ECB took the target most seriously, harshly at a hint of a rise; the RBNZ deal included the Governor facing the sack.[18] A Bank of Canada official argued (in 2004) that the 'target' depended on …

> definitions, which varied. As a 'rule' … it was a balance of reducing inflation (the deviation of inflation from its target) with the expected marginal cost of the inflation reduction (**the negative of the output gap, divided by the Phillips Curve coefficient … multiplied by the weight on the output gap in the objective function**) … The RBNZ used a Taylor-style rule; it was the first [IT-er] in 1989 [agreed 1990 and, from a 0–2 target, by 2002 raised the lower bound to 1] … By 2004 there were 21 central banks using headline annual inflation. The BoE reduced its target to 2% in 2003 with a new CPI price index.
>
> In 2002, the RBNZ also turned to RBA language to place weight on output fluctuations … Changes were more in what central banks chose to report. Norges Bank gave slightly greater 'forecast disclosure' than the RBNZ and, with a few others [gave] forecasts on the output gap; whereas the Bank of Canada, RBA and Bank of Israel are [or were] at the opposite end of the forecast-reporting spectrum, publishing only near-term, often qualitative forecasts for a relatively small set of variables. Israel had the most economic uncertainty … and so was probably not like the intrinsic aversion to reporting a forecast [so evident] in the BoC and RBA …
>
> [As well], a target was always about expectations … that is forecasts, so [BoE] Mervyn King [in 1997] said 'the overall

---

[18] 'Prison yard' is cited in Grenville (1997) my emphasis; comparative data is from a 2004 RBA conference.

transparency associated with inflation targeting effectively removes the possibility of cheating'. King also said no one would admit to being 'an inflation nutter'.

A rule on *output* with *Phillips mangled* (a myth too) was a cover: the targets were citizens, wages and jobs, not assets, to appease bond vigilante expectations (RBNZ on zero inflation!). Critics cited in this revealing 2004 RBA debate, argued that IT were either irrelevant or inflexible; in the US, Janet Yellen opposed IT in 1995, urging a 'wise and humane policy' whenever output was 'unstable'. Others, including Benjamin Friedman, argued that IT is hardly 'ideal optimal' monetary policy. Olivier Blanchard said IT 'rests on the 'divine coincidence' that 'stabilising inflation is equivalent to stabilising output'. Kuttner (Bank of Canada) concluded: 'there seems to be a deeply-ingrained central banking taboo against talking about any sort of short-term trade-off between output and inflation, and not only among IT-ers. One need only recall the controversy surrounding Alan Blinder's 1994 statement that the "central bank *does* have a role in reducing unemployment"' Kuttner said.[19]

Full employment (output) was the tabooed remit; also, half the other (deflation a taboo). In the 1990s, Larry Lindsey and Blinder harped at Greenspan in FOMC meetings; both insisting Greenspan was 'lucky'; Lindsey forcefully urged leaning against the wind of the Dotcom bubble. Greenspan silenced their (deflationary) worries with, for example, 'I've been on Wall Street for 47 years ... and I've a feeling in the pit of my stomach ... that the markets will crack'. He refused Congress's similar requests to raise margin loan requirements. And luck, to the thoughtful Canadian official Kuttner meant this: 'The good luck will inevitably run out, however, and adverse cost-push shocks are sure to appear at some point.' With three years to Northern Rock's fiasco, to *price collapses* and deflation, I mention his comment

---

[19] The BoC official at the RBA Conference, see Kuttner (2004) for this quote, my emphasis [and use of his other points in square brackets]; King, Yellen, Blanchard, Blinder are all cited Kuttner (2004). Phillips is Chapter 6's main topic; see Forder (2014).

not as error, because, contra orthodox training, predictions cannot be made. Instead, facing uncertainty with *one option permitted* shows the poverty of imagination demanded in IT.[20]

Hayek pro-market or quantity views of money, whatever, governments (under pressure from markets) returned many (not all) CBs to harsh 1920s if not 1830s policies; but with farcical complexities of the (above) cited fictional Phillips Curve tool. Few understood them, not even CB Board members. The (silenced) rules were to increase unemployment at a hint of wage rises, to refuse state debt being monetised, and harp against deficits while busily monetising bank debt. Some central banks took the initiative for or against. Alan Greenspan, as Giannini argued too, played what *Barrons* editor called his Wizard of Oz 'cult of personality' (also infuriating Blinder talking to me). Whatever was desired, whether by Congress, banks or FOMC members: a 'new economy', or 'irrational exuberance' or 'perfect' markets, Greenspan was not fake beards, rather the public face of 'maestro' as chameleon or worse.[21] In contrast, the BoC and RBA sensibly refused trader demands to *make predictions* bound to fail (and thus endure more critics), or to take inflation of 3 to 6 per cent very seriously, to preserve jobs. Candid central bank experts dismissed Targets; in 2004, Edwards implied that central bank self-congratulations from *Volcker's intentional recession* and on to the 'Great Moderation', were over-cooked and risked deflation:

> The excellent inflation outcome ... owes a good deal to the anchoring of inflation expectations by central banks, but it was also assisted by supply-side developments ... *nothing to do with central banks*. This is part of the 'divine coincidence' [Blanchard] ... In Australia, low inflation was brought about by

---

[20] Blinder alerted me to the FOMC transcript (we talked about emotions in 2001); see also, citing Greenspan and Lindsey (FOMC), Pixley (2004): note margin loans are subtle ways to reduce market madness, see Palley (2014); and Kuttner (2004).

[21] Goodhart told me about some BoE Board members' over-reliance on 'models'; on Greenspan, see Giannini (2011); also, *Barrons* editor, Alan Abelson, and Blinder, who are all cited interviews in Pixley (2004).

reforms ... and the *unintended* deep recession of 1991, which
for Australia was the equivalent of the *Volcker deflation* ...
There are also global influences. These include a halving of
the real price of oil over the last decade, *constant downward
price pressure in manufacturing as the labour force of China
engages in the world economy,* the lower barriers resulting from
... unilateral reductions in protection, cheap computing and
telecommunication ... and the upswing in productivity growth
in the US, Australia and some other economies, ... as well as
the more flexible labour market ... [Also] for the developed
economies, most of the unfavourable shocks ... have been on
the demand side – the Asian financial crisis, the LTCM/Russian
crisis, the crash in IT equities, September 11, and the Iraq war.
In the developed economies, these crises posed *the risk of lower
output growth and lower inflation simultaneously.* In each ... the
obvious and clear response was for central banks in Australia,
the US, and Europe to *lower* interest rates ... [Earlier, one could]
... think of the inflation target the way in which Goodhart
apparently did ... In the early years of the Bank of England
Monetary Policy Committee he saw it as *a literal and sole
target* to be achieved within a definite and known time frame.
Judgement was important, but only in estimating the path of
the policy interest rate ... It is *also true that inflation targeting
has been complicated by asset-price bubbles* ... continued low
inflation and low interest rates can give *encouragement to
inflation in equity or house prices* which can become speculative
and which can ... cause economic contractions when the bubble
bursts.[22]

---

[22] Edwards (2004) was discussant at that cited RBA conference, my emphases; also see Edey
and Stone (2004) on the early years of IT when the assumption was a two-year inflation
forecast would be a sufficient statistic for determining the required interest rate 'to bring
inflation *to* the target'. They cite Goodhart saying he thought he was doing that. Note that
GATT became the WTO; LTCM was Long-Term Capital Management and IT was here
Information Technology.

Chaos was clearly building in 2004. But few influential CBs looked at asset or bank money inflation; the SE Asian crisis ('faraway' places) barely touched the BoE or ECB. Nixon's dollar float in 1971, after all, was the key step in returning private financial sector plebiscites over central banks and governments (probably not Nixon's intention). States could agree on GATT, Edwards said (aka to mobile capital benefit; not to bank controls after the GFC). How could a central bank 'dove' hold out against financial and state forces aiming 'to club the economy' (another Banca d'Italia official told me)? We saw Friedman was ingenious in reviving harsh views with upbeat Phillips Curve myths, a 'free lunch', and insiders followed Friedman's sloppy tip that a Curve could be 'ground out with Walrasian equations'; tied to the IT 'rule'. The Curve myth gulled even critics like Hyman Minsky. As we see, neither theorists nor states or central bankers succumbed in unison to the 'rational expectations' fiction, 'independence', or the 'efficient market hypothesis' (EMH). There were semi-sociological 'pro-market' commentators, say in London, Samuel Brittan and Peter Jay; the cynical, globally disregarded BoC and RBA saw pitfalls in these alleged 'theories'. Right-wing glee about the EMH was forced to moderate somewhat under the onslaught of ribaldry across countries, if only its sloppy logic.[23] Nevertheless, Figure 7.1 shows, British banking dominated all other UK sectors (like Switzerland). In consequence, both countries' CBs have faced enormous pressures. What can they do about the City or Zurich?

With all targeting's complications, these indecent IT regimes (Phillips Curves thrown in to confuse) were supported with a J. B. Taylor rule, not dissimilar to IT. Allan Meltzer approves of Greenspan applying 'Taylor', saying Bernanke did not. Monetarists were never concerned that Greenspan was a cheerleader for letting banks do what they wanted; finance is innocent. Schularick and *Alan* Taylor point

---

[23] See Chapter 6. Blinder denies he needled Greenspan: but I read FOMC transcripts, not him (he told me) Pixley (2012). Craig Freedman mentioned to me the Peter Jay 'tempering' thesis. See also, rba.gov.au papers rubbishing the EMH; also, in treasury and B. Fraser's speeches against monetarism; political pressure of monetarists; on the EMH see below.

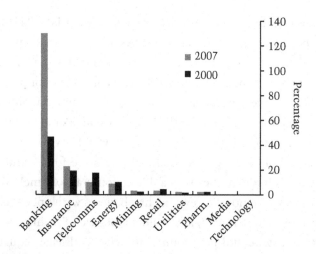

FIGURE 7.1 'Largest companies' assets in each sector relative to annual GDP in the UK: 2000 and 2007
Sources: Haldane 2010: 7 [Annex], from Bank of England data

out, 'the Taylor rule' ignored banks (Figures 7.1 and 5.1 show). Inflation and 'output' were the two *rules*. Pre-democratic orthodoxy separated money as mere 'veil' (save for wage inflation) from 'real' output (substance, not relation). J. B. Taylor differed from Friedman's idea to *strip* the Fed of independence, of political 'importance' and make it a discretion-free 'clerk'. But for all these angles, monetary policy was god. Never matter proponents blundered everywhere in self-contradictions. Blinder says Taylor is a 'conservative' economist (and high official in G. W. Bush's treasury) who blamed the Fed alone for 1929. If pro-independence movements and targets were ill-informed, both were political code against jobs, also versus state repression of *rentiers*, money markets and banks. IT created recessions to suit, and *credibility* of CB independence reassured pecuniary interests in asset inflation, incredibly, in Figure 7.1.[24] I think this 'credibility' is the meaning of CBs' 'Great Moderation'.

---

[24] Schularick and Taylor (2012: 1037; 1051; 1058) on J.B. Taylor's 'Rules'. Friedman, cited in Greider (1987: 87–93); Taylor, to Blinder (2013: 349–5) was inconsistent, see Chapter 8. FOMC records show incessant worries about the Fed's credibility; the public were of zero concern. Burns (weak) and Volcker (scarily tough) were blamed for 'losing' credibility (in Pixley 2004).

Unemployment crushed workers and private banking demanded that states destroy *unpredictable* trade unions.

ICBS AND IT GAVE BANKS *CERTAINTY* – NEVER ENOUGH

Not only rules, a 'model' used in central banks excluded a financial sector. And yet, things are not all as they seem. Some central bankers like Goodhart never accepted this DSGE. Equilibrium means a changeless, timeless situation (magical!) where, Goodhart criticises, banks do not default, 'no one misuses power' or 'uses force'. Any slight (stochastic) change will, in 'the long run', revert to equilibrium. Schumpeter approved equilibrium theory as a starting point despite 'its hopeless discrepancy from any process of real life', which creates 'new problems' ignored in Léon Walras's 'skeleton' (or Friedman's tying this to Curve myths, still applied in central banks). Schumpeter said even if one obeys Walras's equilibrium model and 'excludes' uncertainties [!], with 'a monetary capital market', that is, with something as 'volatile as money' so 'easily *redirected* at a moment's notice', the 'practical value' of his system of a determined and stable economy is 'much reduced'. Such tranquillity in DSGE is soothing (but liable to Ponzi finance, Figure 7.1). *Moralism became louder:* On this, Schumpeter argued some orthodox economists understood bank money creation 'quite clearly'. But Walras 'considered it *an abuse* that ought to be suppressed and refused for this reason, to make it a normal element of his general schema'. Although the 'deposit-creating loan' is old banking practice, it tends to remain a mystery, a secret or 'immoral'. That is no excuse for CBs excluding its mention. Politically though, to acknowledge banks' privilege of money creation (from which they gain assets) is to downgrade the saver's role of political-economic moral superiority as creditor. Bank instability questions might put central banks on the public hook, despite their own activities as banker to banks and (on profits from interest streams) self-financing.[25]

---

[25] Goodhart (2013: 76) a former BoE official on the 'Dynamic Stochastic General Equilibrium', see above. Schumpeter's fence-sitting, on Walras, also Alfred Marshall's efforts to put 'flesh and skin' on it (1954: 1015; 1025–6 and 1116, my

The idea of an 'epistemic community' of central banks is a bit thin. One can see the political reasons to *hide* private bank money 'immorality' from the public with DSGE etc., but that may impute more understanding than is warranted. Clearly some central bankers cultivated banks assiduously yet, an alarmed few were brushed aside. The Fed and BoE (and governments) pushed finance sectors globally, dampened production and cut effective demand. Other CBs, under Wall Street's knock-on global effects, used similar approaches that opened to *market* strategies – quantity of money and equilibrium models that omitted financial sectors; with an idea that *competition* is fine and as applicable for financial assets as exchange of ordinary goods: not so.[26] A low (wage) inflation period – *moderation* – was universalised to timelessness. Counterfactuals never help: even if Greenspan *had* opposed the forces of Wall Street and *laissez faire*-activist Administrations, which he did not, *would it have* mattered? Deregulation-reregulation of banking and finance took place, with which central banks could not cope, another secret some opposed.[27]

In the 'bureaucratic view', administrative and technocratic decisions are not 'politics'. Central bankers can fool or resign themselves, but neutrality is never possible, since *administration cannot reduce decisions about winners and losers to bureaucratic rules*. CB claims to a 'Great Moderation' in the 'IT' period must ignore variable disinflation, aggressive banking, stagnation; growing household debt and democratic public duties. The claim always varies with data

emphasis); see also then RBA Governor Coombs (1971) at after dinner speeches from 1950, joking about how money creation scares everyone (in Chapter 4).

[26] Epistemic community is a worn (too flattering) phrase, I think. On banks' privileged status see Häring (2013); Minsky (2008 [1986]) followed Schumpeter in dismissing equilibrium. Orléan suggests (2014: 233) that Walras introduced 'contingent goods' in the 'market order' equilibrium, of relations to objects; cf. competition is unstable in finance markets since *both sides are buyers and sellers*, quite unlike producers/*sellers* of 'things' to consumers/*buyers*. Central bankers failed to query such substance approaches to money (mostly).

[27] Counterfactuals, mostly in Chapter 3, are over-used (orthodox) tools that wrongly imply they are evidence. 'Laissez faire-activism' is *not* a non sequitur, rather an oxymoronic concept. States enforce laissez faire on specific areas, relinquishing their potential controls and impose 'targets' - aimed at us.

selection. For example, if the starting date is 1970–8, CPI declined thereafter – to 'the moderation' so acclaimed. But in WWI inflation was high, and the Fed, BoE and others savagely cut it back in 1920 until, in the Great Depression it sank to debt-deflation, mass unemployment: a near-death experience to capitalism, and to industrial and small farm sector horror. Rare exceptions – tediously recited as state *profligacy* against 'sound money' orthodoxy – were the short, quickly halted bouts of terrible hyperinflation in mostly the defeated countries of WWI. But they were such weak states that Weimar Germany (for example) was unable to monopolise violence or taxes. The 1990s warnings not to tempt hyperinflation were mendacious. Governor Fraser argued instead, but to little avail, that the financial sector prefers low economic activity. Most central bankers silence *the* great stability story of 1945–70 after WWII. Inflation and state deficits were very low; full employment, decent wages, health and education expanded, the like of which has never been seen before, and not since.[28] Banks were quiet, until 1970, when assets and leverage rapidly expanded, not matched with any increase of banks' equity base. The reverse, if one compares Figure 5.1 with Figure 7.2.

Central bankers largely avoid the 1945–70 bright-eyed inclusive projects; Mervyn King (BoE), wonders if it was a 'success', saying Keynesians are too 'naïve'. That is no answer to the era's social democracy, which was the only progressive counter-example, 'a truly exceptional' change in the balance of money power. Everywhere after that power reversed (Figures 5.1 and 5.2) helped with central bank-induced recessions and stagnation, one thing they can do. The claim of moderation contrasts to social conflicts in the 1970s, or old coin clipping, *the people's* currency debasement said to be exclusively the medieval Prince's fault. Strong states like USA's or UK's hanged or branded people for counterfeiting and clipping, others were weak. After 1980, central banks were to quell hopes and needs, to 'fight

---

[28] See Mannheim (1936: 104), on the 'bureaucratic view'. Fraser is cited in Chapter 4 and in Pixley (2004). I am re-capping Chapters 2 to 4.

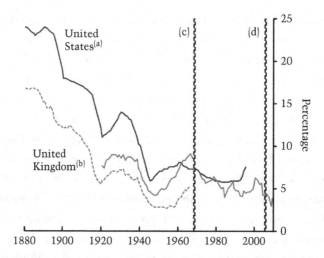

FIGURE 7.2 Long-run capital ratios for UK and US banks
Source: Haldane 2010: 7 [Annex], from Bank of England data
Notes supplied: (a) US data show equity as a percentage of assets;
(b) UK datum was an understatement of banks' capital before 1970;
(c) refers to change in UK accounting standards; (d) to UK's adoption of
International Financial Reporting Standards

inflation first', except none of that applied to the financial sector. Oh,
there was 'plenty of hope, but not for us', to paraphrase Ernst Bloch.
As banks became immoderate and unstable, frantic for certainty, central bank dissonance and internal conflict grew.[29]

TARGETS AND ICBS TOLD CBS TO 'BE KIND TO BANKS'

From this it follows that the 1987 to 2007 period was no moderation but,
to many (at the time, too), a 'great excess'. Why was the finance sector
also allowed to break free from any legitimacy or social justification for
financial activities, and Light Touch authorities became such a proud
slogan (Figures 7.1 and 7.2)? Recall Wall Street's rise with Eurodollars

---

[29] Bank equity is one, much-debated topic. See King (2016: 16); my reply is 1945–70 was
about power too, industrialists (debtors) sided with social justice: ideas and Keynesian
'naïvety' cannot do that. See Ingham (2004), on 'exceptional', and how Louis XV had a
weak, war finance-strapped state, and coins were untrustworthy for ordinary use, thus
clipping (see hanging, in Wennerlind (2001); and Chapter 1 on Law and Louis XV). Bloch's
phrase is cited in Pixley (2004) in my chapter on 'finance utopia'. Kyrtsis (2012) shows
'immoral panic' of frantic banks, mostly reactive, also under competition in Pixley (2016)

in the 1950s, to Nixon's float in 1971–3 under which capital controls disappeared. Central banks thereby lost 'tools'. In many ways, deregulation came with re-regulation of banks towards much evaded, disliked competition, and leverage rose to twenty times equity capital (Figure 7.2) in 2000, more sharply to 2008. Infighting among banks, money funds and shadow banks with financial engineering continues.[30] Competition was pro-market *logic* (village fair), making banks reactive.

The light touch–hard competition movement was embraced even in what Giannini calls 'financially backward' places such as France, Germany and Italy. He gives pride of place to Ronald McKinnon, a monetarist who in 1973 emphasised the concept 'financial repression'. This repression (implying Hayek's preposterous 'serfs' and Friedman's 'freedom lost') referred to the barriers of restrictions on entry to, and steep transaction costs on, the money markets set up by the 'old boys'. It tamed the trading. There had been quantitative controls on credit aggregates, too, if less often on bank deposit or borrowing rates, and a central bank approach to discourage financial engineering and inflations in plural ('taking away the punchbowl') and Glass Steagall (USA). Many governments also had 'massive state ownership in financial institutions' in Germany to Australia. Unthinkable in the USA, even the BoE was nationalised. Postwar LOLR and 'activist macroeconomic policies' had very different crisis dynamics to the long era from 1870 to 1939. Until 2007, no huge collapse of broad money took place in the heartland, just bubbles. We see monetarism cared nothing that bank money is contracted or expanded at financial sectors' will and borrowers' demand and need for money. Oh no, the Fed could do everything. That fraught nature of central banks was, with the GFC, due to paucity of treasury activity, and to illusions and mirages, Haldane showed about banking's 'contribution to economic wellbeing' (little). CB powers can halt inflations (less asset inflation) by inducing recessions and making deflations

---

[30] Often banks copy each other (not compete). The Greenspan 'put' in the 1987, 1998 and 2000 crises, was discussed by central bankers, and to me; in Pixley (2004) – a 'put' is a bet – in the Fed case, it saved huge, copycat banks. Competition assumed lone individuals, bartering goods in markets, not finance markets and M&A in banks.

more likely ('pulling a string'); but reflation is only preventative, not a *remedy*. However much banks logically need base (HPM) money, it 'pushes a string' in deflation.[31]

The social power intrinsic to capitalist money, which compromises central banking possibilities is unknown to most. Thorstein Veblen never assumed capitalism was efficient but destabilizing and disruptive. The actors in Veblen's day were US robber barons, and he attributed the money 'illusion' of 'exaltation' and inflation, and on to a 'depression', as a 'malady' of the *affections of the financier-businessman*. Any slight discrepancy between the 'nominal capitalization which *they have set their heart upon* through habituation in the immediate past' and the 'actual capitalizable value', is the cause of depression, the tiny 'discrepancy which discourages business men'. This malady and depressions, Veblen explained, 'centre on *the metaphysical stability of the money unit*'. Central banks corrupted (crafted) their language around this flighty fiction of belief – to please; to duck and weave. Unemployment and lower wages have enormous social impacts. The chains of interdependencies in money relations are counterintuitive and fragile; cause-effect individualism may be simple but illogical. With money, the solution to deflation that Keynes could see was for governments to act to revive confidence of businesses and not of financial markets. Metaphysical stability of the money unit or 'the fiction of an invariant standard' can need confidence-inducing demand created for all, helped by states, which central banks cannot provide. Austerity (treasuries) only confirms finance sector control whether before or after the GFC.[32]

---

[31] See Giannini (2011: 227–9); McKinnon (1991) – a great sycophant to Friedman; citing Schularick and Taylor (2012: 1031) on the many state-owned banks; and Haldane (2010: 2–3; 14–17). See Figures 5.1 and 5.2 on base to broad money; LOLR is lender of last resort; also, reflation *can* be Greenspan's 'put' to 'boom'.

[32] See Veblen (1904: 237–8); although those workers still in steady employment may enjoy lower prices, thus wage cutting 'losses are more apparent than real', Veblen (1904: 240 his italics); later called the 'worker illusion' but Veblen stressed capitalist illusions. 'Invariant' is Philip Mirowski's (1989) phrase, cited often in Ingham texts. Note that demands for treasury austerity never apply to its war spending The jobless served banks nicely.

Central banks are thus in the unenviable situation initially discussed. Targets kept economies stagnant, state budgets under 'metaphysical' duress and increased unemployment. Yet over 100 years, governments became large, not only from the World Wars and state R&D for economic development, but also democratic activities for education and health, a well-informed public sphere, and considerable state economic activity. After political and social changes in which the finance sector grew dominant, the state's debt might not be accepted unless the 'fictional' stability of money gave *confidence*. States acceded to light touch, to hacking their own democratic potential and depoliticising money, yet with *rules* for (on paper) independent central banks. It suited imperialising US Administrations (if they understood) since states have separate interests in war finance. Unusual arrangements of the Fed spread the process globally. The Fed is so far from formally independent of Wall Street that its District Feds are owned and governed by private local member banks. The NY Fed 'regulates' and bails outs Wall Street; its banks select the NY Fed president who is always on the FOMC. Whether Greenspan was cheerleader or not, Fed Chairs often defer to the NY Fed; whether US Treasury was captured, the US dollar supremacy was a huge bonus and when not, Hank Paulson (former GS&Co chief) G.W. Bush's Treasury head, knew what to do (in Chapter 8). Problems are government 'debt' dependence and, in the US the privately-owned aspect of the central bank. In the UK, Thatcher had 'Big Bang – competition, light touch and reworked BoE's ties with the City. By then, Wall Street had anyway invaded the City.[33]

This is all to suggest, as conservative Philip Coldwell, a president of the Dallas Fed said in the 1970s, the Fed sometimes considered

---

[33] Häring and Douglas (2012: 85–90), discuss one scandal, a NY Fed board member using his insider knowledge in 2009. See Chapter 8 on Paulson. Tim Geithner, schooled by that NY Fed, was NY Fed president then; moved to Secretary of Treasury, not due to direct Wall Street pressure on Obama's administration in 2008, but only that, as Acemoglu et al. (2016) show, the firms Geithner had 'connections' with, did better in market 'value' from his likely appointment. Thatcher had 'big bang' in 1986, 'housewife budget' false analogies and TINA (we saw earlier).

itself as governmen, 'other times, when it serves, it considers itself non-government'. A 1930s–70s critic, anti-bank Congressman Wright Patman summed it up as 'a pretty queer duck'.[34] (I prefer 'chameleon' to the context.). These are structural issues, not mere conspiracies and revolving doors, which show the Fed fulfilling a similar if different role to the BoE, in the Fed's support of the quasi-imperialising US state and globalising Wall Street since the Fed's inception in 1913. The ECB stuck itself on market credibility of its currency, which involved swallowing anti-democratic policies too.

Governments gave orders to the BoC, RBA, RBNZ and others. Aware of bond trader rule, these CBs refused to swallow neoclassical counterfactuals when possible, preferring evidence and judgement in specific contexts. In contrast, one cannot regard the Fed, BoE or ECB as in a miasma of delusions; such CBs happily obeyed Mr. Market; often were market operators. They did anything to support and rescue global finance and to club economic life.[35]

I began fieldwork in 1998 when the cry in big finance centres was liquidity, how 'deep and wide' was this curious liquid, how it was a great sign of stability: not that it subverted productive economic activity before their eyes. Pro-market libertarians and monetarists raved about the freedom of possessive individuals, boosted with a bizarre worship of Wall Street or the Chicago Board of Trade. TV cameras zoomed onto the thickness of Greenspan's briefcase for *clues*; onto talking head shows of (criminal) pump-and-dump analysts. Garish NASDAQ neon signs on Broadway were a fraction of the pathetic rituals of grown-up rich people, ever richer. Orléan's

---

[34] Coldwell and Patman are cited in Greider (1987); also, in Cockburn and Ridgeway (1975); I am grateful to V. J. Carroll on these structural matters. Greider's sociology of the Fed (1987: 71–4) shows none of Volcker's Fed was rich or 'well-connected'. Later the Board's composition was reduced to financiers/bankers, excluding industry mostly, and labour. In January 1932, Patman had spearheaded a movement to impeach Treasury Secretary Mellon (that Stalinist Treasurer); Patman was pushed off the Congress bank committee in 1975.

[35] The Fed and BoE were riven by dissonances though. See Tily (2015: 2–5) on instability; Volcker and 'clubbing', also in Tily (2015: 7); a contrast to DeLong (2000), who says proudly the US was always anti-inflationary, which is correct and grim.

sociological line is that the liberty to sell finance assets is completely reliant on a collective undertaking of each new market to break free of capital immobility. Being free to sell when one wishes or needs, rests on an implicit commitment, argues Orléan, of the entire financial community to hold every security over the long term. Far from lone investors (serfs), an entire (state-supported) structure of stock exchanges, money markets, oligopolistic banks and shadow banks must exist for 'liquidity'. Fears and needs for liquidity are reliant on everyone being *both buyers and sellers*. As soon as everyone is a seller from mimicry, disruptions, fears – a market collapses (such as 1998). The search for liquidity up and down Wall Street, Zurich or the City is a social force of collective, urgent needs externally imposed and felt as 'objectivity'. These sentiments infused central banks; fears in FOMC meetings of 'the market' show CBs' separation into two focal points: one is economic activity (only if wage inflation-free i.e. stagnation) and two, government bond markets and liquidity. (QE is a substitute for market liquidity.)[36]

Praying at this liquidity god was also *the mob*, the standover men from finance economics (often Chicago, which enjoyed lavish business funding for decades), to justify the *rationality* of illiterate security traders versus *bumbling* authorities. 'Rational Expectations' pointed the way spectacularly for the 1990s Dotcom bubble and crash by refusing the existence of bubbles! In this model, one could instantly weed out uncertain prospects. RatEx was answer to the loathed (if right wing) Frank Knight, in leaving uncertainty

---

[36] See Pixley (2004); Orléan the economist-sociologist see (2014: 206; 208–9; 142). Durkheim analysed the 1882 Paris Bourse crash; cited by Wilson in Pixley et al. (2014: 317). Durkheim's study on *Suicide* was to counteract Herbert Spencer's survival of the fittest thesis, so beloved in finance economics. Durkheim took a most isolated act and showed suicide to be subject to social forces and, in financial crashes a societal situation of normlessness, or anomie. A counterpoint to Durkheim is Polanyi 1957 [1944] in that markets are not anomic or norm-free. Instead, social norms of opportunism, price beliefs and conventions shared, dominate, compared to normative systems of redistribution or reciprocity, in hierarchical or proto-socialistic (Indigenous people's) structures. The 1998 collapse was of a US hedge fund; Greenspan saved all, the press spoke 'crash' on my first NYC research and our laughing when the Chicago traders' bell rang was akin to swearing in church. For QE see Chapter 8.

or bubbles to 'psychotics' and 'irrational exuberance', nostrums that many in the Fed or BoE accepted. Oh, no, that Internet ice cream firm would eventually report gains not losses. Forget *Barrons* editor's point that Manhattan has corner shops on every block (selling ice cream). Practically, bubbles are not efficient, nor are they irrational: there is no objective pre-existing value to over-shoot or under-shoot, and all traders must rely on gossip and guesses about each other's sentiments. The rarely admitted trick, well-known as the gamblers' *curse*, is to exit before the fools but make profits up to the last point: this is felt as a force beyond traders' control, just as religion can inspire fervour (to Durkheim). No statistical model can show if 'a stationary system is, in fact, stationary'; RatEx claimed that 'a fairly well defined recurrent event' is 'useful' for probabilistic calculations. The problem of which frequencies to choose became laughably narrow. In FOMC debates during the GFC, the Fed clung to certainty that specific US house price movements were predictive if one excluded those regions of complete price collapse. What? Bernanke (Tooze alleges) assumed a psychotic event.[37]

The prisons designed for CBs (as that renegade RBA official said) had fraught options of resistance, quitting, or craven loyalty. I believe it made decent central banks, and central bankers everywhere (internally) reluctant to talk too loudly. Behind closed doors, using jargon beyond the wit of politicians or bankers, things might be said (I have shown). But dissonances are painful: if one resigns in disgust, another voice is lost to louder voices urging humiliation, greater intolerance and cruelty on innocent people. Can one assume decent individuals can create decent institutions or is it the opposite?[38]

---

[37] US business funding (a longer history) to the 'Chicago School', apparently started around 1965–70 with pharmaceutical firms, which objected to the USFDA food and drug regulations, in (a then) unseemly interference with universities (Nik-Kah 2011). See Knight (1964 [1921]); Pixley (2012) also on RatEx; and citing 'ice creams'; Durkheim cited in Orléan (2014: 232) and RatEx, Mordecai Kurz and Lucas on 'psychotics' are cited (2014:195–6); Tooze (2016), also on 'seat of pants' Fed deliberations at the GFC.

[38] Recapping this chapter so far and asking the conundrum in Markus (2001) that applies to CB mandates: a tough Governor may also humiliate CB members, like meetings anywhere.

THE IMPACTS OF THE EMH

To imagine predictions are possible about tentative collective beliefs, practices and fears of the day belies common sense. Central bankers in their mahogany-panelled boardrooms with leisurely time to trawl over histories of central bank difficulties in controlling private bank money, rarely recalled the Overend-Gurney 1866 scandal in Britain, even the US 1929 crash. Many CBs, not all we saw, were enthralled with finance economists of the 1980s–90s; others endured pressures of the financial industry enjoying these ideas. Inside the Fed, jokes abounded about how people were 'flipping' houses, weeks before the edifice collapsed. Working against this bad faith was the social construction of market institutions, and inability of individuals to set prices due the force of such institutions, and conventions. The collectivity pushes a boom and bust. Central banks' hope for self-regulating markets was based on 'transposing' the haggling in producer-consumer markets onto competition in financial markets, to Orléan, in pursuit of advantage. But in these markets, mimicry prevails. RatEx and light touch enabled the 'financial community' to enlarge its targets.[39]

Another absurd prop to bank legitimacy was the 'Efficient Market Hypothesis'. It was partly derived from Chicago's thin evolution version of Hayek's Darwinian economics. Cybernetics in Hayek's quaint approach, or information searches, only created unreadable maths models and difficulties in defining the concept of cognition. Although biologists had attacked the conflation of natural selection with maximisation, this, as new, 'market hypothesis' conflated gaily; markets were 'efficient' because 'natural selection' would instantly weed out those players who failed to maximize on relevant market information. Any statistically 'exploitable pattern' can be arbitraged away and 'self-destruct'. If that were so, why would central banks

---

[39] See Pixley (2012) citing 'house-flipping' from FOMCs of the fateful 2007–8 and scandals, also my interviews. I again draw on Orléan (2014) and of course 'community' (with ninety-eight definitions) is a self-serving PR word for rip-off merchants in FIRE – Finance, Insurance and Real Estate.

or regulators need to worry? The EMH had various versions; also, it accepted uncertainty unlike RatEx, and later argued 'you can't beat the market'. Neither, Orléan points out, imply 'efficiency'. Anyway, only market traders were clever (or stupidly took on more leverage); state officials were dumb like 'diffusion speculators'. These traders, according to Robert Shiller, the populariser and justifier of a behaviour-type view (with his own financial firm advertised in *The New Yorker* for years), allowed emotions and gossip only to (mum and dad) 'diffusion investor' calculations, unlike cool 'smart traders'. It had a patchy charm.[40]

One can only explain central banker defence, nay promotion to US Congress of such propositions, as due to broader forces, enriched and heartened from Chicago approaches (to scholarly loss). In the attack on financial repression (bankers may as well have been living in hovels), the EMH was a culmination of 'relentless propaganda', partly from the loud-mouthed 'finance economics discipline' ultimately aiming for the creation of financial liquidity on a global scale. This was immensely ambitious, such as Shiller's advocacy of a global housing market as a sure thing. Questions to Shiller at a public lecture showed his ignorance of Frank Knight, but that went nowhere.[41] Securitising proceeded apace, on making student and housing loans liquid, regardless of anyone's job opportunities or wages.

Authorities gave in, some loved it: markets were rational, arbitrage socially useful in 'allocating' investment. One sad story is about how 'leaning against the wind' ('LATW-tilt') became so unfashionable. Sushil Wadhwani recalls his time in Governor Charles Bean's day on the BoE, giving a catalogue of the accepted 1990s fads:

> [Wadhwani thought] 'it possible that some of those who object
> to a LATW-tilt in monetary policy on the grounds that bubble

---

[40] On EMH, Chicago's version of Darwin/Hayek, see Mirowski (2011: 260); note 'cognition' and probability (for HFT below). Orléan (2014: 185) cites Malkiel on 'self-destruct'; 'efficiency'. Pixley (2012) cites Shiller on allegedly 'irrational exuberance'.

[41] Orléan (2014: 258; 60) on propaganda; Pixley questioned Shiller in the early 2000s and, apart from making a fool of himself about Knight at a Sydney University speech, who cares about Sydney?

identification is too difficult are really saying that they would rather carry out inflation forecast-targeting policy on the assumption that financial markets are efficient and there are no bubbles. Indeed, this predisposition to believe that financial markets are efficient on the part of some members was a *frequent source of disagreement* when I was a member of the Monetary Policy Committee at the Bank of England.'

'There are no bubbles'. Other members objected to wage inflation targets on top of trader arbitrage, as not efficient, going nowhere economically useful, indeed bizarrely in UK's 1991 housing bubble and bust in Tory heartland that reduced the wealthy to bed and breakfasts. Labour swept to office soon after. Booms involve social emotions and cognitive dissonances for central banks (not to finance economics). To John Flemming (BoE), no central bank will 'prick a bubble' when it is *nearly* crashing because it will wear a lot of 'odium'. Far better for CB faux strategies to save reputations, he saw, was to earn lots of 'brownie points' in picking up the pieces later (the then Greenspan 'put', he told me). Who wants the odium, when grovelling works so well? The Fed's apparent success (three times) reinforced relaxed views about marvellous economic benefits of the biggest finance centres.[42] And even after the EMH became defunct, post-GFC, its tactics lived in finance centres in a pretence at non-human form that I now discuss.

FROM EMH TO HFT: BUILDING HUMAN 'EFFICIENCY' IN COMPUTER TRADES

The few debates (in the FOMC) on moving against bubbles were either rejected or tortured. In heterodoxy, if CBs use interest rates against bubbles (or CPI rises) that stops economic activity, as in the blunt tool cliché. Arguments to defend the unemployed drowned

---

[42] See Wadhwani (2008) my emphasis on dissonances; note LATW or 'bubble' are less the drunks joke about 'the punchbowl'; all McChesney Martin in Chapter 5. The UK housing bust and Flemming are cited in Pixley (2004).

under inflation targets, predictions and indifference to bank money creation. As well, Goodhart's Law that banks innovate away from any imposed target, fostered heterodox pessimism. Funnily though, among all central banks, only the Fed has control of margin loans (since 1933–4 under FDR) when Wall Street had a reduced role. Whereas once, in the 1950s, the Fed raised margin requirements to 100 per cent: that is, stopping this lending to buy stock to short or go long, and purchase/sell later, Greenspan refused FOMC members and Senate calls to raise it from 50 to 60. Wadhwani suggests that Greenspan's approach of 'doing nothing' did lead CB critics to see the Fed of that time as a 'serial bubble blower' and cites Bernanke's support of Greenspan. Margin loan control is specific to taming bubbles, unlike high rates that savage economic activity. True, banks can avoid using margins, rules are evaded, off-balance sheet leverage grew steadily, but not even margins were raised. Greenspan told Congress it was 'unfair' to modest investors (who lost). More space for cheating modest savers was also made possible because Alan Greenspan, Larry Summers and Bob Rubin silenced serious protests from US agencies, often women like Brooksley Born who opposed structured debt. Put-downs of women deserve noting, since deregulators are still adulated in the finance press. What was Summers' role in the passage of the Gramm-Leach-Bliley Act? When Treasurer and with Fed Chair Greenspan, both pushed for banning derivative *regulation* no less (Blinder recounts). The key enablers of (already) global Wall Street were ultimately Treasury and Congress aided with Fed cheerleading. No surprise, today Summers hectors in the *FT* on 'secular' stagnation (a determinist prime mover from god). These officials helped global finance blast economic activity to the worst collapse since the Great Depression.[43]

With financial recklessness on a grand scale, it was not true that everyone was shocked at the crash. Anyone knowing that money is

---

[43] Goodhart's 'law' as Dow (2006) sees it; on margins and A.G. see Pixley (2012); Wadhwani (2008); Blinder (2013: 63) on Brooksley Born bullied, Summers, and the Act, see Häring and Douglas (2012); Haldane (2010) on 'worst' depression.

a social relation, not a *thing* to be packaged for arbitrage, urged *taming* these unsustainable capitalist bank profits. During the entire era, 1980 to post GFC, cautionary policies were proposed: A huge social movement (in France called ATTAC) demanding taxes on financial transactions (after James Tobin) got nowhere; Thomas Palley urged asset-based reserve requirements (on the margin loan principle) to no avail.[44] With electronic trading and clearing, transaction taxes are cheap to impose. If they *worked*, tax revenues decline because trading is intended to slow down markedly to instil caution. Only governments can impose taxes. Protests at financial firms entrapping the poor, or at governments still privatising banks (in Germany a few banks tried to survive on subprime to manage transitions to private) withered under capitalist-state authoritarianism.[45]

We now know the GFC had little impact on authorities' capacity or willingness to stop evasive, survivalist techniques of the largest centres. One is the rise of 'High Frequency Trading' (HFT), which directly follows (failed) EMH techniques, with algorithms built into computer models. It aims to reduce trading transaction time to zero seconds that a Tobin tax would raise to weeks or months. *HFT accesses* orders to buy or sell *beforehand*. This uninformed but fast trader *human* element built into algorithms is a technically legal form of front running. Why is it legal to arbitrage against Pension Fund selling or buying? Oh, computers get the information! Don't ask who provides it. When a 'flash crash' occurred in 2010, General Electric shares were worth zero for nano-seconds. HFT cannot demonstrate 'efficiency in allocating capital' if GE is worthless momentarily, from algorithms made up of human assumptions. Its purpose is to gain prior advantage with speed. Latest reports (to date) of the BoE and Fed on HFT were in 2015, which talk about the 'dark pool' defence of big pension funds

---

[44] See Pixley (2018) on ATTAC aka the Tobin Tax; see Palley (2014) on discretionary use of reserve requirements.

[45] Dusseldorf was known as easy prey. Rhineland airports were stacked with RBS staff flogging debt, 2007-08; some Landesbanken fell, many regions or rich local councils were gulled, say in Australia, shown in later court cases mainly against GS&Co. It also arranged the 2001 Greek loan secretly when the head of its Europe GS&Co division was Mario Draghi, in Pixley (2012) and on HFT.

to protect their intentions from HFT; central banks promise to do 'further research'. More distractions intervene.[46]

The 1980s to 2007 were the high-water mark of central bank reputations to finance markets. Some, not all, enjoyed orthodoxy's entry-points to club the economy and basked in the favour of fabulously profitable private banking and right-wing governments; harried or infiltrated by strident, uncivil economic 'theorists'. Social democracy was the loser, severely compromised over these decades. How central banks, notably the mighty Fed coped with the GFC is the topic of Chapter 8. The switch was painful and again demonstrates the conflicted situation of very old institutional compromises between the warrior state and capitalist financial power. The EMU without an EU Treasury was merely part of global policies that ignored treasuries, I suggest, to complete this chapter. Namely treasuries have probably lost more than central banks gained: a gain of only mendacious or sly acclaim.

European Monetary Union and Federations in General

Just as financial forces were free to roam the world at will and dictate the terms of loans in the unravelling of the 1970s–90s, the idea of the Euro took off. What bad luck for Europe's social democracies, the strongest in the world. The Euro is a forced marriage to the global CB independence movement, itself based on Bundesbank policies that shaped the European Central Bank's (ECB) model. One can argue the EMU's timing was inauspicious in that events conspired against the ECB design. But against these excuses, the rules of the game the ECB was dealt were brutal. Not 'flawed' or 'mistaken' economic ideas so much as the outcomes of the 1970s money disputes from which central banks gained their destructive orders. Without belabouring the importance of different monetary stories, one can suggest further factors, however, by comparing the EU with other attempts at

---

[46] Haldane (2012) only refers to 'low-level abuse': stock exchange authorities permit 'access'; but King (2016) also says it's front running; the Fed and BoE websites estimate 60 per cent HFT in their finance centres.

federation, or countries that pretend they are not federations, such as the United Kingdom. If a mere plebiscite in 2016 could threaten the 'united' bloc of regions and near-states (Scotland), then the deals for formal federations of the USA, Canada or Australia can give clues about what the nature of monetary union entails in the EU, or Britain too. Calls for secession and social-political divisions are not unknown in the *de jure* constitutional federations.

The overriding reason usually given for the Euro's present problems is from the lack of a fiscal union to match its monetary union. How important is this under *independent* CBs? Though hybrid state-capitalist money is the old rule not explicitly formulated in the Euro (its design ignored bank money), my argument is that an absent EU Treasury is important but not the sole factor. Recall the older federations were experimental, so a 'one best way' for money is questionable. Even if today's EU context is barely comparable, for example, to the 1837 US crisis – its 'great depression' and American humiliation to its primary creditor the City of London – there are logical clues. America's 'manifest destiny' neglects that horror of US dependency on Britain and the monetary factors in 1837.[47]

In effect, this US crisis was not a 'federal' US, but a states-led depression, jump-started by New York state's Erie Canal construction, into a canal and railway 'fever' everywhere. Wall Street entered later, only to bet on canal and railway stock. To be sure, the US Constitution created a political union, and granted power to Congress to issue the currency and bonds, so monetary federation was politically advanced *de jure*, and the EU Parliament in Brussels is no comparison to Congress powers. As well, the ECB stands alone, whereas before 1837 the second CB of the USA was defunct. And yet, the USA was 'a fragile compound' and, after the 1837 Crash and Depression was in no position to wage war against British territorial encroachment from Canada, since Britain was its major creditor.

---

[47] Ingham (2004) summarises the EMU's lack of fiscal policy; on federations see Chapter 1. America was dependent on the City up to 1900.

America's European credit froze in 1843 after defaults of 8 of the then 27 states, which refused to raise property taxes. Each state's hotly defended political sovereignty, after the collapse of their developmental borrowing, led them to self-limit foreign borrowing and tie it (vaguely) to tax raising. But resistance to federal power and its barest capacity to enforce the law threatened the union.[48]

There was indeed no full US Treasury; its revenue (in gold and silver) of tariff taxes and sales of *public land* dried up in 1837 and, to London, America seemed a 'basket-case' of local con-men. Congress was deadlocked (not the only time) over freeing US Treasury from state-located banks that ran and held all its revenue, but which suspended or failed in 1837. Not only this mess but as Galbraith puts it, Americans had not merely aimed for 'no taxation without representation' in the War, but for 'no tax with representation' ever after. Apart from the Civil War's temporary greenbacks and income tax of Lincoln's 1862 legislation, US Congress was only authorized to impose income tax in 1913. FDR's more centralising bank reforms had to wait. Likewise, control over bank note issue was with individual banks, as in Australia (before its federation in 1901) and state-private (PPP) boondoggling was one problem during the nineteenth century in both cases. The other was development of infrastructure in each state. In the US, the constitutional right of states to raise their own militias means that 'the Administration' does not have a monopoly of violence; unheard of elsewhere. After 1837, numerous state-based riots led to state militias, 'civic armies' to quell violence. My point is that US monetary federation took time (and a Civil War). Lincoln's greenbacks raised further acrimonious debates among small farmer (debtor) parties, which did not trust Wall Street and the 'cross of gold': if small farmers 'want more money they cannot bring money into

---

[48] Fraser (2005: 36–9), on the Canal. Much of this and the next par. is from Roberts (2012: 7–11; 35; 75–8; 85–7); he argues the BoE was somewhat lax before 1837: UK investment flooded to the USA for good rates of return. There were two American central banks in the nineteenth century, which were not continued for complex and as ever, disputed reasons, see Galbraith (1975b), Ingham (2004). I have drawn very little for this from Pixley (2018).

existence' as they can 'wheat', said William Jennings Bryan in 1897; Wall Street opposed an inconvertible paper currency (as inflationary). However, the 1837 crash and state defaults were not on 'greenbacks' but overseas state bond issues. The debate was over how all money is credit; not that 'greenbackers' succeeded in the 1913 Federal Reserve after nineteenth century's political diversity became muted.[49]

In sum, federations are hardly 'settled' any more than mono-states. As well, much debate on the Euro was about whether it might rival the US dollar. Politicians of far smaller economies than the EU, like Canada and Australia, never imagined their currencies in that ambitious light. Freedom from the old hegemonic UK was their aim. Their monetary-fiscal management is modest, and federal-state acrimony is part of a game. In Europe's case, a grandiose idea of competing with America took over in the Monetary Union's planning stages: tragically combined as the finance sector's plebiscite was regained aided with the outburst of neoclassical quantity views. The ECB's design put Europe at the mercy of financial markets' estimation of the Euro and member states' bonds (as in 1837 US states), with little thought of war finance (NATO) or French nuclear war power. The bad luck of timing was disastrous though not (inevitably) incurable. It was an effort at civility that descended.

In addition, French and German political differences can make modest, civil solutions difficult, given the stagnation of European economic activity from ECB policies pre-GFC, and worse later. Postwar, France moved from its pre-WWII *laissez-faire* to strong social-state

---

[49] See also Federal tax history section in irs.gov. and Galbraith (1975b); On Federal treasury debates (endless) at the time, against 'states rights' politicians and local banks (also with Bills of Exchange, reams of bank 'paper'), also Mexican war, Roberts (2012:87–112). State violence quelled, e.g. a New York State faced anti-rent wars of former Dutch peasants (in Roberts 2012: 137–74). The American Civil War 1861–65, the first federal (Northern) 'temporary' income tax law passed by Congress (1862), expired a decade later; in 1913, the Sixteenth Amendment of the Constitution was ratified to authorize Congress to impose a tax on income (irs.gov). Like other federations, variations in state taxes cause problems, like the state of Delaware's corporate tax looseness. On greenbacks see Ingham (2004: 8; 44–5); 'cross': Galbraith (1975b: 100) and on the Greenback Party's high tide 1878, later the 'free-silver' Populists Party, which 'captured the Democrats'. The 1867 Paris agreement on the gold standard; and how Bryan lost badly, is in Galbraith (1975b: 94–100).

and Keynesian defences, while Germany disavowed étatism. Post-1945 German concerns included a civilizing transformation of capitalist employers and bankers. Their modest pro-trade union and social commitments remain long after the gangs running the USA or Britain stepped up authoritarian whining. Germany did not turn to *laissez-faire*, either, but to an 'ordo-liberalism' that initially trod a careful path. Its figure-head Walter Eucken was highly critical of *everything* the Reichsbank did: from its 1921 hyperinflation, to Weimar's gift to it in 1924 of autocratic powers and its savage deflation up to 1933. Then the Nazi state apparatus took total control of the Reichsbank in 1939 (or before). For reforms, Eucken proposed in 1946 'a balance of power between the Treasury and central bank'; he suggested for the new 'Bundesbank' monopolistic privileges but with 'precisely specified state control' so it could not 'conduct its own economic policy against the state'. Also, Western Germany designed a decentralised central banking system and early on, there were strong arguments against *the 1924 Reichsbank independence*, given that its deflation fostered Nazism. Arguments against that 1924 Act for the postwar are now 'erased from memory' (argues Bibow): the new Bundesbank was more independent than most, though it required cooperation with the Federal state. Nothing, though, can counteract an authoritarian state prepared and able to destroy CB 'independence' and defences of civil society.[50]

Among other aspects of the EU generally, Schengen (free labour and capital movements: French supported, mid-1980s) highlights

---

[50] On the Euro, as 'rival' see e.g. the Matthijs and Blyth (2015a collection); Germain and Schwartz (2014). See Lanchester (2016) citing others *wrongly* arguing Germany is laissez faire. Schacht of the Reichsbank promoted rearmament, see Chapter 2. Bibow (2015: 13–15) citing Walter Eucken; Bibow calls ordo-liberalism 'peculiar'. Discussions in the Max Planck Institute (Cologne) with notably Jens Beckert confirmed my own impressions: whereas most Australian press barons (e.g. Rupert Murdoch), bank and mining chieftains, were as crude as a Trump by the 1980s, my interviewees in Germany (2007–9) and other EU member countries showed a reasonableness foreign to my interview experiences, since decent bankers were hard to find (not sure why Volcker ignored my request). One ex-Fed official was a bully; my publisher and I dropped his name and trivial points after vitriol I dare ask (as agreed) he check his quotes.

bitter problems for labour to which neoclassical visions were indifferent in assuming 'the jobless' should roam Europe for any low paid work. Lacking a shred of imagination, the powerful insisted further unity would thereby be made possible, as long as one applied 'enough' shock therapy to resisters and workers. Far right backlashes hit Europe later.

Even so, longer perspectives on federations suggest fairer agreements are not impossible, although the USA is hardly comforting. Its Civil War, just after the first 1837–44 Great US Depression and violent aftermath, prevented secession of the South and formally abolished a slave economy, but even with FDR's 1930s reforms, the Jim Crow South refused to accept equal labour laws for 'agricultural and domestic workers', that is, Blacks. Just when that situation improved (with LBJ), things got worse. It is then important to remember that a powerful US federation retains this divide to the despair of many, and its first brilliant (popular) Black President (Obama). As well, Quebec wanted to secede from Canada for about twenty years, Western Australia threatens every time it is booming *or* collapsing (like last year); Scotland's independence hopes are sporadic, but these are peaceful: the European Union aimed for peace at last.[51]

The EU's member-state populations were rarely as neglected as in the US or UK, noting the US 'welfare state' is threadbare and Brexit exposes divisive UK inequalities. EU elite arrogance plays out in disaffection. Yet I doubt that neoclassical or ordo-liberal clubs duped European elites into monetary union unopposed, and notably its currency ambitions. Interviews in 2007–9 showed senior German and French bankers and Paris and Berlin regulators were acutely aware of the threat from the US imposing the 'one best way' in all EU matters financial; but which site of disturbance would emerge? No one can 'pick' an exact point of breakdown, so for example, Europeans worried about US hedge funds. The

---

[51] Katznelson (2013) gives a bleak picture of the New Deal; but the Nazi occupation starved Athens in 1944, later, the Greek Colonels ran a semi-fascist regime aided by Nixon; Eastern Europe had Soviet rule, Portugal and Spain, decades of fascism postwar, to welcome the EU that, so far, is fairly peaceful. See Chapter 5 on post-LBJ.

Fed did not pick subprime either. Neither Germany nor France has populations fully using banks: household debt is low, unlike Spain, Ireland or Greece. Limits on credit cards and mortgages remain in both.[52]

The appointment of Josef Ackerman was a longer concern (in interviews); people (rightly) feared that this new CEO would transpose Wall Street's model onto Deutsche Bank. Paris regulators were bored with the (tax and pay) incentives of London luring their top young bankers to the City. They returned to Paris for free state childcare and superior health services, but with City models too. Management structures in the big French and German banks were changing, then, in the years between the ECB's birth in 2001 to the crisis, also from privatising the modest local banks in these countries. Anyway, national competition for building the most 'free' and biggest financial centre took off globally, the larger of which, as night follows day, put pressure on their governments to slash social welfare and provide tax-free havens. Giannini called EU states 'backward'. Labour markets had much variability, but the opposite to orthodox assertions. All this is to say that reducing every aspect of life to 'the economy' is typical.[53] Countries' traditional cultural or recent fears and hopes do not magically disappear just by imposing a REM model and inflation targets. Against those Anglo-Americans who manage to cite a similar language as a sole cultural point against the ECB,

---

[52] In France credit card *debts* must be paid off in full monthly; in Germany, most people rent; department stores don't accept credit cards, only cash or debit cards: in my 2007–08 time at least. Inequality exists, but less debt inequality, and far less than Anglo-America. My Elite Interviews (2007–9), Germany, France, are anonymous and unpublished.

[53] See Chapter 5; Bibow (2015: 15) says of the early Bundesbank:

> the accumulation of foreign exchange reserves (gold and US dollars) was the foremost factor in the creation of central bank money under the Bretton Woods regime (to the 1980s), when the Bundesbank also lent to the banking system through traditional discount and open-market operations [OMO; later on, repo operations]. On occasion, the Bundesbank also conducted outright purchases (and sales) of long-term government debt securities in secondary markets.

This reserve method is quite common. To Minsky (2008 [1986]), OMO do not allow CB inspection of bank books like the discount window; market moves let private banks free to roam; Admati and Hellwig (2013) slam French and German bank balances post GFC.

in countries like the US or UK, dialects remain (Welsh of course but Geordie is inexplicable as 'English'; or Chicago to New Jersey). Let me briefly note the civilising and decivilising processes facing the ECB first.[54]

Actual Foundation of the ECB

After the twentieth century wars and democratic experiments post 1945, the ECB and its Euro was an extreme example of the general 1980s CB independence movement (ICB). The ICB demand hit on the Bundesbank model, but to exclude Germany's postwar aims of restoring social connections among the social groups and institutions sundered before 1945. Although the ECB's early formulations had civilising and decivilising tendencies (e.g. the Maastricht Treaty of 1992) it is the outlier ICB case. Established by 1999, the ECB lays bare the sociological and democratic issues involved in all ICBs. They attempt to depoliticise money through CBs independent of their Treasury, but the ECB's rules cannot even replicate *informal* relations of other formally independent central banks to central governments. The obvious issue avoided in some of the political science literature is Europe has no 'overarching political sovereignty' from which the ECB would be independent. 'End of story really', BoE John Flemming told me. Serious implications include a lack of a united political body with powers to direct the ECB to break Maastricht (gold-like) rules in a crisis.[55]

The Euro was to be 'pure-private' money. In its 'rules', no individual state could borrow from the ECB (unlike sovereign states from their CB, although Washington DC could not borrow from the 1913 Fed either; and ICBs formally). So 'budget deficits must be financed directly in the money market', like private corporations or California etc. The difference is sovereign states have compulsory taxation: taxpayers are involuntary debtors to states. In democracies, more

---

[54] In the 1950s, the European Economic Community was a customs union, and institutions developed slowly. REM is Rational Economic Man. I mistake lots of dialects/local idiom.

[55] Ingham (2004: 195) on sovereignty; Flemming in Pixley (2004) on independence. But what of the UK troika and "sovereignty"? See below.

so in civilising welfare states, intransigent governments can go via the ballot box (but finance plebiscites make actual voting messy). Ingham and Goodhart ask why these European states agreed to surrender their monetary sovereignty? This is the 'English' or I suggest, a 'mono-state' view. Ingham however also cites Weber, 'for money to be money, it has to be scarce and an autonomous weapon in the economic battle'. It implies money's infrastructural (collective social) power is enfeebled, but does it matter whether in a weak federation or a mono-state?[56]

Like the original US constitution, the Euro rules put 'pseudo-sovereign' (taxing) member-states to the whims of financial markets. This is ironic since the single currency had a non-orthodox (fixed exchange rate) drive, to prevent Forex speculation from destabilising individual members. But it was a 'free-market version'. As Alain Parguez put it in 1999, the Euro was 'a bold plan' to create the soundest and strongest currency in the world. That was the large problem. It required convincing global financial investors, far too early in the EMU, of 'zero expected inflation' through preventing wage inflation, taken as the sole cause of inflation by the ECB and world money markets. Although the ECB regime is harsher than the NAIRU due to different wage structures, the further requirement is that no member state can interfere in the process of money creation, and the ECB is (formally) forbidden to create money. Member states are 'obliged to finance their deficits by selling bonds to commercial banks' and other bond buyers. As Parguez says, the 'ECB should even abstain from acquiring these bonds if it could be an indirect way of financing government deficits'. (Since 2012, the ECB version of QE does that, like other CBs.) Parguez continues this dismal pursuit of 'pure' independence:

> At last, any connection between the Treasury and the Central
> Bank should disappear. Members will have no checking account

---

[56] See Chapter 2 on the FRA 1913 rules; Ingham (2004: 190–1) on independence and citing Weber; and Goodhart (2003a). Gold was often scarce though the standard was lifted in crises. I use 'mono-state' purposefully, as see later on Brexit.

at the Central Bank. This last aspect of the prohibition should prevent states from creating money in the short run to match the discrepancies between flows of expenditure and flows of taxes. They should always spend what they have already received as taxes.[57]

The whole meaning of money as a promise (mutual obligations) into the future, depending on new wealth being created by business firms and states, and the ability of governments to spend their currency and to tax citizens especially if state money is inflating, is totally overturned (as in ICBs). This EMU reverted to aspects of the US 1837 crash (with its states' London Bankers' Ramp). Local states self-limited in the 1840s, and a kind of 'norm' against US Treasury bailouts of states resulted. Canada's and Australia's Treasuries underwrite their provincial states, and/or their CBs lend to them. A (pro-finance) Fed was not until 1913, nor was the IRS; now, all three Treasuries conduct fiscal transfers, but EMU designers did not fully consider these murky federated histories.[58]

The scandalous 1930 class warfare in Britain eventually strengthened Labour greatly after WWII, for example with the National Health Service (NHS), interestingly (in comparing the EU) for the UK's 'four nations', but there's not the automatic yearly fiscal equaliser of the federations. Australian taxes and fiscal transfers, and unified labour institutions is in Chapter 4, so too Canada's. It took two years to reject Norman's BoE 'conquest', in 1938: the BoC would also monetise its federal state debt. Under the Eurozone depression created after 2008, and worse, having kept unemployment and fiscal austerity high and economic activity low since the ECB's 2001 inception, current tax intakes in member states were already weakened before the 2011 speculative attacks (Bankers' Ramps). The ECB kept

---

[57] NAIRU is in Chapter 6. This paragraph draws on and cites Parguez (1999: 63–6; 68).

[58] Mutual obligations as in Tables 1.1 and 1.2. See Matthijs and Blyth (2015b: 250–3) on comparing the US federation, agree that EMU designers did not look to the USA, also mention the 'norm' in US of 1840 (and recall NY state was let go nearly bankrupt in 1974). Thus, all federations have been 'messy' too, not just the EU.

monetary policy tight, ruinously for those countries now blamed for fecklessness. Some suggest that where France, in the 1920s Europe's major creditor, might have engaged in debt forgiveness for the better, so too could Germany in the 2010s. The Euro was a vision of money as 'pure hoarding'.[59]

The pity was the ECB having started as experiment, in hope for more unified institutions to follow, that these could, in logic, proceed. But added was the grandiose hope to be the 'best currency', so the scheme relied on bond vigilantes' estimates of each other's confidence in the 'Euro'. Designers ignored how individual states in federated systems of USA, Canada or Australia remain fitful monetary unions. Judgement is premature.

The likely if not specific mismanagement, to early critics, occurred. Whether the ECB's QE only bailed out big European banks and (US) bond-trading firms that lent or 'invested' (with arbitrage) so prodigiously, is one question. Here the 'hoarders' have a huge ability to bet against Spain or Italy or whomever, due to their holdings of these state bonds.[60]

CB Mistreatment of Locality and Countervailing Possibilities

Other problems with the Euro are not unknown in mono-countries. In addition to weaknesses of all CBs, noted repeatedly, their application of a central interest rate based on averaging indicators, creates or recreates inequality, instability and inefficiency. Induced recessions occur also in the absence of other strong central institutions to counteract disparities in deflation too. Unified labour market–wage

---

[59] NHS Wales came after founding; Scotland and Northern Ireland started separately (NHS website). All are reliant on Whitehall Treasury purse strings. Various *FT* articles suggested debt forgiveness: it enhances Germany's trade (as we saw of Keynes's bancor in Chapters 4 and 5). Parguez (1999: 68) on 'hoarding'.

[60] Fiscal policy 'sharing' (in principle) by these unified federations can help a disaster in Mississippi or a sudden slump in New York. Moody's et al. assess regional states to stricter ratings than their federal sovereign governments. Yet regional areas in the 'UK' are often poorer than Greece and other EU members, see Pixley (2018).

bargaining systems are one. These countervailing examples show up against central bank strength in imposing inequality and creating more impoverished people, to which ICBs must be structurally indifferent. Rate changes can sacrifice slow-growing areas, or suddenly slumped or deprived regions, thereby imposing deflation or inflation to specific sectors. It is less a 'blunt tool' – more a spiked club.

Compare the globally promoted orthodoxy of labour market 'flexibility' and fiscal 'prudence', said to be crucial again after the GFC. Given that unions were tamed after the 1970s, the disparities across Europe beforehand, which hardened with the ECB are marked. Yet they appear in all types of monetary unions. Doubts as to central banks' ability to control money's value without other quasi-monetary institutions are occasionally raised. Central bankers Guy Debelle and Stanley Fischer said, before the Euro was launched, that due to Germany's form of corporatism,

> ... centralized collective bargaining at the industry level (with IG Metall setting the pattern) is at least as much responsible for low inflation in Germany as is the independence of the Bundesbank.[61]

The ECB design ignored that (but so did other ICBs). After the monetary union, and like all, now grandiose central banks, the ECB 'averages' inflation across Europe to set the rates, so that previously sovereign states in Europe cannot use monetary or exchange rate policies to correct either inflation or disinflation. That the ECB kept the entire EU on a restrictive monetary policy is commonly known, but Bob Hancké offers complex explanations of what exacerbated the differences. Hancké says one reason for Germany and other D-Mark bloc countries moving to export dependency and later austerity as a *raison d'état*, is their 'central place for unions'. The IG Metall pattern produced consistent disinflation: With D-bloc productivity gains – and shorter work hours with job security – industrial companies had to

---

[61] Debelle and Fischer (1994: 201) who cite Peter Hall's work on German corporatism. Fischer is well-known, Deputy Chair of the Fed e.g., and Debelle is Deputy Governor of the RBA currently.

train workers and produce up-market, capital-intensive goods. This 'rigidity' and employment stability looks good, both as decent policy and to maintain purchasing power in crisis.

But wage-price inflation in the 'rest of Europe' from 'disorganized', unregulated unions – service sector demands (e.g. surgeons); a decline in industrial productivity – the disinflation of 'D-bloc' countries was forced further down from the 'rest'. The 'rest' moved above the ECB's 2 per cent inflation target, countries which in turn were forced to further price rises to compensate versus the D-bloc. Uncivil ECB interest rates, then, work against solving either divergent problem. Low interest, in wage inflating economies, and high rates in disinflating ones created 'two Europes' (long before Greece's specific Ottoman 'clientelism' was public). As well, PM Berlusconi undermined Italy's economy by deregulating its labour market and ending productivity 'social pacts', which had helped many countries into the EMU. The key is the inconsistency with old national systems of labour relations backed with old *national* central banks adjusting as needed. Thus, the Euro made ECB aims for 'stability' unstable. Mervyn King (BoE) criticises the lack of full 'convergence' of inflation rates before EMU. This is incorrect: strict 'convergence criteria' were met before the EMU, whereas widely variant labour systems, some as disorganized as the UK's, enhanced disparities after the ECB's unifying 'target'.[62] It was a vicious spiral.

Much of Europe went into debt to buy Germany's Department I goods – no creditors without debtors – some with weak, disorganised unions, unable to counteract high inflation. But Italy, Spain and Portugal had low deficits, not Greece (or Germany). Low interest fostered private bank speculation (Spain, Ireland on property; France, Germany on sub-prime, not Greece) and debts on buying German

---

[62] Hancké (2013: 11; 50; 110), points out the Optimal Currency Area OCA approach looks in the wrong direction demanding less organized labour markets and less coordinated wage-bargaining, when *more* of both factors was the most successful. See King (2016: 221; 237) on 'convergence'; ignorant neoconservative governments gaily destroyed most quasi-monetary institutions (and nothing can be taxed on 'wage theft').

stuff (itself not buying from 'the rest'). Capital flowed to Germany after the 1999 Euro launch, an imbalance that grew well before the GFC. And who lends to the 'rest of Europe'? – German and French banks. The ECB created disunity via its structure, and incapacity to cope with, or coordinate regional differences. It was 'independent' of all institutions.[63]

Fiscal transfers were to be a factor in the European Union but went to EU bottom drawers (as German bankers say, 'binned them'), and the UK was little better: commentators attribute a possible breakup (we may well be wrong) of the 'United' Kingdom since 2016's Brexit, to the Brexiteers' stupid ignorance of Ireland's border and of regional disparities. Dow and Montagnoli estimated BoE outcomes before 2007's crash, saying a regional monetary policy in Britain had been possible only to the 1960s, when the BoE had credit controls.

After controls went, disparities grew. They found that 'differential pricing and availability of credit' occurred where some UK regions are more dependent on local credit supply, and there is a relatively high incidence of small and medium enterprises (SMEs) compared to multinational corporations. 'Even where there is a national banking system, SMEs will be more dependent on banks than larger companies, which have access to capital markets' – although better are Bank of Canada SME loans. But, for example, monetary policy designed to dampen a housing boom in SE England has a more lasting negative impact on regions that have not experienced boom conditions. 'The outcome is a choking-off of growth in peripheral regions with the result that monetary policy has a more sustained impact there'. As well, in the unravelling of the 'United' Kingdom, the BoE had a ghastly role, politically sounding too 'pompous' in support of the City against Brexit, both before and after that plebiscite. The RBA

---

[63] Department I goods are the machines/skills to create the Department II goods we buy; mis-called 'capital' goods and consumer goods. Pixley interviews with private bankers in Greece (2013) and in the central Bank of Greece; and personal conversations with Alexandros-Andreas Kyrtsis (University of Athens) and Joseph Halevi (University of Sydney) on the EU; see Pixley (2018) and Kyrtsis (2012).

choked the richest eastern states until 2015; the US Fed choked the 'rust-belts'.[64]

An option Minsky suggested was that the 'useless' private District Feds could foster jobs to ease regional disparities if they acted as lenders through the Discount Window, not via anonymous open market operations (typical now). They could use penal interest to lean against Ponzi finance most, and low rates to 'hedge finance' (i.e. careful, for SMEs notably) which engage most in active business borrowing: recall Mehrling's defence of Real Bills doctrine (Chapter 1). That was not to be. The BoC in contrast for many years supported SME financing, and undertook debt deficit financing for all governments, Canada and provinces. On that, Australia had a constitutional crisis after 1945.[65]

Formal *constitutional* federations of the USA, Australia and Canada (unlike the UK) have 'fiscal equalization' Treasury transfers. The EU started with these ideals but, in the name of attracting global creditors (in the event, hot money), austerity was institutionalized. Keynesians also discuss 'sticky wages' as the means for minimising the worst impact of debt-deflations, and Berlin's central wage guarantee in Germany was a successful backstop to purchasing power (and multiplier) when the GFC hit. Yet the BaFin regulators in Berlin in 2007–8 seemed (to me) more concerned with US hedge funds than its two global banks Deutsche Bank and Commerzbank, or local state and regional banks, with their rash investment in subprime. Bank bailouts came with austerity in German regions (even Frankfurt), and bank supervision needs more thought for the EU. France and Germany had huge bank problems. Available *non-central bank*

---

[64] Dow and Montagnoli (2007: 807; 800, 805) on SMEs and UK's long-ignored periphery (Chapter 3). I cover Brexit's plebiscite more in Pixley (2018). The UK has no written constitution; Parliament, not the people, is 'sovereign' and the 'mono-state' is run from Whitehall Treasury, the BoE and the City. A Tory government decided on a Brexit 'vote'. UK's electorate did not demand it. Australia's latest mining boom ended in 2015, but the RBA's dealing with Western Australia's mining inflation hardly caused angst for this well-off state (with more boring threats to secede without federal top-ups).

[65] See Minsky (2008 [1986]: 364–6) on the Feds, and Mehrling, Chapter 1; on Canada, Ryan-Collins (2015: 17; 25); on USA and Australia, Chapter 4.

means for preventing inflation or deflation in prices/wages are therefore an important separate factor that evidently exists, where labour market regulations are also monetary policy, as in Germany.[66] Yet how does the UK compare?

Post-GFC, the QEs of the Fed, BoE and ECB from 2009 failed to raise growth or price-wage inflation, nor has the BoJ. Egalitarian traditions (often those anti-UK) to influence central banks are not found in the major financial centres but outside the borders: Sweden, India, NZ, Canada and Australia. Central banks of former UK 'Dominions' are understudied. In Canada, Parliament has a strong role in regulating banks and scrutinising bank licences. *Sharing monetary tasks* is a way to relieve central banks of excessive responsibility over money, given so little ability to carry out generative tasks. The return of *rentiers* and ruling elites that only wanted financial deals, not long-term investment and certainly not unions, muted the possibilities of those governments with non-orthodox CBs. The BoC debt financing recalls 300 years of that European tradition, and surely a more 'appropriate use of central bank balance sheet expansion' than QE. After all, capital investment declined once deficit finance was technically banned in 'independence'. Tests of any policy efficacy were forbidden; designers of the ECB refuse to admit banks and free financial markets made fortunes post-GFC. Did they intend to destroy the EMU's and member states' sources of fairly-priced money/bonds? In contrast, a few Governors urge governments to begin with questions not asked at the outset of Independence and Inflation Targets, in which the ECB was enmeshed at its inception. That question of the RBA is:

> ... are *balance sheets in the economy being strengthened or weakened?* If credit is growing quickly, we need to think about whether the credit is being used to *create new productive assets*

[66] Fiscal equalization is an Australian term, calculated per capita and local indicators annually, see Chapter 4; the others appear to be similar. Interviews in Berlin, 2007–8 at the BaFin; and own knowledge or from colleagues at Cologne's Max Planck Institute. This type of 'independent' CB was perfect; no need to examine wage structures, or consensus; last of all any social justice.

or simply to finance current consumption. The implications are quite different.[67]

Such considerations were banned with inflation targets imposed, which left CBs focusing on whether to induce recessions, which are easily done. Given everything else discussed in this chapter to appease financial sectors, the collapses from 2007 resulted. Central bank questions about balance sheet *purposes* for economic activity are necessary; and imply weaknesses without other mechanisms to try to strengthen economies. *Consolidation of monetary policy with fiscal policy* for the better, springs to mind, that hated link banned in CB independence. Not alone, *the EU has a fiscal policy*: austerity. That told *against* post-GFC central banks. The fallout from such treasury policies for the US Fed is explored in the next chapter.

---

[67] See Chapter 8 on QE. Citing Ryan-Collins (2015: 38), on deficit finance. Coombs did his PhD (LSE) on Dominion CBs in the 1930s; Peter Kriesler and I intended to repeat but didn't get around to it. Citation of Lowe (2016) RBA, my emphases; Governor Lowe adds 'strengthening of supervision is at least as important as are the post-crisis regulatory reforms. Rigorous, inquiring supervision that takes a holistic view of the environment is essential to maintaining financial stability and ... for consumers'. www.rba.gov.au/speeches/2016/sp-dg-2016-09-08.html.

8 The State of Monetary Sovereignty

Much has been said about the actual GFC, and this chapter only looks at the involvement of central banks, such as acting jointly with treasuries. Banned for so long, this fiscal-monetary consolidation seemed 'irregular'. No matter the disturbing aspects of CB independence, Targets and worse, how they undermined treasuries – which spend under elected executive orders, with tight legislative reviews. No. Central banks would heroically rescue the benighted social landscape. This science fiction is one reason (so far) why the aftermath has not constrained, democratically, the global finance that created the GFC. Monetary sovereignty needs debate. Financial power seemed divorced from authorities' control and when, after 2007, the global banks called for and received treasury and central bank largesse, there was a furore. Little has happened: rules over bank money production are slight, economic activity is weak. CB relations to their treasuries and banks look deadlocked. The Fed's lending, the cheap money and QE had international impacts, too, but the Fed has only domestic remits. Politics is far more visible although this public attention misses the obvious. Monetary policy is always political, and no amount of pretensions to its technical nature can hide money's divisive character and precariousness so evident in the GFC.

DO BANKS AND STATES SHARE MONETARY SOVEREIGNTY?

Nine years after the Global Financial Crisis, one central banker called for fiscal authorities to act for progressive purposes and admitted monetary policy is limited, given the weak economic activity. The Fed, in contrast, insisted its policies 'will' stimulate economic activity, as has the ECB, BoE, and the Bank of Japan, although against UK's austerity and Japan's 30 years of quasi-stagnation. What a U-Turn that some beg for wage inflation. The global banks and market manipulations are further damaging economies and people's purchasing power, but central banks feed private leverage and profits, and maintain their policies will encourage bank lending to restart business. Global banks limited that decades ago. The uncivil demand a full Depression of the Fed, while punitive disorder fostered disaffection and erratic political leaders. Bank disasters loom from their new schemes for abusing clients and governments; some are worse than before 2007. Surplus countries like Japan, Germany and Saudi Arabia remain defence-dependent (a moot point re Trump) paying on the deficit USA issuing the global currency. China has its own military power; will it stick with the dollar? The obvious spectacle has been decades of dithering in OECD states, scared or unwilling to control global finance. In Japan's deflation, the BoJ seems to push its own agenda, no less, to create more damage. Populations are further impoverished. It is not time for joking while the accumulation of the global financial sector endangers economic life as such. Curzio Giannini assumed a weakening of state sovereignty – the 2016 elections implied worse, but no one knows what.

Monetary sovereignty used to be shared in the early days of capitalist money. There were so many wars to fund and there still are. Private IOUs were flimsy for wealthy merchants. It started as a 'memorable alliance' yet states would 'rule', albeit under strict merchant loan conditions. The deal was exclusive and obscured from populations. Schumpeter, who had little faith in central bank controls beyond stern supervision, was less a realist than is often thought. He argued when 'the theory of credit operations and effects' was understood, 'capitalism ... became analytically conscious of itself'. That drive to dynamic, active economic progress stalled decades ago. Do global banks produce money for any whim, and rule more arbitrarily than governments? Or is the US state and its Fed still sharing in the deal?[1]

---

[1] Some will contest my 'shared' sovereignty idea but see even Giannini (2011), (who ignores war finance) as previously discussed. Weber's state theory (1978, 1981 [1927]) is discussed most in Chapter 1 and see Schumpeter (1954: 318); he thought dynamism stalled in the 1940s.

Control has varied. Today, the meaning of *the state* is little discussed. A generic definition of a 'capitalist state' along Marxian lines of the 'executive committee of the bourgeoisie' suggests too much unity. States compete, they usually have a monopoly over violence, and taxes with which to retire HPM. Moreover, states are large economic actors, inside which tensions exist between state divisions, and with economic 'vested interests', the competitive, monopoly and public sectors. The state's policing, spying and war machine is a different logic to the 'economy' – violent machines that are fairly large employers, so too variable social democratic programmes. Despite capitalism's globalisation, there are specific national class forces inside any territory with strengths and weaknesses, political and cultural divergences. Governments create markets, complement markets or replace markets; armaments industries don't exist without states. Much state-owned economic activity (the 'mixed economy') has been privatised with government underwriting since the 1970s but, however hollowed out, some remain. Deficits are scrutinised so closely that state sell-offs became an accounting trick to forestall bond markets from pushing up state interest payments. Meanwhile corporate taxes are evaded. Bailouts (with few conditions) for banks and money markets were thanked by bond and currency vigilantes applying pressure on state debt.[2] The US global dollar, the safest treasury debt to buy, and largest arsenal by far are all the Administration's imperial weapons. The Fed does consolidate with treasury/banks to fund the military but not overtly and rarely do social programmes meet Wall Street's approval.

The GFC only worsened the constraints. Central banks' ability to reverse stagnation towards jobs is tenuous. Inflation targets of independent central banks, state-designed to give enticing investment *certainties*, cannot get up to a pitiful inflation level to 'induce'

---

[2] Frankel (1979) gives an excellent definition of the state. Some states face powerful financial sectors, others industrial or mining sectors. Public sector service provision, say, the UK's NHS is not lost, though it varies. Bill Clinton was furious about bond traders ruining his health scheme. Disaffection around nationalistic themes, evident in 2016–17's elections, can't be analysed as it unfolds to potential dangers, or disaffection redirects its energies to revive social democracy, a bleak hope.

recovery; negative interest rates are proposed, we see. Authorities fear capital strikes to greener pastures for grazing them dry too. Central banks rarely call states to step in, to start (some) economic activity; private (speculative) investment has ramped up to asset price inflation. Intellectuals and the public are bitterly divided: those dismissing stimulus as 'populist' instead fostered right wing agitators, for years in France, Italy or Australia; then the UK and USA installed populist incompetence. It seems the most explicit statements from any central bank show it knows what is needed. In August 2016, RBA Governor Glenn Stevens, who dropped interest rates to 1.5 per cent with Australian inflation on 1 per cent, said this on retiring:

> I have serious reservations about the extent of reliance on monetary policy around the world. It isn't that the central banks were wrong to do what they could [GFC], it is that what they could do was not enough, and **never could be enough**, fully to restore demand after a period of recession associated with a very substantial debt build-up ... I am not advocating **an increase in deficit financing** of day-to-day government spending. The case [is] for governments being prepared to borrow for the right investment assets – **long-lived assets that yield an economic return.**[3]

In other words, stop screeching about ICBs and Targets. He called on the state to invest via direct deficit finance in a country that avoided the worst of the GFC. Straightaway Australia's current PM Turnbull (and ex-GS&Co partner) preached (down) about 'living within our means'. It is not so much an impasse; daily the situation is dangerous, and then

---

[3] See, Stevens (2016; my emphasis). Wray argues a Stevens-type proposal is fairly 'close' to orthodoxy that taxes 'pay for' state spending (so-called 'sound finance', meaning indecent to populations), whereas states spend the currency into existence and taxes just reduce inflationary trends. I think a renegade like the RBA knows that strict logic but saying it to far right governments is a bad PR move: just get them to spend. Turnbull's Cabinet want tax cuts/trickle down. And cf. Frankel (1979), Herman Schwartz suggested the RBA is calling on the state to act as executive committee of the bourgeoisie (personal email), which is a thought!

the sun rises next morning. In the US, a hostile Congress supported Wall Street, and a gun society, where distinctions between state terrorism or local and global variants are blurred. President Obama said: 'I have a pen and a phone' to make administrative improvements, which can be rescinded with another president's signature. In 2016, allegedly firm governments with austerity budgets and police forces to put down domestic unrest have self-immolated, the Brexit case being a most unusual one sociologically. Everyone asking for more 'political will', that catch cry of economists (even decent ones) and the far right, has only found mendacious billionaires Trump, Farage, et al. Years ago Australian PM Paul Keating argued states are weak over the big things (like mobile capital) and cruelly strong against the weak (like asylum seekers). On the 'big things', state action and inter-state agreements on financial controls are no further to fruition than those on climate change, and they are related (banks are not investing in assets with economic returns). The global finance sector is unhinged from economic activity. Are central banks with warrior states also unhinged? Whether qualitatively worse than past eras, no one can yet say – but trends were depressing years ago.

Monetary sovereignty is heavily weighted against states and towards the private money-creating sector, to bond vigilantes and search for liquid assets. Counter-actions could be taken, but so far have not. Central banks, easy scapegoats, must be bankers to banks. Whether they are state-appointed Leviathans as Geoff Mann puts it, or more feeble, the democratic possibilities are thin. States' 'memorable alliance' is one-sided. It is moot whether the finance sector kind of 'owns' states (or via capture), which direct many central banks implicitly.[4]

---

[4] On Brexit, a bunch of Tories (as though battling on their old Eton footie fields) inaugurated a plebiscite on Brexit, neither wanted, nor about which Tories had a clue. See Mann (2010) and my last sentence here was written before Trump was President: one only needs the term FIRE (Finance, Insurance, Real Estate) to bring Trump Inc. patrimonialism into the picture (or, e.g., Dick Cheney's dubious Iraq War links). Marx had argued the BoE's 1694 'deal' had sold off the state to merchant banks but, as Fernand Braudel protested, war finance and nationalism qualified that dilution or alienation of state power or sovereignty: cited in Arrighi (1994) and Pixley (2013).

CENTRAL BANK PURPOSES SINCE THE GFC: ZERO?

The great silence about central banks is their class-divided power over inflation via maldistribution, and an inability to cure deflation. CBs cannot admit private banks create or destroy the vast bulk of the world's money and profit from deflation. In a nutshell, monetary policy can easily create a recession, ruin debtors (employers and workers), but central banks can do very little to get out of one. Exceptionally, they were unpopular with different, *faux* sufferers in the postwar (in *repressing* banks) and now only please banks. A win for liquidity is producer and household sectors' losses. Rising prices in markets for raw materials, goods and services will normally reduce customers' demand. However, the opposite occurs in markets for financial assets. Here, prices are ruled by expectations (futile predictions) of price rises, which create huge demand for these increasingly 'valuable' assets, leading to upward spirals of rising prices. The result is a precarious 'bubble'.[5] For central banks, it is 'easy' to stop wage-price or state pork barrel inflation, but rarely (save the war to postwar, somewhat) could central banks moderate asset or bank money inflation. When Hartley Withers looked at the problem in 1909, he found the BoE rarely could or would; the Fed has neither the design nor focus. Hyperinflation is cured overnight like 'a miracle' (Orléan) in contrast, as when the Deutsche mark was replaced with the Rentenmark, or Zimbabwe's currency with the US dollar. *We are never told that.* But in debt deflation, the situation is different. Banks profit from deflation because the finance sector enjoys debt's value (money) growing. If that continues down to the last sectors standing, not even banks survive. Some should not. QE averted necessary financial bankruptcies, and, in the name of shareholder value (another fad), banks busily restore market liquidity on asset booms.

Reflation does not achieve much for long, although it's *far preferable* to raising rates further like 1929. Japan is a much-cited counter

---

[5] On liquidity, Bibow (2009: 24); the result is a 'bubble', Ingham (2011: 230); note, sellers *versus* buyers operates in product but not finance markets, a point stupidity might miss.

example on stimulus. In the GFC the Fed acted quickly: whether reflation was based on monetarist counterfactuals to save banks with QE (as many suspect), the result was asset bubbles. As for moving out of depression nothing can happen from central banks. Many say Fed Chair Bernanke's charge to the rescue was a vulgar form of Keynesianism. This is splitting hairs. QE is monetarist – misdirected in deflation. Private bank money is going nowhere beneficial, peaceful or to democratic ends, neither is much state money.[6]

MONETARY POLICY: NEVER EXPLAIN!
NEVER ROCK THE BOAT!

This section suggests that rather than talk of 'an epistemic community', central banks obey orders given from top down by states and global Wall Street, which hardly worry about various ways of knowing (anything). Central bank dissenters are not always silenced, although generally Board members are frightened to rock the boat.[7]

Monetary sovereignty is an uneven and shifting deal over the shared production of capitalist money between states and finance markets. Inside this bargain, the democratic state's problem of keeping social conflict away from public considerations of money's value is crucial yet impossible. A stable value hangs on whether a treasury's debt will be accepted by banks and bond buyers. Yet the grounds of this credit-rating threat over governments will vary, depending on political and social contexts, and anticipations. So, in WWII banks were told to accept the state's war debt on set terms; few people expected all needs for purchases to be met.[8] Later, the grounds for banks and *rentiers* to accept state debt became contested seriously in the democratic 1970s. Mouldy ideas from non-democratic times that blamed

---

[6] See Withers (1918 [1909]), and Chapter 3, counterfactuals and Chapter 4, postwar; Orléan (2013) on hyperinflation miracle cures. See Bhaduri (2014) on 'vulgar' Keynes. Chapter 7 cited Central Bankers like Edwards (2004) on bubbles; Sheila Dow (2013) see below.

[7] Epistemology see further on; I'm grateful to Vic Carroll about CBs 'won't rock the boat'.

[8] Ingham (2004: 144) on money's value. Price controls in WWII: perhaps people's need to live never mobilised Wall Street (or the Chicago School) but, after Pearl Harbour and enemy laws, bank grumbling hardly won friends. Bad enough to FDR was war profiteering.

governments and marginal peoples were lucrative to banks. Central bankers were to depoliticise money partly via independence from monetising state debt; governments gave in to banking's demands to get out of *overt* money production, under threats from the strongest financial centres, yet private bank debt and defence debt is monetised via CBs. Never explain! Most extraordinary, the Fed, ECB and BoE chose to disregard a finance sector despite being Bankers to banks and to states. In 2007 everyone asked what were they thinking?

To central bankers speaking publicly after the GFC's switch to monetary disorder, the 1987–2007 years were the Great Moderation or 'great stability'. Some central banks acted differently, but recent heads of the Fed and BoE reminisced fondly as though the 2007 outcomes were a detached nightmare. They must say that; after all, finance sectors created the GFC. Proof of dangers, more than ever before, lay in assiduously collected details, refined and multiplied in central banks that seemed to be ignored publicly. Central banks were beset with the 'freedom of the prison yard', having kept inflation low and economies stagnant (only appearing stable: unmoving), obedient to states and banks. Their bitter or 'shocked disbelief' at the GFC did not translate to *improved* CB-Treasury relations. Teasing this out is not simple: between state sovereignty and governments' changing perceptions of *their (reduced) possibilities*, and a financial sector becoming detached from, yet abusing certain classes and distressed groups, central banks were in an invidious position. The finance sector had partly replaced the state in maintaining demand (private, debt-driven); moderation of wages did not match 'moderate' banks, as Figures 5.1 and 5.2, and 7.1 show. Since the GFC, central banks doggedly maintain the sector. Change in a heavily weighted power balance to finance is not in sight. Governments are too scared to curb banks and global money trading.[9]

---

[9] See Chapter 7; on claims of 'Moderation' see Chapter 5; Bhaduri (2014: 394) on demand; in 'defence debt', I include policing and spying costs; failure to reform is below.

One way to enter this conundrum is evidence of how central bankers understand this world, and, from that, to ask if changed perspectives *could make* an iota of difference in policies. There are very different ways of knowing and mountains of evidence do not (in my view) present a unified epistemic community.[10] A colleague in economics argues that central banks have 'an almost compulsive obligation to repeat failed policies. This cyclical morass prompts the thought that the learning curve defining economic policy may be perfectly flat ... No theory, [he said] no matter how lame or preposterous, has ever been buried once and for all'. One reason, I think, is central banks are always compromised. The quantity theory of money was dug up although known to be defunct after the European scholastic monks of late medieval times.[11] A starring 'therapeutic role' it gives to monetary policy gave central banks a firmer pedestal before 2007 events crumbled it. Whether *preposterous* theorems defied logic and obvious bank practices is one question, the second is which sectors were responsible or found them congenial. Given the relentless attack on social democracy since 1970, theories had to be old hat ('respectable') with CB appointments to match. Efficacy had nothing to do with choice of semi-feudal approaches. However not all central banks swallowed them, and cognitive and emotional dissonances inside central banks are worth pondering.

Chapter 6 explored the quantity theorem's revival (from 1568) and the 1970s–80s influence of monetarists on governments. States were too generous, too democratic; too inflationary. Central banks

---

[10] In philosophy, epistemology is the study of 'ways of knowing' (put loosely) and a methodology is an entry-point with a set of assumptions embedded in each methodology. (Methods are just tools that can be 'read' in various ways.) These depend on the position of the viewer as any sociology of knowledge argues. My question is whether CBs are in a straitjacket whatever their old/new, conflicting ideas.

[11] On 'lame' quantity theory – not only in the BoJ, see Freedman (2016); and 'dug up' e.g. in the 1870s, 1920s, 1970s, see Schumpeter (1954: 295; 311) who dates the quantity theory to Bodin in 1568 (the Prince's 'money', amid war finance and price revolutions over the fifteenth to seventeenth centuries), but stresses John Law, Louis XV's advisor about 120 years later, was 'in the front rank of monetary theorists of all time' (1954: 321), was no quantity theorist. See Coombs (1971), arguing Law was correct: telling 'the public' caused the disaster.

must stop this wishy-washy kindness to *lower orders*. In 'theory' private banks were innocent go-betweens in lending directly to business, a huge blessing in slogans for finance's 1971 revival. Predictability! Rationality! Another option for central bankers was a 'credit channel', still a 'lame' theory to Schumpeter (JAS). Whereas capitalist 'credit' was difficult to miss from fifteenth century Europe onwards, JAS remained irritated at how – from monastery scholastics accepting that charging interest on loans might no longer be 'usury' for buying food, but to 'compensate' the lender if a capitalist borrower made a profit – this rise in economic activity fell from view as the quantity theory continued 'out of all proportion to its importance'. One theorist, Cantillon, added 'credit' but only 'to draw a sharp dividing line between money *and* the legal instruments that embody claims to money and operations of money'. Bernanke uses that division; others want to 'restore' money's purity, for example, BoE's Mervyn King proposed 'pawnbroker banks' in 2016. However, unlike banks, pawnbrokers *hold* 'money-cash' to lend, on *security* (assets to bid up or down); whereas banks, near banks and central banks create it. The Fed pulls a blanket over bank money.[12]

To insist that credit is *never money* needed only 'auxiliary constructions' for a while (argued JAS). One 'auxiliary' extended the idea of 'velocity' to bankers, who are allegedly not increasing the payment system nor, heaven forbid, 'manufacturing money'. No sir, when bankers 'issue notes' in excess of their cash holdings they are just speeding up the velocity (so lowering interest). *Consequently*, bankers are helpful, innocent intermediaries in lending 'other people's money' (so-called), quickly and efficiently, just as Cantillon said. Also, this money does 'one service at a time'. Of course, 300 years ago, this 'credit channel' was hardly like the electronic transfers of today. Bernanke explained thus his QE deposits in manufacturing money. Whereas Bernanke avoids saying banks also deposit loans

---

[12] Schumpeter (1954: 311, my emphasis) to the credit/money false distinction; Giannini (2011) also has a weird definition of money. A Hayekian, King (2016) devotes a chapter to pawnbrokers: on whom, see Minsky (2008 [1986]).

with keystrokes, King is moralistic and wants banks to be 'innocent'. Both omit money's indubitable and long-proven 'credit' or 'social character' (to JAS). So, more likely, these defunct understandings helped the Fed to solidify its status to Congress, to the *laissez faire*-activist US state from Reagan on, and to Wall Street, *despite* protesters inside the FOMC worrying about the payment system and credit-money's 'social character'.[13]

Although credit is often 'not money' if neither accepted nor used as money by others (anyone can create personal IOUs, non-transferable) – bankers do much more than collect and lend on 'money' from stagnant 'puddles'. This 'velocity' is so 'great' it is 'in different places at the same time'. To Schumpeter, 'you cannot ride on a claim to a horse, but you can pay with a claim to money'. Today, as before, savers gained an undeserved role in investment. Look at how, among many, Adam Smith gave savers a crucial part in the creation of new industry: 'parsimony and not industry is the immediate cause of the increase of capital'. JAS said not one economist who 'swallowed' this 'looked askance at that word "immediately"' or that in depressed conditions, saving (parsimony, thrift) will diminish economic activity, since 'what is saved is not spent' (to Blinder, former Fed Deputy). Yet that politically vaunted role to savers is wedged in as 'loanable funds' so, for example, Bernanke promoted a 'savings glut' idea in 2003, whereby East Asian countries 'flooded' the US capital market and lowered interest rates. Wall Street was innocent of money creation. From this line, the Fed's QE could hope US firms *wanted* to borrow again. Textbooks of 2009 preach how 'the supply of loanable funds comes from people who have some extra income they

---

[13] Schumpeter (1954: 318–20) also, metal money cf. keystrokes; Schularick and Taylor (2012) cite Blinder, Bernanke (and others) on 'financial fragility' or how 'the credit channel' is 'an enhancement mechanism, not a truly independent or parallel channel'. They ridicule this idea; to JAS, this 'auxiliary' is like sticking with Ptolemy, after the Copernican revolution, whereas the theory of credit brought 'capitalism' to be 'conscious of itself' (1954: 318–19). For Bernanke's ideas see Chapter 5.

want to save *and* lend out' like Smith, who assumed that direction 'immediately'.[14]

Just before he died (in 1950) JAS said the idea that all money is credit prevailed. Although he complained: 'even today' with a huge system of credits and debits, text books start with 'legal-tender money and is itself construed from barter'. By 1980 those texts swelled, also to revile state money as the sole source of unpredictability and money's unstable value. Dogmas competed, not social sciences debates of how the postwar social settlement gave diverse questions for central banks. RBA Governor Coombs, one familiar example, strict about government spending over and beyond taxes *and* loans raised, in 1954 criticised the postwar 'dogma' of cheap money in Treasury (not for permanently 'dear money' though). Bank securities purchases and bank loans increase bank deposits, and thus 'increase the total money supply'. Schumpeter's ideal lecturer in taking banks side too, Coombs warned any huge expansion of bank advances, if *'excessive'* for the *'monetary needs of the economy'* can bring 'dangerous inflation'. US Fed chair McChesney Martin's 'leaning against the wind' also assessed the *contexts*, such as capitalist creativity. To the BoC as well, bank advances for full employment with decent redistribution kept social relations in view.[15]

Not all forgotten, yet promoting indecency in CBs has constantly compelled *conformity*, hardly an 'epistemic community'. Few know that bank advances create deposits, or for variable purposes (economic

---

[14] On horse riding, Schumpeter (JAS) (1954: 320–1); – he loathed 'A. Smith' cited (1954: 324); on saved, not investing, JAS (1954: 325–6); 'not spent' is in Blinder (2013: 355) (one can here talk of hoarding); this 'loanable funds' quote of Mankiw is cited in Bibow (2009: 17) my emphasis.

[15] See JAS: Schumpeter (1954: 321; 717) on barter, which he of course disputes. Coombs (1971 [1954]: 14–18); said cheap money was essential in depression and above all in WWII, less for the postwar; Coombs refers to a right-wing government committed to 'cheap money' pork barrels; Coombs publicly stressed the RBA's existing, unusual controls (Butlin 1983); also, difficulties: e.g. Australian banks' intransigence, we saw in Chapters 3 and 4. A perennial problem is defining 'excessive' and arguing that, to control banks. The BoC with slightly different methods also monetised state deficits; lent to small business, qualified with 'independence', in Ryan-Collins (2015) and see Chapter 7. McChesney Martin, see Chapter 1, on 'the social phenomenon' of money in Burns et al. (1979: 26).

activity, consumer *or* financial profits and bubbles). Like Coombs (or JAS) who stressed that context is all-important and monetary policy should beware of 'rigid rules' (that returned, see Chapter 7), Orléan, via the classic sociologists of money, disputes orthodoxy. The claim that 'money is neutral – the idea that a change in the stock of money affects only nominal variables (prices, wages, exchange rates), not real, inflation-adjusted variables (employment, real GDP, real consumption) – [Orléan said] must be abandoned'. As he says, neutrality only appears to be so, in a social context when the value of money is not disputed, questioned, or distrusted. Neoclassical theory can thinly apply (in anti-orthodox terms) when money seems agreeable and dependable. I dispute that. A stable balance of power is needed, which is (now, disagreeably) the opposite from when Coombs could say in 1954 an increase in the money supply is a question about how it is distributed. Friedman's individualistic claim of a neutral 'free lunch' was disproven. *Regressive distribution* to asset booms and not to economic activity became the order in the 1980s–2000s, unspoken in 'Fed speak'. After the GFC, some central banks made a 'helicopter drop' to citizens, but a big drop of CB *lending to states for social ends* is forbidden, not as a result of science but its absence.[16]

The 'epistemic community' idea is rather dubious, then, given informed debate was outlawed by threats, capital strikes and plebiscites. Also, internal divisions. When money is 'dependable' that only means we believe in money. Orléan poses 'turning points' from mobilisation of diverse group interests (a 'critical mass') towards a new monetary norm, from hopes and anxieties, expectations of 'not enough' or 'too much' money, of deflation or inflation. This is not 'ideas' as illusions, but of money *felt* as a stable norm until some disruption. It entailed propaganda to 'savers' (carping until

---

[16] See Coombs (1971 [1954]: 10) on 'rigid'; my colleague Clive Kessler reminds students 'community' has 94 definitions. Orléan (2014: 128–30); also, citing Simmel's great sprawling *Philosophy of* Money (1990 [1907]), who, see also on 'dependable' and 'agreeable' money; and Orléan (2013; 63); who cites other sociologists of money of 1880s–1920s like Simiand (not yet translated) and Durkheim, see Chapter 6.

2007) against the low waged and unemployed. Generally, fears *prevent understanding* of money: we all fear nuclear war so why *seek* another scary unknowable? Former UK Treasury Secretary Nick Macpherson said the GFC proved 'an intellectual disaster' yet preaches austerity dogma. When the 1970s monetary disputes produced a new norm for banks to dictate the terms of accepting state debt through the money markets, to launch their own treadmill of relentless if precarious deals, it gave relief from normlessness, anomie. If lame non-science supported financial sector practices and well-rewarded bonuses, with claims of money's neutrality or the innocent roles of banks, we *wanted* to believe bossy experts, with *certain* reassuring jargon. Ignorance was bliss.[17]

BANK MONEY TOOK OFF

Unlike rosy feelings under stable norms, simple data give no cause for illogical congratulation before the crises or thereafter. As mentioned, Figures 5.1 and 5.2, and 7.1 and 7.2 show excess. State money to bank money changes, over 150 years starting in the 1860s, has a 50:50 ratio of state to bank money up to 1970. Collected by central banks, in 2011 the currency was barely at three to the ninety-seven share of private sector money; with or without QE. Haldane shows inflation of UK bank assets from 1970 grew to 500 per cent of GDP at 2007. He suggests using bank assets (loans and securities) to GDP, as a 'measure' of how far banks departed from funding economic activity since the 1970s. Whether central banks *could* control commercial banks' money creation, or whether they must foster bank profits, is unanswerable. Very few asked though, while bubbles grew. Had states with their central banks withered away? Perhaps Hayek's 'free banking' utopia was at hand: Mervyn King marvelled that electronic private money would replace CBs 'one day'. Bitcoin! Capitalist firms might settle their exchanges with zero-second speed *and* verify who was creditworthy. But Ingham points out private 'near moneys' often operate in

---

[17] See Orléan (2013: 64); Parker and McDermott (2016) on 'disaster' to Macpherson, and new norms, see Chapter 5. Reagan was soothing-appealing; a counterpoint to Thatcher, overseeing the UK's further decline; see Figure 7.1.

exclusive capitalist circles. Early Boston debts between farmers and traders were exchanged and recorded in a money of account, based on pound sterling, which did not circulate. These systems are only cashless (banks adore the idea), not moneyless. The 3:97 ratio only correlates bank money creation being divorced from financing economic development, than before the 1970s. Stronger support is from multiple sources: Haldane's brief UK monetary history lists periodic chaos; Schularick has solid evidence of the *democracies'* efforts to control sovereign debt. WWII reached the highest between 1870 and 2010, but rapidly dropped postwar.[18] The fact that bank money is used as 'money' is evident in chilling details that central bankers who accommodate bank money with HPM could not talk out loud. The claim banks lent 'on' to business reassured diverse audiences.

Was the contrary ignored, or cheered as a jolly good thing? FOMC meetings are not comforting reading. From about 1990, as I said, *the* question was 'what does the market *think*'. Records of transcribed 'laughter' rose also, not implying moderation or *caution*, but fears of unknowables, like when a market (bubble) might 'crack' or whether the Fed might lose credibility to markets. Japan's deflation, Bernanke warned, gave the FOMC pause for thought,

---

[18] It's hard to underestimate the extent my informed experts were alarmed from the 1990s on. See Haldane (2010, 2012); Ingham (2004: 178–9) about King's free banking; and Boston. In contrast, Bitcoin is a Hayekian dream, more deflationary than gold; prone to hoarding and to bubbles. Schularick (2014) refutes Calomiris and Haber (2014) and others, that the democracies are 'too' democratic aka 'too' lavish, populist. Right-wing governments are similar. Many, including Australia (low debt) reduced it from 1980 to date, largely by selling off public assets (and their income stream) – a trick following Thatcher (of poll-tax and Trident infamy, cf. King). See Giannini (2011: 228), on wealth data; also, inequality, see Piketty (2014); Schularick and Taylor (2010: 1031–2) on the ratio public-private debt, in most of OECD: private debt takes off in 1970, social services slashed. Alessandri and Haldane (2009) on BoE balance sheets as per cent of GDP from 1830 to 2007, list BoE peaks at:

> (a) Famine/End of railroad boom (1847); (b) Overextension of credit from 1855-1866; (c) Failure of Overend Gurney (1866); (d) Failure of City of Glasgow Bank (1878); (e) Support for Barings (1890); (f) WWI (1914); (g) Currency and Bank Note Act (1928); (h) WWII (1941); (i) Secondary Banking Crisis (1973); (j) Small Banks Crisis (1991); (k) Current Crisis (2007).

High peaks are WWII 1941 (drops in 1944), far higher in 1973, and GFC, 2007; the 1830–6 /1847 famine/railway bust is the next highest (by per cent).

only in 2003. Critics hoped his was voice of reason, but the Fed steamed full speed to a new bubble. Rules imposed for decades tied above all to job rates, revealed the ugly game: central bankers found a role at last. Stagnation at whatever cost with vicious cycles of high interest adding to state deficits, to prove their independence (popularity) to banks. Governments built prisons that (in California) tracked *de-funding* of universities perfectly. Greenspan's statements calmed Congress, as the Fed foot-dragged to sub-prime, peaking for Bernanke.[19]

Interest in interpreting bank money's incredible growth sank, as precautionary departments in the BoE became 'career graveyards'. By Paulson's reign, US Treasury had not monitored finance markets for some years. Emphasis on wage price stability became hysterical as Greenspan feared *and* blessed the Dotcom asset inflation. Hawks silenced dove intelligence but insider shouting matches were not the sole sources of dissonances; forked tongues of treasuries pleased finance sectors. Honest, publicly horrifying plain speaking from *local* governments, outrage of financial journalists or beleaguered regulators, rose and sank. Usually finance ministries arranged the inflation targets, with austerity under treasuries. Some nefarious deals, such as the Fed-engineered bailout of LTCM in 1998 were hotly criticised everywhere; Governor Alice Rivlin on the FOMC was brushed over; less easy was Congress. The Greenspan 'put' was a public discovery after the GFC, too late! Central bank *targets* about *output* had so little efficacy (if output declined) that, as the Dotcom crumbled, Greenspan and co talked up this old technology relentlessly. Does anyone remember the costly Y2K scare that all computers would crash? Targets for staunching a hint of (wage) inflation, or the ordo-liberalism in the ECB were

---

[19] 'Laughter' data on the FOMC is in Mirowski (2013); in these transcripts, self-interest shines like a red nose; Bernanke (2003) worried about Japan; Pixley (1993; 2004, 2012), with many others, despairingly looked for hopeful signs for years; anyone promoting Tobin taxes on to Bernanke's raising the D-word. Powerful voices made no whatever dent: To President Clinton, Greenspan's insistence he was hobbled by 'f---ing bond traders' ruined his health plan. I visited San Diego during the prison/university reversal. See Tooze (2016: 96) on the Fed's 'oblivious' or 'seat-of-the-pants' business in 2007–8.

also bizarrely combined with 'discretion'. A new mendacious term, 'transparency *to* markets' forced central banks to explain decisions with data chosen to prove what traders needed. Central banks had to predict the future, which no one can do (as the BoC and RBA insisted, and refused) and tell the financial sector exactly their next move – from 'signals' to 'forward guidance', and insider leaking.[20]

And with few contrary concepts permitted in CB remits to jar thought processes, to stress how money creation grew inside banks (secretly too) and rarely directed to economic activity, no danger is seen. Indecent hawks (sycophants) refused to see it. The NY District Fed lost one member to rank insider trading. But with 1990s 'prison exercise yard' decree, only the oldest members, or those schooled in heterodox economic history (banished; erased) tried. Some FOMC members did not stay long, which could imply frustration or futility; and put-downs were constant. The idea laypeople are ill-informed should surely include bankers, the bulk of politicians, and not only citizens. Surveys show few know what central banks do, and for decades most people were unlikely to distinguish credit theories from the quantity theorem on how there is *only* state money or (to Bernanke and Summers), how banks are innocently loaned up. Variations on a broken DVD player.[21]

Central bank claims to moderation do look odd with this bank money and private debt expansion (which CBs kept secret or in unreadable form) with, at the same time, visible decline in economic opportunities and abolition of FE to a swear word. Moralism filled the gap between public animosity about seeing their life chances declining before their very eyes, and the potential reasons, which

[20] On local governments' outrage (e.g. foreclosures), see Blinder (2013). Alice Rivlin, who objected to the LTCM bailout and 'arrogance' of this hedge fund mob, was ignored. Yellen tried; Greider (1987: 455–89; 618; 678) shows Nancy Teeters facing up to Volcker's cruel Fed to no avail. Academics of my age saw dotcom mania as old hat: by 1980 we used internet. Blinder et al. (2001) on transparency; Greenspan hectored the FOMC (not publicly!): don't even tell 'your doorman', cf. Rivlin (FOMC), cited in Pixley (2004).

[21] See Häring and Douglas (2012) on the NY District Fed scandal. See Pixley (2007a): only 5 per cent of Australians I surveyed knew 'a little' of central banks, and that knowledge was pathetic, given their top educations shown in cross-tabs in this large survey.

were not discussed except in impenetrable post-Keynesian texts. To be fair, heterodoxy was hounded out of service to the state, but very few put contrarian claims plainly, to other social science experts or the public. In my experience, many were obsessed with arguing tiny obscure points against neoclassical economics (futilely) or their own colleagues (narcissism of small differences). Too many suffered their own economic imperialism to bother with history, social policy, politics and sociology nobodies. Another conjecture is James Forder's: some doves swallowed the Phillips Curve myth too, making them easy targets of attack. The FE years must be forgotten; FE was too inflationary apparently. The moral bogey to Mervyn King was hyperinflation. Zimbabwe! Politicians hector on the politics of envy (still), yet all economists call for political *will* to use *correct ideas*: their ones. Inside and outside, then, whatever central bank claims to efficacy, nay, moderation, must rest on the CPI index, having approved decades of declining wages, stagnant small business and rise of bank money going nowhere but to property bubbles or internet booms.[22]

GFC TO QE – NOTHING CHANGED! THE SOCIOLOGICAL QUESTION

When the great crisis finally came, it was far worse than the thousands of cynics, informed sceptics and critical journalists imagined. Headlines on likely crashes appeared through the 1990s. Central bankers later feigned amazement, which irritated critics banished for decades. This crunch kept unfolding terribly in money's heartland, not in *faraway backward* places. US and Australian governments lied to citizens over the 1997 SE Asian crash: Wall Street and Sydney had discarded financial protections for hot money to get in and out; bailouts went to these banks (perhaps via Stanley Fischer's IMF role), not

---

[22] Secrecy was evident even in the RBA in 2011, although officials kindly helped with my work on their data on 3:97 ratio (Figure 5.2), it was difficult to locate; and unreadable until one subtracted M1 from M3, then divided to get a per cent of M1 to M3. In the early 1990s, some economic experts in social policy (bemoaning inequality), agreed the unemployed should be congratulated for saving inflation (I heard it); yet mass unemployment does not save economies. See also Forder (2014).

to SE Asian so-called crony capitalists. A 'new financial architecture' was promised. The world waits.[23]

Suddenly in 2008 'cronies' were the world's largest US, UK and EU banks. How could money just disappear? The payment system, tranquilly hidden behind handy exchange, was gravely compromised. Years of everyday thinking that money is a modest add-on with no cognitive or emotional significance, a technical device for exchange, or veil over the real economy where value and its fortunes allegedly arose, were confounded when bank money was not accepted or available as such.[24] People getting by and just surviving – but habituated to dependable stable money as a background *given*, a distant trust far from personal social interactions – were threatened, fearful, angry. Debts grew in value, savings were ransacked; selling anything was pointless as prices tanked; social life and its orderly manner felt abused. The GFC shook the sense of equanimity of the most comfortable moneyed social groups, which promptly blamed the overnight bankrupt, homeless and unemployed. Huge banks, so dogmatic, so righteous, so seemingly legitimate in their teensy linking role to real economic activity ('allocating' was a lie) were mired in intricate dependencies far more than had been imagined or seen: and self-collapsed. The scandal, not merely corruption but highly leveraged evasion of rules, was so vast, the usury so great, the people, institutions, businesses exploited to ruin were so widespread, that general opinion switched. Central bank indifference to money, government praise of (dangerous) banks and support for non-regulated market products, backfired onto seriously battered economies over all those years of *targets*. Surely now, critics hoped, the commodification of money's social relations could be reversed so that money met people's desires and needs, so that money creation might go to decent new jobs in

---

[23] I explored the SE Asian financial crisis, the appalling IMF roles (and switch of 'cronies' to Wall Street in 1998) extensively in Pixley (1999), and (2004).

[24] See Schumpeter (1954: 277) who denied that 'modest' view strenuously. Exchange of goods with money (medium of exchange in the texts) is not like means of payment, for clearing debt obligations. The latter is not a one-to-one or commensurable relation rather, its precondition is a unit of account.

ventures crying out to be started or maintained. Money's infrastructural power might be more public, open to democratic oversight. Its production might be ethically constrained.[25]

Nothing happened of that sort. Treasuries and central banks did not tell populations what banks had really done. Compromised already, the logic of money put to creative ends, its mutual, normative purposes restored, is beyond such tiny reeds as central banks. They saved banks. Alan Blinder hardly tempered his criticism in saying key central bankers were as 'shocked, shocked' as the Captain in the Casablanca gambling den. One political leader who put up a strenuous criticism was UK Prime Minister Gordon Brown: money had become a 'blocked sewer'; this was getting close. Unlike governments which just months before praised the market edifice and fostered 'light touch' *Brown did not try to cover his imprudence.* Banks were near-nationalised, but not *de jure*, another opportunity lost. Northern Rock was the first bank run in Britain since 1866; thereafter the self-referential downward spiral became a frantic panic to sell. But who would buy? The BoE; Treasury; with Gordon Brown's directions.[26]

As we know, Wall Street and the City were saved with few conditions. Counterfactuals set in immediately to silence critics. Not saving banks *would have been* worse; the world *might have* collapsed into anarchy. Are the two not separate issues? If the payment system stops, economic life does too. Central banks had few options against stubborn states. Yet those fewer bank conglomerates to survive continue fanatic trading and gouging after 'conservatorship', the US state's euphemistic failure to nationalise, to run banks

---

[25] To Orléan (2013: 63–4), the symbolic power of money joins people 'objectively' in social interactions, not an 'illusion' but an intense one depending on 'the fabric of the social relations' and expectations of scarcity or availability of money. Fisher (1933) on debt deflation of money growing in value; worse, so scarce that people might not be able to buy goods, services, anything in late 2008. Hyperinflation follows the opposite trajectory in which it was easy to 'blame' the Reichsbank, e.g., we saw in Chapter 2. Ingham (2004) speaks of 'infrastructure'.

[26] Greenspan was only appalled at *individual* bankers; see Blinder (2013:325); Brown was headline news; I see decades of biographies on why opportunities were lost.

professionally for state (public) profit. Depression, rebadged recession is widespread. At the GFC, then, critics hoped for transformation but, thinking sociologically, that was hoping too much. No switch is automatic. Massive upheaval and fear does not give social change (or inevitably for people's improvement) overnight. Determinism mistakes correlations for causes, as in banking. In this great question, political roles of CBs about the now mighty financial sector are the focus: decent states are weakened and compromised; decivilising processes grow.

Above all, there were many money problems not *one*: none was explained to the public. By late 2008, the world's payment system was threatened primarily because serious credit and banking disruptions are 'a standing danger to business', to workers, households, states. When Bernanke said we may have 'no economy on Monday', it was not alarmist. Shut-down was prevented with CB reflation (cheap money), Treasury bailouts and the Fed or BoE buying banks' risky assets, just to maintain ordinary payments, like for food, which is no exaggeration. But thereafter to expanding bank reserves enormously. Second, banks sank; most nearly worthless, with unsellable shares, non-liquid and insolvent. Problems seemed difficult to separate; US Treasury barely tried and *saved banks above all*; the Fed stressed multiple efficacies of its policies. Success is relative to the (money class) definition; later, Bernanke called it his 'courage'.[27]

The chains of interdependencies in money relations (denied in pettifogging models) are too fragile for simplifications. There are thousands of books on lost opportunities, buried under the weight of further hundreds of counterfactuals. Thus, it *would have been* better if underwater mortgage holders, less banks, had been helped; the US had specialist agencies (under Treasury's dimwitted watch) that *would have* given people's purchasing power a boost; indirectly

---

[27] Polanyi (1944: 194), danger to business. To Blinder (2013: 350), Bernanke was 'Keynesian' arguing for monetary policy over 'fiscal' options: I disagree but a Keynesian direction is in Yellen versus Congress intransigence. Tooze takes a harsher line (2016) in a review of Bernanke's *The Courage to Act*.

saving a few stolid banks. Such ideas were not fact-free because FDR had done this very well and, in 2008, Australia's RBA made one sharp, short helicopter drop to all households and Treasury spent effectively on stimulus, putting in bank controls: later, power went to 'austerians' to undo that. Other institutions to a treasury or central bank are, I argue, centralised labour-capital courts or legislatures to set wages publicly; legal rights aid: Obama did raise minimum wages that helped people burdened with debts.[28]

The 1930s Great Depression revisionist histories by economists to the finance sector, harped about central bank opportunities lost from 1929 on. Their anti-democratic approaches dictated a select counterfactual onto the future. 'If' the Fed had increased the money supply in late 1929 or whatever, all *would have been* well. The *Fed's discretionary dear money* caused that Depression (alone!). Therefore, 'history tells us' what *will* cure the GFC, so long as no wage rises occur. Coded as 'long-term' dangers of inflation, claims against citizen needs were posed against Bernanke in 2009. His sad defence was he too 'grasped the mantle of Milton Friedman'. Roosevelt's major 1933–5 reforms were excoriated for so long that options for the public and governments must be reversed: TINA screamed Republicans (mostly) and, naturally, the banks: retain the *status quo ante*. Who cares if Depression ensues. Monetarist counterfactuals reject complex history and wrote out Wall Street banksters. In other countries, trade slowdowns, currency/stock market panics, mass sackings and Bankers' Ramps that sacked civilising social democracies also vanished from 'history'. Ramps were buried with people's lives.

But if the 2007 fallout, refusal to stimulus and stagnation *look like* 1929, and Bankers' Ramp concepts are useful, a specific history

---

[28] Blinder (2013: 320–4) (rightly) stresses that FDR's mortgage *protection* that helped the US from sinking more was barely used in 2008 onwards: usual suspects were Summers, Geithner, et al., for silencing Christina Romer on mortgages; households tried to repay crippling debt; bank foreclosures were often illegal so legal aid needed; spending dropped, few were likely to ask for new loans. Banks ramped up their sniveling excuses. Australia's right-wing government (2013 on) by-passed any GFC to screech 'profligate' Labor.

does not repeat because new constraints arise. True, then and now, US Treasury overlooked bank vindictiveness against banking's own victims in foreclosures. In 1929, however, many capitalist countries had never experienced working democracies with wide electoral participation, full employment, some means to improve life chances – or quiet banks. A Bretton Woods and much that was fair, or shared somewhat equally, are not even memories now, only fascism and WWII. In 2008, governments were the only players left standing, and with *precedents available.*[29]

The conundrums for central bankers in such ambiguous locations instantly came to the fore. In their official capacity, one might say they are in a contradictory class location. The moment routines so biased to the wealthy broke down; nearly ceased in late 2008, no one was blasé. The public blame cast on banks, the anger at 'banksters' – none of this was misdirected. In-coming President Obama told Wall Street CEOs in early 2009: 'My administration is the only thing between you and the pitchforks'. *Laissez faire* was smashed – yet lived. Bankers, with steady-eyed devotion to self-interests, blamed Clinton's Administration for moral hazard, or anyone than their selves.

Let me focus, then, in this unravelling to save banks, on the bedrock of capitalist money, the *memorable alliance* of governments and finance. This suggests the state is 'a controller and also a debtor and a subsidizer dependent on those it subsidizes'. Where do *central banks* stand in this alliance? None wanted to admit to lavishing finance, maybe in self-preservation, or for obeying government 'inflation targets'. Many tried confidence-boosting during 2007 (I don't blame them), to be then accused of missing the severity of banks' mortgage debt; CBs had little idea of off-balance sheet problems. This

---

[29] See Chapter 3 on the 1930s Ramps; answer of Bernanke (2013a) to attacks in Meltzer (2013). Other known measures were rarely used. In Australia, the GFC was less marked: bank deposits *were* guaranteed, yet with RBA cheques to all households, an instant building stimulus to all schools, eased jobs/debts. Banks were to *put the interests of their clients first!* Disregarded the second the ALP Government lost office.

is incredible to outsiders and yes, some knew, being former private bankers or being promoted by bankers - 'You're a brick, Bob' - BoE's Paul Tucker said to Bob Diamond, CEO of Barclays. These dubious connections are as nothing.[30]

What *central bankers did know* was that money markets move between money inflation and debt deflation: Under pressure to slow the Dotcom bubble at a 1996 FOMC, then Fed Chair Greenspan privately admitted (wage-price) 'product' inflation can be conquered - by unemployment he didn't say out loud – but at the cost of *asset inflation* going 'through the roof'. Even to his own colleagues I think, he masked the terms. In ignorance or pressure, or was he mindful of his reputation? Nevertheless, he admitted inflation was in plural, although after *different* answers to Congress, critics said Wall Street had the measure of the man.[31]

Stalling was amply evident in the BoE's and FOMC's decisions late in 2007 to avoid *stigmatising* banks with Lender of Last Resort (LOLR). Weakness or faith, Mervyn King assumes that was essential and fair. Blinder argues the Fed was slow to act, being packed with hawks, although a year ahead of the ECB. The French bank BNP Paribas rang the bell on August 9, 2007; simultaneously Bernanke praised the 'new mortgage market' with its 'more liquid instruments' as a 'textbook' virtue, just as the (classic) destabilising dynamics of a bear market spiralled down. Not until December 2007 did the Fed 'lend', but banks had 'stymied' earlier LOLR attempts 'fearing' bank runs! Bernanke assumed it was a 1907 panic. And yet, central banks operated under *other constraints*. In the 1980s, one global banking 'innovation' was the interbank market (Libor) for allegedly 'a more efficient distribution of funds' so banks could reduce liquid reserves

---

[30] 'Pitchforks' are cited Johnson and Kwak (2011: 3); Amato and Fantacci (2012: 217) on dependent states. The Tucker story is in Pixley (2012).
[31] See Greenspan in the transcripts, FOMC 24 September (1996: 30) his words 'product inflation' not saying 'wage-price'; Pixley (2004) on critics.

by borrowing overnight from each other. Apart from later revelations that banks rigged it, Libor thus avoided scrutiny from their central bank – banks did not need LOLR, its 'stigma' or opening their books. The Fed took this (sociology) seriously because, although mere rumours (stigma) can start a run, this self-fulfilling concept led the Fed to appease banks further. It gave banks less publicly obvious loans (2007), with anonymous auctions, while the *Fed remained in the dark* as to whether banks were in crises. FOMC members seemed scared to know; the Fed also lent to the ECB and BoE.[32] Bank leverage was indeed huge. In 2008, World Bank data in Table 8.1 on total bank liabilities to GDP, the following ratios obtained:

Table 8.1. *Bank liabilities in five countries to GDP, 2008*

Switzerland	629 per cent of GDP
United Kingdom	550 per cent
France	273 per cent
Germany	135 per cent
United States	93 per cent

Sources: Admati & Hellwig 2013: 238 from World Bank

---

[32] See King (2016); Blinder (2013: 90–7) on 'stymied', who criticises *inflation* worries in the FOMC minutes, in early August 2007; to a late August, alarmist Jackson Hole meeting, where Bernanke at last tried to urge FOMC members to act; also Bush's Treasurer Paulson was even slower; Pixley (2012) on Paribas closing its subprime books; on the liquidity/insolvency divide, King's excuse is a fudge; Orléan (2014: 262–3) cites Bernanke saying CDSs 'Collateralized Debt' were a 'textbook' market; on a 1907 analogy, Tooze (2016: 135); Gibson (2009) on Libor's impact; FOMC December 2007 Transcripts; in the 1990s if banks were no longer scrutinising their own borrowers, who *would*? The credit rating agencies had suddenly boomed. None of these reduced dangers of plain default from 'distant and commodified', but actual, borrowers. Gibson shows how the credit rating agencies, like problems with 'syndication' of sovereign loans of the 1980s, 'restricted the range of opinions about the credit-worthiness of borrowers' Gibson (2009: 4) and Gibson and Tsakalotos (2006). Loans to the BoE/ECB suggest US dollar reserves were their key source of money creation.

The data show the GDP order of economies reliant most heavily on finance sectors (see Figures 7.1 and 7.2) through to the diversified USA. Even had central banks looked at banks' books, which the Fed, ECB or BoE had not, the tangled global chains of so many IOUs or near money were so great it was far too late for central banks – control had long gone. Slight differences pertained, I think most to those that acted by 2002 on mortgage scams (the RBA notably alarmed) or, in the 1990s on tougher bank supervision like Sweden, Canada and Australia. But what *dreary outliers* they were, irrelevant to the real business. Thus, in late 2005, FOMC hawk Thomas Hoenig was just thrilled; coded, US wages and jobs were perfect: low pay; casual. Hoenig said 'I'd describe the outlook for the U.S. economy as solid'. Chair Greenspan agreed: 'It's hard to imagine an American economy that is as balanced as this one is.' Did either care the extent that the real business was global finance?[33] Looking at that global picture, Admati and Hellwig criticise prominent bank CEOs for 'invalid' and false claims: Jamie Dimon, head of JP Morgan, and Josef Ackermann, former head of Deutsche Bank. For specious arguments, Dimon's claim that JP Morgan has a 'fortress balance sheet' is a sheet they tear to shreds – it is 'dangerous'; the commitments and 'potential liabilities of the bank are left off the bank's balance sheet'. In 2011, it had 4.5 per cent total equity.[34]

Stepping back, Lehman's collapse in September 2008 exposed heretofore unknown, intricate lending of the actual banks. The Fed and Treasury, dubiously, not positively *consolidated*, saved them with no conditions whatever of merit. Alan Blinder called publicly for Hank Paulson (Treasurer) to be impeached: that he duped Congress. Treasury's second turn at passing a TARP (relief) had not 'a single word' on its 'mutual aims' with the Fed to 'inject capital into banks'. President Bush's Act that passed claimed, it said, to 'mitigate

---

[33] The RBA sent its officers to the suburbs to hear mortgage sales hype, and acted, I was told. Those three countries had late 1980s finance crises and acted. FOMC 13 December (2005: 29; 66), citations of President Hoenig (Kansas City District), and Greenspan, still Chair, very satisfied behind closed doors.

[34] Admati and Hellwig (2013: 83–4; World Bank data: 238), is an outright attack on global finance. Data was calculated under 'stricter' European International accounting rule than the US's.

foreclosure' and 'promote market stability'. Enough, it seems for the Treasury-Fed's first try to 'inject capital' in October 2008. 'Thankful' that three banks 'looked fine' (shown not so later), these chief officials *begged* JP Morgan, Wells Fargo and Goldman CEOs to take TARP loans to hide the stigma of rescuing other banks. Within hours, those three CEOs leaked to, or told the press this, to gain competitive advantage. This to my mind is *one smoking gun*. The US treasury (Paulson), and central bank (Bernanke and Geithner) did not set terms on banks, not even that they stay secret about receiving largesse. Congress was 'thinking it was voting to purchase troubled assets' for people. A needed halt to panic, Blinder concedes, and overall TARP was 'successful'. State controls vanished when Wall Street rose, to a legacy 'troubled' far more than outsiders or Congress guessed. With the Fed and Treasury so compromised away from the public good, their nerve vanished: banks which scorned the largesse kept it.[35]

BLEAK OPTIONS FOR MONETARY AND FISCAL POLICY

The efficacy of monetary policy has never been 'rigorously tested'. After the inordinate self-praise and market-bestowed praise, what can CBs do now? Since QE, lending euphemisms or bold if misleading statements – like Draghi's damagingly late vow that the ECB would do 'whatever it takes!' – there is mainly counterfactual non-evidence (not acting *would have been* worse). The main proof about QE is that the exact same techniques the Fed, BoE and ECB used by the Bank of Japan are 30-year miserable failures. Financial markets govern by panic; in Euroland four countries were blasted economically

[35] TARP was *Troubled Assets Relief Program*. See Blinder (2013: 182–202), also saying Paulson and Bernanke were terrified of Congress (allegedly Gordon Brown too, of the UK troika); Congress rejected the September 2008 TARP I for giving Paulson total discretion; they pulled sums needed from the air; Paulson 'hated' controls on bank executive pay or on dividends with Bernanke's and Geithner's *support*; TARP II, appropriated $700 billion. The three CEOs were Wells Fargo's Dick Kovacevich; GS&Co's Lloyd Blankfein and Dimon, bragging in public they 'neither needed nor wanted' TARP; not of their fears of reduced incomes (!) when meeting Paulson Treasurer, Bernanke Fed Chair and Geithner NY Fed. Also, the non-bank GS&Co was *turned into a bank*. Blinder is truly appalled Congress was duped; however, he perhaps clouds Paulson's potential fear of China; see Helleiner (2015), or British PM Brown's quasi-nationalising between US Treasury's two attempts to pass TARP II in Congress.

before the ECB tried to stop frantic, profitable arbitrage, *secretly saving banks*. The BoJ's negative interest rates (with no impact) were urged on CBs in late 2016. Views differ on central bank efficacy, with sensible arguments that the 1980 monetary policy was not the sole inflation-crushing factor of the 1985 US Recession. Volcker and/ or opportunities took US industrial firms in droves offshore and, as China industrialised to enjoy the US (indebted) consumer of last resort, OECD trade unions declined with firms' offshore moves and oligopolistic employers' change of heart against unions and wage rises. The need for 'discipline' trumped nice profits, and corporate financialising proceeded, with Nixon's dollar float kicking it off. Governments of Thatcher and Reagan were probably worse than Nixon's or the oligopolies in destroying or crippling civil society's defences. Autocratic, warmongering, devoted to banking's triumph, these governments shackled CBs that from 2007, endured the attributions of excessive kindness to banks. As well, states did not change CB mandates to curb cravenness.[36]

With the US dollar, the Treasury-Fed's global role meant other central banks had to respond to the American QE (the BoE and ECB QEs as sideshows). One possibility is that the Fed-Treasury had little option on *specific* domestic bailouts, perhaps more for private banks, however. Foreign governments had massive holdings in the dollar, a sellout of which in 2008 posed huge dangers. In 2003, Bernanke accused 'China' of 'flooding' the US capital market to such an extent that US banks 'could' lend more (or 'too much'). If one talks up the 'loanable funds theorem', one ignores domestic bank money creation or whether it goes to bubbles, not 'business'. The Fed has few controls anyway and Bernanke said the Fed's QE would *'flood' to successful* business recovery. Leaving aside that futile hope, the main impact of cheap money and QE was felt globally with the changed or 'manipulated' US$ that China held passively.

---

[36] 'Efficacy' is in Ingham (2008: 88–91). See Streeck (2014) on the ECB and Roach (2016) on the BoJ; Evans-Pritchard (2016): Japan is discussed below; recall Chapter 7, Edwards (2004) giving CBs a minimal role; see Crotty (2012) on Kalecki (1943) and anti-unionists, and Greider (1988). See Chapter 2 on *bank* war finance.

Eric Helleiner shows Hank Paulson (Bush's head of Treasury) knew something useful (!) – how to appease China from his old GS&Co deals. Bernanke helped the BoE and ECB in late 2007 with swaps and huge loans yet, like Republicans and the IMF, he blamed 'China', unlike Paulson and Treasury itself (one assumes). The secret worry was that China had invested heavily in US institutions (mainly government mortgage insurers) and therefore Treasury bailouts were essential to prevent China starting a run on the dollar. Another excluded point was the Fed loans to the BoE and ECB increased their dependence on the Fed and Wall Street. China needed no loans, the opposite, and it is possible China was entrapped on the grounds if you lend a billion dollars (to the US), it is your problem whereas a hundred is the debtor's problem. QE depreciated the dollar. But how to define 'China'? It is quasi-capitalist; however, the question is whether the US was in hock to China's state and Chinese global finance. An everyday (Republican) exclusion.

A top Chinese official said in early 2009: 'Except for US Treasuries what can you hold? ... [They] are the safe haven. Once you start issuing \$1trillion-\$2trillion [QE] ... we know the dollar is going to depreciate, so we hate you guys but there is nothing much we can do.' Helleiner suggests if the US had copied Nixon's unilateral shut down, China 'might have' dumped the dollar, which is not purely a counterfactual given the PBoC governor suggested a global reserve currency like Keynes's bancor at the G20 in 2009.[37]

Given such interlocking factors, what kind of central bank performance is left to assess? First are absurd claims about the Great Moderation and stability. Second is how CBs dealt with the 2008 events and lengthening aftermath. Potential, often serious slides to debt-deflation and rise in disaffection that can no longer be brushed off blithely, have sharpened public eyes against CBs' obsessive focus on inflation, some more viciously applied than others. The 'state is back' (or the cry) but whatever desired reforms cannot neglect state-treasury

---

[37] See Helleiner (2015: 240): the Chinese official is cited in Helleiner (2015: 241); on the bancor see Chapter 4. Although cf. Schwartz (2009) on the dollar still strong. PBoC is the People's Bank of China.

symbiosis with markets. When 'Main Street not Wall Street' mattered in the postwar era, from 1971 the reverse built up. Wall Street rules, over deflationary austerity Treasuries and nuclear war finance. Central bankers (like Bernanke) imply that 'Main Street' stays in an unwarranted black hole, against their internal hawks using false charges that 'Keynesians' are inflationist. Given bond vigilantes' demands for state stimulus cutbacks, indecent Board members oblige by muffling the *largest pork barrel ever on saving finance*. 'Targets' on output are disproven when today central banks cannot raise 'inflation' to the balmy 2 per cent it was during the full employment years. What of monetary sovereignty? The state as the 'dependent subsidiser' is governed from a global financial 'club'.

Furthermore, there is no point saying public servant Paulson was *personally* weak (accepting the Fed must follow). Consider my *smoking gun*. Treasurer Paulson had national worries about China and met his own formerly tough official persona in a new, similarly swaggering CEO of GS&Co and lost. Paulson's official position switched to weak US Treasury which, with the weaker Fed and the *private bank-owned NY Fed* did not even rescind those three banks' bailouts. At that second, bank vigilante power was low, but state authority did not or could not take away these banks' subsidies. Was the odium Treasurer Paulson gained from letting Lehman fail in 2008 a factor? One can hardly argue the Treasury-Fed teamwork was a measured consolidation of fiscal and monetary powers: it seems reactive.

As well, the Great Moderation was the Great Capitulation to Excess (under orders). Perhaps the 'moral hazard' idea is useful. Sheila Dow argues that the main central bank narrative since the GFC is that banks became too big to fail, had enjoyed bailouts over decades, which meant recklessness arose from expecting more bailouts: 'moral hazard'. After the GFC, banks had 'soft landings'; excessively by *'foaming the runways'*, as Tim Geithner (D.) put it as US Treasurer after Paulson (R.). He ordered one official, Neil Barofsky to throw tax money at banks. Wall Street liked Geithner's appointment – having just been the NY Fed's generous chief to its owners (banks). How brazen of central bankers to ignore decades of Treasury orders to be 'kind to banks', in then accusing banks of moral hazard so that banks are now too big to save. Yes, but Dow asks, whose moral hazard was the more serious? The authorities had expertise and the legitimacy of the state behind them to prevent bank runs (BoE Mervyn King stalled with Northern Rock). CBs must maintain confidence in money *per se*. But so dominant were banks that central bankers could not or would not jawbone and explain money's 'full socioeconomic role'. True. Monetary policy was bereft of conceptions of money or its store of value function, and the dangers of financial instability. Once bank runs threaten, Dow argues, no one is interested in whether money is 'inflating', rather whether banking systems and even states are viable at all.[38]

In answer, inflation targets put central banks in a 'prison'. Yes, many basked in sainthood – the Fed was loved for pleasing Wall Street with routine profit. After the 1970s, banks (bond traders) *asserted further rights to reject the state's debt* at whim. Monetarist central bankers blamed the state and the alleged 'inflationary bias' of democracy (in fact the erratic Nixon's), when (strong) states have no financial interest whatever (in logic) in high interest payments, in enlarging the value of the national debt, or conversely in seeing the value of taxes and fiscal policy strategies decline from inflations. But is evidence and logic hidden because allegedly 'expert' central banks were silent, on purpose to fawn to global finance, or in a hobbled fear and so, refrained from advising states? To Dow, central banks broke the deal as much as private banks, the most important part being that if banks were 'to supply society's money' (Dow) that would be only in exchange for firm regulation with strict and effective supervision. Yet states (not CBs) took supervision away. Ingham and others say that such 'exchanges'

> ... refer to a 'social contract' between banks and the state which
> involves state support for the banks in return for which the state

---

[38] On 'inflationist' allegations, see Chapter 6; Dimon (JP Morgan) not Blankfein is the most swaggering, unrepentant, most threatening: *but*, backed with Morgan's long dubious history; *his position on the NY Fed* of then Geithner. See Dow (2013: 190–1); Barofsky (2013) on 'foaming' and Bair (2012). Schularick (2014: 195) shows finance crises *above all* cause public debt.

imposes regulation. This omits any reference to the basis of the contract that is contained in the state debt and money creation mechanism which is operated by the *state treasury, central bank and banking system*'.[39]

The problem is far deeper. Bank privileges to create state-capitalist money were never about *willingly* accepting supervision. Its lack is always disastrous and cause of huge fiscal costs to save banks and, this time to forestall China et al. from dumping the US dollar. Far more serious is the money creation (memorable alliance) in which banks have control over state debt. It is no matter that states are no longer the main defaulters (400 years ago), instead banks. WWII and industrialists gave FDR and, for example, the ALP's Curtin some scope to put in rules – against perennially *recalcitrant* banks, but in few other wars. Allan Meltzer (a monetarist) predicted 'the interest rate and the exchange rate at which the market will willingly hold the government debt and money', 'will be' the main 'concern' – as if in 2010, making a bold new point. Is this his sole factual statement about state monetary sovereignty dependency with any logic? US Treasury caved in to bond markets in 1971–73. The Fed was founded to do so and the BoE, and to fund war finance. The state is dependent, often erratic.[40]

THE CRASH'S AFTERMATH

When Bernanke later explained the Fed's 'Quantitative Easing' of 2009 and 2010 he said QEs were 'large-scale asset purchases' of government-guaranteed securities. The Fed bought two trillion dollars'

[39] Ingham (2011: 287 my emphasis) is answering Alessandri and Haldane (2010) who take Dow's (2013) line and on state v. bank defaulters. See Chapter 4 on the US Fed and CBA/ RBA in WWII versus banks. FDR couldn't nationalise the District Feds so, Wall Street banks pull strings. Defence can be modest, but not the USA's, and note Obama ramped up nuclear weapons.

[40] Max Weber (1978) repeatedly spoke of threats in a more consistent manner than Meltzer (2013: 224), who criticised Bernanke for looking at banks *at all*, at the conference on Jekyll Island in 2010 on the Fed's hundred years. Meltzer forgets too, as does Congress, that China (not defence dependent), Saudi Arabia, Japan, the Emirates and others remain creditors to the USA.

worth and 'we paid' for them 'by crediting the bank accounts', their 'reserve accounts' with the Fed. This is fine in accounting terms, and just like banking's deposit-creating loans (not that Bernanke said that). There's a 'smoke and mirrors' in Bernanke saying that because these 'electronic entries' just 'sit there' and are not 'cash', this is correct. The Fed is not 'printing money'. They *are* Fed advances (deposited loans not actual currency) to tempt banks to create new money (unsaid). His idea was to see 'expansions in bank lending' – and that is *about all the Fed can do*. The implicit hope (in Fed-provided 'loanable funds') was that commercial banks 'would grant more credit' with their Fed-expanded legal tender deposited reserves, to restart economic activity. But global finance had reduced money-creation for economies for decades.[41]

Here I think is central bankers' dissonance and sorry denial, an unsayable detracting from urging fiscal policy inside the *monetarist asylum* if you prefer. This well-meaning Fed Chair excludes how banks create money just like a central bank (that guarantees bank money), but that can be in any form banks and borrowers privately decide, even if Bernanke's (civil) hope is for a trickle down to the jobs market. Thus, more dependencies came under *carte blanche* QE and Treasury, since trillions went directly to banks, a pitiful few billion to modest lenders and borrowers. Sheila Dow is correct, I think, to say that Bernanke's Fed and King's BoE tried to depoliticise monetary policy in presenting to the public this apparently dramatic QE with monetarist rhetoric, as a 'significant' expansion for banks to restart lending. To monetarism, base (HPM) money is the source of the money supply and of inflation or, conversely, *more* is supposed to cure deflation. On that citizens are duped by states and banks. Given bank money is 97 per cent of the money we use, the bulk is in bank deposits and securities – bank innovations of 'near' money assets. That bank-created money for the property bubble *inflated* and

---

[41] Bernanke (2013: 102–8; 114–15). Ingham and I discussed this; Blinder (2013) says Congress's hysteria at Bernanke 'printing money' was exemplified by Sarah Palin's ignorance, but lots of the men know zero too; see Figure 7.1 on British banks, and Tables 1.1 and 1.2 on bank balance sheets cf. the negative interest idea meant banks would pay the Fed.

turned into the payment system disaster, to be overcome, urgently, with state bailouts, and very low central bank interest rates.

QE became confused or conflated with that (sadly slavish) rescue job in pretending to be a stimulus as well. Dow points out, had banks wanted more liquidity, *central banks always supply it.* Who knows that? Politicians? Authorities have little choice but to facilitate refinancing in all circumstances.[42] It calls in question QE's aim for 'expansion' via helping banks, which can expand their businesses to any other profitable direction; not necessarily if at all to people's economic activity. After the GFC, there was weak aggregate demand for loans, huge household debt repayments (given Main Street had pitiful help) and lack of confidence in the unknowable future. To Dow, there is no 'true' knowledge, only social and political influences on knowledge of the social relations of money. Although the immense size of the QEs made the policy 'unconventional', the technique was conventional CB guarantees of bank money creation whenever needed. It is unknown to the public. Nor was it ever said that QE enabled the private banking sector to keep control of the *production* of money. That is the secret, a political admission of CB defeat. As became evident, QE only shored up bank reserves and financed new asset price bubbles. Was QE a restoration? No, *global finance could dictate the terms to states even more.* Monetarism sees only state money. But witness Senator Elizabeth Warren's calls for jail terms in 2016; asking the Wells Fargo CEO to return his salary, to sack his executives, to resign. One strategy the Fed could try, but has not, is take heavy bets against bond and currency trades. Why not, when no other CB is that mighty and thus capable?[43]

---

[42] To Roach (2016) QE detracted from stressing fiscal policy, and Tooze (2016: 134); Dow (2013: 183; 186): 'accommodation' is another term. And e.g., senior CDO tranches, a good share of which was held by commercial banks, amounted 'to economic catastrophe bonds'. Farhi and Tirole (2009) argue the crisis *could have been* contained ex ante through more careful prudential policies. The question is rather, why it wasn't.

[43] See Dow (2013: 186); Warren is in McGrath (2016) – bank scandals have not abated; and Ingham (2013) on Fed bets.

A 2010 FOMC transcript expresses the many weaknesses of central banks, and to my mind does not prove a bold conspiracy against the public, rather conflicting anxieties of reputations and fears of political derision at the Fed's timidity about finance markets wreaking more world disasters. The political nature of CB decisions is evident, even granted the ever narrower 'prison yard' of divisive options: one wants a catastrophic Depression, others futile hopes. Amidst an *annus horribilis*, in which Bernanke faced Congressional Republican threats to impeach him, at the 2010 December meeting Fed members had to decide whether to continue QE or cut it back. Yellen had pleaded and won at the November FOMC the option of 'boosting the stimulus' of QE further, as the *FT* saw it (swallowing the lame rhetoric). We see less nervous laughter of olden years; members are plain scared about many problems, even of their FOMC colleagues (and the ECB) leaking to hedge funds, incredible to read.

What we see, in so far as outsiders can interpret, is less deluded or muddled thinking nor (too) fraudulent, or (too many) power-hungry members, so much as political clarity over minute options. The immoderate want to let depression ensue to keep the 'long-term' inflation 'target' (unknowable and in debt deflation) – aka give banks all the profits they want. This political decision blithely proposes to destroy people's lives. A scorched earth though, does not necessarily meet global financial interests in abusing those lives. The alternatives, also political decisions, are to keep racking up QE in hope for trickle down effects to jobs, or just to boost (banking) confidence. The FOMC must know QE reduces the state's dividends. It is possible central bankers lost all sense of timing, marking their lack of control. Bernanke refused to study panics or manias, since 'rationality' is assumed, which denies inevitably rational fears of uncertainty. And central bankers' dilemmas are whether to aid banks too early when unnecessary (inviting moral hazard), or too long (unable to retract later), or too dangerously late after all banks are falling (or governments, re the tardy ECB). Few FOMC members discuss the timing of QE (early but too long) a nightmare that creates bank fragility, a path dependency going nowhere but to bank balance sheets, and with no proof that QE was efficacious as 'stimulus'. Apparently, the Fed lacked a choice of exit timing (in global market 'taper tantrums') so it couldn't stop, or think to help households.[44]

At this December 2010 meeting, some worried about paying banks a positive interest rate that 'the public' sees as a subsidy at 'the cost of not fulfilling our dual mandate' (FE). So, the public was not stupid after all, in that only banks were saved. A Mr. Fisher, head of the Dallas Fed thinks expanding QE2 'would be politically suicidal' and, with the Fed targeting government debt yields, Congressional concern about debt 'monetization quickly raises its ugly head' from 'our' most 'volatile critics' (Republicans; world finance probably). Above all he wanted to hear reports from people from 'financial market backgrounds or from the real economy' (why more money creators 'or' the 'real'?). Yellen then Vice-Chair argued Obama's 'fiscal package' (a week before) is positive but sees 'deceleration' and unemployment rising. On the Fed's asset purchases, she thinks new data support the Fed's efficacy in 'stimulating the economy'. In contrast a Governor, Ms. Duke doubts Yellen's propositions, although like others feels that 'whatever' does appear to be working better, nothing should change (yet)! Yellen and others are most concerned about 'the European debt situation'; Yellen is critical the 'European response' to crisis is not stemming 'contagion' (in class terms, not impeding the ruinous bond traders). A Mr. Evans, Chicago District Fed president, also worried about high unemployment and low unit labour costs: a 'dove':

> By lowering real rates, such a development would help us to do better on our employment objective. It would change opportunity costs, and it is difficult to imagine *strongly sustained higher*

---

[44] See Chapter 5 and to paraphrase Kindleberger (1989), also Minsky (2008 [1986]: 364–5) on timing, Pixley (2004) on fears are rational; Minsky's decades' old stress on the Fed leaning *towards* trade and production financing, against Ponzi finance; witness Wells Fargo and Deutsche Bank in late 2016 potential collapses. The taper tantrum is an example of *governing* by panic.

inflation without growth in broad monetary aggregates, bank lending, and growth more generally.[45]

Notice how Mr. Evans has 'and growth', to conclude, perhaps assuming banks do lend to business (quantity views). Those urging dear money is to will a disaster, whereas cheap money may lower the value of underwater mortgages, cheapen interest payments, perhaps raise the price of dwindling assets (QE), but not when banks lifted their earlier 'teaser' rates or foreclosed on impoverished mortgage holders. The FOMC knew and Bernanke had a year before agreed to unconditional bailouts to banks. The problem not mentioned is if money is the only cost, as it is for deals in financial assets, but not for long-term prospects of investment in labour, equipment and property for goods and services, short-term profits can be made in speculative bubbles on assets.

Kansas City District Hoenig, the only dissenter at that FOMC, said agricultural land values were rising somewhat, and asked, 'given that we're trying to affect asset values, what other assets might we be affecting through our current policies?' Later he said extensive deleveraging is taking place, yet he wanted a move away from 'our highly accommodative policy', which is 'inconsistent'. He says 'as we start to raise interest rates, the initial downward effect on asset prices and financial activity will be outsized. The markets will despair'. This was the man thrilled about 2005's numbers, not for populations.

The more decent doves' dubious separation of bank-led bubbles from the 'real' perhaps forestalls 'tongue lashings' (that Blinder said of Summers's) from world destroyers like Hoenig. Members expressed fears of Congress *or* finance and talk of business employment and

---

[45] Note that FOMC transcripts are released 5–6 years after each meeting, freely available on federalreserve.gov. Transcripts record '(laughter)' thus. See the transcript FOMC, December 14, (2010: 96) on bank subsidy; Fisher is on p. 102–4; Yellen p. 59–60; 98; Duke p. 100; Evans p. 46, my emphasis. The refusal to use LOLR with *conditions* (i.e. to maintain or foster business) and via checking bank books, was pointed out years ago by Minsky (2008 [1986]).

confidence measures, as a different question from banks. Dallas District Richard Fisher asked about margin debt rising to 'an extraordinary level' (sadly this once major Fed concern was not discussed as a worry aka routine bubbles) and proposed that a Fed 'dealer survey' be designed to 'keep them guessing' (good): a preferable strategy to giving 'too much' information to financial dealers (ignoring FOMC members were leaking!). Fisher also worried at the March 2008 bailout of Bear Stearns that banks were taking 'advantage' of the Fed – a case of 'too early'. Apparently, Fisher's guidance on rates was from 'regular prayer and pop psychology'.[46]

Outside the Fed, the CEO of Wells Fargo (a 'tarnished' bank in 2016) said in 2008: 'It's interesting that the industry has invented new ways to lose money, when the old ways seemed to work just fine'. This joke (hah, hah) that a GS&Co or a JP Morgan CEO never said publicly, gives pause for thought. By 2010, TARP and QE were huge gifts to banks. The Fed's lack of power is palpable. The most decent it could do was hope for a trickle-down effect on a prayer (not Fisher's). Monetarist pro-market (higher interest) policies, patently defunct to all, are still shouted in public forums. Banks again won, and induced fears of worse knock-on effects, say onto the EMU. Whether Bernanke or FOMC doves *believed* their public explanations is unknowable, the question is why they presented QE as monetarist. Perhaps, to appease the finance sector and ultimately maintain the *memorable alliance* between the state and banking, or to mystify Congress on job creation, or deny 'money printing', or conversely against fiscal deficits: options were miserably starved. Was the Fed utterly beaten?[47]

Rather than (ever) question publicly whether changes in the social relations of money production were necessary – *however unlikely* – the tenor of that FOMC of 2010 was that *monetising the state deficit* is out of court, it is ugly or unmentionable. QE did that

---

[46] Comments at the FOMC, 14 December (2010: 47, 90) of Hoenig. Fisher in (2008) is cited in Jacobs and King (2016: 117); in the FOMC 14 December (2010: 8; 12). See Tooze (2016: 133) on Fisher praying a lot.

[47] The Wells Fargo CEO is cited in John and Saulwick (2008: 45).

inadvertently, but to monetise bank debts. We are in a different world yet some urge policies of the 1920s–30s; we did not design this finance deal. In the 1940s–70s a change occurred, whereby central banks in an era when full employment, with the strength of states to back industry and labour (and vice versa) over *rentiers* and high finance, achieved low inflation. In the US, industrialist associations led by Marriner Eccles, and unions a little, strongly influenced FDR's Administration. These class segments were not fighting Wall Street at 2007.

The option of the state borrowing from CBs in 2008 after global finance took off from 1971 was forbidden, though cannot but help occur *de facto*. Where has the Fed's lending gone? Not in saving mortgagees or creating with treasury 'a level of spending that is sufficient to employ the whole of labour and available resources of the economy'. If the social relations of money are always in a black hole, or mindless land of tranquillity, suddenly the discourse had to change in 2008. Inflation was thereupon desired (after all that hectoring). But, since inflations arise from many sources through decisions made in all sectors, QE's monetarist aspect failed – that is, state-central bank money does not inevitably *cause* inflation if desired. Inflations come from many pressures; the reverse, deflation, only profits banks and *rentiers*. Reducing wage inflation only with a CB-induced major contraction is to risk lower activity for a long time. Monetarists do not care: handmaidens to finance and perhaps/maybe so are CBs.[48] What monetarists cannot or do not want to catch is Dow's point: 'Money arose as a social necessity'. Global finance is the predator on social desires and needs for money. Thrift (in corporate and bank cash piles) is currently driving many countries into depression; that is why a central banker like Alan Blinder urges negative interest rates for bank reserves deposited in CBs. I wonder; banks can place ever more loans (emptying *expensive* reserves) on

---

[48] Coombs (1971 [a speech of 1954]: 9) on the level of spending; Dow on innovation (2006: 39–40 and 42–3). The RBA argues trade unions should ask for higher wages.

asset bubbles. The difference, to Schumpeter on 'creative destruction', is banking was the 'Ephor' or magistrate of capitalist development, but banks can create 'destruction without function' if liquidity is all that is desired.[49]

QE involved Bernanke having to expose to Congress what central banks do, that is, create money. It could even lead to exposing how private banks create most money or how the Fed could intervene in bond markets. The Fed, in those absences about creating money after the Crash, shows to me a *sense of powerlessness*. The BoE's Mervyn King was slow to act and talked of banking's moral hazard but how obvious, with the Royal Bank of Scotland scandal.

The mixed messages are such that Norbert Häring claims 'central bankers never, ever talk about the hugely profitable privilege that the ability to create legal tender means for commercial banks'. Could Bernanke say something about commercial bank money creation and contraction in the Fed's defence? From the way Alan Blinder, former Deputy Chair of the Fed discusses the crisis, perhaps he could. Blinder quotes Sarah Palin's criticism of QE. In 2011 Palin said, 'it's time for us to 'refudiate' the notion that this dangerous experiment in printing $600 billion out of thin air, with nothing to back it up, will magically fix economic problems'. Blinder put it like this: 'It was as if Palin and others had just discovered that central banks create money – and decided they didn't like it.' This fact is generally unknown, and he provided a Charles Dickens quote, but nothing on bank money: 'Credit is a system whereby a person who can't pay gets another person who can't pay to guarantee that he can pay'. That guarantee is not from central banks and HPM solely, but banks' guarantee and is indeed money when accepted, as it was not in 2008 since money markets refused to accept bank money (a run). This is how postwar central bankers talk.[50]

---

[49] Blinder (2013) on rates; Schumpeter (1934 [1911]).
[50] See Häring (2013: 9); Blinder (2013: 252); Dickens is cited Blinder (2013: 237), muted cf. Minsky!

I think a and/or the problem is to explain why central bankers refuse to admit that private banking's loans create deposits, knowing this, being also banks. Financial statements always show equal liabilities and assets (Tables 1.1 and 1.2). Business and households do not. Bank balances change over time: central banks show similar balance sheets (usually not hiding leverage off-balance-sheet like private banks). Why do even critical central bankers like Blinder, who has no qualms in exposing Greenspan his former boss, bury this routine so freely admitted in the 1950s? There were harsher critics on how the finance sector bets on a 'socially useless' future (a term the UK regulator post-GFC used) whether in apparent booms or busts. In a surprising move in early 2014, the Bank of England did explain bank deposit-creating loans. It admitted that all money consists in IOUs. Given the Royal Bank of Scotland (RBS) was the largest bailout the world had ever seen, being, at its crash the largest corporation in the world, disquiet was perhaps more pronounced than in the USA. Perhaps the US dollar hegemony was one cause of backflips, which stayed pianissimo.[51] The *FT* picked up the story earlier: 'loanable funds' theorem does not admit banks deposit loans. Worse, citing Goodhart, if demand is weak, a breakdown in the available central bank reserves of banks for commercial bank lending/deposits can occur: QE is useless.

Can central bankers believe the theorems they chant? Many are not indecent.[52] Finance economists (to banks) told CBs not to act in the public interest; 'neoliberal' states welcome Bankers' Ramps to force austerity on the national debt (its social provisions) – but without that debt, there is less (taxed) HPM. Social democratic states barely endure. Taxes on the wealthy were removed and evaded, while the US nuclear arsenal grows, funded behind a wall of *utter* silence.

---

[51] Socially useless is Turner (2010) then UK finance regulator; the BoE in McLeay et al. (2014) on bank money creation, and Ryan-Collins et al. (2011); on this, Wolf (2014). The Fed made swaps to the ECB and BoE from late 2007, indicating their reliance on US reserves for their money creation (see Chapter 7 on the Bundesbank).

[52] *FT* on money creation, Goodhart in Skypala (2013); and on the Fed in Tooze (2016).

The second Iraq War (at the GFC) relies on the WWI borrowing model. The US Treasury-bond market is enormous and the Fed has a large portfolio of T-bills, multiplied by banks; Treasury the US$'s advantage and nuclear umbrella assets. Not only Pentagon demands, but the rest all cost. Add Bush tax cuts and Obama's nuclear build-up *continuing* to a militarised deep South. US Treasury funds *the biggest war machine ever* (world wars were public) and succumbs to bond vigilantes and (mostly) warmongering Congress on namby-pamby social line items. An implicit trade-off – the Fed monetising state debt for 'free' mobile capital to accept military costs – is divorced from democratic debate.[53]

The thesis of cognitive and emotional dissonance must be involved; a lack of central bank discretionary 'independence', I believe, may impose secrecy or easeful ignorance. The classic structural example of dissonance is the man who believes in female equality but does not (or cannot) practice it. The job claim is bad faith because in public glare, it is difficult to admit the compromised nature of CBs and risk collapse in collective confidence. The time is never ripe. All that BoE open talk died down. Perhaps Libor rigging scandals or Tridents were too close to home.

Blinder, like Riksbank or BoC officials, is a devotee of 'doing the best you can'. He provides voluminous, judicious evidence of double standards in criticisms that Republican Bernanke faced: These are Bankers' Ramps: the banks' betrayals of Treasury and Fed; the 2009 book *End the Fed*, by Texan Congressional, Ron Paul (R.); the Meltzer and JB Taylor-led thundering that Bernanke lost the Fed's *independence* in consolidating with Treasury (omitting *war*). Republicans (not alone) made any government stimulus difficult to pass Congress. It was in

---

[53] In FOMC transcripts, I see no mention of war finance. See Chapters 2, war funding, and 5 on Vietnam to Iraq II. Conjectures are verifiable – Fed officials must know; the Obama Administration; Congress have some clever people. Banks' freedoms boosted – from 'threats'? Treasury debts (unredeemable) are bet on and held globally; the US$ global payments supplement: recorded somewhere (the Fed's balances are easy, not any treasury's); all Defence Departments are greedy. Research is needed, from FoI requests to population surveys on tax. "Umbrellas" are dubious in Australia, say, with US's Pine Gap, an early-warning system.

China's objective interest to see the US consumer machine restored, but China tends to be a US enemy in Congress, like successful Japan was economic enemy, before its now ignored long deflation.[54]

To the left or moderate, it seemed plain the Fed had capitulated to banks. Long before, led by Greenspan's 'cult of personality', the Fed did nothing on bank money inflation in 2005; it approved of bank 'shopping' for the (weakest) regulators up to the eleventh hour; it refused to act on predatory lending. By QE it was too late. Treasury, the SEC et al. were no better on banks illicit foreclosures, as recounted in the Levin Report of 2011. The Fed seldom jawboned banks/Congress to support productive ventures, nor to *keep* bank mortgages, so more people were afloat and active. It watched asset price inflation return as talk of margin loan control withered in 1996. Treasury spent on the Military and, with Greenspan, told Clinton to stop social projects. It makes me feel tired.

HYPOCRITES CHORUS TO SAINTED BANKS

US Treasury gave hardly any stimulus, and trivial help to mortgagees. We saw 'people's fault' moralism from banks and, as Blinder argues, FDR's great scheme to renegotiate mortgages never eventuated. It was 'on the cheap' from Geithner/Summers. Moralism returned in the 1980s but became so deafening after 2008 that Americans were at last cynical: the old term banksters came back. The Mont Pèleron Society founded in 1947, espousing views of Hayek, set up offshoots from Chicago to Melbourne, Tokyo to Mumbai, whose members insult their victims. Like any rigid ideology, neoliberalism (or variants) is not amenable to counter-evidence, particularly the politically cata-strophic outcomes that undercut its *raison d'être*. Its utopian appeal is a degenerated dystopia and opportunity for worse demagogues to shout louder.[55] To Craig Freedman such economic policymakers

---

[54] Blinder is cited in Bibow (2009: 15); and see Blinder (2013).

[55] 'Like 'near money', Banksters' was a take on mafia gangsters, of the 1920s. Recapping Chapter 7 and this chapter; see Levin Report (2011), the Senate's inquiry into the GFC (it never once discussed bank money creation).

double down on their bets. We must try harder, they cry. Into this muddle in Japan's long deflation or Germany's ordo-liberalism, moralism makes things worse with ...

> *morality-like fables allowing decision makers to overlook*
> *the more important and pragmatic role of devising policies*
> *that achieve a degree of* measurable economic improvement.
> *Instead, recession and stagnation are transformed into a justified*
> *retribution for the transgression of bubble induced flightiness*
> *... those who borrowed careless of their ability to repay must*
> *be made to* suffer for their sins. *[Thus]* ... policy makers and
> politicians become obsessed with the idea of fiscal consolidation
> irrevocably drawn by a forced parallel between household
> finances and those of the government ... More dramatically,
> a *personified economy that has gone astray is judged to*
> *deserve a conspicuous retribution for its waywardness. The*
> *appropriateness of economic suffering is seen as apposite, a fit*
> *sentence* parallel to the sense in which a rake should justifiably
> be punished for his destructive behaviour by contracting a
> virulent dose of syphilis.[56]

So, we saw that Léon Walras thought bank-money creation was so 'immoral' he banished it via tunnel vision. David Ricardo saw, but strongly disapproved of, bank money creation and wanted bank power stopped; Ricardo kept on repeating that 'fictitious capital' cannot stimulate industry ('almost unintelligently') as did Marx directly from Ricardo. US Treasurer Mellon in 1929 argued for liquidating everyone (not unlike Stalin). Mervyn King, former Governor of the BoE, has a line uncannily like nineteenth century economists: he calls bank money 'alchemy', an evil that must be stamped out (with a chapter 'Innocence regained', on reaching that nirvana). Hayekian Libertarians say money is far too 'social', a 'disfiguring monstrosity'

---

[56] Freedman (2016) on 'Clueless', my emphases. Fiscal consolidation means austerity. Moralism is hypocritical but the very well-off *prefer* suffering indignities (long airport customs queues), quite apart from blathering Boris Johnson, Trump, Berlusconi (etc.), to maintain wage/job theft and 'the poor' ever poorer.

as Orléan criticises. To excise this social aspect, like fractional reserve banking resting on mutual obligations (*stop right there*), the counterfactual of bank competition was the answer (to disaster), and central banks must be abolished. To harp on immoral 'alchemy' (ordinary money creation) sidetracks pragmatic economic theory. While allegedly charming to all parties, King does not admit his idea for 'pawnbroker banking' undermines the deal of capitalist money. It cannot be improvement, only worse (since the 'value' of pawnbroker 'collateral' is like all value, found in social conflicts of asset bubbles). Does it show incompetence or sad dissonance?[57]

Government and central bank weakness is evident in avoiding how money creation is a hybrid of state and bank debt. It is a pity that treasuries are unable to put this forcefully, but their political masters seem reluctant or, *if they understand*, are fearful that citizens might be horrified. This silence leaves banks alone. When I visited Sicily in 2013, we asked about the Mafia. The answer was 'when the Mafia is quiet they are in control'. *Pianissimo* also marked 2015 appointments to private District Feds of more ex-GS & Co executives. In some countries, *bankers are not permitted near central banks* but, in the US the idea that Wall Street be promoted, and commercial bankers would openly (not secretly) defend banks' interests was assumed in its 1913 founding. That was never a-political. In 1986 Minsky questioned the 12 District Fed's 'reason for being'. Clueless accusations (of Trump), that Obama and Yellen plotted during the 2016 election, apparently urged they promote Depression, yet both needed a positive social settlement.[58]

---

[57] See Blinder (2013: 325) on moralism (etc.); Schumpeter (1954: 723–4) on Ricardo; on 'harsh' Mellon see Bernanke (2013b) and Chapters 2 and 3. Orléan also mentions Jacques Rueff's influence on ECB designers (2014: 159–66); King (2016). Hayek refused to believe that fractional banking was anything than a 'mistake' of individuals 'coalescing'; in Hayek (1945); Heath (1992); Pixley (2014).

[58] The RBA Act forbids bankers/financiers to sit on the Board. Kennedy (2015) on GS&Co on District Feds, also see Minsky (2008 [1986]: 364); Governor Coombs (1971) discussed how people are horrified to know, and gaily told people at after-dinner speeches: perhaps too mellow to worry. Trump was unlike Nixon versus the Fed—Nixon said a Fed-induced downturn wrecked his chances (v. JFK), see Chapter 5.

Perennially, the time is never ripe to tell the public about money (before 'time' goes rotten). With the Bank of Japan story (briefly), it may well be a counter-example central bank that is running a ruling agenda of its own. Freedman says the BoJ shows (like the EMU), 'the continuing confusion between macroeconomic policy and structural reform. Namely that issues affecting an economy's capacity to grow over the long run managed to become somehow identified with those factors impacting an economy's ability to reach something approaching its current productive capacity'. Reflation or deflation was often applied in unsuitable contexts, so the BoJ killed any hints of revival. Others said ZIRP (zero interest rate policy) to negative (NIRP) and QE are 'abject failures' and the BoJ and the Fed are 'woefully disconnected to the economies they have been *entrusted* to manage'.

Also, the BoJ was as uninterested in worrying about asset and property bubbles as the Fed, ECB and BoE. Haldane's 'graveyard' precautionary department at the BoE was matched, with allegedly one lone woman worrying about bubble dynamics who worked on the Fed's research desk between 2006–7. In Europe, no overarching regulator or supervisor of banking existed. Deutsche Bank joined the global credit-creating spree (and Libor and Forex rigging); some Landesbanken and Industriekreditbank were insolvent in 2007 and got bailouts care of German citizens. In my interviews in Germany in 2007–8, some private bank risk officials envisaged a re-assignment to a sub-branch in a 'far away country', *had* they urged their executives to refrain from investing in sub-prime.[59]

The practices of money remains hidden as usual while so-called experts shouted that citizens must be sacrificed, more. CBs were 'entrusted' somehow, contra those who blame Fed activism. However, the problems of war and of letting zombie banks go bankrupt remain. The chances of fair processes are slight with

---

[59] Freedman (2016); on Japan and 'entrusted' my emphasis, in Roach (2016); Admati and Hellwig (2013) on German banks, and quotes on the 'ripe time'. See Tooze (2016). My unpublished interviews in Germany and France had written permission with anonymity; risk managers (said in hindsight).

governments dependent on finance sectors loath to create money directed to citizens' wellbeing, unlike WWII-postwar somewhat. Some zombies are still state-owned *de facto*; nationalising *de jure* is preferable or bank liquidation. Minsky followed Schumpeter's hope for banks' creative destruction role, in that CBs should 'lean against' untoward speculative and Ponzi finance, but too much so might detract from economic expansion and the 'usual ways' of financing that 'spark of creativity' of capitalism. But the productive capitalist corporations are silent about Ponzi finance while FIRE is torching everything. To Volcker, the sole bank innovation of merit was the ATM. Central banks, aiming for credibility to markets, helped spur the GFC, while the monetarist asylum gave justifications via exclusions; silence on how private banks remain in charge of the production of money. Jawboning about dependency on markets argued the crisis needed *consolidation of fiscal-monetary policy* – but it ended favouring banks, not democracy. Disconnected from people's needs for money and, given weak social democracies, banks are liable to breakdown.[60] Of the 'shared' monetary sovereignty, only dangers of rotten bargains appear, to which I turn in concluding these concerns about central banks.

---

[60] On 'creativity' see Minsky (2008 [1986]: 362) that District Feds using a discount window technique (Minsky's preferred, versus Open Market Operations run by the NY Fed) might give them a positive role, since each Fed would act as *lenders* (at a penal rate for Ponzi financing) to the cautious in local district small business. Forget all that; the Fed is inured. RBA Governor Fraser spoke publicly against *dependency on markets*. Today's monetary-fiscal consolidation is obviously against the public under bellicose governments; not only the huge social-fiscal cutbacks.

9 Searching for the Absurd in Central Banking

Money is the predominant contention and social necessity in capitalist life, yet money's promise is mistreated. This book has argued that central banks are compromised in any effort to manage money – they are forced to play an unfair game between two powerful forces, capitalist finance and the warrior state – and when the production of money is under greater control of one or in collusion, central banks must swing to doing the banking for those areas with most control. Does the argument mean we should feel sorry for central banks? Dissonances over central banking's severe powers to curtail economic activity had not existed in pre-democratic days. It was *taken for granted* to impose crushing depressions: states and banks combined to stifle broader political and economic spheres.

The reason this book looks only at the twentieth and the new century is because democratic improvements changed the character of governments. Henceforward, central banks would not favour banks' money creation and/or governments' spending at people's expense alone. Central banks must keep money's value stable while preserving economic stability, so, to price stability was added a second CB mandate of full employment (FE). That was not achieved before terrible suffering, killings, to genocide, and after considerable blame was cast on CBs for *causing* the Great Depression (so, indirectly WWII). This extreme exaggeration only shows it is impossible to treat central banks in glorious isolation. Their role is minor compared to huge global banks that want free reign to direct their money creation to banking's own purposes and likewise to the huge states that aim their spending towards nuclear arsenals and ruthless domestic policing.

So, central bank aims for logical and peaceful outcomes with their twin mandates (FE was often informal) can always be thwarted by anti-social states and banks. Also, peculiarities abound. Governments and private banking are two sides of the same coin of capitalist money. Usually neither is trustworthy, preferring to hoard the promises and obligations of money instead of using them for welcoming projects. The idea that states aim to be socially all-embracing has patchy evidence, this book has tried to show. Central banks are creatures of the state. Only governments can control private banking, which uses *everyone* but with extreme distributional impacts. However, the secretive state usually depends on banks for war finance and provides debtors' prisons. Neither gives the game away that money is an immaterial mutual promise, because these main players either don't know or don't want to know. One exception, when the Allies fought clearly obvious aggressors in WWII, seems to prove the rule.

The full employment era that ensued for thirty to forty years never returned. Central banks are powerless, although far more divided internally since that era when fulfilling their twin mandates was possible. The postwar welfare state and nationalisation 'made the banking system mostly irrelevant', conservatives Calomiris and Haber argue of Britain. But full employment was gone by 1980 and Wall Street never had capital controls under Bretton Woods, so postwar US banks expanded globally away from US Fed controls, while America turned imperial. The denouement is in previous chapters, which I am not repeating here but instead, finishing on what electorates might reasonably expect of central banks. This is where their roles, albeit difficult give slight hope, regardless of things we cannot know of future possible or unimaginable situations.[1]

---

[1] This is not a formal conclusion because I am introducing some new material. See Minsky (2008 [1986]) on the 'unfair game', like Ingham (2004). Ordinary prisons today lock up debtors (etc.), whereas there were debtor jails not so long ago. See Calomiris and Haber (2014: 17; 147–9), where they approve of Thatcher's 'privatizations, labor reforms, and changes in monetary and financial policy'. Ignoring the 1950s City's Eurodollars too, that leaves them unable to explain the GFC, as Ahamed (2014) also argues. They turn a blind eye on wars, and Wall Street pre- and post-1971.

I looked at CB potentials in the first chapter. Modern money is credit that must be exchangeable – depersonalised promises – not a person-to-person IOU for paying obligations later. Nor is money like barter exchange where we swap stuff. Money does not arise between two people – not all credit is the money that is created between three parties. No one accepts transferred IOUs, without a specific 'economic community that guarantees the money'. Money is a three-way relation between the credit and debt obligations of the economically active groups, and (usually) a central power that enforces these promises, unifies and issues a currency and outlaws counterfeiting. Georg Simmel marvelled at money's productive power and felt these credit practices were the source of capitalist dynamism and fantastic new wealth.[2] He said little about the 'economic community' which, over the past 400 years is the modern state that guarantees and bails out these (precarious) promises. Ingham explains that mutual needs became state-capitalist money as a fusion of the two moneys, with the state's monopoly of violence and tax coercion to secure state money (HPM) at the top of money's hierarchy. The two sources of money fused, in a way, into one 'sovereign monetary space', the public debt of state bonds, and the private debt of bills of exchange. Since the fourteenth century, fractional reserve banking has been prone to crises due to its expansion of obligations – liabilities. Central banks give routine guarantees to banks via the state debt that often pays for wars. This is largely unknown.[3]

To emphasise, then, central banks cannot temper the money created in the banking sector or the state, nor its direction: that is, whether bank money is for job-creating ventures or for asset bubbles,

[2] No one can use my scribbled IOU note as *money* at a supermarket. Simmel's sprawling *Philosophy of Money* is a classic, but as Ingham said (at a conference, 2015), Simmel did not specify 'community' (1907 [1990]: 177; 182). Schumpeter (1934 [1911], 1954) is the main defender of banks' magisterial role in capitalist dynamism via depositing loans for development; he soured later, seeing capitalism's dwindling dynamism. Money laundering (of banks now) is a bit like counterfeiting, with notably US$ holdings: rarely considered.
[3] Ingham (2004: 128–9); see herein also Chapters 4–7; and on fractional banking's crises, see Ugolini (2011: 9) and Table 1.1.

or state money is for wars, pork barrelling *or* constructive activity. And the state that imposed dual remits on central banks and looked to the productive economic sectors for allies from labour and capital was a social democratic one (more or less). Full employment was a direction to prevent central banks from *stopping* economic activity and its jobs (down to deflation), and to include bank money inflation in their remit for price stability. Yet in hindsight, the story is shaky. Eisenhower gave the US Fed a sainted role against wages just as it started losing to Wall Street. Social-political forces much larger, more global than the 1930s Bankers' Ramps, rose in the 1970s against social democracy and inserted demands for monetary policies *against* populations and productive ventures. Giannini called this a 'permanent plebiscite' on states. Gradually governments loaded the dice against central banks with (wage) inflation targets and such like.[4]

CENTRAL BANKS AS CHAMELEONS

Moving then, beyond the book's account of CBs' many roles from WWI right through to the GFC, I now consider central bank potentials. It is easy to demonstrate a chameleon switch inside central banks from harsh anti-wage inflation policies since 1980, to their pro-inflation pleas after the GFC. Governments and financial sectors, so far, refuse to accept anything like long-term multiplier effects. My first evidence is the late 1990s, when a group of prominent central bankers tried to formulate what they say in public, during that central banking era of independence from treasuries yet with state-imposed inflation targets. 'Transparency' was their key term and they produced a booklet entitled *How do central bankers talk?* It was a new Style Guide, but its inadvertent agenda was the 'credibility' problems of central banks. There are self-congratulations about central banks no longer

---

[4] Full employment (FE) often de facto, directs treasuries to job creation, stimulus (etc.) that CBs cannot do, and directs CBs away from crushing depressions, by requiring actions to be sparing and brief, if they must raise interest rates against purchasing power. FE counteracts bond-holder interests in dear money that increases debt values for labour-capital producers, and states. See Giannini (2011: 156–7) and Chapter 5 on Eisenhower.

needing to be 'opaque' – instead, under this independence they must now be 'accountable' and 'democratic'. Their idea of *undemocratic* starts from a low base in the absurd 'opacity' and cloak and dagger style guide of a Montagu Norman, the 1920s-30s Governor of the BoE. They instead obsessed about communicating to 'the financial markets'; the booklet worried (rightly) that CBs might seem to be 'too close' to 'markets'. 'Transparency' – this Style Guide hoped – will scotch practices of expert investors (large banks) gaining profitable information just from watching central bank policy changes. A trivial gain – modest 'investors' could play a fairer race armed with carefully crafted policy announcements in Fedspeak, less postwar days jawboning or frank concern for, say, ballooning household debt.[5]

At heart, whatever central bankers mostly do is not something for public debate, said the booklet, or *any democratic scrutiny*. In explaining how they cannot provide transparency to 'the public' they argue that 'greater candour' does not require a central bank to use 'blunt language like, "The Bank of X wants the unemployment rate to go higher". More polite euphemisms have always sufficed in the past and they will continue to do so in the future'. They agree, in subtle jest, that this strategy is not always effective, but hoped for 'quiet acquiescence'.[6]

Euphemisms like that vanished after 2007. *Suddenly*, my contrasting evidence, CBs jawboned in favour of jobs. What? How dare central bankers upset money's neutral role that jaded economics preached? Central banks argued for the wage inflation that, barely months before the near collapse of the payment system in 2008, had been their sole enemy. Right-wing governments are tight-lipped (or loose to incoherent), and orthodoxy revolted publicly against CB's efforts to retrieve the crash. They made any contortion: to save banks; their defunct theories; the *status quo* with

[5] Summarising Blinder et al. (2001). The group comprised mostly well-meaning ECB, BoE, Fed and RBA central bankers, some modest in approach, and a few uncivil monetarists.
[6] Blinder et al. (2001: 31) on 'euphemisms' and acquiescence: to me, this is not singing in uniform - it's discordant or funereal. Thanks to Charles Goodhart for this reference.

austerity. One, J. B. Taylor, argued Bernanke's actions worsened the crisis; all cried out: 'loose money men ... sure to cause inflation'; Taylor, that President Obama's stimulus had no impact. Ignoring its job rise, he perverted his own 'Taylor rule' in calling for tighter money *against* 'output' (which had collapsed). Greenspan 'apparently unrepentant' Alan Blinder says, argued (Obama's) intervention 'hobbled markets ... and hampered recovery', much as Mellon said to President Hoover in the Great Depression, liquidate everything.[7]

Dismissing his own monetarist counterfactuals (even), Allan Meltzer's post-GFC outbursts against those in distress exhibit no qualms about a Recession as bad as the 1930 Depression. In 2014, he said

> The current weak recovery is mainly a real problem that cannot be solved by *printing reserves* or making real interest rates more negative. The main real drag on growth is the uncertainty created by the Obama administration's fiscal and regulatory policies, including his insistence on increasing tax rates, costly regulations, and promoting labor unions ... They avoided permanent tax cuts and favored welfare spending that had small multiplier effects. [Citing J. B. Taylor] the Obama stimulus 'was a triumph of Keynesian wishful-thinking over practical experiences ... [Its impact was] Zero' ... One of the most foolish decisions in the Fed's 100-year history is its current decision to make *the reduction in reserve growth* depend on current labor market data ... [But] the data is noisy and often subject to large revisions ... Volcker added that *the way to reduce unemployment is to lower expected inflation*.[8]

---

[7] Recall Chapters 7 and 8, on Taylor's 'rule' i.e., a copy of Inflation Targets, in which 'output' would be a concern if inflation dropped to 1 per cent. CBs cannot raise output if inflation is in fact deflation at 1 per cent. The 'unrepentant' are cited in Blinder (2013: 353).

[8] Meltzer's ramble is implied in social constructivists, mentioned in Ingham (2004: 84; 145) on performativity as orthodox influence see below; Haldane (2011) cites them admiringly on HFT, although the 'black box' of EMH was empty, its 'construction' was not OK, see Winner (1993). See Haldane (2010) on the 2009 recession, the same 'size' as the 1930's; Meltzer cites himself; all quotes are in Meltzer (2014: 530; 532–4 my emphases).

His evidence? Zero. The 2007–8 property crash and bank collapses brought low output and low inflation simultaneously: deflation. The regressive tax cut movement rages. I think Meltzer knows he is conducting class warfare for this Bankers' Ramp, *giving the neutrality game away*. Note the bogus assertion jobs will rise if *expected* inflation (nowhere in sight, unlike Volcker's watch) is crushed, meaning jobs as Volcker knew. Social spending (indirect boosts to wages and transfers), progressive tax *rises* and unions are abominations. Abandoning his counterfactual tenets, Meltzer forgot markets basked in QE's *certainty* and (profitable) state intervention. Incoherence not 'performativity', was evident too in the 2016 UK anti-Brexit 'Fear Campaign', of bank/BoE 'experts' and 'forecasters' who blandly ignored forty years of stagnation. Wolfgang Munchau grumbled in the *FT*, after Brexit and Trump won:

> The correct course of action would be to stop insulting voters and, more importantly, to solve the problems of an out-of-control financial sector, uncontrolled flows of people and capital, and unequal income distribution.[9]

This implied a plea for social democracy (not what came). Central banks are publicly nervous, wanting some variant to monetarist influences on policies. In October 2016, Fed Chair Yellen tried to supply 'new thinking' to the Fed. She asked, 'how does "heterogeneity" (the fact that people are not all identical, in particular in their access to credit) affect demand and its response to monetary policy;

Craig Freedman denies Volcker would ever say that (personal discussion). The tax-cut/anti-health austerity is not just a US matter.

[9] Münchau (2016), who discusses Brexit, Trump, le Pen, Orbán and other far right European parties. It is unclear if Munchau is anti-migrants and against asylum seekers. To my mind, the 'uncontrolled flows' of migrants refers to the neo-liberal/Friedman project of high entry of peoples forced to take any wage price (or even wage theft). The way to control that is not with harsh borders/detention (Trump and Turnbull), but properly enforced minimum wage rules for all (see Chapter 7) and peace.

how does the financial sector interact with the broader economy; and what really determines inflation?'[10]

Is this a brave question – in exposing the hollowness of CB money *theorems*, targets and so on? The Fed (formally) deploys no theory of the state, class, inequality, gender or race divisions. Yellen challenged neoclassical deduction, from which its sole principle is individual self-interest. Much has been written against this; its *prescriptive intent* never appealed to electorates, but its hectoring has sewn confusion for forty years. Yellen's point is the incentive of self-interest is socially divided. Those who aim for simple survival are unlikely to worry of 'expected inflation' a la Meltzer, or believe joblessness is 'voluntary', far less his advocacy of unemployment that crushes collective desires: dire needs for money and social participation. These views had a few central bankers telling me in 1998 they were proud to be unpopular; coincidentally pop music to banking practices, or the Pentagon, if either thought of the rotten bargain.

Commodification of much of social life proceeds, especially over 'land, labour and money' that Karl Polanyi castigated. In 1944, he hoped those nostrums were gone, but the fictions returned in the 1970s. Few deny that land – the environment – needs care. Who knows how far money is instrumentally abused like labour? Polanyi argued that modern stratification and capitalist class relations had embedded down into social life formerly arranged via hierarchy or reciprocity. Debtor classes lost by 2009, but now what?

This book has looked at central banks' part in decivilising processes that are logically unsustainable, proven so on countless grim occasions. Exceptions are rare. Plain logic and the decency that everyone live dignified, meaningful lives, the civility of refusing to humiliate in destroying these hopes, the logic of treating money's promises

---

[10] Military buildup and corporate tax cuts (Meltzer above wants cuts 'permanent'), imply the US Administration becomes 'more' dependent on banks (for all those failed, patriotic wars for re-election). Yellen is cited in Sandbu (2016) who said of the Fed's global influence: 'The half question, which Yellen only mentions, is how monetary policy spills across borders.' In Chapter 6, Kaldor (1970) made Yellen's points forcibly, with his happy holiday spending example.

with caution are evident in rising dissonances of central bankers aware of these factors. But *they cannot change their roles as bankers* to the indecent social and political forces. Finance centres and erratic governments bleat 'jobs' but refuse the sustainability, logic, peace and democratic values that might hold them to account. CBs must assiduously change tack for state needs to finance their wars and arsenals, too. There will be no moralism against the state with a patriotic war. In tension with that in the 1980s, depoliticisation was fantastically popular to politicians of *democratic* governments, away from trying to manage money, land and labour. Markets 'knew best' (nothing). Governments went international, politicians damned the political classes they interminably *joined*, to wreak havoc and avoid blame – efforts that increased electorates' distrust. As for bank demands for routine 'accommodation' regardless the GFC, central banks rarely jawboned about the possibility that *household debt could never be serviced or paid* once asset prices (like property) collapsed. Those who did were shouted down. Corporate debtors turned to financial tricks. Central banks gave banks *certainty* of low economic activity, predictably to stop wage demands. The US Fed Chair (1979–87) Volcker called it 'wage deceleration': extensively decivilising and logically absurd: he nearly stopped the US economy.[11] Bank traders later gained lucrative step by step clues to how a central bank *will act* beforehand. That was trivial compared to profits from unhindered global roaming, brought care of governments that foolishly pressed competition on the bank money producers. To repeat myself, neither governments nor banks want to understand money.

With regards to CB cognitive and emotional dissonances, FE was abolished not because it lacked logic or normative support. Rather the political collapse of compromises between capital and labour was decisive in coinciding with democracies no longer able to enjoy *respite from money class disputes* and that were, *in lieu*, ramping

---

[11] It even horrified banks, but global crises grew. Volcker's was wage suppression, as corrected by Greider (2014:11); cf. Meltzer (2014) is a scandalous imputation on Volcker, although his 'deceleration' was dissimulating.

up small wars and continual nuclear alert. Without changed social alignments, central bank policy does not change; it mirrors the *status quo* of whatever emerges out of disputations. Money was not democratically controlled, even in that postwar settlement of fair circumstances; only a global totalising empire might control mobile capital, but war complicates that. One problem Giannini saw, slightly like Minsky, was how to 'exploit the magic of credit' for socially beneficial activity without 'inciting banks to imprudent lending practices'. This is insoluble because over the past 400 years, relative bargaining power has shifted and desires for 'liquidity' reasserts a relative dominance over fixed investment in socially useful activities. Thereupon bank money switches to economically useless arbitrage. Workers need opportunities to make liquid their capacity to labour; that 'property' though, is 'attached' to their humanness. Treating labour as a *thing* fosters dissonances from logic and principles, although *money* mistreated wreaks the serious havoc onto workers and those unable to work. It is either endured or welcomed in central banks ever since states were democratic or somewhat so.[12]

Between (war) states and *totalising* financial power, central banks must change from leafy green to hellfire red. Their remits for price stability are political, and the idea inflation can be reduced to wage inflation, when demand for money varies from *many* sources, became the illogicality and scandal of the evidence, primarily of financial power's fights to retain or renew control. Reform of central banks does not occur even if unionists or feminists were on a Board. Yet CB Boards are again crammed with financiers today, and rarely forbidden.[13]

---

[12] Max Weber's remarks on 'mobile capital' see (1978) – and Chapter 1; in a muted Giannini (2011: 255), on 'magic of credit', cf. Ingham (2008: 174); Orléan (2014: 112). Hayek (1945) thought arbitrage was eminently useful.

[13] My argument about totalising is in Pixley (2012). Totalitarianism is over-used; Arendt (1967 [1951]) equated the Soviet system with Fascism, but this was a category error. Both were cruel. Nazi power *never* aimed for any improvement but constant war, plunder and annihilation; if the Soviet autocracies never achieved their desired gains, war/plunder was not required in logic. *Totalising* 'free market' aims are not a huge contrast: a creeping aim for liquidation (in Chapter 6), a war-dystopia just as counterproductive, undemocratic,

Reducing Central Bank Dissonances?

Mandates cannot be improved without serious political-social changes but, since the US Fed has twin remits and yet is so 'flexible', there is no reason why the ECB, BoE and the others should not have FE legislation emulating the Fed and RBA. An extra clause on CBs serving *the public's wellbeing* to avoid savage deflation and asset inflations in plural clarifies that. That would remove deflationary Targets. The main taboo is *actual* (not the pseudo-operational) independence that reinstates CB deficit finance for treasuries spending on publicly declared, socially useful and peaceful purposes. Can it be imagined? In another dark jest, here is my list of *essential and desirable* characteristics for the composition of central bank boards, away from vested interests, so that monetary decisions are not dominated by capitalist bankers with know-nothing (captured) politicians, but by wide sources in the public and global interests. My job criteria preserve central banks from conspiracy lovers who adore blaming them – although from nothing else. It can do little about the whole show of soothing markets and warrior states.

The expertise of the permanent CB officials is enhanced with Board members experienced in recent consumer, service sector and labour market trends, or who scrutinise bank treatment of clients (small businesses; households): with immediate, not time-lagged statistical evidence.[14] Diversity, not the *certainty* of Board Members so wealthy they can evade taxes, ignore (or oppose) public health and childcare systems, *might* look above financiers to the outside edges where fears and anxieties are found. Tax records need scrutiny due to CBs' role in defending HPM. However, imagination and decency cannot democratise state-capitalist money (anymore than legislation can

---

non-dynamic, with non-unionised workers like the Soviet's, *differently* (US guns). Austerity is slow starvation, suicide and divisiveness (prisons; statelessness for many).

[14] Admitting non-US citizens onto the US Fed Board would accept its global impacts. Funnily, it was suggested in the 1977 McCracken Report, in Keohane (1978), but I cannot imagine a Chinese appointment to the Fed Board. Natural science expertise is also desirable.

stop discriminations forever). CB Board members rarely care about crippling work-hours, conditions and pay; just like racial bigots and male supremacists. Class bigots include economic fanatics, ably represented in politics and banking, opposed among those *central bankers trying to save banks or states from themselves.* The manufacturers of bank money own the US District Feds, make decisions; gain insider knowledge and financiers are on CB Boards elsewhere. Treasurers also were/are members, and for that, CBs need *some* independence from states *and* banks.

Counter examples exist: Governor Rajan of the Reserve Bank of India warned of asset bubbles in 2014 and noted how traders were prone to the gamblers' curse. Private banks in Canada must apply to Parliament for license renewals to create money: public scrutiny expands civil society. Bankers are excluded from the RBA Board (*de jure*) whereas producers of goods and services are welcome. Such desiderata, if improbable in the Fed (or other CBs) cannot change money as a 'space of exception', that is not my claim. Of the Fed-induced 1980 depression, Volcker's FOMC Board comprised low to middle income earners; white.[15] Member Lyle Gramley seemed ambivalent about the US suicide rate in a jokey, I hope a dissonant, manner. Women or minorities who reach the top can pull up the ladder of economic opportunity. Technical expertise posing as politically neutral is uncivil and illogically *certain.* 'Wall Street' is indifferent to, and worsens people's life chances. Finance sectors bray for uniformity and predictability of central banks: polite resistance is in order.[16]

---

[15] Desiderata, e.g. Bernie Fraser (cited Pixley 2004) supported an ACTU unionist head, for his help on the RBA Board, which *forbids financiers* in its Act; later a RBA business board member resigned on suspicions of tax evasion; Fraser says it's always hard to find diversity and enthusiasm. The Reserve Bank of India's cautions on bubbles are in Mallet (2014). Greider (1987: 70–2) on FOMC members from mid-west USA; plus, Simon Johnson's (failed) campaign to remove Jamie Dimon (CEO JP Morgan) from the NY Fed Board is in Mirowski (2013: 330–1).

[16] Gramley cited in Pixley (2004): see Rich (2016: 42) on race discrimination; Mann (2013) on 'monetary space' and union CB members not changing that. Banks are shareholders of District Feds. A hundred Congress members and Hillary Clinton, see Fleming (2016), argued the 'Federal Reserve is too "white and male"': yes, but financiers?

The evident dissonance inside CBs today calls in question the postmodern idea of 'performativity' – admired by social studies of finance, amazed at their finding that money is socially constructed (only via monetarists 'framing'). Under orders, CBs 'performed' to a monetarist tune of money's neutrality: Money's value is found in objects (not social conflicts). *Then it wasn't.* Disagreements behind closed doors are veiled from markets (perhaps desirable and it fooled postmodernists, who see money as calculable 'object'). The Fed has margin loan requirements. Greenspan refused to apply them when Board members and Congress *urged*. CBs can question 'light touch'; most didn't. They can ring alarm bells about dangers in the global payment system: some did. They can use their 'bully-pulpit' to inform the public, which is nearly all central banks can do *or* obfuscate on the underlying social divisions; grovel to in-fighting politicians and foul-mouthed bank executives. Many swallowed 'theories' grossly inadequate to understanding money at capitalism's birth, although convenient to the usual suspects. As well, any 'performance' ceased when CBs turned to previous policies post-GFC. Given their revolving doors to status and pomposity, some of the honourable and decent took resignation or retirement 'obliged to be difficult'. I found many like that.

WARRING CLASSES AND WARRING STATES

Against Phillips Curve myths that destroyed most of the Social Class Settlement, CBs could deploy inequality data, even high-quality attitude surveys, since countervailing central bankers know the divisiveness of monetary decisions and need *formal preaching spaces* to alert legislators and the public about trends. For example, the Fed's *rentier*-hawk members were hobbled when for forty years Americans looked on Wall Street as a casino. Australians loathe banks more than the press or unions: the RBA nags against low wages, dubious banks and tax fiddles. The Fed and US Administration faced taxpayer fury at bailing out banks in 2009: but few know why pro-tax arguments are no charity. Retired Alan Budd (BoE) spoke publicly against Thatcher's betrayal of FE; US Congress's last call on the Fed to preserve FE was the Humphrey-Hawkins Act (1978) just as FE lost and bosses won, yet

Bernanke and Yellen *used the FE remit* at last against economic 'framing'. This double mandate is as desirable for a 'decent institution' as is diversity of decent (board member) individuals.[17]

Deference to finance, large employers and state war finance is structural and not a 'Fed power'. Money classes and anti-union politicians outsourced double standards onto central banks. CBs were sainted when modesty should rule. Recent radical-left reformers (even), swallowed monetarists to *separate* Fed roles of 'adjusting the supply of money to stabilise prices and employment' *from* 'stepping in when the financial system is threatened by runs on credit and collapse'. But *banks* 'supply' most money at whim. Congress and White House combined can redirect the US Fed to different ends. Whether they can or will do so, or to what ends is moot.

My anti-hero Joseph Schumpeter explained many apposite points far better than most. One of his social sentiments amply illustrates the thesis of this book. In 1936, of significance since Schumpeter loathed F.D. Roosevelt's reforms, he said:

> The knights of the feudal times were trained to fight and in battle they were superior to everyone else. The only way of defending itself that the bourgeoisie, however, has, 'is to take up the telephone and telephone Senator X and say, "Good God! Good God! Can't you help us"'.[18]

Roosevelt had (briefly) tamed menacing capital strikes and Depression conditions. Influences of decent industrialists (like Eccles' Association) on FDR are underestimated: they might be Schumpeter's target. Similarly postwar Europe, the Dominions, never Britain, thus, (*in lieu* of predatory warrior knights), treasuries and central banks must help.

---

[17] RBA Governors – Coombs was 'difficult' (to Indigenous Rights later) and Fraser (who later resigned from what proved a right-wing non-independent 'Environment' entity), also told me some Board members reliably served public interests, in Chapter 4.

[18] Jacobs and King (2016: 161) on 'reforms'. See Schumpeter (1991 [1936]: 315) on feudal knights. Swedberg, the editor, says this lecture was transcribed with difficulty and remarks JAS was 'more colorful' than most.

Modern war finance is ill discussed if mentioned. Giannini's less parochial central bank text than many (which are nationalistic, and extremist versions recur), suggests central banks cannot last without the 'liberal state', an elitist state that must endure 'the masses'. He loathes Hayek's views. The 'Prince' must logically be Hayek's enemy, however, recent robber baron personas fit Hayek's self-interest universalism perfectly: not Schumpeter's contempt for this class fragment. Giannini granted the neoclassical model a 'great heuristic potential' and 'rigour' (really: minus money!) yet agreed it does not reach toward 'any institution, not just the central bank' beyond being 'almost oxymoronic'. Hayek devotees attribute central banking's 'existence to the prince's greed', to Giannini, 'anachronistic and often blatantly incorrect'. He had little time for monetarism or so-called velocity of 'credit'.[19] Calomiris and Haber cannot stand 'populism' (never Republicans': poor US farmers), ill-defined compared to Giannini's despised 'masses'. Civil society is absent in such tracts, as are industrial giants, service sectors (public and private), entire labour movements' parties, the non-utopian, compromising, non-*populist* constitutionalism of social democratic governments. Evident today too, declining quality – of bureaucracies 'without fear or favour', the press ideally as the Fourth Estate – give less countervailing criticisms of *liberal states*. Calomiris assumes a consensual social settlement would *not* bring stable banking (Roosevelt is a 'populist') and a financial transaction tax (say) is 'autocratic'.[20]

One reaps what is sown. These abusive strategies – indifferent to seriously corrupt, cynical banks, to *established* political parties gaining government by foul means – have results. It is far too

---

[19] Amato and Fantacci (2012) and other honourable exceptions on war finance, see in Chapters, 2, 4 and 5. Giannini (2011: xxi), worryingly described money as a 'payment technology', but lists devotees of Hayek, James Buchanan, Kevin Dowd, etc. He noted that the main European central banks were for 'princes' but the Banca d'Italia, Reichsbank and smaller ones were created for the 'advantages to the community of rationalizing the payments system', not for financing public expenditure (e.g. war); or industry; or social democracy (see Chapters 1 and 2). But, financier Bleichröder gave war finance to Bismarck; see Stern (1977); the Reichsbank was anti-Semitic like others.

[20] I have repeatedly criticised Calomiris and Haber (2014) and Calomiris (2013).

early to tell, but oxymoronic concepts describe the situation (perhaps only temporary) of populist, anti-tax autocrats, the cunning-ignorant who 'treat the state as one's possession'. This feudal Chinese phrase matches Weber's on European feudal patrimonialism. It has a modern catch: A global finance sector to appease for war finance and personal gain: zero for (white) workers sainted only as Englander, Australian or American nationalists.[21]

The Absurd as an Aim

Not only lack of public evidence, but also the *counterfactuals used as illicit evidence* about monetary history have influenced today's central banks. The inconsistency in monetarist recipes (a bizarre U-turn in Meltzer against CBs increasing bank reserves) is unsurprising given their powerful sponsors. Central banks cannot have a prescribed heroic task; they can aim to do their best in whatever ghastly situation is thrown at them. One must ask if any legal, ethical or normative constraints on the creation, use and deployment of money are possible. Reforming central banks is desirable, but it is fanciful to imagine they could ever restrain the powerful forces of states, employers and banks. CBs are rarely allowed to serve the public interest however one might define that awkward phrase. All other CBs are spared the world forces bearing down on the mighty Fed, although are gravely affected by Fed actions.

Only one recent occasion to my knowledge saw seven central banks combine to demolish currency traders' vicious arbitrage against the Yen, when the 2011 tsunami caused a Japanese nuclear power station fallout to spread catastrophically, as far as greater Tokyo (33 million people). The *FT* reported these G7 central banks front page,

---

[21] The Chinese phrase is cited in Osnos (2018); and see Weber's term (1978). The social forces throwing up a Farage, Berlusconi or Trump (or Bush Jnr's team) need thought, so too hard-right governments of Europe to Australia (the latter since 1996; but not in Germany to NZ); the mess in Britain is unclear: the UK High Court pulled up PM May; she could not use 'Royal Prerogative' but needed Parliament which is sovereign, not the people. The lies told in favour of Brexit were abnormal in being driven by the idea that England, whatever that meant, could be an empire again.

only for one day. Was saving Japan due to CBs' deep dissonances, or in support of the Bank of Japan's neo-liberal agenda, or *schadenfreude* gone too far against Japan's decades of debt deflation? Not one CB helped Greece (UK's regions are poorer): the kindly 'straighteners', as Samuel Butler's *Erewhon* put it, did not apply, just Bankers' Ramps; an item for further research.[22]

Geoff Mann is probably correct that money is a space of exception for any social justice, likely to remain so. At my most gloomy, I saw no surprises in the 2016–17 elections, since – after so many normal functioning events of money's inflationary and deflationary tendencies, the high-handed austerity of governments, banking indifference, and this decade's understandable rise of disaffection, but to hostile populist nationalism – one has to ask, what did employers, banks and states expect? Business as usual – shabby braying against pleas and protests for purchasing power, jobs, a modicum of dignity – may continue. Cognitive dissonances inside central banks are part of how the dice is loaded, how absurd is their part. If satire aims for improvement, the absurd has no hope.

I have attempted to take a middle course, firm and not fence-sitting. Central bankers, after so much has gone awry, could beg leave from undue grandeur. They do not labour under irrelevance, because the US Fed is damaging to the world (unintended sometimes). CBs give their democratic state *public advice* about the limits of their positive strengths, when or if they can embrace such logic and decency. Not only treasury policy, but also capital-labour markets with effective wage-work regulators need prominence as decent monetary policy. No government *should* ignore contexts and set a rigid CB path cumquat may; also, any numerate government would return all financial supervisory functions to their *self-financing central banks*. Principles matter: the tragedy of Arthur Burns's US Fed resulted in central banks being

---

[22] References to Japan and G7 CBs solidarity is in Pixley (2012); Garnham et al. (2011). *Erewhon* does a simple reversal, it has banks as churches: the sick go to prison, the embezzlers get the doctors i.e., kindly 'straighteners': could these be CBs?

conductors of a bankers' orchestra that produces discordant, reactive and damaging noises. At any point in time, presidents, industrialists, bankers, US congress have specific strengths. The US unions hardly at all. In the 1970s, the Fed grovelled to bankers one day, Presidents the next: central banker dissonance set in. The dollar floated, Wall Street won. For Volcker's Fed, one option glared: shut down the entire economy. The story descended down to the Feds of Bernanke and Yellen to try their best, foreign to Monatgu Norman's/Strong's grim era.

I mentioned the judiciary has a constitutional place in the separation of powers and faces legislative reviews. Supreme or High Courts always make *political* decisions and appointments matter. In the Fed, take Reagan's preference for Greenspan over reappointing Volcker who is outspoken against 'light touch'. Often judges prove less predictable than, say, the *political* free marketeer Greenspan (under orders, note). Judicial 'black letter' appointments can surprise everyone and, whereas central banks are self-financing, monetary decisions are not 'choices' (about a formal constitution's meaning). Too many private money creators exist, too many authorities support or let CBs down. Treasuries try to keep money believable or, today, do not bother. I cannot see social democracy likely to resurrect but social miracles happen. War finance is the problem since nuclear warfare ends everything. Nuclear capitalist states secretly depend on bank financing and weakened democracy; more became nuclear states. In a cacophony of being pulled and pushed by diverse powerful forces, a modicum of central bank independence from *all sides*, and not uniquely from social democracy (unfairly maligned), could give hope.

Some central banks are open to discussion for various social-political reasons and seem to take their tasks with a healthy dose of black humour, which is sensible given the historical record. The Deputy Governor of the Reserve Bank of Australia plays in *The GFCs*, a Rock Band that performs in the RBA headquarters in Sydney. That may be too macabre for pretentious central bankers. A conference in Boston entitled 'What if the Leader of the Central Bank Told Hilarious

Jokes and Did Card Tricks?' mocked the then adulation, except for a dour monetarist.[23] Central banks like the Bank of Canada or the Reserve Bank of India also see their roles as modest or bleak (absurd), given their democratically auspicious designs and cautious legacies. This lends a dry humour to their operating conditions at any one time to the money-creating masters they are required to help.

[23] My reference is to constitutional courts; states can cut general funding of the court system to hobble separation of powers. Given the absence of any open public airing, it is unlikely people know that banks fund nuclear finance, since most assume wrongly that taxes 'pay for' all state spending. I think Guy Debelle (RBA) plays the sax. The card tricks debate is in Pixley (2007b).

References

Acemoglu, D., Johnson, S., Kermani, A., Kwak, J. & Mitton, T. 2016. 'The value of connections in turbulent times', *Journal of Financial Economics* 121(2): 368–91.

Admati, A. & Hellwig, M. 2013. *The Bankers' New Clothes: What's Wrong with Banking and What to Do about It*. Princeton University Press.

Ahamed, L. 2009. *Lords of Finance: 1929, The Great Depression and the Bankers who Broke the World*. London: Heinemann.

2014. 'How Banks Fail' *New York Times*. 11 April. www.nytimes .com/2014/04/13/books/review/fragile-by-design-by-charles-w-calomiris-and-stephen-h-haber.html?_r=0.

Alessandri, P. & Haldane, A. S. 2009. 'Banking on the State. Bank of England', *Paper to Federal Reserve Bank of Chicago* Conference. November. Available at www.bankofengland.co.uk/publications/speeches

Amato, M. & Fantacci, L. 2012. *The End of Finance*. Cambridge: Polity.

2014. 'Back to which Bretton Woods? Liquidity and clearing as alternative principles for reforming international money', *Cambridge Journal of Economics* 38: 1431–52.

Arendt, H. 1967 [1951]. *The Origins of Totalitarianism*, 3rd edn. London: G. Allen & Unwin.

2006. *Eichmann in Jerusalem: A Report on the Banality of Evil*. New York, NY: Penguin Books.

Arestis, P. & Sawyer, M. (eds.) 2006. *A Handbook of Alternative Monetary Economics*. Cheltenham: Edward Elgar.

Arrighi, G. 1994. *The Long Twentieth Century*. London: Verso.

Bair, S. 2012. *Bull by the Horns*. New York, NY: Free Press.

Barofsky, N. 2013. *Bailout – How Washington Abandoned Main Street While Rescuing Wall Street*. New York, NY: Free Press.

Beggs, M. 2010. 'From the "battle of the banks" to the "credit squeeze": Australian monetary policy in the long 1950s', in L. Chester et al. (ed.), *Proceedings of the Ninth Australian Society of Heterodox Economists Conference: Refereed Papers* Sydney: University of New South Wales, December 2010: 16–45.

Bell, D. 1976. *The Coming of Post Industrial Society*. New York, NY: Basic Books.

Berle, A., & G. Means. 1932. *The Modern Corporation and Private Property*, New York, NY: Macmillan.

Bernanke, B. S. 2000. *Essays on the Great Depression*. Princeton University Press. 2003. 'Why the world's central banks must become more vigilant about falling prices', *Foreign Policy*, November–December: 74–5.

Bernanke, B. S. 2013a. 'Panel discussion' with G.S. Corrigan and Alan Greenspan, in M. D. Bordo, & W. Roberds (eds.), *The Origins, History, and Future of the Federal Reserve: A Return to Jekyll Island*. Cambridge University Press: 405–21.

2013b. *The Federal Reserve and the Financial Crisis*. Princeton University Press.

Bernanke, B. S. (with) Parkinson, M. 2000. 'Unemployment, inflation and wages in the American Depression', in B. S. Bernanke (ed.), *Essays on the Great Depression*. Princeton University Press: 247–54.

Bhaduri, A. 2014. 'What remains of the theory of demand management?', *Economic and Labour Relations Review* 25(3): 389–96.

Bibow, J. 2009. *Keynes on Monetary Policy, Finance and Uncertainty*. London: Routledge.

2015. 'The Euro's Savior? Assessing the ECB's Crisis Management Performance'. Düsseldorf: *Macroeconomic Policy Institute (IMK), Study 42*, June.

Bittman, M. & Pixley, J. F. 1997. *The Double Life of the Family: Myth, Hope & Experience*. Sydney: Allen & Unwin.

Blinder, A. 2013. *After the Music Stopped*. New York, NY: Penguin.

Blinder, A., Goodhart, C., Hildebrand, P., Lipton, D. & Wyplosz, C. 2001. *How Do Central Banks Talk? Geneva Reports on the World Economy 3*. Geneva: International Center for Monetary and Banking Studies.

Blyth, M. 2013. 'Austerity as ideology', *Comparative European Politics* 11: 737–51.

Bok, S. 1978. *Lying: Moral Choice in Public Life*. London: Quartet Books.

Bordo, M. D. & Roberds, W. (eds.) 2013. *The Origins, History, and Future of the Federal Reserve: A Return to Jekyll Island*. Cambridge University Press.

Bordo, M. & Wheelock, D. 2013. 'The promise and performance of the Federal Reserve as lender of last resort', in M. D. Bordo & W. Roberds (eds.), *The Origins, History, and Future of the Federal Reserve: A Return to Jekyll Island*. Cambridge University Press: 59–98.

Boyce, R. 2012. *The Great Interwar Crisis and the Collapse of Globalization*. Houndmills: Palgrave Macmillan.

Burnham, P. 1999. 'The politics of economic management in the 1990s', *New Political Economy* 4(1): 37–54.

Burns, A. F., Milutin, Ć. & Polak, J. J. 1979. 'The Anguish of Central Banking', *The 1979 Per Jacobsson Foundation*. Lecture, Belgrade, Yugoslavia, 30 September: 1–49.

Butlin, S. J. (ed.) 1986. *The Australian Monetary System 1851–1914*. Sydney: The Reserve Bank of Australia.

Butlin, S. J. 1955. *Australia in the War of 1939–1945*, Series 4, Civil, Vol. 3, Part III. Canberra: Australian War Memorial.

   1961. *Australia and New Zealand Bank: The Bank of Australasia and the Union Bank of Australia Limited, 1828–1951*. London: Longmans.

   1983. 'Australian central banking 1945–1959', *Australian Economic History Review* 23(2), September: 95–192.

Butlin, S. J., Critchley, T. K., McMillan, R. B. & Tange, A. H. 1941. *Australia Foots the Bill*. Sydney: Angus & Robertson.

Cain, P. J. 1996. 'Gentlemanly imperialism at work: The Bank of England, Canada, and the sterling area, 1932–1936', *Economic History Review* XLIX(2): 336–57.

Calomiris, C. 2013. 'Volatile times and persistent conceptual errors', in M. D. Bordo & W. Roberds (eds.), *The Origins, History, and Future of the Federal Reserve: A Return to Jekyll Island*. Cambridge University Press: 166–218.

Calomiris, C. W. & Haber, S. H. 2014. *Fragile by Design*. Princeton University Press.

Cannon, M. 2013 [1966]. *The Land Boomers*, 4th edn. Melbourne: Melbourne University Press.

Cassidy, J. 2002. *Dot.con. Greatest Story Ever Told*. London: Allen Lane.

Chernow, R. 1993. *The Warburgs*. New York, NY: Vintage Books.

Cherrier, B. 2011. 'The lucky consistency of Milton Friedman's science and politics', in R. Van Horn, P. Mirowski & T. A. Stapleford, eds. *Building Chicago Economics*, Cambridge University Press: 335–67.

Chick, V. 2008. 'Could the crisis at Northern Rock have been prevented?', *Contributions to Political Economy* 27: 115–24.

Clark, G. 2002. 'Embracing fatality through life insurance', in T. Baker & J. Simon (eds.), *Embracing Risk*. Chicago, IL: University of Chicago Press.

Cockburn, A. & Ridgeway, J. 1975. 'Why they sacked the bane of the banks', *The Village Voice*, February 3.

Colebatch, H. 1927. 'Australian credit as viewed from London', *Economic Record* 3(2): 217–27.

Coleman, W. 2007. 'Milton Friedman on the Wallaby Track', *A Journal of Public Policy and Ideas* 23(2), Winter: 3–7.

Coleman, W., Cornish, S. & Hagger, A. 2006. *Giblin's Platoon*. Canberra: Australian National University Press.

Collison, D. 2002. 'Propaganda, accounting and finance', in G. Frankfurter & E. McGoun (eds.), *From Individualism to the Individual*. Aldershot: Ashgate.

Coombs, H. C. 1971. *Other People's Money: Economic Essays*. Canberra: Australian National University.

1994. *From Curtin to Keating*. Darwin: North Australia Research Unit, Australian National University.

Cornish, S. 2010. *The Evolution of Central Banking in Australia*. Sydney: Reserve Bank of Australia.

2013. 'Review of Susan Howson's 'Lionel Robbins', *Agenda – A Journal of Policy Analysis and Reform, Australian National University Press* 20(1): 97–101.

Crotty, J. 1999. 'Was Keynes a Corporatist', *Journal of Economic Issues* 33(3): 555–77.

2012. 'The great austerity war', *Cambridge Journal of Economics* 36: 79–104.

Cryle, D. 1989. *The Press in Colonial Queensland: A Social and Political History 1845–1875*. Brisbane: University of Queensland Press.

D'Arista, J. 2009. 'The evolving international monetary system', *Cambridge Journal of Economics* 33: 633–52.

de Cecco, M. 1979. 'Origins of the post war payments system', *Cambridge Journal of Economics* 3(1): 49–61.

2009. 'From monopoly to oligopoly', in E. Helleiner & J. Kirshner (eds.), *The Future of the Dollar*. Ithaca, NY: Cornell University Press: 116–41.

Debelle, G. & Fischer, S. 1994. 'How independent should a central bank be?', Conference Series; [Proceedings] Boston, MA: *Federal Reserve Bank of Boston*: 195–225.

Delong, J. B. 2000. 'America's historical experience with low inflation', *The Journal of Money, Credit and Banking* 32(4), Part 2: Monetary Policy in a Low-Inflation Environment, November: 979–93.

Denholm, D. 1979. *The Colonial Australians*. Harmondsworth: Penguin.

Dickens, E. 1997. 'The Federal Reserve's tight monetary policy during the 1973–1975 recession: A survey of possible interpretations', *Review of Radical Political Economics* 29(3): 79–91.

Dow, S. C. 2006. 'Endogenous money: structuralist', in P. Arestis & M. Sawyer (eds.), *A Handbook of Alternative Monetary Economics*. Cheltenham: Edward Elgar: 35–51.

2013. 'The real (social experience of monetary policy)', in J. F. Pixley & G. C. Harcourt (eds.), *Financial Crises and the Nature of Capitalist Money: Mutual Developments from the Challenge of Geoffrey Ingham*. London: Palgrave Macmillan: 178–95.

Dow, S. C. & Montagnoli, A. 2007. 'The regional transmission of UK Monetary Policy', *Regional Studies* 41(6): 797–808.

Down, I. 2004. 'Central bank independence, disinflations and the sacrifice ratio', *Comparative Political Studies* 37: 399–428.

Dymski, G. A. 2006. 'Banking and financial crises', in P. Arestis & M. Sawyer (eds.), *A Handbook of Alternative Monetary Economics*. Cheltenham: Edward Elgar: 385–402.

Dyster, B. & Meredith, D. 1990. *Australia in the International Economy in the Twentieth Century*. Cambridge University Press.

2012. *Australia in the Global Economy*, 2nd edn. Cambridge University Press.

Edey, M. & Stone, A. 2004. 'A perspective of modern policy transparency and communication', *Reserve Bank of Australia*, Conference 9–10 August 2004. www.rba.gov.au/publications/confs/2004/pdf/edey-stone.pdf.

Edwards, J. 2004. 'Discussant', *Reserve Bank of Australia*, Conference 9–10 August 2004.www.rba.gov.au/publications/confs/2004/pdf/

2005. *Curtin's Gift: Reinterpreting Australia's Greatest Prime Minister*. Sydney: Allen & Unwin.

Eichengreen, B. 1990. *Elusive Stability*. Cambridge University Press.

2011. *Exorbitant Privilege*. Oxford: Oxford University Press.

Eichengreen, B. & Mitchener, K. 2003. 'The Great Depression as a credit boom gone wrong', *BIS Working Papers 137*, September.

Elias, N. 1970. *What Is Sociology?* New York, NY: Columbia University Press.

1987. 'The retreat of sociology into the present' *Theory, Culture & Society* 4: 223–47.

2000. *The Civilizing Process: Sociogenetic and Psychogenetic Investigations*, Rev. edition E. Dunning, J. Gouldsblom & S. Mennell, Trans E. Jephcott. Malden, MA: Blackwell.

Epstein, G. 2006. 'Central banks as agents of economic development', *United Nations University (UNU-Wider)*, Research Paper No. 2006/54, May: 1–20.

Evans, R. J. 2016. 'Wait and see', review of The French Resistance, *London Review of Books* 3 November: 19–21.

Evans-Pritchard, A. 2015. 'Crushed Greece leaves the left bereft', *The Daily Telegraph* (London), reprinted *SMH*, 17 July 2015: 32.

2016. 'Negative rates policy is 'fiscal failure', *The Daily Telegraph* (London), reprinted *SMH*, 23 February 2016: 26.

Farhi, E. & Tirole, J. 2009. 'Collective moral hazard, maturity mismatch and systemic bailouts', *National Bureau of Economic Research*, Working Paper No. 15138: 1–49.

Farley, R. 2009. 'Krugman says Bush was first president to lead country into war and cut taxes', November 30, *Politifact*, downloaded 13 July 2016. www.politifact.com/truth-o-meter/statements/2009/nov/30/paul-krugman/krugman-says-bush-was-first-president-lead-country/.

Fisher, I. 1933. 'The debt-deflation theory of great depressions', *Econometrica* 1(4): 337–57.

Fisher, C. & Kent, C. 1999. 'Two depressions, one banking collapse', Reserve Bank of Australia, *Research Discussion Paper* No. 1999-06: ii–54.

Fitzgerald, T. 1990. *Between Life and Economics. The 1990 Boyer Lectures.* Sydney: The Australian Broadcasting Corporation.

Flandreau, Marc and Stefano Ugolini. 2013. 'Where it all began: Lending of last resort at the Bank of England monitoring during the Overend-Gurney panic of 1866', in Bordo & W. Roberds (eds.), *The Origins, History, and Future of the Federal Reserve: A Return to Jekyll Island.* Cambridge University Press: 113–62.

Fleming, S. 2016. 'Federal Reserve is too "white and male" say Democrats' *FT* May 12. www.ft.com/intl/cms/s/0/05f45e66-1850-11e6-bb7d-ee.

Forder, J. 2006. 'Monetary policy', in P. Arestis, J. McCombie & R. Vickerman (eds.), *Growth and Economic Development.* Cheltenham: Edward Elgar: 224–41.

   2014. *Macroeconomics and the Phillips Curve Myth.* Oxford: Oxford University Press.

Frankel, B. 1979. 'On the state of the state: Marxist theories of the state after Leninism', *Theory and Society* 7(1/2), January–March: 199–242.

Fraser, S. 2005. *Wall Street a Cultural History.* London: Faber & Faber.

Freedman, C. 2006. 'Not for love nor money: Milton Friedman's Counter-revolution', *History of Economics Review* 44, Summer: 87–119.

   2007. 'De mortuis nil nisi bonum & middot; Milton Friedman (1912–2006)', *History of Economic Ideas* 2(15): 33–52.

   2016. 'Clueless: How Zombie policies devoured the Japanese economy – A review of Japan's great stagnation and abenomics – Lessons for the world', *Journal of the History of Economic Thought* 38(4): 512–18.

Friedman, B. 2005. *The Moral Consequences of Economic Growth.* New York, NY: Vintage Books.

Friedman, M. 1953. *Essays in Positive Economics.* Chicago, IL: University of Chicago Press.

   1968. 'The role of monetary policy', *The American Economic Review* LVIII(1), March: 1–17.

   1977. 'Nobel lecture: Inflation and unemployment', *Journal of Political Economy* 85(3), June: 451–72.

1997. 'The Euro: Monetary unity to political disunity?', *Project Syndicate* 28 August: 1–3.

Furphy, S. (ed.) 2015. *The Seven Dwarfs and the Age of Mandarins*. Canberra: Australian National University Press.

Galbraith, J. K. 1975a. *The Great Crash 1929* Harmondsworth: Penguin.

1975b. *Money. Whence It Came, Whence It Went*. Boston, MA: Houghton Mifflin Co.

1981. *A Life in Our Times*. Boston, MA: Houghton Mifflin Co.

1986. *A View from the Stands*. Boston, MA: Houghton Mifflin Co.

Galbraith, James K. 1997 'Time to Ditch the NAIRU', *Journal of Economic Perspectives* 11(1), Winter: 93–108.

Garnham, P., Oakley, D. & Harding, R. 2011. 'G7 nations in $25bn yen sell-off', *FT* 19 March: 1.

Germain, R. & Schwartz, H. 2014. 'The political economy of failure: The Euro as an international currency', *Review of International Political Economy* 21(5): 1095–122.

Giannini, C. 2011. *The Age of Central Banks*. Cheltenham: Edward Elgar.

Gibson, H. 2009. 'Competition, innovation and financial crises: A perspective on the current financial market turmoil', *Open Economic Review* 21(1): 151–7.

Gibson, H. & Tsakalotos, E. 2006. 'Narrowing the options: The macroeconomic and financial framework for EU enlargement', in P. Arestis, J. McCombie & R. Vickerman (eds.), *Growth and Economic Development*. Cheltenham: Edward Elgar.

Goldthorpe, J. H. 1978. 'The current inflation: Towards a sociological account', in F. Hirsch & J. H. Goldthorpe (eds.), *The Political Economy of Inflation*. London: Martin Robertson: 186–216.

Gollan, R. 1968. *The Commonwealth Bank of Australia: Origins and Early History*. Canberra: Australian National University Press.

Goodhart, C. A. E. 2003a. 'The two concepts on money', in S. A. Bell & E. J. Nell (eds.), *The State, the Market and the Euro*. Cheltenham: Edward Elgar: 1–25.

2003b. 'Response', in B. Eichengreen & K. Mitchener (eds.), *The Great Depression as a Credit Boom Gone Wrong*, BIS Working Papers 137, September: 88–9.

2013. 'Group-think and the current financial crisis', in J. F. Pixley & G. C. Harcourt (eds.), *Financial Crises and the Nature of Capitalist Money: Mutual Developments from the Challenge of Geoffrey Ingham*. London: Palgrave Macmillan: 70–8.

Goodman, J. B. 1991. 'The politics of Central Bank independence', *Comparative Politics* 23(3): 329–49.

Goot, M. 2010. 'Labor, government business enterprises and competition policy', *Labour History* 98, May: 77–95.

Gould, S. J. 2003. *The Hedgehog, the Fox, and the Magistare's Pox*. London: Vintage.

Greider, W. 1987. *Secrets of the Temple: How the Federal Reserve Runs the Country*. New York, NY: Simon & Schuster.

1988. 'The money question', *World Policy Journal (Duke University Press)* 5(4), Fall: 567–613.

2014. 'Why the Federal Reserve needs an overhaul', in L. R. Wray (ed.), *Federal Reserve Bank Governance and Independence during Financial Crisis*. Kansas, MO: Levy Economics Institute: 8–16.

Grenville, S. 1997. 'The evolution of monetary policy: From money targets to inflation targets', in P. Lowe (ed.), *Monetary Policy and Inflation Targeting*. Sydney: Reserve Bank of Australia: 125–58.

Haldane, A. 2010. 'The contribution of the financial sector: Miracle or mirage?' Speech of the Executive Director, Financial Stability, Bank of England, at the Future of Finance Conference: 1–38. *The LSE Report: The Future of Finance*. London: London School of Economics.

2011. 'The race to zero', *Speech to IEA Congress*, Beijing. 8 July. www .bankofengland.co.uk/publications/speeches.

2012. 'The dog and the frisbee', Speech of the Executive Director, Financial Stability, Bank of England, at the *Federal Reserve Bank of Kansas City's 36th Economic Policy Symposium*. London:1–36. www.bankofengland.co.uk/archive/Documents/historicpubs/speeches/2012/speech596.pdf.

Hancké, B. 2013. *Unions, Central Banks and EMU*. Oxford: Oxford University Press.

Häring, N. 2013, 'The veil of deception over money', *Real-World Economics Review* 63(25): 2–18. www.paecon.net/PAEReview/issue63/Haring63.pdf.

Häring, N. & Douglas, N. 2012. *Economists and the Powerful*. London: Anthem Press.

Hawtrey, R. G. 1921. *The Exchequer and the Control of Expenditure*. London: H. Milford, Oxford University Press.

1962 [1932]. *The Art of Central Banking*, 2nd edn. London: Frank Cass & Co.

Hayek, F. A. 1945. 'The use of knowledge in society', *American Economic Review* XXXV(4): 519–30.

1982. *Law, Legislation and Liberty*. London: Routledge & Kegan Paul.

Hayes, M. 2013. 'Ingham and Keynes on the nature of money', in J. F. Pixley & G. C. Harcourt (eds.), *Financial Crises and the Nature of Capitalist Money:*

Mutual Developments from the Challenge of Geoffrey Ingham. London: Palgrave Macmillan: 31–45.

Heath, E. 1992. 'Rules, function and the invisible hand: An interpretation of Hayek's social theory', *Philosophy of the Social Sciences* 22(1): 28–45.

Heilbroner, R. 2000. *The Worldly Philosophers: The Lives, Times and Ideas of the Great Economic Thinkers*, 7th edn. London: Penguin

Helleiner, E. & Kirshner, J. (eds.) 2009. *The Future of the Dollar*. Ithaca, NY: Cornell University Press.

Helleiner, E. 1993. 'When finance was the servant: International capital movements in the Bretton woods order', in P. G. Cerny (ed.), *Finance and World Politics*. Cheltenham: Edward Elgar.

2010. 'A Bretton Woods moment? The 2007–2008 crisis and the future of global finance', *International Affairs* 86(3): 619–36.

2015. 'The future of the Euro in a global monetary context', in M. Matthijs & M. Blyth (eds.), *The Future of the Euro*. Oxford: Oxford University Press: 223–48.

Henwood, D. 1998. *Wall Street*. New York, NY: Verso.

2003. 'Irresistible temptations', *Left Business Observer*, 104, April: 4.

Herndon, T., Ash, M. & Pollin, R. 2013. 'Does high public debt consistently stifle economic growth? A critique of Reinhart and Rogoff', *PERI Working Paper Series 322*, April. Amherst: University of Massachusetts.

Higgins, B. H. 1949. 'Postwar transition and the future of Lombard Street', in B. H. Higgins (ed.), *Lombard Street in War and Reconstruction*. New York, NY: National Bureau of Economic Research: 70–113.

Howell, M. 2016. 'The amazing career of a pioneer capitalist', *New York Review of Books*, 7 April: 55–6.

Howson, S. 1985. 'Hawtrey and the real world', in G. C. Harcourt (ed.), *Keynes and His Contemporaries*. The Sixth and Centennial Keynes Seminar; University of Kent at Canterbury 1983. London: Macmillan.

Hunter, B. H. & Carmody, J. 2015. 'Estimating the Aboriginal population in early colonial Australia. The role of chickenpox considered', *Australian Economic History Review* 55(2), July: 112–38.

Ingham, G. 1984. *Capitalism Divided? The City and Industry in British Social Development*. Houndmills: Macmillan.

2004. *The Nature of Money*. Cambridge: Polity.

2008. *Capitalism*. Cambridge: Polity.

2011. *Capitalism: With a New Postscript on the Financial Crisis and Its Aftermath*. Cambridge: Polity.

2013. 'Reflections', in J. F. Pixley & G. C. Harcourt (eds.), *Financial Crises and the Nature of Capitalist Money: Mutual Developments from the Challenge of Geoffrey Ingham*. London: Palgrave Macmillan.

Ingham, G., Coutts, K. & Konzelmann, S. 2016. 'Introduction: 'Cranks' and 'brave heretics' rethink money and banking after the Great Financial Crisis', *Cambridge Journal of Economics* 40: 1247–57.

Irwin, N. 2015. 'The 57-year-old chart that is dividing the Fed', *New York Times*, 24 October: BU1.

Isenberg, D. 2006. 'Deregulation', in P. Arestis & M. Sawyer (eds.), *A Handbook of Alternative Monetary Economics*. Cheltenham: Edward Elgar: 365–84.

Jacobs, L. & King, D. 2016. *Fed Power: How Finance Wins*. New York, NY: Oxford University Press.

James, H. 2001. 'The Multiple Tasks of Bretton Woods', *Past and Present*, Supplement 6.

2009. 'The enduring pre-eminence of the dollar', in E. Helleiner & J. Kirshner (eds.), *The Future of the Dollar*. Ithaca, NY: Cornell University Press: 24–44.

Johnson, S. 2011. 'Defaulting to big government' *Project Syndicate*, 18 July. www.project-syndicate.org/commentary/johnson22/English.

Johnson, S. and J. Kwak. 2011. *13 Bankers: The Wall Street Takeover and the Next Financial Meltdown*. New York, NY: Vintage Books.

Jones, E. 2003a. 'Nugget Coombs and his place in the postwar order', *The Drawing Board: An Australian Review of Public Affairs* 4(1), July: 23–44.

2003b. 'Macroeconomic policy and industrial structure: Contested parameters of economic policy in post-World War II Australia', *Working Papers. University of Sydney*, ECOP2003-1, May.

Kaiser, R. G. 2016. 'The disaster of Richard Nixon', *New York Review of Books*, 21 April: 56–60.

Kaldor, N. 1970. 'The new monetarism', *Lloyds Bank Review*, July: 1–18.

Kalecki, M. 1943. 'Political aspects of full employment', *Political Quarterly* 14(4): 322–31.

Katznelson, I. 2013. *Fear Itself*. London: Liveright.

Kaufman, H. 1986. *Interest Rates, the Markets and the New Financial World*. New York, NY: Times Books.

2015. 'You can't go home again', in *Reuters.com* Press Release 24 September 2015. 'Noted economist sees "tectonic shifts" in Economic/Financial landscape'.

Kennedy, S. 2015. 'Wall street is running the world's central banks', *Bloomberg*, 17 November: www.bloomberg.com/news/articles/2015-11-17/what-wall-street-s-return-to-central-banking-may-mean-for-policy.

Keohane, R. O. 1978. 'Economics, inflation, and the role of the state: Political implications of the McCracken Report', *World Politics* 31: 108–28.

Keynes, J. M. 1920. *The Economic Consequences of the Peace*. New York, NY: Harcourt, Brace and Howe.

1940. *How to Pay for the War: A Radical Plan for the Chancellor of the Exchequer*. London: Macmillan and Co.

1964 [1936]. *The General Theory of Employment, Interest, and Money*. New York, NY: Harbinger.

Kindleberger, C. P. 1989. *Manias, Panics, and Crashes: A History of Financial Crises*, 2nd edn. London: Macmillan.

King, J. 2013. 'A case for pluralism in economics', *The Economic and Labour Relations Review* 24(1): 17–31.

King, M. 2016. *The End of Alchemy. Money, Banking, and the Future of the Global Economy*. New York, NY: W. W. Norton & Company.

Knight, F. H. 1964 [1921]. *Risk, Uncertainty and Profit*. New York, NY: A. M. Kelley.

Kriesler, P. & Neville, J. 2003. 'Macroeconomic impacts of globalization', in H. Bloch (ed.), *Growth and Development in the Global Economy*. Cheltenham: Edward Elgar.

Kriesler, P., Halevi. J. & Hart, N. 2013. 'The traverse, equilibrium analysis and post-Keynesian economics', in G. C. Harcourt and P. Kriesler (eds.), *Oxford Handbook of Post-Keynesian Economics Volume 2*. New York, NY: Oxford University Press.

Krippner, G. 2011. *Capitalizing on Crisis: The Political Origins of the Rise of Finance*. Cambridge, MA: Harvard University Press.

Kurzer, P. 1988. 'The politics of central banks: Austerity and unemployment in Europe', *Journal of Public Policy* 8(1), January-March: 21–48.

Kuttner, K. N. 2004. 'A snapshot of inflation targeting in its adolescence', *Reserve Bank of Australia, Conference 9–10 August 2004*. www.rba.gov.au/publications/confs/2004/kuttner.html.

Kuttner, R. 2017. 'The man from Red Vienna', *New York Review of Books*, 21 December: 55–7

Kynaston, D. 1995. 'The Bank of England and the Government'. In R. Roberts & D. Kynaston (eds.), *The Bank of England*. Oxford: Oxford University Press and Clarendon.

Kyrtsis, A.-A. 2012. 'Immoral panic and emotional operations in times of financial fragility', in J. F. Pixley (ed.), *New Perspectives on Emotions in Finance: Sociology on Confidence, Betrayal and Fear*. London: Routledge.

Lanchester, J. 2016. 'Money trap', *The New Yorker*, 24 October: 73–6.

Lane, A. 2016. 'Watching the Trump spectacle overseas', *The New Yorker*, 12 November 2016. www.newyorker.com/news/news-desk/watching-the-trump-spectacle-overseas.

Levin Report. 2011. 'Wall Street and the financial crisis: Anatomy of a financial collapse', Majority and Minority Staff Report, *Permanent Subcommittee on Investigations, United States Senate* (Carl Levin, Chairman; Tom Coburn, Ranking Minority Member), 13 April.

Lloyd, J. 2015. 'Review of "Margaret Thatcher: The Authorized Biography, Vol Two: Everything She Wants"', *FT*, 9 October.

Lowe, P. 2016. 'Remarks to the Asian Development Bank', *Reserve Bank of Australia*, speech of the Deputy Governor.

Macpherson, C. B. 1962. *The Political Theory of Possessive Individualism*. Oxford: Oxford University Press.

Mallet, V. 2014. 'India's Rajan sounds alarm on asset bubbles' *Financial Times* 7 August. www.ft.com/cms/s/0/86629ef2-1dff-11e4-bb68-00144feabdc0.html.

Mann, G. 2010. 'Hobbes's redoubt? Toward a geography of monetary policy', *Progress in Human Geography* 34(5): 601–25.

2013. 'The monetary exception: Labour, distribution and money in capitalism', *Capital and Class* 37(2): 197–216.

Mannheim, K. 1936. *Ideology and Utopia*. London: Routledge & Kegan Paul.

Markus, M. R. 2001. 'Decent society and/or civil society?', *Social Research* 68(4): 1011–30.

Marx, K. 1978 [1852]. 'The 18th Brumaire of Louis Bonaparte', in A. R. Tucker (ed.), *The Marx–Engels Reader*. New York, NY: W. W. Norton & Co: 594–617.

Matthijs, M. & Blyth, M. (eds.). 2015a. *The Future of the Euro*. Oxford: Oxford University Press.

2015b. 'Possible futures, risks and uncertainties', in M. Matthijs & M. Blyth (eds.), *The Future of the Euro*. Oxford: Oxford University Press: 49–269.

May, A. L. 1968. *The Battle for the Banks*. Sydney: Sydney University Press.

McDonald, H. 2016. 'Trump rides the end of the American dream', *The Saturday Paper*, 12–18 November: 12.

McGrath, M. 2016. 'Elizabeth Warren to Wells CEO Stumpf: You should resign and face criminal investigation', *Forbes*, 20 September. www.forbes.com/sites/maggiemcgrath/2016/09/20/wells-fargo-ceo-john-stumpf-to-apologize-to-senate-banking-committee/#4cbd2c7a60da.

McKinnon, R. 1991. *The Order of Economic Liberalization*. Baltimore, MA: Johns Hopkins University Press.

McLean, I. W. 2013. *Why Australia Prospered*. Princeton University Press.

McLeay, M., Radia, A. & Thomas, R. 2014. 'Money creation in the modern economy', *Bank of England Quarterly Bulletin* Q1: 4–27.

Mehrling, P. 2000. 'Modern money: Fat or credit?', *Journal of Post Keynesian Economics* 22(3): 397–406.

Meltzer, A. H. 2013. 'Comments', in M. D. Bordo & W. Roberds (eds.), *The Origins, History, and Future of the Federal Reserve: A Return to Jekyll Island.* Cambridge University Press: 219–25.

  2014. 'Current lessons from the past: How the Fed repeats its history' *Cato Journal* 34(3): 519–39.

Minsky, H. 1992. 'The financial instability hypothesis'. The Jerome Levy Economics Institute, *Working Paper* No 74. Annandale-on-Hudson, New York, NY: Bard College.

  2008 [1986]. *Stabilizing an Unstable Economy.* New York, NY: McGraw Hill.

Mirowski, P. 1989. *More Heat than Light. Economics as Social Physics: Physics as Nature's Economics.* Cambridge University Press.

  2011. 'On the origins (at Chicago) of some species of neoliberal evolutionary economics', in R. Van Horn, P. Mirowski, & T. A. Stapleford, eds. *Building Chicago Economics.* Cambridge University Press: 237–78

  2013. *Never Let a Serious Crisis Go to Waste.* London: Verso.

Moe, T. G., 2014. 'Accord and lessons for central bank independence', in L. R. Wray (ed.), *Federal Reserve Bank Governance and Independence during Financial Crisis.* Kansas, MO: Levy Economics Institute: 64–83.

Moggridge, D. E. 1992. *Maynard Keynes: An Economist's Biography.* New York, NY: Routledge.

Morgan, V. 1943. *The Theory and Practice of Central Banking 1797–1913.* Cambridge University Press.

Münchau, W. 2016. 'The liberal elite's Marie Antoinette moment', *FT,* 28 November.

Nik-Kah, E. 2011. 'George Stigler, the graduate school of business and the pillars of the Chicago school', in R. Van Horn, P. Mirowski, & T. A. Stapleford (eds.), *Building Chicago Economics.* Cambridge University Press: 116–50.

Nordhaus, W. D. 2002. 'The economic consequences of a war with Iraq', in C. Kaysen, S. E. Miller, M. B. Malin, W. D. Nordhaus & J. D. Steinbruner (eds.), *War with Iraq.* Cambridge, MA: American Academy of Arts and Sciences.

Offe, C. 1980. 'The separation of form and content in Liberal Democratic Politics', *Studies in Political Economy* 3: 5–16.

Orléan, A. 2013. 'Money: Instrument of exchange or social institution of value?', in J. F. Pixley & G. C. Harcourt (eds.), *Financial Crises and the Nature of*

Capitalist Money: Mutual Developments from the Challenge of Geoffrey Ingham. London: Palgrave Macmillan: 46–69.

2014. *The Empire of Value*. Cambridge MA: MIT Press Books.

Osnos, E. 2018. 'Making China great again', *New Yorker* 8 January: 36–45.

Packer, G. 2014. 'The uses of division', *New Yorker* 11 & 18 August.

Palley, T. I. 2014. 'Monetary policy in the US and EU after quantitative easing: The case for asset based reserve requirements (ABRR)', *Real-World Economic Review*, Issue No. 68, 5–6 March: 2–9.

2015. 'The critics of Modern Money Theory (MMT) are right', *Review of Political Economy* 27(1): 45–61.

Palma, J. G. 2009. 'The revenge of the market on the rentiers. Why neo-liberal reports of the end of history turned out to be premature', *Cambridge Journal of Economics* 33: 829–69.

Parguez, A. 1999. 'The expected failure of the European and economic monetary union: A false money against the real economy', *Eastern Economic Journal*, 25(1), Winter: 63–76.

Parker, G. & McDermott, J. 2016. 'Sir Nick Macpherson to step down from Treasury', *FT* 5 January.

Pateman, C. 1979. *The Problem of Political Obligation*. Chichester: John Wiley & Son.

Piketty, T. 2014. *Capital in the Twenty-First Century*. Cambridge, MA: Harvard University Press.

Pixley, J. F. 1993. *Citizenship and Employment: Investigating Post-Industrial Options*. Cambridge University Press.

1998. 'Social movements, democracy and conflicts over institutional reform', in B. Cass & P. Smyth (eds.), *Contesting the Australian Way: States, Markets and Civil Society*. Cambridge University Press: 138–53.

1999, 'Impersonal trust in global mediating organisations', *Sociological Perspectives* 42(4): 647–71.

2000. 'Economic citizenship', in W. Hudson & J. Kane (eds.), *Rethinking Australian Citizenship*. Cambridge University Press: 121–35.

2004. *Emotions in Finance: Distrust and Uncertainty in Global Markets*. Cambridge University Press.

2007a. 'How do Australians feel about financial investment?', in D. Denemark, S. Wilson, et al. (eds.), *Australian Social Attitudes 2: Citizenship, Work and Aspirations*. Sydney: University of New South Wales Press.

2007b. 'Central bank leadership', in P. Mehrling, L. S. Moss, J. F. Pixley & G. S. Tavlas (eds.), *What If the Leader of the Central Bank Told Hilarious Jokes and Did Card Tricks? A Panel of Experts, American Journal of Economics and Sociology* 65(5): 876–87.

2010. 'Decency in Anglo-American financial centres?', *Thesis Eleven* 101: 63–71.

2012. *Emotions in Finance: Booms, Busts and Uncertainty*, 2nd edn. Cambridge University Press.

2013. 'Geoffrey Ingham's theory, money's conflicts and social change', in J. F. Pixley & G. C. Harcourt (eds.), *Financial Crises and the Nature of Capitalist Money: Mutual Developments from the Challenge of Geoffrey Ingham*. London: Palgrave Macmillan: 273–99.

2014. 'Uncertainty: The Curate's egg in financial economics', *British Journal of Sociology* 65(1): 200–24.

2016. 'Emotions of uncertainty, competition and cooperation in the international financial sector', in Y. Ariffin, V. Popovski and Jean-Marc Coicaud (eds.), *Emotions in International Politics*. Cambridge University Press: 112–36.

2018. 'Introduction' and 'How mobile capital plays off democracy: The Euro and other monetary federations', in J. F. Pixley and H. Flam (eds.), *Critical Junctures in Mobile Capital*. Cambridge University Press.

Pixley, J. F. & Browne, C. 2010. 'Festschrift for Maria Markus', *Thesis Eleven* 101: 3–5.

Pixley, J. F. & Harcourt, G. C. (eds.). 2013. *Financial Crises and the Nature of Capitalist Money: Mutual Developments from the Challenge of Geoffrey Ingham*. London: Palgrave Macmillan.

Pixley, J. F., McCarthy, P. & Wilson, S. 2014. 'The economy and emotions', in J. Stets & J. Turner (eds.), *Handbook of the Sociology of Emotions, Vol II*. New York, NY: Springer: 307–34.

Pixley, J. F., Whimster, S. & Wilson, S. 2013. 'Central bank independence: A social economic and democratic critique', *The Economic and Labour Relations Review* 24(1): 32–50.

Polanyi, K. 1957 [1944]. *The Great Transformation*. Boston, MA: Beacon Press.

Posen, A. 2008. 'The future of inflation targeting. Interview with Adam Posen', *Challenge*, 51(4), July–August: 5–22.

Prins, N. 2014. 'All the president's bankers', *Financial History*, New York, NY: Spring: 14–16.

Quiggin, J. 2001. 'The people's bank: The privatisation of the Commonwealth Bank and the case for a new publicly owned bank', *Australian Options*. www.uq.edu .au/economics/johnquiggin/JournalArticles01/CBAPrivatisation01.html.

Rich, N. 2016. 'James Baldwin and the fear of a nation', *New York Review of Books*, 12 May: 36–43.

Roach, S. S. 2016. 'Desperate central bankers', *Project Syndicate*, 26 September: 1–4.

Roberts, A. 2012. *America's First Great Depression: Economic Crisis and Political Disorder after the Panic of 1837*. Ithaca, NY: Cornell University Press.

Robinson, J. 1978. *Contributions to Modern Economics*. New York, NY: Academic Press.

Rodrik, D. 2008. 'Second best institutions', National Bureau of Economic Research. *Working Paper* 14050, JEL No. 1: 1–12.

Rowse, T. 2015. 'Coombs the Keynesian', in S. Furphy (ed.), *The Seven Dwarfs and the Age of Mandarins*. Canberra: Australian National University Press: 143–68.

Ryan-Collins, J. R. 2015. 'Is monetary financing inflationary? A case study of the Canadian economy, 1935–1975'. Levy Economics Institute, *Working Paper* No. 848, October: 1–51.

Ryan-Collins, J., Greenham, T. & Werner, R. 2011. *Where Does Money Come From? A Guide to the UK Monetary & Banking System*. London: New Economics Foundation.

Salant, J. 2003. 'US President's family had links to bank with Hitler supporter', *Sydney Morning Herald*, 21 October: 5.

Sandbu, M. 2016a. 'Populists stick to tradition of central bank-bashing', *FT*, 26 October.

2016b. 'The Return of Keynesianism', *FT*, 24 October.

Sawer, M. 2012. 'Andrew Fisher and the era of liberal reform', *Labour History* 102, May: 71–86.

Sayers, R. S. 1949. 'Central banking in the light of recent British and American experience', *Quarterly Journal of Economics* 63(2): 198–211.

Schedvin, C. B. 1992. *In Reserve: Central Banking in Australia, 1945–1975*. Sydney: Allen & Unwin.

Schularick, M. & Taylor, A. M. 2012. 'Credit booms gone bust: Monetary policy, leverage cycles, and financial crises, 1870–2008', *The American Economic Review* 102(2): 1029–61.

Schularick, M. 2014. 'Public and private debt: 'The historical record (1870–2010)', *German Economic Review* 15(1): 191–207.

Schumacher, E. F. 1943. 'Multilateral clearing', *Economica, The London School of Economics*, X(38), May: 150–65.

Schumpeter, J. A. 1934 [1911]. *The Theory of Economic Development*. New Brunswick, NJ: Transaction Publishers, Reprinted 1983.

1954. *History of Economic Analysis*. New York, NY: Oxford University Press.

1991. *The Economics and Sociology of Capitalism*, R. Swedberg (ed.), Princeton University Press.

Schwartz, H. M. 1998. 'Social democracy going down or down under? Institutions, internationalized capital, and indebted states', *Comparative Politics* 30(3), April: 253–72.

2000. *States Versus Markets: The Emergence of a Global Economy*, 2nd edn. (1st edn., 1994). New York, NY: St. Martin's Press.

2005. 'The Australian miracle: Luck, pluck or being stuck down under?', in U. Becker & H. Schwartz (eds.), *Employment 'Miracles'*. Amsterdam: Amsterdam University Press: 157–82.

2009. 'Housing finance, growth, and the US dollar's surprising durability', in E. Helleiner & J. Kirshner (eds.), *The Future of the Dollar*. Ithaca, NY: Cornell University Press: 88–115.

Seccombe, M. 2016. 'Reagan's "voodoo" at the [Australian] budget's heart'. *The Saturday Paper*, May 7: 1, 4

Self, R. 2007. 'Perception and posture in Anglo-American relations: The war debt controversy in the "official mind" 1919–1940', *The International History Review* 29(2): 282–312.

Shull, B. 2014. 'Financial crisis resolution', in L. R. Wray (ed.), *Federal Reserve Bank Governance and Independence during Financial Crisis*. Kansas, MO: Levy Economics Institute: 17–36.

Simmel, G. 1907 [1990]. *The Philosophy of Money*. London: Routledge.

Skypala, P. 2013. 'Pre-school lessons for the bankers', *FT*, 21 January: 20.

Smithin, J. N. 1996. *Macroeconomic Policy and the Future of Capitalism: The Revenge of the Rentiers and the Threat to Prosperity*. Cheltenham: Edward Elgar.

Stapleford T. A., 2011. 'Positive economics for democratic policy', in R. Van Horn, P. Mirowski, & T. A. Stapleford (eds.), *Building Chicago Economics*. Cambridge University Press.

Stern, F. 1977. *Gold and Iron. Bismarck, Bleichröder and the Building of the German Empire*. New York, NY: Alfred A. Knopf.

Stevens, G. 2016. 'An accounting'. *Address to the Anika Foundation Luncheon* by the Governor. Sydney: 10 August (rba.gov.au Speeches).

Streeck, W. 2014. *Buying Time*. London: Verso.

Tallman, E. 2013. 'Comment', in M. D. Bordo & W. Roberds (eds.), *The Origins, History, and Future of the Federal Reserve: A Return to Jekyll Island*. Cambridge University Press: 99–112.

Taylor, J. B. 2015. *Recreating the 1940s-Founded Institutions for Today's Global Economy*. Kansas, MO: Remarks upon receiving the Truman Medal for Economic Policy.

Therborn, G. 1977. 'The rule of capital and the rise of democracy', *New Left Review* I/103, May–June: 3–41.

Tily, G. 2015. 'The long-term rate of interest as Keynes's "villain of the piece"', *Real-World Economics Review*, 73, December: 120–29. www.paecon.net/PAEReview/issue73/Tily73.pdf.

Tooze, A. 2007. *The Wages of Destruction: The Making and Breaking of the Nazi Economy*. New York, NY: Penguin Books.

2014. *The Deluge: The Great War and the Remaking of Global Order*. London: Allen Lane.

2016. 'Just another panic?', *New Left Review* 97, January–February: 129–37.

Turnell, S. & Ussher, L. J. 2009. 'A 'New Bretton Woods': Kaldor and the antipodean quest for global full employment', *Review of Political Economy* 21(3): 423–45.

Turner, A. 2010. 'What do banks do, what should they do and what public policies are needed to ensure best results for the real economy?', *Lecture at CASS Business School*, 17 March 2010: 1–31. www.fsa.gov.uk/pubs/speeches/at_17mar10.pdf.

Tymoigne, E. 2014. 'Coordination between the Treasury and the Central Bank', in L. R. Wray (ed.), *Federal Reserve Bank Governance and Independence during Financial Crisis*. Kansas, MO: Levy Economics Institute: 84–105.

Ugolini, S. 2011. 'What do we really know about the long-term evolution of central banking? Evidence from the past, insights for the present'. *Working Paper* 15. Norges Bank.

Van Horn, R., Mirowski P., & Stapleford, T. A., eds. (2011). *Building Chicago Economics*. Cambridge University Press.

Veblen, T. 1904. *The Theory of Business Enterprise*. New York, NY: Charles Scribner & Sons.

Wadhwani, S. B. 2008. 'Should monetary policy respond to asset price bubbles?', *National Institute Economic Review* 206, October: 25–34.

Watson, D. 2016. 'American politics in the time of Trump', *Quarterly Essay*, 63: 1–74.

Webb, B. 1931. 'Extracts of Mrs Sidney Webb's letter to the women's section of the Seaham divisional labour party; 14th October 1931': From her diary, a permanent LSE holding. digital.library.lse.ac.uk/objects/lse:qux395wip#page/482/mode/2up.

Weber, M. 1978. *Economy and Society*. G. Roth and C. Wittich (eds.), Berkeley, CA: University of California Press.

1981 [1927]. *General Economic History*, Trans. F. H. Knight. New Brunswick, NJ: Transaction Books.

Wennerlind, C. 2001. 'Money talks, but what is it saying? Semiotics of money and social control', *Journal of Economic Issues*, 35(3): 557–74.

Western, B. 2006. *Punishment and Inequality in America*. New York, NY: Russell Sage Foundation.

Wheen, F. 2009. *Strange Days Indeed*. London: Fourth Estate.

Whimster, S. 2009. 'Sociality and pathology in financial institutions', in S. Whimster (ed.), *Reforming the City*. London: Forum Press: 257–82.

White, E. 2013. 'To establish a more effective supervision of banking', in M. D. Bordo & W. Roberds (eds.), *The Origins, History, and Future of the Federal Reserve: A Return to Jekyll Island*. Cambridge University Press: 7–54.

Williamson, P. 1984. 'A "bankers' ramp"? Financiers and the British political crisis of August 1931', *The English Historical Review*, 99(393): 770–806.

Wilson, S. A. 2013. 'The limits of low-tax social democracy? Welfare, tax and fiscal dilemmas for Labor in government', *Australian Journal of Political Science* 48(3): 286–306.

2017. 'The politics of minimum wage welfare states: The changing significance of the minimum wage in the liberal welfare regimes', *Social Policy and Administration* 51(2): 244–64.

Winner, L. 1993. 'Social constructivism: Opening the black box and finding it empty', *Science as Culture* 3(16): 427–52.

Withers, H. 1918 [1909]. *The Meaning of Money*. London: John Murray.

Wolf, M. 2014. 'Only the ignorant live in fear of hyperinflation', *FT*, 10 April.

2016. 'Economic ills of the UK extend well beyond Brexit: Failings include low investment and ... the innumeracy of the elites', *FT*, 29 September.

Woodruff, D. 1999. *Money Unmade*. Ithaca, NY: Cornell University Press.

2014. 'Governing by panic: The politics of the Eurozone crisis', *LSE Europe in Question*, Paper No 81/2014, October: 1–57.

Wray, L. R. 2014a. 'Outside money: The advantages of owning the magic porridge pot', Levy Economics Institute *Working Paper* 821 December.

(ed.) 2014. *Federal Reserve Bank Governance and Independence during Financial Crisis*. Kansas, MO: Levy Economics Institute.

Wray, L. R. 2014b. 'Central Bank independence and government finance', in L. R. Wray (ed.), *Federal Reserve Bank Governance and Independence during Financial Crisis*. Kansas, MO: Levy Economics Institute: 106–27.

Wright, E. O. 1997. *Class Counts: Comparative Studies in Class Analysis*. Cambridge University Press: 1–35.

Index

Printed in the United States
By Bookmasters

Printed in the United States
By Bookmasters